Social Inequality in Canada

Patterns, Problems, and Policies

Fifth Edition

Edited by

Edward Grabb
University of Western Ontario

Neil Guppy
University of British Columbia

PEARSON
Prentice
Hall

Toronto

Library and Archives Canada Cataloguing in Publication

Social inequality in Canada : patterns, problems, and policies / edited
by Edward Grabb, Neil Guppy. — 5th ed.

Includes bibliographical references and index.
ISBN 978-0-13-198475-2

1. Equality—Canada—Textbooks. 2. Social classes—Canada—Textbooks.
I. Grabb, Edward G. II. Guppy, L. Neil, 1949–

HN110.Z9S6 2009   305.0971   C2008-903180-6

ISBN-13: 978-0-13-198475-2
ISBN-10: 0-13-198475-6

Vice President, Editorial Director: Gary Bennett
Editor-in-Chief: Ky Pruesse
Marketing Manager: Sally Aspinall
Developmental Editor: Victoria Spence
Production Editor: Kevin Leung
Copy Editor: Susan Broadhurst
Proofreader: Tara Tovell
Production Coordinator: Avinash Chandra
Permissions Research: Leigh Bennett
Composition: Integra
Art Director: Julia Hall
Cover Design: Anthony Leung
Cover Image: Veer Inc.

13 14   15 14 13

Printed and bound in Canada.

Dedication

TO JAMES ENSIGN CURTIS (1942–2005)

We gratefully dedicate this book to the memory of James Ensign Curtis, who passed away on May 27, 2005. Through close to four decades, we were privileged to know Jim Curtis in many different ways, as an inspiring and dedicated teacher, a generous and gifted colleague, and the dearest and truest of friends. He fulfilled these and other crucial roles in our lives, just as he did in the lives of countless others. Jim was one of the great builders of our discipline, for many of us the finest sociologist that this country has ever produced. It has been a bittersweet task to prepare the new edition of this volume, the first time without Jim's steady hand to help guide it along. We must take solace in knowing that he remains an integral part of it, represented as he is in the chapters and sources that bear his name and in the work of so many of his former students and colleagues, who have contributed to this edition and others over the years. Jim enriched us all with his immense professional accomplishments and with his unparalleled ability to encourage excellence in others. Perhaps most important, though, was Jim's kindness and humanity toward everyone who was fortunate enough to know him. Colleagues, students, friends, and loved ones share the grief of his loss, but also the legacy that Jim Curtis has left to each of us.

Contents

Preface   ix

General Introduction   1

Conceptual Issues in the Study of Social Inequality   *Edward Grabb*   1

Section 1   Power and Class   17

1. Corporate Concentration, Foreign Ownership, and State Involvement in the Canadian Economy   *Edward Grabb and Monica Hwang*   19

2. Corporate Canada, Globalization, and Neoliberal Democracy *William Carroll*   29

3. Working-Class Formation in Canada   *James Conley*   44

4. Affluence, Power, and Strikes in Canada, 1973–2005   *Robert J. Brym*   61

Section 2   Socio-Economic Bases of Social Inequality   77

A. Income, Wealth, and Poverty

5. Changing Income Inequality in Canada   *Peter Urmetzer and Neil Guppy*   82

6. The Distribution of Wealth and Economic Inequality *James B. Davies*   92

7. Defining, Measuring, and Reducing Poverty   *Neil Guppy and Robin Hawkshaw*   106

B. Occupation

8. Social Mobility in Canada: Concepts, Patterns, and Trends *Richard A. Wanner*   116

9. Labour Markets, Inequality, and the Future of Work   *Graham S. Lowe and Wolfgang Lehmann*   133

C. Education

10. Change and Stability in Patterns of Social Inequality in Canadian Education   *Neil Guppy*   150

11. Changing Times, Stubborn Inequalities: Explaining Socio-economic Stratification in Canadian Schooling   *Scott Davies and Vicky Maldonado*   158

12.   Choose Your Parents Carefully: Social Class, Post-secondary Education, and Occupational Outcomes   *Harvey Krahn*   171

Section 3   Ascription and Social Inequality   191

A. Gender

13.   Inequalities of Gender and Class: Charting the Sea Change   *Janet Siltanen*   197

14.   Converging Gender Roles   *Katherine Marshall*   213

15.   Gender at Work: Strategies for Equality in Neo-liberal Times   *Gillian Creese and Brenda Beagan*   224

B. Ethnicity, Race, and Ancestry

16.   The Ebb and Flow of Immigration in Canada   *Monica Boyd and Michael Vickers*   237

17.   The Economic Integration of Visible Minorities in Contemporary Canadian Society: Revisited   *Feng Hou, T.R. Balakrishnan, and Rozzet Jurdi*   253

18.   Racial Inequality, Social Cohesion, and Policy Issues in Canada   *Jeffrey G. Reitz and Rupa Banerjee*   273

19.   First Nations, Inequality, and the Legacy of Colonialism   *Charles R. Menzies*   295

C. Age

20.   Age-based Inequalities in Canadian Society   *Neil Guppy and Robin Hawkshaw*   305

21.   Postponed Adulthood: Dealing with the New Economic Inequality   *John Myles*   317

D. Region

22.   Regional Inequality: Causes and Consequences   *Catherine Corrigall-Brown and Fred Wien*   324

Section 4   Some Consequences of Social Inequality   349

23.   Social Inequality and Health   *Gerry Veenstra*   353

24.   Persistent Inequalities: Homelessness in Canada   *Tracy Peressini*   367

25.   The Effects of Social Status on Beliefs about Individualism and Inequality in Canada   *Edward Grabb and Monica Hwang*   379

26. Inequality and Intolerance: Canada in Cross-national Perspective
   Robert Andersen and Scott Milligan 390

27. Political Involvement, Civic Engagement, and Social Inequality
   James Curtis, Edward Grabb, Thomas Perks, and Tina Chui 409

28. School's Out for the Summer: Should It Be? *Neil Guppy and Scott Davies* 429

Index 433

Preface

Our purpose in this book is to introduce students to key issues in the study of social inequality in Canada. We present a collection of 28 articles that, in varying ways, address virtually all major aspects or dimensions of social inequality. The result is a book dealing with topics that are central to a range of courses, including Social Inequality, Social Class, Social Stratification, Social Issues, Social Problems, and Canadian Society.

This new fifth edition begins from the same approach that guided the earlier versions of the book. Our main premise is that social inequality entails two broad components: *objective or structural conditions* of social inequality (power, poverty and wealth, occupations, and educational attainment, in particular) and *ideologies* that help support these differences. The ideologies—expressed in formal laws, public policies, dominant values, prevailing beliefs, and so forth—provide justification for the objective patterns of inequality that arise in society, as shown, for example, in the income and wealth differences that arise in Canada on the basis of gender, race, region, or education level.

Of course, there are other, less influential, ideologies in society too—"counter-ideologies"—that often reflect the interests of the disadvantaged. These counter-ideologies sometimes are expressed or take shape in the form of social movements that promote the interests of subordinate social groups, such as women, visible minorities, or First Nations peoples. Frequently, these movements call for fundamental changes to existing conditions of inequality, in order to improve the lot of the disadvantaged. A comprehensive analysis of social inequality requires us to understand both the structural and the ideological components of the problem.

In this revised collection we have sought to retain the core strengths of the earlier editions. As before, we have chosen articles with an eye to reflecting the range of theoretical perspectives and research approaches used to address issues of inequality. In addition, we have retained our emphasis on papers that are imaginative and clear expositions of results and theories. Also, we have preserved our commitment in the earlier editions to the historical context of patterns of inequality. Furthermore, we have worked very hard to ensure that various dimensions of inequality—for example, gender and ethnicity—have not been confined exclusively to isolated sections. Although separate sections are maintained for gender and race and ethnicity, we include several articles in other sections that deal with these dimensions as well (e.g., in the sections on education, income, and occupation). Finally, in keeping with the earlier editions, all sections of the book consider politics and ideologies related to inequality.

In this new edition, only 2 pieces from the fourth edition have been retained in unaltered form, while 15 have been revised and updated, and 11 are entirely new. Of the 28 papers, only 5 have been taken from previously published sources, with 23 written expressly for this book. As with the earlier editions, the substantial changes we have made this time illustrate the extensive additions to research on social inequality that have been made in recent years.

While this new edition comprises works by many of the leading experts in the field of social inequality in Canada, space constraints have meant, again, that we could not include a large number of other outstanding studies dealing with the topic. Some of these additional sources are displayed in the lists of "Further References" that appear at the end of each major section of the book, but even these analyses only begin to suggest the growing body of important research that is now available and the difficulty we have had in making the selections for this volume.

The study of social inequality in Canada has moved forward rapidly toward a much better understanding of the phenomenon. Those of us who would prefer to see our society changed to provide greater equality of opportunity and condition can take heart at this improved understanding. It is another matter, though, to turn our understanding into action and achieve social change. The following pages will show that many patterns of inequality are stubbornly resistant to change because they are maintained by formidable forces, especially by the *economic, political, and ideological power* wielded by highly privileged groups. Some of this power and influence operates through the apparatuses of the state, as certain chapters of the book will emphasize.

The studies in this collection demonstrate that some types of inequality are generally becoming more marked over time—as is the case with the high concentration of wealth and corporate control, for example. There are also some forms of inequality that have diminished considerably—as has occurred with differences in the attainment of university degrees by women relative to men, and differences in the earnings and occupations of some ethnic groups, especially those who are not visible minorities. And, finally, there are other patterns, such as the distribution of income, that show little change in recent decades. Thus, those readers who would prefer a more egalitarian society than currently exists in Canada will find reasons for both optimism and pessimism in the research presented here.

We would like to thank many people for their help with this project. First, of course, are the contributors to the volume. The strengths of the book are largely their doing. Second, we are indebted to many individuals for helpful suggestions in improving all of the editions of this book. In particular, we thank the many students, over numerous cohorts, who have given us valuable feedback. People who have provided helpful suggestions regarding this edition or previous editions include Catherine Corrigall-Brown, Gillian Creese, Dawn Currie, Brian Elliott, Dawn Farrough, Martha Foschi, Robin Hawkshaw, and Monica Hwang from the University of British Columbia; Anton Allahar and Jim Rinehart at the University of Western Ontario; Bruce Arai and Paul Maxim of Wilfrid Laurier University; Bill Johnston from the University of Alberta; Kevin McQuillan at the University of Calgary; Monica Boyd, John Myles, and Lorne Tepperman at the University of Toronto; John Goyder, John Hirdes, and Ron Lambert at the University of Waterloo; and Tony Williams from Okanagan University College in B.C. Third, we appreciate the continuing support of personnel from Prentice Hall Canada/Pearson Education Canada, both past and present, including Laura Pearson, David Stover, David Jolliffe, Lisa Phillips, Matthew Christian, Jim Zimmerman, Jessica Mosher, Patti Altridge, Laura Forbes, Alexandra Dyer, Victoria Spence, and Kevin Leung. Additional thanks are also given to a number of helpful reviewers, including Dawn Farough, David Hamilton, and Gregg M. Olsen (if appropriate). Fourth, the support staffs at our respective universities have been extremely helpful with each edition. For their fine work, we are particularly grateful to Denise Baker, Julie Dembski, Joyce D'Souza, Veronica D'Souza, Robin Hawkshaw, Denise Statham, Terry Stewart, Lois Wilbee, and Carol Wong.

Ed Grabb
Neil Guppy

General Introduction

CONCEPTUAL ISSUES IN THE STUDY OF SOCIAL INEQUALITY

Edward Grabb

That human beings are often very different from each other is one of those basic truths about life that we can all recognize. We need only observe the various sizes, shapes, and colours of other people, the different group affiliations they adopt, and the distinct goals or interests they pursue to be reminded of the numerous differences that can be drawn among us. It is also true that many of these differences probably have little or no lasting influence on our existence. And yet, it is clear that certain human differences regularly have significant consequences for the lives we are able to lead in society.

The study of social inequality is really the study of these consequential human differences. In particular, inequality refers to differences that become socially structured, in the sense that they become a regular and recurring part of how people interact with one another on a daily basis. Structured inequality involves a process in which groups or individuals with particular attributes are better able than those who lack or are denied these attributes to control or shape rights and opportunities for their own ends. One major factor in this process is that advantaged groups or individuals tend to obtain greater access to the various rewards and privileges that are available in society. These benefits, in turn, serve to reinforce the control over rights and opportunities enjoyed by the advantaged factions, in a cyclical process that structures and *reproduces* the pattern of inequality across time and place.

In general terms at least, this view of social inequality is held by most theorists and researchers in the social sciences, including many of those who study Canadian society. In this book we have brought together recent exemplary works by some noted Canadian writers, all of whom share an interest in understanding the consequential differences among people and the inequalities they engender.

The main goal of this opening chapter is to provide an integrative background for the papers that have been selected, and a context within which the substance of our selections can be more easily located and comprehended. This is not an entirely straightforward task, since in the study of inequality, as in most vibrant and continuing areas of inquiry, there are clear divergences in theoretical orientations and research traditions.

Given these divergences, there is little possibility at present of establishing a single, universally accepted approach to analyzing the problem. In other words, a complete synthesis of existing thought and knowledge is currently not feasible. Nonetheless, we can arrive at a general understanding of the major theoretical issues and empirical questions that have held the attention of contemporary students of social inequality. This understanding should also help us to appreciate important areas of agreement and dispute among scholars in the field.

The central questions we address in this opening chapter are theoretical in nature. Our discussion here provides the conceptual background for the selection and classification of papers in this volume. In particular, we assess the two most important ideas in most theories of social inequality: the concept of *class* and the concept of *power*, or *domination*. In doing so, we demonstrate that class and power are closely tied to questions of *economic control*, and also to questions of *ideological and political control*. The combined effects of these factors give rise to the key bases for social inequality that operate in Canada and most contemporary societies.

SOCIAL INEQUALITY AND THE CONCEPT OF CLASS

If we were to ask most people what inequality is about, we would probably find that their responses put considerable stress on economic or material distinctions, on differences in economic rights, opportunities, rewards, and privileges between themselves and others. Although such differences might not be their sole focus, people do show a notable interest, for example, in whether they earn as much money as others in different occupations; they might wonder if their own share of society's wealth is growing or shrinking over time; they might even raise such questions as whether it is true that a small number of businesses increasingly controls more and more of their country's economic resources.

In fact, until relatively recently these same kinds of questions—about economic control and material privilege—have also been the predominant concern among most social scientists interested in the topic of inequality. Such a focus is understandable, of course, since economic differences involve the most immediate or fundamental inequality in social settings: people's relative access to the material necessities of life itself. Undoubtedly, this emphasis is at least partly responsible for the central role that the concept of economic class has always played in social analysis, particularly since the early writings of Karl Marx and Max Weber (see Marx 1867; Weber 1922).

Unfortunately, the concept of class has provoked long-standing and still unresolved questions about its precise meaning and significance. Of these questions, five in particular should be raised in this opening section. First, there is the question of whether classes are simply categories of individuals who share similar economic circumstances, or whether the term *class* should refer only to an economic category that is also a real social group, a set of people with a shared sense of common membership or purpose. Second, analysts have debated whether classes are best thought of as simply the same as *strata*— ranked layers of people separated according to income or occupation level, for instance— or whether the dividing lines between classes are less arbitrary, less variable, and more fundamental than such stratum distinctions suggest. Third, some writers contend that classes are best understood as sets of *people*, while others argue they are really sets of *places* or *positions*, like boxes or containers in which the people are located. Fourth, there is the question of whether classes should be defined principally by differences in the amount of material rewards *distributed* to them for consumption purposes, or whether such differences are secondary to, and largely derivative from, structured economic *relationships*, especially relationships that give sustained control over material life to some and not others. For some theorists, such control provides the real means by which classes are defined and delineated. Finally, many writers disagree on how many classes exist in today's societies. Are there just two, a small dominant one and a large subordinate one? Are there instead some intermediate classes between top and bottom and, if so, how many? Or is it the case that there are no easily identifiable classes, but a continuous hierarchy without clear class distinctions?

The difficulties inherent in any attempt to answer all of these questions are obvious from the volume of work that has been generated on the concept of class (for discussion, see Grabb 2007). These differing perspectives cannot be fully incorporated within a single conception or definition of class. Nevertheless, there is sufficient common ground for class to be viewed in a manner that, at least in general terms, is consistent with most major works in the field, including those of the key classical writers, Marx and Weber, and of subsequent writers broadly sympathetic to either or both of these theorists (e.g., Poulantzas 1975; Carchedi 1977, 1987; Wright 1979, 1985, 1989, 1994, 1997, 2005; Wright et al. 1992; Parkin 1979; Giddens 1973, 1981a, 1981b, 1984, 1989, 1994, 1998, 2000; see also Giddens and Diamond 2005).

Our approach to defining the concept of class involves the following answers to the five questions listed above:

1. Classes exist primarily as *categories* of people, and need not be defined as real *groups*. In other words, classes typically will not be sets of people having a common sense of group membership and capability to act in unison toward some collective goal. This is not to say that such united action is never possible; classes sometimes become groups, but only sometimes. As Giddens notes, for example, class systems exist on a national or even international scale in modern times, making such coordination and common purpose exceedingly difficult to generate, at least in the mass of the population (Giddens 1973:84). In those rare instances where simple economic classes also develop these group-like characteristics, some writers find it useful, following Weber, to refer to such groups as social classes (Weber 1922:302–305; see also Giddens 1973:78–79; Grabb 2007:49).

2. While classes normally are not real groups, neither are they merely equivalent to strata, as certain writers seem to suggest (e.g., Johnson 1960:469; see Barber 1957:73; Parsons 1951:172). That is, strata are usually ranked statistical aggregates, for which the criteria used in ranking are quite variable (including such characteristics as income, education, occupation, and general prestige level) and the choice of boundaries is an arbitrary decision made by the researcher. In contrast, class divisions can be traced to more fundamental, deep-seated, and uniform cleavages than the ones implied by these stratum distinctions.

3. Classes are most completely comprehended if we recognize that they are neither just sets of people nor just structural categories, the containers that separate or encapsulate sets of people; they really are both of these things in combination. This double meaning of class is one aspect of a more general process that Giddens has called the "duality" of social structures (Giddens 1979, 1981b, 1984, 1989). Hence, classes exist as structural entities because certain enforceable rights or opportunities—such as the right to own and to exclude others from owning productive property—define them and distinguish them from each other. However, classes have almost no meaning if they are not also seen as real people, for it is people who create the rights or opportunities that define classes in the first place, it is people who enjoy or suffer the consequences of class inequalities, and it is people alone who are capable of changing or consolidating class structures through social action.

4. Classes are most readily defined as *economically based* entities. However, as discussed later, they also have an important part to play in the *political* and *ideological* spheres

of society and can be said to exist, in a sense, within and across all social structures, not just the economic (see Wright 1978, 1980, 1989:343–345; 1997:303–304, 544–545). In delineating classes, we can conform with Marx, Weber, and most leading contemporary theorists by treating one distinction—between those who own or control society's productive property or resources and those who lack this attribute—as the initial and most fundamental division in modern class systems (e.g., Marx and Engels 1848a:58, 92; Weber 1922:927; Giddens 1973:100; Poulantzas 1975:14; Wright 1978:73; Parkin 1979:53).

While this basic division is the crux of most class structures, other forms of social inequality can occur. The relations of domination and exploitation established by this division are the primary factors in class formation, but the distribution of material benefits such as income can also be significant for delineating classes, if only in an indirect way. Such benefits can enhance or blur the division between the dominant and the subordinate classes, depending on whether these benefits are distributed so that the two classes have markedly distinct consumption habits and qualities of life.

In addition, despite what some writers seem to suggest, the distribution of material benefits need not be an insignificant factor in the formation of classes. For example, some Marxist theorists tend to consider all wage and salary employees as simply members of the working class, or *proletariat*, because they depend for their livelihood on the sale of labour power to the propertied owning class, or *bourgeoisie*. However, wage and salary employees sometimes are paid sufficiently high incomes for them to be able to accumulate some surplus funds, over and above what they need for basic survival. These funds can be, and occasionally are, used to gain some control over productive resources, in the acquisition of such holdings as stocks, rental properties, interest-bearing bonds, annuities, pension plans, and so forth. To be sure, these are relatively minor forms of economic control or ownership, and in most cases are somewhat like that of the *petty bourgeoisie*, who own small-scale businesses or farms but employ no workers themselves. Nonetheless, such resources provide a means by which distributive inequalities can give rise to economic categories that are distinct to some degree from both the bourgeoisie and the proletariat (see Wright 1989:325, 333; 1994:45–48).

A related point of note is that those with a distributive surplus have the opportunity to expend these funds in another manner: to help finance special educational qualifications or technical training for themselves or their children. Here again, distributive inequalities need not merely signify consumption differences. Some writers suggest that educational credentials themselves are another form of productive "property." This may be true to the extent that educational certificates are tangible possessions that can generate material dividends of their own and, as a result, provide a basis for economic control otherwise unattainable by those who lack similar credentials (Giddens 1973; Collins 1979; Parkin 1979). Hence, educational advantage or opportunity may be yet another basis on which divisions can arise in the class structure and be passed on or reproduced over generations. The important role of educational certification or "credential assets" in class formation has increasingly been acknowledged by recent Marxist scholars (e.g., Wright, 1985, 1989, 1994, 1997, 2005), in contrast to some earlier Marxists who ignored or downplayed the importance of this factor.

5. The final, and probably most controversial, question to address about class is how many classes actually exist in current capitalist societies. Again, complete agreement

on this question is at present unattainable. Nevertheless, most writers now concur that modern class systems are more complex or pluralist in nature than the traditional Marxist division between bourgeoisie and proletariat is alone capable of representing. On the surface, this may seem to contradict standard Marxist accounts on the subject of class, especially those offered by Marx's early disciples. However, we should note that, on closer inspection, some allowance for a more complex portrayal of modern class systems is really quite consistent with Marx's own analysis and with more recent treatments by Marxist scholars.

At several points in his original writings, it is clear that Marx himself speaks of additional economic groupings that exist in real societies and that complicate the pure two-class model he believes will ultimately emerge in advanced capitalism. Marx refers to these complicating elements in various ways, calling them *Mittelstande* ("middle estates or strata"), *Mittelstufen* ("middle stages or ranks"), and *Mittelklassen* ("middle classes") (Marx and Engels 1848b:472; Marx 1862:368; 1867:673, 688, 784, 791; 1894:892). Most current Marxists describe similar complications in contemporary class structures, although they usually avoid referring to these additional elements as genuine classes (but see Carchedi 1977; Wright and Martin 1987; Wright 1989, 1994, 1997, 2005). Such elements may include the traditional petty bourgeoisie of small-scale owners but also involve a diverse range of salaried personnel that, because of attributes such as educational training, technical knowledge, administrative authority, and so on, persist as "fractions," "contradictory class locations," or similar elements complicating the basic two-class structure of capitalism (Poulantzas 1975:23, 196–199, 297; Wright 1978:90–91; 1979:46–47; 1985:88–89; 1989:301–348; 1994:45–48, 252).

Among most non-Marxists, the existence of intermediate categories in the class structure is readily acknowledged. In fact, some non-Marxists argue that there are so many complexities and fine distinctions in today's economic structure that what we really have is a *continuous hierarchy* with no distinct classes at all (Nisbet 1959; Faris 1972). Other non-Marxists have tried to adhere to this notion of a continuum while simultaneously retaining the concept of class in their analyses. One approach is to conceive of a general social hierarchy that is continuous and yet can also be divided into identifiable class clusters. In contrast to Marxist writers, some non-Marxist analysts, especially the so-called "structural functionalist school," see classes as sets of *occupations* that share a similar level of *prestige* because they are similar in their supposed value to society as a whole (Parsons 1940, 1953; Barber 1957).

Among many recent non-Marxist scholars, however, it is common to reject this conception, primarily because it tends only to confuse classes with statistical categories or strata. Instead, leading contemporary writers outside the Marxist circle now conclude that it is essential to retain key aspects of Marx's original conception of class, provided that these are revamped or supplemented to take account of subsequent developments in advanced class systems.

The latter approach is reminiscent of that adopted by Max Weber, the best known non-Marxist among major classical theorists in the field of inequality. Weber's work entails a constructive critique of Marx's writings. Weber envisions a class structure broadly similar to Marx's, involving a dominant bourgeoisie, or owning class, at the top; a propertyless working class at the bottom; and a mix of "various middle classes" *(Mittelstandklassen)* in between (Weber 1922:303–305). There are several differences between the views of Marx and Weber, of course. Perhaps the most crucial difference concerns their expectations for the eventual fate of the middle categories in the class system. In contrast to Marx, Weber believes that the growing need for intermediate bureaucratic and technical personnel in modern societies means that the middle class will not fall into the proletariat with time, but will continue to endure as a significant force in the future; hence, Weber is far less convinced than Marx that a growing split will emerge between the top and the bottom classes or that an ultimate revolt by the working class against capitalism is likely to occur.

Weber's approach to the study of class has had a notable influence on virtually all current non-Marxist theorists. For example, some recent writers see classes arising because some people are able to gain greater access to certain important "capacities" and "mobility chances" (Giddens 1973:101–103) or to special "resources and opportunities" (Parkin 1979:44–46) that serve to exclude other people from advantaged positions (see also Scott 1996; Tilly 1998). Certainly, these more recent approaches are not identical to one another, nor do they correspond precisely to the views of either Marx or Weber in their subtler details. Still, the class structures they portray are generally akin to one another and to the classical conceptions, for they also arrive at three key groupings: a *dominant class* composed mainly of those who own or control large-scale production; a *working class* made up of people who lack resources or capacities apart from their own labour power; and, in between, a *mixed intermediate range* that mainly includes professional, technical, or white-collar personnel who have some degree of special training or education (Giddens 1973:101–110; Parkin 1979:47–58, 102–110).

Thus, even a brief review of classical and contemporary conceptions of class indicates that what is really at issue among most theorists is not whether complications exist in the class system, but whether the complexities that do occur, especially those found in the centre of the structure, in fact constitute classes in their own right. Marxists usually say no, perhaps because they consider any middle segments to be both transitional and heterogeneous, destined to fall eventually into the proletariat and to blur only temporarily the real two-class system that underlies capitalism. In contrast, non-Marxists routinely treat such central segments as a middle class (or set of middle classes), either because such writers use the term *class* differently or because they genuinely believe these intermediate categories are fundamental and persistent realities within modern class systems.

While no complete resolution of this debate is possible, the view put forth here is that, at least for the current stage of capitalist development, it is reasonable to use the term *middle class* to label these central categories. There are three reasons for taking this position.

First, there is nothing inherent to the word *class* that suggests that it must be reserved solely to refer to permanent and lasting social categories. Thus, while all Marxists treat the bourgeoisie as a real class within capitalism, Marxists also contend that this class is destined for eventual dissolution in future socialist societies. Similarly, then, whether the middle categories in the class system are destined to be transitional entities should not be a crucial concern when deciding whether they form a class at present. Marx clearly saw this himself since, as noted already, he sometimes spoke of the existence of a middle class even though he had no doubt that its days were numbered.

Second, it can be argued similarly that although the middle segments of the class structure are indeed heterogeneous, their diversity is insufficient ground for denying that they form a distinct class. For, as leading Marxists and others acknowledge, the contemporary bourgeoisie and proletariat are also marked by considerable heterogeneity but are deemed to be classes all the same (Poulantzas 1975:23, 139, 198).

Finally, between the proletarian or bourgeois classes, on the one hand, and the set of intermediate categories, on the other hand, there is some conceptual parity that suggests the latter also may be seen as a class. Here the term *conceptual parity* means that the middle class is definable using the very same criteria used to delineate the bourgeoisie and proletariat. These criteria are the measure of people's relative control over society's productive resources and the extent to which such control separates sets of individuals (and the positions they occupy) from one another. What is most distinct about the members of the middle class is their mixed, or hybrid, situation in the productive system relative to people from other classes. As suggested in point 4 above, middle-class incumbents are unlike those in the proletariat and similar to people in the bourgeoisie because they retain some control over productive resources or assets—the acquisition of property and investments or of educational credentials and skills, in particular. However, at the same time, middle-class members are unlike those in the bourgeoisie and closer to people in the proletariat because the resources they control are typically minor in scale and are often derived from a relatively small surplus fund accumulated from salaried or wage-based earnings. That these middle locations tend to commingle characteristics of the other two classes, and yet remain marginal to both of them, is what most clearly identifies the middle class as a separate entity (see Wright 1989:333; Wright et al. 1992:41).

Given these considerations, we can deal with point 5 by provisionally suggesting that Canada, as well as most advanced capitalist countries, retains a class structure that, although highly complex and internally diverse, tends at its core to comprise three basic elements. The first is a predominant class of large-scale owners of productive property, the so-called *capitalist class* or *bourgeoisie* in classical Marxian terminology. The second element is a subordinate class of workers who live primarily through the sale of their labour power to the owning class and who are usually termed the *working class* or *proletariat*. The third major element is a mixed and more heterogeneous middle category of small-scale business people, educated professional-technical or administrative personnel, and various salaried employees or wage earners possessing some certifiable credentials, training, or skills. The latter grouping, while it is for some writers just a set of complicating fractions or fragments within a basic two-class model, can be considered a third or *middle class* for the reasons already outlined (see Grabb 2007:214–215).

Still, as has been pointed out from the beginning of this introduction, this provisional characterization cannot be presented as a universally acceptable conception of modern class structures. Rather, it can best be seen as an approximation, a compromise view with which the differing perspectives that are considered in this book can be compared and contrasted. Such an approximation allows us to recognize some level of agreement on how to think about the concept of class. Even so, other theoretical issues still remain to be addressed. In particular, we should be aware that many analysts believe that a focus on class is too narrow to provide by itself a complete conceptualization of social inequality in all of its forms. Such contentions move us beyond the problems of economic class and control over material or productive resources. They lead to a broader range of concerns that require us to consider the second key idea in most theories of social inequality: the concept of power or domination.

SOCIAL INEQUALITY AS POLITICAL AND IDEOLOGICAL CONTROL

In our opening remarks it was suggested that social inequality is primarily a question of consequential human differences, especially those that become structured and recurring features of our everyday lives. To this point, we have considered what many feel are the most familiar and fundamental illustrations of such differences: the inequalities that derive from differential *economic* control, or people's command over material and productive resources in society. In addition, however, many writers suggest at least two other major mechanisms that are crucial to the creation and continuation of social inequality. The first of these involves control over people and their conduct, over what some might call "human resources." This command over human resources is the essence of *political* control, as broadly defined by various analysts. The third major mechanism can be referred to as *ideological* control. It entails the control of ideas, knowledge, information, and similar resources in the establishment of structured inequality between groups or individuals (Mann 1986, 1993; Runciman 1989; Grabb 2007).

A basic premise of the current discussion is that these two additional forms of control, though they typically occur in conjunction with economic control (and with each other), are not simply reducible to or a consequence of economic control, since both political and ideological control actually have their own distinct origins. In other words, it is possible to gain positions of dominance in society and to establish inequalities between factions without relying purely on control over material resources.

For example, inequality can result from political control when enforceable policies, statutes, or laws are invoked to ensure the compliance of subordinates with the will of others. The government or *state* is most commonly identified with the idea of political control, since it takes primary responsibility for creating the laws that govern the behaviour of people and can ensure compliance, if necessary, through the use of police or military force. However, political control in the broadest sense occurs whenever individuals' actions are constrained by rules of conduct established by others in authority over them in various organizations—when employees obey the work regulations of their jobs or when students comply with the academic regulations of their university, for example. The most extreme or blatant form that political control can take is one usually exercised by the state. This is the use of physical force by one faction on another, what Poulantzas quite literally calls the "coercion of bodies and the threat of violence of death" (Poulantzas 1978:28–29).

In addition to economic and political control, inequalities can also be created through or reinforced by ideological forces. *Ideology* refers to the set of ideas, values, and beliefs that describe, explain, or justify various aspects of the social world, including the existence of inequality (Porter 1965, chs. 15, 16; Marchak 1988). Thus, for example, a belief in racial superiority or inferiority is central to the ideological system that helped create and justify the unequal treatment of blacks by whites in the nineteenth-century southern United States and in the old apartheid system in South Africa. Similarly, the belief in the divine right of kings was important in establishing and maintaining the rule of monarchs and nobles over other people in much of medieval Europe. Of course, it is also possible for ideologies to support *reductions* in inequalities among groups. For example, the Canadian Charter of Rights and Freedoms is one relatively recent attempt in Canada to implement the belief in equal rights and opportunities for all people, regardless of "race, national or ethnic origin, colour, religion, sex, age, or mental or physical disability." In each of these examples, ideas and beliefs about inequality were also converted by governments into official policy or formal laws. This illustrates the often close connection between politics and ideology in society.

We should also recognize, though, that ideology can be fundamental to the third major type of control we have been discussing: economic control. For example, the belief that it is acceptable for people to own private property is clearly an essential ideological pre-requisite for the existence of economic inequalities based on such ownership. Similarly, the belief that people with unequal talents or motivation should also be unequal in the material rewards they receive can be used as both an explanation and a justification for the eco-nomic differences that arise among individuals. In both of these examples, the extent to which people believe or reject ideas about themselves and their society will have an impor-tant bearing on how much inequality exists, and how likely it is to change with time.

POLITICAL AND IDEOLOGICAL FACTORS IN CLASS DIFFERENCES

The recognition of multiple mechanisms of control and the distinct resources they entail suggests that there is some degree of pluralism in the processes that generate social inequal-ity. This, in turn, implies that any investigation based solely on economic class, especially if classes are conceived only in conventional terms as groupings within the structure of material production, is not sufficient by itself to capture and express this pluralism.

Perhaps for this reason, some Marxists have sought to include in their conceptions of class the sense that not only economic control but also political ideological control are cru-cial to the formation of class structures (Poulantzas 1975; Wright 1979, 1985, 1989, 1994, 1997, 2005). The incorporation of these additional elements into conventional conceptions of the class system is a significant innovation. Their inclusion permits us to recognize that classes, although they are primarily economic groupings, can also be important for other reasons and, in a way, may be fundamentally embedded within and across all social struc-tures, both economic and non-economic.

Here we should also note that, in addition to a revised notion of the class system, other complicating elements have come to be recognized in the multifaceted structure of inequality that characterizes most societies. As both Marxists and non-Marxists now gen-erally acknowledge, various patterns of inequality exist that are at least partially inde-pendent of, and not reducible to, class inequality alone. The more prominent examples of these other bases for inequality include gender and race or ethnicity. Other important bases include age, region, and, in some cases, language and religion. Non-Marxists sometimes refer to these factors as different bases for "social closure" (Parkin 1979), while Marxists sometimes call them "multiple oppressions" (Wright 1985:57). Whatever label they are given, however, they represent important additional areas of inquiry for students of inequality and require a conceptual approach that is broader than what the class concept by itself can provide.

SOCIAL INEQUALITY AS THREE FORMS OF POWER

It is primarily for this reason that some writers have recommended that the concept of power be used in conjunction with class theory, in an effort to move us toward a more gen-eral framework for analyzing and thinking about inequality in all of its forms. Some

Marxist scholars have been reluctant to take this approach, especially if it relegates class analysis to a secondary concern (Wright 1985:57; Clement 1982:481). And, indeed, it is essential when analyzing other crucial problems in social inequality that we not ignore or downgrade the continuing importance of class in contemporary societies. Thus, although some now suggest that class may be "dying" as a significant issue or concept in sociology (e.g., Clark and Lipset 1991; Clark et al. 1993), existing research, including many of the studies presented in this book, make it clear that this suggestion is mistaken.

As noted already, however, it can be argued that class analyses are improved significantly by a fuller appreciation of the other forms of inequality and power relations in society. In other words, power can be used as a more generalizable, if not a more fundamental, concept than class, because it can be used to describe and analyze both class and non-class forms of social inequality (Giddens 1981a; Grabb 2007:211–213). Those who adopt the latter perspective contend that class is pivotal in any complete understanding of social inequality, but that class differences represent one manifestation of the more general structure of power that is responsible for generating the overall system of inequality in most societies. Other crucial manifestations of inequality, such as those based on gender and race, can therefore be understood as the results of differential access to the different forms of power or domination in society (see, for example, Blalock 1989, 1991; Wilson 1973; Huber and Spitze 1983; Blumberg 1984; Milkman 1987; Connell 1987; Collins 1988; Li 1988; Mackie 1991; Chafetz 1990, 1997; Walby 1990, 1997; Agger 1993; Andersen and Collins 1995).

However, even if power can serve this more general conceptual purpose, the question still remains: What precisely does the concept of power signify? This is not a simple question to answer since power, like class, is an idea that has stimulated numerous debates over its definition and meaning (see, for example, Lukes 1974; Wrong 1979; Mann 1986, 1993; Runciman 1989; Scott 1996). For our purposes, however, *power* can be defined briefly as the differential capacity to command resources and thereby to control social situations. We have already suggested that there are three major types of resources operating in social settings (material, human, and ideological) and three mechanisms of control corresponding to them (economic, political, and ideological). These three mechanisms can be seen as the key forms of power in society.

Whenever differences in economic, political, or ideological power are sufficiently stable and enduring that they promote regular, routinized relations of ascendance and subordination among people, the resulting pattern of interaction is a case of *structured power*, or what might be termed a *structure of domination* (Grabb 2007). Using abstract imagery, we can think of the overall system of inequality in a society as a kind of framework, involving all three forms of power and the three corresponding structures of domination. In more concrete terms, the structures of domination exist mainly as bureaucratic or corporate organizations: business enterprises in the economic sphere, departments of government in the political sphere, church hierarchies and institutions of higher learning in the ideological sphere, and so forth. It is within all these concrete settings that power differences among people (and among the positions they occupy) become manifested, thereby producing organized patterns of inequality.

Another point to note in this abstract imagery is that there is no perfect one-to-one linkage between each of the three forms of power and each set of concrete structures. These are just the *primary linkages,* since each of the means or forms of power can operate in at least a secondary fashion in any of the three structures. Thus, as noted earlier, political power (control over people or human resources) may indeed be the principal jurisdiction of the set of political or state organizations, but it is also exercised in the control imposed by owners on their workers in the economic structure. At the same time, the various political organizations composing the modern state do not derive all of their power from the capacity to legislate or coerce human behaviour, for they also control material resources through their command over tax revenues, government ownership of some business enterprises, and so on. As for control of ideas or knowledge, this is most obviously identified with ideologically oriented structures such as the mass media, the education system, and the church. However, as mentioned, such ideological control is clearly a means for wielding power elsewhere too. This control is illustrated by the policy-making, information-gathering, and surveillance capacities within the state and by the control over technical ideas and knowledge that occurs in the economic sphere (Giddens 1981b, 1985, 1989).

The combined operation of all structures of domination, or rather the concrete organizations to which they correspond, establishes the major contours of the overall structure of inequality. The organizations themselves are patterned according to formal rules, laws, and rights of office, and their personnel exercise power in accordance with these formal guidelines. In addition, however, the inequalities that may develop within organizations, as well as the inequalities that organizations may engender for people outside them, are at least partly determined by informal practices or traditions, customs or habits, beliefs or prejudices. Not only formal rights or powers, but also informal privileges or advantages, tend to determine the nature and extent of inequality in society. Both act together to designate the key bases of social inequality and how much each will matter.

THE BASES OF SOCIAL INEQUALITY IN CANADA

There is a final conceptual issue to consider. This involves the identification of the central bases of social inequality that arise from the exercise of power in Canada. As already suggested, the notion that there are several distinct bases for inequality in society is one that has achieved increasing acceptance by theorists and researchers in the field, among both non-Marxist and Marxist scholars. It has increasingly been argued that there exists a multiple set of human characteristics or socially defined attributes that are consequential for determining the quality of life of most people. Recall that this is the idea with which we began our introduction to the topic of social inequality.

But what are these major bases for inequality, and why do these particular characteristics matter more than others? While it is difficult to provide answers to these questions that will satisfy all theoretical camps, we can see at least some common ground in the responses that most observers would give to both queries.

Perhaps the more difficult question to deal with is the second: Why are some attributes of people more likely than others to lead to important inequalities? Why, for example, has colour of skin had such a sustained impact on the rights and rewards of people historically, but not colour of eyes or hair? In general terms, it is possible to conceive of this problem by looking once again at the idea of power, or domination, and by considering which factions within the population have historically been the most or the least successful in turning to their advantage the various economic, political, and ideological mechanisms of power that operate within social structures. That is, to the extent that those in positions of ascendancy are able to use the three forms of power to establish and routinize structures of domination, they will be relatively more successful in reproducing across time and place important advantages for themselves and others with similar backgrounds or characteristics. For example, within any capitalist society, those individuals who retain private ownership or control over productive property will clearly enjoy special advantages and may well attempt to use their strategic position to encourage the further institutionalization of property rights in law, to foster belief systems favourable to such rights, and to employ other comparable means to help ensure that the privileges of property are maintained for themselves and succeeding generations of capitalists. In a similar fashion, those who have recognized training and skills, notably those who possess formal credentials or degrees in areas such as medicine and law, will themselves benefit from the advantages such exclusive accreditation brings and will also tend to favour the continuation of the system of special certification (and attendant privileges) for themselves and the cohorts who follow.

In both of these illustrations, we have noted important bases for inequality—property and educational credentials—that also happen to correspond to two of the key types of economic or productive resources that are in demand in most societies. In the present context, however, these are not simply resources but socially defined human attributes, or capacities of real people. In this form, they become recognized by others as crucial characteristics for differentiating some individuals or factions from others and for determining the rights, opportunities, rewards, and privileges of those who do or do not have them. We should note that this distinction, between resources on the one hand and human attributes on the other hand, illustrates once again what has elsewhere been referred to as the duality of social structures. In addition to these attributes, though, is a whole range of other consequential human differences that should be identified. Gender and race/ethnicity are probably the best contemporary examples. Inequalities based on gender and race/ethnicity are neither identical to nor reducible to class inequality. Nevertheless, like class inequality, these two bases of inequality can be conceived of as the product of long-standing factional antagonisms, struggles, or contests in which economic, political, and ideological mechanisms of power have played significant roles in establishing and structuring advantages for one grouping of people relative to others.

In fact, a full range of attributes or capacities can be delineated, comprising all major bases of inequality. In the contemporary Canadian context, these include the set of class-related bases—property ownership, education, occupation, and possession of wealth or income—as well as the key non-class bases—gender, race, ethnicity, language, region, and age (see Grabb 2007). As the papers in this volume will show, there is evidence to indicate that social groupings that are distinguishable from others on these dimensions have often been able to maintain significant advantages within the system of social inequality in Canada, and have done so largely because of superior access to economic, political, and ideological power.

In considering such a list, of course, we should also be aware that not all of these factors will be equally influential in shaping the general patterns of inequality in Canadian society. It is also important to acknowledge that other factors may matter, in different historical periods or different places, and that there may be considerable variability over time in the importance of prevalence of some bases of inequality relative to others. One example is religious affiliation. This is one social characteristic we have not listed here, but that in the past was a significant basis for inequality in Canada. Nevertheless, most analysts would agree that religion, while still notable, is now probably of less consequence in influencing the power or rank of Canadians than it was in centuries past. At the same time, though, it is clear that religious differences continue to play a major part in shaping the structure of inequality in other countries—in contemporary Northern Ireland or the Middle East, for example.

PLAN OF THE BOOK

The selections in this book reflect rather clearly the central role that the study of class and power has played in theory and research on inequality in Canada (see, in particular, Sections 1 and 2). Various chapters also discuss the array of social characteristics that have arisen as important bases for inequality in this country (in particular, Sections 2 and 3). As the subtitle of the book suggests, we have attempted within each section to attend not only to the patterns of social inequality and some of the problems these patterns pose for our society but also to the policies and ideologies involved in inequality. Section 4 outlines some of the varied consequences of inequality for individuals.

Our choice of "Power and Class" as the topic of our first section is meant to underscore that control over productive property provides a fundamental context within which the other bases for inequality operate in Canada and other capitalist societies. This section, therefore, provides necessary groundwork for understanding the patterns of inequality discussed in the other sections.

We have stated that certain key inherited or attained socio-economic characteristics are very important in defining the contours of inequality in our society. This issue is the principal focus of Section 2, which deals with the distribution of personal wealth or income, occupational status, and educational attainment. These three bases for inequality are distinct from each other and from the ownership factor itself, but are also involved in shaping the system of economic classes. Ownership of productive property is the essential basis for class inequality, particularly inequality that exists between the owning class and the working class. At the same time, however, educational credentials and surplus wealth or income are, as we have seen, potentially important for distinguishing the "middle class," or comparable intermediate categories, from the two major classes. The reason for including occupation in the same section is perhaps less obvious, but follows from two considerations. First, occupation has long been used in social research as an approximate indicator of class location, although methodological problems associated with this have been of some concern to many writers, especially Marxists. Second, the analysis of occupational inequality is useful in a supplementary or residual sense, because occupation subsumes such phenomena as skill level, manual versus non-manual labour power, and so on, that are not fully captured in research restricted to the study of ownership, wealth or income, and education.

In Section 3, the central concern is factors of social ascription. In Canada, these include gender, race, ethnicity, language, age, and region of residence. This third set of attributes is discussed separately from class and the socio-economic status characteristics for two reasons. First, these bases for inequality are conceptually independent of class distinctions, although, as we shall see, they may be correlated with class location and may give rise to important divisions *within* classes. Second, these attributes are ascriptive in nature, involving statuses that are not achieved or attained by people, but rather given to them. The ascriptive process is most clear in such characteristics as gender, race, and ethnicity, which are all assigned to people essentially at birth. Age is another social characteristic that, though constantly changing, is assigned and essentially beyond personal control. Language and region of residence are also assigned characteristics. For adults, there is some reason to dispute the ascriptive label for these last two attributes, because adults can elect to alter the language they speak or move to another place. However, even in adulthood, these attributes are more ascriptive than they appear because of the pressures on many Canadians to retain the language and place of residence they are born into. Language barriers and regional divisions tend to reproduce themselves over time, in spite of any policy efforts to change or reduce them.

The first three sections of the volume concentrate on structural questions: the character of class divisions and the other key bases of social inequality, and the ways in which such inequalities have been developed and maintained. The final section serves a different purpose, by providing a broad sampling of evidence to show that all of the various bases of inequality can influence the quality of life enjoyed or endured by Canadians. Of course, the earlier parts of the book also deal with the consequences of inequality, to the extent that these sections examine the effects of class, gender, or ethnicity on education, occupation, or income, for example. Section 4, however, goes beyond this to show the wide-ranging impact that social inequality can have on aspects of life as diverse as health and mortality, the incidence of domestic violence, and people's beliefs about the causes of inequality. Taken together, the collection of papers in this volume should give the reader a good sense of the array of important issues that Canadian researchers have addressed in the study of social inequality.

REFERENCES

Agger, Ben 1993. *Gender, Culture, and Power*. Westport, CN: Praeger.

Andersen, Margaret, and Patricia Collins (eds.) 1995. *Race, Class, and Gender*. Belmont, CA: Wadsworth.

Barber, Bernard 1957. *Social Stratification*. New York: Harcourt Brace and World.

Blalock, H.M., Jr. 1989. *Power and Conflict: Toward a General Theory*. Newbury Park, CA: Sage.

Blalock, H.M., Jr. 1991. *Understanding Social Inequality*. Newbury Park, CA: Sage.

Blumberg, Rae Lesser 1984. "A general theory of gender stratification." In R. Collins (ed.), *Sociological Theory 1984*, pp. 23–101. San Francisco: Jossey-Bass.

Carchedi, Guglielmo 1977. *On the Economic Identification of Social Classes*. London: Routledge.

Carchedi, Guglielmo 1987. *Class Analysis and Social Research*. Oxford and New York: Basil Blackwell.

Chafetz, Janet Saltzman 1990. *Gender Equity: An Integrated Theory of Stability and Change*. Newbury Park, CA: Sage.

Chafetz, Janet Saltzman 1997. "Feminist theory and sociology: Underutilized contributions for mainstream theory." *Annual Review of Sociology* 23:97–191.

Clark, Terry Nichols, and Seymour Martin Lipset 1991. "Are social classes dying?" *International Sociology* 6:397–410.

Clark, Terry Nichols, Seymour Martin Lipset, and Michael Rempel 1993. "The declining political significance of class." *International Sociology* 8:293–316.

Clement, Wallace 1982. "Corporations, power, and class." In D. Forcese and S. Richer (eds.), *Social Issues: Sociological Views of Canada*, pp. 469–485. Scarborough, ON: Prentice-Hall Canada.

Collins, Randall 1979. *The Credential Society*. New York: Academic Press.

Collins, Randall 1988. *Theoretical Sociology*. San Diego, CA: Harcourt Brace Jovanovich.

Connell, R.W. 1987. *Gender and Power: Society, the Person and Sexual Politics*. Cambridge, UK: Polity Press.

Faris, Robert E. L. 1972. "The middle class from a sociological viewpoint." In G. Thielbar and S. Feldman (eds.), *Issues in Social Inequality*, pp. 26–32. Boston: Little, Brown and Company.

Giddens, Anthony 1973. *The Class Structure of the Advanced Societies*. London: Hutchinson.

Giddens, Anthony 1979. *Central Problems in Social Theory*. Berkeley, CA: University of California Press.

Giddens, Anthony 1981a. "Postscript (1979)." In *The Class Structure of the Advanced Societies,* 2nd ed., pp. 295–320. London: Hutchinson.

Giddens, Anthony 1981b. *A Contemporary Critique of Historical Materialism. Vol. 1: Power, Property, and the State*. London: Macmillan.

Giddens, Anthony 1984. *The Constitution of Society*. Berkeley and Los Angeles: University of California Press.

Giddens, Anthony 1985. *A Contemporary Critique of Historical Materialism. Vol. 2: The Nation-State and Violence*. Berkeley and Los Angeles: University of California Press.

Giddens, Anthony 1989. "A reply to my critics." In D. Held and J. Thompson (eds.), *Social Theory of Modern Societies*, pp. 249–301. Cambridge, UK: Cambridge University Press.

Giddens, Anthony 1994. *Beyond Left and Right: The Future of Radical Politics*. Stanford, CA: Stanford University Press.

Giddens, Anthony 1998. *The Third Way: The Renewal of Social Democracy*. Cambridge, UK: Polity Press.

Giddens, Anthony 2000. *The Third Way and Its Critics*. Cambridge, UK: Polity Press.

Giddens, Anthony, and Patrick Diamond (eds.) 2005. *The New Egalitarianism*. Cambridge, UK: Polity Press.

Grabb, Edward G. 2007. *Theories of Social Inequality*, 5th ed. Toronto: Thomson Nelson.

Huber, Joan, and Glenna Spitze 1983. *Sex Stratification: Children, Housework, and Jobs*. New York: Academic Press.

Johnson, Harry M. 1960. *Sociology: A Systematic Introduction*. New York: Harcourt, Brace and World.

Li, Peter S. 1988. *Ethnic Inequality in a Class Society*. Toronto: Wall and Thompson.

Lukes, Steven 1974. *Power: A Radical View*. London: Macmillan.

Mackie, Marlene 1991. *Gender Relations in Canada*. Toronto: Butterworths.

Mann, Michael 1986. *The Sources of Social Power, Vol. 1*. Cambridge, UK: Cambridge University Press.

Mann, Michael 1993. *The Sources of Social Power, Vol. 2*. Cambridge, UK: Cambridge University Press.

Marchak, M. Patricia 1988. *Ideological Perspectives on Canada*. Toronto: McGraw-Hill Ryerson.

Marx, Karl 1862. *Theories of Surplus Value, Vol. 2*. Moscow: Progress Publishers.

Marx, Karl 1867. *Capital, Vol. 1*. New York: International Publishers.

Marx, Karl 1894. *Capital, Vol. 3*. New York: International Publishers.

Marx, Karl, and Friedrich Engels 1848a. *The Communist Manifesto*. New York: Washington Square Press.

Marx, Karl, and Friedrich Engels 1848b. *The Communist Manifesto* (German version). In *Marx Engels Werke, Vol. 4*. Institut fur Marxismus-Leninismus Beim Zk Der Sed. Berlin: Dietz Verlag.

Milkman, Ruth 1987. *Gender at Work*. Urbana and Chicago: University of Illinois Press.

Nisbet, Robert A. 1959. "The decline and fall of social class." *Pacific Sociological Review* 2:11–17.

Parkin, Frank 1979. *Marxism and Class Theory: A Bourgeois Critique*. London: Tavistock.

Parsons, Talcott 1940. "An analytical approach to the theory of social stratification." In T. Parsons, *Essays in Sociological Theory*, pp. 69–88. New York: The Free Press.

Parsons, Talcott 1951. *The Social System*. New York: The Free Press.

Parsons, Talcott 1953. "A revised analytical approach to the theory of social stratification." In T. Parsons, *Essays in Sociological Theory*, pp. 386–439. New York: The Free Press.

Porter, John 1965. *The Vertical Mosaic: An Analysis of Social Class and Power in Canada*. Toronto: University of Toronto Press.

Poulantzas, Nicos 1975. *Classes in Contemporary Capitalism*. London: New Left Books.

Poulantzas, Nicos 1978. *State, Power, Socialism*. London: New Left Books.

Runciman, W.G. 1989. *A Treatise on Social Theory. Vol. 2: Substantive Social Theory*. Cambridge, UK: Cambridge University Press.

Scott, John 1996. *Stratification and Power*. Cambridge, UK: Polity Press.

Tilly, Charles 1998. *Durable Inequality*. Berkeley, CA: University of California Press.

Walby, Sylvia 1990. *Theorizing Patriarchy*. Oxford: Basil Blackwell.

Walby, Sylvia 1997. *Gender Transformations*. London: Routledge.

Weber, Max 1922. *Economy and Society, Vols. 1–3*. New York: Bedminster Press.

Wilson, William Julius 1973. *Power, Racism, and Privilege*. New York: Macmillan.

Wright, Erik Olin 1978. *Class, Crisis, and the State*. London: New Left Books.

Wright, Erik Olin 1979. *Class Structure and Income Determination*. New York: Academic Press.

Wright, Erik Olin 1980. "Class and occupation." *Theory and Society* 9:177–214.

Wright, Erik Olin 1985. *Classes*. London: Verso.

Wright, Erik Olin 1989. *The Debate on Classes*. London: Verso.

Wright, Erik Olin 1994. *Interrogating Inequality: Essays on Class Analysis, Socialism, and Marxism*. London: Verso.

Wright, Erik Olin 1997. *Class Counts: Comparative Studies in Class Analysis*. Cambridge, UK: Cambridge University Press.

Wright, Erik Olin (ed.) 2005. *Approaches to Class Analysis*. Cambridge, UK: Cambridge University Press.

Wright, Erik Olin, Andrew Levine, and Elliott Sober 1992. *Reconstructing Marxism*. London: Verso.

Wright, Erik Olin, and Bill Martin 1987. "The transformation of the American class structure, 1960–1980." *American Journal of Sociology* 93:1–29.

Wrong, Dennis 1979. *Power: Its Forms, Bases and Uses*. New York: Harper and Row.

Power and Class

We begin our look at social inequality in Canada with a series of papers dealing with the interplay of power and class structure in our society. This is a logical starting point because, as was discussed in the General Introduction, the concepts of class and power are pivotal to any general understanding of social inequality. In this section, we are especially interested in the power that derives from ownership and control of productive property and resources, and the nature of the class structure that is defined by such power. Some of the selections also explore the connections between economic classes and the state, most notably the roles that government activities and policies play in shaping the pattern of both ownership and class inequality in Canada.

In capitalist countries like Canada, and perhaps in all societies, ownership of property is arguably the key defining criterion for those who wish to understand the nature of material inequality and the emergence of economic classes. But what is really meant by the notion of property ownership in this context? Most theorists agree that property does not refer to the simple possession of material resources that are used only for personal consumption, such as food, clothing, shelter, and the like. This is not to say that the distribution of these and other consumer items is unimportant to the study of inequality, nor is it to deny the tremendous significance of such items for those who experience a shortage or abundance of them in their daily lives. Rather, it is to recognize that the possession of material benefits or products is not only, or even primarily, what constitutes property ownership. Ownership of property, in its most crucial sense, entails the *right of disposition over the economic process in general*.

The essence of property ownership is having the capacity to command the various activities and organizational processes that are involved in producing, accumulating, investing, or expending society's material or economic resources. Ultimately, it is from this capacity that decisions are made about the distribution of economic benefits to people, and it is through this capacity that some groups and individuals can exclude others from economic control or influence. Perhaps the most important outcome of this process is that the class of people who own society's productive property is in a position to establish relations of domination and exploitation over the class of non-owners, who in turn must sell their labour in order to survive. The non-owners, or working class, may resist this pattern of relationships through political organization, unionization, and other forms of collective action. However, as both classical and contemporary social theorists have often pointed out, the owning class is typically able to override or limit the success of such opposition, given the rights of this class to private productive property and the protection of these rights by the state or government.

The first chapter in this section, by Edward Grabb and Monica Hwang, assesses evidence on the concentration of economic power in Canada, in order to answer three related questions: Has the share of Canada's economy that is controlled by private-sector corporations increased in recent decades?; what part do foreign-controlled companies play in Canada's ownership structure?; and how does the state's power and influence compare with that of private business interests when it comes to owning and directing the contemporary Canadian economy?

The second paper in this section, by William Carroll, offers an extensive assessment of several issues relating to the concentration of economic ownership in Canada and the nature of the Canadian capitalist class. He also links this discussion to the increasingly crucial problem of understanding the global capitalist economy and the role of Canada's corporate leaders and large-scale businesses within this broader international context. For many observers, the high concentration of economic control in relatively few hands is a potentially serious problem. The main concern is that far too much power has been

wielded historically by the owners of productive property. Any further centralization of ownership, both within Canada and internationally, enhances the likelihood that such power could be abused, with the rest of the population facing increased exploitation and domination by the owning class.

In the third article, James Conley considers the processes and forces that have been involved in the formation of the Canadian working class. Beginning with Marx's and Weber's classical approaches to understanding capitalist class structures, Conley then focuses on a review of Canadian evidence relating to a number of key topics. These include the alleged tendency for increased class polarization in modern capitalism, the changing organization of the workplace and its possible effects on working-class solidarity, the likelihood of increasing class awareness or class consciousness within the working class, and the prospects for mobilization, formal organization, and collective action among workers in Canada today.

The final chapter in this section, by Robert Brym, looks at power and class primarily from the point of view of the working class, especially the struggles over power that give rise to workers' strikes. Brym finds that, in contrast to the pattern in earlier times, the strike has not been a particularly effective mechanism for improving the situation of workers relative to the capitalist owning class. He suggests that this change, which has been in place since the mid 1970s, reflects a major redistribution of power away from workers and in favour of employers.

The overall message conveyed by this section of the book is that ownership of productive property or resources, especially through the mechanism of giant private-sector business enterprises, is perhaps the most fundamental force generating the overall pattern of social inequality, both in Canada and in the larger global arena. Moreover, the available evidence suggests that this will continue to be true for some time in the future.

chapter one

Corporate Concentration, Foreign Ownership, and State Involvement in the Canadian Economy

Edward Grabb and Monica Hwang
(An original chapter written
for this volume.)

INTRODUCTION

One of the central issues to consider when assessing the structure of economic power in Canada is the part played by those who own or control large-scale business enterprises. Although researchers addressed this question in the early part of the twentieth century (e.g., Myers 1914; Creighton 1937), it was John Porter's extensive analyses in the 1950s and 1960s that provided the first detailed evidence on the high concentration of economic ownership and control in this country (Porter 1956, 1957, 1965). One of Porter's main conclusions was that fewer than 200 large corporations, controlled by governing boards comprising roughly 1000 individual directors, dominated much of Canada's economic power structure at that time.

Porter's findings set the stage for subsequent attempts to understand Canadian patterns of ownership and control. The next major body of research was Wallace Clement's analysis of Canada's "corporate elite" (Clement 1975, 1977a, 1977b), which suggested that, by the 1970s, economic control in Canada was probably even more concentrated than in the period Porter considered. Clement found that only 113 powerful companies, under the control of approximately 1000 directors, accounted for the majority of business activity.

In recent decades, William Carroll has conducted a series of studies suggesting that economic power is even more concentrated than previous research indicates.

Carroll's research shows that, by the late 1990s, the Canadian corporate elite or "dominant stratum" included only 426 people; these individuals sit as directors on the boards of multiple companies and together generate the entire interlocking system of enterprises at the top of Canada's corporate structure (Carroll 2004:17; see also Carroll 1982, 1984, 1986; Carroll, Fox, and Ornstein 1982; Carroll and Alexander 1999).

Other academics, commentators, and journalists have also contributed to what is now a sizable body of literature on the workings of the Canadian economy (e.g., Newman 1979, 1981; Marchak 1979; Niosi 1981; Ornstein 1976; Brym 1985; Antoniou and Rowley 1986; Francis 1986; Veltmeyer 1987; Laxer 1989; Fox and Ornstein 1986; Grabb 1990; O'Connor 1999; Brownlee 2005). Virtually all of this research suggests that the concentration of economic power continues to be very high, with a small group of powerful, often interconnected, and mainly private-sector corporations at the centre of Canada's ownership structure.

In the past, many of these powerful companies were owned or effectively controlled by a small number of people. For much of our history, in fact, a few prominent and long-established families formed a major component of Canada's economic elite (see Newman 1979; Antoniou and Rowley 1986; Francis 1986). In the past, these included such well-known names as the Eatons, the Molsons, the Westons, the Irvings, and the McCains. These have since been joined or replaced by the Stronachs, the Rogers, the Aspers, and others. Another component of our economic elite includes individual entrepreneurs who, through what are commonly called "conglomerates" or "holding companies," control interrelated sets of large and often quite diverse businesses. A good illustration is Paul Desmarais who, through Power Corporation, has maintained interests over the years in such areas as financial services,

life insurance, steamship lines, newspapers, communications, oil and gas, and forestry. As the principal investors and shareholders in many of Canada's biggest businesses, these families and individual business leaders have tended to enjoy an inordinate amount of influence in determining the general nature and overall direction of our economy.

Apart from private-sector companies and their owners, most writers have identified two other principal components that are believed to be integral to Canada's economic power structure. The first of these is foreign-owned private businesses, which have played a significant part in our economy for some time but became especially prominent during the latter half of the twentieth century. The degree to which our economy has been controlled by such outside interests has occupied the attention of researchers and observers over the years (e.g., Levitt 1970; Clement 1977a; Laxer 1989). The ways in which foreign ownership links the Canadian economy to the larger global capitalist system is an increasingly central element in this discussion (Carroll 2004; see also Chapter 3 in this volume).

The final key factor to consider when assessing who controls or directs the Canadian economy is the role of the government or state. Especially since the 1970s, contemporary social scientists in various countries have shown a sustained interest in the amount of state involvement in economic activity (e.g., Miliband 1973; Poulantzas 1978; Wright 1978; Offe 1984). In Canada, as well, observers have debated the extent of state intervention in business activity and its implications for shaping our system of economic power (e.g., Panitch 1977; Calvert 1984; Banting 1986; Fox and Ornstein 1986; Carroll 2004).

The goal of this chapter is to build on previous research and analysis on these topics by assessing the pattern of ownership and economic control in Canada, with a particular focus on the 1990s and 2000s. We are primarily concerned with three related questions. First, what does the available evidence tell us about ownership concentration in recent decades, especially in regard to the role of Canada's large-scale private-sector businesses and corporations? Second, what part do foreign or non-Canadian companies play in our economy, and has the level of involvement by foreign-controlled corporations changed? Finally, how does the level of ownership by major private-sector companies compare with that of state-controlled agencies or enterprises? The answers to these questions will provide a clearer picture of the nature of economic power and ownership concentration in Canada in the contemporary period.

ANALYSIS

Concentration of Corporate Ownership

Our first concern is to assess the current level of economic concentration among privately owned corporate enterprises. Research has shown that there was a high degree of economic centralization in Canada in the past. For example, one study reported that, although some 400 000 companies were operating in Canada in 1987, the largest 25 enterprises by themselves accounted for more than 41% of all corporate assets in that year (O'Connor 1999:36). Previous research also indicated that the level of ownership concentration was significantly greater in the mid 1980s than it had been just 10 years before (e.g., Francis 1986:3; Grabb 1990:77).

More recent evidence suggests some changes in the structure of corporate ownership. First, a number of the established family "dynasties," including the Eatons, the Reichmanns, and the Bronfmans, have experienced the loss or sale of some of

their corporate holdings and some reduction in their overall influence (see Francis 1997:38; Associated Press 2000, 2002). Nevertheless, other family-based enterprises continue to be very important. For example, the Westons, who are best known for their vast food empire; the Stronach family, whose Magna International is a major force in vehicle parts manufacturing; and the Bombardier family, who have long been leaders in the manufacture of trains, recreational vehicles, and other transportation equipment, continued to control three of the top 20 corporations operating in Canada as of 2005, and were still among the major decision makers on the Canadian economic scene (*Financial Post* 2006:64). Some influential entrepreneurs have also continued to thrive and expand. A prime example is Paul Desmarais, who is the majority owner of Power Corporation. As mentioned earlier, this company is a large conglomerate with investments in a number of business endeavours. It has consistently ranked among the top 15 or 20 companies in Canada over the years (see, e.g., *Financial Post* 1985, 1995, 2006).

It may not be surprising, then, that government statistics and other evidence suggest a sustained pattern of high economic concentration. Between 1987 and 1998, the share of Canada's corporate assets controlled by the largest 25 enterprises continued to represent more than 40% of the national total (Statistics Canada 1995:50; 1998:38–40). It has also been reported that, by the year 2000, large companies (those with assets above $25 million) accounted for almost 80% of all business assets held in Canada (Statistics Canada 2001:37, 44; see Carroll 2004:201; Brownlee 2005:31–32). These figures suggest exceptionally high levels of ownership concentration and are also consistent with the increase in mergers and acquisitions involving major companies. Corporate takeovers in Canada have occurred at an unprecedented rate in recent times. In 1997, there were 1274 mergers and acquisitions involving more than $100 billion of assets (Greenwood 1998). In 2000, the asset value of corporate takeovers was more than double the 1997 figure (Arab 2000). Although there was a brief decline in merger "fever" beginning in 2001 (Canadian Press 2001), activity has since risen to record levels. In 2006, 1968 mergers and acquisitions occurred, representing $257 billion in assets (Alexander 2007). These figures almost certainly signal an even higher degree of ownership concentration in the present day compared with previous years.

Ownership concentration is apparent throughout most of the economy, but one area that has always stood out is the financial sector. Only a handful of banks, trust companies, and insurance firms have long predominated (e.g., Francis 1986:242). Recent mergers and acquisitions in the financial sector have only added to this centralization. Prominent examples include the 1997 purchase of National Trust Company by the Bank of Nova Scotia, the 1997 takeover of London Life Insurance by Great West Life Assurance (which in turn is controlled by Power Corporation), the 2000 takeover of Canada Trust by the Toronto-Dominion Bank, and the 2002 acquisition of Clarica Life Insurance by Sun Life Insurance (Statistics Canada 2000:25; Newman 1997:54; Ferguson 2000; Arab 2002). The evidence of ownership concentration in the financial sector is truly striking. Data from Statistics Canada indicate that financial and insurance industries in Canada owned assets worth $2.214 trillion in 2005 (Statistics Canada 2007a). The *Financial Post* (2006:64) reported that $1.727 trillion of these assets, or more than 78% of the total for 2005, were held by the five largest Canadian banks alone: Royal Bank, Canadian Imperial Bank of Commerce, Toronto-Dominion Bank, Bank of Nova Scotia, and Bank of Montreal.

Despite concerns about the high level of concentration in Canada's financial sector, some government officials have recently spoken in favour of even more mergers and centralization, so as to make Canadian banks large enough to compete for business in the global economy (Friend 2006).

The mass media represent another area of the economy that has seen high levels of ownership concentration. A good illustration is provided by the Asper family, who own CanWest Global and other media enterprises. As of 2002, the Aspers by themselves controlled 60% of Canada's newspapers and television outlets (Worthington 2002; Canadian Press 2002). Another example is Thomson Company, which as of 2007 held interests in such well-known media outlets as CTV Broadcasting, CHUM Broadcasting, and *The Globe and Mail*. There is also considerable centralization in the related field of telecommunications, with BCE (Bell), Telus, and Rogers accounting for the vast majority of economic activity in this area.

Concentration has also been high in resource industries. For example, Silverberg found that the top five forestry companies in Canada, which in 1972 controlled 26% of that industry, had raised their ownership share to 43% by the year 2000. He also showed that the largest five mining companies increased their assets substantially, from 49% to 72% of the total, during this same period (Silverberg 2001:152, 191). A number of major mining mergers in recent years, several of them involving foreign takeovers, have only added to the level of concentration in this industry (Olive 2007).

Changes in Foreign Economic Influence

From Canada's beginnings as a colony, first of France and then of England, our economy has been marked by a considerable amount of foreign control and influence.

While Canada in the modern era has evolved into one of the most prosperous and industrialized nations in the world, we still experience a relatively high level of foreign involvement in the economy, at least in comparison with other developed countries. For example, the United Nations Conference on Trade and Development reported that, in 2005, foreign direct investment in Canada represented about 32% of the nation's Gross Domestic Product. This figure is comparable to that of the European Union (34%) but is higher than the average of 21% for the world's developed economies as a whole (United Nations 2006).

Much of the early research on foreign ownership in Canada focused on the influx of American-based transnational corporations during the twentieth century (e.g., Levitt 1970; Clement 1975, 1977a; Laxer 1989). Evidence indicates that this American involvement developed in a series of stages, but became especially important during a period of about 25 years after the Second World War. Between 1970 and the mid 1980s, however, Canada witnessed a decline in the general level of American and other foreign ownership (Niosi 1981:31–33; Grabb 1990:78).

More recent evidence shows that, although foreign involvement is still a prominent feature of the Canadian economy, the level of influence has continued to decline. For example, foreign companies accounted for 34% of the assets of all companies operating in Canada in 1970. This proportion had dropped to about 26% by 2000, and to just 21% by 2005 (Statistics Canada 2005, 2007a). It is also notable that Canadian companies themselves have a more significant role as investors in other countries than was true in the past. In the period 2003 to 2005, for example, the dollar value of Canadian investments outside Canada surpassed the value of investments made by foreign enterprises within Canada

(United Nations 2006). On the other hand, since 2005 a spate of large-scale acquisitions of Canadian firms by outside interests has occurred, suggesting that a new round of foreign takeovers is in process. These developments, which have involved many countries from around the globe, are especially evident in the mining sector. For example, companies such as Alcan, Inco, and Falconbridge have been purchased by foreign investors from Britain, Australia, Brazil, and Switzerland (Olive 2007; Canadian Press 2007). Some observers suggest that these signs of a renewed increase in foreign ownership in Canada could put our economic sovereignty at risk, while others see foreign involvement, both in Canada and elsewhere, as a natural consequence of the global expansion of the capitalist economy in the current era (for discussion, see Carroll 2004; Brownlee 2005; also Erman 2006; Olive 2007).

Over the years, some of the strongest evidence of foreign control in our economy could be found at the very top of the non-financial sector, where a few major non-Canadian corporations tended to predominate. In the mid 1980s, for example, 6 of the top 10 companies operating in Canada were foreign owned. These included the Canadian subsidiaries of the three American automotive giants (General Motors of Canada, Ford of Canada, and Chrysler Canada), as well as two American-owned oil subsidiaries (Imperial Oil and Texaco Canada) and one Dutch-controlled oil company (Shell Canada) (*Financial Post* 1985). By 2005, there was evidence of a reduced foreign presence among the very largest businesses, with only 3 non-Canadian companies among the top 10. These were General Motors of Canada, Daimler Chrysler Canada, and Imperial Oil (*Financial Post* 2006:68).

Despite this decline in foreign enterprises in the top 10 in recent years, the influence of foreign companies continues to be substantial. For example, as of 2005, 23 of the leading 100 companies in Canada were wholly owned or majority owned by non-Canadians. Moreover, if only non-financial companies are considered, this number rises to 28 out of the top 100 (*Financial Post* 2006:68–71). Of the top 50 foreign-controlled companies doing business in Canada in 2005, 33 were American, with 9 based in Europe, 5 in Japan, and 1 each in Brazil, the Bahamas, and China (*Financial Post* 2006:121). The predominant American role in the foreign sector of the economy is also confirmed by recent government statistics, which show that companies based in the United States accounted for 59% of the total assets and 63% of the total operating revenues for foreign companies in Canada in 2005 (Statistics Canada 2007b:Table 24). These proportions are down somewhat from previous years but still indicate a substantial American influence. Companies from European nations accounted for another 31% of the foreign-controlled assets and 24% of foreign-controlled revenues in 2005, and both of these figures are higher than in previous years (see Statistics Canada 2007b:Table 24).

The State and Economic Power

The next question to address is the role of Canada's various levels of government in the contemporary Canadian economy. Historically, business activities have often been influenced by state involvement, although sometimes in contradictory ways. At certain times, for example, governments have lent money to Canadian capitalists and imposed tariffs or other trade restrictions on foreign competitors in order to promote and protect Canadian companies. At other times, however, governments have offered tax reductions and other incentives to encourage foreign business ventures in

Canada, and have also established state-run enterprises that compete directly with Canada's private-sector firms (Clement 1975, 1977b; Traves 1979; Marchak 1979; Laxer 1989).

Some of the discussion on the role of the Canadian state has centred on whether government intervention in the economy has become excessive in recent decades. Certain researchers question this claim, and suggest that the state's role in the Canadian economy is actually rather small. These analysts usually acknowledge that the state spends a considerable portion of the national wealth, with governments covering the costs of providing and maintaining public education, health care, a wide range of social services, transportation facilities, and the like. However, most of these writers also contend that, otherwise, the state has normally been a limited player in the Canadian economy, with private business interests still acting as the pre-eminent force (e.g., Calvert 1984; Fox and Ornstein 1986; Brym 1989; O'Connor 1999). It is argued, as well, that a good deal of government activity has been directed toward assisting private-sector businesses, especially in their attempts to be more competitive in the global capitalist economy (Carroll 2004:45–46).

Other observers, however, have alleged that the various branches of the state have become too influential within our economic system. These writers argue that governments at all levels have too often used their considerable taxation and spending powers to fund a number of poorly conceived endeavours, including expensive, loosely administered social programs and unprofitable, inefficient government enterprises (see, e.g., Horry et al. 1992; Francis 1995:13; Walker 1997). Similar views appear to be found among many private-sector capitalists, who view the government as an intruding competitor in the business arena (Ornstein 1985, 1999).

Added to these perceptions is the belief that state-owned companies usually have an unfair advantage over private businesses, which need to turn a profit to survive and cannot rely on government financial assistance to bail them out of difficulty.

One direct means for measuring state economic power is to determine the proportion of major enterprises that are government controlled. Previous research found that, in both 1975 and 1985, only 4 of the top 25 non-financial corporations operating in Canada were state owned, and less than 10 of the top 100 (Grabb 1990:79). More recent business rankings suggest an even smaller government presence at the highest level. For example, in 2005, there were no government-directed enterprises among the leading 25 companies, and just 8 in the top 100 enterprises. These included two utilities—Hydro-Québec and British Columbia Hydro and Power Authority—three financial services organizations—Canadian Mortgage and Housing Corporation, Caisse de dépôt et placement du Québec, and Insurance Corporation of British Columbia—as well as Canada Post, the Ontario Lottery Corporation, and the Canadian Wheat Board (*Financial Post* 2006:64–66; see also Carroll 2004:51–52). On this basis, it is difficult to argue that government enterprises dominate the Canadian economy.

Perhaps a more comprehensive gauge of government economic influence is the share of the nation's total assets held by the various branches of the state. One earlier study, using government data on the "national balance sheet," estimated that the share of total assets in Canada owned by the government or public sector stood at 18.0% in 1961, and declined to just 10.6% by 2001 (Grabb 2004:26). More recent data indicate that, by 2005, the asset value of government businesses and enterprises represented only 6.9% of total corporate assets held within Canada (Statistics Canada 2007b). Such findings reveal that government economic control in Canada is not nearly as great as some observers have argued, is far lower than that enjoyed by the private business sector, and has been declining for a number of years.

Although numerous factors probably account for declining state involvement, a major cause has been the changing policies of the federal government and many provincial administrations in recent years. In particular, state leaders have been increasingly motivated to encourage private-sector economic expansion and also to sell off various government-run enterprises to private interests. This pattern began in the mid 1980s, around the time of the election of the federal Progressive Conservatives under Brian Mulroney. However, despite suggestions to the contrary prior to their election in 1993, the federal Liberals, led by Jean Chrétien, adopted much the same set of policies and followed them to the early 2000s. The current government of Stephen Harper appears to be following the same course.

SUMMARY AND CONCLUSION

Our review of recent evidence of economic control and ownership in Canada has revealed that many of the same patterns of ownership that existed in previous decades are still in place. That is, we have found a relatively high concentration of economic power in a small group of giant private-sector corporations operating at the top of the ownership structure. Moreover, the recent and unprecedented evidence of mergers and acquisitions involving major corporations suggests that this high level of concentration is likely to continue, or even increase, in the future. It seems clear that large-scale financial and non-financial business enterprises, along with the principal shareholders and directors that control them, are as powerful as they have ever been in the Canadian economy.

We have also considered the level of foreign involvement in Canada's ownership structure. In this case, we determined that non-Canadian businesses play a substantial role in the economy, though somewhat less so than they did in the peak years of foreign activity around 1970. Even so, many of the most powerful and profitable enterprises currently operating on the Canadian scene still show a notable foreign presence, with close to a quarter of the top 100 companies owned by non-Canadian, mostly American, transnational corporations.

The final major issue we addressed was the degree of state control over Canada's economic affairs. In keeping with earlier research from previous decades, we have seen that the government role, though notable in some respects, is really quite minor in comparison with that played by private corporations. Moreover, the government's presence on the economic scene has declined in the past several decades, both in regard to its role as a director of large-scale business enterprises and in its control over national assets. Now very few of Canada's largest enterprises are government owned, and the proportion of Canadian assets owned by all branches of government is down to less than one-tenth of the total. In addition, during the 1990s and 2000s, we have seen concerted drives by the federal and provincial governments to cut back on services in the interest of eliminating government deficits and reducing the nation's debt. These policies make it evident that there has been some curtailment of state economic activity in the spending area as well. The government strategy for the future clearly appears to be one in which political leaders look primarily to the private sector, and not to state-sponsored programs, to promote economic activity. Overall, the current climate is one in which private-sector businesses continue

to determine the major contours and direction of Canada's economic power structure.

REFERENCES

Alexander, Doug 2007. "Canadian mergers soared to record in 2006, bank says." *Bloomberg News*, February 23.

Antoniou, Andreas, and Robin Rowley 1986. "The ownership structure of the largest Canadian corporations, 1979." *Canadian Journal of Sociology* 11:253–268.

Arab, Paula 2000. "Corporate takeovers reach fever pitch." In the *London Free Press*, October 7:D8.

Arab, Paula 2002. "Sun Life swallows Clarica to become No. 1." In the *London Free Press*, October 7:C3.

Associated Press 2000. "Seagram dead at 76." In the *London Free Press*, June 21:A1, A3.

Associated Press 2002. "Deal allows Vivendi to avoid bankruptcy." In the *London Free Press*, August 20:C6.

Banting, Keith 1986. *The State and Economic Interests.* Toronto: University of Toronto Press.

Brownlee, Jamie 2005. *Ruling Canada: Corporate Cohesion and Democracy.* Halifax: Fernwood Publishing.

Brym, Robert 1985 (ed.). *The Structure of the Canadian Capitalist Class.* Toronto: Garamond.

Brym, Robert 1989. "Canada." In T. Bottomore and R. Brym (eds.), *The Capitalist Class: An International Study*, pp. 177–206. New York: New York University Press.

Calvert, John 1984. *Government, Limited.* Ottawa: Canadian Centre for Policy Alternatives.

Canadian Press 2001. "Corporate takeovers down 39% this year." In the *London Free Press*, April 25:D3.

Canadian Press 2002. "CanWest reduces media assets." In the *London Free Press*, July 11:C6.

Canadian Press 2007. "Alcan deal bittersweet." In the *London Free Press*, July 13:D7.

Carroll, William 1982. "The Canadian corporate elite: Financiers or finance capitalists?" *Studies in Political Economy* 8:89–114.

Carroll, William 1984. "The individual, class, and corporate power in Canada." *Canadian Journal of Sociology* 9:245–268.

Carroll, William 1986. *Corporate Power and Canadian Capitalism.* Vancouver: University of British Columbia Press.

Carroll, William 2004. *Corporate Power in a Globalizing World: A Study in Elite Social Organization.* Don Mills, ON: Oxford University Press.

Carroll, William, and Malcolm Alexander 1999. "Finance capital and capitalist class integration in the 1990s: Networks of interlocking directorships in Canada and Australia." *Canadian Review of Sociology and Anthropology* 36:331–354.

Carroll, William, John Fox, and Michael Ornstein 1982. "The network of directorship links among the largest Canadian firms." *Canadian Review of Sociology and Anthropology* 19:44–69.

Clement, Wallace 1975. *The Canadian Corporate Elite.* Toronto: McClelland and Stewart.

Clement, Wallace 1977a. *Continental Corporate Power.* Toronto: McClelland and Stewart.

Clement, Wallace 1977b. "The corporate elite, the capitalist class, and the Canadian state." In L. Panitch (ed.), *The Canadian State,* pp. 225–248. Toronto: University of Toronto Press.

Creighton, Donald 1937. *The Commercial Empire of the St. Lawrence.* Toronto: Macmillan.

Erman, Boyd 2006. "Hot Canada draws buyers." *The National Post,* March 15:FP1.

Ferguson, Rob 2000. "Ottawa expected to go slow on bank mergers." In the *Toronto Star,* June 4: B4, B5.

Financial Post 1985. *The Financial Post 500,* Summer 1985.

Financial Post 1995. *The Financial Post 500,* Summer 1995.

Financial Post 2006. *The Financial Post Business FP500: Canada's Largest Corporations,* June.

Fox, John, and Michael Ornstein 1986. "The Canadian state and corporate elites in the postwar period." *Canadian Review of Sociology and Anthropology* 23, 4 (November):481–506.

Francis, Diane 1986. *Controlling Interest.* Toronto: Macmillan.

Francis, Diane 1995. "The need for laws to limit spending." *Maclean's,* February 13.

Francis, Diane 1997. "When famous families lose touch." *Maclean's,* March 17.

Friend, David 2006. "Let banks merge, Dodge says." In the *London Free Press,* December 12:D1.

Grabb, Edward 1990. "Who owns Canada? Concentration of ownership and the distribution of economic assets, 1975–1985." *Journal of Canadian Studies* 25:72–93.

Grabb, Edward 2004. "Economic power in Canada." In J. Curtis, N. Guppy, and E. Grabb (eds.), *Social Inequality in Canada: Patterns, Problems, Policies,* 4th ed., pp. 20–30. Toronto: Pearson Education Canada.

Greenwood, John 1998. "Corporate takeovers soar to record." In the *London Free Press,* January 10:D8.

Horry, Isabella, Filip Palda, and Michael Walker 1992. *Tax Facts 8.* Vancouver: The Fraser Institute.

Laxer, Gord 1989. *Open for Business.* Toronto: Oxford University Press.

Levitt, Kari 1970. *Open for Business.* Toronto: Oxford University Press.

Marchak, Patricia 1979. *In Whose Interests? An Essay on Multinational Corporations in a Canadian Context.* Toronto: McClelland and Stewart.

Miliband, Ralph 1973. *The State in Capitalist Society.* London: Quartet Books.

Myers, Gustavus 1914. *A History of Canadian Wealth.* Toronto: James Lewis and Samuel.

Newman, Peter 1979. *The Canadian Establishment.* Toronto: McClelland and Stewart–Bantam.

Newman, Peter 1981. *The Acquisitors.* Toronto: McClelland and Stewart–Bantam.

Newman, Peter 1997. "How Power trumped the Royal Bank." *Maclean's,* September 1.

Niosi, Jorge 1981. *Canadian Capitalism: A Study of Power in the Canadian Business Establishment.* Toronto: Lorimer.

O'Connor, Julia 1999. "Ownership, class, and public policy." In J. Curtis, N. Guppy, and E. Grabb (eds.), *Social Inequality in Canada: Patterns, Problems, Policies,* 3rd ed., pp. 35–47. Scarborough, ON: Prentice-Hall Allyn Bacon Canada.

Offe, Claus 1984. *Contradictions in the Welfare State.* Cambridge, MA.: MIT Press.

Olive, David 2007. "Another big bite out of Canada?" *The Toronto Star,* May 8:A1, A8.

Ornstein, Michael 1976. "The boards and executives of the largest Canadian corporations:

size, composition, and interlocks." *Canadian Journal of Sociology* 1:411–437.

Ornstein, Michael 1985. "Canadian capital and the Canadian state: Ideology in an era of crisis." In R. Brym (ed.), *The Structure of the Canadian Capitalist Class,* pp. 129–166. Toronto: Garamond.

Ornstein, Michael 1999. *Politics and Ideology in Canada.* Montreal and Kingston: McGill-Queen's University Press.

Panitch, Leo (ed.) 1977. *The Canadian State.* Toronto: University of Toronto Press.

Porter, John 1956. "Concentration of economic power and the economic elite in Canada." *Canadian Journal of Economics and Political Science* 22:199–220.

Porter, John 1957. "The economic elite and the social structure of Canada." *Canadian Journal of Economics and Political Science* 23:377–394.

Porter, John 1965. *The Vertical Mosaic.* Toronto: University of Toronto Press.

Poulantzas, Nicos 1978. *State, Power, Socialism.* London: New Left Books.

Silverberg, Shane 2001. "Concentration of ownership in Canada's resource industries: Historical and recent trends in mining, petroleum, and forestry." Unpublished master's thesis, University of Western Ontario.

Statistics Canada 1995. *Corporations and Labour Unions Returns Act. Preliminary 1993.* Catalogue 61–220.

Statistics Canada 1998. *Corporations and Labour Unions Returns Act. Preliminary 1998.* Catalogue 61–220.

Statistics Canada 2000. *Inter-Corporate Ownership 2000.* Catalogue 61–517.

Statistics Canada 2001. *Canada's International Investment Position, 2000.* Catalogue 67–202.

Statistics Canada 2005. "Study: Trends in foreign investment and foreign control." *The Daily,* November 18.

Statistics Canada 2007a. "Foreign control in the Canadian economy." *The Daily,* June 14.

Statistics Canada 2007b. *Corporations Returns Act 2005.* Catalogue no. 61-220-XWE.

Traves, Tom 1979. *The State and Enterprise: Canadian Manufacturers and the Federal Government, 1917–1931.* Toronto: University of Toronto Press.

United Nations 2006. *The World Investment Report 2006.*

Veltmeyer, Henry 1987. *Canadian Corporate Power.* Toronto: Garamond.

Walker, Michael 1997. "The law of diminishing returns applies to government." In the *London Free Press,* January 2:B7.

Worthington, Peter 2002. "Asper chain redefines 'loopy.'" In the *London Free Press,* March 16:F5.

Wright, Erik Olin 1978. *Class, Crisis, and the State.* London: New Left Books.

Corporate Canada, Globalization, and Neoliberal Democracy

William Carroll

(Abridged from William Carroll 2004.
"Corporate power and neoliberal
democracy." In William Carroll,
*Corporate Power in a Globalizing
World: A Study of Elite Social
Organizations*, pp. 200–218.
Don Mills, ON: Oxford University Press.
Reprinted with permission.)

In the last quarter of the twentieth century, Canada's corporate elite underwent a number of significant changes—some of them closely associated with recent globalization and its political handmaiden, neoliberalism, and all of them at least conditioned by those worldwide developments. Yet in some ways the scene remained familar.

Corporate power is Janus-faced. It is ultimately rooted in the economic relations of advanced capitalism—the organization of life around a system of commodity production and exchange in which giant corporations and massive pools of money capital concentrate enormous social power in the control of the capitalist class's top tier, placing workers, communities, and states in a relation of unilateral dependence.

But the exercise of corporate power is not simply a matter of commanding the heights of industry and finance. Its other face, no less important for elite organization and less fateful for capitalist democracies, is cultural and political. In a way of life deeply marked by class inequality, by the juxtaposition of Rosedale and Regent Park, by the presence of homeless people living on the street within blocks of the First Canadian Place, the corporate elite must struggle to maintain hegemony. The consent of subordinates can never be taken for granted, and although much of the work of organizing that consent might be delegated to intellectuals of various stripes—in the media, policy planning, public relations, academe, etc.—the corporate elite, that small group at the apex of the dominant class, must exercise active leadership. This is not to say that the corporate elite, or the dominant class, "controls" the political process and its outcomes. Fred Block's (1977) famous claim that "the ruling class does not rule" is still entirely apposite, even after three decades of a neoliberal globalization that has diminished the relative autonomy of national states, which Block took for granted as he wrote in the closing days of the Keynesian class compromise.

Even if "the ruling class does not rule," business leadership *does reach* into civil society and into the institutions of the state, recruiting support for a world view within which the interest of capital in profitable accumulation becomes universalized as the general interest of society, or even humanity. To reach effectively, to be a leading cultural and political force, the corporate elite must achieve and maintain a certain social cohesiveness as a business community—an internal basis of solidarity, with a shared perspective on what is to be done.

CONCENTRATION OF ECONOMIC POWER

To begin with the obvious, large, increasingly globalized corporations concentrate enormous economic power in the hands of those controlling the business strategies of dominant firms. There are approximately 1 million incorporated businesses in Canada, yet the top 25 enterprises account for 41.2% of all business assets. Across all economic sectors, large companies (firms generally with assets greater than $25 million or annual revenue greater than $100 million) claim 79.4% of all business assets (Statistics Canada 2001:37, 44). The sheer concentration of corporate assets is

not a new development, however. In Canada, capital has been highly concentrated, and a small elite of finance capitalists has wielded considerable economic power, ever since the era of the National Policy, under which the state facilitated investment in industrial capacity. Even at the dawn of the post–Second World War era, the largest corporate survival of the National Policy, the Canadian Pacific Railway, towered above all other corporations in the country, accounting in itself for one-tenth of total industrial assets (Carroll 1986:65–6).

What was new in the ensuing half-century was the further *geographical concentration* of corporate head offices into a very few metropolitan command centres. Of course, even half a century ago Montreal and Toronto were the cities that mattered for the corporate elite (and particularly for the financial sector); yet a good many industrial corporations had their head offices and physical plants outside the Toronto–Montreal axis. As the century closed, the spatial organization of corporate power had been simplified into a bipolar configuration with two major urban centres and two lesser ones in the far west. Although nearby secondary centres hosted a few head offices and thereby figured peripherally in the national network, there was little involvement of outlying areas, and Toronto had decisively eclipsed Montreal as the country's corporate metropolis and terminus for many continental and transnational interlocks. Consistent with a consolidating organized capitalism, this shift in the locus of power meant the *further centralization of strategic control over capital* in the form of large, multidivisional corporations in which plant-specific, operational aspects of management were subordinated to extra-local corporate strategies issuing from metropolitan head offices.

In a globalizing world, the concentration of economic power cuts across national borders. Transnational investment is an important means through which capital becomes concentrated, and the most powerful corporations are transnationals (TNCs) whose multifarious holdings enable them to play one national or regional workforce (or state) off against another. In late twentieth-century Canada, transnationalization bore several meanings. In the financial sector it meant in part the entry of major European companies—though these did not establish elite-level ties to major Canadian companies. In industry the flagging presence of U.S.-based TNCs was accompanied by an increased complement of subsidiaries of Japanese-based TNCs, again with little in the way of elite-level connections. Meanwhile, Canadian-based companies, both industrial and financial, continued their own process of transnationalization, an important aspect of economic concentration. By the closing years of the century, domestically controlled TNCs outnumbered large companies of purely "national" scope and Canadian direct investment abroad outweighed foreign direct investment (FDI) in Canada. At the same time the corporate network became recentred around a core of transnational banks and corporations, controlled by capitalists based in Canada. Although TNCs were central to this loose network, on the boards of transnational banks sat many outside directors of companies whose operations remained sub-transnational. We concluded that "transnational financial capital" has radiated from Canada in a way that has *not* disorganized the national network but has *embedded* it more extensively in a circuitry of global accumulation. Following the Swiss example (Rusterholz 1985), the Canadian network has become recentred around an expanding sector of Canadian-based TNCs, both industrial and financial. In this transition, Canada's business community participated with other nationally-based corporate elites in a global process of capital concentration and centralization. According to Peter Dicken, 1985 marked a major shift in the growth of world FDI to unprecedented levels, as FDI consistently outpaced world GNP. By the mid 1990s the advanced capitalist countries were the source of 92% of world FDI. The same countries were host to three-quarters of all FDI in the world, underlining the fact that most transnational corporate investment takes the form of a cross-penetration of capital among developed national economies (Dicken 1998:42–5).

STRATEGIC CONTROL

Corporate power is not wielded by a monolithic elite. It inheres in specific agents controlling capital concentrations and flows. At the higher reaches of the Canadian economy, family capitalism has not succumbed to the technocratic rationality of the managerial revolution; nor, by the late 1990s, had state capital been very widely privatized into new accumulation vehicles for capitalist investors. Major shareholders—wealthy families—have continued to make up a substantial fraction of the corporate elite, and family control at the "ultimate" level actually increased after 1976 as more capitalist families resorted to intercorporate ownership as a means of control. By 1996 major shareholders were often central players in the network of thick ties knitting together strategically aligned firms. Yet at the same time the presence of institutional investors expanded, so that both a "depersonalization of capital" and a "repersonalization" seemed under way. If in Scott's (1997) view, depersonalization of control is one sign of a transition to "disorganized capitalism," the robustness of family empires suggests that his thesis needs qualification in the case of Canada. The well-known tendency for many Canadian companies to be controlled by other corporations continued through the 1990s, contributing further to the concentration of economic power. Major enterprise groups, organized around inter-corporate ownership, associated capitalists, and thick interlocks, continued to claim space within the corporate network even if the specific companies and controlling agents changed. The larger of these ensembles—the Brascan and Power groups—became increasingly transnationalized, although in rather different ways. But even if major shareholders and institutional investors gained a bigger piece of the action, as U.S.-based TNCs came to play a somewhat smaller role in the control of Canada's largest firms, the growth of credit unions and similar kinds of non-proprietary economic organizations at the margins of corporate power presented alternatives to that power, and member-elected directors of these organizations remained detached from the corporate elite.

Despite neoliberalism's commitment to getting government off the backs of business, the Canadian state has continued to exercise agency in the control of corporate capital, with a slightly lower profile after the privatization of such crown jewels as Air Canada and the CNR. Certain ties between state enterprises and private-sector corporations even strengthened—notably in Quebec, which continued to follow an industrial strategy of sorts. In other cases, elite-level ties between state enterprises and the business community may have facilitated privatization initiatives. Whatever the case, the state has not renounced all agency in the economic field, and in some respects neoliberal programs to commercialize operations such as the post office have increased the state's "presence" among the largest corporations, even if government-controlled firms remain on the whole marginal to the corporate network.

CORPORATE GOVERNANCE REFORM

Governance reforms have had the same two-faced quality as the corporate power they seek to regulate "from within." Arising out of heightened international competition, the frantic search for profit, and the financial crises and scandals that accompany this search, they have sought to pulverize traditional elite practices in the service of a "higher morality" that, above all, portends even fatter financial returns. The reforms' impact on the structure of finance capital was dramatic, as interlocks involving corporate officers (and especially lower-level executives) disappeared from the network. Most significantly, bankers left the boards of industrial corporations and banks slimmed their elephantine directorates. This left a looser network of weak ties, in which the banks continue to figure prominently (particularly in the transnationalized segment) even if their boards are no longer quite the central hubs they once were.

A looser network, carried by outside directors, built more around information ties and business scan than around primary interlocks and patient money, and centred increasingly on transnational corporations, suits this new relation between finance and industry. Finally, the state has figured significantly in this transition. Deregulation has led not only to a more concentrated yet less socially integrated financial sector dominated by universal banks, but to increased involvement of institutional investors in equity markets, augmenting the power of funds within controlling constellations.

VECTORS OF CORPORATE POWER

Capital, as David Harvey (1982) reminds us, never entirely escapes the material actualities it is anchored in. Within Canada, the changing social spatial terrain has seen not only a concentration of corporate head offices in four major urban centres, but also a *westward drift* of corporate power, tracking the flow of capital itself. Notably, Calgary rose from obscurity to become an important command centre for the energy/ petrochemical sector. By the late 1990s, this reconfigured structure of finance capital continued to be centred on the Toronto–Montreal axis, home to most of the major financial institutions and many major industrial corporations, particularly in the high-tech sectors, but in contrast to the 1970s, let alone the 1940s, it now extended to the emerging command centres of Calgary and Vancouver. Still, the western cities remained for the most part industrial outposts. Reflected clearly in the network is the continued financial hegemony of Toronto and Montreal as sites of allocative power, and the vital role of "finance capitalists" whose interlocking directorships stitched together industry and finance, east and west. And while Toronto ascended to the status of a second-tier global city, the Montreal-based segment underwent its own recomposition with the coming-of-age of a Québécois fraction integrated into the national network.

The north–south vector of corporate power is more difficult to characterize. As Stephen Clarkson (2002:214) has observed, "there is no single template that can capture all corporate responses to continentalism." We can safely say that the last quarter of the twentieth century witnessed no blending of Canadian and American corporate elites, at least not via interlocking directorships. Already sparse, "continental connections" grew sparser. Canadian and American corporations are organized in two separate national networks, with very few ties traversing the border. Among the largest corporations, Canada–U.S. interlocks are no more profuse than, say, Canada–Europe interlocks. Moreover, across the two decades fewer firms and fewer directors

participated in continental interlocks. In particular, interlocks reflecting U.S. strategic control of Canadian companies disappeared from the network, in part because of the declining number of large American branch plants and in part because of changes in the structure of transnational management. By the late 1990s the continental network was a sparse collection of cross-border ties—relatively few of which entailed strategic control of capital— carried by perhaps threescore capitalists and corporate advisers. For some of the largest Canadian-based transnationals, such as Nortel, the sort of cross-border interlocking that was in play seemed compatible with the weakly organized financial–industrial relations that have come to prevail with the partial "disorganization" of national economies.

But if continentalism has been in decline at the level of corporate interlocking, in other ways it has been developing apace. Corporations rely increasingly on networked business processes, which Schiller and Mosco (2001:1) identify with the coming of cybercapitalism. The decline of continental directorship ties, particularly those linking American parents to their Canadian subsidiaries, may actually reflect more extensive networking at an operational level, as new communications technologies render the Canadian subsidiary simply one among various subunits within a single economic zone. This interpretation is speculative but other examples of continental integration can easily be cited. Even though they remain domestically controlled, many of Canada's best-known companies are now run by Americans, and many of Canada's top capitalists themselves now have residences in Phoenix and other sunbelt cities (Newman 1998:136, 141). Some Canadian corporations have moved their executive offices to the U.S. and their shares now trade on the NYSE and NASDAQ. Most major Canadian corporations own subsidiaries in the U.S., and between 1976 and 1996 there was a doubling of large Canadian firms with subsidiaries exclusively in Canada and the USA. Indeed, according to Bill Burgess "it is Canadian investors who have been the more aggressive 'continentalizers,'" a state of affairs that hardly suggests a process of "silent surrender." Burgess goes on to note that levels of continental foreign direct investment between the U.S. and Canada are comparable to levels among 14 western European countries. He concludes that Canadian economic integration with the United States is "consistent with the broader pattern of interpenetration of 'core' countries, however unequal in size and power" (2002:205).

The changing perspectives of Canadian corporations with major stakes in the American economy raise the issue of corporate "nationality"—a question made more salient with the advent of North American free trade. As the agreements of 1989 and 1994 took effect, the east–west axis of Canada's home markets was further eroded. In the later 1990s north–south trade flows grew by an estimated 10% to 11% a year while east–west flows expanded by only 3% to 4% annually (Scoffield 1998:B4). What was consolidated in all this was an "attitude change" among Canadian capitalists, a shift toward continental business strategies according to which companies were increasingly focused on north–south trading opportunities, and "restructured their operations to take advantage of big U.S. markets" (Scoffield 1998:B4). Overall, trade—always a key aspect of capital accumulation in Canada—gained importance, rising from 25% of GDP in 1991 to 41% in 1997; and Canada's trade with the U.S. increased from approximately 77% in 1985–87 to 82% in 1996–98 (Du Boff, 2001:43). Thus we find by the late 1990s a Canadian corporate elite whose social organization remained "national" at the level of corporate governance, but whose business strategies were increasingly continental, if not more fully "global." Ironically, the weakening of elite-level continental connections may coincide with and even reflect a deeper form of continentalism: an amalgamation of Canadian and American economies.

In conceptualizing continental relations it is crucial to keep in mind that regionalization is to globalization as a part is to the whole. We have suggested that the Free Trade agreements of 1989 and 1994 have had important implications for the structure of corporate power in North America.[1] But as Schiller and Mosco (2001:3) note, these are not simply regional agreements; they form an integral part of the globalization process. For instance, NAFTA provisions to protect foreign investors, enabling them to sue a government for compensation against regulations that retard their profits, were quickly picked up by the WTO as a new prospective norm for international governance. And, in integrating the North American market, NAFTA has stimulated an enormous inflow of foreign investment, further integrating the world economy. Driven by the complementary interests of American, Canadian, and Mexican corporate capital, "NAFTA is part of, facilitates, and advances globalization—the restructuring of economic and financial capital through international flows of production, trade, investment, and assets" (Du Boff 2001:58).

When we look beyond this continent to the global corporate network, for the most part we again find only sparse and weak ties connecting Canada's corporate elite to the rest of the world. To the close of the twentieth century, transnational interlocking remained no more than a sideline for Canadian corporate capitalists, most of whose network affiliations remained nationally organized. Most of the ties that did embed Canada within the global network reached from other countries into Canada, not vice versa. The loose network we mapped for 1996 did contain one major transnational enterprise group based partly in Canada. The Desmarais-Frère empire—a Euro-Canadian partnership of two fabulously wealthy families—is a unique ensemble stitched together via family shareholdings, intercorporate ownership, and interlocking directorships that span the North Atlantic. Although other major transnational family empires can be cited, Desmarais is the only Canadian finance capitalist controlling a set of world-class corporations in other countries.

Apart from the Desmarais-Frère group, most of the interlocks joining Canadian corporations to the global network involve either the strategic control of Canadian subsidiaries by parents based in Japan or the U.S., or outside directorships that often feature a large financial institution on one side of the relationship, and that terminate in Europe or the U.S. With its interlocks extending primarily to the European and American networks, corporate Canada most closely resembles a middle power within an "American ruling class" (van der Pijl 1984). Canada's corporate elite is positioned in the centre of the global network, even if its status is secondary to the major Euro–North American powers—the U.S., the UK, Germany, and Europe.

As with continental connections, however, directorship interlocks represent only one aspect of global corporate power. There are several "transnational practices" (the term comes from Sklair 1995) that serve to knit the component parts of the world economy together—transnational strategic alliances, intercorporate ownership, collaborative ventures, subcontracting relationships, and so on (Dicken 1998:223–40). Canada's top corporations have been busy enlarging their own transnational reach, and although their foreign branches do not rank among the world's largest corporations, there is a growing network of parent–subsidiary control relations extending from Canada to a wide range of countries. Some heirs to major family fortunes have also internationalized their investments. For instance, Charles Bronfman has invested heavily in Israel in recent years, and now chairs Israel's largest industrial conglomerate (Adams, 2002).

What our mapping of the Canadian corporate elite within the global network reveals is, first, that Canada's corporate network is one of the most integrated. Second, and consistent with Dicken's (1998:193) observation that most transnational corporations remain nationally embedded, Canadian corporate capital has retained a predominantly "national" base even as finance capital has become increasingly transnational in scope. Dense and thick ties tend to knit national corporate networks together, while a sparse set of weak ties links hands across the borders.

However, there are structural forms of globalization that are not evident at the level of corporate elites, and since the early 1970s the elaboration of these forms has been fateful for world capitalism. Among the most important is growth in the volume of stateless, mobile financial capital—foreign-held portfolio investment. By 2000, the total stock of Canadian direct investment abroad had reached $301 billion, slightly more than the total stock of foreign direct investment in Canada ($292 billion). Yet the figures on portfolio investment suggested a different story. The value of foreign bonds held in Canada ($35 billion) was less than one-tenth of the value of Canadian bonds held abroad ($381 billion), mostly in the form of state debt. This contributed to a net international investment deficit of $346 billion (Statistics Canada 2001), placing stateless financial capitalists in a position of allocative power vis-à-vis the Canadian state. This shift in capital structure can be read as having provided somewhat of a practical economic basis for promoting neoliberal policies. The grave images evoked by a succession of finance ministers in the 1980s and 1990s—depicting the state deficit as Public Enemy Number One and warning Canadians of the international humiliation and effective trusteeship they would face if the debt was not brought under control—were the most visible political response to the global capital's enhanced structural power (Workman 1996). The corporate elite played an active role in this political-cultural construction project.

A CULTURE OF ACTIVISM

The corporate elite develops and maintains itself as a "business community" in much the same way that any community does. There will be fractional divisions of interest and perspective over one matter or another, but communicative ties and joint activities continually recreate a collective sense of solidarity. If we consider the period from the 1970s through the 1990s, what is striking is the extent to which the cultural basis for elite solidarity shifted from the sphere of leisure to that of activism.

In the early 1970s, private clubs, mainly in Montreal and Toronto, were the key sites for building class cohesion. Such clubs existed specifically to provide a space for comradely conversation among an exclusive membership, and leading directors of dominant corporations routinely belonged to several of them, knitting the elite into a centralized old boys' network. Before the Fraser Institute launched in 1974, with the Business Council on National Issues (BCNI) following soon after, in 1976, the culture of solidarity that sustained the business community was primarily one of leisure, befitting an oligarchic elite. Corporate capitalists and their advisers did participate in policy groups such as the

Conference Board, but these groups also included representatives of other parts of the society, such as labour. The venues they provided did more for class collaboration than for the development of an elite community. Sectoral organizations such as the Canadian Manufacturers Association played an important role in constructing and expressing the sectional interests of certain fractions of the business community, but were not suited for articulating the general interests of corporate capital. It was in the dense, centralized network of private clubs, and also on the capacious boards of the big five banks, that the elite found its collective identity as an exclusive "confraternity of power."

In the 1970s, corporate elites created agencies of business activism—"councils," "roundtables," "institutes"—that brought leading capitalists and organic intellectuals together for explicitly political purposes. The Canadian case is no different from what Michael Useem (1984) found in his study of corporate business's proactive contribution to the rise of neoliberalism in Britain and the U.S. Indeed, the Anglo-Saxon world has "led the way" in constructing and implementing the neoliberal paradigm. In Canada, business leaders recognized the need to legitimate a dramatic transition in the policy paradigm, from the Keynesian welfare state and associated state regulation of capital to the market-drive politics of neoliberalism. With the founding of the BCNI the corporate elite's basis for community began to shift from the sphere of leisure to that of political activism. Business activism has mimicked social-movement activism. Typically, a movement develops as a collection of organizations, some practising a more flamboyant or extremist politics than others. The more extremist groups—and here the Fraser Institute comes to mind—attract the media coverage that puts political ideas into circulation, enabling more moderate groups to make similar claims from a more "respectable" footing (Gamson and Wolfsfeld 1993:122). The same holds, of course, beyond the arena of Canadian politics. Groups like the Trilateral Commission and World Economic Forum now constitute a transnational policy bloc that promotes neoliberalism both within nations and in the programs of supranational agencies such as the WTO and IMF. The participation of Canadian business leaders in global policy groups has reinforced a certain worldly political solidarity within Canada's corporate elite, while contributing to the emergence of what Robinson and Harris (2000) call a transnational capitalist class (see Carroll and Carson 2003).

In the field of corporate political party donations, the key transition was from a long-standing bipartisan corporate consensus to a more diverse pattern as of 1997. The flow of funds favoured the incumbent party offering "the greatest political and indeed economic return" for the contributor-investor (MacDermid 2001:19). Of course, the policy frameworks of governments and parties alike had, by the mid 1990s, been strongly conditioned by two decades of well-organized business activism. The CEO of the Business Council on National Issues, Thomas d'Aquino, summed matters up nicely:

> If you ask yourself, in which period since 1900 has Canada's business community had the most influence on public policy, I would say it was the last twenty years. Look at what we stand for and look at what all the governments, all the major parties . . . have done, and what they want to do. They have adopted the agendas we've been fighting for in the past two decades (quoted in Newman, 1998:151).

The new culture of activism that d'Aquino personifies has extended to university governance boards. The corporate elite gained more of a national presence in

university governance, and there was a complementary traffic in the other direction, as university CEOs joined the corporate elite.

These kinds of activism, whether in policy formation or in higher education and research helped to compensate for the loss of the integrative mechanisms formerly provided by the culture of leisure and significantly extended the reach of corporate power into civil society.

THE GROWING IMPORTANCE OF ORGANIC INTELLECTUALS

A more activist corporate elite relies extensively on an expanding corps of organic intellectuals. It is clear that intellectuals make up an important, and growing, element of corporate power. Even in the mid 1970s, the corporate elite included a varied assortment of advisers—retired corporate capitalists, lawyers, consultants, and so on. With the thinning of corporate interlocks—which also reduces the number of ties across enterprise groups—the contributions that such well-connected advisers make to elite integration become more critical.

As higher education became increasingly integrated into the process of capital accumulation in the late twentieth century, academics—particularly university CEOs—made up an increasingly large fraction of the corporate elite. But the corporatization of universities has value beyond the economic domain. According to Antonio Gramsci (1971:10), one of the most important aspects of a dominant class's hegemony "is its struggle to assimilate and to conquer 'ideologically' the traditional intellectuals, but this assimilation and conquest is made quicker and more efficacious the more the group in question succeeds in simultaneously elaborating its own organic intellectuals."

Meanwhile, as outside directors have gained profile in the interlock network, the wisdom of retired capitalists (and retired politicians) has also been put to good commercial use on the boards of the largest corporations. In the 1990s, as their corporate affiliations cut across different enterprise groups, partly compensating for the decline of bank centrality, advisers such as former premiers Peter Lougheed and William Davis further integrated the elite. Many of the women recruited into the elite since the 1970s have also taken up advisory positions. If their widespread exclusion from high-level authority points up the resilience of male domination at the higher reaches, the tenfold increase in the elite's female complement indicates a shift toward a culture of meritocracy.

DIVERSITY, MERITOCRACY, DEMOCRACY

With the advance of bourgeois society, aristocratic forms of closure have been rendered culturally archaic, and the years since the mid 1970s have witnessed an acceleration of that trend. This period is one of *moral reform* within the corporate elite, of a transition to greater diversity and openness. These democratizing developments went hand in hand with the development of business activism and the decline of the culture of leisure as the key basis for community.

Driven by heightened international competition, financial deregulation, and the enhanced power of institutional investors, corporations have sought to empower boards as independent, rational agencies. Open recruitment of directors would populate boards with dynamic, capable directors. Enhanced autonomy from management would help create conditions for effective discussion leading to rational strategic choices. Smaller, leaner boards following

"best practices" would further sharpen the competitive edge.

It would be difficult, however, to argue that these reforms had any demonstrable success in resolving capitalism's tendencies toward crisis and uneven development, and here the sorry case of Nortel provides a fine exemplar. Canada's best hope as a world-class transnational in the late 1990s, Nortel adopted the governance reforms of 1995 and proceeded to build shareholder value through a series of artful acquisitions that left it at the brink of bankruptcy when the dotcom-telecom bubble burst in 2000–01. Nortel's rise and fall demonstrates that aggressive pursuit of shareholder value is hardly a cure for capitalism's ills.

This is not to say that the new governance regime had no implications for elite organization. Among the most significant was a weakening of the interpersonal network that knits leading corporate directors into a business community. The life-world of the elite became less closely integrated via corporate cross-affiliations. The contraction of corporate directorates (especially bank boards) and the reduced number of directorships per director made the core of the network less of a densely woven old boys' network. A looser, less centralized network, with less representation of corporate insiders on directorates, may support more open communication among directors in the service of maximizing shareholder value. Yet even as the elite's social organization became less centralized, the banks retained a presence at the heart of the network, as most directors in the core of the interpersonal networks sat on the directorates of the big banks. With the weakening of the old boys' network came an increase in the number of women and non-British (but almost exclusively European) ethnicities at the upper echelons of corporate power. For example, between 1976 and 1996, the proportion of women in the Canadian corporate elite grew from 0.6% to 9.2%, while the proportion of non-British grew from 22.1% to 36.2%, including a rise from 12.7% to 18.3% among French members (Carroll 2004:18). The corporate elite became less monocultural and less petrified, although its composition in terms of ethnicity and gender still contrasted sharply with that of the general population. By the late 1990s, the elite was regrouping around an Eurocentric multiculturalism that encompassed an emerging Québécois elite segment based primarily in Montreal. Although women remained almost a token minority consigned to the lower strata as advisers and vice presidents, and almost entirely removed from continental and transnational interlocking, the elite's composition was becoming somewhat less patriarchal. In its social profile, educational credentials came to figure more importantly than exclusive club memberships, and advisers from academic and other fields of expert knowledge constituted a larger subgroup. These developments modernized the face of Canadian corporate capital, and provided for a more persuasive business leadership, more in tune with contemporary society.

CORPORATE POWER AND NEOLIBERAL DEMOCRACY

Multiculturalism, meritocracy, the reform of corporate governance—these are elements of an elite-level democratization that has curiously coincided with an increase in the importance of markets in people's lives resulting from both globalization and the implementation of a neoliberal policy paradigm. On the surface, this paradoxical medley seems consistent with the notion, championed by Francis Fukuyama (1992), of the "end of history." For Fukuyama, advanced liberal democracy—a system of free markets and liberal states toward which all human societies are evolving

(1992:48)—is ideally suited to meet the human needs of self-esteem, reason, and desire.

However, "corporate democratization" has clear limits. "Multiculturalism," for instance, has been largely the project of the Canadian state. Prior to the 1960s, a modernist state discourse valorized the British group exclusively. But from the Report of the Royal Commission on Bilingualism and Biculturalism (1968) onward, the framework shifted to a new form of "multicultural discipline." Instead of trying to transform its Others through assimilation, the new discourse "articulates them with regimes of rational-bureaucratic discipline" (Day 200:205). As ethnic difference is acknowledged and accommodated within larger social hierarchies that remain unchallenged, individual members of minority groups learn to accommodate themselves to the apparatuses of power. From the standpoint of ethnic and racialized minorities, this liberal multiculturalism is a co-optative tool for what Himani Bannerji (2000:27) calls the "salad bowl corporate view of difference." The modest growth of ethnic diversity within the Canadian corporate elite fits comfortably within this pattern. Lacking any political dimension, it simply expresses the Eurocentric cosmopolitanism of an Atlantic ruling class.

By the same token, the structure of property ownership limits the scope for meritocracy. Mechanisms of closure associated with the old boys may have weakened after the 1970s, but the most powerful form of closure—ownership of capital—shows no sign of weakening, even if certain concentrated holdings now accumulate under the control of funds rather than families. In July 2002 the Toronto Stock Exchange reported a decrease in corporate share ownership among Canadians, reversing the upward trend that had been building since tracking began in the 1970s (Market Trend

Canada 2002). Ownership of most shares is extremely concentrated within a tiny segment of the population.[2] For the most part, corporate democratization is restricted to the principal actors within the business community itself, and extends only begrudgingly to minor shareholders.

The stark limits to corporate democratization help to account for the hollowness of claims about the rise of "popular capitalism" put forward by neoliberals in the 1980s. However dramatic the shift *within the corporate elite* from oligarchy to democracy may have been (and in areas such as gender and ethnic representation the gains have been modest), it should not be mistaken for democratization of economic relations. This transition seems integral to a new form of hegemony—a more porous elite social organization offering greater possibilities for the ruling class's reach into civil society, for civil society's reach into the ruling class, and thus for more effective business leadership.

It is significant that the new regime of corporate power coincides with the turn of neoliberalism, a policy paradigm that has been identified with the hollowing-out of democracy. One result is "a decline in the relative autonomy of the state from transient capitalist class will and ideology" (Ross and Trachte, 1990). What neoliberal democracy offers is a market-driven politics in which the mobility of investment shifts power from voters to capital, obliging states to serve the needs of global market forces. This does not render states impotent, but it does constrain them to use power "to advance the process of commodification" (Leys 2001:3).

The enormous concentrations of capital that dominate the world market ensure that the shift in control over public affairs from citizens to markets affords at best "'a democracy of the few', of the rich and powerful" (Ewan, McBride, and Shields 2000:81). Petras and Veltmeyer (2001:70)

exaggerate only slightly when they call these politics a "new authoritarianism," distinct from the old-style militarism that denied electoral competition and individual liberty to those on the margins of world capitalism. The new authoritarianism, evident at both centre and periphery, combines formal features of liberal democracy with market-driven decision making within elite transnational structures shielded from popular electorates. This helps explain a paradox in the 2002 UN Human Development Report, which bore the title "Deepening democracy in a fragmented world." Observing that since the 1980s a "global shift from authoritarian to democratic regimes" has brought the world "more democratic countries and more political participation than ever" (UN Development Programme 2002:15, 14), the Report noted that "people around the world seem to be losing faith in democracy" (2002:63).[3] As welfare states and old-style authoritarian regimes give way to neoliberal democracy, strategic decisions are made in "centralized headquarters by non-elected officials who rule by decree and without popular representation, deliberation or consultation" (Petras and Veltmeyer 2001:158).

Liberal democracy, Ellen Wood reminds us, arose within modern capitalism in a long process whereby "certain *political* powers were gradually transformed into *economic* powers and transferred to a separate sphere" as a national state with "an unprecedented *public* character" were forged (1995:36, 40). Standing apart from the economy, the state could "belong to everyone" even as the class power of capital, mediated by markets and the pressures of competition, organized economic life (1995:40–1). In this way, "democracy could be confined to a formally separate 'political' sphere while the 'economy' followed rules of its own" (1995:203). With recent globalization, liberal democracy has very nearly "reached its limits" (Wood, 1995:235).

Democratization will have to await more coherent and sustained initiatives "from below" that will champion human development, ecological well-being, and the expansion of public spheres beyond the narrow, elitist confines of neoliberal democracy. Whether the anti-corporate globalization protests that began to build in the mid 1990s and attained spectacular visibility in the 1999 "Battle in Seattle" can be translated into a cumulative movement for global democracy remains to be seen. Meanwhile, Canada's corporate elite, both in its pursuit of profit and in its extensive cultural and political activism, continues to exert a dominant influence that extends beyond state-defined boundaries. The "national identity" of corporate capital becomes ambiguous as capitalist practices become transnational. Against claims that globalization betokens a "hollowing out of corporate Canada" (Arthur 2000), my research confirms the continued existence of a robust nationally organized business community. Yet that community, its business strategies, and its political vision are embedded within institutional structures of an increasingly global character.

The implications of corporate power in the international field are clear enough. Statistics on global corporate concentration cited at the beginning of this chapter are reflected in massive and widening disparities in wealth and income worldwide. In 1960 the 20% of the world's people in the richest countries had 30 times the income of the poorest 20%. By 1997 the former's income was 74 times the latter's (Lee 2002). World inequality did not increase much from the mid 1960s to the early 1980s, but began to rise sharply as neoliberal policies were imposed worldwide, often at the insistence of the IMF and World Bank.[4] Anthropologist Wade Davis,

who characterizes global disparities and dislocations as a "ticking bomb," points out that behind the statistics are human lives of destitution and oppression (Davis 2002).

Ultimately, in a globalizing world corporate power grows at the expense of workers, communities, and the ecosystem itself. Recent transitions in the Canadian corporate elite give us a window—a view from the top—on a malleable structure of power that is also a contested terrain. In coming years, as the Canadian corporate elite's dominion becomes even more globalized and as other globalizing elites extend their reach further into Canada, we can expect its political vision to blend the "national interest" with "regional" North American and "global" interests. It was not by chance that late in 2001 the Business Council on National Issues relaunched itself as the Canadian Council of Chief Executives, voicing a new commitment "to the shaping of sound public policy in Canada, North America and the world." To contest corporate power, its critics in Canada will need to move well beyond the old preoccupation with "the survival capacities of the Canadian state" (Clarkson, 2002:420). The stakes are higher than ever before, and the struggle epochal. The ticking bomb can be defused only by transfiguring corporate power into economic democracy.

NOTES

1. As an example, there is evidence that Canada–U.S. free trade has begun to weaken the controlling positions of wealthy families in Canada by ratcheting up competitive pressures and "thereby raising the price that families must pay to maintain corporate control" (Morck, Stangeland, and Yeung, 2000:361–2).

2. In 1999, 94% of all stocks held outside RRSPs (which are vehicles of passive investment) was owned by the richest 20% of Canadian family units. The poorest 60% claimed a total of only 1%. Even within the

richest quintile, share ownership was highly concentrated. Only 27% owned stocks outside RRSPs—that is, approximately 5% of family units owned 94% of stocks outside RRSPs (Kerstetter, 2002).

3. The results of Gallup International's Millennium Survey of more than 50 000 people in 60 countries, summarized in the UN Report (p. 63), are instructive. When asked, "Does government respond to the will of the people?" only 10% answered affirmatively.

4. In just five years, between 1988 and 1993, nearly 4% of world income was redistributed upward into the top income decile, so that by 1993 this stratum claimed 50.8% in comparison to the 22.3% claimed by the poorest 75% (Lee, 2002).

REFERENCES

Adams, Paul 2002. "'Peace has a cost,' Bronfman says." *Globe and Mail* (Toronto), May 30: A11.

Arthurs, Harry W. 2000. "The hollowing out of corporate Canada?" In J. Jenson and B. de Sousa Santos (eds.), *Globalizing Institutions*, pp. 29–51. Burlington, VT: Ashgate.

Bannerji, Himani 2000. *The Dark Side of the Nation: Essays on Multiculturalism, Nationalism and Gender*. Toronto: Canadian Scholars' Press.

Block, Fred 1977. "The ruling class does not rule: Notes on the Marxist theory of the state" *Socialist Revolution* 7, 3:6–28.

Burgess, Bill 2002. "Canada's location in the world system: Reworking the debate in Canadian political economy" Ph.D. diss. University of British Columbia.

Carroll, William K. 1986. *Corporate Power and Canadian Capitalism*. Vancouver: University of British Columbia.

Carroll, William K. 2004. *Corporate Power in a Globalizing World: A Study in Elite Social Organizations*. Don Mills, ON: Oxford University Press.

Carroll, William K. and Colin Carson 2003. "The network of global corporations and elite policy groups: A structure for transnational capitalist class formation?" *Global Networks* 3, 1:29–57.

Clarkson, Stephen 2002. *Uncle Sam and Us: Globalization, Neoconservatism and the Canadian State*. Toronto: University of Toronto Press.

Davis, Wade 2002. "The ticking bomb." *Globe and Mail* (Toronto), July 6.

Day, Richard J.F. 2000. *Multiculturalism and the History of Canadian Diversity*. Toronto: University of Toronto Press.

Dicken, Peter 1998. *Global Shift*, 3rd ed. New York: Guilford Press.

De Boff, Richard B. 2001. "NAFTA and economic integration in North America." In V. Mosco and D. Schiller (eds.), *Continental Order? Integrating North America for Cybercapitalism*, pp. 35–63. New York: Rowman and Littlefield.

Evans, B. Mitchell, Stephen McBride, and John Shields 2000. "Globalization and the challenge of Canadian democracy." In M. Burke, C. Mooers, and J. Shields (eds.), *Restructuring and Resistance: Canadian Public Policy in an Age of Global Capitalism*. Halifax: Fernwood Publishing.

Fukuyama, Francis 1992. *The End of History and the Last Man*. New York: Free Press.

Gamson, William A. and Gadi Wolfsfeld 1993. "Movements and media as interacting systems." *Annals of the American Political Science Society* 528:114–127.

Gramsci, Antonio 1971. *Selections from the Prison Notebooks of Antonio Gramsci*. New York: International Publishers.

Harvey, David 1982. *The Limits to Capital*. Chicago: University of Chicago Press.

Kerstetter, Steve 2002. *Rags and Riches: Wealth and Inequality in Canada*. Ottawa: Canadian Centre for Policy Alternatives.

Lee, Marc 2002. "The global divide: Inequality in the world economy." *Behind the Number* 4, 2 April 18. http://www.policyalternatives.ca.

Leys, Colin 2001. *Market-Driven Politics: Neo-Liberal Democracy and the Public Interest*. London: Verso.

MacDermid, R. 2001. "Toward an investment theory of Canadian electoral politics." Paper presented at the Annual General Meeting of the Canadian Political Science Association, Quebec, May 27–29.

Market Trend Canada 2002. *Canadian Shareowners Study July 2002*. Toronto: Toronto Stock Exchange.

Morck, Randall, David A. Strangeland, and Bernard Yeung 2002. "Inherited wealth, corporate control, and economic growth: The Canadian disease?" In R.K. Morck (ed.), *Concentrated Corporate Ownership*, pp. 319–372. Chicago: University of Chicago Press.

Newman, Peter C. 1998. *Titans: How the New Canadian Establishment Seized Power*. Toronto: Viking.

Petras, James, and Henry Veltmeyer 2001. *Globalization Unmasked: Imperialism in the 21st Century*. Halifax: Fernwood Publishing.

Robinson, William I., and Jerry Harris 2000. "Towards a global ruling class? Globalization and the transnational capitalist class." *Science and Society* 64, 1:11–54.

Ross, Robert J.S. and Kent C. Trachte 1990. *Global Capitalism: The New Leviathan*. Albany, NY: SUNY Press.

Rusterholz, Peter 1985. "The Banks in the centre: Integration in decentralized Switzerland." In F.N. Stokman, R. Ziegler, and J. Scott (eds.), *Networks of Corporate Power*, pp. 131–147. Cambridge: Polity Press.

Schiller, Dan, and Vincent Mosco 2001. "Introduction: Integrating a continent for a transnational world." In V. Mosco and D. Schiller, *Continental Order: Interpreting North America for Cybercapitalism*, pp. 1–34. New York: Rowman and Littlefield.

Scoffield, Heather 1998. "Canada adjusts to free trade realities." *Globe and Mail* (Toronto), December 31:B1, B4.

Scott, John 1997. *Corporate Business and Capitalist Classes*. New York: Oxford University Press.

Sklair, Leslie 1995. *Sociology of the Global System*. Baltimore: Johns Hopkins University Press.

Statistics Canada 2001. *Canada's International Position, 2000*. Cat. No. 67–202. Ottawa: Ministry of Industry.

United Nations Development Programme 2002. *Human Development Report*. New York: Oxford University Press.

Useem, Michael 1984. *The Inner Circle*. New York: Oxford University Press.

van der Pijl, Kees 1984. *The Making of an Atlantic Ruling Class*. London: Verso.

Wood, Ellen Meiksins 1995. *Democracy Against Capitalism*. Cambridge: Cambridge University Press.

Workman, Thom 1996. *Banking on Deception: The Discourse of Fiscal Crisis*. Halifax: Fernwood.

chapter three

Working-Class Formation in Canada

James Conley
(An original chapter
written for this volume.)

INTRODUCTION

Near the end of May 2007, rallies were held in Windsor, Oshawa, and Ottawa to protest the loss of manufacturing jobs. Organized by unions and addressed by labour leaders such as Buzz Hargrove of the Canadian Auto Workers and Ken Georgietti of the Canadian Labour Congress, the rallies were attended by tens of thousands of workers. Hargrove blamed government trade policy and car imports from Asia and Europe for thousands of jobs that have been lost at automakers and parts manufacturers.

What is the relationship between protests by unionized workers and the sociological study of social inequality? Conflicts such as these, the social conditions on which they are based, and the social changes that sometimes result from them are related to inequalities of power, which have always been central components of sociological inquiry into social inequality. Who has power? What are its institutional bases? How is it used? These are among the many questions asked by sociologists, and addressed in other chapters of this volume. The classical theories of class, which still define most theoretical debates and empirical research in this area, concentrated on identifying sources of power and conflicts of interest in the ownership of productive property (Marx) or in positions in markets and organizations (Weber).

The identification of inequalities of power and antagonistic interests in structured social relationships is only the first step to understanding social conflicts and social change, however. Intervening between structural inequalities of class power and class conflict are processes of class formation and mobilization. These processes involve consideration of the sources of conflict and the resources available to members of classes, the existence of solidarity within classes, the awareness of class interests and dispositions to act on them by class members, the mobilization of classes by organizations, and the forms of collective action that class members undertake.

The resources, social organization, dispositions, and mobilization of dominant classes are often taken for granted, for their power is firmly institutionalized. Attention here will focus on the working class. Like most studies of working-class formation and collective action, this chapter starts from the ideas of Marx and Weber before turning to the dynamics of working-class formation in Canada.

CLASS FORMATION AND CLASS CONFLICT IN THEORY

The power of the capitalist class rests on its control over society's productive resources. Ownership of property gives business owners the right to exclude others from the use of those resources, to allocate them to different uses, to move them, to choose production technologies, and so on. These powers also give the capitalist class leverage on the state. But what are the bases for opposition to capitalist class power?

Marx

For Marx, the reasons for working-class opposition to the power of the capitalist class lie in workers' experiences of exploitative and alienating work, and in the consequences of capitalist profit-making strategies for working-class standards of life. The "general law of capitalist accumulation," Marx argues, is "that in proportion as capital accumulates, the lot of the labourer, be his pay high or low, must grow worse . . . accumulation of wealth at one pole is, therefore, at the same time accumulation of misery, agony of toil, slavery, ignorance, brutality, mental degradation, at the opposite pole" (Marx 1867:604). Either in absolute terms or relative to that of the capitalist class, the standard of living of workers falls as capitalism develops, and the conditions of work become more toilsome (Grabb 2007; Braverman 1974).

Marx believed that capitalism created not only grievances among workers, but also the conditions of class formation and class power for workers to act to eliminate the sources of their distress. Specifically, Marx expected capitalism to create three conditions giving workers the organization and resources to resist capitalist power. First, changes in the production process would bring workers together in larger workplaces, and a more co-operative production process would lead to solidarity between workers. Marx differed from Durkheim (1893), who expected the increasing division of labour to lead, at least under certain circumstances (e.g., the absence of large inequalities in wealth and other obstacles to equality of opportunity), to organic solidarity between occupational groups in modern societies. Instead, Marx expected that changes in production would obliterate skill differences, making all workers into what are today called semi-skilled labourers. Mechanized production would also reduce the importance of physical strength, and gender differences between workers would cease to be significant. This process of homogenization would in effect create mechanical solidarity within the working class (Sørensen 1994), and increase the possibility of and necessity for workers to organize on a broad, inclusive basis. The changing character of production also gave workers power: even as the demise of craft production and the introduction of machine pacing deprived workers of control over the process of production as individuals, they gained power as a collectivity.

Second, Marx emphasized the power that derives from class size. The class structure in capitalism would polarize as the petty bourgeoisie of small proprietors disappeared, and the capitalist class would grow smaller and more concentrated as large capitalists swallowed up smaller capitalists. As a consequence, the working class would become the largest class in capitalist societies, confronting a small capitalist class in a conflict without any intermediaries.

However, structural tendencies in capitalism toward homogenization of the working class and polarization of the class structure only furnish preconditions for working-class power. The problem of collective action remains: individual workers do not have the resources to counter the power of capitalists,[1] and size is not enough for power unless it is organized. Marx expected that, in the course of conflict with capitalists, workers would develop increasingly broad levels of organization: unions would form on local, then on industrial, and finally on national levels, at the same time as political parties advancing the interests of workers would grow (Marx and Engels 1848). In other words, out of the experience of conflict, increasingly inclusive and politicized forms of organization of workers would result, and increasingly broad struggles would follow between workers, on the one hand, and capitalists and the state, on the other hand.

Weber

Weber is often described as involved in a debate with Marx's ghost. This certainly applies to Weber's thoughts on social inequality, which assume much of what Marx had to say but go on to add to and amend Marx's views (see Grabb 2007). Unlike Marx, who almost exclusively emphasized class, Weber considered classes, status groups, and parties as "phenomena of the distribution of power" within societies (Weber 1922:927). Weber expected that, in addition to or instead of conflict occurring on class lines, there would be organized conflict based on status groups and factions competing for power in organizations, especially the state.

Like Marx, Weber thought that property was central to the concept of class. However, unlike Marx, Weber conceived of classes as based on positions in markets, not in production. From this perspective, classes are distinguished by differences in the possession of marketable, income-producing goods and services. Thus, Weber's analysis points to possible lines of differentiation among workers based on possession of skills and other advantages in labour markets. Such differentiation in labour markets need not promote the general impoverishment of the working class that Marxian theory seems to suggest, because there would be distinct segments or strata within the working class, with different experiences, different interests, and different capacities for organization and collective action.

Even more importantly, Weber believed that the development of a new middle class of white-collar employees, technical specialists, and professionals, due to the expansion of bureaucratic forms of administration in modern times, would provide an avenue for mobility out of the working class, and give people in these positions a distinct identity and interests (Weber 1922:304). The existence of a middle class between the working class and the capitalist class contradicts the Marxian expectation that the class structure in capitalism would become polarized over time.

Weber's concept of status identifies the second aspect of power that affects class formation. The existence of status groups that cut across different classes may also complicate the increasing homogeneity of the working class that Marx envisioned. Moreover, rather than arising purely on the basis of class location, groups may form around status-related issues, including shared consumption patterns and styles of life. Thus, status groups based on gender, sexual orientation, ethnicity, region, or education can divide members of one class, and create solidarity between members of different classes. Finally, relations of domination between such status groups are typically more "transparent" than class relations, and therefore may be a more readily available source of group identity than class.

Party is the third key aspect of power that Weber distinguishes. With respect to problems of class formation, Weber's insight here is that when groups organize to pursue power and its rewards in organizations, and above all in states, they may do so on bases other than class or status. The best example may be forms of political party organization. The history of party systems and of political cleavages in societies can thus be expected to have effects on working-class formation and the organization of class conflict, especially insofar as success in attaining power results in the distribution of benefits (such as patronage or welfare benefits) to supporters belonging to different classes.

The ideas of Marx and Weber continue to provide a basis for the way sociologists think about class formation and class conflict. Marx tended to see working-class formation and collective action as a series of steps toward an end point, a terminus on the road to a revolution that would overthrow capitalism. Weber, in contrast, presents a more complex and contingent view of class formation, as one of several possible lines along which groups in conflict might form.

CLASS FORMATION AND CLASS CONFLICT IN CANADA

What do we know about class formation and class conflict in Canada in the early twenty-first century? Evidence on working-class formation and conflict will be presented with respect to the following issues: (1) the structural tendencies of class formation, with particular attention to the process of polarization expected by Marx, (2) the changes in social organization in workplaces and labour markets that have affected working-class solidarity, (3) the dispositions of members of different classes, and (4) levels of mobilization in unions and political parties, along with conflict in social movements and strikes.

Class Structure: Polarization?

As we have seen, Marxists have expected that working-class formation would be facilitated by a polarization of the class structure. This polarization has three aspects: decline of the petty bourgeoisie, polarization of incomes, and polarization of skills. While generally agreeing on the demise of the petty bourgeoisie, Weber and his followers are less sure about the other two predictions. What does the Canadian evidence show?

Marx expected that the petty bourgeoisie, comprising self-employed artisans, farmers, shopkeepers, and the like, would disappear under the pressure of competition from larger, more efficient capitalist enterprises. The result would be a class structure polarized between workers on the one hand and capitalists on the other hand. Weber, in contrast, did not expect a polarization, because a new middle class of salaried employees with educational credentials would develop in tandem with bureaucratic organizations and interpose itself between the capitalists and the workers.

In Canada, evidence on levels of self-employment over the course of the twentieth century largely bears out expectations about the decline of the petty bourgeoisie.[2] The self-employed declined from about 25% of the total labour force in 1931 to about 12% in the 1970s. Since then, however, the trend has reversed, both in Canada and in other countries. In the first decade of the twenty-first century, the percentage of Canada's workforce in the self-employed category hovered around 15%, fluctuating according to the fortunes of the industries in which self-employment is concentrated (Statistics Canada 2006a, 2007). Approximately two-thirds of the self-employed do not have any employees.[3]

Most of the historical decline of the petty bourgeoisie in Canada was due to falling employment in the agricultural sector, where levels of self-employment have always been very high, and continue to be over 60%.[4] Recent increases have occurred across all industries. In addition to farming, levels of self-employment have remained higher than average in construction, professional, scientific and technical services, and business support services. As Marx would have expected, manufacturing has a very low level of self-employment (between 4% and 6% in the last two decades) and self-employment is virtually non-existent in utilities, public administration, and education (Gardner 1995; Crompton 1993; Arai 1997; Statistics Canada 2006a, 2007).

Despite its recent growth, the petty bourgeoisie has nonetheless declined in prominence over the longer term, much as Marx expected. Has this polarized the class structure, making class conflict and working-class formation more likely? As noted earlier, Weberian understandings of the class structure point to the growth of a new middle class of employees characterized by authority within bureaucratic organizations, including the state, and by the possession of educational credentials.

Although the causes, characteristics, conceptualization, and future prospects of the new middle class have been the subject of considerable theoretical debate by neo-Marxist and neo-Weberian theorists (see Grabb 2007), there is agreement that the numbers of middle-level administrators and managers, professionals, and skilled technical employees constitute a significant and generally growing part of the post-industrial class structure, one that is relatively distinct from the bourgeoisie, the petty bourgeoisie, and the working class (Myles and Turegin 1994). In the only large-scale Canadian study to use neo-Marxist class categories, the new middle class, defined as lower-level managers and supervisors with authority to impose sanctions on other employees, was found to represent about 25% of the labour force in the early 1980s, compared to nearly 60% for the working class, more than 10% for the petty bourgeoisie, and 6% for employers (Clement and Myles 1994). Since then, however, it has been suggested that the middle class has been in decline. This position was given credibility by the wave of "downsizing" during the 1980s recession, involving well-publicized layoffs of middle managers in large corporations, and reductions in the public sector. Public-sector employment declined from nearly one-quarter of the labour force in 1976 to one-fifth in 2005, even after several years of early twenty-first century growth in education, health care, and social assistance jobs (Statistics Canada 2006a).

Nevertheless, based on census data on occupations, those occupations that have the closest fit to what Marxists and Weberians consider the new middle class have grown steadily over the last several decades. For example, as Table 3-1 shows, the proportion of the labour force in what have been called "knowledge occupations"—professional, management, and technical occupations—grew from less than 14% of the employed labour force in 1971 to nearly 25% in 2001. More than 40% of employees in the non-market service sector (government, educational, and health and social services) are "knowledge workers" (Baldwin and Beckstead 2003). The science and engineering workforce alone grew from less than 10% in 1981 to nearly 14% in 2001 (Beckstead and Gellatly 2006). In addition, rising levels of post-secondary education point to growth in the new middle class, despite the existence of a gap between the employees' educational credentials and the tasks that many actually perform on the job (Guppy and Davies 1998; Livingstone 1999).

The economic restructuring that has occurred in Canada and other advanced capitalist societies since the 1970s has spawned another debate about the new middle class. The debate concerns whether this class has declined, not in numbers but in income and quality of working conditions. First, some writers suggest that the long-term processes of routinization, deskilling, and loss of autonomy that occurred with manual and clerical workers in previous stages of industrialization are now extending to professional employees and middle-level administrators in the post-industrial period. However, evidence since the early 1980s has not shown any decline in skill requirements in new middle class occupations; instead, the shift to a post-industrial service economy has created both skilled and unskilled jobs, but the former have grown more than the latter, as shown by the data on knowledge workers in Table 3-1 (see also Clement and Myles 1994).

The possible effects of further changes since the 1980s have yet to be determined. It may be that at least some of the recent increases in self-employment stem from members of the new middle class going into business for themselves, because of the reduced job security produced by large companies either downsizing or contracting out work. Technological changes, especially computer technologies, make such arrangements possible, and also provide opportunities for self-employment in consulting work (Arai 1997). It has been suggested that this shift to self-employment represents a form of "precarious work," along with part-time and temporary work (Vosko et al. 2003). Nevertheless, regardless of its consequences for individuals' job security and well-being, to the extent that it represents a shift from the new middle class (employees) to the petty bourgeoisie (self-employed), it does not indicate a polarization of the class structure.

The third possible pattern of class polarization to receive attention in recent

TABLE 3-1 Knowledge Workers in Canada, 1971–2001				
	Share of employment* (%)			
	1971	1981	1991	2001
All knowledge-based occupations	13.8	17.5	21.5	24.7
Management occupations	1.6	3.6	5.4	6.1
Professional occupations	8.7	9.9	11.3	14.3
Technical occupations	3.5	4.0	4.7	4.4
All other occupations	86.2	82.5	78.5	75.3
All occupations	100	100	100	100

*Defined as the employed labour force using the 1971 Census labour force concept.
Source: Baldwin and Beckstead 2003:5, Table 1.

decades concerns the polarization of earnings and income. In this case, the middle class is conceptualized in a gradational, distributive way, and is represented by those individuals in the middle categories of the income structure. Any shrinkage among middle-income earners could have important implications for class formation, because this group would include not only many members of the new middle class, as defined in Marxist or Weberian terms, but also the more affluent part of the working class. In Canada, increases in average real incomes for men began after the Second World War, came to a stop in the early 1980s, and have been largely stagnant since. Among women, both labour force participation and earnings have slowly risen, with the increasing prevalence of dual-income households helping to prevent declines in economic circumstances for many families. Income polarization has occurred, but it is mainly on the basis of age and marital status, with declines in the earnings of younger workers relative to older workers, and the earnings of lone-parent families headed by less educated young females relative to two-parent families and lone-parent families headed by more educated women over 40 (Galarneau 2005; Myles et al. 2006; Morissette 1998; Heisz et al. 2001; Morissette and Johnson 2005). Although the latter patterns represent increased hardship for part of what might be considered the working class, they do not appear to represent a squeezing out of the middle of the income range. One example of income polarization that does correspond to Marx's expectations, however, is the increase in very high incomes. This has been caused in large part by the extremely high levels of compensation for chief executives of large corporations and others in the top income percentile, a pattern that has not been as pronounced since before the Second World War (Mackenzie 2007; Saez and Veall 2005).

What, then, can we conclude from the evidence on polarization in the class structure? First, Marx and Weber were broadly correct about the decline of the petty bourgeoisie, but its decline has not been uniform across all sectors of the economy, and the long-term trend has been reversed somewhat in the last 25 years. Second, there has been growth in new middle-class positions in the class structure, as Weber expected, and they have not been subject to the deskilling expected by many neo-Marxists. Moreover, although there has probably been a decline in job security for many middle-class workers in both the private and the public sectors since the 1980s, neither the absolute numbers nor the proportions of such jobs have decreased. Third, polarization of earned incomes has occurred, but only at the very top of the income distribution has this happened along class lines. For most of the labour force, polarization has involved falling incomes for workers in the most vulnerable labour market positions, with others in more secure positions being somewhat better protected. The result has been a more complex class structure than classical Marxism tends to suggest.

Social Organization: Homogenization of the Working Class?

Marx expected capitalism to facilitate working-class solidarity through the concentration of workers in larger workplaces, with a more co-operative labour process and fewer skill differences among workers. He also expected the significance of gender differences within the working class to decline. What has happened in Canada?

Marx saw the concentration of industrial workers in large factories as a source of class solidarity and power. On average, workplaces grew for much of the twentieth century, especially in manufacturing, but in

TABLE 3-2	Employees by Size of Establishment (Manufacturing) 1925–2005		

A.

Year	Employees (%)		
	<100	100–499	500+
1925	40.8	35.4	23.8
1930	39.3	35.0	25.7
1940	35.3	34.5	30.2
1950	34.5	31.8	33.7
1960	35.7	32.4	31.9
1970	30.5	37.1	32.5

B.

Year	Employees (%)		
	0–100	101–500	>500
1975	30.7	38.6	30.7
1980	32.0	37.8	30.2
1985	34.9	37.9	27.2
1990	39.4	36.2	24.4
1995	36.8	39.5	23.7

C.

Year	Employees (%)		
	<100	100–500	>500
2000	44.7	35.4	20.0
2005	46.5	36.1	17.4

Sources:
A. *Historical Statistics of Canada*, revised ed., Series R795-811, 812-825.
B. Baldwin et al. 2002:Table 1, Distribution of Manufacturing Employment and Shipments by Plant Size Class: Canada.
C. Statistics Canada 2005. *Labour Force Historical Review* (Catalogue 71F0004XCB).

the last 25 years this trend has reversed and the proportion of workers employed in manufacturing and other goods-producing industries has declined. Table 3-2 shows that, between 1925 and 1970, the proportion of manufacturing employees working in establishments with fewer than 100 workers dropped from 40% to 30%. At the same time, the proportion of employees in large establishments (500 and over) rose from less than 24% to more than 32%. From 1975 to 1995, however, the share of employment in small plants rose, while employment in large plants fell back to less than 24% of manufacturing employment. More recent figures, for 2000 and 2005, show a continued increase for small plants, to more than 46%, and a continued decline for large plants, to less than 18%. Although not treated as part of manufacturing, the closely related utilities industry is characterized by large workplaces: about 30% of workers are employed in large establishments with more than 500 employees (Statistics Canada 2007). Not all of this shifting has involved blue-collar production workers. Consistent with Weber's expectations, evidence suggests that the proportion of professional and managerial employees has generally risen with increases in workplace size (Morissette 1991:37).

Levels of manufacturing employment have followed the business cycle in the last few decades, falling precipitously in recessions in the early 1980s and 1990s then rising again during economic upswings, and are currently contracting again because of problems in the high technology sector and the high value of the Canadian dollar (Yates and Leach 2007; Ferrao 2006).

Overall, though, there has been a clear trend to smaller workplaces in manufacturing. Also, despite manufacturing's continuing importance (Yates and Leach 2007), the share of total employment represented by manufacturing has declined over the last 20 years, from 18.5% in 1987 to 14.5% in 2006 (Statistics Canada 2007).

Outside of manufacturing and utilities, average workplace size tends to be smaller, especially in the private sector of the economy. Between 1997 and 2006, in the service sector as a whole, more than 70% of employees worked in establishments with fewer than 100 employees, and more than half of those with less than 20 employees. If we exclude services in education, health care and social assistance, and public administration, which are predominantly public-sector occupations, then about three-quarters of service workers were employed in establishments with fewer than 100 employees, and well over half of those worked with fewer than 20 other employees. Fewer than 10 percent were in establishments with more than 500 employees (Statistics Canada 2007).

The public-sector services, in contrast, are characterized by large workplaces: one-fifth or more of workers in health care and social assistance, public administration, and education are in establishments with more than 500 employees. These include jobs in government departments, hospitals, schools, and universities (Statistics Canada 2007).

Thus, we find that the social organizational conditions for class formation envisaged by Marx have been only partly met in the sectors where he expected them to develop (e.g., in manufacturing and utilities, areas where the share of total employment has declined). These conditions have also been partly met in the public sector, but not in the expanding service industries in the private sector.

As noted earlier, since the 1980s, the share of private-sector employment accounted for by small establishments has risen. This increase has potentially significant implications for working-class formation, since workers in small firms and establishments (workplaces) receive less pay and fewer benefits than workers in larger firms, are less likely to receive on-the-job training, and are more likely to be laid off (Clement and Myles 1994:57–59; Baldwin et al. 2002; Statistics Canada, Labour Statistics Division 2004). Given these considerations, we might expect workers to be more class conscious in small firms. However, as Stinchcombe (1990) points out, the social relations and employment relationship in small firms tend to reduce class solidarities. This is partly because the social distance between employer and employee is likely to be smaller than in larger firms, the employer is more likely to work alongside the employee, and employees can perceive opportunities for themselves to move up to the role of small employer. In smaller firms, there are also likely to be more individualized labour contracts and less routinized production. By comparison, larger companies tend to have more bureaucratized labour relations, with internal labour markets, standardized employment conditions, and extensive quasi-judicial procedures for grievances. In recent years, some large employers have adopted new forms of workplace organization such as Japanese-style approaches to production management and flexible specialization. These forms of organization recreate, to some extent, the social relations of small firms, and are also supposed to empower workers through multi-tasking, job rotation, and reduction in status distinctions between workers and management. According to some analyses, however, these new forms of control are simply "old wine in new bottles," and have not reduced either work-place conflict or worker solidarity (Rinehart et al. 1997). More recent evidence suggests that large establishments continue to make organizational innovations: in 2001, "downsizing," or reducing the number of employees to save on costs, occurred in approximately one-quarter of large workplaces (those with more than 100 employees), and large workplaces were also more likely to exhibit increased reliance on temporary and part-time workers, increased overtime work, and self-directed work groups (Statistics Canada, Labour Statistics Division 2004).

Gender and Ethnicity

Two of the most important changes in the Canadian labour force in the last 50 years have been the increased participation of women in paid work, and the rise in immigration from non-European nations. Both of these processes are well documented in other chapters in this volume. Here our main concern is to consider their implications for working-class formation.

Although the importance of physical strength has declined in modern production, as Marx expected, the social significance of gender has not disappeared. Women are more likely than men to occupy working-class positions in the paid labour force, they are more likely to be employed in the service sector of the economy than in the goods-producing sector, and they are more likely than men to work in the public sector and for non-profit organizations in the private sector (Clement and Myles 1994; Drolet 2002). There is not only gender segregation by industry, but also segregation between women and men within occupations, so that women and men tend not to work in the same workplaces at the same jobs. Women's experiences at work are consequently different from men's. In addition, the continuing

greater responsibility of women for household labour and child care further distinguishes their experience of the labour market and paid work from that of men. Women's average earnings are also less than those of men, although the gap decreases at higher levels of education. Consequently, despite the shared interests that men and women may have as employees, women's interests may diverge from those of their male co-workers over issues such as maternity leaves, child care, pay equity, employment equity, and sexual harassment. One important trend that works in the opposite direction, however, is an increase in educational homogamy—that is, for people with similar levels of education to marry each other (Hou and Myles 2007). Although education is related to class position, it is not identical, so it cannot be taken as an indicator of class formation per se. Indeed, following Weber, education might be better seen as a basis for status group formation, because education has typically been a source of status honour or prestige (Milner 1994; Weber 1922).

The changing gender composition of the Canadian working class has been accompanied by changes in its ethnic and racial composition, as immigration levels have increased from outside the traditional European sources. In the past, ethnic affiliations rooted in segregated residential communities and their institutions, and in exclusion from and competition for jobs, may have been a source of both ethnic and class solidarity (see, e.g., Frager 1992). The assimilation of previous generations of European immigrants and their children has reduced the salience of ethnic differences within the working class, but the linguistic-regional differences between anglophone and francophone workers have a long history in Canadian society. As well, differences in occupation and income between those of European ethnic origin, on the one hand, and visible minority immigrants and Aboriginals, on the other hand, have continued to be significant.

As Weber long ago suggested, status differences involving gender, race, ethnicity, language, and region have often been features of working-class social organization, and have not disappeared with capitalist development. All of these differences tend to cut across class allegiances, reducing the sense of shared or common experience. Located within different relations of power, status differences can be double-edged swords, contributing to working-class solidarities when class and status interests are congruent, but acting as sources of division at other times, as when men and women or immigrants and the native-born compete with each other for scarce employment opportunities.

Class Consciousness

Both class polarization and the changing social organization of workplaces and labour markets entail structural conditions that affect the broad patterns of social cleavage in capitalist societies, as well as the solidarities of workers within them. The third feature of class formation to consider is people's interpretations of these structural conditions, and the extent to which class-based outlooks follow from them. Despite some acknowledged methodological limitations, sample surveys of attitudes have provided a good deal of the evidence for assessing and measuring class consciousness in previous sociological research, although they have fallen out of fashion at times in recent decades. These survey measures range from people's estimates of their own class locations to their attitudes toward the role of corporations in the economy, to their feelings about unions and strikes, and so on. With this wide variety of attitude items, investigators seek to understand and to study different dimensions of the class consciousness

of members of the various classes. Conceptually, researchers influenced by Marx have generally used a typology involving three types or degrees of class consciousness: class awareness or identity, oppositional class consciousness, and revolutionary or counter-hegemonic class consciousness (Giddens 1973; Livingstone and Mangan 1996). Class identity has been defined as awareness of membership in a distinct class, class opposition as the belief that the interests of the workers and capitalists are opposed, and counter-hegemonic consciousness as a belief in the possibility and desirability of a society organized along non-capitalist lines.

Assessment of the results of attitude surveys is complicated by the variety of measures that have been used for both class position and class consciousness. Although members of the working class and petty bourgeoisie are more likely than members of other classes to choose a working-class identity, most studies suggest that the class identity adopted by the majority of respondents in all classes is "middle class" (Livingstone and Mangan 1996, Johnston and Baer 1993).

As for oppositional class consciousness, surveys have found that, on such issues as the rights of labour unions and the redistribution of income from rich to poor, the attitudes of workers and capitalists diverge: members of the capitalist class and the petty bourgeoisie express more pro-business and less pro-labour attitudes than do industrial and service workers. The findings for the new middle class are inconsistent, with some studies showing them to be little different from workers, and other studies showing them to have more pro-business attitudes. Gender further complicates this picture, for studies also show that women have less pro-labour attitudes than do men, although in other respects women are more likely to adopt left-wing positions than men. The organization of workers also has an effect on oppositional consciousness: most studies find that membership in a union is positively associated with pro-labour attitudes (Clement and Myles 1994; Livingstone and Mangan 1996; Langford 2002). Nonetheless, the differences between classes have tended to be small.

Finally, while little research has been conducted on hegemonic class consciousness, it generally shows that most people in all class positions rarely see an alternative to a capitalist economy. Members of the working class are somewhat more likely to do so, but even in this class the proportion represents a tiny minority (Livingstone and Mangan 1996; Johnston and Baer 1993).[5] It is difficult to avoid the conclusion that class understood as an economic category is subjectively meaningful to the majority of Canadians, including members of the working class (Gidengil, 2002).

Mobilization and Collective Action

For Marx and subsequent Marxists, class polarization, growing working-class solidarity based on changing workplaces, and oppositional and counter-hegemonic consciousness should all go hand in hand with increasing levels of working-class organization and, ultimately, power. In Canada, more workers have become organized, but the effects have not always been clear-cut.

Although it is not all that they do, labour unions exist to defend the economic interests of their members. These interests include wages and benefits, working conditions, fair treatment by employers, and job security. Unions have largely succeeded in protecting these interests, for union jobs typically have higher wages and better benefits than do non-union jobs. This is not all that unions do, however. Many unions are also involved in movements and campaigns for broader objectives affecting working people more generally. Examples include support for

the social programs of the welfare state, the organization of non-unionized workers, and sometimes support for social democratic political parties, such as the New Democratic Party.

As Marx expected, unions have grown from small local organizations, based mainly on skilled craft workers, to large national and international bodies, often encompassing workers from a wide variety of different occupations. These include many members of the new middle class, such as some of the more than one-in-five union members who have a university degree. The growth of unions in Canada occurred in three major waves: the organization of craft unions in the late nineteenth and early twentieth centuries, the spread of industrial unions in manufacturing in the 1940s, and the rapid growth of public-sector unionism in the 1960s. Union membership has expanded from 133 000 in 1911 to 4.1 million in 2006. In Canada, union density, or the percentage of paid workers who belong to unions, has ranged between 30% and 33% since the late 1960s, and is currently less than 30%. In the majority of other advanced capitalist societies, union density has fallen, sometimes to very low levels. In the United States, for example, union density has declined from 23% to 16% in recent years (Galarneau 1996; Akyeampong 2001a; Western 1995; Statistics Canada 2006b).

Canadian unionization rates have not suffered such declines largely because of the strength of unionism in the public sector (e.g., civil servants, hospital workers, university professors). At more than 70%, union density in the public sector is more than four times that in the private sector (17%). Members of the public sector make up more than half of all union members in Canada. However, even in Canada, union growth has not kept pace with the general growth in employment, for several reasons. First, there is the shift of private-sector employment from goods-producing industries, such as manufacturing, forestry and mining, and construction, in which union density is higher (but declining), to service industries, in which union density is lower. Unions have had little success in organizing new growth industries and occupations such as those connected with information technology, and "knowledge workers" in management and professional occupations. Second, there is the trend toward decreases in establishment size in goods-producing industries, since unionization rates are generally lower in small firms, although union density has even declined in larger enterprises (those with more than 100 employees). Third, there is the growth in part-time and temporary jobs, which still remain somewhat less likely to be unionized (Galarneau 1996; Akyeampong 2001a, 2006; Morissette et al. 2005). Partly as a consequence of declining levels of unionization in goods-producing industries, union density has fallen among men, and despite the slowness of unions to take up women's concerns in the past, women's unionization rate now exceeds men's. By 2000, women made up more than 49% of union members, up from approximately 33% in 1982 and only 16% in 1962 (Akyeampong 2001a; White 1993; Statistics Canada 2006b). Just as there has been polarization in earnings between younger and older workers, so there has been divergence in unionization between younger and older workers: gains in unionization for women have largely been from increased employment of women over 45 in the highly unionized public sector, while unionization rates for younger women fell; unionization fell for all male workers, but more so for younger ones. Indeed, these declines help to explain the earnings gap between younger and older workers (Morissette et al. 2005).

Unions in Canada have often supported left-leaning political parties, in particular the New Democratic Party. Even so, such parties have never achieved more than third-party status in national politics, although they have formed several provincial governments. Also, the fortunes of the NDP have declined in the past decade, and in Canada there has never been a strong tendency for members of the working class to vote for left-wing political parties; gender and region have often been stronger predictors of voting than has class (Gidengil 2002; Gidengil et al. 2003). Consequently, most of the opposition of workers to the power of capitalism or big business has been manifested in strike activity and political protest campaigns.

Surges of union organization have corresponded historically with periods of heightened industrial conflict, with the two feeding off each other. The expansion of industrial unions in the 1940s and the rise of public-sector unionism in the 1960s both occurred amid waves of strikes that, at times, gave Canada among the highest rates of industrial conflict in the world (Cruikshank and Kealey 1987). In recent times, the number of strikes and the time lost to strikes have fallen to historically low levels, although the number of workers involved has remained high (Akyeampong 2001b, 2006).

Not surprisingly, given the high rate of unionization in the public sector, unions have played prominent roles in protest campaigns against government cutbacks and attempts to restrict union power. Some examples are the opposition to the federal government's imposition of wage controls in the 1970s, the Solidarity movement in British Columbia in the 1980s, opposition to the Harris government's "Common Sense Revolution" in Ontario in the 1990s, and conflict with the Campbell government in British Columbia in the early years of this century. At present, an important concern for unions, and for working-class organizations more generally, is the threat of increasing capital mobility in today's global economy. Such possibilities have meant that unions, often in alliance with other groups, have fought against free trade agreements and international institutions promoting corporate globalization. The combination of neo-liberal governments, globalization, and shifts in employment has weakened unions in all countries, though in Canada less than most. Labour strife and protests are likely to continue in the future as unions try to preserve what they have gained in the past, and seek to find ways to organize in industries where they have been weak (see Warskett 2007). The rallies against the loss of manufacturing jobs, which were noted at the beginning of this chapter, illustrate such conflicts, but they also suggest the obstacles to class mobilization in a country as large and diverse as Canada. The loss of manufacturing jobs primarily affects Ontario and Quebec, and has little impact on the burgeoning natural resources and construction industries elsewhere in the country (Ferrao 2006). It is therefore not surprising that the rallies were limited to several cities in Ontario.

CONCLUSION

In this chapter, we have found that, although Marxist theory furnishes many of the key ideas for an understanding of class formation and class conflict, the history of these two processes, in Canada and elsewhere, is more variable, contingent, and dependent on other conditions than Marx anticipated (see Katznelson 1986; Somers 1997). At the very least, modifications of the Marxian view are also required, including those provided by Weber, such as the role of status groups and the development of a new middle class. Although it may still be premature to proclaim "the death of class," as some have done (e.g., Pakulski and Waters 1996), sociologists increasingly

seek new ways to understand class formation and conflict (see Wright 2005). Even Emile Durkheim, the classical sociological theorist who has typically been treated as a precursor of functional theories of stratification, has been enlisted in the ranks of class theorists (for discussion, see Grabb 2007). The occupational groups that Durkheim thought were essential for organic solidarity, the argument goes, also fulfill the criteria for class, as they are based on the technical division of labour in production, are socially institutionalized in the labour market and society, are an important source of identity, and are a basis for collective action (Grusky 2005). It remains to be determined in future studies if such a disaggregated view of classes, whether alone or in combination with Marxist, Weberian, or other conceptions of class, will provide a better basis for understanding social changes and social conflicts.

NOTES

1. The power of individual and small-group "resistance," such as restriction of output, should not be ignored. This resistance has sometimes led to changing managerial strategies to deal with problems such as high rates of turnover.

2. The concept of self-employment does not correspond strictly to Marx's concept of petty bourgeoisie, as it includes both self-employed people who do not employ paid help and those who do (i.e., employers or capitalists). There is some debate in the literature about how many paid employees are required before a self-employed person becomes a member of the capitalist class. For example, Clement and Myles (1994) use three as a threshold.

3. Marxists would argue that many of these people are not really self-employed, insofar as they are actually dependent on a buyer of their product or service. Thus, they are employees in all but name, without many of the benefits and legal protections to which

employees are entitled. An example would be newspaper carriers.

4. This pattern may be due less to capitalist competition than to technological changes, which have made possible larger scales of production, even for family farms. Although often feared, large-scale corporate farming has not been a major factor in Canadian agriculture. In fact, the rate of self-employment in agriculture has declined only marginally since 1931 (Gardner 1995). However, the forces that Marx expected to lead to the demise of the petty bourgeoisie have been at work: declining numbers of small producers; increased average farm size; larger capital investments in farm machinery and equipment; and narrow margins between expenses and revenues, which require many farm households to combine farm and off-farm employment. In fact, all but the very largest family farms (those with revenues of more than half a million dollars) rely on off-farm employment income for more than half of their total income (Bowlby 2002; Statistics Canada, Agriculture Division 2007).

5. This pattern might be expected to vary according to the level of class conflict, but even in an industrial city such as Hamilton, Ontario, in a period of high strike activity, Livingstone and Mangan (1996) found that there was not much spontaneous recognition of class conflict. In his study of a postal workers' strike in the same city in the same time period, Langford (1994) found little enduring change in class consciousness as a result of participation in the strike.

REFERENCES

Akyeampong, Ernest B. 2001a. "Fact sheet on unionization." *Perspectives on Labour and Income* 13, 3:46–54

Akyeampong, Ernest 2001b. "Time lost to industrial disputes." *Perspectives on Labour and Income* 13, 3:14–16

Akyeampong, Ernest 2006. "Increased work stoppages." *Perspectives on Labour and Income* August:5–9

Arai, Bruce 1997. "The road not taken: The transition from unemployment to self-employment in Canada." *Canadian Journal of Sociology* 22:365–382.

Baldwin, John R., and Desmond Beckstead 2003. "Knowledge workers in Canada's economy, 1971–2001." Statistics Canada Micro-economic Analysis Division, Insights on the Canadian Economy Analytical Paper No. 4.

Baldwin, John R., Ron S. Jarmin, and Jianmin Tang 2002. "The trend to smaller producers in manufacturing: a Canada/U.S. comparison." Statistics Canada Economic Analysis Research Paper Series No. 003.

Beckstead, Desmond, and Guy Gellatly 2006. "Innovation capabilities: Science and engineering employment in Canada and the United States." Statistics Canada Micro-economic Analysis Division, The Canadian Economy in Transition Series Research Paper No. 011.

Bowlby, Geoff 2002. "Farmers leaving the field." *Perspectives on Labour and Income* 14, 1: 23–28.

Braverman, Harry 1974. *Labor and Monopoly Capital*. New York: Monthly Review Press.

Clement, Wallace, and John Myles 1994. *Relations of Ruling: Class and Gender in Postindustrial Societies*. Montreal and Kingston: McGill-Queen's University Press.

Crompton, Susan 1993. "The renaissance of self-employment." *Perspectives on Labour and Income* 5, 2:22–32.

Cruikshank, Douglas, and Gregory S. Kealey 1987. "Canadian strike statistics, 1891–1950." *Labour/Le Travail* 20:85–145.

Drolet, Marie 2002. "The 'who, what, when and where' of gender pay differentials." The Evolving Workplace Series, No. 4, Statistics Canada and Human Resources Development Canada.

Durkheim, Emile 1893. *The Division of Labor in Society*. Translated by George Simpson. New York: The Free Press, 1933.

Ferrao, Vincent 2006. "Recent changes in employment by industry." *Perspectives on Labour and Income* January:5–10.

Frager, Ruth 1992. *Sweatshop Strife: Class, Ethnicity, and Gender in the Jewish Labour Movement of Toronto, 1900–1939*. Toronto: University of Toronto Press.

Galarneau, Diane 1996. "Unionized workers." *Perspectives on Labour and Income* 8, 1: 43–52.

Galarneau, Diane 2005. "Education and income of lone parents." *Perspectives on Labour and Income* 6, 12:5–16.

Gardner, Arthur 1995. "Their own boss: The self-employed in Canada." *Canadian Social Trends* 37:26–29.

Giddens, Anthony 1973. *The Class Structure of the Advanced Societies*. London: Hutchinson.

Gidengil, Elisabeth 2002. "The class voting conundrum." In D. Baer (ed.), *Political Sociology: Canadian Perspectives*, pp. 274–287. Don Mills, ON: Oxford University Press.

Gidengil, Elisabeth, André Blais, Richard Nadeau, and Neil Nevitte 2003. "Women to the left? Gender differences in political beliefs and policy preferences." In M. Tremblay and L. Trimble (eds.), *Gender and Electoral Representation in Canada*, pp. 140–159. Don Mills, ON: Oxford University Press.

Grabb, Edward G. 2007. *Theories of Social Inequality* (5th ed.). Toronto: Nelson.

Grusky, David, in collaboration with Gabriela Galescu 2005. "Foundations of a neo-Durkheimian class analysis." In Erik Olin Wright (ed.), *Approaches to Class Analysis*, pp. 51–81. Cambridge: Cambridge University Press.

Guppy, Neil, and Scott Davies 1998. *Education in Canada: Recent Trends and Future Challenges*. Ottawa: Statistics Canada.

Heisz, Andrew, Andrew Jackson, and Garnett Picot 2001. "Distributional outcomes in Canada in the 1990s." In K. Banting, A. Sharpe, and F. St-Hilaire (eds.), *The Review of Economic Performance and Social Progress: The Longest Decade: Canada in the 1990s*, pp. 247–272. Montreal: The Institute for Research on Public Policy.

Hou, Feng, and John Myles 2007. "The changing role of education in the marriage market: Assortative marriage in Canada and the United States since the 1970s." Statistics Canada, Business and Labour Market Analysis, Analytical Studies Branch Research Paper No. 299.

Johnston, William, and Douglas Baer 1993. "Class consciousness and national contexts: Canada, Sweden and the United States in historical perspective." *Canadian Review of Sociology and Anthropology* 30, 2:271–295.

Katznelson, Ira 1986. "Working-class formation: Constructing cases and comparisons." In I. Katznelson and A. Zolberg (eds.), *Working-Class Formation*. Princeton: Princeton University Press.

Langford, Tom 1994. "Strikes and class consciousness." *Labour/Le Travail* 34:107–137.

Langford, Tom 2002. "Does class matter? Beliefs about the economy and politics in postindustrial Canada." In D. Baer (ed.), *Political Sociology: Canadian Perspectives*, pp. 307–324. Don Mills, ON: Oxford University Press.

Livingstone, David, and J. Marshall Mangan (eds.) 1996. *Recast Dreams: Class and Gender Consciousness in Steeltown*. Toronto: Garamond.

Livingstone, D.W. 1999. *The Education–Jobs Gap: Underemployment or Economic Democracy*. Toronto: Garamond Press.

Mackenzie, Hugh 2007. "Timing is everything: Comparing the earnings of Canada's highest-paid CEOs and the rest of us." Toronto: Canadian Centre for Policy Alternatives. http://www.growinggap.ca/files/Timing%20is%20Everything.pdf (accessed June 26, 2007)

Marx, Karl 1867. *Capital: A Critical Analysis of Capitalist Production*. Vol. 1. Moscow: Progress Publishers, 1953.

Marx, Karl, and Frederick Engels 1848. "Manifesto of the Communist Party." In Marx and Engels, *Selected Works in Three Volumes*, Vol. 1. Moscow: Progress Publishers, 1969.

Milner, Murray, Jr. 1994. *Status and Sacredness: A General Theory of Status Relations and an Analysis of Indian Culture*. New York: Oxford University Press.

Morissette, René 1991. "Canadian jobs and firm size: Do smaller firms pay less?" Analytical Studies Branch, Statistics Canada, Research Paper No. 35.

Morissette, René 1998. "The declining labour market status of young men." In Miles Corak (ed.), *Labour Markets, Social Institutions, and the Future of Canada's Children*, pp. 31–50. Ottawa: Minister of Industry.

Morissette, René, and Anick Johnson 2005. "Are good jobs disappearing in Canada?" Analytical Studies Branch, Business and Labour Market Analysis Division, Statistics Canada, Research Paper No. 239.

Morissette, René, Grant Schellenberg, and Anick Johnson 2005. "Diverging trends in unionization." *Perspectives on Labour and Income* 6, 4 (April):5–12.

Myles, John, Feng Hou, Garnett Picot, and Karen Myers 2006. "Why did employment and earnings rise among lone mothers during the 1980s and 1990s?" Statistics Canada, Business and Labour Market Analysis, Analytical Studies Branch, Research Paper Series No. 282. Ottawa: Minister of Industry.

Myles, John, and Adnan Turegin 1994. "Comparative studies in class structure." *Annual Review of Sociology* 20:103–124.

Pakulski, Jan, and Malcolm Waters 1996. *The Death of Class*. London: Sage.

Rinehart, James, Christopher Huxley, and David Robertson 1997. *Just Another Car Factory? Lean Production and Its Discontents*. Ithaca, NY: ILR Press.

Saez, Emmanuel, and Michael R. Veall 2005. "The evolution of high incomes in northern America: Lessons from Canadian evidence." *American Economic Review* 95, 3 (June): 831–849.

Somers, Margaret R. 1997. "Deconstructing and reconstructing class formation theory: Narrativity, relational analysis, and social theory." In John R. Hall (ed.), *Reworking Class*, pp. 73–105. Ithaca, NY: Cornell University Press.

Sørensen, Aage B. 1994. "The basic concepts of stratification research: Class, status, and power." In David B. Grusky (ed.), *Social Stratification in Sociological Perspective: Class, Race and Gender*. Boulder, CO: Westview.

Statistics Canada 2006a. *The Canadian Labour Market at a Glance 2005*. Ottawa: Minister of Industry.

Statistics Canada 2006b. "Unionization." *Perspectives on Labour and Income* August: 18–42.

Statistics Canada 2007. CANSIM Table 282-0012—Labour force survey estimates (LFS), employment by class of worker, North American Industry Classification System (NAICS) and sex, annually (persons).

Statistics Canada, Agriculture Division, Whole Farm Data Projects Section 2007. *Statistics on Income of Farm Families 2004*. Ottawa: Minister of Industry.

Statistics Canada, Labour Statistics Division 2004. *Workplace and Employee Survey Compendium 2001*. Ottawa: Minister of Industry.

Stinchcombe, Arthur L. 1990. *Information and Organizations*. Berkeley, CA: University of California Press.

Vosko, Leah F., Nancy Zukewich, and Cynthia Cranford 2003. "Precarious jobs: A new typology of employment." *Perspectives on Labour and Income* October:15–26.

Warskett, Rosemary 2007. "Remaking the Canadian labour movement: Transformed work and transformed labour strategies." In V. Shalla and W. Clement (eds.), *Work in Tumultuous Times: Critical Perspectives*, pp. 380–400. Montreal and Kingston: McGill-Queen's University Press.

Weber, Max 1922. *Economy and Society: An Outline of Interpretive Sociology*. Edited by Guenther Roth and Claus Wittich. Berkeley, CA: University of California Press, 1968.

Western, Bruce 1995. "A comparative study of working-class disorganization: Union decline in eighteen advanced capitalist countries." *American Sociological Review* 60:179–201.

White, Julie 1993. *Sisters and Solidarity: Women and Unions in Canada*. Toronto: Thompson Educational Publishing.

Wright, Erik Olin (ed.) 2005. *Approaches to Class Analysis*. Cambridge: Cambridge University Press

Yates, Charlotte, and Belinda Leach 2007. "Industrial work in a post-industrial age." In V. Shalla and W. Clement (eds.), *Work in Tumultuous Times: Critical Perspectives*, pp. 163–191. Montreal and Kingston: McGill-Queen's University Press.

chapter four

Affluence, Power, and Strikes in Canada, 1973-2005

Robert J. Brym

(An original chapter written for this volume. I thank Jonah Butovsky, John Fox, Morley Gunderson, Alan Harrison, Reza Nakhaie, Gregg Olsen, and Michael Shalev for helpful comments on a draft of this chapter.)

AFFLUENCE, UNEMPLOYMENT, AND STRIKES

Common sense suggests that affluence breeds contentment. On this assumption, people with secure jobs, good working conditions, and high wages are happier than people who face the prospect of unemployment, poor working conditions, and low wages. Moreover, according to the common-sense view, happier workers are less likely to strike. After all, compared with unhappy workers, their needs and demands seem closer to having been met. They appear to lack the deprivations that would motivate them to strike.

It follows from the common-sense view that there ought to be an observable association between measures of strike activity and measures of economic well-being. Figure 4-1, covering the 1973–2000 period, seems to suggest there is such an association.[1] The graph's horizontal axis shows GDP per capita (GDPpc), or the total value of goods and services produced in Canada in a year divided by the number of people living in the country at year end. GDPpc is an indicator of the economic well-being of the average Canadian. It is measured in constant (1992) dollars to eliminate the influence of inflation. In effect, this indicator of economic well-being shows the purchasing power of the average Canadian in a given year. Meanwhile, the graph's vertical axis shows weighted strike frequency, or the number of strikes that took place in Canada

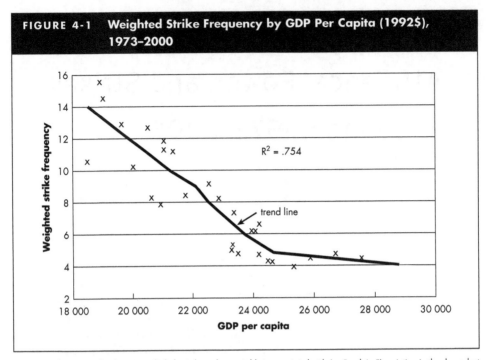

FIGURE 4-1   Weighted Strike Frequency by GDP Per Capita (1992$), 1973–2000

Notes: (1) R^2 measures the degree to which the independent variable is associated with (or "explains") variation in the dependent variable. If the independent variable accounts for none of the variation in the dependent variable, the value of R^2 is 0. If it accounts for all of the variation, its value is 1. The R^2 given here is adjusted for the number of cases. (2) The "trend line" is a LOWESS curve. LOWESS stands for "locally weighted scatterplot smoothing." After dividing the values of the independent variable into a number of equal parts, the LOWESS curve computes least squares regression lines for each part and then smoothes the lines. This reveals patterns in the data that may be obscured by a single linear regression line computed over all values of the independent variable.

each year divided by the number of non-agricultural workers in the country. The curve formed by annual scores on these two variables slopes downward. This suggests that when well-being is low, propensity to strike is high; and when well-being is high, propensity to strike is low. Affluence, it seems at first glance, does breed contentment.

Case closed? Hardly. GDPpc is an average, and averages can mask more than they reveal. For instance, GDPpc could conceivably rise when the purchasing power of high-income earners (a minority of the population) rises a lot and the purchasing power of middle- and low-income earners (a majority of the population) falls a little. In that case, rising GDPpc would mask the fact that most people are worse off.

Because workers who strike are unlikely to be rich, we need a better measure of workers' well-being than GDPpc. One candidate is the *unemployment rate*. Unemployment is more likely to affect ordinary workers than the well-to-do. Doctors rarely lose their jobs, and business executives, even if they are fired, can live relatively comfortably off savings in the typically short period before they find work again. On the other hand, unemployment is likely to result in a sharp decline in living standards for ordinary workers, and sometimes the period before they find a new job is protracted.

How then does strike activity vary with the unemployment rate? Figures 4-2 and 4-3 provide the surprising answer. During the first half of the 1973–2000 period, weighted strike frequency fell when the

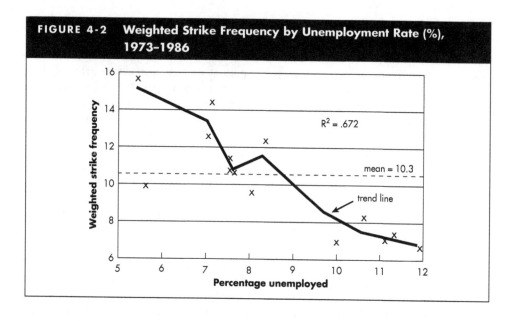

FIGURE 4-2 Weighted Strike Frequency by Unemployment Rate (%), 1973–1986

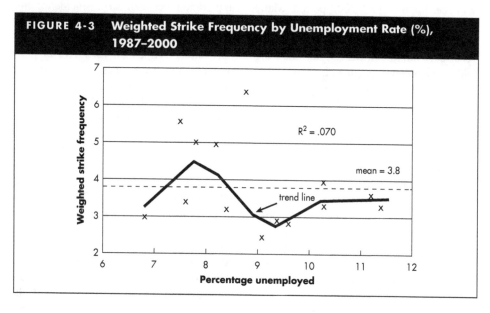

FIGURE 4-3 Weighted Strike Frequency by Unemployment Rate (%), 1987–2000

unemployment rate rose, and rose when the unemployment rate fell (see Figure 4-2). In other words, when workers were most economically deprived, they were *least* inclined to strike, and when they were most secure in their jobs, they were *most* inclined to strike. This is just the opposite of the common-sense view outlined above. Equally unexpected are the results for the second half of the 1973–2000 period (see Figure 4-3). After 1986, the relationship between the unemployment rate and weighted strike frequency virtually disappeared. Thus, the trend line summarizing the association between weighted strike frequency and the unemployment rate shows little trend. What accounts for the inverse association between the unemployment rate and weighted strike frequency in the 1973–1986 period? What accounts for the near disappearance of this inverse association after 1986? These are the intriguing questions I address in the remainder of this chapter.

STRIKE RESEARCH ON THE EFFECT OF THE BUSINESS CYCLE

The existing body of strike research goes a long way toward explaining the trend for the 1973–1986 period, although not, as you will see, for the 1987–2000 period. Many strike researchers begin with the observation that capitalist economies undergo recurrent "boom and bust" cycles. During bad times, unemployment is high and business profitability low. During good times, unemployment is low and business profitability high. They then note the existence of an association between the business cycle and strike frequency (Rees 1952). They argue that, as unemployment falls, strike incidence rises. That is because workers are in a better bargaining position during good economic times. Accordingly, at the peaks of business cycles workers are more likely to enjoy higher savings and alternative job opportunities. At the same time, workers know employers are eager to settle strikes quickly since business is so profitable. Strikes are therefore relatively low risk. In contrast, during economic downturns, workers are less well off and have fewer job alternatives. They understand that employers have little incentive to meet their demands because profitability is low and inventories high. Workers avoid strikes during troughs in the business cycle since they are riskier than in economic

good times. From this point of view, workers' contentment, levels of felt deprivation, and other states of mind are unimportant as causes of strike activity. What matters is how *powerful* workers are. Their bargaining position or their ability to get their own way despite the resistance of employers is what counts. Said differently, strike research suggests we can arrive at superior explanations for variations in strike activity by thinking like sociologists, not psychologists.

The association between strike incidence and the business cycle (or its proxy, the unemployment rate) was first demonstrated empirically for the United States (Ashenfelter and Johnson 1969) and shortly thereafter for Canada (Smith 1972). Since then, researchers have shown that the association between strike incidence and the business cycle was a feature of most advanced capitalist countries in the twentieth century (Hibbs 1976). However, later research also introduced three important qualifications to the argument.

First, before the Second World War, the North American *system of collective bargaining* between workers and employers was not well institutionalized. In Canada, for example, the legal right to organize unions, bargain collectively, and strike with relatively little constraint dates only from 1944. Before then, strikes were often fights for union recognition. They were therefore less responsive to economic conditions (Cruikshank and Kealey 1987; Jamieson 1973 [1957]:102; Palmer 1987; Snyder 1977). As a result, in Canada and the United States, the effect of the business cycle on strike incidence is stronger for the post–Second World War period than for the pre–Second World War period.

The second important qualification concerns the fact that, in much of Western Europe, *the institutional environment* mitigates the effect of economic conditions on strike frequency. One important aspect of the institutional environment is the degree of centralization of bargaining units. Strikes are negotiating tools. They are therefore more frequent during periodic contract renewals than between contracts. In much of Western Europe, however, centralized, nationwide bargaining among workers, employers, and governments means that entire sectors of the workforce come up for contract renewal and negotiation at the same time. Thus, aggregate measures of strike frequency are affected not just by the phase of the business cycle but by the periodicity of contract renewal schedules. In contrast, the absence of a centralized bargaining structure in Canada and the United States makes aggregate measures of strike frequency more sensitive to the business cycle in North America (Harrison and Stewart 1994; Snyder 1977; Franzosi 1989).

Union density, or the proportion of the non-agricultural labour force that is unionized, is another aspect of the institutional environment that influences strike activity. Unions educate workers and enable them to speak with one voice. Their organizational assets allow unions to mobilize workers. It follows that union density will influence strike action, although strike frequency is often less affected than are strike duration and the average size of strikes (Shorter and Tilly 1971).

Finally, the third condition limiting the impact of the business cycle on strike frequency is political. In many Western European countries, left-wing or social democratic parties have formed governments or at least achieved representation in cabinets. This has the effect of moving negotiations over the division of rewards in society from the labour market, where strikes are important bargaining tools, to the political sphere. Where labour is powerful enough to negotiate favourable income redistribution and welfare policies at the political level, industrial conflict tends to

recede.[2] Agreeing to limit strike action has even been used as a bargaining chip in exchange for income redistribution and welfare concessions in Sweden, Germany, and other Western European countries. Thus, in the 1970s and 1980s, strike frequency in Sweden, for example, was relatively insensitive to the business cycle (Franzosi 1989; Hibbs 1978; Korpi and Shalev 1980).

In sum, a substantial body of research demonstrates an association between the business cycle and strike frequency. Moreover, it shows that the association is strongest in North America in the post–Second World War era because that is the setting least influenced by mitigating institutional and political variables (Paldam and Pedersen 1982).

In the context of this research, Figure 4-2 is as ordinary as Figure 4-3 is puzzling. The strong inverse relationship between the unemployment rate and strike frequency for the 1973–1986 period is wholly in line with expectations derived from the research literature. However, contrary to what we are led to expect by the research literature, there is little discernible trend for the 1987–2000 period. The unemployment rate is very *weakly* associated with strike frequency in the latter period. Said differently, cyclicality appears to have been largely wrung out of Canada's labour relations system in the last 14 years of the twentieth century, at least in terms of its influence on the incidence of industrial disputes. With respect to its impact on strike incidence, the business cycle was somehow repressed—and this occurred in precisely the setting (post–Second World War North America) where its impact was previously the greatest.

Why? What accounts for the repression of the business cycle as a determinant of the incidence of Canadian industrial disputes? That is the question on which the remainder of this chapter turns. An intimation of my answer lies embedded in my decision to divide the recent history of Canadian industrial disputes into two 14-year periods, as in Figures 4-2 and 4-3. Inspection of scatter plots suggested that a shift in the direction of the relationship between the unemployment rate and weighted strike frequency took place after 1986. Since data were available for 14 years following 1986, I chose to examine the relationship for a period of equal duration before 1987. That period starts in 1973.

Using 1973 as the cut-off is also justifiable on historical grounds, for 1973 was the year of the first oil shock. In that year, due to war in the Middle East, the price of oil on world markets tripled, intensifying already high inflation and galloping wage demands. As a result, a strike wave that had been growing since the mid 1950s gained force and crested in 1974–1975. In the entire history of Canadian labour, the only strike action that matched that crest was the Winnipeg General Strike of 1919 and the ensuing sympathy strikes that stretched all the way from Amherst, Nova Scotia, to Victoria, British Columbia (see Figure 4-4). Understandably, therefore, the strikes of 1974–1975 caused a strong reaction among government and corporate leaders. They soon took measures to make it substantially more costly for workers to strike. Thus, 1973 marks the beginning of an historical era, one aspect of which is the substantive focus of this chapter.

In the balance of this chapter, I outline how, from the mid 1970s to the 1990s, government and corporate leaders weakened unions and made it more difficult for workers to achieve their goals. These actions had the effect of making strikes less frequent and repressing the effect of the business cycle on the propensity to strike. As you will see, they explain the near-trendless trend line in Figure 4-3.

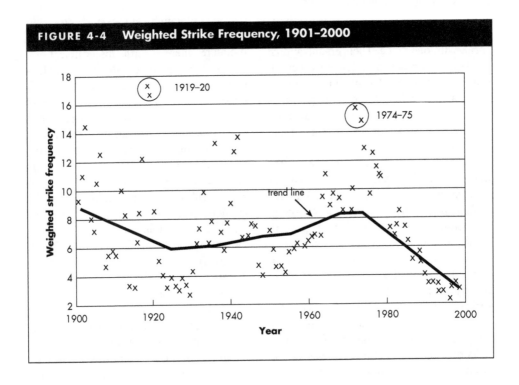

FIGURE 4-4   Weighted Strike Frequency, 1901–2000

A NEW ECONOMIC AND POLITICAL CONTEXT

Government and business leaders reacted to the 1919–1920 strike wave by sending in troops to restore order, throwing union leaders in jail, legislating strikers back to work, and changing laws to allow the deportation of British-born immigrants, who were thought to dominate the strike leadership (Bercuson 1990 [1974]). Faced with a strike wave of similar proportions in 1974–1975, government and business leaders again felt that drastic action was necessary. However, the political, institutional, and cultural environment had changed between these two extraordinary episodes of labour unrest. As a result, strategies for controlling labour were different. In 1944, Canadian workers had won the right to organize, bargain collectively, and strike with relatively little constraint. In the context of three decades of post-war prosperity, their new rights allowed them to win substantial gains in real earnings and a massive expansion of state supports and services. In the mid 1970s, business leaders and governments sympathetic to business felt they had to control labour unrest while fighting wage gains and the growth of the welfare state. To accomplish these tasks, they organized a neo-conservative "counter-revolution" that continues to this day.

The neo-conservative counter-revolution was, however, motivated by more than just the strike wave that crested in the mid 1970s. Rising government debt and global competition also contributed to the decision to go on the political offensive (Johnston 2001).

Government borrowing rose quickly in the 1970s and 1980s. By the end of that period, interest payments were consuming a quarter of the federal government's annual budget. With indebtedness threatening to cripple government programs, the neo-conservative claim that debt reduction is sound public policy made sense to more and more people.

At the same time, global competition was becoming fiercer. By the early 1970s, Japanese and West German industry had fully recovered from the destruction of the Second World War. Manufacturers in these countries were exporting massive quantities of finished goods to North America and other markets. In the 1980s, South Korea, China, and other countries followed suit. With growing global competition threatening the welfare of Canadian industry, big business had to develop new strategies to survive and prosper. One such strategy involved restructuring: introducing computers and robots, eliminating middle-management positions, outsourcing parts manufacturing, and so forth. Another strategy was to increase business opportunities and to bring about job growth by creating a free trade zone encompassing Canada and the United States (MacDonald 2000).

Controlling labour while cutting debt, restructuring, and promoting free trade required deep ideological change. Business leaders therefore set about the task of redefining in the public mind the desirable features of the market, the state, and the relationship between the two. From roughly the end of the Second World War until the mid 1970s, labour demands focused on improving wages and state benefits. Now, an imposing ideological machine sought to convince the public that high wages and generous state benefits decrease the ability of Canadians to compete against workers in other countries. Massive job losses will result (the neo-conservative argument continued) unless wages are held in check and state benefits slashed. That was the main message of Canada's two neo-conservative, corporate-funded think tanks and pressure groups, the Fraser Institute, founded in 1974, and the Business Council on National Issues (BCNI), founded in 1976. The creation of these bodies in the mid 1970s signalled that, like its counterpart in the United States, the Canadian business elite was becoming more ideologically and politically organized and unified (Akard 1992; Langille 1987).

One important sign of neo-conservative success was the outcome of the 1988 "free trade" federal election (Richardson 1996). Just four days before the election, a Gallup poll showed the pro–free trade Progressive Conservatives with the support of only 31% of Canadians intending to vote. The anti–free trade Liberals enjoyed a commanding 43% of the popular vote while the anti–free trade New Democratic Party stood at 22%. At about the same time, an Angus Reid poll disclosed that most Canadians opposed free trade by a margin of 54% to 35%. A majority of Canadians apparently sensed that free trade might open the country to harmful competition with giant American companies, thus leading to job losses and deteriorating living standards.

Then, a mere 100 hours before the first votes were cast, a little-known organization, the Canadian Alliance for Trade and Job Opportunities (CATJO), swung into high gear. CATJO was funded exclusively by the BCNI. With a campaign budget larger than that of the two opposition parties combined, CATJO bankrolled a media blitz promoting the PCs and their free trade policies. A barrage of brochures, newspaper ads, and radio and television commercials supported the idea that Canadian prosperity depends on the removal of all taxes and impediments to trade between Canada and the United States. CATJO argued that if goods and services could be bought and sold across the border without hindrance, and capital invested without restraint, good jobs would proliferate and Canada's economic future would be

assured. The CATJO onslaught succeeded in overcoming some of the public's fears and drawing attention away from the opposition. On election day, the PCs won with 43% of the popular vote. The free trade agreement with the United States was signed just six weeks later.

The free trade agreement, later broadened to include Mexico, sharply increased competition for investment between jurisdictions, leading to a "downward harmonization" of labour policies (Gunderson 1998). Just as water seeks its lowest level, capital that is allowed to flow freely between jurisdictions will seek the jurisdiction with the lowest costs and therefore the highest profit potential, all else being the same. Increasingly, jurisdictions will compete for investment by offering outright tax concessions to investors and ensuring competitive labour costs in the form of lower state benefits, wages, and rates of labour disruption due to strikes. As Canadian workers learned, persistent demands for higher wages—indeed, failure to make wage and other concessions—increase the prospect of plant closings. Where capital mobility is unrestricted, it is only a short hop from southern Ontario to "right to work" states like Georgia or the Maquiladora free trade zone of northern Mexico. In this context, unions lose bargaining power and strikes become riskier actions with a lower probability of achieving their aims.[3]

The slew of government budget cutbacks that took place in the 1990s also had a negative influence on strike incidence. Since workers who go out on strike sometimes quit or lose their jobs, declining income-replacing state benefits make strikes riskier for them. In other words, many of the cutbacks of the 1990s increased the potential cost of job loss to workers and therefore ensured that strike incidence would drop. Restricting eligibility for employment insurance and welfare were two of the most important policy measures affecting the readiness of workers to strike.

High government debt, intense global competition, and neo-conservative publicity and lobbying continued to push the Canadian electorate to the right in the 1990s. The Reform Party became the official opposition, its popularity aided by the defection of members of the working class, most of them non-unionized, from the Liberals and the NDP (Butovsky 2001). The ruling Liberals, meanwhile, adopted much of the neo-conservative agenda. To varying degrees, all major parties supported the new industrial relations regime that had begun to crystallize in the mid 1970s.

A NEW INDUSTRIAL RELATIONS REGIME

Beginning in the mid 1970s, governments adopted a series of measures aimed at better controlling labour (Panitch and Swartz 1993 [1985]). Among them was the establishment of "wage and price controls" that, in practice, limited only wages but claimed to require equal sacrifices from labour and business. That strategy was followed by the Trudeau government in 1975 when it established the Anti-Inflation Board for a three-year period. Blessed by business and condemned by the labour movement, the anti-inflation program suspended collective bargaining for all workers in Canada. By undermining the ability of strikes to achieve wage gains, it also dampened labour militancy. A similar approach was taken in 1982, when the federal government passed the Public Sector Compensation Restraint Act. The Act imposed a two-year wage limit on federal employees, eliminating their right to bargain and strike. The provinces soon passed similar laws. In some cases, provincial cutbacks were even more draconian than those implemented at the federal level. Public employees in Quebec, for example,

took a 20% pay cut. In 1991, the federal government announced a one-year wage freeze for federal employees followed by a 3% limit on wage increases for the next two years. By 1993, even the Ontario NDP was backing wage restraint. In that year, the government of Bob Rae introduced a "Social Contract" that overruled the provisions of existing collective agreements and effectively reduced the wages of all 900 000 provincial employees for a three-year period.

A second method of labour control involved amending a variety of laws and regulations. For example, governments persistently broadened the definition of "management" and "essential service," thereby denying many public-sector workers the right to strike. Thus, in 1984 nearly 76% of public-service workers negotiating contracts were designated as providing managerial or essential services. In the preceding set of negotiations, fewer than 47% of those workers were so designated. In addition, and to varying degrees, governments imposed restrictions on political strikes and secondary picketing (picketing beyond the plant or department affected by a strike). They increased employers' rights to fight organizing drives and employees' rights to attempt decertification. They banned strikes in designated work sites, weakened the ability of unions to discipline members who carried out anti-union activities, permitted unions to be sued, and, in most jurisdictions, allowed the use of replacement workers. One result of these actions was that, beginning in 1984, union density began to decline (see Figure 4-5).

Finally, throughout the 1980s, and particularly after Brian Mulroney's Progressive Conservative government was elected in 1984, federal and provincial governments increasingly adopted ad hoc back-to-work legislation to weaken workers' bargaining position and thereby limit strike action. Used on average only 0.2 times per year in

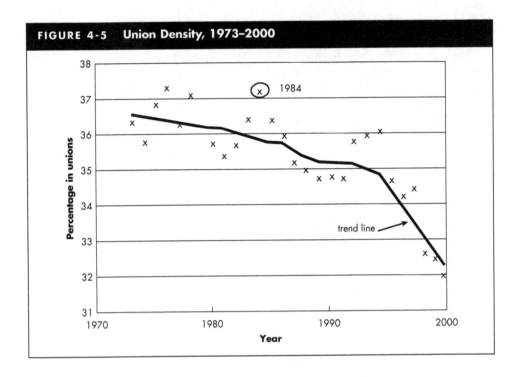

FIGURE 4-5   Union Density, 1973–2000

the period 1950–1954, back-to-work laws were passed on average 5.0 times per year in the period 1975–1979 and 5.4 times per year in the period 1985–1989.

At first, limiting the right to strike was widely viewed as a temporary measure necessitated by fear of a resurgence of the strike wave of 1974–1975, the highest inflation rates Canada had ever seen, and the deep recessions of 1981–1982 and 1991–1992. However, limiting the right to strike became a matter of an enduring, if unstated, public policy, largely because economic and political conditions required a less expensive and less militant workforce. By the mid 1980s, a new labour relations regime had crystallized. One of its main purposes was to render labour's ultimate bargaining tool—the strike—increasingly superfluous as a means of bargaining for improved terms of employment.

CONCLUSION: THE WITHERING AWAY OF THE STRIKE?

About 1960, some influential social scientists predicted that the strike was "withering away." The working class, they wrote, had become "embourgeoisified" due to growing affluence. Class conflict was supposedly becoming "institutionalized" in stable systems of collective bargaining. These developments were viewed as a sort of natural evolutionary process, part of the peaceful unfolding of the "inner logic of industrialization" (Ross and Hartman 1960; Dahrendorf 1959).

In the 1960s and 1970s, an international strike wave caught these social scientists by surprise. It cast doubt on the validity of their generalizations. Now, however, amid an international "resurgence of labour quiescence" (Shalev 1992) that has lasted more than two decades, some observers may be tempted to argue that affluence has at last caused the strike to wither away. For them, the generalizations of 1960 may appear valid after all.

My analysis suggests we should avoid this conclusion. I have shown that a measure of average affluence (GDPpc) is inversely associated with weighted strike frequency but is a poor measure of the economic conditions that shape the lives of Canadian workers. The unemployment rate is a much better indicator of workers' economic conditions; and for the 1973–1986 period, the unemployment rate varied inversely with weighted strike frequency. This suggests that the relative power or bargaining position of workers—not their level of affluence—determined their propensity to strike. Complicating the story, however, is a fact most researchers have overlooked. In the 1987–2000 period, the inverse relationship between the unemployment rate and weighted strike frequency nearly disappeared.[4] The business cycle had little effect on workers' propensity to strike. The reason? Actions taken by employers and governments from the mid 1970s to the late 1990s—introducing free trade, cutting budgets for a wide range of government assistance programs, passing laws and regulations that undermined unions—disempowered workers and rendered the strike a less effective weapon.

In sum, the history of Canadian industrial relations since the mid 1970s suggests that the "inner logic" of industrial capitalism is driven by power, not alleged evolutionary imperatives such as the rising average level of affluence. Industrial relations systems are institutionalized forms of class conflict—that is, enduring legal resolutions of historically specific struggles between workers and employers. But "enduring" does not mean "permanent." Trends lasting a few decades should not be

confused with the end of history. Industrial relations systems change when power is massively redistributed between classes. In Canada, for example, a massive redistribution of power in favour of workers took place from the mid 1940s on, when workers won the legal right to unionize and strike and were in a position to extract increased disposable income and benefits from employers and governments. Another massive redistribution of power, this time in favour of employers, took place after the mid 1970s. The Canadian industrial relations regime was transformed on both occasions. The transition from the first regime to the second was marked by a change in the relationship between strike frequency and the business cycle. It follows that, however difficult it might be to imagine in the current industrial relations climate, another massive shift in the distribution of power in society could once again help the strike regain its former popularity.

POSTSCRIPT: AN UPDATE AND SOME COMPARISONS

In Canada, strikes continued to decline in frequency in the first years of the twenty-first century. Between 2000 and 2005, weighted strike frequency fell nearly 30%. Moreover, the non-association between the unemployment rate and weighted strike frequency persisted until 2005, the most recent year for which data are available as of this writing.

Is Canada unique? The United States also exhibited a strong association between the unemployment rate and weighted strike frequency in the decades after the Second World War. Did that association disappear after the mid 1980s, as it did in Canada? And what about Western European countries such as Sweden, where, for reasons described earlier, the association between the unemployment rate and weighted strike

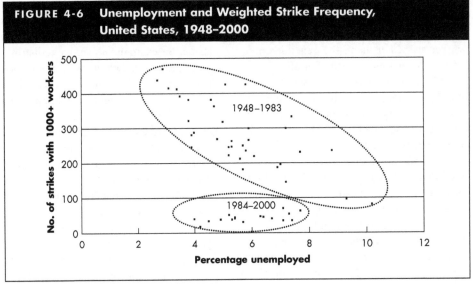

FIGURE 4-6   Unemployment and Weighted Strike Frequency,
United States, 1948–2000

Source: U.S. Department of Labor (2000a; 2000b; 2000c).

frequency was weaker than in North America? Are rich countries outside North America influenced by social forces that have shaped the Canadian pattern of strike activity in recent decades?

Figure 4-6 helps to answer the first set of questions. Change in the association between the unemployment rate and weighted strike frequency in the United States was evident three years earlier than in Canada, but the direction of change was identical in the two countries (Rosenfeld 2006). In the mid 1980s, both Canada and the United States saw the negative association turn into a non-association as employers and governments took concerted action to suppress strike frequency. The changing association between the unemployment rate and weighted strike frequency is thus a North America–wide pattern.

Figure 4-7 helps to answer the second set of questions. Strike frequency declined even more rapidly in Sweden than in Canada over the past two decades.

In Canada in 2005, weighted strike frequency was one-third as high as it was in 1987, but in Sweden it was just one-fifth as high.

These observations suggest that patterns of Canadian strike activity are not made entirely or even largely in Canada. They are strongly influenced by regional and global forces. Specifically, the consolidation of power by the owners and chief beneficiaries of multinational corporations that began in the 1970s was a worldwide phenomenon. By the 1980s, it resulted in the imposition of a host of new arrangements, including free trade agreements, liberal economic policies, and restrictive labour relations regimes on a large part of the world's population. It follows that if the decline in strike activity that has taken place in Canada and other countries in recent decades is in substantial measure an effect of globalization, the prospects for a revival of strike activity may be bound up with the movement to resist globalization in its present form.

FIGURE 4-7   Index of Weighted Strike Frequency, Canada and Sweden, 1987–2005 (1987 = 100)

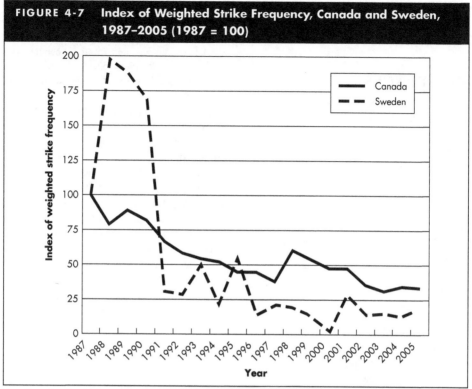

Note: The index of strike frequency is the number of strikes divided by the size of the active paid labour force, with the value for 1987 set at 100. U.S. data, not shown here, closely track the Canadian trend.

Source: International Labour Organization (2007).

NOTES

1. Data sources for this chapter are as follows:

    Population: CANSIM (2002b).

    Gross Domestic Product per Capita: CANSIM (2002a).

    Strikes: Statistics Canada, "Series E190-197 . . . " (2001); Human Resources Development Canada (2002).

    Union membership: Statistics Canada, "Series E175-177 . . . " (2001); Human Resources Development Canada (2001); Union Membership (2000).

    Non-agricultural workers (1902–10 and 1912–20 interpolated): *Fifth Census . . .* (1915), Table 1, p. 13; *Labour Organizations . . .* (1973) pp. xxii–xxiii; *1994–1995 Directory . . .* (1995) p. xiii; Union Membership (2000).

    Unemployment: CANSIM (2001).

2. That is why the influence of union density on strike action peaks at intermediate levels of union density and then tapers off. In countries with the highest proportion of unionized workers, unions tend to exert considerable political influence.

3. As Morley Gunderson commented on a draft of this chapter, the argument developed here is also an argument about wage concessions. Moreover, for strike incidence to fall, the *joint* cost of strikes to both workers and employers must increase. In the present case, the cost of strikes to employers has increased, partly because strikes threaten the loss of global market share.

4. See, however, Cramton and Tracy (1994), who reach similar conclusions about the United States in the 1980s.

REFERENCES

Akard, Patrick J. 1992. "Corporate mobilization and political power: The transformation of U.S. economic policy in the 1970s." *American Sociological Review* 57:587–615.

Ashenfelter, Orley, and George Johnson 1969. "Bargaining theory, trade unions, and industrial strike activity." *American Economic Review* 59:35–49.

Bercuson, David Jay 1990 [1974]. *Confrontation at Winnipeg: Labour, Industrial Relations, and the General Strike* (rev. ed.). Montreal: McGill-Queen's University Press.

Butovsky, Jonah 2001. *The Decline of the New Democrats: The Politics of Postmaterialism or Neoliberalism?* Ph.D. dissertation, Department of Sociology, University of Toronto.

CANSIM 2001, "Unemployment rate age 15+ SA CDA." Retrieved April 4, 2001 (http://dc2. chass.utoronto.ca/cansim2/English/index. html).

CANSIM 2002a. "G.D.P., expenditure-based, 1992$/gross domestic pr at market prices." Retrieved January 7, 2002 (http://dc2.chass. utoronto.ca/cansim2/English/index.html).

CANSIM 2002b. "Population of Canada, by province/Canada." Retrieved January 7, 2002 (http://dc2.chass.utoronto.ca/cansim2/ English/index.html).

Cramton, Peter C., and Joseph S. Tracy 1994. "The determinants of U.S. labour disputes." *Journal of Labor Economics* 12:180–209.

Cruikshank, Douglas, and Gregory S. Kealey 1987. "Strikes in Canada, 1891–1950." *Labour/Le Travail* 20:85–145.

Dahrendorf, Ralf 1959. *Class and Class Conflict in Industrial Society.* London: Routledge & Kegan Paul.

Fifth Census of Canada, 1911 Vol. VI. 1915. Ottawa: Census and Statistics Office, Department of Trade and Commerce.

Franzosi, Roberto 1989. "One hundred years of strike statistics: Methodological and theoretical issues in quantitative strike research." *Industrial and Labor Relations Review* 42:348–362.

Gunderson, Morley 1998. "Harmonization of labour policies under trade liberalization." *Industrial Relations* 53. Retrieved April 9, 2001 (http://www.erudit.org/erudit/ri/v53no1/ gunder/gunder.html).

Harrison, Alan, and Mark Stewart 1994. "Is strike behavior cyclical?" *Journal of Labor Economics* 12:524–553.

Hibbs, Douglas 1976. "Industrial conflict in advanced industrial societies." *American Political Science Review* 70:1033–1058.

Hibbs, Douglas 1978. "On the political economy of long-run trends in strike activity." *British Journal of Political Science* 8:153–175.

Human Resources Development Canada 2001. "Special tabulation on union membership, 1960–2000."

Human Resources Development Canada 2002. "Chronological perspective on work stoppages in Canada (work stoppages involving one or more workers), 1976–2000." Retrieved March 27, 2002 (http://labour-travail.hrdc-drhc.gc.ca/doc/wid-dimt/eng/ws-at/table.cfm).

International Labour Organization 2007. "Yearly data." Retrieved May 18, 2007 (http:// laborsta.ilo.org/).

Jamieson, Stuart 1973 [1957]. *Industrial Relations in Canada* (2nd ed.). Toronto: Macmillan.

Johnston, William A. 2001. "Class and politics in the era of the global economy." In Doug Baer (ed.), *Political Sociology: Canadian Perspectives*, pp. 288–306. Don Mills, ON: Oxford University Press.

Korpi, Walter, and Michael Shalev 1980. "Strikes, power and politics in the Western nations, 1900–1976." *Political Power and Social Theory* 1:301–334.

Labour Organizations in Canada 1972 1973. Ottawa: Economics and Research Branch, Canada Department of Labour.

Langille, David 1987. "The business council on national issues and the Canadian state." *Studies in Political Economy* 24:41–85.

MacDonald, L. Ian (ed.) 2000. *Free Trade: Risks and Rewards.* Montreal and Kingston: McGill-Queen's University Press.

1994–1995 Directory of Labour Organizations in Canada 1995. Ottawa: Minister of Supply and Services Canada.

Paldam, Martin, and Peder Pedersen 1982. "The macroeconomic strike model: A study of seventeen countries, 1948–1975." *Industrial and Labor Relations Review* 35:504–521.

Palmer, Bryan D. 1987. "Labour protest and organization in nineteenth century Canada, 1820–1890." *Labour/Le Travail* 20:61–83.

Panitch, Leo, and Donald Swartz 1993 [1985]. *The Assault on Trade Union Freedoms: From Wage Controls to Social Contract* (2nd ed.). Toronto: Garamond Press.

Rees, Albert 1952. "Industrial conflict and business fluctuations." *Journal of Political Economy* 60:371–382.

Richardson, R. Jack 1996. "Canada and free trade: Why did it happen?" In Robert J. Brym (ed.), *Society in Question*, pp. 200–209. Toronto: Harcourt Brace Canada.

Rosenfeld, Jake 2006. "Desperate measures: Strikes and wages in post-accord America." *Social Forces* 85:235–265.

Ross, Arthur M., and Paul T. Hartman 1960. *Changing Patterns of Industrial Conflict.* New York: Wiley.

Shalev, Michael 1992. "The resurgence of labour quiescence." In Marino Regini (ed.), *The Future of Labour Movements*, pp. 102–132. London: Sage.

Shorter, Edward, and Charles Tilly 1971. "The shape of strikes in France, 1830–1960." *Comparative Studies in Society and History* 13:60–86.

Smith, Douglas A. 1972. "The determinants of strike activity in Canada." *Industrial Relations* 27:663–677.

Snyder, David 1977. "Early North American strikes: A reinterpretation." *Industrial and Labor Relations Review* 30:325–341.

Statistics Canada 2001. "Series E175-177: Union membership in Canada, in total, as a percentage of non-agricultural paid workers, and union members with international affiliation, 1911 to 1975 (thousands)." Retrieved March 29, 2001 (http://www.statcan.ca/english/freepub/11-516-XIE/sectione/sectione. htm#Unions).

Statistics Canada 2001. "Series E190-197: Number of strikes and lockouts, employers and workers involved and time loss, Canada, 1901 to 1975." Retrieved March 29, 2001 (http://www.statcan.ca/english/freepub/11-516-XIE/sectione/sectione.htm#Unions).

Union Membership in Canada—2000 2000. *Workplace Gazette: An Industrial Relations Quarterly* 3, 3:68–75.

U.S. Department of Labor 2000a. "Labor force statistics from the current population survey." Retrieved December 31, 2000 (http://146.142. 4.24/cgi-bin/surveymost).

U.S. Department of Labor 2003b. "Where can I find the unemployment rate for previous years?" Retrieved August 8, 2003 (http://www.bls.gov/cps/prev_yrs.htm).

U.S. Department of Labor 2000c. "Work stoppage data." Retrieved August 8, 2003 (http://data.bls.gov/labjava/outside.jsp?survey=ws).

FURTHER REFERENCES— SECTION 1: POWER AND CLASS

Baer, Douglas (ed.) 2002. *Political Sociology: Canadian Perspectives.* Don Mills, ON: Oxford University Press. This collection includes a number of papers that deal with issues of political power and inequality, the role of the state in contemporary Canadian society, and related questions.

Brownlee, Jamie 2005. *Ruling Canada: Corporate Cohesion and Democracy.* Halifax: Fernwood Publishing. This monograph critically examines Canada's economic elite. The author argues that, over recent years, the nation's richest and most powerful business leaders have become more integrated and politically unified, asserting considerable influence over government policy and the distribution of wealth.

Carroll, William 2004. *Corporate Power in a Globalizing World: A Study in Elite Social Organization.* Don Mills, ON: Oxford University Press. This book considers the structure of corporate business ownership in Canada and the patterns of connection linking large-scale enterprises both within Canada and internationally. The role played by Canada's corporate elite in shaping these structures and patterns is given special consideration.

Clement, Wallace, and Leah Vosko (eds.) 2003. *Changing Canada: Political Economy as Transformation*. Montreal and Kingston: McGill-Queen's University Press. This edited volume examines political transformations, welfare state restructuring, international boundaries and contexts, the new urban experience, and creative resistance. The authors question dominant ways of thinking and promote alternative ways of understanding and explaining Canadian society and politics that encourage progressive social change.

Evans, Bryan, and John Shields 1998. *Reinventing the State: Public Administration Reform in Canada*. Halifax: Fernwood Publishing. This book looks at the trend toward a shrinking role for government in Canadian society in the 1990s and links this trend to such contemporary developments as globalization and the state economic crisis. The authors suggest alternatives to this reduced role of government in the lives of Canadians.

Global Transformations Website. Retrieved September 4, 2007 (http://www.polity.co.uk/global/research.htm). This website provides good background for researching issues related to globalization. Readers should know that this is hosted by a publisher (Polity Press) in England. However, it is a useful and comprehensive resource.

Held, David, and Aysa Kaya (eds.) 2007. *Global Inequality: Patterns and Explanations*. Cambridge: Polity Press. This is an edited volume that includes recent analyses by numerous writers on problems of income inequality, poverty, and related issues around the world.

McMullin, Julie 2004. *Understanding Social Inequality: Intersections of Class, Age, Gender, Ethnicity, and Race in Canada*. Don Mills, ON: Oxford University Press. In this analysis, the author explores how various forms of social inequality, including class, age, gender, race, and ethnicity, all intersect and simultaneously shape the power structure, the ideological system, and the distribution of resources in Canada.

Ornstein, Michael, and Michael Stevenson 1999. *Politics and Ideology in Canada*. Montreal and Kingston: McGill-Queen's University Press. This book examines the question of ideological power in Canada. The analysis compares the perspectives of Canada's elite leadership with those of the general public on a range of important issues, such as state power and support for government welfare programs.

Socio-Economic Bases of Social Inequality

A. INCOME, WEALTH, AND POVERTY
B. OCCUPATION
C. EDUCATION

In the previous section we saw that the private ownership of productive economic property contributes to a fundamental social division in Canadian society. For a very small number of Canadians, variously defined as an elite or as a ruling, upper, or capitalist class, ownership provides power and privilege. However, beyond ownership there are many other dimensions of social inequality, three of which are explored in this section. These include inequalities that are tied to *income, wealth, and poverty*; *occupation*; and *education*.

These three bases of inequality are closely interrelated. A causal connection runs from education through occupation to income, in that schooling typically affects job prospects, and a person's job largely determines income. Furthermore, income has consequences beyond an individual's own lifetime, influencing, for example, the educational opportunities of one's children, and thus their jobs and incomes too. Several issues involved in this complex interrelationship should be emphasized.

First, in the study of these forms of inequality, it is necessary to clarify whether the focus is on individuals or families. When seeking to explain the occupations or incomes of people, sociologists normally study individuals. However, when looking at intergenerational job mobility or the inheritance of wealth, the focus is mainly on families. Thus, the unit of observation (individuals or families) should be made clear.

Second, discussions about inequality often involve the idea of transmission across generations. To what degree is social inequality *reproduced* over time? Research of this type investigates how family origin or family background influences the attainment of education, occupation, or income levels. Questions of the openness or rigidity of opportunities in society are central here, as is the awareness that inequalities endure across generations.

Third, the relations among the three dimensions—income or wealth, occupation, and education—are not fixed and, although they are intertwined, the associations among them are not perfect. That is, even though these forms of inequality are closely tied in Canada, some people with little education do earn large incomes, for example. Such individuals are relatively rare, however, as are people who live in poverty or lack jobs despite having high levels of education. In other words, the connections linking these three types of inequality are not deterministic, but *probabilistic* (although often quite strong).

Fourth, while social inequality is a feature of all societies, the *degree of inequality is variable*. At different times and in different societies the amount of inequality varies. Sociologists studying inequality in Canada, therefore, have been concerned with how inequality here compares with that in other countries, and also with how levels of inequality may be changing over time.

Explanations for the levels of social inequality in Canada often vary. While this section of the book stresses facts about inequality, issues of interpretation are equally important. Contrary to popular wisdom, facts do not speak for themselves. For example, how are we to understand or explain the consistent finding that women on average earn less money than men? As the selections in Section 3 indicate (see, e.g., Chapter 15 by Creese and Beagan), there are several competing and even conflicting reasons that sociologists have put forward to explain gender inequality.

Throughout this book, you will encounter certain ideas that are consistent touchstones for interpreting social inequality. Two of these basic perspectives are raised here, so that you will recognize, compare, and assess them when you think about the reasons behind social inequality in Canada.

One way people try to explain inequality is by pointing to its positive consequences for societal well-being. This line of reasoning holds that people will only be motivated to acquire useful skills and to work at responsible jobs if they receive high rewards for doing so. In this way, people with drive, talent, and ability will be encouraged to use these attributes for the benefit of both themselves and the society in general. From this perspective, tangible incentives, including high incomes, prestige, and influence, must go to those occupying key positions in society. The *achievement* principle is central to this explanation for differences in income, prestige, or rank (see Davis and Moore 1945 for more detail).

A very different argument is taken by those who emphasize that certain groups in society benefit more than others from the way in which social structures are organized. Tensions and disputes over aspects of inequality are seen to stem from the opposing interests of different groups, as one group attempts to control profit or privilege at the expense of another group. For some researchers, these interest groups are class-based, while for others they are defined by non-class factors such as gender or ethnicity. In all of these instances, however, the interpretation is that conflict or struggle is the key to understanding social inequality. The struggle for control over economic resources, power, and privilege is understood as the key motor of social change (see, e.g., Wright 1985 for a class-based account of this perspective).

The tension between these two perspectives underlies much of the writing on inequality, although there are several variants of each approach. In general, though, those who stress achievement tend to focus on equality of opportunity. They also emphasize the freedom of individuals to pursue their own goals, interests, and destiny. However, an emphasis on equality of condition or outcome, for all people, usually comes from those who argue that the control and accumulation of power and profit by one group gives them (and their children) an unfair advantage in society. These competing ideas continue to inform much of the discussion about the causes of social inequality in the present day.

INCOME, WEALTH, AND POVERTY

We begin this section by exploring the distribution of money. At the extremes of the income distribution are affluence and poverty, the rich and the poor. The readings in this section examine how economic rewards are distributed in Canadian society, how that distribution has changed over time, what governments have and have not done in attempting to influence the distribution, and what arguments are made for and against income redistribution.

The first reading, by Peter Urmetzer and Neil Guppy, explains that while the economic pie has grown bigger in the post–Second World War era, the sizes of the slices apportioned to various income groups have remained remarkably stable. What makes this surprising is that these decades since the Second World War have often been described in terms of a growing welfare state. Whatever else the state may have done during this period, it is not true that the government played Robin Hood, taking from the rich and giving to the poor. The state looked after everyone's welfare equally, such that very little, if any, redistribution of income occurred. More recently—that is, in the 1980s and 1990s—

the size of the economic pie has not grown, for wages and salaries have been stubbornly stable. For many people this has meant working harder and longer just to keep pace with inflation. One consequence is the resistance of Canadians to any tax increases.

Many believe that the government uses the tax system to collect from the rich to give to the poor. As Urmetzer and Guppy describe, the poor do receive some transfer income, but so too do the rich. The result is that little income redistribution occurs. To understand this, it is important to realize that we pay tax in many forms: sales tax, income tax, gasoline tax, excise tax, and so forth. Some of these are progressive taxes, where the size of the tax bite increases with your income, while others are regressive, in that the tax bite is bigger for those with less income. People with large incomes are also able to use tax shelters (and to hire well-paid tax accountants to find such shelters). The net result is that the overall rate of tax paid by all Canadians varies surprisingly little over the entire income scale.

Income, however, is only one part of the material resources Canadians possess. For some—the super-rich—income is far less important than are assets. Wealth is accumulated and stored in land, buildings, stock, precious metals, art, and so on. As James Davies demonstrates in his paper on the distribution of wealth in Canada, there are some extremely rich families in this country. In fact, comparisons with the United States show that there are more rich families per capita in Canada. Furthermore, the distribution of wealth is far more unequal than is the distribution of income, with inheritance of wealth being the major cause of this pattern.

At the other extreme of the distribution of economic resources is poverty. The chapter by Guppy and Hawkshaw addresses this important question. Their analysis begins with thoughts on defining poverty. They consider conceptual definitions of poverty, including a look at how Statistics Canada calculates their "low-income lines" (a phrasing that avoids the word poverty!). An examination of the trends in the extent and distribution of poverty in Canada follows and the article finishes with a look at various poverty reduction strategies.

OCCUPATION

People's occupations are of fundamental importance, because working is what many of us do with most of our waking lives. Our jobs or careers are often at the core of our personal identities, frequently defining who we are in our own minds and in the eyes of others. And, of course, our occupations generate the incomes on which most of us make a living. Occupations also provide at least an approximate measure of where we stand on a wide variety of other inequality dimensions. These include income, education, skill level, degree of responsibility in the workplace, amount of authority over other workers, prestige ranking, and so on.

Perhaps for these reasons, occupation has been viewed by some researchers as the best overall indicator of a person's general social class location or socio-economic rank. The relevance of occupation to the field of social inequality is revealed in the range of problems involving work or occupation that researchers in this field have addressed. These include, for example, the changing composition of the labour force, the extent to which occupational status depends on the attainment of educational credentials, the degree to which the occupational backgrounds of parents influence the occupational attainments of their children, and the problems posed by the changing nature of work in technologically advanced societies.

Such issues form the focus of the two papers chosen for our section on occupational inequality. In the first chapter,

Richard Wanner assesses the question of occupational mobility and occupational status attainment in Canada. He considers the extent to which occupational advantages or disadvantages of parents are inherited by their children when the latter eventually enter the labour force as adults. He also looks at whether the amount of occupational mobility and overall patterns of status attainment have changed over time. These analyses address some of the key debates about the evolving nature of inequality in this country.

In the second chapter on occupation, Graham Lowe and Wolfgang Lehmann provide a detailed analysis of Canada's occupational structure, with special concern for the nature of present-day labour markets and the future of work. Among the major issues considered are the movement to a service-based economy in recent decades; the trend toward more "non-standard" work, including temporary and part-time employment; and the prospects for a growing gap between "good" jobs and "bad" jobs. This selection also addresses the question of gender segregation and gender inequality in the Canadian labour force, including the gap in earnings between male and female workers. Throughout the chapter, the author considers the possible implications of several of these issues for policy-makers in business and government.

EDUCATION

How much education a person attains is arguably the most important of the three inequality dimensions under discussion in this section on income, occupation, and education. The argument would be that education is the most important because educational credentials are among the best predictors of attainment of the other two rewards. Studies of social mobility show this to be the case

(Wanner 1999). Education is very often the sole avenue to the best jobs and the highest salaries.

It is little wonder, then, that academic researchers, educational practitioners, and politicians have devoted substantial attention to the question of providing equality in the opportunity to acquire education. The first selection, by Neil Guppy, asks how a child's educational attainment is affected by class, gender, ethnicity, race, and ancestry. If there was complete equality of educational opportunity in Canada, the effect of these factors would be minimal, so that schooling attainment would depend only on people's own effort and ability. Conversely, if these other factors do affect educational attainment, this suggests that equality of educational opportunity is not prevalent in Canada. Guppy demonstrates that class continues to affect educational attainment, but that the effects of gender as well as ethnicity and race are more muted now then they were several decades ago. However, the story for ethnicity and race is nuanced because the educational fortunes of First Nations peoples and some visible racial minorities do not match the positive experiences of other visible minorities or immigrant Canadians. Hence, for people from less privileged classes, and for First Nations and some other groups, educational disadvantages have changed very little in recent decades.

Scott Davies and Vicky Maldonado take up the theme of explaining how class inequalities in educational attainment come about. Why, they ask, does family socio-economic status have such an important impact on schooling destinies? They examine numerous explanations, from purely economic to cultural. If money, for example, were the key, then we would expect that the link between parents' education and their offspring's education would be greatly reduced, if not eliminated, in countries where post-secondary schooling is free. There is no evidence to support this, however, suggesting that money is not the key factor. Another explanation could relate to the expectations of working-class versus middle-class parents. Perhaps, social organization of family life is the major explanatory factor. Working-class families have more rigid working lives, buffeted by shift work, tiring commuting schedules, moonlighting, and so forth, all of which make it harder for them to contribute to school-related activities than is the case for middle-class parents. As Davies and Maldonado conclude, explaining the link between family origin and educational destination has proven to be a very difficult issue. This paper makes a significant contribution to such explanations, however, by showing us some promising lines of argument.

In the final selection on education, Harvey Krahn provides evidence to show that family socio-economic status and the educational attainments of an individual's parents have strong predictive effects on that individual's own educational aspirations, occupational aspirations, and chances of achieving these aspirations. Using a research design that allowed him to follow people from school into the workforce, Krahn shows how powerful a factor family background is in affecting the occupational outcomes of Canadians.

REFERENCES

Davis, Kingsley, and Wilbert E. Moore 1945. "Some Principles of Stratification." *American Sociological Review* 10:242–249.

Wanner, R. 1999. "Expansion and ascription: Trends in educational opportunity in Canada, 1920–1994" (electronic version). *Canadian Review of Sociology*, August.

Wright, Erik Olin 1985. *Classes*. London: Verso Books.

chapter five

Changing Income Inequality in Canada

Peter Urmetzer and Neil Guppy
(An original chapter written
for this volume.)

INTRODUCTION

Misconceptions about income inequality are widespread. Frequently, information is tainted by personal impressions and media accounts. Thus, while the homeless have become a common and all too visible feature of the urban landscape, they comprise only a small portion of Canada's population. The same is true of sports stars and executives earning the seven-figure salaries reported in the media: only a small number of Canadians fall into this million-dollar club. These impressions, although powerful in influencing our perceptions about inequality, are unrepresentative. The fact is that most Canadians fall outside the extremes of excessive poverty and wealth. The majority of people in this

country have such typical incomes that they remain inconspicuous to both the average observer and the sensationalist eye of the media.

Nevertheless, inequality does exist. Canada's economy has historically followed a cycle of bust and boom, and not all Canadians are affected equally by these cycles (see Chapter 7 on poverty). For example, an economic downturn creates a slowdown in new housing construction, causing layoffs in the building industry, while universities and colleges may benefit from the same downturn as more people upgrade their skills, translating into more jobs for teachers. Examples such as these illustrate that we need a more comprehensive way of looking at inequality, an approach that does more than focus narrowly on the rich and the poor. We need to move beyond personal and journalistic accounts, which gravitate toward the unusual.

INCOME

Some people may question the relevance of asking questions about income inequality, especially in a wealthy country such as Canada. From a social science perspective, patterns of economic inequality are important because they reveal the consequences of various social processes and political decisions. Although seldom acknowledged, many political debates directly address issues of economic distribution since these kinds of policies have consequences benefiting some while disadvantaging others. We need some way of assessing these outcomes. We need ways of evaluating claims about the superiority of market forces over government intervention. Evidence of how these policies affect income distribution becomes an indispensable evaluation tool. Invariably, a cut in social programs or a change in tax structure or monetary policy makes some people richer and some people poorer.

The abolition of minimum wage legislation, resulting in higher profits for employers and lower pay for workers, does not affect everyone equally. The increased cost of borrowing suggests that a policy of high interest rates also has diverse consequences, as the borrower's larger interest payments end up as increased profits for investors. One person's loss is another person's gain. This holds true for the majority of economic policy decisions Canadians have grappled with over the past few decades: the struggle over the welfare state, free trade, the deficit, and globalization. Rarely are the consequences of these decisions neutral.

Statistics on income distribution serve to illuminate, at least indirectly, the outcome of these policies. Careful examination of trends in income distribution reveals patterns about the organization of Canadian society. It is this question, then, that provides the primary focus of this chapter: How has income inequality changed in Canada in recent decades? We begin by tracing changes in income.

Subsequent to the poverty and hardship of the Depression years in the 1930s, Canadians have experienced relative affluence. From the 1950s through the late 1970s, Canadians, whether as individuals or in families, enjoyed rising incomes and general economic prosperity. This is true even after inflation is taken into consideration.[1] Figure 5-1 charts the average real income of Canadian families from 1951 through 2005, showing two distinct periods: (1) rising real incomes year upon year from 1951 to 1979, and (2) income stagnation from 1980 through 1996, with a modest rise in the late 1990s and early 2000s. Notice, too, that this is the average income of families, not individuals.

The growth of real income for families from the 1950s through the 1970s reflects a period of sustained and unprecedented expansion in the Canadian economy. Throughout this period, levels of productivity rose, largely based on technological advances and an increasingly highly skilled labour force. Organized labour succeeded in tying wages to productivity and, consequently, earnings grew. However, beginning in the early 1980s, family earnings began to stagnate. This occurred despite the increasing number of married women entering the workforce (from 50% in 1980 to about 80% in 2002). Earnings of married women have done much to keep family poverty rates down. Figure 5-1 shows that although average earnings fluctuated somewhat, family purchasing power

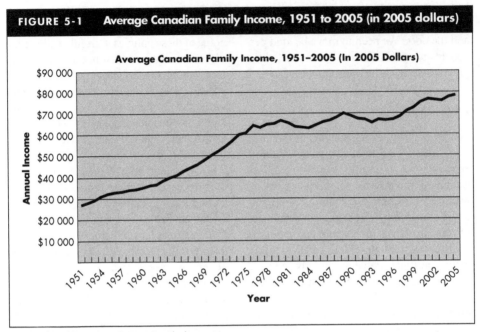

FIGURE 5-1   **Average Canadian Family Income, 1951 to 2005 (in 2005 dollars)**

Source: Adapted from various Statistics Canada documents.

remained essentially flat from 1980 to 1996. In the late 1990s and the early 2000s, family incomes rose more quickly, but even then not as fast as in the decade just after the Second Word War.

Averages, however, suffer from a major shortcoming: they only measure what statisticians call "central tendency" and are silent about dispersion or variation around that central point.[2] To gain a better understanding of these variations, we need an easy method of examining the *distribution* of earned income.

Distribution of Income: Quintiles

A common way to measure income distribution is to divide the population into a small number of equal-size groups, usually fifths, and then examine each group's relative share of the total income. An intuitively appealing way of doing this is to imagine a queue that contains all families in Canada. At the head of this line is the family that earns the highest income; at the tail is the family that earns the lowest income. This line is then divided into five equal-size groups called fifths or quintiles (or 20% of the population). Next, the sum of the income of each of the five groups is calculated. The resulting sum for each group is then presented as a portion of the total income of all five quintiles (or the total income of all families and unattached individuals in Canada).

As Table 5-1 shows, for the top quintile this turns out to be 46.7% in 2005. In other words, of all money earned in Canada in 2005, 46.7% of it was earned by the wealthiest 20% of families. Such disproportion means that only 53.3% was left for the remaining 80% of families. The lowest income earners, the 20% of families at the end of the line, shared a meagre 4.1% of all income.

TABLE 5-1	Percentage of Total Before-Tax Income Going to Families and Unattached Individuals by Quintile, 1951–2005						
Income quintile	**1951**	**1961**	**1971**	**1981**	**1991**	**2001**	**2005**
Lowest quintile	4.4	4.2	3.6	4.6	4.5	4.1	4.1
Second quintile	11.2	11.9	10.6	10.9	10.1	9.7	9.6
Middle quintile	18.3	18.3	17.6	17.6	16.5	15.6	15.7
Fourth quintile	23.3	24.3	24.9	25.1	24.7	23.8	23.9
Highest quintile	42.8	41.4	43.3	41.7	44.2	46.8	46.7

Source: Adapted from Statistics Canada publications *Income in Canada,* various years, and *Income Distributions by Size in Canada,* various years.

If income were distributed perfectly equally in Canada, every group would be allotted an identical share of income (i.e., 20%). As the table shows, the highest quintile is successful in acquiring more than double its 20% share, while the lowest quintile receives less than a quarter of its fifth.

Table 5-1 also tracks how income shares have changed between the years 1951 and 2005. At first glance, there appears to have been little change in the proportion of income that each quintile receives. Closer examination, however, reveals a gradual shift of approximately 4.2% from the second and middle quintiles to the two highest quintiles. Surprisingly, perhaps, it is not the lowest of the quintiles, the point of focus of most poverty studies, where the majority of losses have occurred, but in the second and middle quintiles. The top quintile, which arguably needs it the least, has experienced the biggest increase since 1951, an increase of 3.9 percentage points. Between 1981 and 2005 this increase is especially evident, amounting to 5 percentage points.

As a matter of fact, between 1981 and 2005, the top quintile is the only one that can lay claim to a substantial increase in its share of the national income, with all other quintiles losing ground. This confirms what many middle- and lower-income Canadians are feeling: that it is increasingly difficult to make a living. A 3.5 percentage point gain for the top quintile may appear to be a trivial amount, but given that the total annual income generated in Canada surpasses $1 trillion, this increase translates into more than $50 billion. If this share were given to the lowest quintile, its share would increase to 7.6% of national income, effectively eliminating poverty in Canada.

Canada, compared to other industrialized countries, has fared relatively well with respect to income inequality, particularly when compared to Great Britain and the United States (Olsen 2002). However, as the data in this chapter illustrate, this has recently changed as gains associated with the economic expansion of the 1990s went mainly to higher-income families (Picot and Myles 2005). The reasons for this upward redistribution are not entirely clear. Armine Yalnizyan (2007) documents that this increase cannot be traced to high-income earners working longer hours; quite the contrary, high-income earners are working fewer hours now than in the 1980s, whereas all other income groups are working more. Investment income is also unlikely to explain this increase, as incomes for top income earners kept growing throughout 2000 and 2001 even when the stock market underwent a major correction. The answer may be simple mathematics, as a 3% increase in salary for someone making

$100 000 a year is double that for someone making $50 000 a year. Over even a short period of time, this would explain a considerable amount of divergence in incomes. Another explanation could be a change in the labour market. As the baby boomers start to retire, fewer high-skilled workers are available to fill these jobs, resulting in even higher wages for high-income earners. Since high-income earners are also more likely to retire early, worker shortages will be felt first in this sector.

Transfers and Taxes

The figures in Table 5-1 reflect all forms of income. For example, for those families in the top quintile, earnings from stock market dividends, real estate holdings, pension plans, and professional salaries would be included. By comparison, earnings in the bottom quintile primarily consist of income from employment insurance, pension plans, wages, and social assistance (often informally referred to as "welfare"). The crucial difference to note here is between market income and government transfers. That is, income is either market-based (wages, return on investment, etc.) or collected in the form of transfers (payments designed to assist people who are out of work or retired, including social assistance, employment insurance payments, and government pensions). Once we acknowledge this important distinction, the distribution of income

changes dramatically. As shown in Table 5-2, when only market income is considered, the lowest quintile receives only 2.1% of all income, while the highest quintile earns more than half (51.1%).

The second column of Table 5-2 shows that after transfer payments are taken into account, the lowest quintile sees an income increase from 2.1% of all market income to 4.1% of total income.[3] The highest quintile has a smaller share of the total income (46.7%) than of market income (51.1%).

Beyond the transfer system, the tax system can also be used to aid redistribution. Income tax, at least in theory, is a progressive tax in that high-income earners are taxed at a higher rate than low-income earners.[4] The government then takes these revenues and redistributes them in favour of lower-income families. In other words, what high-income earners pay in the form of proportionally higher taxes goes into the pockets of poorer families as proportionally higher transfers. The end result is a more equitable distribution of income.

For 2005, the most recent data available, the redistributing effect of income taxation is apparent, albeit only minimally (see the far-right column in Table 5-2). Only the highest quintile experienced a decrease in its share (from 46.7 to 44.0%), with all other quintiles gaining. Comparing the columns Income Before Transfers and Income After Taxes shows the effect income tax has on national income, and the

TABLE 5-2	Percentage of Different Income Concepts Going to Families and Unattached Individuals by Quintile, 2005		
Income Quintile	**Income Before Transfers**	**Total Money Income**	**Income After Taxes**
Lowest quintile	2.1	4.1	4.7
Second quintile	7.6	9.6	10.6
Middle quintile	14.8	15.7	16.5
Fourth quintile	24.4	23.9	24.2
Highest quintile	51.1	46.7	44.0

Source: Adapted from the Statistics Canada publication *Income in Canada*, various years.

redistribution characteristic of the welfare state becomes obvious. Here is good evidence of the state acting as the legendary Robin Hood, taking from the rich and giving to the poor.

But this is not the full picture. At this point, we have only examined income taxes, and the bulk of government revenues comes from consumption (e.g., sales taxes, excise taxes) and property taxes. In theory, consumption taxes are flat since everyone pays exactly the same rate, regardless of income (e.g., the 5% Goods and Services Tax). However, many economists and sociologists have argued that in practice consumption taxes are effectively regressive; that is, low-income earners end up paying a higher proportion of their income in consumption taxes than do high-income earners. This conclusion is based on two related arguments.

One line of argument points out that sales taxes constitute a higher proportion of the income of a poor family than a rich one. This is best illustrated by an example. Compare two families, the Browns and the Greens, similar in many respects, with the exception of income. After income tax, the Greens earn half ($30 000) what the Browns do ($60 000). Now both families purchase a used car costing $10 000. The sales tax on this purchase, including GST and Provincial Sales Tax (PST), would amount to around $1500 in most of Canada's provinces. In effect, the Greens pay one-twentieth of their income in sales taxes ($1500/$30 000) while the Browns pay only one-fortieth ($1500/$60 000).

The argument can be made, though, that the wealthier family is likely to spend more on a car, say $20 000, and thus end up paying the equivalent proportion of sales tax. And this is a major shortcoming of this argument: It rests on hypothetical examples that can easily be countered using equally convincing hypothetical examples. The argument that consumption taxes are

regressive, however, gathers steam once spending patterns are taken into consideration. This second criticism focuses less on hypothetical examples and more on outcomes.

Families in lower-income brackets are forced, out of necessity, to spend most of their income and therefore contribute a higher proportion of it to taxes. For example, a family earning $30 000 a year is likely to spend all of its income on food, shelter, clothing, and other basics. By contrast, a family earning $300 000 a year can afford to save or invest a considerable portion of its income in mutual funds or real estate holdings. Money saved is not subject to consumption taxes.

Moreover, not all products and services are taxed equally. For example, the purchase of a home is not subject to PST, and post-secondary tuition fees are taxed by neither the provincial nor the federal government. We know that high-income earners are more likely to be homeowners and send their children to university, thus benefiting from these exemptions. Low-income earners, on the other hand, have less opportunity to take advantage of these tax breaks and therefore end up paying proportionally more of their income in taxes. Thus, with consumption taxes the proportion of tax paid increases as earnings decrease, the direct opposite to the relationship found with income tax. As we saw above, income tax is structured in such a way that high-income earners pay a higher proportion of tax than do low-income earners, a structure that is considered progressive. Applying similar reasoning reveals consumption tax to be regressive.

Once both income and consumption taxes are taken into consideration, the overall redistributing effect of the Canadian taxation system becomes less apparent. As Hunter (1993:104) explains, "what taxes on income give, . . . taxes on spending take away." In other words, income taxes help to redistribute money, but consumption taxes erode much of this redistributive effect. The final outcome is that after different taxes (and tax breaks) are considered, very little Robin Hood remains in the welfare state.

Income Distribution in Other Countries

How fair is the distribution of income in Canada? In the abstract, this is a difficult question to answer, and a response depends on all kinds of philosophical assumptions about merit, human rights, and property relations. On a more practical level, though, we can answer this question by comparing Canada's income distribution to that found in other countries. Table 5-3 shows that Canada distributes its income more equally than the United States, Australia, or the United Kingdom, countries that share cultural ties and economic philosophies that date back to the colonial days of the British Empire (with the exception of Quebec, of

course). Canada, however, does less well when it comes to the lower quintiles. This is true in comparison to Western European countries in general and Scandinavian countries in particular. Not surprisingly, Sweden, often heralded as the exemplar of the welfare state, also has the most equitable distribution of income found in the West. What is surprising is that Japan, a country that cannot even boast a welfare state (but has very low unemployment), has the most generous distribution toward the lowest quintile.

Table 5-3 demonstrates that income can be distributed in a variety of ways and follows no overall or consistent pattern. Income is least equally distributed in South Africa, Mexico, and Brazil. In these countries, a wealthy top quintile occurs at the expense of an impoverished bottom quintile.

In comparison to countries in South America or Asia, Canada's distribution is more equitable. But this could change, especially as the assault on government social programs continues. The elimination

TABLE 5-3	**Income Distribution According to Quintiles in Selected Countries (Various Years)**				
	Lowest Quintile	Second Quintile	Middle Quintile	Fourth Quintile	Highest Quintile
Sweden	9.1	14.0	17.6	22.7	36.6
Japan	10.6	14.2	17.6	22.0	35.7
Germany	8.5	13.7	17.8	23.1	36.9
Canada*	7.2	12.7	17.2	23.0	39.9
Korea (Rep.)	7.9	13.6	18.0	23.1	37.5
Australia	5.9	12.0	17.2	23.6	41.3
UK	6.1	11.4	16.0	22.5	44.0
USA	5.4	10.7	15.7	22.4	45.8
Russian Federation	6.1	10.5	14.9	21.8	46.6
Malaysia	4.4	8.1	12.9	20.3	54.3
Hong Kong	5.3	9.4	13.9	20.7	50.7
Mexico	4.3	8.3	12.6	19.7	55.1
Brazil	2.8	6.4	11.0	18.7	61.1
South Africa	3.5	6.3	10.0	18.0	62.2

* Figures for Canada vary from those presented in Table 5-1 because they are categorized differently (after tax and adjusted for family size).

Source: World Bank, *The World Development Report,* various years.

or reduction of social programs would dramatically alter the distribution of income in this country, no doubt most directly affecting those in the lower quintiles. The contagion of cuts that has swept Canada in recent decades has raised concerns about the "Brazilianization" of our economy, a term that is meant to reflect the stark inequities that plague Brazil, a country completely lacking a welfare state (Therborn 1986). The fear is that by investing too much faith in markets, some governments, including Canada's from time to time, have turned their backs on social programs and ignored the poor. But the stability of income shares in Canada suggests that this view may be overly pessimistic.

Given the dramatic changes that Canadian society has undergone since the Second World War, it is remarkable how stable the distribution of income has remained. In addition to an increase in the participation of women in the labour force and a decline in industrial jobs, these changes include a marked increase in government expenditures on social programs. The fact that income distribution has remained more or less constant alongside the increase in government involvement has led some commentators to question the efficacy of the welfare state as a mechanism for the redistribution of income (e.g., Teeple 2000). An often-quoted study by Hewitt (1977) argues that the redistributive effect of the welfare state is minimal at best. Hewitt's study also shows that the Canadian welfare state lags behind in its redistributive effectiveness, particularly when compared with Western European countries. Given the monumental and pervasive presence of the welfare state in Canadian society—in the form of employment insurance, pensions, education, health services, and other services too numerous to mention—most Canadians would, no doubt, find such a conclusion surprising.

On the face of it, it seems almost inconceivable that Canadian society would be identical in the absence of the welfare state. Yet the quintile approach shows precisely that: between the early 1950s and 2005, a period that saw an explosion of welfare state services, income shares changed relatively little. Does this mean that the seemingly interminable political wrangling over social programs in Canada is essentially about nothing? The answer to this is a resounding no. Those who claim that the welfare state is ineffective must take note that the quintile approach itself does not reveal important changes in Canada's income composition. As we saw, the most common way to present quintiles is by total income—that is, market and transfer income combined. This approach ignores how the composition of income has changed over the years, specifically the ratio of market income to government transfers. Were it not for these transfers, the poorest quintile would receive very little income (see Table 5-2, column 1).

Another change that quintiles ignore is that Canada's most costly social programs, such as health and education, are not included in income statistics because they are received in kind (i.e., as a service) rather than as monies. Nonetheless, this has an effect on income distribution, in that not having to pay for health care or education translates into a decrease in expenditure. This saving rises proportionally as income declines. For example, $1000 for an operation represents a bigger portion of income saved for someone in the bottom quintile (average income for individuals and families was $12 900 for 2005) than someone in the top quintile ($146 500, same category, same year) and therefore can be considered as contributing toward equality.

These observations are not consistent with views that perceive little utility in the welfare state. The reason income shares have stayed so consistent over the years is precisely because of social programs (transfers) that have steadily kept pace with a decline in market income. In short, income distribution has remained relatively uniform because of the welfare state, not despite it.

CONCLUSION

Because this chapter is an introduction to the subject, we have just scratched the surface of the various ways one can study income inequality. We have examined only how income varies among the different quintile groups and neglected the effects on income attainment of important sociological variables such as sex, ethnicity, and region. Another intriguing question asks who occupies the different quintiles. Individuals may occupy the lowest quintile, but do so only on a temporary basis (e.g., retired individuals drawing a small pension [counted as income], but relying on extensive savings accumulated over a lifetime [not counted as income]). Many people occupy the lowest quintile at some point in their lives—as students, when learning a trade, when retired or unemployed—without suffering the consequences normally associated with poverty, such as inadequate diet or shelter. This dynamism is not reflected in the figures. Conversely, some individuals are permanent occupants of the lower quintiles. This includes the homeless, who have increased their presence in most Canadian cities yet are not included in this type of study, primarily because they are notoriously difficult to track in income surveys.

This chapter is more descriptive than theoretical, and we do not dwell on why income inequality has changed (e.g., in market versus transfer aspects). Even a cursory inventory shows that theories abound: the advent of neo-liberalism, changes in the labour market, a change in income tax structure, globalization, and so on. Whatever the issue, it is worthwhile to adopt a critical stance and ask who is likely to benefit or lose.

And who benefits is not beyond empirical verification. In this chapter we have learned that although income has risen substantially since the early 1950s, income distribution has stayed relatively stable. Closer inspection, however, showed that, as no doubt many middle-class Canadians can attest, the middle quintiles have been less successful at holding on to their share. Much of this income has escaped upward to the highest quintile, giving some credence to the claim that the rich are getting richer.

We also saw that the primary statistic used to compare incomes, income quintiles, is not without its problems. Its primary shortcoming is that it obscures how the composition of income has changed over the past few decades (market income versus transfer income). One reason for the stability of incomes is that social programs have done a remarkable job of subsidizing the incomes of those in the lower quintiles, thus preventing their fall into absolute poverty.

Canada has a fairly typical distribution of income for an industrial economy. As study after study shows, Canada is a wealthy country, and how to divide that wealth continues to stimulate much political debate. In the end, definitive answers about what is fair continue to elude us, and we are no closer to an answer today than when Karl Marx and Adam Smith debated this issue more than a century and a half ago. The lack of a conclusive answer, however, should not deter us from asking this question. Once we fail to do so, someone else's version of "what is fair" is sure to win out.

NOTES

1. Inflation refers to rising prices. To remove the effect of inflation we use "real" or "constant" dollars, a common procedure applied to historical comparisons of this sort. This method better reflects the purchasing power of money; that is, what a dollar can buy. A bottle of Coke that cost 10 cents in the

1950s costs a dollar or more now. The purchasing power of our money has decreased. What once cost a dime now costs a loonie. But then our incomes have increased, so the question becomes, "Is a Coke more affordable now than in the 1950s?" In Canada, we use the consumer price index (CPI) as a method of evaluating price changes (and inflation). By purchasing a similar basket of goods and services (e.g., milk, haircuts) month after month, we can calculate how much prices are increasing because of inflation. Incomes can then be adjusted so that we subtract or remove the effect of inflation, and examine real purchasing power, as shown in Figure 5-1.

2. When Statistics Canada presents its findings on income, it provides both average (total earnings divided by the number of cases) and median incomes (the amount earned by the family located midway between the highest and lowest incomes). Statistics Canada tracks both types of income because averages can be unduly inflated by even a small number of very high incomes. For example, the average of a bank president earning $1 million a year and 100 bank clerks earning $12 000 a year would be close to $22 000, vastly overstating the salary of the average bank employee. For that reason, some argue, median income is a better indicator of what the "typical" family or individual earns (which, by the way, would be $12 000 for the bank employees in our example).

3. Between 1990 and 1999 (in constant 1999 dollars), market income for low-income families dropped from $5276 to $4590, while transfers remained almost constant at $6732 and $6703, respectively (Statistics Canada, *Income in Canada*, 2000). For evidence of the growing proportion of market income flowing to the highest quintile, see any of the recent issues of *Income in Canada*, Statistics Canada Catalogue 75-202-XIE.

4. The precise amount of income tax that people pay depends on a complex array of factors, including the amount of money earned and the methods by which the money was earned (e.g., wages, interest, capital gains). The following information includes federal tax only. Each province also collects its share of income tax. In the 2006 tax year, all Canadians paid no federal income tax on the first $8839 they received. After that, any additional earnings below $36 378 were taxed at a rate of 15.25%. Between $36 378 and below $72 756, income was taxed at 22%. Between $72 756 and below $118 285, income was taxed at 26%. Earnings starting at $118 285 were taxed at 29%. In effect, as your income rises, you pay higher rates of income tax. This is progressive taxation.

REFERENCES

Hewitt, Christopher 1977. "The effect of political democracy and social democracy on equality in industrial societies: A cross-national comparison." *American Sociological Review* 42:450–464.

Hunter, Alfred 1993. "The changing distribution of income." In Curtis, Grabb, and Guppy (eds.), *Social Inequality in Canada* (3rd ed.). Scarborough, ON: Prentice Hall.

Olsen, Gregg 2002. *The Politics of the Welfare State: Canada, Sweden, and the United States.* Toronto: Oxford University Press.

Picot, Garnett, and John Myles 2005. *Income Inequality and Low Income in Canada: An International Perspective.* Ottawa: Statistics Canada.

Statistics Canada various years. *Income in Canada.* Catalogue 75-202-XIE. Ottawa.

Statistics Canada various years. *Income Distributions by Size in Canada.* Catalogue 13-207-XPB. Ottawa.

Teeple, Gary 2000. *Globalization and the Decline of Social Reform.* Toronto: Garamond Press.

Therborn, Göran 1986. *Why Some People Are More Unemployed Than Others.* London: Verso Books.

World Bank various years. *The World Development Report.* Washington.

Yalnizyan, Armine 2007. *The Rich and the Rest of Us: The Changing Face of Canada's Growing Gap.* Ottawa: Canadian Centre for Policy Alternatives.

chapter six

The Distribution of Wealth and Economic Inequality

James B. Davies
(An original chapter written
for this volume.)

INTRODUCTION

This paper addresses a series of questions about the distribution of wealth and economic inequality in Canada. First, what is wealth and how is it distributed among families in Canada? Second, how does this compare with the picture elsewhere in the world? Third, what determines how wealth is distributed? Fourth, why should we care? And, finally, how does wealth mobility affect our views about wealth inequality?

WHAT IS WEALTH?

A person's wealth equals the value of all of his or her assets minus debts at a moment in time. This concept is also referred to as "net worth." The assets that must be included cover a wide range. They include, for example, cash, bank deposits, owner-occupied housing, guaranteed investment certificates (GICs), registered savings plans (RSPs), stocks and shares, bonds, mutual funds, consumer durables, real estate, and machines and equipment used in unincorporated businesses. There is also a wide variety of debts: mortgages, credit card balances, personal loans, small business loans, and so forth.

Table 6-1 indicates the relative importance of the different forms of wealth at the end of 2006. Note, first, that 35.7% of the total value of assets is made up of real estate, the most important form of which is residential housing. Financial assets have been increasing in relative importance in recent years and now, at 57.4% of the total, are more important

TABLE 6-1 Year-End National Balance Sheets at Market Value, Persons and Unincorporated Business, Canada, 2006		
	Assets (in millions)	**% of Assets**
I. Non-financial Assets		
Residential Structures	$1 271 026	19.5%
Non-residential Structures	30 794	0.5
Land	1 057 955	16.2
Consumer Durables	386 824	5.9
Machinery, Equipment, and Inventories	31 658	0.5
Total	2 778 257	42.6
II. Financial Assets		
Currency and Deposits	713 650	10.9
Canada Savings Bonds	15 465	0.2
Other Canadian Bonds	57 885	0.9
Life Insurance and Pensions	1 396 073	21.4
Shares	1 417 190	21.7
Miscellaneous	140 853	2.2
Total	3 741 116	57.4
TOTAL ASSETS	6 519 373	100.0
III. Debt		
Mortgages	654 954	10.0
Other Debt	430 104	6.6
Total	1 085 058	16.6
NET WORTH	5 434 315	83.4

Source: These data originate from the CANSIM II Database, Series V28368579-608. CANSIM is an official Mark of Statistics Canada.

than non-financial assets. Among financial assets, shares and bonds (other than Canada Savings Bonds), whose ownership is relatively concentrated, make up 22.6% of total assets. More widely distributed assets like cash, bank accounts, life insurance, and pensions make up the bulk of the total.

Some urge the use of a broader definition of wealth—one that would include, for example, the value of unfunded pension rights. Although such wealth is illiquid, people with pension rights are better off than others. The amounts involved are also substantial. The value of funded pension plans does appear in Table 6-1, on the life insurance and pensions line. But the value of rights to old age pension benefits (both Old Age Security and Guaranteed Income Supplement) and Canada Pension Plan/Quebec Pension Plan (CPP/QPP) benefits should also be included. Estimates of such "social security wealth" in the United States vary from about 40% to 200% of conventional net worth.[1]

Finally, it is often argued that the present value of future labour earnings—that is, "human wealth"—should be included.

As for social security wealth, data availability is a barrier. Estimating human wealth requires projecting future earnings. A wide range of estimates of aggregate human wealth is available (see the appendix to Davies and Whalley 1991). A best-guess estimate is that the total value of human wealth equals about three times that of non-human, or "physical," wealth.

HOW IS WEALTH DISTRIBUTED IN CANADA?

The best answer to the question "How is wealth distributed in Canada?" may be "We don't know." In Canada, the major sources of information on the distributions of income and wealth among families are from Statistics Canada's household surveys. The most recent wealth survey, the Survey of Financial Security (SFS), was conducted in the early summer of 2005. There was one earlier SFS, in 1999, and before that wealth data were provided by the Survey of Consumer Finance (SCF) for 1970, 1977, and 1984. All surveys are subject to sampling and non-sampling error. These sources of error are especially important in wealth surveys.

Sampling error is the difference between the sample value of a statistic—for example, average wealth—and its true *population* value. The larger the sample, the smaller this error is likely to be. For characteristics like national medians, it is generally small, since the sample sizes used by Statistics Canada are large. Without the application of special sampling techniques, however, estimating the mean or the shape of the *distribution* of a highly skewed variable like wealth can involve significant sampling error.[2] Most samples will select too few rich households, although a few samples will have too many. This problem can be addressed by oversampling in the upper tail. This approach was not generally followed by the SCF, but the SFS does oversample in the upper tail (see Statistics Canada 2007a; Morissette and Zhang 2007).

Non-sampling error is an especially serious problem in wealth surveys. It takes two forms. First, some people refuse to be interviewed. Studies indicate that the likelihood of this non-response varies with age, region, and income. These problems can be corrected through weighting families according to their likelihood of being in the sample. Differential response across age groups, for example, can be almost entirely corrected. However, it is only when differential response according to wealth is highly correlated with differential responses according to observable characteristics (age, region, size of urban area, etc.) that this type of error can be adequately corrected by weighting. Since the correlation is far from perfect, differential response remains a problem.

Another form of non-sampling error—misreporting—occurs because people sometimes refuse to report certain items, or make mistakes. In cases where people report that they own an asset but do not report its value, an imputed value can be assigned. However, no correction is possible if the interviewers do not know that the family owns an asset. Studies in the United States indicate that, on average, assets like bank accounts are underreported by 40% to 50%. Other assets are more accurately reported. The value of owner-occupied houses, for example, is, on average, reported with surprising accuracy (see Davies 1979b).

Some of the results of these combined errors are well known for the *income* distribution. While wages and salaries are, on average, reported fairly accurately, SCF estimates of average transfer payments were about 20% lower than the true figures, and the shortfall was about 50% for investment income. The situation is worse for wealth surveys. The Spring 1984 SCF estimates of share ownership, for example, were only about 14% of the year-end 1983 national balance sheet totals. Estimates for other assets are not as bad, and some, such as housing, are fairly accurately represented.

Keeping all of these reservations in mind, let us look at Table 6-2, which shows estimates of the 1984, 1999, and 2005 wealth distributions in Canada. These data, provided by Morissette and Zhang (2007), use a consistent wealth definition for the 1984 SCF and 1999/2005 SFSs. Unfortunately, to achieve this consistency it is necessary to leave out some interesting and important assets that are in the SFS surveys but were not included in the SCF. They include household contents, collectibles, annuities, and registered retirement income funds (RRIFs) as well as some other assets. The result of this omission is to push up

estimated inequality significantly. Some results, in the form of quintile shares, are provided by Statistics Canada (2007a) using the full SFS range of assets.

The table suggests that the real wealth of Canadian families has risen quickly in recent years, which is probably quite true. From 1984 to 2005, mean wealth rose from $148 500 to $251 700, which is an increase of 69.5%, or 2.5% per year. In the most recent years, from 1999 to 2005, the annual increase averaged 3.7%, which is a reflection of buoyant stock markets, increasing house prices, and other factors.

As expected, we find that wealth inequality is high. In 2005, using the restricted definition of wealth employed by Morissette and Zhang (2007) as shown in Table 6-2, the share of the top 10%, or top decile, was 58.2%, and the top two deciles—that is, the top quintile—had a total share

TABLE 6-2	Distribution of Wealth, Families and Unattached Individuals, Canada, 1984, 1999, and 2005		
	1984	**1999**	**2005**
Decile Shares	%	%	%
1	−0.5	−0.6	−0.6
2	0.1	0.0	0.0
3	0.5	0.4	0.2
4	1.7	1.3	1.1
5	3.5	2.8	2.5
6	5.6	4.7	4.4
7	8.2	7.4	6.9
8	11.5	11.0	10.5
9	17.5	17.4	16.8
10	51.8	55.7	58.2
Gini Coefficient	0.691	0.727	0.746
Mean ($2005)	$148 500	$202 900	$251 700
Median ($2005)	67 300	74 400	84 800

Note: Wealth here omits home contents, annuities, registered retirement income funds (RRIFs), and some other assets in order to achieve the same definition in all three years. Wealth inequality is lower if these assets are included, which may be done for 1999 and 2005 (see Statistics Canada 2007a:Table 1).

Source: Morissette and Zhang (2007). Decile shares are from Table 1, means and medians are from Table 4, and the Gini coefficients are from the text on p. 7.

of 75.0%. While these numbers are pushed up somewhat by the wealth definition used here, even when the full range of SFS assets is included the share of the top quintile is still 69.2% (Statistics Canada 2007a:Table 1). Another indicator is the Gini coefficient, which would equal 0.0 if everyone had the same wealth and 1.0 if there was complete inequality (one person having all assets). The Gini for 2005 in Table 6-2 is 0.746, which can be compared to the Gini for total income, which stood at just 0.364 in 2005 for Canadian families with two or more members (Statistics Canada 2007b:Table 9-2).

Table 6-2 also suggests that wealth inequality may have been rising over the last two decades in Canada. For example, there is a large jump in the share of the top decile between 1984 and 1999, from 51.8% to 55.7%; there was also a smaller increase from 1999 to 2005, when this share rose to 58.2%. Morissette and Zhang conducted sensitivity tests to determine whether the rise from 1984 to the later two years could simply reflect the SFS doing a better job at capturing the extreme upper tail of the distribution. Leaving out the top 1%, and then the top 5%, which removes the truly rich from the picture, they found that there is still an increase from 1984 to 1999, although the jump is smaller than in Table 6-2. These authors also performed computations to investigate the impact of changes in age structure and family composition from 1984 to 2005. They found that rather than helping to explain the rise in inequality, these factors acted to slow down the increase in wealth inequality to a small extent. The most likely reasons for the increased inequality are rises in house and share prices, and increased saving in financial assets, especially via registered retirement savings plans (RRSPs) and other tax-sheltered savings vehicles. These factors push up the wealth of upper-middle- and higher-income groups, but they have less impact on people at middle- or low-wealth levels.

One advantage of the SFS over the earlier SCF surveys is that it has inquired into the value of employer-based pension rights in the form of registered pension plans (RPPs). When these are included, the share of the top 10% in 2005 is 50.9%, which is considerably less than the figure of 58.2% shown in Table 6-2. This difference indicates the considerable equalizing power of pension rights for the wealth distribution, which has been found in previous research for other countries as well. Pensions tend to be equalizing since they are most important for middle- and upper-middle-income groups rather than for the truly wealthy. It is also found that, when pensions are included, the 1999 and 2005 wealth distributions are quite similar. The importance of the observation of rising wealth inequality between 1999 and 2005 in Table 6-2 should therefore not be exaggerated. It is unclear whether there really was any true increase in wealth inequality between those dates. As we see below, this is consistent with a general lack of a strong trend in wealth inequality in other countries in recent years.

It is interesting to know as much as possible about the very highest wealth-holders. So far, not much information on the top 5% or top 1% of families is available from the SFS, but their situation was examined in the 1984 SCF. In that survey, there were approximately 100 000 families in the top 1%, and their average wealth was $2 508 000 in 2005 dollars. In 1999, there would have been about 125 000 families in the top 1%, and if their assets had increased by the average amount since 1984, their mean wealth would have been $4 251 000. This amount is still not what most people would consider a great fortune. Thus, the "top 1%" and the "super rich" are not the same thing. The latter are a small minority of the top 1%.

For the reasons discussed above, the figures shown in Table 6-2 are affected by important sources of error. Although Statistics Canada tries very hard to reduce these errors, and in particular now over-samples the upper tail in its SFS survey, in view of the limitations of sample surveys we ought to look at other sources of information when studying wealth in order to get a complete picture. Davies (1993) examined a number of alternative sources, including both journalistic accounts and studies by private firms.

Various magazines and newspapers publish lists of the seriously wealthy. A world list of billionaires is provided annually by *Forbes* magazine, and attracts great attention around the world. Indications are that *Forbes* works quite hard to achieve accuracy, although it is naturally difficult for it to make estimates of the net worth of individuals whose wealth is not in the form of shares in publicly traded companies. In 2007, Forbes listed 946 billionaires around the world, of whom 23 were Canadian. The wealthiest Canadians were David Thomson at $22 billion and Galen Weston at $7.9 billion, ranking tenth and ninety-third in the world, respectively. An indication of Canada's relative showing on this list is that the U.S., with about 10 times Canada's population, had 405 entries on the list, or about 20 times as many billionaires as Canada. The implication is that Canada has a somewhat less unequal distribution of wealth than the U.S., a point that is corroborated by other data, as discussed below.[3]

There is also journalistic evidence on the sub-billionaires. Newman (1975) attempted to provide a complete list of all Canadian families with wealth greater than $20 million, or about $60 million in today's dollars. There were 160 families on his list. The list of the corporate wealthy provided by Francis (1986) indicated 32 families with wealth greater than $100 million. Using this evidence, Davies

(1993) "guesstimated" that the share of the top 1% in the Canadian wealth distribution in the 1970s and 1980s was probably around 25%. This proportion implies significantly more concentration than suggested by the SCF wealth distribution, which placed the share at about 18%.

INTERNATIONAL COMPARISONS AND THE WORLD DISTRIBUTION OF WEALTH

It is useful to put the Canadian wealth distribution in international perspective. The UN University's World Institute for Development Economics Research (WIDER) in Helsinki has helped to make that possible through its recent research program on household assets from a global perspective. A centrepiece of that research is a study by Davies, Sandstrom, Shorrocks, and Wolff (2006), hereafter referred to as DSSW. This is the first study that has attempted to estimate the *world* distribution of wealth. As is true within countries, DSSW find that world wealth is distributed less equally than world income. They estimate that the wealth share of the top 1% of households globally is 32%, and of the top 10% is 71%. The corresponding Gini coefficient is 0.802, which is getting close to the maximum Gini value of 1.0, and is significantly above the values estimated for the world distribution of income. For example, Milanovic (2005) estimated a world income Gini of 0.642 in 1998. Globally, median wealth per adult is estimated at $8400, and $523 300 is required to be in the top 1%.

Levels of wealth inequality are not systematically higher or lower in developing countries than in developed countries. Some developed countries, like the U.S. and Switzerland, have almost as much wealth inequality as seen for the world as a whole. The Gini coefficient for the U.S. in

2001 was 0.801, and the share of the top 10% was 69.8%. On the other hand, countries like Japan, Canada, Australia, Germany, and France have more moderate levels of wealth inequality, as typified by a 2001 Gini for Canada of 0.663 and a top decile share of just 53.0%.[4]

Among developing countries, DSSW find that some of the highest levels of wealth inequality are in Latin America, where estimated Ginis range up to 0.748 in Mexico and 0.783 in Brazil (see also Davies and Shorrocks 2005). Inequality is also high throughout Africa and in much of Asia. China, on the other hand, still had moderate wealth inequality in the year 2000, according to official data, with a Gini of 0.550 and a share of the top decile of just 41.4%. However, wealth dispersion has increased rapidly from a very low level in the early 1980s, when freer markets and more private property were first allowed. It was recently reported that the number of billionaires in China is now second only to that in the U.S. (*Globe and Mail* 2007).

Also noteworthy is that the ratio of wealth to income is estimated to be lower in most developing countries than in rich countries. The ratio of household wealth to GDP in the G7 countries is estimated to average 4.32, for example, which compares with an average value of 2.53 for China, India, South Africa, and Brazil. This is interesting because having adequate assets is likely more crucial in poor countries, where life is often precarious and there are few social safety nets.

Finally, there is always much interest in trends in wealth inequality over time. As reported in Davies and Shorrocks (2000) and Ohlsson et al. (2006), several developed countries—not including Canada, unfortunately—have long-time series on wealth starting in the early years of the twentieth century. With the exception of Switzerland, they all show a pattern of a long and very substantial decline in wealth inequality from the 1920s to the 1970s, with the share of the top 1% declining from figures as high as 60% to 70% to 20% to 30%. Since the 1970s, wealth inequality has increased somewhat in Sweden, the United Kingdom, and the United States, but the increase has been small. This pattern contrasts with the strong rise in income inequality seen over the last three decades in the U.S., the UK, and many other countries. Suggested explanations for this recent trend are that changes in wealth naturally lag behind those in income, and that the increase in the number of very high incomes reflects, for example, increases in executive salaries, rather than a rise in income due to wealth. It has also been pointed out by Atkinson (2006) that the wealth of the rich has in fact been rising quickly (and has become more concentrated), but this has not raised relative wealth inequality much because ordinary people have also seen a rise in their wealth due to rising house prices and other factors.

WHAT DETERMINES HOW WEALTH IS DISTRIBUTED?

Wealth is the result of past accumulation, and comes from two main sources: labour income ("earnings"), or gifts and inheritances. Both provide resources that can be either saved or consumed. Resources that are saved can accumulate at different rates. Wise or lucky investors earn high rates of return, while others earn lower rates. Finally, given the lifetime path of earnings, savings, etc., up until retirement, the older the consumer, the greater tends to be his or her wealth. Thus, current wealth depends on past earnings, inheritances (including gifts), savings rates out of earnings and inheritances, rates of return, and age.

It is sometimes suggested that a large part of wealth differences might simply be explained by age. To illustrate this possibility, examples of societies that are egalitarian but that also display considerable wealth concentration are sometimes devised. For instance, consider a society with zero population growth and a zero rate of interest, in which everyone works for 40 years and then retires for 10 years. Assume that, while earning a constant amount during their working years, people save at a constant rate, and then *"dissave"* at a constant rate during retirement, ending life with zero wealth. The wealthiest people would be those who were at stages just before and just after the retirement age. In this world, the share of the top 10% of wealth-holders would be about 19%.

At first glance, the fact that a 19% share for the top 10% could be generated from age differences alone might seem impressive. However, this does not mean that a large part of wealth concentration is explained by age in the real world, for at least two reasons. First, if we look at the top 1% in the example, we find that their wealth share is just 2%. By altering the details of the example, one could get this share to 3% or 4%, but this would still be far short of the estimated real-world shares. Second, the assumed variation of wealth with age is not realistic. In the real world, there is a less extreme pattern. On average, people save for the first few years after retirement and only dissave slowly beyond that point (see Burbidge and Robb 1985).

In Davies (1979a), I developed a micro-simulation model that can be used to *decompose* wealth inequality (see Davies 1982 for a summary). That is, it is possible to see how wealth inequality would be reduced if we eliminated differences in earnings, inheritances, savings rates, rates of return, and age. The most important factor was inheritance, followed by differences in savings rates. Differences in earnings, rates of return, and age were of

lesser importance and similar to each other in impact (see Davies 1982:489, Table 1[5]).

There is other evidence on the importance of inheritance. First, Wedgwood (1929) investigated the sources of wealth held by rich British decedents in a 12-month period during 1924–1925. Of 99 persons dying with at least £200 000, which was a fortune at the time, about 60% had a predecessor, usually a parent, who had died leaving at least £50 000, and about 70% had predecessors who left at least £10 000 (Wedgwood 1929:138–139). This work was updated by Harbury and Hitchens (1979), who found similar results for the 1950s, 1960s, and 1970s. As reported by Brittain (1978:Chapter 1), studies by *Fortune* magazine in the U.S. on top American wealth-holders concluded that about half were "self-made." However, sample surveys of the entire population indicate that a larger fraction—as many as 60%—of those in top wealth groups had received some inheritance (Brittain 1978:18). The implication of these studies is that in both the UK and the U.S. at least half of the genuinely wealthy have benefited to some extent from inheritance.

While the distribution of wealth is more unequal than that of income, the distribution of inherited wealth is much more unequal than that of wealth in general. Sample surveys indicate that the majority of people have never received an inheritance (see, e.g., Brittain 1978:18), and a majority will likely never receive significant amounts in gifts or bequests. On the other hand, a small minority receive truly spectacular amounts. It is this extreme concentration, rather than the total amount being passed on, that makes inheritance an important determinant of wealth inequality.

What makes inherited wealth so concentrated? Ironically, part of the answer lies in the great importance of human wealth. The majority of families find that investing in their children's human capital, via upbringing and education, is more effective than providing gifts and bequests. But some families are in a position to provide more. First, some provide for their heirs by passing along family businesses, including farms. Second, some exhaust the attractive opportunities for investing in their children's education and upbringing before their benevolence has been used up. Third, the lure of bequests may be used to elicit attention from children in a form of exchange (see Sussman et al. 1970; Cox 1987). The genuinely wealthy would almost all be in one of these three categories, and we therefore expect to see them making considerable use of bequests.

The extent of concentration in inheritance depends on practices of estate division, fertility, and choice of marital partner (see Atkinson 1983:183–189). At one extreme, in some societies *primogeniture* is practised. Under this arrangement, the entire estate passes to the eldest son (or daughter, in the absence of a son). This keeps large estates intact, and preserves wealth inequality over time. At the opposite extreme, many families practise equal division of estates. Especially where families are large, which was true in North America in the nineteenth and early twentieth centuries, this contributes to the rapid breakdown of wealth concentration. It appears that, in North America today, equal division of estates is the norm, although departures from this norm are observed.

Differences in fertility according to wealth can also have a sizable effect. If the wealthy had smaller families than others, their wealth would be broken up relatively slowly by division among heirs, and wealth concentration would tend to be preserved. While this factor may have been important in some societies at some times, in Canada today, fertility differences across income and wealth groups are not large, so that it likely has a relatively small effect.

Finally, the extent of assortative mating is important. If wealthy sons marry wealthy daughters, inherited wealth can remain confined to a small minority of families. While there is positive sorting of mates according to wealth and income, the correlation in mates' backgrounds is far from perfect. Thus, there is a tendency for inequality to be broken down through wealthy children marrying non-wealthy spouses, as well as through division of estates.

WHY SHOULD WE CARE HOW WEALTH IS DISTRIBUTED?

One reason some people are concerned about the distribution of wealth is that they believe it has much to do with the distribution of power in society. This concern has several facets, since power can take political, social, or economic forms. As an economist, I am not especially qualified to comment on the first two forms of power, but it is important not to exclude them entirely from the discussion.

Some believe that the wealthy exert vastly greater political influence than others. This could be achieved through funding political campaigns, by bribing politicians and civil servants, by control of media, and through funding researchers who obtain congenial findings. Similarly disproportionate *social* power may accrue to the wealthy, for example, through the impact of advertising and media content on values and attitudes.

While not all would agree about the extent of political and social power conferred by wealth in Canada today, there is little doubt that the wealthy can exert considerable influence by the channels mentioned. But what of the economic power created by the concentration of wealth? At first blush it might appear that the concentration of corporate wealth observed in our society must imply great concentration of economic power. However, to the extent that we maintain internationally open and competitive markets, the power of even large corporations is limited by the rigours of the marketplace.

In competitive markets, business initiatives are governed by the logic of profit and loss. In order to survive, firms have to strive to make as much profit as possible. If they do not take advantage of opportunities, someone else will. Factors like technology, consumer preferences, supplies of productive inputs, the regulatory environment, and taxes and subsidies really determine what happens. The preferences of individuals who control even large corporations may ultimately be unimportant.

One should not be complacent about the limitations that competitive and open markets place on individuals' economic power. The wealthy do not like such limitations and, like other groups, such as trade unions and professional associations, they can be expected to use their political power to try to achieve protection from competition. It is important for the electorate to be critical of weak competition policy, subsidies to private firms, special tax breaks, and other preferential treatment for private firms and wealthy individuals. In the long run, such vigilance may be more effective in preventing unhealthy concentration of power in society, and indeed in preventing undue concentration of wealth itself, than a strategy that attacks wealth concentration directly.

I turn now to a discussion of the second reason why wealth inequality may matter—that is, due to its implications for differences in economic well-being.

What determines the distribution of economic well-being at a moment in time? Often we attempt to summarize this distribution by looking at households' incomes over the calendar year. This is informative, but has its limitations. If two families have equal incomes, but one has $1 million in non-human capital and the other just $100 000, their well-being is likely to be quite different. This realization has prompted many observers to argue that we should look at wealth as well as income.

Wealth differs from income in that it is a store of purchasing power for the future. While most income is consumed in the year it is received, consumption of wealth usually takes place gradually over the lifetime of the consumer or, possibly, by his or her heirs. Thus, when we turn to wealth, we must change our focus to the long run.

The long-run differences in well-being of a cohort of Canadians of similar age are determined largely by the sum of their human and non-human resources—that is, by "total wealth." We might try to estimate the distribution of this total wealth among people aged 20–24, 25–29, 30–34, and so on up through the age spectrum. Knowing net worth, including the net value of pension rights and social security wealth, would be an important component of this exercise, but so also would be knowledge of the distribution of human wealth.

Since human wealth, on average, is considerably larger than non-human wealth, we might ask whether there is much point in studying the distribution of non-human wealth by itself. The answer is that, while looking at the distribution of wealth alone is a limited exercise, it is an important one. Although there is not a perfect correlation, people with high labour income also tend to have high wealth, so that, overall, wealth differences tend to reinforce differences in earnings. Also, the extremes reached by wealth in the upper tail are not matched by the distribution of human wealth. Thus, at the highest reaches, one can almost say that the distribution of non-human wealth *is* the distribution of total wealth. Looking at the top of the wealth distribution gives us unique and valuable information about the upper extremes of individual economic resources in our society.

Finally, we may ask a deeper question about whether the observed differences in wealth are really important. To what extent are these differences inequitable? In other words, do they represent true *inequality*? There is a wide range of possible answers to this question. Perspectives range from those of libertarians, on the right, to socialists, on the left.

Libertarians believe that, as long as wealth has been accumulated honestly, differences in wealth-holding are fair. Nobody has any superior right to that of the individual to enjoy the fruits of his or her past accumulation. Since there is no injustice, there is no "inequality." This is a highly individualistic approach.

Socialists have a very different viewpoint. First, the component of wealth that can be traced to inheritance is considered undeserved, and certainly indicative of inequality. Second, some of the differences in past earnings and rates of return, which led to current differences in wealth, are regarded as unfair. In other words, aside from differences that are due purely to age, savings rates, or "reasonable" differences in rates of return and labour earnings, all wealth differences would be regarded as unjustifiable by a true socialist.

Between the libertarian and socialist positions is a large gap. What would a representative or "typical" Canadian think about wealth differences? It would be interesting to answer this question by means of a sample survey. In the absence of such evidence, one can only conjecture. My guess is that the typical Canadian probably believes that differences in inheritance are less justified than those in labour earnings. However, I would also guess that he or she does not believe that differences in inheritance have *no* justification. Parents' rights to pass on to their children the fruits of their labour are

considered important by many. Public concern about tax loopholes is also widespread, so it is likely that the typical Canadian is also not entirely happy with differences in self-accumulated wealth. Thus, the average Canadian probably thinks that there is some true inequality involved in wealth differences.

HOW DOES WEALTH MOBILITY AFFECT OUR PERCEPTIONS OF INEQUALITY?

Wealth mobility exists if people change their relative position in the wealth distribution over time. Such mobility can take place both within lifetimes and from generation to generation. Within a lifetime, it is important to look at a person's wealth relative to others of about the same age. If this changes over time, and the change is not offset by changes in human wealth, then there is meaningful wealth mobility.

In fact, there is considerable wealth mobility both within lifetimes and across generations (see, e.g., Menchik 1979). While the majority of the rich have benefited from inheritance, there are many well-known, true-life "rags to riches" stories. Conversely, there are many wealthy heirs who have squandered their fortunes. And, over successive generations, there is even more mobility. It is sometimes claimed that "shirtsleeves to shirtsleeves in three generations" is typical. While this claim is exaggerated, the work by Wedgwood, Harbury and Hitchens, Menchik, and others does show that there is substantial intergenerational wealth mobility.

It is sometimes asserted that, given any level of wealth concentration, there will be less concern about inequality when there is a great degree of wealth mobility. But this is not obvious. It may depend very much on what kind of mobility we are talking about. For example, although there is wide respect for those who build up their wealth by working hard, and by saving and investing wisely, there can be great resentment of those who get rich via exploitative, questionable, or illegal activity. And, while the public probably doesn't have much sympathy with the downward mobility of spendthrift heirs, people may feel concern for those who have been forced out of business by unexpected technological change, recession, or international trade shocks.

It seems likely that people regard wealth mobility as desirable only when it occurs for good reasons. This comes back to the earlier discussion. Upward mobility that occurs through moderate inheritance, working hard, saving carefully, and perhaps also bearing risk and having good luck in investments may be considered healthy and acceptable, just as the wealth differences created by these factors may not be resented. However, people may disapprove of mobility that stems from what are regarded as excessive inheritances or earnings differences, unequal tax treatment, and so on, just as they disapprove of wealth differences that are caused by these factors.

Summing up, a reasonable degree of wealth mobility may be necessary, if the mechanisms that determine wealth differences in a society are to be regarded as fair. However, it is not *sufficient*. Hence, the fact that there is considerable wealth mobility in Canada and other Western countries shows that these societies are not caste-ridden, but it does not imply that the people of these nations should not be concerned about wealth inequality.

CONCLUSION

This chapter has tried to make clear the concept of wealth, has summarized the available evidence on how it is distributed in Canada and also to an extent in other countries, has discussed the determinants of wealth differences, and has asked whether these matter. The analysis has emphasized that, ideally, a comprehensive concept of wealth needs to be used—one that includes pension rights and social security wealth in addition to more narrowly defined net worth. The chapter has also stressed that even this broad concept of wealth leaves out the bulk of people's economic resources, which take the form of expected future labour earnings or human wealth.

We have seen that wealth differences are much greater than differences in income, although the *precise* shape of the wealth distribution is unknown both in Canada and in other countries. Concentration in wealth-holding is the result of differences in inheritances, savings rates, labour earnings, rates of return, taxes paid, and age. Inheritance and the high rates of return earned by some entrepreneurs and investors together provide most of the explanation for the extreme length of the upper tail of the wealth distribution. The great stock market booms of the 1990s and the early twenty-first century drew particular attention to the role of investment returns. They created a new crop of billionaires in Canada and lengthened the upper tail of the wealth distribution. Therefore, there may be a tendency at the moment to think of investment as the main source of riches in our society. However, stock market booms come and go. In 2002, there was a "meltdown" in high-tech and internet share values, and the North American stock market overall lost all of the gains it had created since 1997. In 2007, there was another sharp downturn associated with the "sub-prime" mortgage crisis in the U.S. With such downturns it perhaps becomes easier to appreciate the role of more stable factors, most notably inheritance, in creating the long upper tail of wealth-holding.

The chapter concluded by discussing why wealth differences matter. There are at least three key answers. The first is that great wealth may spell disproportionate power in our society. Although public vigilance and participation in democratic political institutions can reduce this power difference, these activities are unlikely to eliminate it completely. A second reason is that, particularly in the upper tail, differences in non-human wealth have an important influence on the distribution of economic well-being. Finally, while some wealth differences reflect factors that are widely regarded as justifiable—such as age, accepted differences in labour income, and voluntary differences in savings rates—other wealth differences, such as inheritance, unequal treatment by the tax system, and extreme differences in labour income do not win such uniform approval.

NOTES

1. Feldstein (1976) estimated aggregate social security wealth in the U.S. in 1962 at $382 billion. This was 54% of conventional net worth ($711 billion) in his study. Wolff (1987) obtains a range of figures for 1969, when conventional net worth had risen to $2904 billion. The estimates for social security wealth vary from $1194 billion (41% of net worth) to $5649 billion (195% of net worth), depending on assumptions about future growth in earnings, and social security contributions and benefits. (See Wolff 1987:219, Table 9.1.)

2. A variable is skewed if its frequency histogram has one "tail" longer than the other. Distributions of income and wealth are highly positively skewed, meaning that they have very long upper tails. (A negatively skewed distribution has a long lower tail.)

3. Note that we would not expect Canada to have 10% of the number of billionaires compared to the U.S., even if it had the same degree of wealth inequality. This is because average wealth in Canada is lower, so that those in the top 0.01%, for example, would be less wealthy than the top 0.01% in the U.S., even if relative inequality was the same within the two countries.

4. These figures are lower than we saw in Table 6-2 since a broader concept of wealth, which is more equally distributed, is used in the DSSW study.

5. At about the same time that I was developing my simulation model, Michael Wolfson built another model, which he used to address similar questions. The Davies and Wolfson models differ in many respects, but they agree in ascribing the most important role in explaining the concentration of wealth in the extreme upper tail to differences in inheritance. See Wolfson (1977, 1979). Interestingly, the conclusions from the Davies and Wolfson studies are consistent with the assessment of the famous University of Chicago economist Frank Knight, who devoted considerable thought to the determinants of personal wealth. As Knight wrote in 1923, "the ownership of personal or material productive capacity is based upon a complex mixture of inheritance, luck, and effort, probably in that order of relative importance" (Brittain 1978:1).

REFERENCES

Atkinson, Anthony B. 1983. *The Economics of Inequality* (2nd ed.). Oxford: Clarendon Press.

Atkinson, Anthony B. 2006. "Concentration among the rich." UNU-WIDER Research Paper No. 2006/151. http://www.wider.unu.edu/publications/publications.htm

Brittain, John A. 1978. *Inheritance and the Inequality of Material Wealth*. Washington: The Brookings Institution.

Burbidge, J.B., and A.L. Robb 1985. "Evidence on wealth–age profiles in Canadian cross-section data." *Canadian Journal of Economics* XVIII (November):854–875.

Cox, Donald 1987. "Motives for private income transfers." *Journal of Political Economy* 95: 508–546.

Davies, James B. 1979a. *Life-Cycle Saving, Inheritance, and the Personal Distribution of Income and Wealth in Canada.* Ph.D. thesis, London School of Economics.

Davies, James B. 1979b. "On the size distribution of wealth in Canada." *Review of Income and Wealth* 25 (September):237–259.

Davies, James B. 1982. "The relative impact of inheritance and other factors on economic inequality." *Quarterly Journal of Economics* 47:471–498.

Davies, James B. 1993. "The distribution of wealth in Canada." In Daniel J. Slottje and Edward N. Wolff (eds.), *Research on Economic Inequality,* Vol. 4. Greenwich, CN: JAI Press.

Davies, James B., Susanna Sandstrom, Anthony Shorrocks, and Edward N. Wolff 2006. "The world distribution of household wealth." Helsinki: UNU-WIDER. http://www.wider.unu.edu/

Davies, James B., and A.F. Shorrocks 2000. "The distribution of wealth." In A.B. Atkinson and F. Bourguignon (eds.), *Handbook of Income Distribution,* pp. 605–675. Amsterdam: North-Holland/Elsevier.

Davies, James B., and A.F. Shorrocks 2005. "Wealth holdings in developing and transition countries." Paper presented at the Luxembourg Wealth Study conference on Construction and Usage of Comparable MIcrodata on Wealth, Perugia, January. http://www.lisproject.org/lws/perugia.htm

Davies, James B., and John Whalley 1991. "Taxes and capital formation: How important is human capital?" In D. Bernheim and J. Shoven (eds.), *National Saving and Economic Performance.* Chicago: University of Chicago Press.

Feldstein, M. 1976. "Social security and the distribution of wealth." *Journal of the American Statistical Association* 71:800–807.

Francis, Diane 1986. *Controlling Interest: Who Owns Canada?* Toronto: Macmillan.

Globe and Mail 2007. "China's year of the billionaire." October 11:B1.

Harbury, C.D., and D.M.W.N. Hitchens 1979. *Inheritance and Wealth Inequality in Britain.* London: George Allen and Unwin.

Menchik, Paul L. 1979. "Inter-generational transmission of inequality: An empirical study of wealth mobility." *Economica* 46:349–362.

Milanovic, Branko 2005. *Worlds Apart: Measuring International and Global Inequality.* Princeton and Oxford: Princeton University Press.

Morissette, René, and Xuelin Zhang. 2007. "Revisiting wealth inequality." *Perspectives on Labour and Income* 19, 1:5–16. http://www.statcan.ca/english/freepub/75-001-XIE/11206/art-1.pdf.

Newman, Peter C. 1975. *The Canadian Establishment,* Vol. 1. Toronto: McClelland and Stewart.

Ohlsson, Henry, Jesper Roine, and Daniel Waldenstrom 2006. "Long-run changes in the concentration of wealth: An overview of recent findings." UNU-WIDER Research Paper No. 2006/103. http://www.wider.unu.edu/publications/publications.htm

Statistics Canada 2007a. "The wealth of Canadians: An overview of the results of the Survey of Financial Security 2005." Pension and Wealth Research Paper Series. Catalogue No. 13F0026MIE.

Statistics Canada 2007b. "Income in Canada." Catalogue No. 75-202-XWE.

Sussman, Marvin B., Judith N. Cates, and David T. Smith 1970. *The Family and Inheritance.* New York: Russell Sage Foundation.

Wedgwood, Josiah 1929. *The Economics of Inheritance.* London: George Routledge & Sons.

Wolff, Edward N. 1987. "The effect of pensions and social security on the distribution of wealth in the U.S." In Edward N. Wolff (ed.), *International Comparisons of the Distribution of Household Wealth.* Oxford: Clarendon Press.

Wolfson, Michael 1977. *The Causes of Inequality in the Distribution of Wealth: A Simulation Analysis.* Ph.D. thesis, Cambridge University.

Wolfson, Michael 1979. "The bequest process and the causes of inequality in the distribution of wealth." In J.D. Smith (ed.), *Modeling the Intergenerational Transmission of Wealth.* New York: NBER.

chapter seven

Defining, Measuring, and Reducing Poverty

Neil Guppy and Robin Hawkshaw
(An original chapter written
for this volume.)

INTRODUCTION

Images in popular culture frequently extol the virtues of money. Wealth and fortune are goals to which many aspire: owning yachts, diamonds, lavish homes, and vacation properties. TV shows glamorize the rich and famous, and magazines portray lifestyles of affluence and opulence. Lottery corporations promote these dreams of richness and luxury. The flipside of wealth—poverty—evokes images that are demonized, and many shrink from even reflecting on such misfortune. Homelessness, poor nutrition, ill-fitting clothes, cold and damp households, these images of squalor and poverty are for most of us scenarios to avoid and living conditions that are repulsive. Many aspire to

prosperity and fame, but no one aspires to poverty.

Moving beyond images to considering seriously either wealth or poverty is harder work. Money is important, a message reinforced repeatedly in our society. And money is unevenly distributed, as these images document. But if money makes the world go round, as surely it does, then what is the fate of those with little of it?

In this chapter we focus on "too little," the issue of poverty. We begin by asking, Why care? Why does knowing about poverty matter? Why ask about its extent, or form, or explanation? Answering these questions requires that poverty be defined. This, though, is complicated, because any attempt to define "too little" entails some arbitrariness. Poverty lines, however defined, are social constructions. After reviewing conceptual complexities, we provide evidence pertinent to trends in the extent of poverty in Canada. Finally, we examine poverty reduction strategies, and particularly the role of government.

WHY DEFINE AND MEASURE POVERTY?

A set of interrelated ideas supports the rationale for systematically monitoring how income is distributed among citizens, and especially how the financially less well-off are faring. These arguments have to do with compassion, democracy, investment, and social policy. We review each in turn, while also arguing that public policy commitments to reducing poverty often are linked with how people explain poverty.

Compassion

Community underlies this rationale. Framed variously by different commentators, this rationale is about being "our brother's keeper" or about being "as strong as our weakest link." No matter the strength of individualism, as social animals we thrive in groups. Our identity and sense of self is shaped and maintained by those around us, by our community of others. As social beings it makes perfect sense that compassion toward others matters because *they are us* in the sense of being members of our community.

Democratic Citizenship

Democracy is based on the principle of active voices influencing outcomes. In a democracy, decisions should not be solely the views of an aristocracy or a corporate elite. Democracy rests on the full participation of all citizens in the political community—the social inclusion of all who are born into or

become members of the community. This is an argument about providing both equality of opportunity and freedom from coercion or discrimination (see Arneil 2006). This idea is well captured by a definition of poverty used in recent decades throughout Europe: "the poor [are those] whose resources (material, cultural and social) are so limited as to exclude them from the minimum acceptable way of life in the Member State in which they live" (EEC 1985).

Investment

Enhancing the welfare of citizens, and especially children, encourages the development of strong cognitive abilities. Such abilities pay individual dividends to those who succeed economically in our increasingly strong knowledge-based economies. But investing to enhance child welfare also contributes an important social dividend by stoking societal well-being through productivity gains and economic successes. Societies able to activate the productivity of more citizens will advance economically, and simultaneously spend less time attending to frictions exacerbated by sharp internal income and wealth disparities.

Policy

Poverty is not something simply to define or measure, but something to ameliorate. Nevertheless, if we are to craft social policies that help those who are poor, and prevent others from slipping into poverty, then we need some method of targeting action. The purpose of poverty measurement is, therefore, to enhance societal well-being by increasing the effectiveness of public policy.

The definition and measurement of poverty is also linked to how it is explained. For those viewing the causal processes underlying poverty as rooted inside the individual (e.g., deviant, lazy), there is less concern with measuring poverty and more attention to policies of law and order aimed at reforming or motivating targeted individuals (e.g., prison training programs, work-for-welfare schemes). For those who understand poverty as the outcome of social forces (e.g., job losses through plant closures, family breakdowns), measuring poverty is important in order to determine whether social policies are working (e.g., welfare measures, re-education efforts).

DEFINING POVERTY

As the images in the opening paragraph highlight, poverty and wealth occupy the opposite ends of a single continuum, the distribution-of-money continuum. No natural point on that continuum defines where poverty or wealth begins and ends.[1] This means that all poverty lines are arbitrary or subjective. Based in part on this arbitrariness, scholars have long debated whether an absolute or a relative definition of poverty is better (political views also influence this definitional debate).

Absolute poverty refers to the amount of money necessary to purchase the basic goods essential to survival. This has an intuitive appeal since when hunger gnaws or when a home is not an option, poverty is easier to understand as a lack of basics. Nevertheless, exactly what is necessary is not obvious, nor is it obvious what amount of money should be devoted to such essentials as food, shelter, and clothing. What does a nutritious meal cost? Is indoor plumbing or electricity a necessity?

Adam Smith (1776) addressed this question by arguing that basic needs were not limited to things "indispensably necessary for the support of life," but included also things like leather shoes and linen shirts which were "rendered necessary" by "established rules of decency." In effect, leather shoes and linen shirts were essential if people were to be full community participants, or "creditable persons" in Smith's language. His understanding of basic needs included an appreciation of dignity.

This latter argument turns on the concept of social inclusion and exclusion. If it is wrong to exclude women or visible minorities from community engagement, so too is it wrong to exclude the poor. Even though an individual or a family might not be undernourished, that is not sufficient in defining poverty. Poverty arises when people do not have the full complement of essentials necessary to meet a community standard of decency or credibility. As the World Bank (2001) has argued, "poor people live without fundamental freedoms of action and choice that the better-off take for granted." This line of argument urges moving beyond absolute essentials to recognizing community standards as well.

Such reasoning has led to the development of relative poverty lines. Perhaps best understood as a disparity approach or as comparative disadvantage, here poverty is defined in relation to community standards. Poverty can be defined relatively, for example, as including all people with incomes falling below 50% of the average income in a country.[2]

Absolute and relative poverty lines also differ in how they are adjusted over time. Typically, an absolute poverty line is corrected annually by the rate of inflation (i.e., if inflation rises by 2% then the poverty line rises by 2%). Conversely, a relative poverty line is adjusted to take into account changed standards of living such that if everyone else is better off (or worse off) because of economic change, the poverty line should reflect this.

One final complicating factor intrudes: poverty *lines*, however defined, ignore the depth of poverty. A poverty line is a threshold but the poor are not homogeneous; some experience much deeper levels of poverty than do others (because they are further below the line). Measuring poverty requires both defining a threshold and understanding how people fare relative to that threshold.

The definitional debate between absolute and relative poverty ought not to be considered as though one is right and the other wrong. Each definition highlights different aspects of poverty and calls for different policies of poverty reduction. For example, the absolute definition of poverty has greater applicability in developing countries where starvation and homelessness are more widespread. Conversely, in advanced industrial countries like Canada, the relative definition focuses attention on social cohesion and inclusiveness, where policies of income redistribution have greater policy appeal.

MEASURING POVERTY

Unlike the United States, where a definition of poverty is sanctioned by the federal government, Canada has no official definition of poverty. Consequently, in this country measures of poverty compete, with none recognized as authoritative. Statistics Canada has produced a non-intuitive, complicated Low Income Cut-Off (LICO) line. First constructed in 1961 by Jenny Podoluk (1968), her measure estimates the percentage of Canadians living in what she called "straitened circumstance." This is effectively a hybrid absolute and relative

poverty line, calculated to reflect the income required for a family to purchase the basic essentials necessary to survive in a modern society.[3] It has attributes of an absolute line in that its original focus, which remains, is on the income needed to meet the essentials of daily living. It is relative, however, in that it calculates such expenditures relative to an average family.

Table 7-1 shows 2006 LICO lines with adjustments for both family and community size. So, for example, in large cities like Montreal, Toronto, and Vancouver, a family of four with a gross (pre-tax) income at or below $39 399 would be considered as living in "straitened circumstance." To put that number in perspective, the median family income in 2006 in large cities was approximately $61 000.

Christopher Sarlo (2006), in collaboration with the Fraser Institute, has produced an alternative poverty line for Canada. This line is defined by a basic-needs approach, calculating the money required to purchase a basket of goods comprising the basic necessities of life. Similar to the LICO, Sarlo creates multiple lines reflecting the needs of people in different regions, in centres of different population sizes, in families of different size, and who have different health/disability statuses.

TABLE 7-1	Low Income Cut-Offs (LICO) Before Tax, 2006				
Family Size	Population of Community of Residence				
	500 000+	100 000 to 499 999	30 000 to 99 999	Less than 30 000	Rural
1	$21 202	$18 260	$18 147	$16 605	$14 596
2	$26 396	$22 731	$22 591	$20 671	$18 170
3	$32 450	$27 945	$27 773	$25 412	$22 338
4	$39 399	$33 930	$33 721	$30 855	$27 122
5	$44 686	$38 482	$38 245	$34 995	$30 760
6	$50 397	$43 402	$43 135	$39 469	$34 694
7+	$56 110	$48 322	$48 024	$43 943	$38 626

Source: Statistics Canada (2007).

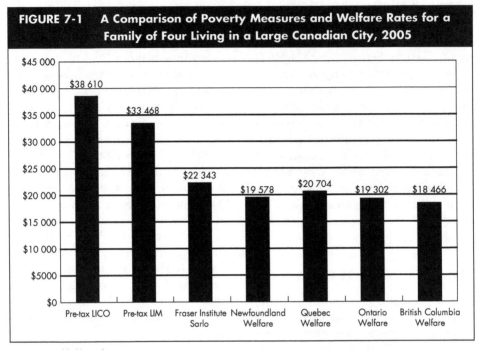

FIGURE 7-1   A Comparison of Poverty Measures and Welfare Rates for a Family of Four Living in a Large Canadian City, 2005

Source: Assembled by authors.

Figure 7-1 compares the Statistics Canada LICO (pre-tax) to the Fraser Institute Sarlo line (also pre-tax). As you can see, for a family of four, the two methods provide poverty thresholds that differ by about $17 000. The difference highlights what occurs when you take a basic-needs, absolute approach (Sarlo) and compare it with a line that reflects, at least in part, community standards. Another of the poverty lines in Figure 7-1 is more akin to the definition and measurement of poverty in Europe. This is the Statistics Canada Low Income Measure (LIM), which is based on a threshold defined as one-half of the median income of a Canadian family (showing a poverty line of $33 468 for a family of four).

Figure 7-1 also includes 2005 welfare rates. These rates are based on what a family of four would receive in each of the provinces noted. These fall below any of the poverty lines, signalling that while Canada does have a social safety net, it hangs very, very low. Another standard with which to compare poverty lines uses minimum wages. In 2005, minimum wages, which are set provincially, ranged between $7 and $8 per hour. Using $8 an hour, someone who worked 35 hours a week for 52 weeks would earn $14 560. If this person were the sole earner in the family, the family would be well below the Statistics Canada low-income lines and about $8000 below Sarlo's line.

Using the LIM definition, Figure 7-2 adds a more historical dimension, showing that over the last 30 years the poverty rate in Canada has changed very little (between 10% and 14% of all Canadians). Although our collective standard of living has generally risen over this period, and while the rich have become even better off than before, the incidence of poverty in Canada has remained stubbornly stable.

Important, too, is the depth of poverty. It is not enough merely to calculate a poverty line. Substantial numbers of people fall below this line, and so a measure of the gap

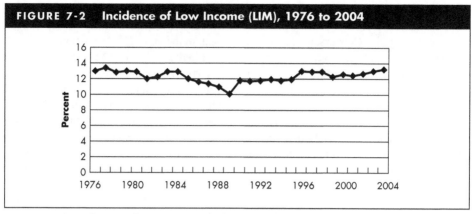

FIGURE 7-2   Incidence of Low Income (LIM), 1976 to 2004

Sources: Statistics Canada, Survey of Consumer Finances and Survey of Labour and Income Dynamics, various years.

between what people actually receive as income and the poverty line is important. Indeed, as shown in Figure 7-3, in 2005 the average low-income family was living in deep poverty, fully $6700 dollars below the poverty threshold (as calculated using LICO). Expressed differently, the average depth of poverty would be almost 20% below the poverty threshold.

Experiencing poverty is stressful, demeaning, harmful, and debilitating, especially when it persists. Therefore, the length of time individuals experience conditions of inadequate housing, poor access to health care, and chronic nutrition problems is important. Most Canadian estimates note that poverty is a transient experience for about half of Canada's poor (Heisz 2007).

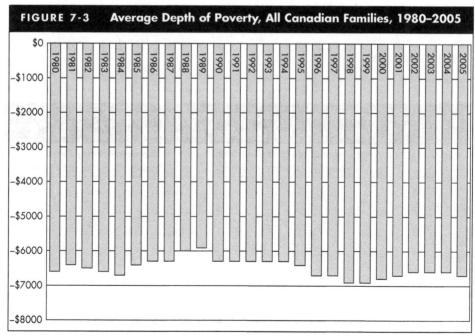

FIGURE 7-3   Average Depth of Poverty, All Canadian Families, 1980–2005

Source: Statistics Canada, CANSIM Series, V25746674.

In other words, every second person living in poverty this year is likely not to be living in poverty next year. Conversely, persistent poverty over at least five years is experienced by about one-quarter of all poor Canadians (which amounts to more than 1 million Canadians!).

Comparing poverty across countries is difficult given the definitional points raised above, but it is possible to gain some insight by using Statistics Canada's LIM measure (half of median income). This is done in Table 7-2. In Finland, just over 5% of people were living in poverty in the late 1990s, whereas in the U.S. the comparable figure was 17%. About 12% of Canadians were living in poverty based on this definition of half of median income. In general, European countries, save for the United Kingdom, have lower rates of poverty than either Canada or the U.S. In large measure, the reason for this can be deduced from the final column in the table, which shows how much poverty is reduced if gross income (pre-tax) is compared to net income (post-tax/transfer). To the extent that the percentage of people in poverty is reduced, this implies that income redistribution, via a strong welfare state, is working to alleviate poverty. Notice that the reductions are greater in

Europe, only slightly less redistributive in Canada (52% reduction), and comparatively weak in the U.S. (28% reduction).

Finally, who is likely to experience poverty? Here the patterns are very clear, and it matters not how poverty is measured. Although some emphasize the "feminization of poverty" (Duffy and Mandell 2001), the likelihood of women (11.2%) and men (10.5%) living in poverty is almost identical (post-tax/transfer). However, single-parent families, the majority of which are headed by women, are much more likely to be poor (33% are poor post-tax/transfer) than are married or common law families (8% post-tax/transfer). Aboriginal Canadians also suffer from higher rates of poverty than do other Canadians, rates that have been characterized as "third world." Unattached individuals, especially those aged 45 to 64, are more likely to be poor than are people who are married or living common law. Given Canada's relatively good pension coverage, both public and private, poverty rates among the elderly have declined in recent years, although elderly women (8% post-tax/transfer) are more likely to be poor than elderly men (3% post-tax/transfer). Finally, recent immigrants to Canada have increasing

TABLE 7-2	Comparisons by Country of Poverty Rates and Poverty Reduction via Redistribution (circa 2000)	
Country	Poverty Rates (% below half of median pre-tax income)	Percent Poverty Reduction, Before vs. After Tax/Transfer
United States	17.0	28
United Kingdom	12.3	61
Canada	11.9	52
Netherlands	8.9	59
Germany	8.2	71
Belgium	7.9	75
Sweden	6.4	78
Finland	5.4	70

Source: Adapted from Picot and Myles (2004).

difficulties finding good paid employment, and the rate of poverty among new
arrivals has increased recently.

Popular images often portray the poor as
lazy welfare dependants. As with many
other groups, there are no doubt some
among the poor who are lazy. However,
fully 30% of people living in poverty in
Canada work full-time, full-year (Fleury
and Fortin 2006). They suffer from being in
low-wage jobs with pay rates that, despite
their working long hours, provide incomes
below the poverty threshold. Many other
individuals who live in poverty also work,
although not full-time, full-year (see above
on minimum wages and poverty levels).
Clearly, the solution to poverty is not as simple as giving everyone a job.

REDUCING POVERTY

Defining and measuring "too little" is typically understood as a first step in ameliorating persistent poverty. In reducing poverty,
an official definition would help. If policy
is to be effective, there must be tangible,
identifiable goals, and without a consistent,
authoritative definition of poverty, Canada
lacks one of the core elements critical to
policy success. With no demonstrable
measure of poverty, it is very easy for all
Canadians to avoid responsibility. The failure of Statistics Canada to provide leadership here is difficult to explain, especially
since the agency is involved in measuring a
variety of other social parameters that are
also laden with value judgments (e.g.,
unemployment, consumer price index).

Of course, it would be naive in the
extreme to assume that an official definition
would jump-start a movement to ameliorate
at least the worst excesses of poverty (e.g.,
the persistent poverty in some of our inner
cities or in some First Nations communities).
Nevertheless, any progress on reducing
poverty is fraught with difficulty if the measurement is constantly shifting. That said,

Canada has been successful in reducing
poverty in some delimited areas, and in particular with respect to the elderly. Several
decades ago, one could point to poverty
among the elderly, and especially elderly women, as a national concern. More
recently, both private and public pensions
have provided higher levels of support to
more and more elderly Canadians (Duffy
and Mandel 2001).

It is also increasingly clear that social
welfare mechanisms work, with provisions
for the elderly being one good example.
However, it is also the case that welfare is
increasingly subject to ideologically motivated criticism. Welfare programs are
doomed to failure, it is often argued, for
three reasons. Long ago, de Tocqueville
(1997 [1835]:70) wrote that "any permanent, regular administrative system whose
aim will be to provide for the needs of the
poor will breed more miseries than it can
cure." While it is true that income redistribution requires administrative support, and
while it is also true that some redistribution of income goes to the middle class,
Table 7-2 clearly shows that social welfare
mechanisms in many European countries
are relatively successful at reducing
poverty (as they are also in Canada,
although not as strongly).

A second complaint is that welfare
programs create a poverty trap. The argument is that giving handouts to the poor
breeds reliance rather than independence.
However, we see this as an easy claim to
make but a difficult one to support with
plausible evidence. Welfare rates in
Canada, as shown in Figure 7-1, keep people below even the lowest poverty lines, so
it is hard to imagine how this fosters welfare dependence. No doubt escaping
poverty is difficult for some, but it is not
clear that the welfare system is the key
causal factor at work. We need only recall
the large proportion of Canadians who are
poor despite working full-time, full-year.

The third argument against welfare programs is that income redistribution requires taxation of those who are better off, and this creates a disincentive for the economically successful to invest and work hard themselves. That redistribution actually creates onerous disincentives is difficult to prove. Still, while this dampening effect may occur to some extent, other factors help to counterbalance it. For example, even a small taste of economic success may encourage people to invest further in training, be more productive, and consume more, all factors beneficial to everyone in society. Furthermore, not ameliorating poverty can be expensive, since excessive inequality can breed tension, increasing crime and social unrest. The end result could lead to higher taxes to pay to enforce law-and-order measures.

These three arguments each frame poverty reduction as bad public policy. However, in the final analysis, whether social welfare programs work to reduce the incidence of poverty is an empirical question. Several recent studies have compared the extent of social welfare provisions across industrial nations to determine whether these provisions have reduced poverty over time (see Kenworthy 1999; Brady 2005). They have. As Brady (2005:1349) concludes, "the welfare state effectively reduces poverty." This is in keeping with the results in Table 7-2 and with Canada's experience in pension provisions, but Brady's conclusion has behind it the weight of more comparisons over more countries and for more years, with controls for other possible factors that might influence this relationship (e.g., unemployment rates, economic cycles). The bottom line is that well-designed welfare systems work to reduce poverty.

Welfare payments do help to ameliorate some of the worst excesses of poverty, but other laws and practices actually work against income redistribution and poverty reduction. These are important to recognize,

especially at a time when many middle and higher income earners are bemoaning high rates of taxation. The phrase "legislated poverty" captures the effect of some laws that act to reinforce low income for some. Minimum wages, as noted above, are far below even the lowest poverty lines in every province; in their design, they consign some individuals to poverty wages. Tax breaks for higher income earners, such as through registered retirement savings plans or registered education savings plans, effectively allow the better-off among us to shelter some money from tax, money that could be devoted to redistribution if the political will were sufficiently strong.[4]

Finally, some argue that income poverty ignores other important dimensions of poverty (World Bank 2001). Poor health or well-being, relative to that of one's contemporaries, could be considered a separate dimension of poverty. Similarly, lack of housing or substandard housing could also be used to signal poverty. However, poverty continues to be measured as income poverty, although there is growing awareness that this is only one dimension of a large social problem (see Iceland 2005).

CONCLUSION

Images of opulence and squalor are one thing. Understanding how unequally money is distributed, and why, is another. For those among us with little money, for whom hunger and shelter are everyday concerns, life is cold and heartless. This is especially so when poverty is persistent, reinforcing a daily grind of humility and struggle. The organization of our social world could be different (it might even include an official definition of poverty!). While inequality is a feature of all societies, evidence also shows that the depths of poverty experienced in any of the rich industrial nations can be ameliorated via sensible, well-planned welfare provisions.

NOTES

1. A simple analogy may avoid confusion. Temperature ranges along a continuum from hot (boiling) to cold (freezing). The boiling and freezing points of a fluid (e.g., water) are defined by physical changes (e.g., liquid to either gas or solid). By way of comparison, no naturally occurring points define for us poverty (freezing) or wealth (boiling).

2. A line of argument followed by Statistics Canada, for example, is that the definition of low income (poverty, in everyone else's language!) should relate to purchases or expenditures rather than to incomes. A relative definition might then be any person or family whose purchases of food, shelter, and clothing are above 50% of the mean level of such expenditures for the country in which they live. That is, they spend substantially more on these three elements than would a typical person or family.

3. Currently, the technical calculation for the LICO is as follows. If a family unit spends 20 percentage points more of their gross income on food, shelter, and clothing than the average Canadian family, they fall below the LICO. In 2006, and using pre-tax income, this constituted spending more than 63% of their income on food, clothing, and shelter.

4. Tuition fees in Canada cover a small portion of the cost of higher education. Fewer children from poor families attend college and university. The subsidized part of higher education therefore disproportionately benefits students from families in higher-income categories. This highlights how tax breaks like registered educational savings plans reinforce existing patterns of inequality.

REFERENCES

Arneil, Barbara 2006. *Diverse Communities: The Problem with Social Capital* Cambridge: Cambridge University Press.

Brady, David 2005. "The welfare state and relative poverty in rich Western democracies, 1967–1997" *Social Forces* 83, 4:1329–1364.

de Tocqueville, Alexis 1997 [1835]. *Memoir on Pauperism.* Translated by S. Drescher. Chicago: Ivan R. Dee.

Duffy, Ann, and Nancy Mandell 2001. "The growth in poverty and social inequality: Losing faith in social justice." In D. Glenday and A. Duffy (eds.), *Canadian Society: Meeting the Challenges of the Twenty-First Century*, pp. 77–114. Toronto: Oxford University Press.

EEC 1985. On specific action to combat poverty (Council decision of December 19, 1984). Retrieved June 4, 2007. http://eurlex.europa.eu/smartapi/cgi/sga_doc?smartapi!celexplus!prod!CELEXnumdoc&numdoc=31985D0008&lg=en

Fluery, Dominique, and Myriam Fortin 2006. "When working is not enough to escape poverty: An analysis of Canada's working poor." Policy Research Group, Human Resources and Social Development Canada, Working Paper SP-630-06-06E.

Heisz, Andrew 2007. "Income Inequality and redistribution in Canada: 1976 to 2004." Analytical Studies Branch Research Paper Series, 11F0019MIE No. 298.

Iceland, John 2005. "Measuring poverty: Theoretical and empirical considerations." *Measurement* 3, 4:199–235.

Kenworthy, Lane 1999. "Do social-welfare policies reduce poverty? A cross-national assessment." *Social Forces* 77, 3:1119–1139.

Picot, Garnet, and John Myles 2004. "Income inequality and low income in Canada." *Horizons* 7, 2:9–18.

Podoluk, Jenny R. 1968. *Income of Canadians.* Ottawa: Census Monograph, Dominion Bureau of Statistics.

Sarlo, Christopher 2006. "Poverty in Canada update 2006." Retrieved May 1, 2007. http://www.fraserinstitute.ca/admin/books/files/PovertyinCanada2006.pdf

Statistics Canada 2007. "Low income cut-offs for 2006 and low income measures for 2005." Income Research Paper Series, Statistics Canada Catalogue no 75F0002MIE, no. 004. Retrieved June 1, 2007.http://www.statcan.ca/english/research/75F0002MIE/75F0002MIE2007004.pdf

Smith, Adam 1776 [1991]. *An Inquiry into the Nature and Causes of the Wealth of Nations.* New York: Knopf.

World Bank 2001. *World Development Report, 2000/2001: Attacking Poverty.* New York: Oxford University Press.

chapter eight

Social Mobility in Canada: Concepts, Patterns, and Trends

Richard A. Wanner
(An original chapter written
for this volume.)

Seymour Martin Lipset (1963) once said that Horatio Alger[1] has never been a Canadian hero. He was correct in that the myth of unlimited opportunity for ambitious young persons never became as much a part of the folk wisdom in Canada as it did in the United States. Indeed, as Lipset (1989) himself has shown, some attitude surveys find that Canadians are more likely to favour equality of result than equality of opportunity.

Nevertheless, like most industrial societies, Canada increasingly relies on educational credentials to sort persons into jobs. As recently as 1961, just 2.9% of all Canadians had earned a university degree. By 2001, this had risen to more than 15%, with nearly 44% having had at least some post-secondary education. During the same period, the proportion of professionals in Canada's labour force increased by more than 2.5 times to over 20%, while the proportion of workers in agriculture dropped by two-thirds to less than 3% of the labour force. Has this massive transformation of the labour force resulted in an increase in opportunity in Canada? Are young persons less likely to inherit the status position of their parents than they were a generation ago? Has the increased availability of higher education led to more rapid career advancement? Has a greater reliance on educational credentials in hiring created more opportunities for women and members of minority racial and ethnic groups? Sociologists have long studied issues like these under the rubric of "social mobility" or "status attainment."

CONCEPTUAL ISSUES

Social mobility has been broadly defined as the upward or downward movement of individuals or groups into different positions in a social hierarchy based on wealth, income, occupation, education, power, or any other scarce social resource. Societies with high rates of social mobility are generally regarded as more open societies, while those with lower rates are deemed to be more closed. Social mobility may be either upward, as in the daughter of a welder becoming a lawyer, or downward, as in the son of a Ph.D. dropping out of high school. This movement assumes that occupations or other status characteristics are ranked from highest to lowest in terms of status or prestige and movement is up or down the status or prestige hierarchy. Mobility may also be classified as either intergenerational, in which movement is from parents' status to the status of their children when they become adults, or intragenerational, in which movement takes place within a person's own career, sometimes known as career mobility.

Although social mobility is possible along all of the hierarchies mentioned, most research on the phenomenon by sociologists has focused on occupational mobility. This is because occupational standing is generally agreed to be closely related to other behaviours and to other indices of general social standing, such as income and education. Occupation is also relatively easy to measure in surveys, and occupational rankings have been shown to be quite consistent both over time and across societies (see Treiman 1977). Many mobility researchers (e.g., Erikson and Goldthorpe 1993) regard occupation as primarily an indicator of social class position when combined with a measure of class of worker, which refers to one's status as either employer, self-employed, or employee. Those adopting such a class-structural

approach do not regard class positions as inherently ordered and are thus uninterested in movement of individuals up or down a social hierarchy (see Erickson and Goldthorpe 1993:29–35).

Until recently, most research on social mobility was restricted to men. Indeed, the large-scale mobility surveys carried out through the 1970s only rarely included interviews with women, although the 1973 Canadian Mobility Study (CMS) did so. It is not that women were simply excluded from the research by predominantly male sociologists; their exclusion was justified theoretically. The argument commonly goes as follows: stratification theory is mainly concerned with explaining inequalities that arise out of the economic and prestige structures of society, and these structures are embodied in the occupational structure; women are peripheral to the occupational structure because of their interrupted employment patterns, attachment to part-time work, and family responsibilities. Therefore, their social class or status position is determined by the occupation of the male head of household.

A major assumption underlying this argument was that the family and not the individual is the relevant social unit, and that the class or status position of the unit must be determined by its (usually male) head (Erikson and Goldthorpe 1992). As we shall see, however, since the 1970s this conventional view has been challenged, and women in their own right are increasingly incorporated into social mobility research and stratification research more generally.

Social mobility is typically studied by means of mobility tables that cross-classify a set of categories of the occupations of respondents with a survey of their fathers', or more rarely mothers', occupations. The marginal distribution of parents' occupations is termed the occupational "origin," while the marginal distribution of respondents' occupations is known as the occupational "destination." More recently, a technique called log-linear modelling has been used to examine the underlying structure of such tables and make comparisons of tables for different groups or different countries. Later in this chapter I will describe briefly how such models have been applied in mobility research.

From data gathered for the 1973 CMS by Statistics Canada and reported in Boyd et al. (1985), we know that there has been a great deal of upward occupational mobility in Canada up to the early 1970s, but most of it has been between occupations that are very close together in terms of their relative statuses. A father who is a labourer is much more likely to have a son who becomes a machine operative than to have a son who becomes a lawyer. We have also learned that much of this upward mobility is due to the expansion of some occupations and the contraction of others over time. As described above, occupations at the top of the hierarchy, such as professionals, have been growing dramatically in the twentieth century, while occupations at the bottom, particularly farm occupations, have been declining. The result is that much social mobility has been induced by the opportunities created by this change in the occupational structure. Mobility of this kind is known as structural mobility. The mobility in a society that exceeds that permitted by shifts in its occupational structure is known as exchange mobility, or sometimes as circulation mobility or social fluidity. Most mobility research has concentrated on exchange mobility, since it is regarded as the true measure of the openness of a social system.

Although we will only deal with it briefly here, status attainment research is complementary to mobility research. Using regression models instead of log-linear models, it attempts to identify the variables intervening between parents' status and their offspring's status. Paying particularly attention to educational, occupational, and income attainment, the status attainment researcher focuses on the process that results in people ending up where they do in status hierarchies.

Mobility research is not simply descriptive, serving only to measure a society's relative openness. From its beginnings (Sorokin 1927), the study of occupational mobility has been concerned with the impact of the process of industrialization on occupational structures and occupational mobility. Two contrasting theoretical positions have emerged. The first, tracing its origins to the work of Lipset and Bendix (1959), maintains that mobility rates, or at least exchange mobility rates (Featherman et al. 1975), should be similar in all industrial societies because of broad similarities in their occupational structures and the status structures that underlay them. The second, with roots in Sorokin's work and partially elaborated by Treiman (1970), argues that mobility rates should increase as a result of continued industrialization, the expansion of educational opportunities, the presence of certain political ideologies, particularly socialist and democratic socialist ones, and the diminution of status differences between classes over time. This theory has been variously termed the "industrialism thesis" (Kerr et al. 1960) or the "liberal theory of industrialism" (Erickson and Goldthorpe 1993).

A second major theoretical concern in mobility research is derived from Marx's recognition that social mobility may be inimical to the process of class formation and Weber's definition of the social class structure as "composed of the plurality of class statuses between which an interchange of individuals on a personal basis or in the course of generations is readily possible and typically observable" (Weber 1947:424). This theme of class formation and class boundaries shows up particularly in the work of European sociologists such as John Goldthorpe (1987), but is also apparent in the concern with barriers to intergenerational movement evident in the status attainment literature (Blau and Duncan 1967). Theorists such as Giddens and Parkin have both used the results of mobility studies in their attempt to understand class formation and class relationships. Giddens (1973) has explored the role of mobility processes in the institutionalization of persons in similar market positions into structurally significant social class categories and relationships.

SOURCES OF CANADIAN MOBILITY DATA

Four large-scale sample surveys conducted in Canada have obtained the measures required for mobility and status attainment research. The 1973 CMS was a survey of nearly 45 000 men and women originally conducted to investigate rates and patterns of intergenerational occupational mobility in the Canadian population.[2] The data were collected by Statistics Canada as a supplement to the July 1973 Labour Force Survey. Though measures for some of the variables come from the survey interviews, the bulk of the measures were included in a self-administered questionnaire left with respondents and picked up several days later by field workers (see Boyd et al. 1985).

The 1986 mobility data were collected as part of Statistics Canada's General Social Survey (GSS) program[3] and based on telephone interviews with 16 390 respondents using random digit dialling methods. The main sample was a national sample, excluding residents of institutions and the Yukon and Northwest Territories, consisting of 9946 persons aged 15 and over. A supplementary sample of 6444 was also drawn in certain regions of New Brunswick, Quebec, and Ontario with high concentrations of francophones because of

the language knowledge and use module of the survey. All social mobility questions were also asked of members of this supplementary sample. Adjustment for oversampling is included in the weights used to estimate population counts at the national level.

The 1994 (Cycle 9) GSS was designed partially to replicate the education, work, and retirement items from the 1989 (Cycle 4) survey, but added new sections on the transition into retirement, social origins, and work interruptions. The sample design and interviewing methods were essentially the same as those applied in earlier GSS surveys. In 1994, the sample included approximately 11 500 respondents, with 10 000 persons in the main sample and a supplementary sample of 1500 persons aged 55 to 74.

Most recently, Cycle 15 of the GSS collected data during 2001 on 24 310 respondents. The theme for this cycle was Family History, and data were collected not only on respondents, but also on their marriage or common law partner, children, parents, and brothers and sisters. While measures of both respondents' and their parents' occupations are available from this survey, the occupational measure used is somewhat different from those available in the earlier surveys, as described below.

The analysis reported in this chapter is restricted to men and women born in Canada and aged 25 to 64 at the time of the surveys. Only native-born Canadians are included because most immigrants' status origins, their education and parents' occupations, are from another country and do not reflect Canada's opportunity structure. Both anglophone and francophone Canadian men and women are included in the analysis despite the evidence that linguistic group is often an important dimension of stratification in Canadian society. However, Boyd (1981) found no substantial difference between anglophones and francophones in the patterns of effects of paternal education and occupation or respondents' education on attainment of first job, prompting her to conclude that "there is little difference between the two groups with respect to the *process* of stratification [emphasis in original]" (1981:666). However, she did observe differences between linguistic groups in the average levels of the status variables. Wanner (2005) arrived at a similar conclusion using data from the 1986 and 1994 GSS cycles in addition to data from the 1973 CMS.

In the tables that follow, I use a simple occupational classification for the Canadian labour force based on collapsing the 16-category classification used in the 1973 CMS (see Pineo et al. 1977) and used again in the 1986 and 1994 surveys. Unfortunately, for the 2001 GSS, Statistics Canada did not code the occupations of respondents and their parents into the Pineo et al. classification used in previous surveys. Instead, they used a collapsed version of the 1991 Standard Occupational Classification, which does not use skill level as a classifying criterion and is in some respects more of an industry than an occupational classification.[4] However, the eight-category classification available in the public-use version of the data is quite similar to my collapsed version of the Pineo et al. classification. Both classifications preserve the conventional manual/non-manual distinction to make these results comparable to those for other countries, as well as a distinction between higher and lower professionals. The occupational categories are rank ordered in the sense that those at the upper end (e.g., professional or managerial occupations) have higher educational requirements, produce greater earnings, and have higher occupational prestige scores than those at the lower end (e.g., lower manual or primary-industry occupations). Thus the terms *upward* or *downward* mobility refer to the direction of movement along the status

hierarchy on which the occupational categories are ranked.

The remainder of this chapter will be devoted to exploring patterns of intergenerational occupational mobility in Canada as well as trends between the initial survey of 1973 and the most recent 2001 survey. First, I examine changes in Canada's occupational structure, or the distribution of workers over occupational categories both over generations and between the surveys, since the structural component of total mobility is determined by these distributions. I then use some simple methods based on percentages to explore patterns and trends in mobility tables for both men and women. I next introduce briefly the concept of a mobility model and offer some results that shed further light on the question of trends in equality of opportunity. I conclude by comparing the Canadian results to mobility patterns in other countries.

TRENDS IN THE CANADIAN OCCUPATIONAL STRUCTURE

Figure 8-1 shows trends in Canada's occupational structure from 1891 to 2001 using a limited set of occupational categories.[5] Trends are shown separately for men and women to emphasize both historical differences between them and the different patterns of change they have experienced over time. These changing occupational distributions represent the marginal distributions of our mobility tables—that is, the Canadian occupational structure. Differences between the distributions of parents and those of their adult children represent structural mobility brought about by shifts in the availability of occupations over time. It is particularly evident in Figure 8-1 that the proportion of men engaged in farming declined dramatically since 1891, from more than half of

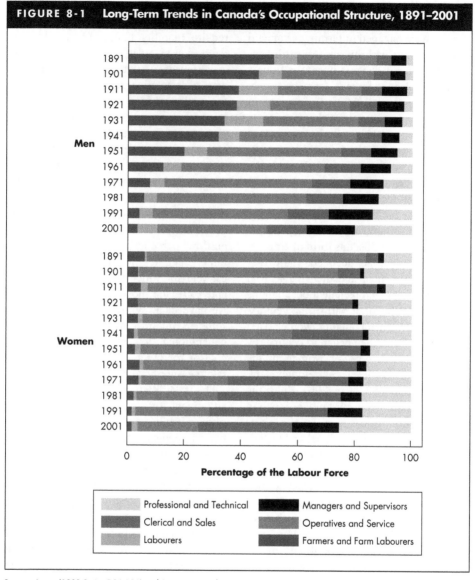

FIGURE 8-1 Long-Term Trends in Canada's Occupational Structure, 1891–2001

Sources: Leacy (1983:Series D86-106) and Statistics Canada (1981, 1993, 2001)

the male labour force to less than 3.5% by 2001. As farming declined among men, growing numbers of them were employed in operative and service occupations up to 1961, reflecting mainly the growth in manufacturing employment. Since 1951, an increasing proportion of men have been found in both managerial and professional and technical employment, consistent with Bell's (1973) forecast for post-industrial societies. At the same time, unskilled manual occupations declined after reaching a peak of nearly 14% of the male labour force in the 1930s, although some 6% of men were still found in such occupations by 2001.

The story for women is considerably different. While a substantial proportion of women were engaged in farming as unpaid family workers early in the twentieth century, they do not show up in census figures on the paid labour force as farmers; hence, we see a very small fraction of women in farming occupations throughout the century. Before the 1950s, a higher proportion of women were found in the amorphous operative and service category. Early in the twentieth century, this meant mainly domestic service employment, while during and after the Second World War many women were employed as factory operatives. Since the 1950s, this form of employment for women has declined, while first clerical employment and then managerial and professional and technical occupations expanded. In the latter half of the century, clerical employment among women first grew rapidly, and then began to decline: by 1981, more than 43% of women in the labour force were in clerical employment, declining to about 33% by 2001. Since the 1960s, there has been substantial growth in the proportion of women employed as managers or in the professional and technical category. A substantial amount of sex segregation remains in Canada's occupational structure, but it is clear that women are increasingly found in higher-status, higher-wage occupations. Nevertheless, the large differences in the male and female occupational distributions predispose women to considerably more "structural" mobility than is typical of men when mobility is measured based on father's occupation.

BASIC PATTERNS OF MOBILITY

Although the trends observed in Figure 8-1 describe the evolution of Canada's opportunity structure, they tell us nothing about the inheritance of occupational status from generation to generation. For this we require mobility tables. These tables are quite simply created by cross-classifying an origin status (e.g., father's occupation) with a destination status (e.g., daughter's occupation). If a mobility table is percentaged across the rows, the results are termed "outflow percentages," representing distributions of respondents flowing from common status origins. If the mobility table is percentaged down columns, the results are inflow percentages, representing distributions of respondents into common status destinations. Tables 8-1 and 8-2 display outflow percentages for father–son and father–daughter mobility in 1973, the earliest year for which we have mobility data, and 2001, the most recent year for which we have data. While these tables provide some useful information about the intergenerational flow of labour, they do not control for other processes related to the relative supply and demand for workers, such as differential fertility, educational attainment, or technological change. One of the advantages of the more complex statistical models often applied in mobility analysis is their ability to control for such factors. As mentioned above, the occupational classifications in the two years are similar, but not strictly comparable in all categories.

The first place to start in examining the welter of data available in these tables is with their diagonals, which represent status inheritance[6] or immobility. That is, along the diagonals are respondents to the surveys whose occupations are in the same category as those of their parent. These are quite consistently the highest percentages in the table, indicating that movement from origin to destination is by no means a random process, but is characterized by a sizable amount of inheritance. Near the upper left corner of the top panel of Table 8-1, we see that in 1973, 21.2% of sons who came

TABLE 8-1 Outflow Percentages from Father's Occupation to Respondent's Occupation, Native-Born Canadian Men and Women Aged 25-64, 1973

Father's Occupation	Son's or Daughter's Occupation							
	Upper Professional	Manager	Lower Professional	Upper Non-manual	Lower Non-manual	Upper Manual	Lower Manual	Farm
Men								
Upper Professional	31.4	20.2	12.6	12.0	7.9	10.1	5.3	0.5
Manager	19.8	21.2	10.7	13.3	9.0	13.3	11.1	1.5
Lower Professional	14.8	12.9	19.2	11.7	9.6	17.4	12.2	2.2
Upper Non-manual	16.6	15.0	8.2	21.8	9.6	17.1	11.0	0.7
Lower Non-manual	11.3	11.2	6.8	19.1	11.3	20.2	18.8	1.3
Upper Manual	8.0	8.8	6.2	13.4	9.3	31.5	21.5	1.2
Lower Manual	5.5	6.7	4.7	11.5	8.7	27.9	33.3	1.6
Farm	4.7	4.5	3.3	7.4	5.6	25.0	26.5	23.0
Women								
Upper Professional	24.7	5.2	22.8	28.3	14.9	0.8	3.3	0.0
Manager	16.1	2.3	15.5	32.8	24.2	4.4	4.7	0.0
Lower Professional	9.8	3.8	16.6	30.9	30.6	3.3	5.1	0.0
Upper Non-manual	11.4	3.0	14.9	32.5	28.9	2.4	6.4	0.4
Lower Non-manual	7.4	2.2	13.4	30.5	33.9	1.4	10.6	0.5
Upper Manual	6.5	2.0	11.0	29.5	36.1	2.0	12.3	0.7
Lower Manual	4.4	1.1	9.9	25.9	38.6	1.8	18.1	0.2
Farm	10.0	2.1	12.3	20.4	32.3	1.2	17.9	3.8

Note: Totals of all rows should equal 100%, but may not due to rounding error.

TABLE 8-2 Outflow Percentages from Father's Occupation to Respondent's Occupation, Native-Born Canadian Men and Women Aged 25–64, 2001

Father's Occupation	Son's or Daughter's Occupation							
	Professional	Manager	Technical	Clerical	Sales and Service	Trade and Transport	Processing	Primary
Men								
Professional	41.3	9.8	10.2	5.2	13.9	12.0	6.1	1.6
Manager	29.9	18.4	5.6	6.9	14.8	13.8	7.4	3.2
Technical	25.0	8.5	17.3	4.9	17.4	14.2	9.2	3.5
Clerical	20.1	14.4	7.9	11.1	16.8	23.6	5.5	0.4
Sales and Service	18.9	13.6	7.5	9.6	24.4	17.9	6.4	1.8
Trade and Transport	14.1	10.6	6.7	6.7	14.7	33.4	9.9	4.0
Processing	13.2	8.9	8.5	10.3	14.9	26.8	15.3	2.1
Primary	8.7	8.0	4.7	3.6	11.0	29.5	11.2	23.5
Women								
Professional	41.9	9.1	8.9	23.0	15.6	0.3	0.8	0.5
Manager	26.6	9.7	9.6	22.5	24.6	1.9	3.7	1.6
Technical	25.3	8.0	12.2	25.6	23.5	1.4	3.3	0.7
Clerical	24.4	8.8	5.3	34.3	23.9	0.0	2.2	1.2
Sales and Service	22.7	9.3	7.4	29.6	23.1	1.8	5.0	1.1
Trade and Transport	18.0	7.2	7.3	29.3	30.9	3.0	3.4	1.1
Processing	15.4	6.9	6.6	28.2	31.0	4.7	6.4	0.9
Primary	18.3	7.8	6.3	26.5	29.1	2.2	4.5	5.3

Note: Totals of all rows should equal 100%, but may not due to rounding error.

from managerial origins became managers themselves, that is, inherited a managerial status. By the 2001 survey, shown in Table 8-2, this figure had dropped to 18.4%, suggesting that the amount of inheritance of this sort of occupational status had declined.[7] Among the men, even stronger inheritance appears among both higher and lower manual workers as well as farm or primary workers, implying that the manual/non-manual distinction represents a real barrier to mobility, and one that has remained strong over the 28-year period covered by these data.

The lower panels of Tables 8-1 and 8-2 present outflow percentages for father–daughter mobility in 1973 and 2001. Here, the most obvious feature is not so much concentration along the diagonal, though there is a considerable amount of that, but the extent to which daughters are likely to end up in upper or lower non-manual occupations in 1973 (clerical and sales and service occupations in 2001) regardless of their origins. Since this would constitute downward mobility from professional and managerial origins and upward mobility from manual origins, there is considerably more mobility and less immobility from

father's occupation among women than among men. By 2001, however, the proportion of women ending up in clerical occupations declined considerably if they came from higher-status origins. Over time, there also appears to be a much greater propensity for women to be upwardly mobile to both professional and managerial occupations.

SUMMARIZING MOBILITY TABLES

Some basic summary statistics comparing relative flows in mobility tables for 1973, 1986, 1994, and 2001 are presented in Table 8-3. In this table, the percent immobile is computed as the percentage of the cases lying on the diagonal of each mobility table. Upward mobility is the percentage of cases below the diagonal; downward mobility is the percentage of cases above the diagonal. Structural mobility is computed simply by summing the positive percentage differences between origin and destination statuses and may be interpreted as the percentage of cases that would have to be reallocated to make the origin and

| TABLE 8-3 | Measures of the Components of Total Mobility from Father's Occupation, Native-Born Canadian Men and Women Aged 25–64, 1973–2001 |

	Men				Women			
	1973	**1986**	**1994**	**2001**	**1973**	**1986**	**1994**	**2001**
Immobile	26.8	26.8	27.6	26.2	13.3	12.1	13.5	13.1
Mobile								
Upward	56.3	50.3	47.5	50.4	71.5	69.7	66.5	67.6
Downward	16.9	22.9	24.9	23.3	15.2	18.2	20.0	19.3
Structural Mobility	21.6	20.3	16.5	15.6	56.0	55.7	50.5	48.0
Exchange Mobility	51.6	52.9	55.9	58.2	30.7	32.2	36.0	38.9

Note: These measures are based on frequency counts from 8-by-8 mobility tables for the years listed.

destination distributions identical. Exchange mobility is movement in the table not accounted for by marginal differences and equals the sum of the percentages of immobility and structural mobility subtracted from 100%.

In the case of mobility from father's occupation shown in Table 8-3, the proportions of both men and women who are immobile have remained remarkably constant between 1973 and 2001, despite differences in the occupational classification for 2001 noted above. Another way of putting it is to say that the volume of total mobility (the "upward" plus the "downward" percentages) has also remained quite constant. Nevertheless, a net increase in exchange mobility can be observed for both men and women, largely the result of a decline in structural mobility.

The most impressive change to be observed in Table 8-3 is the shift over time in the relative balance of upward and downward mobility, with the latter increasing to a considerable extent over the 20-year period under consideration here. Up to 1994, this can be accounted for largely by the substantial decline in farm origins over the period, which has had the effect of eliminating a major source of upward structural mobility. Specifically, for men in 1973 virtually all structural mobility was driven by movement out of farming. By 1994, only about 60% of this structural mobility was farming-related, with about 11% of all upward mobility originating in farming occupations.

As mentioned, for women, structural mobility from their fathers' occupations is a qualitatively different phenomenon compared to that for men, involving as it does a gender shift in the transition from origin to destination distributions. As a consequence, we see considerably more structural than exchange mobility among women than among men, and also considerably less immobility. What is perhaps surprising is the preponderance of upward over downward mobility among women, although this is largely the result of daughters of manual fathers finding themselves in lower non-manual occupations. If we were to use mother's occupation as our origin distribution for women, the ratio of upward to downward mobility would be similar to that of men (see Wanner 1993).

MODELS OF MOBILITY

While we have gleaned a fair amount of information about patterns and trends in occupational mobility from an examination of some simple percentage tables, it rapidly became apparent to researchers in the field that these results could be misleading in a number of respects. What is required is a statistical model that reflects these patterns and trends. Such a statistical model consists of one or more equations expressing the relationship between two or more variables. These equations must be capable of being compared to observed data so that the fit between the model and the data may be evaluated. Statistical models are an expression of hypothetical statements derived from social theories and assume that the observable world works in the way predicted by the theory. If the model can be shown to fit observed data well, it lends support to the theory. A poor fit casts doubt on the theory.

By the late 1960s, Leo Goodman (1969) had developed an approach to modelling data organized as frequencies in cross-tabulations that closely resembled regression analysis for continuous variables. In these so-called log-linear models, the dependent variable is the logarithm of the frequency count of cases in cells of such tables, while the independent variables are membership in certain rows or columns or row-column combinations in the table. Such log-linear models were immediately applied to mobility tables and developments have been rapid since (see Breen and Whelan 1994; Goodman and Hout 1998; Hout 1983).

One form of log-linear model that has become popular with mobility researchers was developed by Xie (1992). His "log-multiplicative layer effect model"[8] is particularly useful because it provides a single parameter value that indexes the overall strength of association between occupational origins and destinations across time periods or countries, assuming that the basic pattern of association between origins and destinations is the same for the time periods or countries. The larger the value of these parameters, the stronger is the association between origin and destination statuses. Alternatively, a mobility table exhibits more openness if the association is weaker. The advantage of using these parameters to index association is that their value is not affected by the marginal distributions. That is, they reflect mobility rates relative to the occupational structure, not the absolute rates shown in Table 8-3.

Table 8-4 shows the parameters indexing association from two separate log-multiplicative layer effects models, one for men and one for women. In both cases, there is evidence of a sharp decline in the association between father's occupation and respondent's occupation between the 1973 survey and the 1986 survey. Between 1986 and 1994, we can observe little change in the magnitude of the association for either

men or women, implying that the trend toward an increase in the openness of the system failed to continue into the early 1990s. However, the association between origin and destination declines still further by the 2001 survey for both men and women, although a portion of this may be related to the slightly different occupational classification used in that year.

The finding that the Canadian system of occupational stratification is becoming more open over time stands up when more rigorous methods incorporating controls for other variables are used. Wanner (2005) applied cohort methods to the 1973 through 1994 GSS data to assess trends in the effect of father's occupation on son's or daughter's occupation, while controlling for such factors as education, labour force experience, and mother tongue. Using both ordinary least squares regression models and a multinomial conditional logit model, which is a form of log-linear model permitting the inclusion of controls, he found that the effect of father's occupational status on off-spring's status declined considerably during the course of the twentieth century.

Why has the Canadian system of occupational stratification been more open in recent decades than it was in the 1970s? These results are quite consistent with Hout's (1988) findings for the United States using

TABLE 8-4 **Measures of the Strength of Association* Between Father's Occupation and Respondent's Occupation for Native-Born Canadian Men And Women Aged 25–64, 1973, 1986, and 1994**

Year	Men	Women
1973	1.000	1.000
1986	0.868	0.779
1994	0.890	0.720
2001	0.739	0.659

*Based on normed φ parameters from Xie's (1992) log-multiplicative layer effect model applied to observed frequencies from mobility tables for 1973–2001.

data assembled from a series of U.S. General Social Surveys between 1972 and 1986. He interprets the sizable decline in the association between men's and women's occupational origins and destinations that he observed as the result of increasing proportions of university graduates in the American labour force, a group for which he finds virtually no association between origin status and destination status. The strong association between origin and destination among those with less than a university education accounts for nearly all of the overall association. Given the strong educational expansion in Canada between the 1950s and the 1970s (see Wanner 1999), it is likely that a similar interpretation would apply to this country. The continued decline of the association after 1994 and into the twenty-first century suggests that the expansion of university education has likely continued, though at a slower rate than during the earlier period.

CANADA IN COMPARATIVE PERSPECTIVE

How do the trends and patterns of occupational mobility we have observed for Canada compare to those for other countries? As mentioned earlier, the theories underlying mobility research can only be tested by means of longitudinal comparisons within a single society, cross-sectional comparisons of two or more societies, or both. Relatively little cross-national research has included Canada, because Statistics Canada will not make available outside its Research Data Centres a detailed occupational code identifying unique occupational titles that would make it possible to create occupational categories equivalent to those available for other countries. However limited, the available research indicates that Canada is by no means the "low mobility" society some commentators have claimed it to be, and the trend in Canada toward greater

openness is shared with most other post-industrial societies.

McRoberts and Selbee (1981) compared exchange mobility from father's occupation to son's occupation in Canada and the United States using 1973 data from both countries and found no significant differences between the two countries. Wanner (1986) examined both structural and exchange mobility from father's to son's occupation in comparing Canada to the U.S. and found that, while exchange mobility rates are similar, structural mobility into higher-ranking occupations is less pronounced in Canada than in the U.S. This implies that, while equality of opportunity is similar in the two societies, a combination of the supply and demand for labour in Canada produces fewer actual opportunities for upward mobility. In another comparison, Wanner and Hayes (1996) used data from the 1980s to compare mobility rates and patterns among men in Australia and Canada. They found that not only are structural mobility effects far stronger in Australia, but also there is a greater association between occupational origins and destinations there (i.e., Australia is a less open society than is Canada).

Just one of the major studies comparing mobility rates and patterns in many countries has included Canada. Ganzeboom et al. (1989) undertook the huge task of analyzing 126 mobility tables from 32 countries, including four tables from Canada. Their results suggest that the association between status origins and destinations in Canada is fairly low, indeed lower than in such countries as Sweden, the United Kingdom, France, and the Netherlands. Consistent with trends in Canada described above, Ganzeboom et al. report that "the overall trend in association between father's and son's class position is *down* in nearly all countries we could include in our analysis [emphasis in original]" (1989:31).

Since the appearance of the work of Ganzeboom et al. (1989), a large number of studies of social mobility have confirmed the prediction of the industrialism thesis that the association between origin status and destination status will decline. This decline in class-based ascription has been documented in Australia (Marks and Jones 1991), Canada (Wanner 2005), Hungary (Luijkx et al. 1995), the Netherlands (de Graaf and Luijkx 1992; Hendrickx and Ganzeboom 1998), Norway (Ringdal 1994), and France (Vallet 1999). In a recent volume reporting on trends in social fluidity in several European countries since the 1970s (Breen 2004), 7 of the 10 countries studied were found to have become more open for men, while 6 of 9 were more open for women.

Although sociologists have concentrated their efforts on occupational mobility, a number of economists have more recently studied intergenerational income or earnings mobility (see Corak 2004). This is done by predicting the income of children, as adults, from the income of a parent, expressed either in percentile terms or through the construction of income mobility tables by cross-tabulating parent's and offspring's incomes expressed in deciles or quartiles. Since income tends to be highly correlated with occupational status, results from both lines of research tend to be similar. In the case of Canada, the finding of Ganzeboom et al. (1989) that Canada has a fairly open mobility regime compared to other more developed countries is confirmed by Corak's (2005) finding that the effect of father's earnings on son's earnings in Canada ranks with the low effects found in the Scandinavian countries, and is less than half the effect found in such countries as France, the United States, and the United Kingdom. In this context, a lower effect implies less intergenerational inheritance.

SUMMING UP

This chapter has attempted to provide a basic introduction to contemporary research on social mobility by presenting some definitions of basic terms, a brief survey of theoretical and methodological issues, and an analysis of patterns and trends in intergenerational occupational mobility among Canadian men and women. The basic message I have attempted to convey is that understanding a system of stratification involves not only examining the distributions of scarce resources and how those distributions change over time, but also understanding the process whereby individuals arrive at a particular location in those distributions. This is the role of mobility and status attainment research: to understand the physiology of social inequality rather than its anatomy.

Although we have seen that Canadian society has become more open and the availability of opportunities less driven by shifts in the occupational structure since the early 1970s, Canada is still a stratified society characterized by a considerable amount of inheritance of privilege. Theoretically derived models of mobility tables provide rich detail that pinpoints exactly where mobility and immobility are taking place in the social structure. Mobility research is well suited to studying the problem of class formation by viewing the occupational hierarchy as discrete, with barriers to movement forming and dissolving over time. This affords insights into the processes whereby systems of inequality are historically reproduced and transformed. That being said, since the early 1990s many scholars of social inequality have shifted their efforts from the study of social mobility by means of the intensive analysis of mobility tables using log-linear models to issues such as gender, racial, and ethnic inequities. These problems are linked to the incorporation of ethnically diverse immigrants into industrial societies, structural barriers to mobility in labour markets, and education both as a form of stratification and as a mechanism facilitating mobility. Far from abandoning the key issues raised by social mobility research, these new lines of inquiry serve to broaden our understanding of systems of inequality and movement within them.

NOTES

1. In the late nineteenth century, Horatio Alger, Jr., published a series of books for young people, the "Luck and Pluck" series, that featured poor but ambitious young men who always seemed to move from rags to riches by dint of their own efforts and a series of fortuitous events. The "Horatio Alger myth" has since then been synonymous with equal opportunity for all.

2. The CMS was funded by the Canada Council. Monica Boyd, Hugh A. McRoberts, and John Porter, all of Carleton University at the time, Frank Jones and Peter Pineo, both of McMaster University, and John Goyder, University of Waterloo, served as principal investigators on the original project. See Boyd et al. (1985) for a discussion of the CMS and its methodology.

3. The GSS has, since 1985, been a national survey conducted by Statistics Canada on a nearly annual basis and designed to monitor Canadian social trends and provide data to address social policy issues. See Norris and Paton (1991) for a detailed description of the GSS program and survey methodology.

4. Even the detailed data from GSS Cycle 15 available in Statistics Canada's Research Data Centres, with 47 major groups, does not contain sufficient detail to reproduce the Pineo et al. categories.

5. The occupational classification used here is somewhat different from those used in the remainder of this chapter, since I was constrained by available historical statistics for the period up to 1961.

6. The term *inheritance* is used here in the very loose sense that occupational destinations are in the same category as origins. The term is not meant to imply some sort of direct bestowal of a position. Although this still happens in advanced industrial societies, as when children inherit their parents' businesses, most people are employed by others.

7. It must be pointed out that all data used here come from samples of the Canadian population. As a result, all figures reported here, whether percentages or coefficients of mobility models, are estimates of the actual corresponding value in the Canadian population. Because the samples are large, the estimates are probably good ones, but the estimates are subject to some error nevertheless. To keep our discussion as simple as possible, I do not report the inferential statistics necessary to determine how accurate our estimates may be.

8. Erickson and Goldthorpe (1993:91–93) describe a similar model they term a "uniform difference" model.

REFERENCES

Bell, Daniel 1973. *The Coming of Post-Industrial Society: A Venture in Social Forecasting.* New York: Basic Books.

Blau, Peter M., and Otis Dudley Duncan 1967. *The American Occupational Structure.* New York: Wiley.

Boyd, Monica 1981. "Status attainment in Canada: Findings of the Canadian Mobility Study." *Canadian Review of Sociology and Anthropology* 18:657–673.

Boyd, Monica, John Goyder, Frank E. Jones, Hugh A. McRoberts, Peter C. Pineo, and John Porter 1985. *Ascription and Achievement: Studies in Mobility and Status Attainment in Canada.* Ottawa: Carleton University Press.

Breen, Richard (ed.) 2004. *Social Mobility in Europe.* Oxford: Oxford University Press.

Breen, Richard, and Christopher T. Whelan 1994. "Modelling trends in social fluidity: The core model and a measured-variable approach compared." *European Sociological Review* 10: 259–272.

Corak, Miles (ed.) 2004. *Generational Income Mobility in North America and Europe.* Cambridge: Cambridge University Press.

Corak, Miles 2005. "Equality of opportunity and inequality across the generations: Challenges ahead." *Policy Options/Options Politiques* 26: 78–83.

de Graaf, Paul M., and Ruud Luijkx 1992. "From 'ascription' to 'achievement'? Trends in status attainment in the Netherlands between 1930 and 1980 (*Van 'ascription' naar 'achievement'? Trends in statusverwerving in Nederland tussen 1930 en 1980*)." *Mens en Maatschappij* 67:412–433.

Erikson, Robert, and John H. Goldthorpe 1992. "Individual or family? Results from two approaches to class assignment." *Acta Sociologica* 35:95–105.

Erikson, Robert, and John H. Goldthorpe 1993. *The Constant Flux: A Study of Class Mobility in Industrial Societies.* Oxford: Clarendon Press.

Featherman, David L., F. Lancaster Jones, and Robert M. Hauser 1975. "Assumptions of social mobility research in the United States: The case of occupational status." *Social Science Research* 4:329–360.

Ganzeboom, Harry B.G., Ruud Luijkx, and Donald J. Treiman 1989. "Intergenerational class mobility in comparative perspective." *Research in Social Stratification and Mobility* 8:3–84.

Giddens, Anthony 1973. *The Class Structure of the Advanced Societies.* New York: Harper and Row.

Goldthorpe, John H. 1987. *Social Mobility and Class Structure in Modern Britain* Oxford: Clarendon Press.

Goodman, Leo A. 1969. "How to Ransack Social Mobility Tables and Other Kinds of Cross-Classification Tables." *American Journal of Sociology* 75:1–39.

Goodman, Leo A., and Michael Hout 1998. "Statistical methods and graphical displays for analyzing how the association between two qualitative variables differs among countries,

among groups or over time." *Sociological Methodology* 28:175–230.

Hendrickx, John, and Harry B.G. Ganzeboom 1998. "Occupational status attainment in the Netherlands, 1920–1990: A multinomial logistic analysis." *European Sociological Review* 14:387–403.

Hout, Michael 1983. *Mobility Tables.* Beverly Hills, CA: Sage.

Hout, Michael 1988. "More universalism, less structural mobility: The American occupational structure in the 1980s." *American Journal of Sociology* 93:1358–1400.

Kerr, Clark, John T. Dunlop, Frederick H. Harbison, and Charles A. Myers 1960. *Industrialism and Industrial Man.* Cambridge, MA: Harvard University Press.

Leacy, F.H. (ed.) 1983. *Historical Statistics of Canada.* Ottawa: Statistics Canada.

Lipset, Seymour Martin 1963. *The First New Nation.* Garden City, NJ: Anchor Books.

Lipset, Seymour Martin 1989. *Continental Divide: The Values and Institutions of Canada and the United States.* Toronto: C.D. Howe Institute.

Lipset, Seymour Martin, and Reinhard Bendix 1959. *Social Mobility in Industrial Societies.* Berkeley, CA: University of California Press.

Luijkx, Ruud, Peter Robert, Paul M. de Graaf, and Harry B. G. Ganzeboom 1995. "From Ascription to achievement: The status attainment process in Hungary (*A szarmazastol a teljesitmenyig: A statuszmegszerzes folyamata Magyarorszagon*)." *Szociologiai Szemle* 4:3–27.

Marks, Gary N., and F.L. Jones 1991. "Change over time in father–son mobility in Australia." *Australian and New Zealand Journal of Sociology* 27:315–331.

McRoberts, Hugh A., and Kevin Selbee 1981. "Trends in occupational mobility in Canada and the United States: A comparison." *American Sociological Review* 46:406–421.

Norris, D.A., and D.G. Paton 1991. "Canada's General Social Survey: Five years of experience." *Survey Methodology* 17:227–240.

Pineo, Peter C., John Porter, and Hugh A. McRoberts 1977. "The 1971 census and the socioeconomic classification of occupations."

Canadian Review of Sociology and Anthropology 14:91–102.

Ringdal, Kristen 1994. "Intergenerational class mobility in post-war Norway: A weakening of vertical barriers?" *European Sociological Review* 10:273–288.

Sorokin, Pitirim 1927. *Social Mobility*. New York: Harper & Brothers.

Statistics Canada 1981. *Census of Canada: Population: Labour Force—Occupation Trends.* Cat. No. 92-920 (Volume 1, National Series).

Statistics Canada 1993. *1991 Census of Canada: The Nation: Employment Income by Occupation.* Cat. No. 93-332.

Statistics Canada 2001. *2001 Census of Canada.* Retrieved June 2007. http://www12.statcan.ca/english/census01

Treiman, Donald J. 1970. "Industrialization and social stratification." In E.O. Laumann (ed.), *Social Stratification: Research and Theory for the 1970s*, pp. 207–234. Indianapolis, IN: Bobbs-Merrill.

Treiman, Donald J. 1977. *Occupational Prestige in Comparative Perspective*. New York: Academic Press.

Vallet, Louis-Andre 1999. "Forty years of social mobility in France: Temporal trends in social fluidity illuminated by recent models (*Quarante années de mobilité sociale en France: L'Evolution de la fluidité sociale a la lumiere de modeles recents.*)." *Revue Francaise de Sociologie* 40:5–64.

Wanner, Richard A. 1986. "Structural and exchange mobility in Canada and the United States: A comparison." Meeting of the Research Committee on Social Stratification of the International Sociological Association, Rome.

Wanner, Richard A. 1993. "Patterns and trends in occupational mobility." In J. Curtis, E. Grabb, and N. Guppy (eds.), *Social Inequality in Canada: Patterns, Problems, Policies* (2nd ed.), pp. 153–178. Scarborough, ON.: Prentice-Hall.

Wanner, Richard A. 1999. "Expansion and ascription: Trends in educational opportunity in Canada, 1920–1994." *Canadian Review of Sociology and Anthropology* 36:409–442.

Wanner, Richard A. 2005. "Twentieth-century trends in occupational attainment in Canada." *Canadian Journal of Sociology* 30:441–467.

Wanner, Richard A., and Bernadette C. Hayes 1996. "Intergenerational occupational mobility among men in Canada and Australia." *Canadian Journal of Sociology* 21:43–76.

Weber, Max 1947. *The Theory of Social and Economic Organization*. New York: Oxford University Press.

Xie, Yu 1992. "The log-multiplicative layer effects model for comparing mobility tables." *American Sociological Review* 57:380–395.

Labour Markets, Inequality, and the Future of Work

Graham S. Lowe and Wolfgang Lehmann
(An original chapter written
for this volume.)

INTRODUCTION

Debate and controversy surround the present and future of work. Canadians entered the twenty-first century having experienced two decades of profound changes in their working lives. The labour market turmoil of the 1980s and 1990s provided particularly fertile ground for futurists who seized on these trends, offering conflicting images of where work is headed. Just compare, for example, Jeremy Rifkin's (1995) image of a technology-dominated "workerless world," William Bridges' (1994) entrepreneurial "dejobbed world" of flexible work, and Richard Sennett's (1998) "new capitalism" where the sense of purpose and commitment in work has eroded. As with

many futurist predictions, some of these have shown enduring value—such as Sennett's concern with flexible work and commitment—while others have been, at least for the time being, put into question. Rifkin's prediction of massive job losses has been replaced by a concern with the exact opposite: labour shortages. Nowhere has this been more pronounced than in Alberta's resource-driven economy in the second half of the first decade of the twenty-first century.

Sociologists also are concerned about the changing work world and the implications of these trends for society. However, they reject futuristic predictions in favour of a careful consideration of evidence, explanations, and public policy options. A sociological analysis of work is rooted in a firm understanding of labour markets. This chapter examines labour markets: what they are, how they operate, major Canadian labour market trends, and the implications of these trends for social inequality.[1]

A labour market can be defined as the processes and institutions through which workers are allocated to paid jobs. Because jobs provide income and other rewards—such as pensions, paid vacations, opportunities for career advancement, and personal development and fulfillment—they have a direct bearing on an individual's living standard and quality of life. Sociologists use information about a person's job or occupation to locate that person in the class structure. Thus, labour markets are central to understanding broader issues of how inequality is structured in a society (Van den Berg and Smucker 1997).

A POST-INDUSTRIAL SOCIETY?

We will begin by examining changes in jobs in the context of debates about an emerging post-industrial society. The post–Second World War expansion of white-collar occupations and service industries, along with increasing living standards, gave rise in the 1970s to a theory of "post-industrial society." Daniel Bell (1973) argued that the industrial phase of capitalism was over, replaced by a post-industrial society that was based on knowledge production rather than goods production. While industrialization had brought increased productivity and living standards, post-industrial society would usher in reduced class conflict and less concentration of power. Bell underscored the importance of knowledge, suggesting that it was the new basis of power. Knowledge workers, such as technicians, scientists, and other professionals, would become the new elite.

An alternative, critical view is provided by neo-Marxist scholars (Braverman 1974; Rinehart 2006). Examining changes in the "labour process"—how work is actually performed—these researchers suggest that work under corporate capitalism has become more alienating and that class divisions are widening. The growing numbers of non-managerial white-collar workers in offices, shops, or the public sector form, in this view, a new working class. More sophisticated managerial control techniques and computer technology extended the degradation of working conditions from the factory into offices and other white-collar settings.

A close inspection of labour market trends reveals a far more complex and contradictory picture than that portrayed by either the post-industrial or the labour process perspective. In the United States, Robert Reich (1991) points out that the real winners in the high-tech, global economy are the symbolic analysts: Bell's knowledge workers. Reich argues, however, that their rise to power and wealth has created even greater inequality. In Canada, John Myles (1988) has found some support for both theoretical positions. Myles shows that shifts in employment patterns across industries, coupled with changing skill requirements within industries, has created jobs at the top and the bottom of the occupational ladder, and a decline in middle-level blue-collar jobs in the manufacturing sector. In sum, the shift to a service-based economy has been accompanied by growing signs of polarization in the labour market.

EXPLAINING LABOUR MARKETS

The debates about post-industrialism draw our attention to how, and why, certain individuals or groups occupy particular locations in the labour market. Who gets to be a corporate executive, a computer technician, or a parking lot attendant? Are these jobs allocated based on ability, other personal characteristics (such as age, gender, ethnicity, or social class), luck, or some combination of these factors? These are key sociological questions, given that one's job determines one's "life chances." Furthermore, an understanding of how the labour market operates is essential to designing public policies that can shape the future of work, thereby addressing concerns about a lack of good jobs.

There are two major theoretical perspectives on labour markets. Human capital theory comes from economics, while labour market segmentation theory is more sociological. Both recognize that some jobs are better than others, in terms of pay and benefits, career opportunities, personal rewards, and social status. Beyond this similarity, the two perspectives offer alternative views of how labour markets are organized and operate.

Human Capital Theory

Human capital theory draws on neo-classical economics (Becker 1975). It assumes that the labour market is one large, open arena in which everyone with similar qualifications competes on the same basis for available jobs. The market rewards those individuals who have the greatest "human capital," as measured by education, training, experience, and ability. A job's rewards are based on its economic contribution to society. By focusing on the supply of labour, in terms of workers' characteristics, this theory does not address the influence of employers' hiring practices or the organization of work on inequality. The theory simply assumes that employers make rational hiring and promotion decisions based on ability.

Human capital theory presents a consensus view of society; issues of class and

power are ignored. However, human capital theory does accurately predict the returns on education. There is solid evidence that, on average, individuals with university degrees have higher incomes, greater lifetime earnings, a lower risk of unemployment, and a generally higher probability of being in a "good" job, in comparison with individuals who have lower levels of education. This was starkly clear in the 1990s, when the vast majority of new full-time jobs went to university graduates.

Nevertheless, human capital theory can't explain why some groups get better jobs than other groups, regardless of ability or education (Blau and Ferber 1986), or why it is easier for some groups to attain high levels of education (Lehmann 2007). For example, young people from poor families often don't even get the opportunity to apply to a university and are at risk of dropping out of high school. In 2004, the chief executive officers of the top 160 corporations listed on the Toronto Stock Exchange received an average compensation package worth approximately $6 million (Krahn, Lowe, and Hughes 2007:111). In contrast, equally able and educated individuals in socially useful occupations—say, primary school teachers or managers of community food banks—earn far less. In addition, members of recent immigrant groups often end up working in low-status jobs, such as taxi drivers or security guards, even though they may be highly educated and experienced.

Labour Market Segmentation Theory

Such inequalities among different jobs provide the starting point for labour market segmentation theory (Kalleberg 1988). This perspective rejects human capital theory's assumption of a homogenous labour market, in which all people compete on the basis of their education and other human-capital attributes. Instead, it depicts the labour market as comprising unequal segments, where movement to a better or "primary" labour market segment from a worse or "secondary" segment is often difficult. The segmentation perspective examines the barriers that many qualified individuals face in trying to enter the primary labour market.

There are different versions of this basic labour market segmentation perspective. A dual economy model highlights the uneven development of economic sectors in industrial capitalist societies (Hodson and Kaufman 1982). This model distinguishes between core and periphery industries, with the majority of better jobs found in organizations located in core sectors, which include mainly large corporations and government. Large corporations like Toyota or General Motors provide good careers and benefits to their workers, while subcontracting for parts and services to an extensive network of small firms in which wages and working conditions are poor.

Small firms tend to have lower profit margins, to invest less in new technologies and worker training, to require less skilled workers, and to be more labour intensive than large organizations. Hence, there is greater pressure to keep wage costs down, and workers are considered to be easily replaceable. Unions and professional associations also influence labour market outcomes. The majority of public-sector workers in Canada belong to unions. Unionization also is much higher in large than in small firms. The concentration of professionals in the primary labour market creates "shelters" that limit access only to individuals with recognized credentials, increasing the bargaining power of professional associations (Krahn, Lowe, and Hughes 2007:Chapters 3, 7). The size, profitability, and market dominance of core firms (those in primary labour markets) enable them to use stable employment conditions to gain the co-operation of workers. This employment system is known as an internal labour market (Althauser 1989) and it also applies to governments and other public sector organizations across Canada. These organizations are pyramid-shaped bureaucracies that recruit at specified entry-level positions and then provide security, career paths, and training to workers once inside, as long as they meet management's expectations for hard work and commitment to the organization's values. Most job openings therefore are filled internally, essentially creating a sheltered organization-based labour market.

Until recently, the internal labour market has been a hallmark of core sector organizations. In the last decade, however, widespread downsizing has shaken internal labour markets. Staff cuts, a "delayering" process whereby the bureaucratic hierarchy is flattened, and a shift to contracting out and temporary workers have all reduced internal career mobility and shaken the employee commitment that these organizations once cultivated. A growing number of large private-sector and public-sector organizations are adopting "flexible" approaches to employment, using lower-paid part-time or temporary workers in place of full-time employees. For example, in the retail sector, grocery and department stores rely on a "just-in-time" workforce. In many hospitals, unionized cleaning, laundry, and food preparation jobs have been contracted out to firms that employ lower-wage, non-union labour. Another example is the fast-food industry, in which multinational fast-food chains recruit staff from secondary labour markets populated by students, middle-aged women, and recent immigrants (Reiter 1991).

WORK IN A SERVICE ECONOMY

The post-industrialists and their critics would agree that Canada is a service-based economy. From the perspective of human capital theory, the rise of a service economy poses questions about possible changes in the relationship between education and jobs, and the relative "payoffs" of investing in education. For labour market segmentation theory, the recent restructuring of industries and labour markets raises questions about which groups have or have not benefited from these changes.

Changing Industrial Patterns of Employment

To understand these changes, we need to look at industrial patterns of employment over time. Industry classifications focus on the type of economic activity occurring within the workplace. We can distinguish three major sectors: primary (agriculture, mining, forestry, and other resource extraction industries), secondary (manufacturing and construction), and tertiary (industries that create services rather than products). The service sector includes a wide range of industries, from finance and retail trade to education, government, and health and social services.

Much of Canada's industrialization initially entailed a drop in primary sector employment and a growth in manufacturing jobs. Service industries also expanded in this period, accounting for almost half of all jobs by 1951 (Picot 1987:11). Since then, the proportion of the workforce in both the primary and the secondary sectors has declined steeply, although through technological change and new production methods these sectors still contribute significantly to national economic output. As shown in the far-right column of Table 9-1, by 2005, the service sector accounted for almost three-quarters of all employment. Agriculture accounted for only 2.1% of all employment, while manufacturing accounted for 13.5%. In contrast, in 1961, these two sectors accounted for 11% and 24%, respectively, of all jobs.

Table 9-1 also reveals the extent of industrial restructuring in the Canadian economy between 1985 and 2005. The table reports two crucial pieces of information necessary for understanding changing industrial patterns of employment. First, we need to examine the actual numbers of jobs gained or lost in each industry during the 1985–2005 period. Note that, in absolute terms, employment losses occurred in the primary sector, and especially in agriculture, largely because of global trends in commodity markets. The lowest net gain in jobs occurred in the utilities and public administration sectors. Although this is a reversal of the job-loss trend in public employment in the 1990s, the modest increase still reflects the declining government budgets, service cuts, and privatization that were evident throughout most of the 1990s. It is also interesting that a large number of new jobs were created in professional, scientific, and technical services and the health care and social assistance sectors, which are both associated with the knowledge and technology-intensive "new economy." Nevertheless, at the same time, the manufacturing and construction industries of the "old economy" also added jobs.

A second important pattern concerns the rates of employment growth or decline. Public discussions of employment trends often mistakenly focus only on these percentage changes, and this can be misleading if the actual number of jobs involved is not taken into account. For example, the 34.3% increase of jobs in trade (retail and wholesale) in the two decades is much smaller than, for example, the 70.1% increase in the information, culture, and recreation sector. Because trade is such a large sector, however, the actual number of jobs created was higher than in any other sector.

TABLE 9-1	Changes in the Distribution of Employment between 1985 and 2005, Canada (in thousands)			
	Actual 2005	**Net**	**% change**	**2005**
Total	17342.6	4330.0	33.3%	
Goods-Producing Sector	4267.9	345.3	8.8%	24.6%
Agriculture	364.2	−180.7	−33.2%	2.1%
Forestry, fishing, mining, oil and gas	334.1	−46.6	−12.2%	1.9%
Construction	1102.2	328.6	42.5%	6.4%
Manufacturing	2339.7	236.2	11.2%	13.5%
Utilities	127.6	7.7	6.4%	0.7%
Services-Producing Sector	12694	3975.9	45.6%	73.2%
Upper Tier:				
Transportation and warehousing	823.7	164.1	24.9%	4.7%
Information, culture and recreation	778.6	320.8	70.1%	4.5%
Finance, insurance, real estate and leasing	1011.7	280.9	38.4%	5.8%
Professional, scientific and technical services	1086.4	632.5	139.3%	6.3%
Business, building and other support services	716.2	411.4	135%	4.1%
Educational services	1145.4	367.3	47.2%	6.6%
Health care and social assistance	1770.9	657.5	59.1%	10.2%
Public administration	857.1	46.2	5.7%	4.9%
Lower Tier:				
Trade	2696	688.8	34.3%	15.5%
Accommodation and food services	1085.5	334.9	44.6%	6.3%
Other consumer services	722.4	71.4	11%	4.2%
Unclassified Industries	380.6	9	2.4%	2.2%

Source: Statistics Canada (2006).

Given the size and diversity of the service sector, it is useful to divide it into an upper tier, which tends to include the service occupations with the highest pay and educational qualifications, and a lower tier, which includes jobs that generally involve lower incomes and educational requirements (Krahn, Lowe, and Hughes 2007:Chapter 2). Currently, 47% of the employed are located in the upper-tier services and approximately 26% have jobs in lower-tier service industries, while 24.6% of employed Canadians work in the goods-producing sector. If we look again at the sectors that have seen the largest net job growth, we realize that they reflect either end of the spectrum of jobs in the new, service-driven economy: (1) jobs in the knowledge-intensive professional services sector, (2) jobs in the scientific and technical service sectors, and (3) jobs in the trade sector, which are often the temporary, part-time, low-paid jobs we refer to as McJobs. This finding lends support to the notion of an increasingly polarized labour market in Canada. We will return to this distinction between upper-tier and lower-tier service industries in our later discussion of "good" and "bad" jobs.

Occupational Changes

We can also examine employment by looking at occupations, or the kind of work that individuals perform in their jobs. Most workers in primary and secondary industries would be classified as blue-collar (or manual) workers, while the growth of service industries is directly related to the expansion of white-collar occupations. Historically, white-collar occupations tended to be viewed as having higher status. However, as service industries grew and diversified, the white-collar occupational category came to include well over half of Canada's workers, some of whom performed less desirable jobs. Because many of the new white-collar positions—especially clerical, sales, and personal service jobs—have been filled by women, the term *pink-collar* has often been applied to these occupations.

Another related change in the labour force is the rising educational level of workers. Canadians are becoming increasingly well educated. The proportion of the workforce with a university degree increased from 7% to 22% between 1975 and 2005, and over half of all workers have now completed some form of post-secondary education (Statistics Canada 2006). As Table 9-1 documents, many new jobs have been created recently in upper-tier service industries that would require some form of post-secondary education. However, the rising educational level raises the question of underemployment: are well-educated workers, especially recent graduates, able to find jobs that adequately reward their investment in education? (See Livingstone 1999.) Using 2001 Census data, Statistics Canada (2003a:7) estimates that in 2001, 16% of the labour force (or 2.5 million) were in highly skilled occupations that normally require a university education. This number represents

a 33% increase compared to 10 years earlier in 1991. Nonetheless, Livingstone (2005) argues that underemployment has been on the rise in the past two decades and estimates that 34% of Canadians experience underemployment at work.

NON-STANDARD WORK

Despite public concerns about declining job security, the majority of employed Canadians still have a full-time, year-round, permanent job. Public insecurity on this issue is fuelled by the recent waves of downsizing, but perhaps more so by the spread of alternatives to the standard type of employment (Lowe 2000). Non-standard work takes four main forms: part-time employment, multiple job-holding, own-account self-employment (i.e., those who work for themselves but have no employees), and temporary work. These four types of non-standard work accounted for 28% of all employed Canadians (ages 15 to 64) in 1989, and one-third of all employed Canadians by 2002 (Krahn, Lowe, and Hughes 2007:88–94).

The non-standard work trend is double-edged. It has advantages, to the extent that it provides some individuals with greater choice and flexibility in how they organize their work life. For example, parents (especially mothers) with young children, university students, older workers wanting to ease out of a full-time career, or highly skilled professionals seeking the continual challenge of new projects may seek out part-time or contract work. Given women's generally greater family responsibilities compared to men, it is perhaps not surprising that 40% of female workers in 1994 were in non-standard jobs, compared with 27% of men. Often, though, this choice involves trade-offs. The main disadvantage of non-standard work is that it tends to offer lower wages and fewer benefits than full-time work, because employers use non-standard employment as a "flexible" strategy for reducing labour costs. Obviously, temporary and part-time employment provides job incumbents with much lower annual salaries compared to standard employment. It is also important to point out that average hourly earnings of non-standard workers are substantially lower than those of individuals in standard jobs. While an individual in a standard job earned an average of $18.89 per hour in Canada in 2004, a permanent part-time worker earned only $13.20 per hour and a temporary part-time worker only $11.58 per hour (Kapsalis and Tourigny 2004:7). In addition to salary and benefit disadvantages, finding oneself in non-standard work also may have repercussions for one's ability to move into standard employment. Of all non-standard workers in 1999, more than half (54%) were still employed in non-standard work two years later and an additional 10% had returned to non-standard work, from either standard work or not working in the two intervening years (Kapsalis and Tourigny 2004:8).

Part-time work is defined as working less than 30 hours per week in one's main job. It is the most common type of non-standard employment, accounting for approximately 18% of all employment in 2005 (Statistics Canada 2006). This is a modest increase from 1977, when part-time employment was 13% of the total. About three-quarters of part-timers are women, and youth of both genders are also concentrated in these jobs. An important measure for our understanding of labour market inequalities is involuntary part-time employment, whereby people have to accept part-time jobs because suitable full-time jobs are not available. In 1975, the involuntary part-time rate was 11%. In 2005, this rate was 7.4% (Statistics Canada 2006). Although this appears to be a substantial decline, which may be explained by the strong performance of the Canadian economy in the

2000s, it also reflects a change in how Statistics Canada collects involuntary part-time information. Unlike in 1975, Statistics Canada now separates those who were and were not actively looking for full-time work. The involuntary part-time rate is calculated by using only the number of people who were actively looking for full-time work. There were, however, another 18.2% of part-time workers in 2005 who stated that they worked part-time because of business conditions and because they could not find full-time work (rather than for personal reasons), but had settled into their part-time work schedules without looking for full-time work (Statistics Canada 2006). This suggests an actual increase of part-time work for non-personal reasons from 1975 and indicates that despite a strong economy, a sufficient number of full-time jobs to meet the needs of workers are not being created.

HOURS OF WORK

We can gain a more complete picture of how labour market restructuring affects employment opportunities by examining trends in work hours. Canada established a standard 40-hour workweek in the late 1950s. Despite expectations of more leisure time due to the productivity gains of computers and other new technologies, by 2000 the average length of the workweek was still just under 37 hours. However, a substantial polarization in work hours has occurred, as part-time jobs increased at the same time as did jobs with long hours.

By 2004, only 59% of paid workers put in 35 to 40 hours weekly (Krahn, Lowe, and Hughes 2007:85–88). Young workers (ages 15 to 24) experienced the largest drop in work hours, resulting in a sharp decline in real earnings (i.e., adjusted for inflation) since the 1980s (Betcherman and Leckie 1997). Over the same period, many adult workers, especially men, have put in longer hours. This has been mainly due to organizational downsizing, which tends to increase the workloads (usually without more pay) for remaining employees, and also has occurred because of a rise in multiple job-holding. Thus, by 2000, 16% of the labour force worked more than 40 hours weekly, and in some management and professional occupations, a 50-hour workweek has become common (Canadian Policy Research Networks 2002).

The fact that some people don't have enough work while others have too much is a reflection of a more polarized labour market (Duffy et al. 1997). In this context, it is not surprising that a growing number of policy analysts and interest groups are calling for a reduced workweek. Shortening the workweek to 35 or 30 hours is seen as a way of redistributing work. This policy would redistribute income, because those with no job or with too few hours would see increased incomes, while groups of full-time workers would experience small cuts in both income and hours (Human Resources Development Canada 1994). It appears, however, that work redistribution is unlikely to strike a chord with Canadians. In a 1999 survey, only 9% of Canadians agreed that they would prefer to work fewer hours for less pay, while 20% wanted more hours for more pay and 71% liked their hours and pay just as they were (Canadian Policy Research Networks 2002). Nonetheless, work redistribution has attracted interest in other countries because of persistently high unemployment. Unionized German auto workers have negotiated shorter work hours in order to create more jobs and, in France, there is widespread popular support for a legislated 35-hour workweek to help reduce high unemployment.

In contrast, Canada has witnessed record-breaking low unemployment rates. In April 2007, for instance, the Canadian unemployment rate was at a 30-year low of 6.1% (Statistics Canada 2007a:4). Just a few years ago, during 2000, more than 1 million Canadians were unemployed (i.e., out of a job but actively seeking one). Since the end of the Second World War, the long-term trend in unemployment rates had been upward, from an average of 4% in the 1950s to between 7 and 8% in the early twenty-first century. Recent changes in economic conditions coupled with the demographic reality of an aging population have led to a shift away from discussions about unemployment and work redistribution and toward concerns about labour shortages.

GOOD JOBS AND BAD JOBS

There is considerable debate about whether the service economy has created more good jobs than bad ones, and how public policy can encourage the creation of better-quality jobs in the future (Banting and Beech 1995; Osberg et al. 1995; Duffy et al. 1997). The language of "good" and "bad" jobs refers to widening disparities on a range of job characteristics: wages, benefits, skill requirements, security, working conditions, and intrinsic rewards, such as the experience of challenging and satisfying work. The good jobs–bad jobs dichotomy seems to capture the basic difference between standard and non-standard jobs. In the 1980s, 44% of all employment growth was in non-standard jobs (Economic Council of Canada 1991:81), a trend that continued in the 1990s. However, not all of these non-standard jobs are what critics call "McJobs". Some of these positions earn high incomes and require high levels of skill and education; business consultants and project engineers are two good examples.

Income is an obvious criterion for identifying jobs that may be more or less desirable. If we are looking at the incomes of paid employees (i.e., excluding the self-employed), individuals in the service sector earn about 20% less than people in the goods-producing industries. However, there is wide variation in income within the service sector, with workers in the upper-tier industries earning much more than those in the lower-tier industries. For example, paid employees in engineering, architectural, and computer-related services earned an average of about $800 per week in the mid 1990s, almost four times as much as those in food and beverage services (Grenon 1996).

Despite the overall positive developments in the Canadian labour market, at least as far as unemployment is concerned, incomes nonetheless have become increasingly polarized. As CEO compensation continues to grow, the average salaries for new employees have declined in the past two decades. Young men without a university education have been particularly affected by this decline in relative wages (Statistics Canada 2003b). This is most likely due to the disappearance of traditional, unionized, well-paying blue collar jobs in the manufacturing sector.

Employment benefits are another measure of job quality. Benefits such as employment insurance, the Canada/Quebec Pension Plan, and workers' compensation are part of the "social safety net." Although they are mandatory, such government-funded benefits only provide a minimum level of support. In addition, however, some jobs come with employer-provided benefits, which therefore give some workers much better security and living standards than others, and which again reinforce the distinction between good and bad jobs. Figure 9-1 reports the proportion of employees in 1999 and 2003, by age and gender, who did not receive non-wage benefits, which include dental plans, supplementary health insurance, pension plans, or life insurance. Although we do see a slight decline in the percentage of employees who do not receive these kinds of benefits (which suggests that more employees in 2003 receive them), we also notice that women and young employees are still more likely to be shut out of employee benefit programs. This is mostly explained by their work status and where they work. Part-time

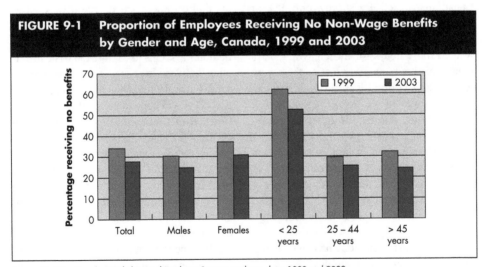

FIGURE 9-1   Proportion of Employees Receiving No Non-Wage Benefits by Gender and Age, Canada, 1999 and 2003

Source: Statistics Canada, Workplace and Employee Survey, employee data, 1999 and 2003.

and temporary employees are less likely to receive benefits, as are workers in the lower-tier services, which is where we find more women and young people. Benefits are more common in large organizations and in unionized workplaces, which also tend to be larger.

Training can also be an important job benefit; however, only about one in five workers receive work-related training that is paid for by the employer (Human Resources Development Canada 1997) and only about one in ten Canadian firms is involved in substantial, formal employer-supported training (Peters 2004). Increasingly, training is viewed by workers as a personal "safety net" that increases their employability in a volatile labour market. Furthermore, workers who receive employer-sponsored training already have labour market advantages, to the extent that they are better educated, work in large firms, and often have full-time positions. For instance, more than 50% of workers with university credentials received formal job-related training in 2002, compared to less than 20% of workers with only a high school diploma or less, just as managers were substantially more likely to participate in job-related training than were blue-collar workers (Peters 2004:5, 15).

LABOUR MARKET GENDER INEQUALTIES

One of the most profound changes in Canadian society over the last three decades has been the sharp rise in female employment. In 1976, 42% of women over the age of 15 in Canada had jobs; in 2000, this figure had reached 58%. During the same period, the proportion of men employed dropped from 73% to 68% (Statistics Canada 2007b). Deeply rooted barriers to female employment have been eroding. Many factors underlie this change, particularly feminism's

critique of traditional female stereotypes, women's rising educational levels, and economic pressures for women to support themselves or their families.

Most wives in the 1950s and 1960s left the labour force to raise families. By the 1980s, however, a growing proportion of mothers with young children were also employed, greatly increasing the female labour force participation rate (Logan and Belliveau 1995). Dual-earner families now account for 3 out of 5 families. As well, 15% of all mothers in the workforce are single parents. Sociologists use terms like the *double day*, or the *second shift*, to denote the tendency for most married women to spend their days in paying jobs, yet still assume most of the responsibilities of child care and domestic chores when they get home (Hochschild 1989). Most workplaces have not adapted to this social change by becoming more flexible and family friendly.

Gender-Segregated Employment

The concept of occupational gender segregation describes the concentration of men and women in different occupations. Gender-role socialization and education reinforce this pattern. Consequently, many women end up in occupations that are predominantly female, such as clerical work or nursing. The concept of a female "job ghetto" emphasizes the unequal rewards and opportunities built into the labour market on the basis of a worker's gender. Women in job ghettos lack easy access to the more challenging and lucrative occupations that traditionally have been dominated by men. These male segments of the labour market (e.g., senior management and some professions such as engineering) often set up success criteria that are male-biased (Kanter 1977).

FIGURE 9-2   Women's Employment by Occupational Group, Canada, 2006

Women as percentage of total employment in occupation

Occupational Group	Percentage
All occupations	47.1
Managerial	36.3
Business/finance	51.6
Natural Science/engineering/mathematics	22
Social sciences	71.3
Teaching	63.9
Doctors/dentists/other health	55.3
Nursing/therapy/other health related	87.4
Artistic/recreational	54.1
Clerical/administrative	75
Sales/service	56.8
Primary occupations	20.5
Processing/manufacturing/utilities	31.1
Trades/transport/construction	6.5

Source: Statistics Canada (2007b).

Figures 9-2 and 9-3 describe two major trends associated with occupational gender segregation. Figure 9-2 identifies the percentage of employees in each occupation who are women. In 2006, women comprised 47% of the total labour force. Although women have made substantial inroads into previously male-dominated professional occupations (e.g., 55% of doctors, dentists, and other health workers were women in 2006), they continue to be overrepresented in what we consider traditional female occupations. For instance, clerical and administrative jobs, along with nursing and health-related occupations, have the highest concentrations of women (75% and 87%, respectively). Teaching, social sciences, and sales and service occupations (e.g., jobs in restaurants, bars, hotels, tourism, hairdressing, child-care facilities, and domestic and building cleaning) are between 56% and 71% female. All of these could be labelled job ghettos in the sense that the majority of employees are women, although pay and other working conditions in some positions (particularly nursing and teaching) are relatively good. By contrast, 22% of jobs in natural sciences, engineering, and mathematics, and just 6% of trades, transportation, and construction occupations, are held by women. Even in the previously male-dominated professions that women have entered in greater numbers, such as medicine or law, women tend to be found in the less lucrative and less prestigious areas; while men dominate in corporate and criminal law or in surgery, women are more likely to be found in family law and working as general practitioners.

Figure 9-3 shows the distribution of the female labour force across all occupations. Clerical and administrative occupations employed almost one-quarter of all female workers in 2006, although this proportion is down from one-third two decades earlier.

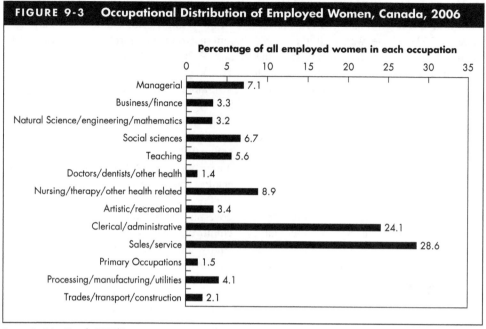

FIGURE 9-3 Occupational Distribution of Employed Women, Canada, 2006

Percentage of all employed women in each occupation

Occupation	Percentage
Managerial	7.1
Business/finance	3.3
Natural Science/engineering/mathematics	3.2
Social sciences	6.7
Teaching	5.6
Doctors/dentists/other health	1.4
Nursing/therapy/other health related	8.9
Artistic/recreational	3.4
Clerical/administrative	24.1
Sales/service	28.6
Primary Occupations	1.5
Processing/manufacturing/utilities	4.1
Trades/transport/construction	2.1

Source: Statistics Canada (2007b).

More than half of the female labour force is in service, sales, and clerical jobs. These numbers demonstrate women's continued overrepresentation in lower-status occupations, or what we have referred to as job ghettos. Less than 10% of female workers are in traditional male areas of work, such as primary occupations, manufacturing, and other manual occupations.

Despite these patterns, however, occupational gender segregation is slowly being reduced as women move into a broader range of occupations. Over the past 20 years, more women have entered non-traditional jobs in which men historically predominated, especially in management and some professions (Hughes 1995). Nevertheless, Figure 9-3 shows that only 7% of employed women are managers, even though this is a growing area of female employment. It appears that many women still encounter a "glass ceiling." This concept refers to the often-invisible barriers to women's advancement that persist despite formal policies, such as employment equity, that are designed to eradicate these obstacles.

The Gender Wage Gap

Male–female wage differences reveal how gender is a major source of labour market inequality. For example, female managers reported average annual earnings in 1995 of $32 306, two-thirds the earnings of their male counterparts ($48 753) (Statistics Canada 1997). Similar differences are observed in all major occupations. The average 1995 earnings of all employed women in Canada ($20 219) represented only 65% of the average earnings of all employed men ($31 053). Examining only full-time, full-year workers, which is perhaps a more appropriate comparison, given women's higher level of part-time employment, we see that male average earnings increase to $40 610, compared with $29 700 for females. Expressed as a female-to-male earnings ratio, or gender wage gap, in 1995 full-time working women received an average of 73% of the wages of their male counterparts. Sadly, this earning ratio has declined again somewhat in the past decade. In 2003, women in full-time, full-year employment received 70.6% of the wages of their male counterparts, but this is still up from 60% in 1970 (Krahn, Lowe, and Hughes 2007:194).

Women's rising incomes can be explained partly by their rising educational attainment and access to better-paying jobs. Another factor, however, is that, since 1975, real earnings for men have fallen slightly (Krahn, Lowe, and Hughes 2007:Chapter 3). During this period, women were moving into intermediate-level professions and junior and middle-level management positions. At the same time, males were losing ground in well-paying (often unionized) manual jobs, and in some professional and managerial occupations due to downsizing and industrial restructuring. While different factors affected male and female employment, the overall result was rising wages for some women and falling wages for some men.

Women can face two key forms of labour market discrimination. Employers could pay women less than men for performing the same jobs, a form of wage discrimination that is rare in Canada today. More common, however, is an indirect type of discrimination, which results from the gender-segregated structure of the labour market, and from the gender-based stratification within organizations that gives men greater access to jobs with the highest rewards. Thus, when statistical models are applied that take into account male–female differences in various characteristics— education, training, and work experience; occupation and industry of employment; and geographic location—the wage gap shrinks. Applying this type of analysis to

men and women employed in the same jobs within a single establishment, the earnings ratio narrows even further, to between 90% and 95% (Gunderson 1994; Coverman 1988).

Another important point in this regard is that most of the reduction in occupational gender segregation has resulted from women moving into male-dominated jobs, and not from men moving into female-dominated jobs. Public policy has been a catalyst for these changes. Since the mid 1980s, the federal and some provincial governments, as well as a number of large employers, have implemented employment equity and pay equity policies. The goal of employment equity policies is the elimination of barriers to the recruitment or advancement of four social groups that historically have been disadvantaged in the Canadian labour market: women, visible minorities, Aboriginal peoples, and persons with disabilities. Pay equity promotes the principle of equal pay for work of equal value. This policy uses job evaluation systems to compare predominantly female jobs with predominantly male jobs within the same organization, in an attempt to redress any undervaluing of women's work. Both approaches are good examples of how public policy can positively influence employer practices, by promoting gender equality in the labour market. Of course, employment equity policies address more than just gender-based inequities in the labour market. While our focus in this chapter has been on gender, it is important to apply the same kind of labour market analysis to other groups. Despite the positive developments in the Canadian economy, young Canadians continue to experience much higher levels of unemployment compared to adults (Statistics Canada 2006) and those with low levels of education are finding it increasingly difficult to obtain and keep good jobs (Lehmann 2007).

Visible minorities continue to face discrimination in hiring practices. And recent immigrants to Canada are disproportionately found in low-wage and low-skill jobs (Chung 2004), despite arriving here with average levels of education that surpass those of the Canadian-born population (Canadian Education Statistics Council 2003). Such analyses are discussed in other chapters of this volume.

CONCLUSION

Many of the concerns that Canadians have about the future of work are, in fact, concerns about present labour market trends (Lowe 2000). Widespread feelings of economic insecurity among Canadians are common reactions during periods of high unemployment and underemployment, as non-standard work spreads, real incomes decline, and the labour market becomes more polarized into clear winners and losers. A paradox is that despite the overall current boom in Canada's economy, many of these problems have continued (e.g., the spread of non-standard work) and polarization has intensified. Some regions in Canada experience massive labour shortages (e.g., Alberta), while other parts of the country continue to see a large portion of the population unemployed (e.g., Newfoundland). And even in booming provincial economies, many workers juggle multiple low-paying jobs to make ends meet while other workers earn record-breaking incomes. Finally, an increasing number of workers are putting in longer hours than they consider ideal. These developments have a direct impact on society, as more of the risks associated with economic change are transferred to individuals, families, and communities, and as the divide between "haves" and "have-nots" widens. The study of labour markets can inform public policies to address these problems.

This chapter has focused on paid work in the formal economy. Such an emphasis makes sense if we consider that, directly or indirectly, the vast majority of Canadians rely for their daily living on earned income from employment. Still, it is important to recognize that a fully comprehensive discussion of work would have to include unpaid work performed in households and in volunteer-based community organizations, as well as paid work in the "informal" or "underground" economy that operates outside government regulation (e.g., the backyard mechanic who fixes your car for cash). Hence, while the paid labour market is a crucial element in the world of work, it does not account for all important labour performed by Canadians. Looking into the future, it is interesting to speculate about changes in how Canadians value and participate in all forms of work.

NOTE

1. This chapter relies extensively on data and analysis from Statistics Canada. Useful sources in this regard are two quarterly publications, *Perspectives on Labour and Income* and *Canadian Social Trends*; *The Labour Force* (monthly); and the *Labour Force Historical Review* CD-ROM. Students are encouraged to visit Statistics Canada's website (www.statcan.ca) for regular updates and extensive background information on labour market, demographic, economic, and social trends.

REFERENCES

Althauser, Robert P. 1989. "Internal labor markets." *Annual Review of Sociology* 15:143–161.

Banting, Keith G., and Charles M. Beach (eds.) 1995. *Labour Market Polarization and Social Policy Reform.* Kingston, ON: School of Policy Studies, Queen's University.

Becker, Gary S. 1975. *Human Capital: A Theoretical and Empirical Analysis with*

Special Reference to Education (2nd ed.). Chicago: University of Chicago Press.

Bell, Daniel 1973. *The Coming of Post-Industrial Society.* New York: Basic Books.

Betcherman, Gordon, and Norm Leckie 1997. *Youth Employment and Education Trends in the 1980s and 1990s.* Ottawa: Canadian Policy Research Networks Inc., Working Paper no. W03.

Blau, Francine D., and Marianne A. Ferber 1986. *The Economics of Women, Men and Work.* Englewood Cliffs, NJ: Prentice-Hall.

Braverman, Harry 1974. *Labor and Monopoly Capital: The Degradation of Work in the Twentieth Century.* New York: Monthly Review Press.

Bridges, William 1994. *Job Shift: How to Prosper in a Workplace without Jobs.* Don Mills, ON.: Addison-Wesley.

Canadian Education Statistics Council 2003. *Education Indicators in Canada: Report of the Pan-Canadian Education Indicators Program 2003.* Toronto: Canadian Education Statistics Council.

Canadian Policy Research Networks 2002. Job Quality website, work hours section. www.jobquality.ca

Chung, L. 2004. "Low-paid workers: How many live in low-income families." *Perspectives on Labour and Income* 5(12):5–14.

Coverman, Shelley 1988. "Sociological explanations of the male–female wage gap: Individual and structuralist theories." In Ann Helton Stromberg and Shirley Harkess (eds.), *Women Working: Theories and Facts in Perspective* (2nd ed.). Mountain View, CA: Mayfield.

Duffy, Ann, Daniel Glenday, and Norene Pupo (eds.) 1997. *Good Jobs, Bad Jobs, No Jobs: The Transformation of Work in the Twenty-first Century.* Toronto: Harcourt Brace Canada.

Economic Council of Canada 1991. *Employment in the Service Economy.* Ottawa: Supply and Services Canada.

Grenon, Lee 1996. "Are service jobs low-paying?" *Perspectives on Labour and Income* (Spring):29–34.

Gunderson, Morley 1994. *Comparable Worth and Gender Discrimination: An International Perspective.* Geneva: Organization for Economic Cooperation and Development.

Hochschild, Arlie 1989. *The Second Shift: Working Parents and the Revolution at Home.* New York: Viking Penguin.

Hodson, Randy, and Robert L. Kaufman 1982. "Economic dualism: A critical review." *American Sociological Review* 47:727–739.

Hughes, Karen D. 1995. "Women in non-traditional occupations." *Perspectives on Labour and Income* (Autumn):14–19.

Human Resources Development Canada 1994. *Report of the Advisory Committee on Working Time and the Distribution of Work.* Ottawa: Supply and Services Canada.

Human Resources Development Canada (and Statistics Canada) 1997. *Adult Education and Training in Canada: Report of the 1994 Adult Education and Training Survey.* Ottawa: Supply and Services Canada.

Kalleberg, Arne 1988. "Comparative perspectives on work structures and inequality." *Annual Review of Sociolgy* 14:203–225.

Kanter, Rosabeth M. 1977. *Men and Women of the Corporation.* New York: Basic Books.

Kapsalis, C., and P. Tourigny 2004. "Duration of non-standard employment." *Perspectives on Labour and Income* 5(12):5–13.

Krahn, Harvey, Graham S. Lowe, and Karen D. Hughes 2007. *Work, Industry & Canadian Society* (5th ed.). Toronto: Thomson Nelson.

Lehmann, Wolfgang 2007. *Choosing to Labour? School–Work Transitions and Social Class.* Montreal & Kingston: McGill-Queen's University Press.

Livingstone, D.W. 1999. *The Education–Jobs Gap: Underemployment or Economic Democracy.* Toronto: Garamond Press.

Livingstone, D.W. 2005. *Basic Findings of the 2004 Canadian Learning and Work Survey.* Paper presented at the Future of Lifelong Learning and Work Conference, June 20, 2005, Toronto.

Logan, Ron, and Jo-Anne Belliveau 1995. "Working mothers." *Canadian Social Trends* (Spring):24–28.

Lowe, Graham S. 2000. *The Quality of Work: A People Centred Agenda.* Toronto: Oxford University Press.

Myles, John 1988. "The expanding middle: Some Canadian evidence on the deskilling debate."

Canadian Review of Sociology and Anthropology 25:335–364.

Osberg, Lars, Fred Wien, and Jan Grude 1995. *Vanishing Jobs: Canada's Changing Workplace.* Toronto: Lorimer.

Peters, V. 2004. *Working and Training: First Results of the 2003 Adult Education and Training Ssurvey.* Ottawa: Statistics Canada & Human Resources and Skills Development Canada. Catalogue No. 81-595-MIE2004015.

Picot, W. Garnett 1987. "The changing industrial mix of employment, 1951–1985." *Canadian Social Trends* (Spring):8–11.

Reich, Robert B. 1991. *The Work of Nations: Preparing Ourselves for 21st-*Century Capitalism. New York: Alfred A. Knopf.

Reiter, Ester 1991. *Making Fast Food: From the Frying Pan into the Fryer.* Montreal and Kingston: McGill-Queen's University Press.

Rifkin, Jeremy 1995. *The End of Work: The Decline of the Global Labor Force and the Dawn of the Post-Market Era.* New York: Putnum.

Rinehart, James 2006. *The Tyranny of Work: Alienation and the Labour Process* (5th ed.). Toronto: Thomson Nelson.

Sennett, Richard 1998. *The Corrosion of Character: The Personal Consequences of Work in the New Capitalism.* New York: W. W. Norton & Company.

Statistics Canada. *The Labour Force.* Catalogue No. 71-001, monthly.

Statistics Canada. *Perspectives on Labour and Income.*

Statistics Canada. *Canadian Social Trends.*

Statistics Canada 1997. *Earnings of Men and Women 1995.* Catalogue No.13-217.

Statistics Canada 2001. *Labour Force Historical Review 2000.* Catalogue No. 71-F004-XCB.

Statistics Canada 2003a. *2001 Census Analysis Series: The Changing Profile of Canada's Labour Force.* Catalogue No. 96F0030XIE2001009.

Statistics Canada 2003b. *2001 Census Analysis Series: Earnings of Canadians: Making a Living in the New Economy.* Catalogue No. 96F0030XIE2001013.

Statistics Canada 2006. *Labour Force Historical Review 2005.* Catalogue No. 71F0004XCB.

Statistics Canada 2007a. *The Daily,* May 11. Catalogue No. 11-001-XIF.

Statistics Canada 2007b. *Women in Canada: Work Chapter Updates 2006.* Catalogue No. 89F0133XIE.

Van den Berg, Axel, and Joseph Smucker (eds.) 1997. *The Sociology of Labour Markets: Efficiency, Equity, Security.* Scarborough, ON: Prentice Hall, Allyn and Bacon Canada.

c h a p t e r   t e n

Change and Stability in Patterns of Social Inequality in Canadian Education

Neil Guppy
(An original chapter written
for this volume.)

INTRODUCTION

Social inequality is a pervasive feature of all modern societies. Privilege and power are unequally distributed. Many people endure a life of stigma and poverty while others reap the rewards of wealth and prestige.

Very frequently, the education system is understood as a social institution with the power to alter an individual's position in this unequal distribution. The argument is as follows. First, education is understood as an important arena for honing the skills and abilities that are helpful for success in life. An individual's educational accomplishments, or lack thereof, facilitate social mobility either up or down this distribution of inequality (e.g., good jobs or bad jobs). In contrast to societies with little mobility, where a person's fate is determined at birth (e.g., an inflexible caste system), in more open societies an individual's position in the hierarchy of inequality can be altered significantly by education.

However, for education to influence upward and downward mobility, a second premise of the argument is important. If schooling is fair and neutral—that is, if it promotes equality of opportunity—then children from all backgrounds should have relatively equal likelihoods of moving up or down the inequality hierarchy, independent of their family origins. Put simply, people's adult destinations (e.g., job, income, residence) should be at most only modestly related to their childhood origins. The converse, in which adult destinations are determined mainly by childhood background, means that the system of social inequality is largely reproduced over time.

Decades of social research suggest that, along some dimensions, a person's background matters less today than it did previously in influencing adult destination. On other dimensions, though, there has been relatively little change. In this chapter, I argue and provide supporting evidence that for women and many ethnic groups, educational attainment is much more equally distributed now than it was in previous decades. However, with regard to social class or socio-economic background (which are used interchangeably here), there has been virtually no change over time. Education still serves to reproduce class inequality, even though it has simultaneously contributed to a fairer and more just distribution of outcomes by gender, ethnicity, and race.

EDUCATIONAL ATTAINMENT BY SOCIO-ECONOMIC BACKGROUND

Young people spend more time in school now than was the case historically. More specifically, average years of schooling have increased and high school dropout rates have diminished. But averages can deceive. In this case, the averages conceal differences in years of schooling or dropout rates for people with different social class or socio-economic backgrounds. Parental education, income, and occupation, all of which are good indicators of class background, still are strongly related to children's school success, and the educational inequality that results from this relationship has persisted both in Canada and in most other Western nations (see Blossfeld and Shavit 1993; Wanner 1999). Rather than support an argument for equality of opportunity, this evidence points to the social reproduction of inequality. That

is, over generations, education does little to alter the position of family members along the hierarchy of inequality.

Table 10-1 provides recent Canadian evidence demonstrating this pattern. For those individuals whose parents did not complete high school, the likelihood of attending university is less than 1 in 5 (17.6% for women and 13.0% for men in 1991, with similar figures for 2000). However, among those that had even one parent who attended university, the likelihood of attending university is about 1 in 2. For women, this likelihood increased from 50.4% in 1991 to 61.7% in 2000. For men, the corresponding percentages were slightly lower but in the same range: 48.7% and 52.5%. In either case, the probability of individuals pursuing a university degree is more than three times greater if they have one parent who attended university, as compared to people whose parents did not complete high school.

Table 10-1 also supports the argument that inequality of educational opportunity, at least based on socio-economic background, is getting worse, not better. Notice that, for men and especially for women, the likelihood of attending university increased most over time for young people who had at least one parent completing university (a 3.8% increase for men and an 11.3% increase for women). These findings undermine any strong sense that for Canadians from disadvantaged class backgrounds, education serves as a great equalizer or as a means to promote equality of opportunity. There is some evidence, however, that post-secondary access in Canada is more equitably distributed across classes than in the United States (Frenette 2005).

There are many possible explanations for finding a strong link between the education levels of parents and children. Perhaps it is a function of family structure, or maybe it differs by ethnicity, or it could be a consequence of work ethic or academic achievement. While there are numerous possibilities,

TABLE 10-1	Percentage Attending University by Parents' Highest Education Level and Sex, 1991 and 2000		
	SLS*	YITS*	%
Parental Education	1991	2000	Difference
Women			
No high school	17.6	17.9	0.3
High school graduate	27.1	27.8	0.7
College	38.9	39.5	0.6
University	50.4	61.7	11.3
Men			
No high school	13.0	12.4	–0.6
High school graduate	19.8	18.3	–1.5
College	28.9	27.9	–1.0
University	48.7	52.5	3.8

* SLS is the School Leavers Survey and YITS is the Youth in Transition Survey, both national surveys conducted by Statistics Canada. Only young people from two-parent families are included. Education level is coded as highest school achievement of either parent.

Source: Author calculations based on Finnie et al.(2004).

even when all of these other factors are taken into account, the strong class-based parent–child link persists. Using definitions slightly different than those in Table 10-1, Finnie et al. (2005) state that "the relative university attendance rates for those whose parents have a high school diploma and those with at least some university education are 29 versus 53 percent in the case of men, and 37 versus 65 percent for women (*holding other factors constant*)" [emphasis added].

Hertzman (2000:14) has argued persuasively that this pattern of higher educational attainment by children of more educated parents represents a "socio-economic gradient." As we move up the gradient—along dimensions of education, or income, or wealth, for example—the children of families of higher socio-economic status generally attain higher levels of education.

Three important factors underlie this socio-economic gradient. First, the gradient represents a *causal* linkage between family background and educational attainment. No matter how many other factors are taken into account (e.g., ethnicity, region, family structure), the effect of socio-economic level on educational attainment persists. Second, the gradient is *robust* across different measures of education or schooling. For example, if instead of university attendance we were to look at high school dropouts, we would find that parents' education has a causal influence on high school completion rates. Furthermore, the linkage between family origin and school attainment is *robust* across different measures of socio-economic status or social class (i.e., comparing working, middle, and upper classes, or contrasting people with different family income levels). Finally, the gradient *persists* through time and across place. That is, it exists in all industrial countries and has endured through time, although its steepness varies both cross-nationally and -historically.

Another way to understand this gradient is to consider the skills and abilities that children bring with them to their first days of schooling. We know that children's readiness to learn at school is influenced by their home and neighbourhood environments. These environments are in turn linked to family socio-economic status. For example, Verdon (2007) has shown that, among five-year-old children, there are differences in readiness to learn by family income: "When it came to receptive vocabulary, communication skill, knowledge of numbers, copying and using symbols, attention, and co-operative play, children from lower-income households scored lower than those from more affluent households." This is yet another example of the socio-economic gradient in action.

A final way to understand this gradient is displayed in Table 10-2. Using data from the Statistics Canada Youth in Transition Survey, Krahn and Taylor (2007) examined the options for post-secondary study that are open to grade 10 students. Taking the right English, mathematics, and science courses is critical for college and university admission. These researchers found that family income influences the likelihood that students choose courses in their early high school years that will allow them to pursue post-secondary education. For example, in Ontario, only 49% of grade 10 students from families with incomes below $30 000 enrolled in high school courses that will permit them to enrol in future post-secondary programs. Among students in families with incomes of $90 000 or more, the corresponding figure is 73%. In each province, the socio-economic gradient is evident: the higher the family income, the higher the proportion of students who are eligible to pursue post-secondary credentials.

In summary, there is consistent evidence that educational attainment in Canada differs systematically by social class or socio-economic status. Moreover, this distribution of educational inequality shows no sign of significant change in recent decades.

EDUCATIONAL ATTAINMENT BY GENDER

Reporting in 1970, Canada's Royal Commission on the Status of Women argued that "education opens the door to almost

TABLE 10-2	Percentage of Grade 10 Students with Post-Secondary Access Options Open, by Family Income and Province, 2000			
Family Income	**British Columbia**	**Alberta**	**Saskatchewan**	**Ontario**
Less than $30 000	59	50	83	49
$30 000 to $44 999	60	52	83	52
$45 000 to $59 999	60	53	88	59
$60 000 to $74 999	70	56	93	65
$75 000 to $89 999	69	62	89	70
$90 000 or more	73	68	89	73
Total	66	59	87	64

Source: Krahn and Taylor (2007).

every life goal. Wherever women are denied equal access to education, they cannot be said to have equality" (1970:161). In previous decades, far fewer women than men had been advancing to higher education, but that began to change such that by 1982 more women than men were earning undergraduate degrees. The women's movement and greater labour force participation among women were critical factors in explaining these changes. Now, as Figure 10-1 shows, there are over 100 000 more women than men pursuing full-time undergraduate degrees at Canadian universities.

Explaining this inversion in university attendance rates over the last half-century has people asking why most university students are women (see Frenette and Zeman 2007). The answer lies in women's higher scholastic achievements relative to men (both in school grades and on standardized tests such as for reading), women's study habits and school engagement, and parental expectations. Another factor is that high-paying jobs are more plentiful for men who

do not have university credentials than for women with the same education, especially in resource-based provinces.

By and large, schools are now places where traditional gender roles have been challenged and changed. Indeed, Arnot, David, and Weiner (1999:150) call these changes "one of the most extensive inversions of social inequality in contemporary times." The labour market and its associated workplaces are far more segregated and gendered than are schools. Certainly, some gender segregation and stereotyping still occurs in schooling, but the massive changes that have occurred within education should not be ignored. For example, when the Royal Commission Report was published in 1970, women were still a minority in both medical schools and law schools. Now women comprise the majority of students in both law and medicine. The more equitable balancing of women in these professional schools is symptomatic of the massive change in educational attainment by gender.

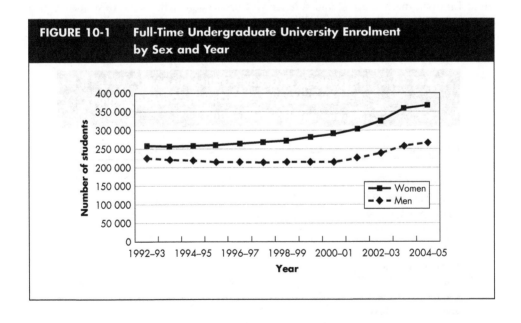

FIGURE 10-1   Full-Time Undergraduate University Enrolment by Sex and Year

EDUCATIONAL ATTAINMENT BY ANCESTRY, ETHNICITY, AND RACE

One approach to examining educational attainment by ethnicity is to contrast the educational outcomes of young people from visible minority and non-visible minority backgrounds. Shaienks and Gluszynski (2007) present evidence on this question, as summarized in Table 10-3. Their findings show, first of all, that the likelihood of having attended some form of post-secondary education for those aged 24 to 26 is higher among those from visible minority backgrounds (87%) than among those not in visible minority families (78%). Examining the type of institution attended makes it clear that visible minority Canadians are more likely to have attended university (62%) than are people who are not from visible minority backgrounds (49%).

Another approach to examining the same question—that is, is educational attainment unevenly distributed by ethnicity or race?—is to examine the educational experiences of children born in families who emigrated to Canada, as opposed to children born into families of Canadian residents (i.e., non-immigrants). Both McMullen (2004) and Worswick (2004) have demonstrated that while children from immigrant families are more likely to start school with less developed educational abilities, especially in reading and writing, rapid gains by immigrant children in the early years mean that the performances of immigrant and Canadian-born students converge fairly quickly. Although the educational system cannot take all of the credit for this pattern, the convergence is good evidence that the experiences in school of immigrant children are positive with respect to developing key scholastic abilities.

Nevertheless, both of the comparisons provided above are problematic in one key way. By creating two broad dichotomies—visible minority and others—the comparisons effectively lump together many different groups, and imply that the experiences of all people within a particular group are similar. For example, First Nations people are not members of a visible minority (as officially defined by the Canadian government) and so are treated as non-visible minorities and as native-born Canadians. However, it is clear that their experiences could be quite different from other individuals subsumed under these two categories. Similarly, the visible minority category includes people from the West Indies, Japan, and India, yet the experiences of young people from these three distinct ethnic groups may be very different.

TABLE 10-3	Post-secondary Participation Rates of Canadians Aged 24 to 26, by Visible Minority Status, December 2005			
	Participation Rate	Type of Post-secondary Institution Attended		
	Attended Post-secondary	University	College/Cégep	Other Type of Post-secondary
Visible Minority	87	62	27	11
Not Visible Minority	78	49	34	17

Source: Shaienks and Gluszynski (2007).

Other chapters in this book address the links between education and ethnicity, race, and ancestry. Schools may be institutions in which many immigrant children have found success, but this is not the case for most First Nations people. While some Aboriginal people have done exceptionally well in schools, as Menzies discusses in Chapter 19, school success has not been the modal experience for the vast majority of First Nations people. In Chapter 17, Hou, Balakrishnan, and Jurdi show how education is unequally distributed across ethnic and racial minorities in general. Their analysis reveals, as well, that translating education credentials into labour market success is another potential hurdle that minority groups must face in Canada.

CONCLUSION

This review and presentation of recent evidence should make it apparent that education has important consequences for the lives of Canadians (see Davies and Guppy 2006 for a fuller discussion). Among students who drop out of high school, finding sustainable work that pays well is very difficult over the course of their lifetimes. Among students who graduate from law or medical school, on the other hand, secure and well-paid employment is much easier to attain. In present-day Canada, children from different social classes have quite different likelihoods of dropping out of school or attaining a professional educational credential. For women, school attainment is now much more equitably distributed than it was for previous generations. Finally, school success is also a reality for members of many immigrant and visible minority groups, but far less so for others, including First Nations people.

REFERENCES

Arnot, Madeleine, Miriam David, and Gaby Weiner 1999. *Closing the Gender Gap: Postwar Education and Social Change* Cambridge, UK: Polity Press.

Blossfeld, H.P., and Y. Shavit 1993. *Persistent Inequality: Changing Educational Attainment in Thirteen Countries.* Boulder, CO: Westview Press.

Davies, Scott, and Neil Guppy 2006. *The Schooled Society: An Introduction to the Sociology of Education.* Toronto: Oxford University Press.

Finnie, Ross, Christine Laporte, and Eric Lascelles 2004. "Family background and access to post-secondary education: What happened over the 1990s?" Statistics Canada, Analytical Studies Branch Research Paper Series, Catalogue No. 11F0019 No. 226.

Finnie, Ross, Eric Lascelles, and Arthur Sweetman 2005. "Who goes? The direct and indirect effects of family background on access to post-secondary education." Statistics Canada, Analytical Studies Branch Research Paper Series, Catalogue No. 11F0019MIE No. 237.

Frenette, Marc 2005. "Is post-secondary access more equitable in Canada or the United States?" Statistics Canada, Analytical Studies Branch Research Paper Series, Catalogue No. 11F0019MIE No. 244.

Frenette, Marc, and Klarka Zeman 2007. "Why are most university students women? Evidence based on academic performance, study habits and parental influences." Statistics Canada, Analytical Studies Branch Research Paper Series, Catalogue No. 11F0019MIE No. 303.

Hertzman, Clyde 2000. "The case for an early childhood development strategy." *ISUMA: Canadian Journal of Policy Research* (Autumn):11–18.

Krahn, Harvey, and Alison Taylor 2007. "Streaming' in the 10th grade in four Canadian provinces in 2000." *Education Matters: Insights on Education, Learning and Training in Canada* 4, 2. Statistics Canada 81-004-XIE.

McMullen, Kathryn 2004. "Children of immigrants: How well do they do in school?" *Education Matters: Insights on Education, Learning and Training in Canada* 1, 2. Statistics Canada 81-004-XIE.

Royal Commission on the Status of Women 1970. *Report of the Royal Commission on the Status of Women in Canada*. Ottawa: Information Canada.

Shaienks, Danielle, and Tomasz Gluszynski 2007. "Participation in postsecondary education: Graduates, continuers and drop outs—results from YITS Cycle 4." Statistics Canada, Research Paper, Catalogue No. 81-595-MIE No. 059.

Verdon, Lisa 2007. "Are 5-year-old children ready to learn at school? Family income and home environment contexts." *Education Matters: Insights on Education, Learning and Training in Canada* 4, 1. Statistics Canada 81-004-XIE.

Wanner, Richard 1999. "Expansion and ascription: Trends in educational opportunity in Canada, 1920–1994." *Canadian Review of Sociology and Anthropology* 36:409–442.

Worswick, Christopher 2004. "Adaptation and inequality: Children of immigrants in Canadian schools." *Canadian Journal of Economics* 37, 1: 53–77.

chapter eleven

Changing Times, Stubborn Inequalities: Explaining Socio-economic Stratification in Canadian Schooling

Scott Davies and Vicky Maldonado
(An original chapter written
for this volume.)

INTRODUCTION

Schools are the central arena for social inequality; a setting in which children compete from early ages to be eventually sifted and sorted into highly stratified career paths. For decades, social scientists have demonstrated that students' socio-economic status (SES) strongly shapes their educational success, from primary grades to post-graduate studies. On average, poor or working-class youth have fared less well than their more affluent peers, whether on standardized test scores, high school completion rates, or university attendance. Within any socio-economic category there has been a range of outcomes, and thousands of underprivileged youths have enjoyed success in

Canadian schools, but on average these disparities have been remarkably durable. Indeed, this repeated finding across time and space is as close as sociologists have come to discovering a scientific law. To explain these patterns, sociologists from the 1950s through to the early 1990s examined a combination of cultural and structural forces that posed barriers to working-class youth and discouraged them from developing high educational expectations (for a comprehensive review, see Karabel and Halsey 1977; for Canadian examples, see Anisef 1974; Guppy 1984; Murphy 1979; Porter et al. 1979).

This chapter takes these durable empirical trends and classic explanations as its point of departure. We review trends in Canadian educational attainment since the early 1990s, establish a framework for understanding disparities, re-examine classic explanations, and ponder which explanations need to be revised to fit emerging trends. We draw not only on Canadian research, but also on research from Britain and the United States, where socio-economic patterns of educational inequality are fairly similar and where research has been internationally influential.

RECENT TRENDS IN EDUCATIONAL ATTAINMENT

A striking cumulative trend in Canadian schooling over the past few decades has been the rising attainments of Canadians from all walks of life. By 2003, 62% of young Canadians had attended a post-secondary institution (Zeman 2007). Most young adults, regardless of social origin, possess more school credentials than their parents or grandparents (Corak et al. 2003). Indeed, many Canadians from *all* SES categories now attend some form of post-secondary schooling (Finnie et al. 2005). Recent surveys show that the overwhelming majority (more than 80%) of Canadian parents from even the lowest income and educational categories expect their children to attend college or university (Davies 2005). While higher education was once thought to be foreign territory to most youth from humble origins, attending some form of higher education is increasingly becoming the norm, even among the disadvantaged. This Canadian trend is part of broader international expansion of higher education that has permeated all corners of the globe (Schofer and Meyer 2005).

However, an equally striking trend has been the durability of educational inequality. While all groups are attaining more and

more years of schooling, educational gaps between the more and less affluent persist, as the attainments of advantaged youth have easily kept pace with the less advantaged. This can be seen in a wide variety of indicators from primary, secondary, and post-secondary levels. For instance, young children from low-income households are four times more likely to experience delays in vocabulary development than are more affluent children (Hertzman 2000). Elementary schools that have larger proportions of students living in affluent and stable neighbourhoods fare much better on standardized tests (Johnson 2005). Teenagers with university-educated parents score considerably higher on reading, math, and science tests compared to their peers with less educated parents (Willms 2002; Statistics Canada 2005). These development trends tend to shape later attainments. Youth from the lowest family income quartile are three times more likely to drop out of high school than those from the highest quartile (Zeman 2007). While half (50.2%) of youth hailing from the top income quartile of families attended university, only 31% from the bottom quartile did so (Frenette 2007). Likewise, about 50% of youth with university-educated parents attended university themselves in 2001, compared to only 18% of those with parents having high school education or less (Drolet 2005).

These current trends illustrate that even though Canadians from all socio-economic strata are generally staying in school longer, long-standing patterns of educational inequality are robust, despite decades of educational expansion and reform. This pattern of persisting inequality amid expansion has been found in many nations beyond Canada (Shavit et al. 2007). A challenge is thus posed: how can we explain persisting inequality in an era of expanding and rising attainment?

A FRAMEWORK FOR EXPLAINING DISPARITIES:

The sprawling literature on school attainment can be fruitfully organized into a framework that distinguishes between resources, contexts, and expectations. *Resources* refer to tangible possessions (i.e., finances) or attributes of people (i.e., skills) that offer advantages in school competitions. *Contexts* refer to characteristics of schools and neighbourhoods that can influence attainment over and above those resources. Finally, *expectations* refer to the processes by which people make educational decisions. We introduce the latter concept to align with a lengthy theoretical tradition that attempts to understand how individuals convert social structure into social action, and by which social action aggregates into concrete social structures (see van den Berg 1998).

Resources

The most elemental explanation for socio-economic disparities in school rests with economic resources. Porter et al. (1979) concluded in an earlier era that "money matters" in education because even though K–12 public schools do not charge tuition, school performance can require additional money, whether to pay for optional field trips, for books and other learning materials, for school uniforms (in schools that require them), and perhaps for private tutors. Further, non-religious private schools, which send most of their graduates to universities, are largely unaffordable to lower-income families. More important, those researchers showed that students' SES backgrounds affected their decisions to attend university, even controlling for their academic ability, likely due to the requirement of paying tuition fees (Porter et al. 1979). Recent Canadian studies continue to show that access

to higher education is conditioned by parental income (Frenette 2007) and, not surprisingly, American research shows that a family's wealth, net of their income, strongly shapes their children's odds of attending a post-secondary institution (Conley 2001). Another economic factor is the quality of public schooling. While data are not conclusive, students from more affluent neighbourhoods do achieve at higher levels, net of their family resources, likely because their schools enjoy superior resources and attract better teachers (Boyle et al. 2007). Though it has been difficult for researchers to demonstrate that superior school resources directly raise learning outcomes, better-funded schools may generally nurture an environment that promotes better academic climates and higher expectations among students.

Nevertheless, the role of money did not figure strongly in classic explanations of education disparities for several reasons. Socio-economic gaps in student performance appear from the earliest primary grades, before most families are required to pay any extra tuition fees or bear additional expenses for schools. Most Canadian high school students who take part-time jobs have done so not out of dire necessity, but for extra disposable income. For much of the post–Second World War era, post-secondary tuition fees in Canada were relatively affordable, and nations like Great Britain, France, and Australia that had abolished those fees still had comparable (or worse) socio-economic inequalities in university participation. Further, researchers have long found that parental education is a more powerful predictor of a variety of student outcomes than is parental income. While financial resources— whether used for tuition, transportation, private tutors, or to avoid the need for part-time work—affect school outcomes, they do not fully determine student success. Thus, classic studies usually pursued other explanations.

Many sociologists from the 1950s through to the early 1990s instead explained educational disparities through a combination of cultural forces and the structure of schooling. The stronger predictive power of parental education over parental income or class position suggests the explanatory importance of non-material resources passed on from parents to their children. One such explanation examined how children informally learn academic skills from their families. For years, researchers have discussed how more educated parents pass on to their children "human capital"—basic reading, writing, and vocabulary skills, and disciplined work habits—giving them a distinct advantage in school. A variety of classic studies showed that exposure to reading material in households, for instance, improved the chances of an individual completing high school and attending university (reviewed in Sewell and Hauser 1980). Recent research has vindicated those views, as newer data show that socio-economic disparities in skills such as the ability to read, write, and reason can be detected among students from the earliest school years (Alexander et al. 1997). Moreover, SES learning gaps, as measured by standardized tests, actually *widen* during the summer months when youth are not in school (Downey et al. 2004). Researchers are now concluding that out-of-school summer learning experiences serve to widen SES gaps in test scores, high school completion, and university attendance (Alexander et al. 2007). This line of research reasons that family differences in skills and related resources fuel SES disparities, while schools actually serve to shrink those gaps to some degree during the regular school calendar.

Do youth from higher SES origins enjoy other, less skill-based advantages? Some sociologists have focused on cultural aesthetics as another type of family resource. "Cultural capital," the signature concept of

French sociologist Pierre Bourdieu (Bourdieu and Passeron 1990), refers to the possession of sophisticated (as opposed to merely competent) conversational abilities and tastes for literature and the arts. Bourdieu contends that schools reward children who possess a certain type of cultural sophistication that is less likely to be found among the working class. For Bourdieu, schooling is conducted according to styles of speech, dress, and cultural references that are drawn from the professional middle class, and are thus largely foreign to working-class youth. Teachers are seen to value the kinds of aesthetic know-how and vocabulary possessed by middle-class children, mistaking a cultural style as a badge of intelligence and natural ability. In essence, schools reward middle-class culture.

To test this theory, sociologists have attempted to correlate statistically school outcomes with various indicators of cultural capital, such as whether students have attended art galleries or museums or have engaged in a variety of extra-curricular lessons. But a variety of studies suggest that the link between cultural capital and class background is not exactly as Bourdieu imagines. Some find that the possession of cultural capital does not boost school performance or teacher evaluations net of those activities that enhance literacy or good work habits (Dumais 2006; Kingston 2001). Further, not all middle-class youth participate in high-status culture—far from it— and not all lower SES children are excluded from this culture (Kingston 2001). Finally, the contention that North American school curricula reflect a class-based culture, as Bourdieu contended in the French context, has yet to be established.

Partly in response to this research, Lareau (2000, 2003) suggests that middle-class cultural advantages lie not in their aesthetic dimensions, but instead in their superior knowledge of school requirements and their ability to develop competitive strategies to facilitate academic success. She suggests that successful middle-class parents "activate" their resources by using their knowledge of how to choose good schools and good teachers, and knowing how to intervene effectively on behalf of their children (see also Looker 1994). Indeed, children enjoy academic advantages when their parents spend time with them and actively monitor their homework (Ho and Willms 1996; Schneider and Coleman 1993). Conversely, families that lack advantages in some areas can compensate by excelling in other areas. For instance, many Asian immigrant parents possess little of the dominant cultural capital, few English skills, and have relatively little direct contact with teachers, yet compensate by enrolling their children in private tutoring and monitoring their children's homework at higher-than-average rates (Schneider and Coleman 1993). In contrast, families with impressive resources "on paper" may spend little time interacting with their children, or may not know how to guide their children through crucial educational contests. Knowledge that a high LSAT score is crucial to one's chances of acceptance into law school, for example, is especially helpful if one can already afford the books and study courses that can improve such scores. Exposing one's children to music, art galleries, and world travel may offer some advantages, but that potential needs to be actualized through strategic action.

Contexts

Given these family resources, how do different surrounding contexts affect school attainment? While at one level motivation is an individual, idiosyncratic matter, sociologists know that individual effort does not occur in a social vacuum, but is embedded in broader social contexts. The formal structure of schools, along with informal relationships among students, teachers, parents, and neighbours, can channel an individual's actions.

One key aspect of school structure is the practice of streaming. In Canada, as in many countries, lower SES youth are more likely than their middle-class counterparts to be streamed into less challenging, terminal programs in high school (Krahn and Taylor 2007). The very existence of these streaming systems, critics contend, disadvantages working-class students (Curtis et al. 1992). These youth would fare better in a non-streamed high school environment that offered the same curricula and expectations, but being stuck in lower tracks steers them to less challenging work and lowers their expectations and aspirations. Once in different tracks, fatalistic frames of reference are reinforced, as opportunities to rise in school and learn are limited. The incentives of available jobs and/or impending domestic roles, when combined with streaming, lead these youth to perceive school as irrelevant to their future. It becomes a pointless dress rehearsal for their upcoming roles.

In support of this line of thinking, researchers have continually found that American Catholic schools place far fewer students in lower streams, and as a result more of their working-class students score well on standardized tests, graduate from high school, and attend post-secondary institutions (see Morgan 2001). Such findings have encouraged a "de-streaming" movement, which seeks to abolish differential grouping and to mix students of all abilities. In the early 1990s, Ontario removed streams in grade nine, and planned eventually to phase out all streaming. However, for a variety of reasons—but largely due to teacher complaints about the practical difficulties imposed by heterogeneous ability groups—the government ended the experiment. Nevertheless, American research suggests that de-streaming may be a valid tool for easing class disparities in schooling if practical problems associated with student heterogeneity can be overcome.

This thinking about streaming extends to a broader issue: how the complexity of school systems may shape attainment. Even when students from humble origins have lofty aspirations and are academically gifted, other factors mitigate against their success. The daunting variety of choices available in modern post-secondary education, such as the distinctions between community colleges and universities, different types of degrees, the informal ranking of institutions, and the wide variety of programs available within any institution, creates an elaborate system of selection with many ports of entry. To make wise choices and maximize one's benefit, one must understand how the system operates; for example, what are the efficacious strategies for success or the informal rankings of programs and institutions? While research on this issue is not decisive, it is probable that such navigational savvy is held disproportionately by students from middle-class origins. Data show that schools in nations with more differentiated and complex secondary structures greatly shape student aspirations, while families and peers are more influential in nations with less complex systems (Buchmann and Dalton 2002). By international standards, Canadian K–12 schooling is not particularly hierarchical (see also Kerckhoff 2001). The vast bulk of Canadians attend comprehensive secondary schools, rather than purely academic institutions (such as British grammar schools) or purely vocational schools (as in Germany's *Hauptschule*). Streaming in Canadian schools occurs relatively late, and our provincial systems offer many opportunities for high school dropouts

to re-enter schooling. Further, access to university is more equitable in Canada than in the United States (Frenette 2005b), perhaps due to the latter's large private sector and astonishing variety of institutions. But while the Canadian system does offer broad opportunities for working-class youth, informal processes can create advantages for middle-class youth, who may have superior information about the academic marketplace and are more likely to know which fields offer lucrative rewards and how to find competitive advantages.

This research on streaming and school structures is complemented by a broader strand of theorizing about "social capital." Social capital refers to sets of social relationships within a community that can produce educational success, independent of its resources (see Coleman 1988). Communities are seen to create social capital by forging norms of reciprocity and mutual obligation among parents, youth, and schools. Such norms breed strong bonds of trust, co-operation, and mutual respect, and can channel motivation and effort, while communities with weak obligations and expectations can foster less commitment to educational goals. Importantly, communities with greater social capital are seen to have fewer socioeconomic disparities. As Coleman (1988) contended, lower SES students fare better in Catholic schools not only because they were less often placed in vocational streams, but also because they enjoyed thicker feelings of school community in which teachers and parents cared not only for their own children, but for others' children as well. Such environments, Coleman argued, lend greater support to otherwise disadvantaged students. This research on social capital links to recurrent findings that schools and neighbourhoods with higher-than-average SES have superior educational outcomes, net of family resources (Boyle et al. 2007), presumably because those settings expose low SES students to an enriched academic environment, to high-status role models, and to aspiring peers.

Culture and Expectations

Our consumer-driven, success-striving society encourages people to pursue the "North American dream" of a prestigious, well-paying job, and so everyone "values" education in an abstract sense. Whether through surveys, interviews, or policy statements, virtually all Canadians claim to place great importance on education. But while expressing an appreciation for education is one thing, converting desires into reality is another.

The process by which our educational desires become firm and motivating expectations is the bridge between an individual's resources and his or her surrounding social contexts. We develop expectations by comparing ourselves to similar people, aligning our aspirations and efforts accordingly. Our significant others shape our frames of reference for the kinds of jobs and lifestyles we want, and the role school plays in our desires. For instance, when asked what they would like to be when they grow up, very young children often reply "police officer," "nanny," or "teacher." But as they grow older, learning about the jobs of their parents' friends, these choices change. Their choices change again as young people hear others encouraging or remaining mute about their occupational dreams.

Sociologists apply ideas about expectations in two broad ways. One tradition, known as a "rational choice perspective," assumes that people make educational decisions by calculating its costs, its anticipated benefits, their probability of success, and the attractiveness of alternative options (see Goldthorpe 1996; Morgan 2005). Student's SES origins shape the degree to which they view schooling as desirable, since different social locations give rise to unequal costs,

benefits, and chances of success. While average attainments have risen for all groups, SES disparities are seen to persist because cost–benefit balances for different strata have remained stable. Low SES youths may deem the prospect of paying high tuition fees for university only to suffer a bout of unemployment to be very costly, since their families would likely be less able to subsidize them, and since they likely lack social connections that could land them a white-collar job.

A second tradition, associated with Pierre Bourdieu, emphasizes that people's perceptions are rooted in their pre-existing dispositions and surrounding influences. This tradition de-emphasizes the strategic and calculating aspect of social action, and instead focuses on its more habitual and instinctive qualities. According to Bourdieu, people are oriented by cultural repertoires and social scripts, which themselves are historical products of groups internalizing their objective conditions. For instance, the decision of a young people from lower SES origins to not attend university may stem not from any rigorous cost–benefit calculation on their part, but instead they may feel that university is alien territory, particularly if no family members have ever attended such an institution. Rather than systematically calculating the costs and benefits of paying post-secondary tuition fees and the odds of landing a good job, this perspective emphasizes how youths' job aspirations tend to mirror the kinds of jobs held by their parents or other people like themselves (for a Canadian example, see Lehmann 2007). So a youth from a lower SES background may view a relatively secure blue-collar job that requires few educational credentials as a viable option, while more affluent students might reject such a choice out of hand, and would instead seek entree into elite universities, largely because they feel that only such locations are worthy of them (Mullen 2007).

In general, this perspective emphasizes how our social upbringing shapes our preferences, and which life options we may find enticing, impossible, or unacceptable. In Bourdieu's terms, people's past experiences and current social positions (or "habitus") encourage them to "come to terms" with their circumstances and adjust their expectations to what is "realistic." We learn to desire largely only what we can expect, Bourdieu emphasizes.

While these two traditions are not entirely incompatible, they offer differing emphases on whether actors' schooling decisions are based on a knowing assessment of their probable costs and benefits, or based on prevailing group norms, scripts, and cultural values. Both acknowledge that people's sense of desirable yet possible and realistic life options influence their educational expectations, and that immediate family and friends greatly influence our mental horizons.

Systematic research on educational expectations suggests a nuanced reality. While research on "status attainment" has long found that student aspirations are influenced by family and friends, net of their own economic and academic resources (Morgan 2005), SES only partly influences people's educational expectations. Some poor and working-class students do develop high expectations. These studies portray middle-class versus working-class families as having only incrementally different outlooks, as opposed to profoundly dissimilar values or norms. Today, rational choice theorists would comprehend the rising postsecondary expectations of Canadians from all walks of life as reflecting how the changing economy is shifting the relative costs and benefits of schooling, replacing solid blue-collar opportunities with jobs that require school credentials. Rational choice perspectives are useful for understanding rising absolute levels of school attainment.

But what about persisting disparities? In previous eras, sociologists tended to embrace more habitual explanations. For decades, sociologists have proclaimed a fundamental mismatch between the cultural orientations that schools require and the culture of lower socio-economic groups. In the 1950s and 1960s, many sociologists held that modern schools require students to embrace a set of "middle-class" orientations that value achievement, competition, and aspirations for upward social mobility, and that families from lower socio-economic strata failed to embrace those needed orientations. Working-class families were seen to be behind the times, mired in a pre-modern value set (see Hyman 1953).

In the 1970s through the 1990s, sociologists redefined these working-class orientations as instances of cultural "resistance." In the most popular version of this idea, Paul Willis (1977) argued that class disparities in school stem from the working class's rejection of the ethic of status striving in favour of working-class mores of solidarity, mores that were historically forged through struggles with capitalist employers. A working-class upbringing was said to instill (at least in boys) a pride in heavy manual labour, a preference for solidarity over competitiveness, a disparaging stance toward the kind of "pencil-pushing" that pervades schoolwork, and a general antagonism to institutional authority. In Willis's account, these habits encouraged working youth to reject school and eagerly anticipate the "real world" of factory employment. Yet, today's economy forces us to confront a key question: if fewer youth today can look forward to traditional blue-collar jobs, are such stances still prevalent among lower SES youth? If not, is there still a working-class "habitus" that can help us understand persisting disparities in educational expectations? We return to this issue in the conclusion.

A flip side to research on student expectations is the classic notion that teachers, themselves middle class, tend to hold higher expectations for middle-class students than for working-class students. Teachers are said to generalize, perhaps unconsciously, from the physical and social attributes of students (e.g., dress, demeanour, and speech style) to their abilities. According to this argument, teachers subtly expect well-dressed, presentable, and articulate children to be good students, and expect those with the opposite traits to be poorer students. This typecasting is also said to create a self-fulfilling prophecy. Whether via body language or the attention they give to students, teachers are said to treat students differently, and students are said to internalize these subtle messages. Thus, students for whom teachers have low expectations are said to eventually develop poor self-images, which in turn lead to poor academic performance. However, while proof for this thesis was originally said to be provided by the famous "Pygmalion in the classroom" experiment (Rosenthal and Jacobson 1968), subsequent analyses suggest that the conclusions drawn from that study far overshot its data, and later attempts at replication have produced mixed results at best (see Wineburg 1987; Raudenbusch and Bryk 2002).

CONCLUSION: THEORIZING PERSISTING INEQUALITY IN A CHANGING SYSTEM

SES gaps persist, albeit at higher average rates of attainment. Documenting these trends is relatively easy, but devising convincing and well-grounded explanations is more difficult. Sociologists have long explained these disparities by pointing to unequal resources, contexts that advantage some groups over others, and how both of these factors shape student expectations.

But the relative weight of these factors is changing, as rising levels of attainment are stimulating new government policies and new family strategies. We end this chapter by discussing how prevailing explanations may need to be revised.

Are some resources becoming more important with time? We argued that research confirms the importance of middle-class parents' ability to pass on skills and to strategically intervene for their children, but is less supportive of more aesthetic understandings of class culture. Further, while sociologists in previous eras understandably downplayed the role of finances, the past decade has seen a steep rise in university tuition fees, and in some provinces, tuition for professional programs has been deregulated. While some argue that these hikes have had little impact on access to university, there is evidence that deregulation is indeed discouraging lower SES groups from entering professional programs (Frenette 2005a, 2005b). This suggests that family finances may re-emerge as a prime factor that shapes educational outcomes, at least in terms of accessing some university fields. Policy-makers are attempting to counteract this effect by making loans and bursaries more readily available, but it is too early to judge their impact.

Understanding inequality requires that we recognize not only the barriers faced by working-class youth, but also the evolving advantages and strategies of middle-class families. Even if working-class frames of reference change and school biases are removed, which would render working-class students more competitive, middle-class families appear to be developing new strategies to keep ahead. Research is showing marked rises in the use of private tutors, private schools, educational consultants, and educational toys, suggesting that middle-class families are also using the marketplace to retain their educational advantages (Aurini 2006; Davies and Quirke 2007), perhaps reflecting a broader rise of increasingly intensive and competitive parenting (Lareau 2003; Quirke 2006).

In what ways are contexts changing? Policy-makers want colleges and universities to expand and differentiate. To encourage more post-secondary attendance, Canadian policy-makers are lessening the amount of non-academic streaming in high schools, and are devising policies to allow more flexibility for dropouts to re-enter school systems at various levels. To encourage post-secondary expansion, governments are allowing tuition to rise, placing more of the financial onus on families. To encourage differentiation, governments and market forces appear to be creating more structural hierarchy within programs in colleges and universities. Politicians are encouraging programs and institutions to raise more of their own funds independently and governments are creating pools of research monies that are far from evenly distributed among Canadian institutions. These phenomena may be triggering a steeper prestige pecking order among universities (Davies and Zarifa 2006). In combination, all of these trends may shift more and more "streaming" from secondary to post-secondary levels.

If middle-class families are responding to these trends with new competitive strategies, what will be the response among lower SES groups? While sociologists have long seen "working-class culture" as an enduring and coherent entity that discouraged its young from aspiring to post-secondary studies, that particular cultural form is likely fading in Canada. De-industrialization is transforming the very job structure that helped forge that culture. Until the mid 1980s, blue-collar jobs in resources and manufacturing that required few educational credentials attracted many of the working class, particularly males, out of school. But the stock of such jobs is now

smaller. More school leavers now encounter service sector jobs (often requiring educational credentials, even if not high levels of skill). Further, on average, women are marrying and bearing children at later ages and, perhaps as a result, female educational attainments among all classes have shot upward. Thus, two viable alternatives that previously attracted many working-class students out of school have been recently undercut. In response, working-class families have boosted their attainments substantially, though gaps between them and the middle class persist. But in an era in which 80% of parents in even lower income groupings expect their children to attend a college or university (Davies 2005), it is less and less plausible to presume that working-class families are alienated from the education system, or that their children will follow the habits of their parents and opt for factory work.

The theoretical challenge, therefore, is to combine rational choice and habitual understandings of educational decision making in an era of change. As our society embraces the "knowledge-based economy," lifetime learning is being hailed as the next source of educational expansion. People of all descriptions, so the argument goes, will return to school numerous times over their employment lifetimes to upgrade their skills. Middle-class families, it appears, are largely discounting any options they deem to be inferior (a reflection of their "habitus"), yet they are also consciously devising new competitive strategies to pass on educational advantages. Fewer working-class children will be employed in settings that are similar to those of their parents, and are coming of age in an era in which formerly plentiful proletarian employment is on the wane. Even if these youth are not very upwardly mobile, they will work in non-farm and non-factory settings. It is difficult to imagine that strong anti-school attitudes will survive in this coming era.

In sum, to understand persisting inequalities in education, we need to acknowledge important social changes. Parental resources like cognitive skills and competitive strategies are increasingly vital, and family finances may re-emerge as an important determinant of post-secondary participation. Contexts will evolve, as more and more "streaming" of students migrates upward from high schools to the expanded and increasingly differentiated post-secondary sector. This context will elicit high educational expectations among the vast bulk of families, weakening traditional blue-collar ambivalence toward schools. Yet, disparities among families according to their possession of key resources will likely continue to make educational outcomes highly unequal.

REFERENCES

Alexander, Karl L., Doris R. Entwisle, and Carrie S. Horsey 1997. "From first grade forward: Early foundations of high school dropout." *Sociology of Education* 70, 2: 87–107.

Alexander, Karl L., Doris R. Entwisle, and Linda Steffel Olson 2007. "Lasting consequences of the summer learning gap." *American Sociological Review* 72, 2:167–180.

Anisef, Paul 1974. *The Critical Juncture*. Toronto: Ministry of Colleges and Universities.

Aurini, Janice 2006. "Crafting legitimation projects: An institutional analysis of private education businesses." *Sociological Forum* 21, 1: 83–112.

Bourdieu, Pierre, and Jean-Claude Passeron 1990. *Reproduction in Education, Society and Culture* (2nd ed.). London: Sage.

Boyle, Michael H., Kathy Georgiades, Yvonne Racine, and C. Mustard 2007. "Neighbourhood and family influences on educational attainment: Results from the Ontario Child Health Study Follow-Up 2001." *Child Development* 78, 1: 168–189.

Buchmann, Claudia, and Ben Dalton 2002. "Interpersonal influences and educational aspirations in twelve countries: The importance of institutional context." *Sociology of Education* 75:99–122

Coleman, James S. 1988. "Social capital in the creation of human capital." *American Journal of Sociology* 94:s95–s120.

Conley, Dalton 2001. "Capital for college: Parental assets and postsecondary schooling." *Sociology of Education* 74, 1:59–72.

Corak, Miles, Garth Lipps, and John Zhao 2003. "Family income and participation in post-secondary education." Analytical Studies Branch Research Paper Series, no. 210. Accessed October 26, 2007. http://www.statcan.ca/english/research/11F0019MIE/11F0019MIE2003210.pdf

Curtis, Bruce, David W. Livingstone, and Harry Smaller 1992. *Stacking the Deck: The Streaming of Working Class Kids in Ontario Schools.* Toronto: Our Schools/Our Selves.

Davies, Scott 2005. "A revolution of expectations? Three key trends in the SAEP data." In Robert Sweet and Paul Anisef (eds.), *Preparing for Post Secondary Education: New Roles for Governments and Families*, pp. 149–165, Chapter 6. Montreal: McGill-Queens University Press.

Davies, Scott, and Linda Quirke 2007. "The impact of sector on school organizations: The logics of markets and institutions." *Sociology of Education* 80, 1:66–89.

Davies, Scott, and David Zarifa 2006. "The stratification of universities: Comparing Canada and the United States." Paper presented at the annual meeting of the American Education Research Association, San Francisco.

Downey, Douglas B., Paul T. von Hippel, and Beckett Broh 2004. "Are schools the great equalizer? Cognitive inequality during the summer months and the school year." *American Sociological Review* 69:613–635.

Drolet, Marie 2005. "Participation in post-secondary education in Canada: Has the role of parental income and education changed over the 1990s?" Analytical Studies Branch Research Paper Series, no. 243. Accessed October 23, 2007. http://www.statcan.ca/english/research/11F0019MIE/11F0019MIE2005243.pdf

Dumais, Susan A. 2006. "Children's cultural capital and teachers' assessments of effort and ability: The influence of school sector." In Maureen T. Hallinan (ed.), *School Sector and Student Outcomes*, pp 201–222. Notre Dame, IN: Notre Dame University Press.

Finnie, Ross, Eric Lascelles, and Arthur Sweetman 2005. "Who goes? The direct and indirect effects of family background on access to post-secondary education." Analytical Studies Branch Research Paper Series, no. 237. Accessed October 25, 2007. http://www.statcan.ca/english/research/11F0019MIE/11F0019MIE2005237.pdf

Frenette, Marc 2005a. "Is post-secondary access more equitable in Canada or the United States?" Analytical Studies Branch Research Paper Series, no. 244. Accessed November 22, 2007. http://www.statcan.ca/english/research/11F0019MIE/11F0019MIE2005244.pdf

Frenette, Marc 2005b. "The impact of tuition fees on university access: Evidence from a large-scale price de-regulation in professional programs." Analytical Studies Branch Research Paper Series, no. 263. Accessed October 26, 2007. http://www.statcan.ca/english/research/11F0019MIE/11F0019MIE2005264.pdf

Frenette, Marc 2007. "Why are youth from lower-income families less likely to attend university? Evidence from academic abilities, parental influences, and financial constraints." Analytical Studies Branch Research Paper Series, No. 295. Accessed October 28, 2007. http://www.statcan.ca/english/research/11F0019MIE/11F0019MIE2007295.pdf

Goldthorpe, John H. 1996. "Class analysis and the reorientation of class theory: The case of persisting differentials in educational attainment." *British Journal of Sociology* 47, 3:481–505.

Guppy, Neil 1984. "Access to higher education in Canada." *Canadian Journal of Higher Education* 14, 3:79–93.

Hertzman, Clyde 2000. "The case for an early childhood development strategy." *ISUMA: Canadian Journal of Policy Research* (Autumn):11–18.

Ho, Esther, and Doug Willms 1996. "Effects of parental involvement on eighth-grade achievement." *Sociology of Education* 69:126–141.

Hyman, Herbert H. 1953. "The value systems of different classes: A social psychological contribution to the analysis of stratification." In Reinhard Bendix and Seymour Martin Lipset (eds.), *Class, Status and Power: A Reader in Social Stratification*, pp. 426–442. Glencoe, IL: Free Press.

Johnson, David 2005. *Signposts of Success: Interpreting Ontario's Elementary School Test Scores*. Toronto: C.D. Howe Institute

Karabel, Jerome, and A.H. Halsey 1977. "Introduction." In Jerome Karabel and A.H. Halsey (eds.), *Power and Ideology in Education*. New York: Oxford University Press.

Kerckhoff, Alan C. 2001. "Education and social stratification processes in comparative perspective." *Sociology of Education* (extra issue):3–18.

Kingston, Paul 2001. "The unfulfilled promise of cultural capital theory." *Sociology of Education* (extra issue):88–99.

Krahn, Harvey, and Alison Taylor 2007. "'Streaming' in the 10th grade in four Canadian provinces in 2000." *Education Matters: Insights on Education, Learning And Training in Canada* 4, 2. Accessed October 30, 2007. http://www.statcan.ca/english/freepub/81-004-XIE/2007002/stream.htm

Lareau, Annette 2000. *Home Advantage: Social Class and Parental Intervention in Elementary Education* (2nd ed.). London: Falmer.

Lareau, Annette 2003. *Unequal Childhoods*. Berkeley, CA: University of California Press.

Lehmann, Wolfgang 2007. *Choosing to Labour: School–Work Transitions and Social Class*. Montreal and Kingston: McGill-Queens University Press.

Looker, E. Dianne 1994. "Active capital: The impact of parents on youths' educational performance and plans." *Sociology of Education in Canada: Critical Perspectives on Theory, Research and Practice*. Toronto: Copp Clark Longman.

Morgan, Stephen 2001. "Counterfactuals, causal effect heterogeneity, and the Catholic school effect on learning." *Sociology of Education* 74:341–374.

Morgan, Stephen 2005. *On the Edge of Commitment*. Stanford, CA: Stanford University Press.

Mullen, Ann 2007. "Elite destinations: How social background shapes educational choices." Unpublished paper, Department of Sociology, University of Toronto.

Murphy, Raymond 1979. *Sociological Theories of Education*. Toronto: McGraw-Hill Ryerson.

Porter, Marion, John Porter, and Bernard Blishen 1979. *Does Money Matter?* Downsview, ON: Institute for Behavioural Research.

Quirke, Linda 2006. "'Keeping young minds sharp': Children's cognitive stimulation and the rise of parenting magazines, 1959–2003" *Canadian Review of Sociology* 43, 4:387–406.

Raudenbush, Stephen W., and Anthony S. Bryk 2002. *Hierarchical Linear Models*. Thousand Oaks, CA: Sage Publications.

Rosenthal, R., and L. Jacobson 1968. *Pygmalion in the Classroom.* New York: Rinehart and Winston.

Schneider, Barbara, and James S. Coleman 1993. *Parents, Their Children, and Schools.* Boulder, CO: Westview Press.

Schofer, Evan, and John W. Meyer 2005. "The world-wide expansion of higher education in the twentieth century." *American Sociological Review* 70:898–920.

Sewell, William, and Robert Hauser 1980. "The Wisconsin longitudinal study of social and psychological factors in aspirations and achievements." *Research in Sociology of Education and Socialization* 1:59–99.

Shavit, Yossi, Richard Arum, and Adam Gamoran 2007. *Stratification in Higher Education: A Comparative Study.* Palo Alto, CA: Stanford University Press.

Statistics Canada 2005. "Student achievement in mathematics—The roles of attitudes, perceptions and family background." *Education Matters* 2, 1. Accessed October 26, 2007. http://www.statcan.ca/english/freepub/81-004-X1E/2005001/math.htm

Van den Berg, Axel 1998. "Is sociological theory too grand for social mechanisms?" In Peter Hedstrom and Richard Swedberg (eds.), *Social Mechanisms*, Chapter 9. Cambridge, UK: Cambridge University Press.

Willis, Paul 1977. *Learning to Labour.* Farnborough, UK: Saxon House, Teakfield.

Willms, J. Douglas 2002. *Vulnerable Children.* Edmonton: University of Alberta Press.

Wineburg, Samuel S. 1987. "The self-fulfilment of the self-fulfilling prophecy: A critical appraisal." *Educational Researcher* 16, 9:28–37.

Zeman, Klarka 2007. "A first look at provincial differences in educational pathways from high school to college and university." *Education Matters: Insights on Education, Learning and Training in Canada* 4, 2. Accessed October 30, 2007. http://www.statcan.ca/english/freepub/81-004-X1E/2007002/provdiff.htm

Choose Your Parents Carefully: Social Class, Post-secondary Education, and Occupational Outcomes

Harvey Krahn
(An original chapter written for this volume.)

INTRODUCTION

Rapid advances in the science of genetics over the past decade have made it possible for parents to pre-select the sex of their children with little chance of error (Boseley 2002). And, with cloning specialists shifting their attention from the animal world to the human species, it may be only a matter of time before someone chooses to bring a perfect copy of her- or himself into existence (Radford 2002). While the ethical implications of such actions need to be seriously debated, science has brought us to the point where parents literally can choose their children.

What if the laws of time and physics could be reversed, and we could choose our parents? Given the opportunity, whom would you choose? Famous parents?

Gorgeous parents? A loving, caring mother and father? Someone who would get off your back? This chapter concludes that, if you are concerned about your own educational and career future, and if you really could select your parents, you would clearly benefit from making them better educated and more affluent.

SOCIAL CLASS AND LIFE CHANCES

Throughout much of the twentieth century, sociologists from different theoretical camps have debated the extent to which *social class*—one's position in an economic hierarchy defined by occupation, education, or income—affects people's life chances (Grabb 2002). There has generally been

171

agreement that, compared with their working-class counterparts, middle-class North Americans enjoy a more comfortable and worry-free existence, tend to live longer and healthier lives, and are more likely to pass such advantages on to their children (Forcese 1997; Allahar and Côté 1998; Corak 1998). Even so, since at least the Second World War, counterarguments about the decline in importance of social class have also frequently been heard.

For example, it has been argued that the affluence generated by the post-war economic expansion in Western democracies has essentially eliminated the large pockets of perpetual poverty and the huge income disparities that had seemed so inevitable in earlier eras (Lenski 1973). Related to this, the rapid expansion of post-secondary institutions in Canada and the United States during the 1960s and 1970s (Clark 2000) allowed many more talented young people, even those born into poorer families, to acquire post-secondary credentials and, thus, move into better-paying professional careers. Daniel Bell (1973) proposed that, in post-industrial society, rigid social inequalities based on accidents of birth (e.g., were you born into a wealthy or a poor family?) were replaced by more fluid and less severe income differences based on educational attainment.

More recently, several European social theorists (Giddens 1991; Beck 1992) have suggested that the rapid social and economic change characteristic of globalized, post-modern society have provided young people with more opportunities to shape their own destinies, even though post-modern society has also generated more risks. In short, the argument goes, social class is no longer as relevant an explanation of social inequality as it once was; it is "an increasingly outmoded concept" (Clark and Lipset 1991:397).

However, researchers examining the connections between individuals' educational accomplishments and career outcomes and their family of origin continue to see persistent intergenerational patterns. Young people from more advantaged backgrounds are more likely to succeed in school and, subsequently, in the labour market (Looker 1997; Davies and Guppy 1997; de Broucker and Lavallée 1998; Davies 1999; Butlin 1999; Knighton and Mirza 2002). The most obvious explanations for such social class effects is that wealthier parents can pay for better and more secondary and post-secondary education.

In addition, children from more advantaged backgrounds are less likely to participate in non-academic (vocational) secondary school programs that typically leave graduates without the high school credits required for university entrance (Wotherspoon 1995; Andres and Krahn 1999). This "streaming" may be a function of teachers and advisers providing more encouragement and advice to middle-class youth compared with their less advantaged peers. It may also reflect the educational choices of working-class youth, who typically report lower educational and occupational aspirations (Andres et al. 1999) than their middle-class peers. The latter are more likely challenged by their parents and teachers to "aim higher."

Related to these patterns is the differential distribution of *cultural capital* (Bourdieu 1986). Children from more affluent backgrounds are more likely to have been exposed to the experiences (e.g., preschool education, a "book" culture in the home, exposure to the fine arts) and beliefs (e.g., "You have to get a university degree to be successful in life") that are valued in the formal education system and, therefore, are more likely to enjoy and do well in school (Andres 1994; Looker 1994; Davies 1999). In contrast, working-class youth without such advantages are more likely to do poorly and may, sometimes, even reject the values of an educationally focused society (Willis 1977).

Thus, despite the observations of social theorists who describe the declining relevance of social class, research findings clearly demonstrate that social class continues to matter. The most convincing evidence comes from longitudinal studies that track individuals as they move into, through, and out of the formal educational system into their adult occupational careers. The research results discussed below are taken from such an over-time study that monitored the educational and occupational ambitions and experiences of a large sample of Canadian youth over a 14-year period.

RESEARCH DESIGN AND METHODS

The Edmonton School–Work Transition Study began in 1985 as part of a larger longitudinal study of high school and university graduates in three Canadian cities (Edmonton, Toronto, and Sudbury).[1] Since this paper focuses only on the experiences of the Edmonton high school "class of 1985," the following discussion of research methods will be restricted to this educational cohort.

The original 1985 sample included 983 high school seniors from six different Edmonton high schools representing both middle- and working-class sections of the city. Survey participants completed questionnaires in class in May and early June of that year. Follow-up surveys were conducted by mail in 1986, 1987, 1989, and 1992. In each follow-up survey, attempts were made to contact only those individuals who had participated in the previous

wave of data collection (e.g., in 1987, no attempt was made to contact those who had not completed the 1986 survey). By 1992, cumulative sample attrition had reduced the sample to 404 of the original members of the class of 1985 (41% of the baseline 1985 sample).[2]

The 1999 follow-up survey was conducted by telephone since many of the postal addresses recorded in 1992 were out of date. In addition, the 1999 survey attempted to contact as many of the original 1985 respondents as possible, whether or not they had participated in all four intervening waves of data collection. Ultimately, after many telephone calls to locate and interview the study participants, 509 interviews were completed with original members of the Edmonton high school class of 1985 (about 5% completed questionnaires that they had asked to be mailed to them). This represented 52% of the original 983 respondents, and 57% of the 894 who had provided follow-up information in 1985. Almost all of the original sample members who did not participate in the study in 1999 could not be located or, if located, could not be reached by telephone, despite repeated call-backs. Very few (only 6% of the potential respondents) refused to participate in the 1999 survey.[3]

1985 Sample Characteristics

Fifty-one percent (n = 261) of the 509 respondents were female, and 49% (n = 248) were male. Two-thirds (65%) were born in 1967, making them either 17 or 18 at the time they were first interviewed in 1985. One in four (26%) were one or more years older (born pre-1967) while 9% were younger (born in 1968). All but three of the 509 respondents (99%) were single when first interviewed in 1985.

Eighty-five percent of the sample members were born in Canada, while 15% were immigrants, a proportion very similar to the proportion of immigrants in the city of Edmonton in the mid 1980s. Twelve percent of those who answered the survey question about race indicated that their mother was either Aboriginal or a member of another visible minority group. The same response pattern was observed for a second question about the racial origin of respondents' fathers.[4] On average, sample members had lived in Alberta for 14.8 years and in Edmonton for 13.7 years.

Two-thirds (65%) of the respondents' mothers were employed (either full-time or part-time) when the baseline survey was conducted in 1985, as were 86% of the fathers of sample members. Six percent of the fathers were unemployed at the time, as were 2% of the mothers. A considerably higher proportion (15% of fathers and 11% of mothers) had been unemployed at some time in the previous year. In total, 22% of the 509 sample members indicated that one or both of their parents had been unemployed at some point in the previous 12 months.

When surveyed in 1985, 38% (of those who answered the question) indicated that their mother had acquired at least some post-secondary education, with 18% saying their mother had a university degree. A full 50% (of the respondents who answered the question) noted that their father had participated in the post-secondary system following high school, with 28% indicating that their father had a university degree.[5] In total, 29% of the sample members reported that at least one of their parents had completed a university degree. In the following analyses, this simple binary variable—whether or not at least one parent had completed a university degree—is used to measure family socio-economic status (SES), a proxy for the concept of social class.

It is important to remember that all of the respondents in this study had managed to get to grade 12. Thus, high school dropouts are absent from the sample. Since the probability of dropping out of high school is inversely correlated with family socio-economic status (Gilbert et al. 1993; Tanner et al. 1995), it is likely that the very poorest sector of Edmonton's population (in 1985) was underrepresented in the study. Even so, there is still considerable variation in socio-economic status within the sample.

SOCIO-ECONOMIC STATUS (SES) AND HIGH SCHOOL EXPERIENCES/ PERFORMANCE

In total, two-thirds (64%) of the 1985 survey participants were enrolled in academic high school programs that should, if successfully completed, provide graduates with the course credits needed for university entrance. The remainder was enrolled in a range of non-academic programs. Using parents' university education as our basic measure of socio-economic status (SES), it is apparent that there is a strong relationship between family social status and the type of high school program in which youth participate (see Table 12-1). Five out of six (84%) students from higher SES families were enrolled in academic high school programs, compared with only a small majority (55%) of students from families in which neither parent had completed university. While this study cannot explain the process whereby "streaming" into different high school programs occurs, it can tell us whether it makes a difference for educational and occupational attainment.

TABLE 12-1 High School Program and Grades by Parents' University Education, Edmonton High School Seniors, 1985			
Parent(s)' Education	No Degree	Degree	Total
High school program			
Academic	55	84	64
Non-academic	45*	16	36
Grades in past year			
< 60%	16	12	15
60–69%	49	37	45
70–79%	28	34	30
80%+	7*	17	10
Total %	100	100	100
(N)	(360)	(149)	(509)

* Differences in percentages are statistically significant (p < 0.05; chi-square test).

Table 12-1 also demonstrates a strong relationship between family SES and students' performance in high school. One-half (51%) of the survey respondents from families where at least one parent had acquired a university degree reported average grades of 70% or higher in their senior year in high school, compared with only 35% of the young people from less advantaged family backgrounds. Again, this study cannot clearly identify the determinants of these grade differentials. However, other research suggests that the greater "cultural capital" available to middle-class youth is part of the explanation. In addition, as Table 12-2 suggests, young people from university-influenced households probably learn to place more value on higher education and, hence, may put more effort into doing well in high school. As university students know, higher high school grades improve one's chances of being accepted into university and, furthermore, into programs that lead to higher-paying careers and into "better" (higher- status) universities.

SOCIO-ECONOMIC STATUS (SES) AND EDUCATION VALUES

When first surveyed in 1985, the Edmonton high school seniors in the study were asked to indicate how much they agreed or disagreed with a wide array of statements about different aspects of education and work. Table 12-2 displays average responses to four of the education-related statements, broken down by our measure of SES (parents' university education). Only a minority of these young people agreed that "most of the classes at school are a complete waste of time" (mean score = 2.29 on a 1–5 scale) while a majority agreed that "overall, I have enjoyed my time in high school" (mean = 3.79). Differences by socio-economic status were inconsequential. These findings reinforce those reported by other researchers (Tanner et al. 1995; Davies 1999) who have concluded that there is very little evidence of

TABLE 12-2   Education Values by Parents' University Education, Edmonton High School Seniors, 1985

	Mean Scores*		
Parent(s)' Education	**No Degree**	**Degree**	**Total**
"Most of the classes at school are a complete waste of time."	2.26	2.36	2.29
"Overall, I have enjoyed my time in high school."	3.78	3.83	3.79
"Continuing my education will help me get a good job."	4.12	4.25	4.16
"For the sort of job I'm likely to get, you don't really need much education."	1.83[†]	1.61	1.76
(N)	(360)	(149)	(509)

* Respondents were asked to agree or disagree with each statement on a five-point scale, with "1" representing "strongly disagree" and "5" representing "strongly agree."

[†] Differences in means are statistically significant ($p < 0.05$; F-test).

"resistance" to formal education among high school students in Canada or of greater "resistance" among young people from less advantaged backgrounds.

However, we observe a somewhat different pattern of responses to the remaining two statements featured in Table 12-2. A very large majority of high school seniors agreed that "continuing my education will help me get a good job" (mean = 4.16), while a very small minority agreed that "for the sort of job I'm likely to get, you don't really need much education" (mean = 1.76). Sample members from higher SES families were somewhat more likely to agree with the first statement and significantly more likely to disagree with the second. Thus, while we find no evidence of outright "resistance" to the idea of formal education among less advantaged Canadian youth, we do see that, to some extent, they are less convinced of the ability of post-secondary education to improve their future labour market position. Nevertheless, even among grade 12 students from families where neither parent had completed university, a solid majority acknowledged

the career value of investments in post-secondary education.

SOCIO-ECONOMIC STATUS (SES) AND EDUCATIONAL/ OCCUPATIONAL ASPIRATIONS

The hints in Table 12-2 that middle-class youth are somewhat more confident of their ability to translate formal education into career success suggest that we might want to examine the post-secondary education plans and future occupational aspirations of these high school seniors. When asked in 1985, virtually all of the sample members indicated that they intended to acquire some post-secondary education— only 7% of the total sample said they intended to finish high school and nothing more (see Table 12-3). One-half (51%) planned a college (or technical school) education,[6] while four out of ten (42%) expected to acquire a university degree, including 17% who intended to complete a second degree. Knowing that, by 2000, only about 60% of all Canadian labour

TABLE 12-3	Post-Secondary Education Plans and Occupational Aspirations by Parents' University Education, Edmonton High School Seniors, 1985		
Parent(s)' Education	**No Degree**	**Degree**	**Total**
Post-secondary education plans			
Finish high school	9	1	7
1–2 years college	58	34	51
3–4 years university	22	34	25
5+ years university	11*	31	17
Occupational aspirations			
Managerial/professional	55	69	59
Other	45*	31	41
Total %	100	100	100
(N)	(360)	(149)	(509)

* Differences in percentages are statistically significant (p < 0.05; chi-square test).

force participants had at least some post-secondary education (Krahn and Lowe 2002:46), it would appear that not all of these 1985 study participants would, eventually, reach their educational goals.

These 1985 survey participants were also asked, "What kind of job or career do you want eventually?" and answered with responses such as "teacher," "mechanic," "rock star," "engineer," "hairdresser," and "lawyer." Recognizing that many high school seniors may not have firm career plans, their answers to a question like this still signal general preferences for employment in the future. To simplify the analysis, the many different specific occupational aspirations recorded by sample members in 1985 have been collapsed into two basic categories: "managers/professionals" (managers of all kinds and professionals such as nurses, lawyers, teachers, engineers, and artists) and "other occupational aspirations" (included here are all other lower-status occupations as well as the "don't know" responses provided by a

small minority of respondents). Table 12-3 demonstrates that well over half (59%) of the total sample hoped to someday be in a managerial or professional occupation, the type of job that typically pays better, provides more fringe benefits, and is generally more rewarding (Krahn and Lowe 2002). Since, by 2002, only 34% of all employed Canadians were in managerial or professional occupations (Krahn and Lowe 2002:67), it is again apparent that not all of these high career aspirations would have been attained.

Along with the high educational and occupational aspirations of the total sample, what stands out in Table 12-3 are the statistically significant SES differences. Specifically, two-thirds (65%) of the survey respondents from university-educated families expected to acquire one or more university degrees, compared with only one-third (33%) of those from families where neither parent had completed a university degree. The SES differences in occupational aspirations are not quite as large, but are still pronounced: 69% of the grade 12 students from more advantaged backgrounds hoped to become a manager or professional someday, compared with only 55% of the high school seniors from lower SES backgrounds. Thus, class background does matter for education and career plans.[7] Does it also matter for post-secondary education and career outcomes?

SCHOOL–WORK TRANSITIONS BY 1992

Only 404 of the original 1985 sample members participated in the 1992 follow-up survey. By this time, seven years after high school graduation, most of the study participants had effectively completed their transition from school to work, although a minority were still involved (mainly full-time) in the post-secondary system and a small proportion were continuing with (part-time) training relevant to their current jobs. Figure 12-1 shows

that 6% of the total sample (n = 404) had completed an apprenticeship by 1992, while 37% had acquired a college or technical school diploma. Within this category, two-thirds had received their diploma from a technical school and one-third had obtained a college diploma. Almost one-third of the study participants (32%) had obtained a university degree, and a small proportion (3%) had acquired a second degree. In total, 69% of the sample had acquired at least one post-secondary credential by 1992 (some had obtained several credentials—for example, a first and second degree, or a degree and a diploma).

With the exception of apprenticeships, an area where female respondents were conspicuously absent (2%, compared with 11% of males), Figure 12-1 reveals only small gender differences. Male sample members were somewhat more likely to have obtained a college or technical school diploma, while female study participants

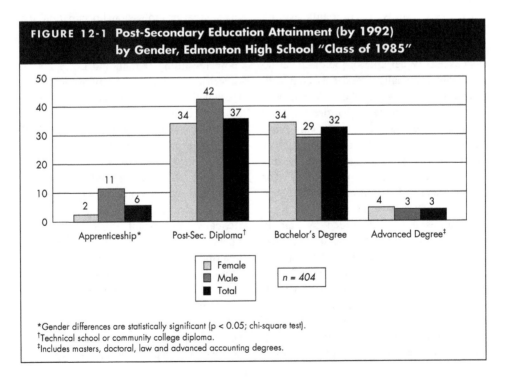

FIGURE 12-1 Post-Secondary Education Attainment (by 1992) by Gender, Edmonton High School "Class of 1985"

Female / Male / Total

n = 404

*Gender differences are statistically significant (p < 0.05; chi-square test).
†Technical school or community college diploma.
‡Includes masters, doctoral, law and advanced accounting degrees.

were a bit more likely to have received a university degree by 1992. Obviously, a more detailed analysis of the type of diploma or degree would have highlighted more distinct patterns of gender segregation (e.g., females with education degrees and males with engineering degrees). Overall, 67% of the young women in this study had acquired some kind of post-secondary credential by 1992, compared with 71% of the men who participated in the 1992 follow-up survey.

SCHOOL–WORK TRANSITIONS BY 1999

By 1999, the Edmonton grade 12 students who had first participated in the study 14 years earlier were now 32 years of age, on average. Two-thirds (66%) were married or in a long-term relationship, one-half (52%) were raising children, and six out of ten (61%) had purchased a home. One in six

(18%) were still participating in some kind of formal education, but most of this activity was part-time and much of it was career training relevant to current occupations. Figure 12-2 reveals that, by 1999, sample members had acquired some additional post-secondary credentials.

Twelve percent had completed an apprenticeship by 1999 (8% of the women and 17% of the men in the sample). Forty-three percent now had a college or technical school diploma. While the proportion with university degrees had not increased since 1992, by 1999, 5% of the total sample reported a second degree. Thus, it is apparent that the bulk of the school–work transition (and virtually all of the undergraduate university education) of these Edmonton youth had been completed within the first seven years following high school. In the next seven-year period, some study participants acquired additional non-university credentials and a few more went

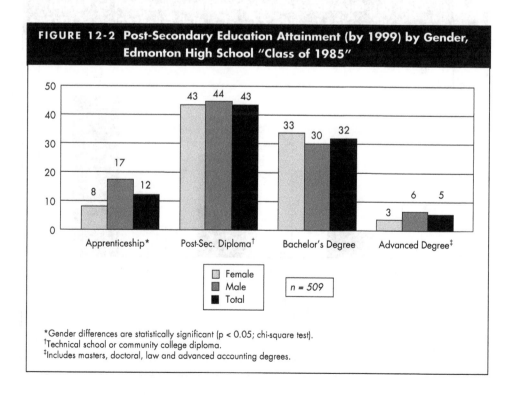

FIGURE 12-2 Post-Secondary Education Attainment (by 1999) by Gender, Edmonton High School "Class of 1985"

*Gender differences are statistically significant (p < 0.05; chi-square test).
†Technical school or community college diploma.
‡Includes masters, doctoral, law and advanced accounting degrees.

on to post-secondary training. In addition, gender differences in the acquisition of post-secondary credentials declined.

SOCIO-ECONOMIC STATUS (SES) AND SCHOOL–WORK TRANSITIONS

In total, 71% of the sample members reported at least one post-secondary credential by 1999. Fourteen years earlier, 93% had planned to obtain such credentials (see Table 12-3). The central question addressed in the following analyses is whether family SES—or, in other words, class background—had an impact on post-secondary educational attainment. Figure 12-3 demonstrates, very clearly, that the answer is "yes."

By 1999, 14% of the sample members from lower SES families had completed an apprenticeship, compared with 9% of the respondents from more advantaged backgrounds. Similarly, we see a small SES difference in the acquisition of post-secondary diplomas (46% versus 37%). However, we see a much larger difference in the opposite direction with respect to university education.[8] Figure 12-3 shows that, if at least one parent had completed university, the odds of children in this family completing university are almost three times as high as they are for children from families without a university tradition (56% compared with only 21%).

These findings document the huge impact of class background but cannot directly explain the differences. However, it is very likely that education values and ambitions, as well as familiarity with academic issues and discourse, differed significantly in

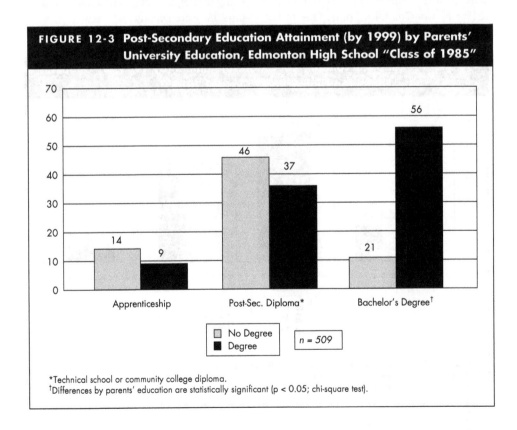

FIGURE 12-3 Post-Secondary Education Attainment (by 1999) by Parents' University Education, Edmonton High School "Class of 1985"

*Technical school or community college diploma.
†Differences by parents' education are statistically significant (p < 0.05; chi-square test).

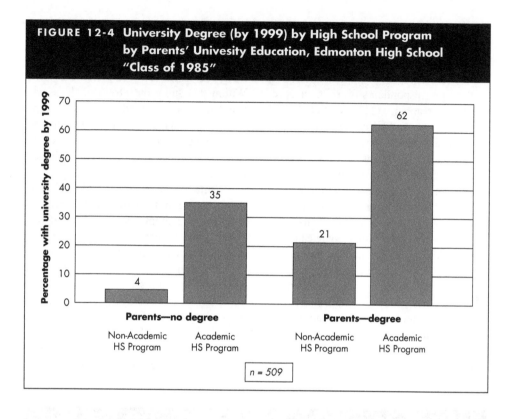

FIGURE 12-4 University Degree (by 1999) by High School Program by Parents' Univesity Education, Edmonton High School "Class of 1985"

the two types of families. Furthermore, as already noted in Table 12-1, children from more advantaged backgrounds were much more likely to complete an "academic" high school program that provided all of the necessary prerequisites for university education. Thus, Figure 12-4 reveals that only 4% of the 1985 sample members whose parents had not completed university and who had been enrolled in "non-academic" high school programs had completed a university degree by 1999. In sharp contrast, 62% of the higher SES graduates who had been enrolled in "academic" high school programs had a degree by 1999 (a ratio of 15 to 1). These differences in "cultural capital" were no doubt augmented by differences in parents' financial resources, the result being that middle-class youth were much more likely to have obtained university credentials by 1999.

SOCIO-ECONOMIC STATUS (SES) AND OCCUPATIONAL OUTCOMES

How well had the class of 1985 turned its post-secondary credentials into satisfactory employment? By 1999, 87% of the sample members (n = 442) were employed. Only 4% (n = 19) were unemployed, while the remaining 9% (n = 48) were out of the labour force, frequently for family-related reasons. Almost half (48%) of the employed study participants were in managerial or professional jobs, including 15% in managerial positions, 11% in science or engineering professional positions, and 10% in professional positions in the health care sector. Seven percent of the employed sample members were teachers, while the remaining 5% were in a range of other professional occupations. Just over

one-third (36%) were in lower-status clerical, sales, or service occupations, while
16% reported a variety of skilled and semi-
skilled blue-collar occupations.

Female respondents were overrepresented in teaching (11% versus 4% of
males), health-related occupations (16% versus 4%), and clerical jobs (30% versus 6%).
In turn, male respondents were significantly
overrepresented in science and engineering
occupations (17% versus 4% of females) and
blue-collar jobs (26% versus 4%). However,
when all of the different higher-status occupations are combined into a single category,
gender differences in managerial/profes-
sional employment were non-significant.

Figure 12-5 documents the extent to
which family background (SES) and
respondents' own educational attainment
had influenced their career outcomes.
While 48% of all employed sample members
were in managerial/professional occupations,

the odds of having acquired a higher-status
occupation were considerably higher (66%)
for young people from families where at
least one parent had completed university.
Within this sub-group, 89% of those who
had themselves acquired a university degree
were in a managerial or professional position when surveyed in 1999, compared with
only 38% of sample members without a
degree.

While a much lower proportion of
sample members from non-university
families had themselves completed university (see Figure 12-3), those who had
acquired a degree despite their disadvantaged background were still highly likely
(78%) to be in a higher-status occupation
by 1999. In contrast, only 30% of lower
SES sample members without a degree
were in managerial or professional positions. Looking at Figure 12-5 in another
way, when we focus on only those sample

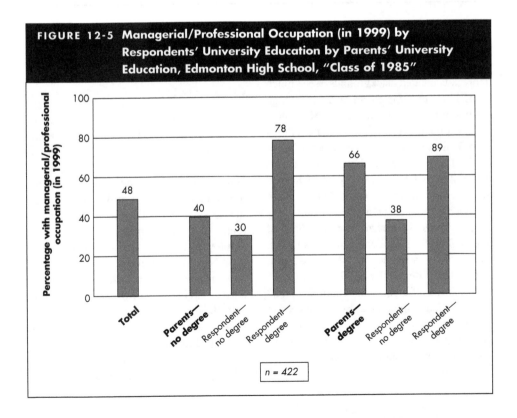

FIGURE 12-5 Managerial/Professional Occupation (in 1999) by Respondents' University Education by Parents' University Education, Edmonton High School, "Class of 1985"

n = 422

members with a degree, or on only those without a degree, in each case we see a class advantage. For example, among university graduates, 89% from a higher SES background were in managerial/professional occupations in 1999, compared with 78% from lower-status families. Thus, taking educational attainment into account, individuals from higher SES families still do somewhat better than their less advantaged counterparts.

SOCIO-ECONOMIC STATUS (SES) AND THE FIT BETWEEN ASPIRATIONS AND OUTCOMES

In Table 12-3 we observed that 59% of these young people had aspired to managerial or professional occupations when completing high school in 1985. The 1999 follow-up study revealed that very few (only 12%) were in exactly the same job they had mentioned 14 years earlier (e.g., nurse, auto-mobile mechanic). Less than one-third (30%) were in the same general type of occupation (e.g., health-related occupations, science and engineering). Using an even broader category, we find that only 36% had both aspired to a managerial/professional occupation and then, eventually, moved into such a career. Having observed that SES strongly influences both educational attainment and occupational outcomes, we now turn to a final research question: Does SES also influence one's chances of finding the type of employment that one had hoped to obtain?

Figure 12-6 provides a clear answer. A total of 268 respondents (59% of the total longitudinal sample) had aspired to managerial or professional occupations in 1985

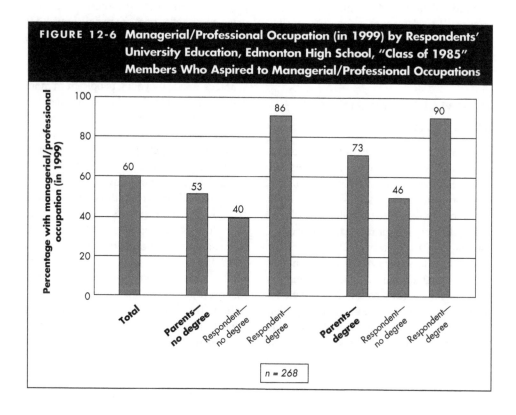

FIGURE 12-6 Managerial/Professional Occupation (in 1999) by Respondents' University Education, Edmonton High School, "Class of 1985" Members Who Aspired to Managerial/Professional Occupations

n = 268

(see Table 12-3). Sixty percent of these "high-goal" individuals had attained these goals by 1999 (see Figure 12-6). However, by the age of 32, only 53% of "high-goal" sample members from less advantaged families were employed in a managerial or professional occupation, compared with 73% of "high-goal" study participants from higher SES families. This big difference is largely explained by the previous findings that the children of university-educated parents were almost three times as likely as their less advantaged peers to themselves obtain a university degree (see Figure 12-3), and that a university degree significantly enhances one's chances of employment in a professional or managerial occupation (see Figure 12-5). Because of the latter, within both the lower and the higher SES groups the acquisition of a university degree doubled the odds of obtaining the higher-status employment to which one had aspired when leaving high school (see Figure 12-6). However, as we saw earlier (in Figure 12-3), lower SES sample members were much less likely to obtain a university degree.

SUMMARY AND POLICY IMPLICATIONS

Summarizing the findings from this longitudinal study of school–work transitions, we have seen that middle-class youth (1) typically do better in high school and are more likely to complete academic high school programs that will improve their chances of gaining entry to university; (2) are somewhat more likely to recognize the labour market value of post-secondary education; and (3) have higher educational and occupational aspirations. In the 14 years following high school completion, (4) members of this cohort acquired an impressive array of post-secondary credentials. (5) They were somewhat more likely to obtain college and technical school diplomas compared with university degrees. The over-time survey data clearly show that (6) children of university-educated parents were much more likely to obtain a university degree themselves; and, as a result, (7) were much more likely to move into managerial or professional employment and (8) to find the type of higher-status employment to which they had originally aspired when leaving high school. In short, these data analyses clearly demonstrate that social class, as measured by SES or parents' university education, continues to matter. In fact, it matters a great deal. So choose your parents carefully!

Class matters as a result of "streaming" into academic and non-academic programs in high school. It matters because of the different education values, and the different education and occupational aspirations, of teenagers from lower and higher SES families. It matters because more affluent parents can provide more financial support for their children's post-secondary education. Ultimately, class matters the most because of the different post-secondary educational "choices" made by young people from more and less advantaged backgrounds since, in our credential-focused society, a university degree continues to be the prerequisite required to compete for most of the better-paying, higher-status, and often more satisfying types of employment.

If social class matters this much, should we, as members of society, do something to reduce these SES-based differences in education and career opportunity? If you begin with the premise that public policy interventions are always inappropriate, then the answer is "no." Alternatively, you might argue that unequal education and employment opportunities as a result of family background are unfair.

You might also propose that an economy in which some potentially very talented people do not have equal opportunity to compete for the best jobs is an economy that is less productive than it could be. In that case, your answer would be "yes." Either argument invites suggestions for public policy responses.

Having observed the impact of "streaming" in the high school system—and, specifically, the much higher probability of obtaining a university degree if one completes an "academic" high school program—we should look carefully at how high school programs are organized and how young students are channelled into them. On one hand, it is difficult to reject the argument that some young people may not have the ability or aptitude to complete highly challenging high school courses that lead to university entrance. High school programs that lead to non-university careers are a useful and important alternative. On the other hand, it is possible that some young people who could complete "academic" high school programs are not encouraged to try, or are even actively discouraged, perhaps because of cultural capital deficits.

High school counsellors and others involved in advising young people about educational and career choices need to be acutely conscious of the significant impacts they can have on students' futures. In addition, high school programs, both "academic" and non-academic, need to be designed in such a way that young people in them can continue to make choices. For example, several Canadian provinces have designed youth apprenticeship programs that allow high school students to apprentice for trades while still obtaining the high school credits needed for university entrance, should they decide to go this way in the future (Lehmann 2000).

The longitudinal survey data examined in this paper highlight a substantial class effect on occupational outcomes, via post-secondary educational attainment. In other words, children of university-educated parents are much more likely to complete university themselves and, as a result, are more likely to obtain higher-status and more rewarding occupations. Greater access to cultural capital among middle-class youth is part of the explanation, but material capital—money—also plays an important role. Most of the Edmonton youth in this study had completed university by the late 1980s or early 1990s. As we might expect, many had taken out student loans, and many were still paying back these loans in 1999 when they were last surveyed. And, no doubt, many had relied heavily on parents to help finance their post-secondary education.

However, the cost to students of a university education in the late 1980s was relatively low compared with the situation today. In 1980, Canadian universities received only 13% of their total revenue from students' tuition fees. By 1995, this had risen to 24% (Little 1997:2), and tuition fees have continued to rise steadily in almost all provinces since then. In a number of larger universities, professional faculties have more than doubled their tuition fees in the past several years. As tuition costs continue to increase across the country, universities and provincial governments are promising to put in place funding programs to assist the less advantaged to attend university and other post-secondary institutions. It remains to be seen whether these new sources of financial assistance will be sufficient and, furthermore, whether they will really be directed toward the most needy. If not, we can expect to see an even more pronounced impact of social class on educational and occupational attainment in the future. As we have observed, class already matters a great deal with respect to post-secondary education. Without appropriate policy interventions of the type discussed above, it may matter even more in the future.

NOTES

1. The author of this chapter and Dr. Graham S. Lowe have been co-principal investigators in this study since 1985. The Population Research Laboratory, Department of Sociology, University of Alberta, has been responsible for data collection and processing. The largest funding source for this study has been the Social Sciences and Humanities Research Council of Canada (SSHRC). Alberta Learning has also provided significant amounts of funding.

2. Only 894 of the original 983 respondents provided their names and addresses for follow-up purposes. Hence, the 1992 sample of 404 represented 45% of the original respondents who might have participated.

3. Additional analysis of attrition bias in this longitudinal study (not reported here) indicates that female respondents were somewhat more likely to remain in the study from start to finish, as were 1985 respondents with higher educational aspirations.

4. Fourteen percent of the sample members did not answer these questions (or respond to the 1986 follow-up survey when the question was first included).

5. Ten percent of the 509 sample members did not answer these questions, presumably because they were unsure about how much education their parent(s) had acquired.

6. Included in this category are about 5% of the total sample who stated that they expected to complete one or two years of university.

7. Additional analyses (not reported here) checked for gender differences in high school experiences/performance, education values, and education and career plans. No statistically significant gender differences were observed.

8. Since only 5% of the total sample had completed a second degree by 1999, these results are not examined in this and subsequent analyses.

REFERENCES

Allahar, Anton, and James Côté 1998. *Richer and Poorer: The Structure of Inequality in Canada.* Toronto: James Lorimer.

Andres, L. 1994. "Capital, habitus, field, and practice: An introduction to the work of Pierre Bourdieu." In L. Erwin and D. MacLennan (eds.), *Sociology of Education in Canada*, pp. 120–135. Toronto: Copp Clark Pitman.

Andres, Lesley, Paul Anisef, Harvey Krahn, Dianne Looker, and Victor Thiessen 1999. "The persistence of social structure: Cohort, class, and gender effects on the occupational aspirations and expectations of Canadian youth." *Journal of Youth Studies* 2, 3:261–282.

Andres, L., and H. Krahn 1999. "Youth pathways in articulated post-secondary systems: Enrolment and completion patterns of urban young women and men." *Canadian Journal of Higher Education* 19, 1:47–82.

Beck, Ulrich 1992. *Risk Society: Towards a New Modernity.* London: Sage Publications.

Bell, Daniel 1973. *The Coming of Post-Industrial Society.* New York: Basic Books.

Boseley, Sarah 2002. "Call for ban on sex choice clinics." Special Report: The Ethics of Genetics. Retrieved December 13, 2002 (http://www.guardian.co.uk/guardian/).

Bourdieu, Pierre (R. Nice, trans.) 1986. "The forms of capital." In J.C. Richardson (ed.), *Handbook of Theory and Research for the Sociology of Education*, pp. 241–158. New York: Greenwood Press.

Butlin, George 1999. "Determinants of post-secondary participation." *Educational Quarterly Review* 5, 3:9–35.

Clark, Terry Nichols, and Seymour Martin Lipset 1991. "Are social classes dying?" *International Sociology* 6:397–410.

Clark, Warren 2000. "100 years of education." *Canadian Social Trends* (Winter):3–7.

Corak, Miles (ed.) 1998. *Labour Markets, Social Institutions, and the Future of Canada's Children.* Ottawa: Statistics Canada and Human Resources Development Canada.

Davies, Scott 1999. "Stubborn disparities: Explaining class inequalities in schooling." In James Curtis, Edward Grabb, and Neil Guppy (eds.), *Social Inequality in Canada: Patterns,*

Problems, and Policies (3rd ed.), pp. 138–150. Toronto: Prentice Hall.

Davies, Scott, and Neil Guppy 1997. "Fields of study, college selectivity, and student inequalities in higher education." *Social Forces* 75, 4: 1417–1438.

de Broucker, Patrice, and Laval Lavallée 1998. "Getting ahead in life: Does your parents' education count?" *Canadian Social Trends* (Summer):29–41.

Forcese, Dennis 1997. *The Canadian Class Structure* (4th ed.). Toronto: McGraw-Hill Ryerson.

Giddens, Anthony 1991. *Modernity and Self-Identity: Self and Society in the Late Modern Age.* Oxford: Polity Press.

Gilbert, Sid, L. Barr, W. Clark, M. Blue, and D. Sunter 1993. *Leaving School: Results from a Longitudinal Survey Comparing School Leavers and High School Graduates 18 to 20 Years of Age.* Ottawa: Minister of Supply and Services.

Grabb, Edward G. 2002. *Theories of Social Inequality: Classical and Contemporary Perspectives* (4th ed.). Toronto: Harcourt Canada.

Knighton, Tamara, and Sheba Mirza 2002. "Postsecondary participation: The effect of parents' education and household income." *Educational Quarterly Review* 8, 3:25–32.

Krahn, Harvey, and Graham S. Lowe 2002. *Work, Industry and Canadian Society* (4th ed.). Scarborough, ON: Thomson Nelson.

Lehmann, Wolfgang 2000. "Is Germany's dual system still a model for Canadian youth apprenticeship initiatives?" *Canadian Public Policy* 26, 2:225–240.

Lenski, Gerhard 1973. *Power and Privilege: A Theory of Social Stratification.* New York: McGraw-Hill.

Little, Don 1997. "Financing universities: Why are students paying more?" *Education Quarterly Review* 4, 2:10–26.

Looker, E. Dianne 1994. "Active capital: The impact of parents on youths' educational performance and plans." In Lorna Erwin and David MacLennan (eds.), *Sociology of Education in Canada: Critical Perspectives on Theory, Research and Practice*, pp. 164–187. Toronto: Copp Clark Longman.

Looker, E. Dianne 1997. "In search of credentials: Factors affecting young adults' participation in post-secondary education." *The Canadian Journal of Higher Education* 27, 2:1–36.

Radford, Tim 2002. "Italian promises cloned human baby in January." Special Report: The Ethics of Genetics. Retrieved November 28, 2002 (http://www.guardian.co.uk/guardian/).

Tanner, Julian, H. Krahn, and T.F. Hartnagel 1995. *Fractured Transitions from School to Work: Revisiting the Dropout Problem.* Don Mills, ON: Oxford University Press.

Willis, Paul 1977. *Learning to Labor: How Working Class Kids Get Working Class Jobs.* New York: Columbia University Press.

Wotherspoon, Terry 1995. *The Sociology of Education in Canada: Critical Perspectives.* Toronto: Oxford.

FURTHER REFERENCES— SECTION 2: SOCIO-ECONOMIC BASES OF SOCIAL INEQUALITY

Income, Wealth, and Poverty

Blais, Francois, and Jennifer Hutchinson 2002. *Ending Poverty: A Basic Income for All Canadians.* Toronto: James Lorimer & Company. The authors explore the idea of a universal basic income for all Canadians.

Halli, Shiva S., and A. Kazemipur 2000. *The New Poverty in Canada: Ethnic Groups and Ghetto Neighbourhoods.* The authors present a picture of urban poverty in Canada.

Hurtig, Mel 1999. *Pay the Rent or Feed the Kids: The Tragedy and Disgrace of Poverty in Canada.* Toronto: McClelland and Stewart. Hurtig documents the indicators of poverty and the growing disparity among Canadians.

Milanovic, Branko 2005. *Worlds Apart: Measuring International and Global Inequality.* In this book, the author compares patterns of income inequality in more than 100 countries. The analyses are often technical but provide a wealth of information on levels of inequality and how these have changed over time in different regions of the world and in different types of societies.

National Council of Welfare (http://www. ncwcnbes.net/). The Council has produced publications such as *Poverty Profile, The Child Poverty Profile* and, most recently, *Solving Poverty.*

Poverty Reduction (http://www.acdi-cida.gc.ca/ poverty). Information about Canada's efforts at national and international poverty reduction.

Raphael, Dennis 2007. *Poverty and Policy in Canada.* Toronto: Canadian Scholars' Press. This volume provides a unique perspective on poverty and its importance to the health and quality of life of Canadians.

Statistics Canada. *Perspectives on Labour and Income.* Ottawa: Statistics Canada. Published four times a year, this is an excellent source of up-to-date information on various topics related to the study of inequality, including income patterns. This source is also available online through the Statistics Canada website (http://www.statcan.ca). Catalogue 11-008-XIE.

Statistics Canada 2007. *Income in Canada.* This annual publication presents highlights and summary statistics on income and low income of families. The income concepts covered are market income, government transfers, total income, income tax, income after tax, and low income. This source is also available online through the Statistics Canada website (http://www.statcan.ca). Catalogue 11-202-XIE.

The Vanier Institute of the Family (http://www. vifamily.ca/). Publications about important issues and trends critical to Canadian families. This site has a Virtual Library with current readings and reports.

Occupation

Betcherman, Gordon, and Graham Lowe 1997. *The Future of Work in Canada: A Synthesis Report.* Ottawa: Canadian Policy Research Networks Inc.

Canadian Labour Congress (http://www.clc-ctc.ca). This site provides information on work from the unionized worker's perspective.

Canadian Policy Research Networks. Research Area: Labour Market and Vulnerable Workers (http://www.cprn.org/theme.cfm?theme=62 &l=en). A non-profit, charitable policy think-tank based in Ottawa. Its products are available for free at this website.

Duffy, Ann, Daniel Glenday, and Norene Pupo (eds.) 1997. *Good Jobs, Bad Jobs, No Jobs: The Transformation of Work in the 21st Century.* Toronto: Harcourt Brace Canada. In this collection of papers, the editors provide a range of analyses dealing with the apparent polarization of occupations into "good" and "bad" categories in recent years, and also of the problems of unemployment and underemployment for many workers.

Industry Canada (http://www.ic.gc.ca). This site provides information on the Canadian economy, trade, and jobs.

Krahn, Harvey, Graham Lowe, and Karen Hughes 2007. *Work, Industry, and Canadian Society* (5th ed.). Scarborough: Thomson Nelson. This text provides a comprehensive review of employment, the labour market, and workplace trends in Canada, and helps students to interpret these trends using different theoretical perspectives.

Lowe, Graham 2000. *The Quality of Work: A People-Centred Agenda.* Toronto: Oxford University Press. This monograph considers a number of important issues in the analysis of work in the contemporary era, including the future direction of occupational growth and the crises and problems posed for young people, the less educated, the unskilled, and others in their attempts to integrate themselves into the changing "new economy."

Rinehart, James 2006. *The Tyranny of Work* (5th ed.). Toronto: Thomson Nelson. This monograph explores the nature of work in Canada from a critical perspective, with a particular emphasis on the labour process and the alienating nature of work under capitalism.

Statistics Canada. *Perspectives on Labour and Income* and *Canadian Social Trends.* These two quarterly publications are invaluable sources of information on Canadian labour market and employment trends and issues. They are also available online through the Statistics Canada website (http://www. statcan.ca). Catalogue 11-008-XIE and 75-001-XIE.

Van den Berg, Axel, and Joseph Smucker (eds.) 1997. *The Sociology of Labour Markets:*

Efficiency, Equity, Security. Scarborough, ON: Prentice Hall Allyn and Bacon Canada. This collection of essays covers the major theoretical perspectives on labour markets and presents research findings from various studies of how labour markets operate.

Education

Canadian Policy Research Networks. Research Area: Education and Learning. (http://www.cprn.org/theme.cfm?theme=62&l=en). A non-profit, charitable policy think-tank based in Ottawa. Its products are available for free at this website.

Castellano, Marlene Brant, Lynn Davis, and Louise Lahache (eds.) 2000. *Aboriginal Education: Fulfilling the Promise.* Vancouver: UBC Press. The authors document the significant gains made in Aboriginal education in recent years.

Council of Ministers of Education, Canada (http://www.cmec.ca/). CMEC is the national voice for education in Canada. For example, see *The Transition from Initial Education to Working Life: A Canadian Report for the OECD Thematic Review.*

Davies, Scott, and Neil Guppy 2006. *The Schooled Society: An Introduction to the Sociology of Education.* Don Mills, ON: Oxford University Press. An examination of the intersections between Canadian society, education, and the labour market.

Guppy, Neil, and Scott Davies 1998. *Education in Canada: Recent Trends and Future Challenges.* Ottawa: Statistics Canada and Nelson Publishing. An assessment of Canadian education, from Confederation to the present, using materials from the Canadian Census. Recent decades are stressed.

Pocklington, Tom, and Allan Tupper 2002. *No Place to Learn: Why Universities Aren't Working.* Vancouver: UBC Press. The authors cast a critical eye on how Canadian universities work—or fail to work.

Programme for International Student Assessment (PISA) 2000 (http://www.cmec.ca/pisa/2000/indexe.stm). *Measuring Up: The Performance of Canada's Youth in Reading, Mathematics, and Science. First Results for Canadians Aged 15.* PISA, conducted in 2000 by the Organisation for Economic Co-operation and Development (OECD), tested more than 250 000 students from 32 countries.

Robertson, Heather-Jane 1998. *No More Teachers, No More Books: The Commercialization of Canada's Schools.* Toronto: McClelland and Stewart. The author reports on the increasing commercialization of education in Canada.

The Society for the Advancement of Excellence in Education (http://www.saee.bc.ca/). Provides non-partisan education research and information to policy-makers, education partners, and the public.

Statistics Canada 2007. *Education Matters: Insights on Education, Learning, and Training in Canada.* Catalogue 81-004-XIE. This is an online publication that regularly provides studies on a variety of topics of interest to students of education and social inequality.

section three

Ascription and Social Inequality

A. GENDER
B. ETHNICITY, RACE, AND ANCESTRY
C. AGE
D. REGION

A n historic moment was signalled by the signing in 1948 of the Universal Declaration of Human Rights (a United Nations initiative), which proclaimed the rights of all citizens. In the next decade, inspired principally by Martin Luther King, Jr., the U.S. civil rights movement riveted attention on the plight of blacks in North America. Throughout this era, the promotion of equality in human rights spread to include other ethnic, linguistic, and religious groups. Based also on equal rights for groups defined by sex, nationality, region, and physical ability, powerful social movements arose in the aftermath of the Second World War, transforming politics, economics, and culture the world over.

Many grievances of these disadvantaged groups were long-standing, with, for example, the struggles of women and Aboriginal peoples having had a tortuously long history. But in the late 1940s and early 1950s, following a world war

in which millions had died battling Hitler's racism, a new surge of human energy focused on promoting and advancing the opportunities of oppressed people. The racial bigotry of fascism had been crushed at immense cost, and a world sensitized to the brutality of human hatred was more accommodating to the idea of equal opportunity.

Perceiving a maturing of industrial capitalism in the post-war era, some social thinkers came to believe that the political fault lines of society, in the past often based on territory, religion, race, and ethnicity, would dissolve as democratic freedoms and economic opportunities flourished. With economic prosperity would come political modernization. An era of equal opportunity would follow, in which merit and effort would determine the distribution of social resources. Traditional social cleavages would pale in the face of a growing meritocracy, in which competence, achievement, and motivation would determine individual life chances.

In sharp contrast to this modernization view, other social thinkers foresaw growing conflict along class lines. Rather than a maturing of competitive capitalism, these theorists saw a period of monopoly capitalism, in which a class of wealthy owners prospered at the expense of others. The gap between the rich and the poor would widen, they believed. As consciousness of class interests grew, the eclipse of traditional cleavages would result, and class antagonism would obliterate old hostilities. The significant fault line of modern society now would be based on class interests grounded in the differential ownership of private property. Traditional conflicts among religious, racial, or regional groupings would be forgotten.

Neither of these two perspectives has served us particularly well in understanding the most recent social movements dominating the Canadian political scene. Neither view fits closely with the facts. The women's movement, the quest for native self-government, the rise of Quebec nationalism—these are all phenomena whose emergence, and magnitude, theorists of class antagonism or political modernization did not anticipate. People from a diversity of class backgrounds expressed group rights with vigour and dedication in a variety of "modern" countries.

At the core of any of these particular movements is a collective membership based on birthright. The women's movement or the black civil rights movement focuses on social groups defined by birth. Sex, for example, is not attained or achieved; it is determined at conception, and individuals have no say in the matter. However, as an ascribed attribute, sex is important sociologically only to the extent that people use it as a significant marker. Others react to us, make judgments about us, and generally orient themselves to us based on a variety of ascribed features, including our sex, race, age, ethnicity, and region.

Although distinctions involving sexes, races, or age groups are based on birthright, notice that it is the socially constructed distinctions around these birthrights that are significant for sociologists. The concept of "race" perhaps best illustrates this point. In apartheid-era South Africa, "race" was established by committee (under the Population Registration Act). This occurred because no group was "pure-blooded," no genetic differentiation could separate "white," "mixed," and "black" South Africans—such was the history of sexual mixing.

This is true more widely, in that all human groups are genetically mixed populations. The distinctions we make are based on those observable physical characteristics that we collectively choose to use as group markers. Race is not a biological construct, but a socially created system of classification. No "pure" racial groups exist.

Not only a process of social differentiation is at work here, but also invariably a hierarchical structuring, a stratification of dominant and subordinate groupings, occurs. Races were not only separated (differentiated) in South Africa; they were also ranked (stratified). The degree and the strength of this hierarchy vary across societies, but inequality based on ascription is a common feature of all societies. Ascriptive attributes are correlated with different scarce rewards: income, power, prestige. This is the context—the "vertical mosaic," as John Porter (1965) labelled the phenomenon of ascriptive inequality in Canada—within which various social groups have rallied to press for increased human rights.

In Canada, these social movements have found expression in an array of formal agencies and organizations, including the Assembly of First Nations, the National Action Committee on the Status of Women, the Canadian Human Rights Commission, and the National Advisory Council on Aging. Government policy initiatives in such areas as multiculturalism, bilingualism and biculturalism, non-traditional job training for women, and regional development have reinforced these movements.

GENDER

Social scientists distinguish between sex and gender. Sex is a biological concept referring to physiological differences between women and men (e.g., reproductive functions, hormonal variation). Gender is a social concept referring to socially constructed differences between women and men (e.g., femininity and masculinity).

In modern Canada, masculine traits entail being adventurous, forceful, and stern, whereas more feminine attributes include being gentle, sensitive, and warm. What it means to act or to think in a feminine, as opposed to a masculine, way depends on social expectations that vary both in time and space (see, e.g., Mackie 1991:1–7). As you will know from your own experience, although gender roles are social creations that we learn, there are powerful social expectations that allow relatively little deviation (which is why we treat gender here as ascribed).

The importance of this distinction for us is to underscore the idea that many differences between women and men are more the result of gender roles than of biological destiny. In modern Canada, women occupy a disadvantaged position on a variety of inequality dimensions, but this ought not to be regarded as some immutable, unchangeable fact of human nature. Although women who work full-time, full year, earn only about 71% of what men do and typically find themselves in jobs with relatively little power and responsibility, this does not mean that such inequalities are unalterable. Instead, as we noted in the preface to this volume, it means that the economic, political, and ideological control of privileged groups plays a formidable role in structuring and maintaining inequality.

Sociology has played an important role in addressing gender inequality. In the first chapter of this section, Janet Siltanen uses the discipline of sociology as a focus to show how women's experiences and gender inequalities have been addressed by different scholars. From a period in which women were largely invisible in scholarly research, two more recent stages have occurred. Beyond stage one, where women's experience was made visible, stage two was a period in which analysts and researchers sought to understand and explain that experience. In a third and more recent stage, the concept of gender, along with the related question of sexual identity, has become more contested.

In her chapter on who does the housework in Canadian households, Katherine Marshall looks at recent Canadian evidence that confirms that gender differences in the division of labour are still evident, if diminishing. Today's couples aged 25 to 54 have a more equal partnership in the sharing of financial, child-care, and household responsibilities but women continue to do significantly more housework than men. Even more interesting, although more people are doing housework, the time they spend doing housework has decreased. In dual-earner families, men's participation in housework has grown from 70% in 1992 to 74% in 2005, whereas women's has dropped from 94% to 90%. Men are doing more housework and women are doing less and so we see a convergence of gender roles beginning.

Gillian Creese and Brenda Beagan, in the final chapter in the Gender subsection, review trends in women's employment opportunities between 1930 and 2005, pointing to specific policy changes of particular significance to women. Their empirical evidence considers employment rates, earnings ratios, and occupational segregation, and they especially highlight policies dealing with both pay and employment equity.

ETHNICITY, RACE, AND ANCESTRY

As much as any country in the world, Canada has developed as a nation of immigrants. In the first paper in the Ethnicity, Race, and Ancestry section, Monica Boyd and Michael Vickers provide us with detailed evidence on the changing nature of immigration in Canada over the past 100 years. Among the many important patterns they identify is the movement away from European immigration and toward larger proportions of non-white or visible minority immigrants in recent decades, as well as the shift away from individual male immigration and toward more female and family-based immigrants in the latter decades of the 1900s. The authors also note the considerable ebb and flow in the number of immigrants that came to Canada in different stages or time periods. Interestingly, the amount of immigration at the end of the twentieth century was very nearly back to the highest level experienced at any time within that century—that is, to the level that occurred at the beginning of the 1900s. Boyd and Vickers spell out the various factors that have made for the ebb and flow, most of them rooted in politics and public policy. This chapter provides one of several illustrations in the book of how social status distributions and public policy are closely related.

What are the implications for inequality of the ways in which ethnicity, race, and ancestry are socially constructed? The next selection, by Feng Hou, T.R. Balakrishnan, and Rozzet Jurdi, starts to address this question. The analyses of recent census data in this article demonstrate that educational attainment, occupational status, and income level vary considerably across ethnic groups. The data show particularly that some "visible minorities" have lower levels of income than other ethnic groups, and have lower incomes than would be expected from their education levels. Further, some "non-visible minorities"—for example, certain European-origin groups—have approached income parity with the majority "charter groups," the British and French. This has occurred despite the fact that several European-origin groups have somewhat lower educational attainment levels than the average for the total population. Most visible minorities have higher educational attainment, and in a number of cases higher occupational status, but lower incomes than the average for the population.

Hou, Balakrishnan, and Jurdi go on to speculate about the causes of these patterns. They hypothesize that some groups may have better incomes than their educational credentials suggest they should because of "economic mobilization within the ethnic community." The ethnic community provides social support by providing employment and business opportunities for ethnic group members. Further, the authors believe that the earnings disadvantages of some visible minorities are likely related, at least in part, to employment discrimination. Programs intended to compensate for discriminatory practices against ethnic and racial group members have helped to lessen income inequality, but the effects of discrimination have not been completely erased (cf., e.g., Agocs and Boyd 1993).

The problem of racial discrimination is one of the important issues addressed in the next chapter, by Jeffrey Reitz and Rupa Banerjee. These researchers provide a detailed assessment of problems related to racial inequality and discrimination in Canada, based in part on their analysis of the 2002 Ethnic Diversity Survey. Much of their discussion considers the effects that racial and ethnic inequalities can have on social cohesion, and the social policy implications that flow from trying to enhance a sense of inclusion and shared citizenship among all Canadians.

In the final selection dealing with ethnicity, race, and ancestry, Charles Menzies examines the relations of Aboriginal peoples with the rest of Canadians, and shows that racial injustice toward this group is still evident in Canada today. Ancestry matters, and it matters as much now for First Nations people as it did at the time of first European contact. He enumerates forms of disadvantage in socio-economic attainment and important life chances experienced by Aboriginal peoples in Canada. He traces some of the history of dislocation that has beset the Aboriginal peoples of Canada, pointing out that this dislocation has its origins in the imperialist encroachment of European nations in pursuit of riches from North America's resources. For several centuries Aboriginal peoples have been placed in an increasingly dependent position, with their protests over land claim settlements or their calls for greater self-determination going unheeded. More recently, while these old demands remained unresolved, a new Canadian constitution was signed that contains no statements on the Aboriginal rights of the indigenous population. These rights, including self-government, have remained a basic demand of the Aboriginal peoples. Menzies describes how some progress toward self-determination has been made in recent years. However, he cautions us that this process will be particularly helpful for Aboriginals only if it is built on a sound economic base.

AGE

Gender and ethnicity/race/ancestry are but two ascribed attributes that have served to unite people around social issues. Age is a third. Consider this: Is it reasonable to have a minimum wage policy specifying that people under a certain age—often 16, 17, or 18—should be paid a lower wage rate than people a few weeks or months older? Should people be forced out of the labour force once they reach the age of 65, even if they are willing and able to continue working? Especially in the last decade, age discrimination has become a rallying point for

social protest. One particularly dramatic incident occurred in 1985, when Canadian pensioners successfully organized to oppose legislation proposed by the federal government to reduce pension benefits for seniors. Using the concepts of age grading and dependency, Guppy and Hawkshaw show how age relates to a variety of dimensions of social inequality.

The next chapter, by John Myles, examines the life courses of today's postindustrial cohorts and examines the differences in their lives, from the generation that matured in the 1960s and 1970s. Today's labour market is more knowledge-based and requires young people to attend school longer, which then delays their entry into the labour force and adulthood. It is also worth noting that the relative earnings of young adults have been falling for more than two decades. Postponed adulthood, combined with declining entry-level wages, means that both the cumulative earnings and the accumulated wealth of adults in their mid-thirties have fallen dramatically since the end of the 1970s. But these are the very people who are forming new families; often individual wage earners are making less money, although because of dual-earner households some families have increased their yearly income. This increases inequalities between singleearner families and dual-earner families. Myles states that postponed adulthood is the reason society has made so little progress in reducing child poverty. Coupled with the increase in the number of elderly, the postponed adulthood of post-industrial cohorts has decreased their expected socio-economic stability.

REGION

The last subsection on ascription shifts our attention from individual attributes to the community and regional contexts in which Canadians live. The chapter by Catherine Corrigall-Brown and Fred Wien provides considerable information on the extent of regional inequality in Canada with regard to unemployment, income, and related social indicators such as health, life expectancy, and educational attainment. The authors also review key explanations for regional inequalities and discuss some of the policies that governments have implemented to alleviate problems of regional disparity.

On first consideration, it might seem odd to include region as an issue under the topic of ascription. After all, people can choose to move from region to region. Thus, region of residence could be viewed as an achieved or attained status, because it can be changed by individual choice in a way that ascribed statuses like gender or race cannot.

Nevertheless, there clearly are ascribed aspects to the region variable. Region of birth, for example, is not a matter of personal choice and, moreover, is a good predictor of a person's ultimate place of residence. That is, people who are born in a particular region often stay in the same locality during their adult lives, because of the strong community allegiances, regional identities, and social ties that arise in early life and that constrain people to stay where they are, in spite of pressures or opportunities to go elsewhere. This may be especially true in a region like Quebec, where the French language is another strong bond keeping a large proportion of the population in that part of the country. However, the holding power of regional ties is apparent throughout the entire country— in the Atlantic provinces, the West, and elsewhere.

Region can also have lasting effects on people's stratification position and life chances. This occurs for at least two reasons. First, some Canadians have developed stereotypes about regional cultures and personality traits. We hear some people speak of "rednecks" from the West, "laid-back" Vancouverites, "unsophisticated" Newfoundlanders, and "anti-Canadian" Quebecers, for example. Certain expectations are then formed and judgments are made on the basis of what are typically misleading perceptions or impressions. Such attitudes, in turn, can have negative effects on how we deal with and relate to each other. Second, and equally important, inequalities of reward and opportunity are also structured by the communities and regions in which Canadians live. The regional disparities of the country often reinforce many of the structural inequalities that arise within the larger population, including the differences in corporate economic power, wealth, income, occupation, education, and so on that were discussed in Sections 1 and 2 of the book.

The central concern of this section on Social Ascription is the degree to which social inequalities are related to ascriptive factors. Despite the optimistic view of those who believe that ascribed statuses are becoming less and less important in contemporary Canadian society, the evidence reviewed in this section reveals that people's life chances continue to be affected in significant ways by race, ethnicity, ancestry, gender, age, and region. We are still a long way from the elimination of ascriptive inequalities.

REFERENCES

Agocs, Carol, and Monica Boyd 1993. "The Canadian ethnic mosaic recast for the 1990s." In J. Curtis, E. Grabb, and N. Guppy (eds.), *Social Inequality in Canada: Patterns, Problems, Policies* (2nd ed.), pp. 331–352. Scarborough, ON: Prentice-Hall.

Mackie, Marlene 1991. *Gender Relations in Canada.* Toronto: Butterworths.

Porter, John 1965. *The Vertical Mosaic.* Toronto: University of Toronto Press.

chapter thirteen

Inequalities of Gender and Class: Charting the Sea Change

Janet Siltanen
(An original chapter written
for this volume.)

If we date the women's movement in Canada from the late 1960s, it becomes possible to speak about "before" and "after" on virtually every topic that has been raised by feminists. This does not mean that everything changed in the way that the participants and supporters of the movement intended. But there was a sea change. . . .

(Hamilton 1996:42)

INTRODUCTION

Second-wave feminism was a movement for intellectual as well as political change. As the quote from Hamilton identifies, a vast range of topics was affected by its challenge to take seriously women's experience and gender inequality.[1] Sociology and, within it, the study of inequality were not exempt from this challenge. As people turned to existing traditions of stratification analysis, looking for intellectual resources and inspiration to address women's experience, they found little of either. Worse, they often found exactly the same male-oriented ideas and practices they were trying to challenge outside of academia.

In "before" forms of stratification analysis, men are the main characters of interest, and if women appear at all, it is usually in peripheral, supporting roles. The "sea change" in sociology, and in the study of inequality specifically, has meant that women's lives, and the inequalities between women and men, are less likely to be ignored or marginalized as topics relevant to the study of inequality. In the "after" forms of stratification analysis, women's experience and issues of gender are more frequently in the foreground. It is possible to observe some of this "sea change" by looking at how prominent Canadian collections of stratification research positioned women's experience and, more generally, issues of gender inequality.

Social Stratification: Canada, edited by Jim Curtis and Bill Scott and published in 1973, was the first collection of research wholly dedicated to the study of inequality in Canada. It was, and remains, an important landmark in Canadian sociology. At the same time, it has definite "before" characteristics—women's experience, and the analysis of inequalities between women and men, are absent from the stratification agenda. The themes organizing the book are, the editors say, an expanded list of the dimensions of the "Canadian Social Stratification System": occupational prestige, authority, income or wealth, education, ethnicity, and religion. A footnote to this list (Curtis and Scott, 1973:4, 7n) notes that while it "includes [the] most important dimensions of stratification in industrial societies it is not necessarily complete (for example, age and sex stratification might be included in a longer list)." In the collection as a whole, only 1 of the 21 articles addresses women's experience in any extensive fashion, and it focuses on low income and poverty.

This relegation of "sex stratification" to the end of a long list of inequality topics was to end. With the sea change, stratification analysis began to open up to the significance of women's experience, and gender, for the analysis of inequality. Twenty years on and in the first (1993) edition of the book you are currently reading, gender appears as a dimension of stratification significant enough to warrant its own section of articles. In a later edition, the gender section remains but in addition it is recognized that gender inequality cannot be segregated from other stratification issues. The 1999 editors (Curtis et al. 1999:v) draw attention to the fact that they "have worked very hard to ensure that various dimensions of inequality, for example, gender and ethnicity, have not been confined exclusively to isolated sections. While separate sections . . . are maintained, we include several articles in other sections that deal with these dimensions as well." There is a definite "after" taste to this later presentation of gender as a form of inequality that is important, not ghettoized as a specialized interest, and incorporated into other aspects of stratification analysis.

Incorporating gender has been a significant advance in the sociological study of inequality. Over the course of the last 30 or so years, there has been a close and critical engagement with conventional theories of inequality, and methods of stratification analysis, over the appearance and representation of women's experience and gender inequality. Earlier engagements often focused on the inclusion of women, or the sexual division of labour, as analytical considerations. The beginning of a more elaborate sociological interest in "gender" itself is usually attributed to Oakley (1972), who advocated distinguishing between the biologically given features of "sex" and the socially constructed characteristics of "gender"—a formulation that shaped the interest in gender inequality for at least two decades.[2] Thus, while earlier arguments addressed stratification by "sex," later formulations used the concept of gender.

It is important to realize that the conceptualization of gender has its own history. Early analyses of stratification regarded being male or female as an "ascriptive" characteristic: that is, a "natural" attribute beyond the influence of individuals or societies. However, the concept of gender was introduced as a challenge to the idea that feminine and masculine characteristics are natural and not subject to change. A gender perspective regards being masculine or feminine as a very social achievement that requires intense effort and scrutiny on the part of individuals and societies. Further, inequalities associated with being male and female came to be seen as socially created consequences of the way society is organized around gendered identities. For example, the gap in earnings between women and men is not a consequence of natural abilities or chromosome patterns. It is a result of how ideas of gender enter into the social organization of paid and domestic work. Later, the division between the natural and the social started to break down as the conceptual foundation for gender, and questions of race, sexuality, and sexual orientation emerged to confront the tendency to define gender in universal terms. This development in how we think about gender has had a significant impact on how we think about gender inequality.

As the theorization of gender developed, incorporating gender into theories of inequality posed tougher challenges. My purpose here is to show how challenges to stratification theory have intensified as the conceptualization of gender underwent its own development and critique.

The "after" era of stratification analysis has had many trajectories of theoretical elaboration and change, and feminist sociologists have had a go at just about all of them.[3] As an introduction to this important and lively area of scholarly work, we can identify three levels in the challenge to theories of inequality in the Canadian context. The challenges are distinguished as levels, rather than phases or stages, for two reasons. First, higher levels imply more extensive challenges to revise and rethink stratification approaches. The challenge intensifies with each level. Second, while we will see some chronological sequencing as we move from level one to three in the examples discussed in this chapter, challenges at levels one and two are not historically obsolete.

In this chapter, I use examples from the challenges to Marxist class analysis. I do this because it is in this area of scholarly work that some of the sharpest and most interesting debates have occurred, both

within Canada and internationally. Not all forms of stratification analysis have witnessed such intense scrutiny, nor provoked such profound questioning about the foundational dynamics of society.[4] As gender itself becomes a contested concept, as has happened recently in some quarters of analysis, contesting stratification on behalf of gender becomes a more elaborate and complex task. Marxist class theory has faced the toughest challenges yet—a testament to people's attachment to it despite its explanatory vulnerability in the face of women's experience and gender inequality.

THE THREE LEVELS OF CHALLENGE

The first level of challenge is to make women visible. The challenge of recognizing the existence of two genders involves the basic but fundamental argument that the study of stratification in sociology cannot be about men only. The inclusion of women, and women's experience, in the analysis of stratification is an essential condition for the credibility and validity of theories of inequality. One response to this challenge has been to see how women would fit into already developed theoretical concepts and arguments of class analysis. While this gives women an analytical presence, fitting women in can mean providing only a description of the inequality between women and men, and not an explanation of it. Or, it can sometimes mean gender inequality actually disappears from view. As significant as this level of challenge is, it leads somewhat inevitably to questions of *how* women's experience is to be included and *how* inequalities between women and men are to be addressed.

At the second level of challenge, inclusion of women into existing theoretical frameworks is not sufficient, and the focus shifts to the need to identify and examine gender inequality. Here arguments take issue with what counts as inequality and the ability of existing theoretical concepts to explain gender inequality. At this level, the insistence on the visibility and explanation of gender inequality forces a more substantial revision of class analysis. However, as we shall see, there has been a range of responses to this challenge, depending on how gender inequality is conceptualized.

At the third and most challenging level, the concept of gender is itself unsettled. Just as gender challenged class in terms of its claim to represent general experience, the possibility that gender has a single, unified meaning is challenged. Class and gender, it is argued, can no longer confront each other as if they each defined a homogeneous terrain of inequality. Inequalities cohering around, for example, sexuality and race cut through and specify gender as well as the relationship between gender and class. The need to particularize the meaning of gender (to say where, when, and how it is significant), as well as the configuration of class/gender relations, leads to further, deeper, questioning about the significance of class. At its strongest, this third-level challenge calls for a major repositioning of class and a fundamentally new approach to theories of inequality.

Let us consider now some examples of how Canadian and other scholars have worked through the three levels of challenge.

Level One: The Challenge of Acknowledging Women's Experience

In the "before" studies of stratification in Canada, many research projects and reports were exclusively and explicitly about men's experiences only. Canadian sociology was by no means unique in this regard, and feminist sociologists in Canada joined a chorus of voices, including those from the United States, Australia, and Britain, objecting to

the exclusion of women from the realm of stratification inquiry.

Marxist approaches to a class analysis of capitalism were very male-oriented. A Y chromosome seemed to be a prerequisite for entry into the work sites and industrial disputes of class action! For example, in *Class, State, Ideology and Change*, a "before" anthology bringing together Marxist scholarship throughout the 1970s in Canada, women's experience is discussed in 1 article out of 22 (Grayson 1980). Significantly, that one article is an examination of "institutionalized practices of excluding women" (Smith 1980:264).

In Marxist analysis more generally, however, scholars did find some attention to women's experience, particularly in terms of their oppression within the family. The classic reference point in Marxist scholarship for the discussion of women's position within capitalist society is Engels' late-nineteenth-century classic *The Origins of the Family, Private Property and the State*. In this work, Engels argues that women are essentially excluded from the central dynamic of capitalist commodity production. They are locked away in a privatized family form to ensure clear inheritance lines for accumulated private property. Indeed, at the time of Engels' writings, women were themselves part of the private property of fathers or husbands. Women's liberation, Engels asserted, requires release from this privatized existence, and rests with their full entry into the public world of productive relations.

Analysts in the mid twentieth century found some much-valued company in Engels' recognition of and objection to women's unequal position within the family. However, this analysis did not travel easily into contemporary arrangements. Two aspects concern us here. First, people were not content to see housework and child care as simply a private service to the husband. As Zaretsky pointed out (1976:94), "Engels fails to specify the place of women, as housewives and mothers, in relation to capitalist production." Second, by the 1960s the double shift was well established as the main profile of women's work. Women were not only labourers in the domestic sphere, but were now proletarianized as wage labourers. They were heading for "liberation" in Engels' sense of the term, although for women it often felt like anything but. So, Marxist analysis needed to consider how to include in the analysis of contemporary capitalism women's position as both domestic and wage labourers.

Marx's own writings are not helpful in this regard. His argument is that the dynamic of capitalism would do away with any distinctive social features of the labourers themselves. While women did work as wage labourers during Marx's time, and did have some distinguishing characteristics in terms of where and how they were employed, these divisions within wage labour were in his view antithetical to the dynamic of capitalism and destined to fade away. He also paid little attention to the activities of social reproduction located within the household. Although the reproduction of the working class was an important concept that entered into calculations of the value of labour-power and into the reproduction of capital, Marx was not interested in analyzing directly how this was accomplished. These matters can, he said (1976:718), be "safely" left "to the worker's drives for self-preservation and propagation."

Despite this limited assistance from Marx and Engels in determining how women might be included in the analysis of late-twentieth-century capitalism, there was a concerted effort to incorporate women's contemporary experience into Marxist class analysis. Two areas received special attention in Canadian scholarship: incorporating women's domestic labour via the labour theory of value, and incorporating women's wage labour via the concept of the reserve army of labour.

To bring domestic labour into the dynamics of capitalist production, many attempts were made to understand domestic labour in terms of Marx's labour theory of value. The "domestic labour debate" was about whether and how women's domestic labour could be seen as contributing to the extraction of surplus value, which is the basis of the exploitative relationship between capitalists and the proletariat. As Fox noted (1986:182), "the explicit aim of the domestic labour debate . . . was to come to an understanding of the relationship of the private household to capitalist commodity production."[5] When it came to fitting women's waged labour into Marxist theory, people argued that capitalists used women's wage labour as a form of reserve. Women are, in Connelly's (1978) formulation, "last hired and first fired." While the experience of the Second World War is often referred to as the prime example of using women as a reserve of labour, it was argued that this practice continued subsequently as a feature of the organization of the capitalist labour force. A reserve of (female) labourers willing, for whatever reasons, to be employed with substandard wages, benefits, and working conditions creates competitive pressure on the (male) employed population to accept degradations in their employment conditions and remuneration in order to keep their jobs.

Limitations of the "Stretch to Fit" Strategy

At this level of challenge to conventional theory, the interest is to recover women's experience, giving it visibility and relevance. This in itself is an important strategy and achievement. Obviously, those who responded positively by attempting to fit women into existing formulations of class analysis recognized the claims of the feminist critique, and saw the significance of the need to have women's experience included.

As additional motivation, a theory of class that has no place for women's experience was going to lose relevance as an explanation of contemporary inequality. While there was considerable debate about whether Marxist categories could be "stretched to fit" aspects of women's experience, there was, even among those who initially saw value in the attempt, a recognition that to address the inequality in women's and men's experience comprehensively, concepts and ideas needed to be derived from the problematic of gender inequality itself. Further, many analysts were concerned that the aim of addressing the oppression of women was being subsumed by an agenda to salvage Marxist theory. Attempts to bring feminism and Marxism together were producing, in Hartmann's (1981) well-known metaphor, an "unhappy marriage," with the identity of feminism becoming obscured by the partnership.

Responding to the critique of neglect by fitting women into existing frameworks leaves unanswered the question of why women were not there in the first place. This is not an accidental absence—it's not that people just forgot to put them in. As Crompton and Mann archly comment, "It is not the case ... that gender has been simply omitted from stratification analysis by default" (1986:2). The exclusion of women's experience is a reflection of the particularity of the theoretical framework. While claiming it to be a *general* theory, it was in fact a *gendered* theory—from the vantage point of, and primarily about, male experience.

Several commentators of the time insisted that such practices of active exclusion amounted to a form of intellectual sexism in academic approaches to the analysis of inequality. As an early American commentator observed, "sex has rarely been analyzed as a factor in stratification processes and structures, although it is probably one of the most obvious criteria of social differentiation and one of the most obvious bases of economic, political

and social inequalities" (Acker 1973:340). Indeed, the "before" analysis of stratification fits many of the criteria Eichler (1988) identifies as "sexist" research.

Women's experience was not in stratification theory and research because it was thought to be irrelevant to the identification and location of the processes of inequality as defined by Marxist analysis. It's not surprising, then, that many aspects of what was identified as women's oppression, and gender inequality, both within the experience of labour and outside it, were just not being captured by the Marxist analysis of class. This includes, for example, issues of sexuality, the medical domination of women's reproductive health, the experiences of violence, and the silencing of women's creative and political voices. It was, in part, discontent with how the "stretch to fit" strategy narrowed the conceptualization of what counts as gender inequality and women's oppression that prompted some to move to the second level of critique.

Before moving on to examine the next level of challenge, it is important to observe briefly that the need to be alert for this first level of challenge has not diminished. While much has changed, theories of inequality, including neo-Marxist ones, continue to emerge that construct their vision of society aligned with the centrality of male experience. A recent example is theories of the development of welfare states that identify working-class politics, the compulsion of wage labour, and class struggle as the central dynamics in the formation of welfare states. Again, much of this struggle and politics is focused on men's experience. What feminists have argued, repeatedly, is that this historical story leaves out women and "women's issues" from the development of the welfare state. Almost 20 years ago, Andrew (1984) was motivated by the absence of women from this area of work to insist that the history of welfare state development needed reinterpreting in order to bring women's experience and contributions to light. And, more recently, similar arguments have had to be made against formulations in the comparative welfare state literature, which excludes much of women's experience through its "focus on male workers' decommodification" (O'Connor et al. 1999:19). As we seem fated to continually discover, the privileging of men's experience is by no means an obsolete feature of sociological accounts.

Nevertheless, having won, for the most part, the argument about the necessity of including women's experience, the manner of inclusion becomes a key area of attention. For many this raised significant questions about the conceptualization of gender, and its explanatory status vis-à-vis class.

Level Two: The Challenge of Explaining Gender Inequality

At this level of challenge, the inclusion of women's experience is a necessary but not sufficient response to the interest in inequalities between women and men. As identified by Maroney and Luxton (1987:9, 11), there is a need to move "beyond the stage of 'adding women on' to make a genuine attempt to theorize gender." The general challenge is to include a concept of gender in the analysis of inequality, and there have been many discussions about how this might be done. In all responses to this second-level challenge, class is not abandoned as a central explanatory concept. Discussions are about how gendered experience is to be positioned with respect to class processes. As we shall see, there have been different interpretations of just how challenging it is to conventional frameworks to think about inequalities of gender *and* class. In part, this rests on how people conceptualize gender in their analysis. This conceptualization can range from, at one end of the spectrum, an empirically identified

dichotomous variable to, at the other end, a theoretical concept referring to a systematic and socially structured relationship of inequality. There is a fairly broad consensus that some sort of revision to Marxist class analysis is required; the disputed question is, how much?

Starting in the 1980s, there emerged in Canadian scholarship a debate about the appropriate positioning of gender inequality in relation to theories of class inequality. There were two related questions: (1) is there a uniquely identifiable structure of social processes responsible for producing gender inequalities; and (2) if there is such a structure, how does it connect with the structure and dynamic of capitalism?

One position in the debate advocated using Marx's method of analysis—dialectical materialism—to revise class analysis in ways that better reflect the historical and contemporary reality that the working class has two sexes. In doing so, Armstrong and Armstrong (1986) answered "no" to the first question. They argue that both gender inequality and class inequality are products of the capitalist system. "Patriarchy and capitalism are not autonomous, not even interconnected systems, but the same system. As integral forms, they must be examined together" (1986:226). In this view, a sexual division of labour is a definitive feature of capitalism and, therefore, class is gendered and gender classed. A key aspect of the Armstrongs' argument is that all aspects of class, at all level of analysis, are gendered.[6]

This contrasted with the positions of Connelly (1986:241) and Jensen (1992:201), who both argued that the significance of gender is specified by the level of analysis. The abstract analytical level of capitalism is gender-free, but specific formations of capitalist societies must be analyzed as forms of gendered class. Jensen (1992:215) argues, "a system of gendered power can be acknowledged and resisted without immediately requiring that it be articulated at the highest level of abstraction to the capitalist mode of production." In her formulation, gender and class would not have the same analytical status. We can accept, Jensen argued, that gender relations are not reducible to class relations without sacrificing the analytical primacy of class.

For Connelly, a similar specification of levels of analysis resolves the need to acknowledge gendered relational forms that pre-existed, and went into the formulation of, capitalist relations. She takes issue (1986:245) with Armstrong and Armstrong's notion that "the sexual or gendered division of labour is essential at the level of the capitalist mode of production." Similar to Jenson, Connelly argues that it is at the level of concrete social formations that capital exists alongside and in competition with other forms, including gender. "At this level the focus is on how the relations of production intersect, combine and conflict with the relations of gender in different classes and within different historical periods within one society, and in different societies" (Connelly 1986:246).

Although there is some disagreement in these three positions as to the exact formulation of the gender and class relation, all agree that a theory of capitalism can be revised to encompass gender inequalities. A different position is adopted by those analysts who identify gender inequality as having a more autonomous relation to capitalism. They answer "yes" to question 1 (Is there a unique gender structure?) and go on to explore answers to question 2 (How does this gender structure relate to capitalism?). Class and gender are historically connected, but independent processes also affect the trajectory of each. Whereas the previous arguments limited the contemporary operation of gender to within levels of capitalist class formations, this alternative approach is premised on the more limited operation of class.

For example, in *Relations of Ruling*, Clement and Myles adopt something akin to a "dual-systems" approach in setting out

the relationship between gender and class. Dual systems theory (Hartmann 1981) was developed in response to the observation that the categories of capitalism are "sex-blind." They could identify the "empty places" of capitalist social organization but could not give an explanation of who filled those places. A theory of gendered hierarchy, or patriarchy, was needed to identify the positioning of individuals within the structure of capitalism. In setting out their orientation to the contemporary configuration of class and gender, Clement and Myles state (1994:35): "The significant fact about the postindustrial division of labour, then, is not so much that the working class of industrial capitalism has come to an end. Rather, a new working class employed in services has grown up alongside it. And superimposed on this material division of labour is a social division based on gender."

One aim of their analysis is the gendering of class theory, and they conclude that the "class structures of the developed capitalist economies are also neo-patriarchal structures . . . " (1994:140). They refer, ultimately, to the "feminization of the class structure" which occurs "not despite, but because of patriarchy" (1994:243, 245).

One way to think about the turn to dual systems theory is that it involves the recognition that class categories cannot be the basis of a general theory of inequality. However, that the dynamics of capitalism cannot account for patterns of inequality that have been thought of as central to the operation of capitalist relations of production— patterns such as who fills what positions and what people earn—is a major blow to any claim that the general structuring principle of industrial or post-industrial society is the market relations of the capitalist mode of production.

This possibility provides the framework for an investigation by Li (1992) into the extent to which race and gender "fractionalize" class categories. He asks (1992:492), "what are the consequences of race and class as bases of class fractions on earnings within each specific class?" The dependent variable in Li's analysis is earnings from employment and self-employment. The independent variables include the main three that are of interest—social class, race, and gender—plus controls for industrial sector, education, and hours of work. Li uses the neo-Marxist class scheme developed by Erik Olin Wright to define social class. This means using five class categories (employers, managers, professionals, petty bourgeoisie, and workers), with each distinguished on three dimensions: (1) ownership of capital, (2) control of capital and, (3) control of labour.

In the analysis, Li finds that "race and gender fractionalizations operate more strongly among wage-earners than among those who own and control capital" (1992:503). He concludes that his analysis says something to the debate about the relative importance of class, gender, and race in processes of inequality. At least in the case of income inequality, his results suggest that class carries no ultimate explanatory weight. Processes producing race and gender as lived experiences of differentiation and inequality carry equal, if not more, weight.

The growing recognition of the significance of race and ethnicity in identifying different experiences of inequality *among* women led analysts to realize that they could not be content with a simple, dichotomous presentation of gender. Detailed investigations of women's experiences of inequality showed the importance of recognizing differences among women. Ng's (1986) investigation of a community-based employment counselling and placement agency reveals the minute acts and assumptions that come together to create "immigrant women" as a distinct category of labour. Research into patterns of employment in the garment industry (Gannagé 1987) showed a form of work organization etched by ethnic, gender, and skill distinctions creating complex networks of solidarities and feelings

of division. Research on work within the domestic sphere also exposed inequalities among women. Arat-Koc (1989) examined the lives of immigrant women working as live-in domestic workers in Canada, a situation in which housework "becomes the responsibility of *some* [women] with subordinate class, racial and citizenship status, who are employed and supervised by those who are liberated from . . . physical burdens" (1989:53). She concludes that the domestic service relationship, between female employer and female employee, is one that adds class and race complexities to gender inequalities.

This research on patterns of inequality within gender categories foreshadows the shift to the third level of challenge. It is evidence that a dichotomous concept of gender, with a single fixed meaning, is too limited a formulation for the many variations and possibilities of gendered experience. The recognition of variation within gender, race, and class categories, and of different patterns of relations between these forms of experience, sets the scene for a more nuanced and complex picture of the inequality to be explained.

Level Three: The Challenge of Multiple Genders, and Complex Inequality

As attempts to develop an understanding of the relationship between class and gender proceeded, debates within feminism and feminist sociology were beginning to unsettle previously held ideas about gender. The notion that we could separate sex from gender started to break down, as people came to accept the impossibility of separating the "natural" and the "social." Delphy, Stanley, and others shook the foundations of the sex/gender division by inverting what had become the common formulation and suggesting that our understanding of biological sex is a consequence of gendered thinking.[7] Analysts were on the lookout for tendencies to essentialize gender—that is, to use concepts of femininity and masculinity as if they had singular, fixed, and ahistorical social meanings.[8] More dramatically still, the fissures within women's experience—the differences and inequalities between women themselves—were demanding their due attention. Authors argued that the naturalizing process challenged by feminists in terms of gender identities was noticeable in the case of race, even within feminist analysis itself (Kobayashi and Peake 1994). Racialized difference and inequality had been erased in most approaches to gender and class. As Bannerji (1995:31) expresses it, "the type of difference encoded by 'race' adds a peculiar twist to gender. In societies such as ours in Canada not only is all labour gendered . . . but all forms of gendered labour are 'raced.'" Recent research continues to demonstrate deep and deteriorating racial divisions in where Canadians labour and with what rewards—divisions that distinguish, for example, white, native-born men from all others, and white women from their Aboriginal sisters (Creese 2007, White et al. 2003).

In addition, and in part inspired by postmodernist approaches, researchers became increasingly aware that the meanings of gender and class, and even their salience, can be highly varied depending on context and the particular circumstances being investigated. There is, in other words, a trend toward regarding the relevance and substance of dimensions of stratification as questions for, and not assumptions of, research.

As theoretical work around the concept of gender starts to confront the need to be more specific about the meaning and significance of gendered experience, a similar contextualizing is being suggested in terms of class.[9] In effect, the claim that class has meaning as an abstract, general process of inequality is abandoned, and its place in explanations of inequality becomes more open to investigation. One strategy has been to focus on intersections of inequality dimensions, including class, gender, race, dis/ability, and sexuality, with commitments to investigate the potential relevance of all dimensions.

In Canadian scholarship, the main development that builds on the problematizing of gender challenges the practice of assuming the validity of theoretical (including class) perspectives. There is a move to a multidimensional approach to inequality with no presumption of the *relative importance* or *particular configuration* of any dimension. As Creese and Stasiulus (1996:8) set it out, "When we shift our theoretical lens to the intersections between and among relations of gender, race, class and sexuality, we extend the boundaries of political economy by challenging the 'categorical hegemony' attempted by many Marxists with class, many feminists with gender." As they note, however, care must be taken not to regard patterns of intersectionality as socially or historically predetermined.

This position is echoed in several other attempts in Canadian research to grasp inequality as a complex phenomenon that may have a unique configuration in specific circumstances. For example, Parr's historical analysis of the variable gendered pattern of labour in two Ontario manufacturing towns prompts her to urge us to adopt an approach of "presuming less" about the relevance of theoretical categories and their relation to configurations of daily life in specific settings (1990:231). She summarizes the current intellectual challenge as needing to think beyond the "assertion of an ahistorical hierarchy of oppressions . . . to rethink the categoricalism that canonizes gender, class, race, ethnicity and nationality" (1990:8). In Evans and Wekerle's approach to the development of the Canadian welfare state, they reject "a position that placed gender in contestation to, or ranked in a hierarchy with class and race" and commit themselves to promoting a perspective that examines "variability over time and place" (1997:9). This position is also adopted by Seccombe and Livingstone (1996) in their proposed development of a materialist understanding of group consciousness in the context of work. They aim to "break with a 'class first' framework that treats gender, generational and race relations as subsidiary to, or somehow derived from, class relations" (1996:131). More recently, a collection of Canadian research on work aligns the premise of the centrality of gender and race in the analysis of work in neo-liberal capitalism, with the recognition that precise patterns of inter-relations show considerable complexity and variation within and across public and private workplaces (Shalla 2007).

A very significant current question for the analysis of the complexity of inequality, however, is one of methodology. How are we to analyze inequality as a complex, multi-dimensional social process whose exact configuration varies across time and place? An earlier answer to this question (as in the dual systems theory approach) was to regard each dimension as simply additional information about the pattern of inequality. Known as an "additive model," this approach is where one would add, to an analysis of class, considerations of gender, race, disability, age, minority status, citizenship, and so on. The problem with an additive approach is that it cannot cope with the complex connections and interactions between various dimensions of oppression. It is the complexity of intersectional analysis that lies behind both its appeal and its methodological challenge.

Recently, an American sociologist has suggested a way to think about the complexity of intersectionality and a way to approach it analytically. McCall (2005) identifies two forms of analysis that can focus on the categorical complexity of intersecting dimensions of inequality and

oppression: intracategorical analysis and intercategorical analysis.

The main focus of intracategorical analysis is to reveal the experiential realities of individuals and groups positioned at specific intersections of oppression. This is probably the most common form of intersectional analysis done in Canadian academic and government-sponsored research. For example, one of the research reports in the Status of Women's Integration of Diversity initiative (Côté et al. 2001) looked at the experiences of French-speaking, family-sponsored immigrant women living in Ontario—an intersection of disadvantages along dimensions of gender, language, immigration class, and visible minority status. Another (Kenny et al. 2002) examined experiences of culture, education, and work among Aboriginal women—not considered as an undifferentiated group, but distinguished by diversity in their Aboriginal ancestry (Inuit, First Nations, Metis) and regional circumstances. Bruckert's analysis of the strip trade is also an excellent example of an intracategorical analysis. She highlights the intersecting dimensions of gender and class experienced by women whose livelihood is a form of sexualized labour (Bruckert 2002).

As McCall notes, the exploration of intracategorical complexity is typically qualitative, and draws on the rich developments within feminist and sociological research practices designed to reveal and express the depth and complexity of lived experience. McCall argues, however, that this offers an important but limited view of intersectionality. She makes the point that in this form of analysis "complexity derives from the analysis of a social location at the intersection of single dimensions of multiple categories" (McCall 2005:1781). For an analysis that examines the full range of possible intersections, she recommends an intercategorical approach.

To appreciate the systemic and structured nature of intersecting multiple dimensions of inequality, it is important to examine complexity as a feature of relationships between as well as within *all* categories of the dimensions of interest. If gender is operating in a particular context as a structuring mechanism of inequality, we need a comparison between men and women to establish this. If we are then interested in the intersection of gender and visible minority status, we need to contrast and compare the experience of men and women within each category of visible minority status, as well as contrast and compare the experience of all visible minority groups within each gender category. Such an inter-categorical analysis would be able to tell us which dimensions are having a structuring effect and whether any existing effects are modified or contextualized by their intersection with other dimensions. This type of approach can only be conducted in practice with forms of analysis that can handle inter-categorical complexity. Typically, this form of analysis is quantitative.

There is talk in discussions of feminist methodology in Canada of revisiting quantitative methodologies to find ways of claiming them for feminist purposes (for example, see Rose 2001). In a recent review of American trends in feminist methodology, an emerging interest in the possibilities of quantitative analysis is also noted (Fonow and Cook 2005). In this light, McCall's argument is very timely. She presents a strong case for the value of certain forms of quantitative research in advancing the analysis of intersectionality. The report of her own quantitative intercategorical analysis of the relative weight of gender, class, and race on wage inequalities in four American cities piques one's interest in the possibilities of this approach, as it supports the need for place-specific and contextualized policy development that much recent feminist research in Canada is calling for. For example, the need for policy to be more specific and contextualized is a comment that features prominently in the Status of Women papers produced for the Integration of Diversity initiative.[10] This is also the direction of recent efforts to develop an intersectional framework to inform inequality policy analysts and activists (CRIAW 2006).[11]

CONCLUSION

One major achievement of the analysis of inequalities between women and men is acceptance of the idea that these are socially created and amenable to change. Class analysis, too, broke with previous explanations that argued that there was something inevitable and natural about the presence of inequality in society. The analysis of Canadian society in terms of class presents a view that inequality is the result of a system of organization in which the production of profit is given priority over the needs of people. As radical as this view was, and still is, in challenging the dominant idea of Canada as a just and gentle society, class analysis produced its own set of analytical limitations and theoretical exclusions. While not entirely silent on the question of inequality between women and men, many came to accept that the categories of class analysis were indeed "sex-blind." The investigation of how class and gender inequalities relate to one another has been a huge effort among those who seek to understand the complexity of inequality in order to bring it to an end.

This chapter has set out a progression of challenges to class analysis from the position of women's experience and gender inequality. The first level of challenge came from the realization that traditional forms of analysis were ideological constructions that excluded women's experience. At this basic but essential level, there is the insistence that women's lives be recognized and included in stratification analysis. As attention shifts from the fact of exclusion to the manner in which women's experience and gender inequality are to be included, the conceptualization of class comes under more intense scrutiny. Attempts to stretch existing components of class analysis to fit gender inequality are found wanting. There is a wish to consider a full range of gender issues and experiences of inequality. At its most developed, this second level of challenge sees limits in the explanatory capacity of class categories. Class continues to be given pride of place in explaining inequality, but there is a recognition that other structures and processes, such as gender, are needed to fill in significant aspects left unexplained. As the conceptualization of gender itself becomes contested, the direction of theory and research is toward more complex understandings of how the multiple forms of gender, including racialized forms, are embedded in a dynamic of inequality. Researchers working at this third level of challenge abandon explanations that put class first, and try to examine both the meaning and the salience of intersecting dimensions of inequality. As with all other potentially relevant forms of inequality, the significance of class in any specific investigation must be established, not presumed.

These analytical developments bring Canadian work on inequality into conversation with more iconoclastic positions on the future of class as an analytical concept. There are exciting and dramatic arguments, inspired by the gender critique of class, that challenge the entire narrative of "capitalism" and ask us to consider whether current circumstances require a completely new framework for analysis. For example, Gibson-Graham (1996), while continuing a commitment to Marxism, and to the analysis and struggles against exploitation, nevertheless wants to "divorce Marxism from one of its many and problematic marriages—the marriage to 'the economy' in its holistic and self-sustaining form." They would like to see an end to capitalism "as we knew it," for in their view, our form of knowing has created

a more unitary, total, and powerful entity than exists. Bottero (1998) is equally radical in her suggestion that the legacy of class analysis is a separation of the social and the economic that continues to distort attempts to analyze inequality. Her provocative assertion is that explanations of gender inequality have accepted the general "market nature of society—and it is this which must be rejected, if gender is to be theorized in structural terms. To do so, however, involves fundamental revision of both class and gender theory" (Bottero 1998:485). At the same time, Irwin (2005) demonstrates in a very compelling way the gains in explaining women's and men's everyday lives that are possible when a suitably complex, experientially embedded, and relational concept of class is used in sociological research.

The hope of many is that there is a way to continue the immensely creative, critical, and politically progressive impulses of the legacy of Marx's theory of class, without remaining caught in conceptual snares that conceal and distort significant aspects of the history and organization of society. For some of those interested in pursuing explanations of gender inequality, this means continuing to work with the concept of class; for others, it means cutting these ties and heading further out to sea toward as yet uncharted territory

NOTES

1. Hamilton (1996) gives a detailed description of first-wave and second-wave feminism in Canada. First-wave feminism is associated with struggles in the late eighteenth and early nineteenth centuries, particularly the fight for legal recognition, voting rights, and the breaking down of barriers in education and employment. Second-wave feminism reached its height between the 1960s and 1980s. Primary issues were inequalities in the family, reproductive choice and control, equal pay, pornography, and domestic violence. The distinction between liberal, radical, and socialist feminists is associated with

second-wave feminism. Of course, we are now in the period identified as third-wave feminism (or more contentiously, post-feminism). See Marshall (2000) and the new edition of Hamilton (2005) for discussions of current forms of feminism and their relation to sociology.

2. Jackson and Scott (2002), Davies et al. (2006), and Biggs and Downe (2005) give a good indication of the current state of research on gender in Canada and internationally. See also Siltanen and Doucet (2008).

3. See Hamilton (2005) for a quick overview of contemporary Canadian feminist interests. Vosko (2002) provides an informative account of the development, and current interest, of feminist political economy in Canada.

4. In this chapter, the terms *inequality* and *stratification* are used interchangeably. In the sociological literature, the two have been distinguished, although there are different presentations of what the two terms mean. I follow here the practice of regarding the sociology of stratification as the analysis of structured social inequality, including class analysis. Inequality is, of course, a much broader phenomenon than class, as this chapter discusses. See Grabb (2007) for a discussion of the two terms, which contrasts stratification and class analysis.

5. See Hamilton and Barrett (1986) for some retrospective thoughts from key participants on the longer-term contribution of this debate.

6. For consistency, I use *gender* here, although the Armstrong and Armstrong did not frame their argument in this way.

7. These arguments from both Delphy and Stanley are reprinted in Jackson and Scott (2002).

8. For an example of this argument in the area of gender inequalities in paid work, see Siltanen (1994) and Pratt and Hanson (1993).

9. Stasiulis (1999) also examines this issue in the case of race.

10. Papers by Rankin and Vickers (2001), Bakan and Kobayashi (2000), and Kenny et al. (2002) are particularly strong on this point.

11. For further discussion of efforts to address diversity within gender in the context of policy analysis, see Siltanen (2006)

REFERENCES

Acker, Joan 1973. "Women and social stratification: A case of intellectual sexism." *American Journal of Sociology* 78:936–945.

Andrew, Caroline 1984. "Women and the welfare state." *Canadian Journal of Political Science* 17:667–683.

Arat-Koc, Sedef 1989. "In the privacy of our own home: Foreign domestic workers as solution to the crisis of the domestic sphere in Canada." *Studies in Political Economy* 28:33–58.

Armstrong, Pat, and Hugh Armstrong 1986. "Beyond sexless class and classless sex: Towards feminist Marxist." In Roberta Hamilton and Michel Barrett (eds.), *The Politics of Diversity*, pp. 208–37. Thetford, UK: Thetford Press Limited.

Bakan, A. B., and A. Kobayashi 2000. "Employment equity policy in Canada: An interprovincial comparison." Paper prepared for the Status of Women Canada's Policy Research Fund initiative on the Integration of Diversity into Policy Research, Development and Analysis. (http://www.swc-cfc.gc.ca/pubs/pubspr_e.html).

Bannerji, Himani 1995. *Thinking Through: Essays on Feminism, Marxism, and Anti-Racism.* Toronto: Women's Press.

Biggs, L., and P. Downe (eds.) 2005. *Gendered Intersections.* Halifax: Fernwood Press.

Bottero, Wendy 1998. "Clinging to the wreckage? Gender and the legacy of class." *Sociology* 32, 3: 469–490.

Bruckert, C. 2002. *Taking it Off, Putting it On: Women in the Strip Trade.* Toronto: Women's Press.

Canadian Research Institute for the Advancement of Women 2006. *Intersectional Feminist Frameworks.* (http://www.criaw-icref.ca).

Clement, Wallace, and John Myles 1994. *Relations of Ruling: Class and Gender in Postindustrial Societies.* Montreal & Kingston: McGill-Queen's University Press.

Connelly, Patricia 1978. *Last Hired, First Fired: Women and the Canadian Work Force.* Toronto: The Women's Press.

Connelly, Patricia 1986. "On Marxism and feminism." In Roberta Hamilton and Michel Barrett (eds.), *The Politics of Diversity*, pp. 241–254. Thetford, UK: Thetford Press Limited.

Côté, A. et al. 2001. "Sponsorship . . . for better or worse: The impact of sponsorship on the equality rights of immigrant women." Paper prepared for the Status of Women Canada's Policy Research Fund initiative on the Integration of Diversity into Policy Research, Development and Analysis. (http://www.swc-cfc.gc.ca/pubs/pubspr_e.html).

Creese, G. 2007. "Racializing work/reproducing white privilege." In V. Shalla and C. Clement (eds.), *Work in Tumultuous Times*. Montreal & Kingston: McGill-Queen's University Press.

Creese, Gillian, and Daivia Stasiulis 1996. "Intersections of gender, race, class and sexuality." *Studies in Political Economy* 51(Fall):5–14.

Crompton, Rosemary, and Michael Mann (eds.) 1986. *Gender and Stratification*. Cambridge, UK: Polity Press.

Curtis, James, Edward Grabb, and Neil Guppy (eds.) 1999. *Social Inequality in Canada: Patterns, Problems, and Policies* (3rd ed.). Scarborough, ON: Prentice Hall Allyn and Bacon Canada.

Curtis, James E., and William G. Scott (eds.) 1973. *Social Stratification: Canada* (3rd ed.). Scarborough, ON: Prentice-Hall.

Davies, K., M. Evans, and J. Lorber 2006. *Handbook of Gender and Women's Studies*. London: Sage.

Eichler, Margrit 1988. *Non-sexist Research Methods*. Wellington, NZ: Unwin Hyman.

Engels, F. 1972 [1884]. *Origin of the Family, Private Property and the State*. New York: International Publishers.

Evans, Patricia M., and Gerda R. Wekerle (eds.) 1997. *Women and the Canadian Welfare State: Challenges and Change*. Toronto: University of Toronto Press.

Fonow, M.M., and J.A. Cook 2005. "Feminist methodology: New applications in the academy and public policy." *Signs* 30, 4: 2211–2236.

Fox, Bonnie 1986. "Never done: The struggle to understand domestic labour and women's oppression." In Roberta Hamilton and Michel Barrett (eds.), *The Politics of Diversity*, pp. 180–189. Thetford, UK: Thetford Press.

Gannagé, Charlene 1987. "A world of difference: The case of women workers in a Canadian garment factory." In H. J. Maroney and M. Luxton (eds.), *Feminism and Political Economy:*

Women's Work, Women's Struggles. Toronto: Methuen.

Gibson-Graham, J.K. 1996. *The End of Capitalism (As We Knew It): A Feminist Critique of Political Economy*. Cambridge, UK: Blackwell Publishers.

Grabb, Edward G. 2007. *Theories of Social Inequality* (5th ed.). Toronto: Thomson Nelson.

Grayson, J. Paul 1980. *Class, State, Ideology and Change: Marxist Perspective on Canada*. Toronto: Holt, Rinehart and Winston.

Hamilton, Roberta 1996. *Gendering the Vertical Mosaic: Feminist Perspective on Canadian Society*. Toronto: Copp Clark Ltd.

Hamilton, Roberta 2005. *Gendering the Vertical Mosaic: Feminist Perspectives on Canadian Society* (2nd ed.). Toronto: Pearson Education Canada.

Hamilton, Roberta, and Michele Barrett (eds.) 1986. *The Politics of Diversity*. Thetford, UK: Thetford Press.

Hartmann, Heidi 1981. "The unhappy marriage of Marxism and feminism: Towards a more progressive union." In L. Sarpent (ed.), *Women and Revolution*, pp. 1–41. London: Pluto Press.

Irwin, S. 2005. *Reshaping Social Life*. London: Routledge

Jackson, S., and Sue Scott 2002. *Gender: A Sociological Reader*. London: Routledge

Jensen, Jane 1992. "Gender and reproduction, or babies and the state." In M. Patricia Connelly and Pat Armstrong (eds.), *Feminism in Action: Studies in Political Economy*, pp. 201–236. Toronto: Canadian Scholars' Press.

Kenny, C., et al. 2002. "North American Indian, Métis and Inuit women speak about culture, education and work." Paper prepared for the Status of Women Canada's Policy Research Fund initiative on the Integration of Diversity into Policy Research, Development and Analysis. (http://www.swc-cfc.gc.ca/pubs/pubspr_e.html).

Kobayashi, A., and L. Peake 1994. "Unnatural discourse: Race and gender in geography." *Gender, Place and Culture* 1, 2:225–243.

Li, Peter S. 1992. "Race and gender as bases of class fractions and their effects on earnings." *Canadian Review of Sociology and Anthropology* 29, 4:488–523.

Maroney, Heather Jon, and Meg Luxton 1987. "From feminism and political economy to feminist political economy." In Heather Jon Maroney and Meg Luxton (eds.), *Feminism and Political Economy: Women's Work, Women's Struggles*, pp. 5–50. Toronto: Methuen.

Marshall, Barbara L. 2000. *Configuring Gender: Explorations in Theory and Politics*. Peterborough, ON: Broadview Press.

Marx, Karl 1976. *Capital*. Middlesex, UK: Penguin.

McCall, L. 2005. "The complexity of intersectionality." *Signs* 30, 3:1771–1800.

Ng, Roxanna 1986. "The social construction of immigrant women in Canada." In R. Hamilton and M. Barrett (eds.), *The Politics of Diversity*. London: Verso.

Oakley, Ann 1972. *Sex, Gender and Society*. New York: Harper and Row.

O'Connor, Julia S., Ann Shola Orloff, and Sheila Shaver 1999. *States, Markets, Families: Gender, Liberalism and Social Policy in Australia, Canada, Great Britain and the United States*. Cambridge: Cambridge University Press.

Parr, Joy 1990. *The Gender of Breadwinners: Women, Men, and Change in Two Industrial Towns 1880–1950*. Toronto: University of Toronto Press.

Pratt, G., and S. Hanson 1993. "Women and work across the life course." In C. Katz and J. Monk (eds.), *Full Circles: Geographies of Women over the Life Course*, pp. 27–54. London: Routledge.

Rankin, L.P., and J. Vickers 2001. "Women's movements and state feminism: Integrating diversity into public policy." Paper prepared for the Status of Women Canada's Policy Research Fund initiative on the Integration of Diversity into Policy Research, Development and Analysis. (http://www.swc-cfc.gc.ca/pubs/pubspr_e.html).

Rose, D. 2001. "Revisiting feminist research methodologies: A working paper." Paper prepared for the Status of Women Canada's Policy Research Fund initiative on the Integration of Diversity into Policy Research, Development and Analysis. (http://www.swc-cfc.gc/pubs/revisiting).

Seccombe, Wally, and David Livingstone 1996. "'Down to earth people': Revising a materialist understanding of group consciousness." In David Livingstone and J. Marshall Mangan (eds.), *Recast Dreams: Class and Gender Consciousness in Steeltown*, pp. 131–194. Toronto: Garamond Press.

Shalla, V. 2007. "Theoretical reflections on work." In V. Shalla and C. Clement (eds.), *Work in Tumultuous Times*, pp. 3–29. Montreal & Kingston: McGill-Queen's University Press.

Siltanen, Janet 1994. *Locating Gender: Occupational Segregation, Wages and Domestic Responsibilities*. London: UCL Press.

Siltanen, Janet 2006. "Gender, diversity and the shaping of public policy: Recent aspects of the Canadian experience." *Scottish Affairs* 56 (Summer):88–101.

Siltanen, Janet, and Andrea Doucet 2008. *Gender Relations*. Toronto: Oxford University Press.

Smith, Dorothy E. 1980. "An analysis of ideological structures and how women are excluded: Considerations for academic women." In J. Paul Grayson (ed.), *Class, State, Ideology and Change: Marxist Perspective on Canada*, pp. 252–267. Toronto: Holt, Rinehart and Winston.

Stasiulis, D. 1999. "Feminist intersectional thinking." In Peter Li (ed.), *Race and Ethnic Relations in Canada*. New York: Oxford University Press.

Vosko, Leah F. 2002. "The pasts (and futures) of feminist political economy in Canada: Reviving the debate." *Studies in Political Economy* 68 (Summer):55–83.

White, J., P. Maxim et al. 2003. "Labor force activity of women in Canada: A comparative analysis of Aboriginal and non-Aboriginal women." *The Canadian Review of Sociology and Anthropology* 40, 4:391.

Zaretsky, Eli 1976. *Capitalism, the Family, and Personal Life*. London: Pluto Press.

chapter fourteen

Converging Gender Roles

Katherine Marshall
(Adapted from the Statistics Canada
publication *Perspectives on Labour and
Income* 7, 7 (July 2006). Catalogue
no. 75-001-XIE. Retrieved online at
http://www.statscan.org/english/freepub/
75-001-XIE/10706/art-1.htm)

Families are the cornerstone of any society. Their supply of paid labour is vital to the economy, as is their unpaid labour in raising the next generation. The dynamics of who does which type of labour within families continue to change. Women's expanding economic role has been the main impetus for eroding the cultural idea that men should be primarily responsible for paid work while women look after unpaid household and family duties. Today's couples have a much more equal partnership in the sharing of financial, child care, and household responsibilities.

Understanding the changing division of labour within families is crucial in developing effective policies. Employers may be well over the idea that women's earnings are simply "pin money" for the family, but accepting that men's work schedules are increasingly affected by home responsibilities, such as picking up children from daycare, staying home with a sick child, or taking parental leave, is relatively new. Changing workplace practices, such as on-site daycare and flexible work arrangements, as well as labour legislation such as parental, maternity, and compassionate care leave confirm that "WLB (work–life balance) has emerged as a critical public policy issue in Canada" (HRSDC 2005). The increasing number of dual-earner families and a heavier overall workload make balancing a job and home life that much more difficult.

The division of labour within families is also of interest from a sociological point of view. Women's entrenched participation in the labour market was expected to launch "a revolution in the gendered division of labor," but the rate of change has been slow (Cooke 2004). Tension from multiple daily demands and a longer workday can arise when "second-shift" duties are discussed and divided. An imbalance in the division of household labour has been linked to marital conflict, reduced physical and mental well-being, and lower wages (Cooke 2004; Coverman 1983).

Time-use surveys can illuminate overall trends in the hours men and women spend on paid work and housework, as well as on child care and other unpaid household labour. Time-use diaries permit analysis of the types of activities done on a daily basis, and for how long. The study targets those aged 25 to 54 as they are the most likely to be employed and have dependent children at home, leaving them challenged for time. The latter part of the article focuses on the hours of work, the division of labour, and the well-being of dual-earner families (see Data Sources and Definitions).

MORE TIME AT THE OFFICE, PARTICULARLY FOR WOMEN

The average daily time spent on paid work, housework, and other unpaid household duties (including child care) for those aged 25 to 54 has increased steadily over the past two decades, rising from 8.2 hours in 1986 to 8.8 hours in 2005. All of the increase comes from paid labour, which rose from an average of 4.7 hours per day in 1986 to 5.4 hours in 2005, while unpaid work dropped slightly. These findings refute the theories that advanced technology and growth in productivity capacity would invariably lead to increased leisure time.[1]

Both men and women have added to their overall workday since 1986 (see Figure 14-1). Most of the 0.6-hour increase for men has come from unpaid work, rising

from 2.1 to 2.5 hours, although their paid labour also rose (from 6.1 to 6.3 hours). The 0.7-hour increase for women has come entirely from paid work (3.3 to 4.4 hours), despite a half-hour drop in unpaid work (4.8 to 4.3 hours). Although gender differences in the division of labour are still evident, they are slowly breaking down.

CONVERGING LABOUR FORCE PARTICIPATION RATES

The jump in the average time women spend in paid labour is attributable not only to time spent on the job, but also to an increase in their participation rate. Canadian women have one of the highest participation rates in the world, a rate that is converging with men's. For example, while the difference in labour force participation rates for men and women aged 25 to 54 was 44 percentage points in 1986 (94% for men versus 50% for women), in 2005 it stood at 10 points (91% versus 81%) (see Figure 14-2). Time-use data on average daily participation rates show a similar trend, with the women's rate rising from 44% in 1986 to 51% in 2005, and men's decreasing from 68% to 65% (see Table 14-1).[2]

MEN'S PARTICIPATION IN HOUSEWORK UP, WOMEN'S DOWN

The proportion of those doing some housework daily, be it making sandwiches for lunch, vacuuming, or taking out the garbage, increased from 72% in 1986 to 79% in 2005. However, this increase is entirely attributable to men, whose participation rose from 54% to 69%, while women's remained steady at around 90% (see Figure 14.3). Changes in the daily participation rate for core housework (meal preparation, meal clean-up,

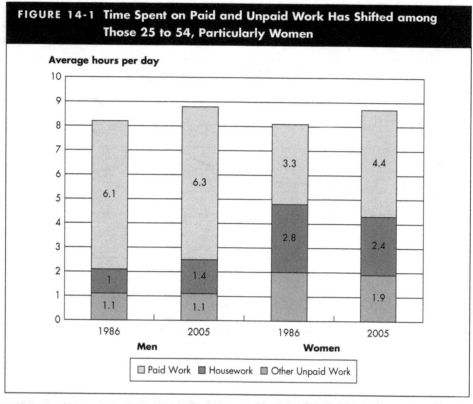

FIGURE 14-1 Time Spent on Paid and Unpaid Work Has Shifted among Those 25 to 54, Particularly Women

Notes: Average hours may not add due to rounding. Other unpaid work means primary child care and shopping for goods and services.
Source: Statistics Canada, General Social Survey, various years.

indoor cleaning, and laundry) are the most noticeable—40% to 59% for men, and 88% to 85% for women.

Even though the proportion of people doing housework of some kind has increased, the amount of time spent at it has decreased (from an average of 2.7 hours per day in 1986 to 2.5 hours per day in 2005) (see Figure 14-3). All of the decrease comes from core housework. Labour-saving devices such as dishwashers, and semi-prepared or pre-packaged food items (such as pre-washed bags of salad, already peeled carrots, or frozen dinners) as well as numerous take-out options, may be helping to cut down the time spent in kitchens.

Still, given the trend toward ever bigger homes,[3] it seems puzzling to witness a reduction in time spent on housework. Canadians are not alone in this; a remarkably similar trend has been observed in the United States. Between 1975 and 1995 the average weekly hours Americans spent on housework dropped from 15.5 to 13.7. Furthermore, "women's and men's hours spent in housework have converged over the period, primarily due to the steep decline in women's hours of housework" (Bianchi et al. 2000). One reason for the overall decline could be today's service-oriented economy. From take-out meals to snow removal, groundskeeping, and housecleaning, people buy many goods and services once produced in the home. Housework standards may also be falling and people are less bothered if their house fails the

FIGURE 14-2 Women Have Increased Their Labour Force Participation Dramatically

Source: Statistics Canada, Labour Force Survey.

TABLE 14-1 Time Spent on Paid Work, Housework, and Other Unpaid Work

	Men 25 to 54				Women 25 to 54			
	1986	1992	1998	2005	1986	1992	1998	2005
Total paid and unpaid hours	6.3	8.6	8.9	8.8	8.1	8.4	8.5	8.8
Paid work and related	6.1	6.1	6.3	6.3	3.3	3.6	4.0	4.4
Work	4.9	5.1	5.1	5.3	2.8	3.0	3.2	3.7
Related activities	0.7	0.6	0.6	0.4	0.3	0.3	0.4	0.3
Commute	0.5	0.5	0.5	0.6	0.3	0.3	0.3	0.4
Housework	1.0	1.4	1.4	1.4	2.8	2.9	2.6	2.4
Core	0.4	0.5	0.7	0.7	2.5	2.3	2.2	1.9
Non-core	0.6	0.9	0.7	0.7	0.3	0.6	0.5	0.5
Other unpaid	1.1	1.1	1.2	1.1	2.0	1.9	2.0	1.9
Child care	0.4	0.4	0.5	0.5	0.9	1.0	1.0	1.0
Shopping and services	0.7	0.6	0.7	0.6	1.1	0.9	1.0	0.9

Note: Figures may not add due to rounding.
Source: Statistics Canada, General Social Survey, various years.

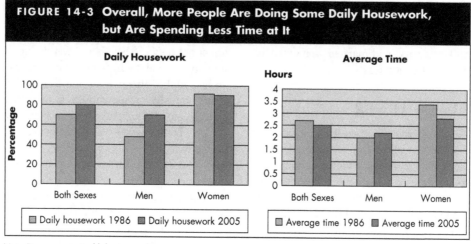

FIGURE 14-3 Overall, More People Are Doing Some Daily Housework, but Are Spending Less Time at It

Note: Figures may not add due to rounding.
Source: Statistics Canada, General Social Survey, various years.

"white-glove" dust test. In the same vein, people's priorities may have changed as to how they want to spend their time (Bianchi et al. 2000).

Overall, participation rates for other types of unpaid labour—primary child care and shopping for goods and services—have remained relatively stable over the past 20 years. The average time spent has trended upward for child care and downward for shopping. However, the participation rate and time spent on child care for those with children at home shows a more noticeable increase, particularly among men.

MORE MARRIED MEN NOW DOING HOUSEWORK

In all family types, daily participation rates for housework continue to be significantly higher for women than for men. However, the gap is narrowing. For example, among married men with children, the participation rate rose from 54% to 71%. Furthermore, while the presence of a wife lessened men's involvement in housework in 1986 (single

men had a participation rate of 61%, and married men 53%), 2005 saw roughly 7 in 10 married men, both with and without children, participating in housework. The increase in husbands' participation is a logical reaction to the reality that most wives are now engaged in paid labour, and for longer hours, and therefore have less time to do housework. The significant increase in participation among men living alone may be partly attributable to changing cultural norms, whereby both men and women have been taught life skills formerly reserved for the opposite sex. "It is likely more acceptable for men to cook and clean, indeed, welcomed, for men to show competence at making a home-cooked meal, for example" (Bianchi et al. 2000).

From the standpoint of time, married women, particularly those with children, continue to do significantly more housework than married men, but the overall difference has lessened. In 1986, women with children did 2.2 hours more per day than their male counterparts (3.3 versus 1.1 hours), with the difference decreasing to 1.3 hours by 2005 (2.8 versus 1.5 hours). This narrowing is the result of married men with children spending significantly more time on housework, and married women spending significantly less.

DUAL-EARNERS

The steady rise in women's labour force participation means that in most couples, even those with dependent children at home, both spouses are now employed. The proportion of dual-earners among husband-and-wife families with children under 16 at home rose from 36% in 1976, to 58% in 1992, to 69% in 2005. Without a doubt, juggling home and work responsibilities is more challenging when both parents are employed. Society has

a vested interest in ensuring that these individuals are able to meet this challenge, since the consequences of being overburdened affect not only the health and well-being of individuals and their family, but also the ability to be effective in the workplace. Unmanageable responsibilities in either sphere can have negative spillover effects, such as inattentiveness at home or lack of productivity at the workplace (Daly 2004).

Not only has the number of dual-earners increased since 1992, so too has the average daily amount of time these couples spend on paid work and housework combined (up 0.5 hours per day, a result of 0.7 hours more paid work but 0.2 hours less housework) (see Table 14-2).[4] This net change within couples was due to an increase in husbands'

TABLE 14-2   Participation in and Time Spent on Paid Work and Housework in Dual-Earner Families

	Participation		Time per day	
	1992	2005	1992	2005
	%		Hours	
Total				
Both	99	99	15.3	15.8
Husband	99	98	7.7	7.9
Wife	100	99	7.6	7.8
Paid Work				
Both	72	72	11.5	12.2
Husband	71	73	6.3	6.6
Wife	72	70	5.2	5.6
Housework				
Both	82	82	3.8	3.6
Husband	70	74	1.3	1.4
Wife	94	90	2.4	2.2
Wife's Share	50	50		
Paid work	45	46		
Housework	65	62		

Note: Figures may not add due to rounding.
Source: Statistics Canada, General Social Survey, various years.

paid work and housework (0.3 hours and 0.1 hours, respectively), and an increase in wives' paid work and decrease in housework (0.4 hours and –0.2 hours, respectively).[5]

In both 1992 and 2005, each partner in dual-earner couples did 50% of the combined paid work and housework each day. However, wives did 45% of total paid work but 65% of housework in 1992. By 2005 these proportions stood at 46% and 62%.

As in the general population, men in dual-earner families have increased their participation in housework (from 70% in 1992 to 74% in 2005), while the women's rate has dropped (from 94% to 90%).

CHILDREN WIDEN THE GAP . . .

Several factors are associated with who does what in a dual-earner family, and how much time they spend. For example, school-aged children at home add an average of 1.2 hours to a family's workday, pushing it to more than 8 hours for both parents. However, fathers tend to add both paid work and housework (0.4 and 0.3 hours, respectively) compared with men without children at home, whereas women add only housework (0.6 hours more than women without children).

. . . AND EDUCATION NARROWS IT

When only the wife in a couple has a university degree, her share of housework decreases to 59%, compared with 62% overall. Although not a strong finding, this is consistent with other studies, which have found that "increases in wife's education, as a proxy for wage rate, tend to be associated with an increased share of housework for the husband" (Anxo and Carlin 2004:30). Also, lower levels of education for both partners add to the length of the total workday (paid work and housework). Families in which neither partner graduated from university worked an average 16.3 hours per day compared with 15.2 hours for those in which both had a university degree. Most of the added time came from housework.

PARITY IN LABOUR WHEN WIVES HAVE HIGH INCOME

High personal income, for either sex, is associated with spending more time at a job and less on housework. For example, compared with women whose annual income was less than $30 000, those with $100 000 or more did one hour more of paid work, and one hour less of housework per day. (Both did an average of 8.1 hours of total work per day.)

Longer job hours often bring higher earnings, which in turn can offer some relief from housework by providing the means to hire someone else to do it. In 2004, only 7% of households with income less than $40 000 paid for domestic help, spending an average of $813. This compared with 43% of households with $160 000 or more, who spent $2150.

When wives have an income of $100 000 or more, the division of paid labour and housework between partners is more likely to be split equally. In these couples, each partner spent about 6.5 hours per day on paid work and 1.5 hours on housework.

Furthermore, a wife's income is likely to influence the husband's time spent on housework as well as her own. For him, time spent doing housework rises along with her income, while for her, the time falls. On the other hand, regardless of her husband's income level, a wife's time spent on housework stays the same. These findings partly support the "relative resources" theory of the division of housework, which suggests that partners with relatively high education and income have more power to get out of doing housework (Bianchi et al. 2000). Other research has shown that high-income households are more likely to buy domestic help, especially if the wife is the primary earner. The latter are twice as likely to hire help than high-income households in which the husband is the main earner (Palameta 2003).

Finally, even though dual-earner partners working full-time both contribute 8 hours of total labour each day, husbands are more likely than wives to spend more time at a job (6.6 versus 5.9 hours) and less time on housework (1.4 versus 2.1 hours). Past research has found that not only are wives in these families more likely to do most of the housework, but they also feel most responsible for anticipating, planning, and organizing what needs to be done (Marshall 1993). Findings show that husbands or wives who work part-time and have a spouse working full-time have a shorter overall workday (paid work and housework) than their spouse. However, many are likely spending a considerable amount of time on child care.

ALTHOUGH TIME-STRESSED, EMPLOYED PARENTS SATISFIED WITH LIFE OVERALL

Both children and work arrangements within families influence work–life balance (WLB) satisfaction and stress caused by lack of time. Sole earners in couples with children at home had some of the lowest WLB satisfaction rates (69% for sole-earner fathers and 73% for mothers). Dual-earner fathers reported the highest satisfaction rate (77%), significantly higher than dual-earner mothers, who had the lowest (67%).

Men and women in dual-earning families, with and without children, feel most stressed about not having enough time. Given that children require a great deal of time and energy, it is not surprising to find that when both parents are employed, only 58% of fathers and 45% of mothers did not feel stressed for lack of time. Except in couples with dependent children and the husband as sole earner, women reported being significantly more stressed for time than men.

Interestingly, compared with other women, those in dual-earner couples and working part-time express the highest WLB satisfaction (86%), are some of the least time-stressed (65%), and have a high overall life satisfaction rate (88%).

PARENTING AND LONG HOURS MORE BURDENSOME FOR WOMEN

Not surprisingly, the longer a couple spends on an average weekday working at their jobs and doing housework, the more difficult it is to find balance in life with time enough to accomplish everything.[6] Women generally tend to feel more time-stressed than men, regardless of length of workday or presence of children

Longer workdays and the presence of children also affect women more than men in terms of WLB satisfaction. Only 52% of women with children in couples with long hours felt satisfied with their WLB, the lowest rate overall. In contrast, 71% of their male counterparts were satisfied. However, although overall life satisfaction fell somewhat as the workday lengthened for both men and women in dual-earner families (with or without children), the difference was not significant, and the vast majority (80% or more) felt satisfied with their life as a whole.

CONCLUSION

While women's entry into the job market has been dramatic, men's entry into housework has been gradual, prompting some to call the latter a "stalled revolution" (Cooke 2004). However, this study shows that, although gender differences persist in the division of labour, they are steadily diminishing. Since 1986, of the total time spent on paid and unpaid work, women aged 25 to 54 have proportionally increased their average daily time at a job (4.4 hours of 8.8 in 2005), while men have increased their time on housework (1.4 of 8.8 hours in 2005). As women's job attachment has increased, so too has men's involvement in housework and child care. Women's increasing hours in paid labour (and thus income), combined with "normative changes in the direction of equality and sharing" (Beaujot 2006:24) is likely to further reduce gender differences in the division of labour in the future.

However, not only are more men and women sharing the economic and domestic responsibilities in families, but most are also increasing the length of their paid workday. This has helped position work–life balance among the top 10 issues in collective bargaining. It has risen in importance because of the "increased recognition of the costs of work–life imbalance in terms of workplace injury rates and the general health of workers, as well as the development and well-being of children and aging parents" (Canadian Association of Administrators of Labour Legislation 2002:4). Dual-earner couples who worked long days doing their job plus housework and who had dependent children at home were less satisfied with their work–life balance. They also felt more time-stressed, particularly women. However, despite these stage-of-life pressures, the majority of dual-earner husbands and wives felt satisfied with their life as a whole.

Increasingly, employees are legally entitled to various kinds of paid and unpaid leave for family responsibilities. As well, more workplaces are offering flexible work arrangements, health promotion and employee assistance programs, and other family support such as on-site child care. It has been shown that employees with flex-time arrangements feel considerably less time-stressed than those without this benefit (Fast and Frederick 1996). In short, changing work arrangements in the home are inspiring alternative work arrangements at the office.

DATA SOURCES AND DEFINITIONS

Every year since 1985, the General Social Survey (GSS) has interviewed Canadians aged 15 and over living in the 10 provinces on a wide range of social issues. Using a 24-hour diary, the GSS collected detailed information on time use in four different years using varying sample sizes: 1986 (16 400), 1992 (9800), 1998 (10 700) and 2005 (19 600). Individual activities were recorded sequentially throughout the day and subsequently coded to an international listing. Each day of the week is sampled. Therefore, calculations are usually averaged over a seven-day period (see below). While the 1986 survey collected data during the months of November and December, the remaining cycles covered a 12-month period. Most time-use surveys include sections on the perception of time and indicators of well-being.

The Labour Force Survey (LFS) collects information on labour market activity every month during a one-week period from all persons 15 years and over. It includes questions about the usual and actual weekly hours spent at a person's main job and any other job. The LFS participation rate for a particular group (for example, women aged 25 to 54) is the labour force in that group expressed as a percentage of the population for that group.

Replacing the Family Expenditure Survey in 1997, the annual Survey of Household Spending (SHS) collects data on the expenditures, income, and characteristics of families and individuals living in private households. The SHS category "domestic help" includes, for example, housekeepers, cleaners, paid companions, and housesitters.

Paid work (time use) includes the work activities of all jobs or businesses, while related paid activities include looking for work, delays at work, and coffee breaks. Commute to work is the total time spent travelling to and from the workplace. Total paid work covers paid work, related paid activities, and commuting.

Core housework (time use) includes meal preparation, meal clean-up, indoor cleaning, and laundry. Core activities are those that are most likely done on a daily basis and generally demand the most time. Non-core housework includes things such as outdoor cleaning, mending or sewing, interior or exterior maintenance and repair, gardening, pet and plant care, household paperwork, or unpacking groceries. Total housework consists of core and non-core activities.

Primary child care (time use) consists of activities directly involving children, such as feeding, helping, teaching, reading to, talking or playing with, medical care, and any related travel such as taking children to school or driving them to sports or other activities.

Activity participation rate (time use) indicates the proportion of the population (or sub-population) that reported spending some time on the activity on diary day. The participation rate is a daily rate and, unless otherwise specified, is an average over a seven-day week.

Average time spent on activities (time use) of the population or a sub-population refers to the total time all respondents reported spending on a given activity divided by the population, and averaged over a seven-day week. The time spent by participants refers only to those who participated in that activity on diary day, but again averaged over seven days.

Dual-earners are defined here as married or common-law couples in which the main activity of both partners in the previous seven days was "employed." Both partners had to be currently living in the same household and not on vacation from their job during the previous week. Since the analysis focuses on the division of labour by sex, same-sex couples were excluded.

Total paid work and housework time within couples is the sum of minutes both partners spent on paid work and related paid activities, and on core and non-core housework, on diary day. This calculation uses the 24-hour diary reporting for the respondent's time, and the time-related questions asked of the respondent for their partner's time. For example, if the respondent reported that their partner worked on diary day, a follow-up question asked the exact start and end times of all shifts worked on that day. (Since respondents were not asked to report any commute time for their partners, commute time for both partners is excluded from the total paid work calculation.)

Respondents were also asked to estimate the total number of hours their partner spent on core and non-core housework in the previous week. Therefore, average daily time spent on housework by the partner was calculated by adding the total weekly core and non-core hours, dividing this amount by 7, and then (based on established housework activity patterns), multiplying by 0.11 if diary day was a weekday, and 0.22 if diary day was a Saturday or Sunday. Calculations of the average time both partners spent on paid and unpaid work at the household level are very consistent with individual level data—that is, using only diary data for respondents by sex. Knowing the work dynamic within a couple is important for understanding the individual work pattern and well-being of each of the partners.

The target population includes all respondents aged 25 to 54 at the time of the survey. This is the core working-age group and also the group most likely to have dependent children living at home, thus increasing the likelihood of their having significant employment and home responsibilities. In order to clearly examine the amount of paid and unpaid labour done by those living alone or in a couple, households with extra members, such as grandmothers or boarders, were excluded.

Statistics Canada information is used with the permission of Statistics Canada. Users are forbidden to copy the data and redisseminate them, in an original or modified form, for commercial purposes, without permission from Statistics Canada. Information on the availability of the wide range of data from Statistics Canada can be obtained from Statistics Canada's Regional Offices, its World Wide Web site at www.statcan.ca, and its toll-free access number 1-800-263-1136.

NOTES

1. For a discussion of the different theories of leisure, see Gershuny and Fisher (2000).

2. While both the GSS and the LFS show women's average hours at paid work increasing, the LFS shows men's hours falling but the GSS shows them increasing. It is difficult to explain this difference, but some of it may be due to the different collection methods of the two surveys (see Data Sources and Definitions).

3. According to the census, the average number of rooms per dwelling increased from 5.8 in 1986 to 6.3 in 2001. Although square footage is not collected, this increase does suggest larger homes.

4. A comparison of dual-earner couples from the first time-use survey in 1986 was not possible since information about spouse's main activity was not collected.

5. The increase in paid work between 1992 and 2005 would have been larger if commuting to work had been included. This activity increased during this time but was not part of the calculation of work time within dual-earner couples (see Data Sources and Definitions).

6. This section looks at the total paid work and housework time couples do on an average weekday (Monday through Friday). This is arguably the most hectic part of the week. Women's total labour as a proportion of the couple's total workday (paid work and housework combined) was around 50% for all lengths of days (6 hours of a 12-hour day, or 10 hours of a 20-hour day).

REFERENCES

Anxo, Dominique and Paul Carlin 2004. "Intra-family time allocation to housework: French evidence." *International Journal of Time Use Research* 1, 1 (August):14–36.

Beaujot, Roderic 2006. "Gender models for family and work." *Horizons* 8, 3 (April):24–26.

Bianchi, Suzanne M., Melissa A. Milkie, Liana C. Sayer, and John P. Robinson 2000. "Is anyone doing the housework? Trends in the gender division of household labor." *Social Forces* 79, 1 (September):191–228.

Canadian Association of Administrators of Labour Legislation (CAALL) 2002. *Work–Life Balance: A Report to Ministers Responsible for Labour in Canada.* Gatineau, QC: CAALL.

Cooke, Lynn Prince 2004. "The gendered division of labor and family outcomes in Germany." *Journal of Marriage and Family* 66 (December):1246–1259.

Coverman, Shelley 1983. "Gender, domestic labor time, and wage inequality." *American Sociological Review* 48, 5 (October):623–637.

Daly, Kerry 2004. *The Changing Culture of Parenting.* Contemporary Family Trends series. Ottawa: The Vanier Institute of the Family.

Fast, Janet E., and Judith A. Frederick 1996. "Working arrangements and time stress." *Canadian Social Trends* (Statistics Canada, Catalogue No. 11-008-XPE) (Winter):14–19.

Gershuny, Jonathan, and Kimberly Fisher 2000. "Leisure." In A.H. Halsey with Josephine Webb (eds.), *Twentieth-Century British Social Trends* (3rd ed.), pp. 620–649. London: Macmillan.

Human Resources and Social Development Canada (HRSDC) 2005. "Addressing work–life balance in Canada." http://www.hrsdc.gc.ca/asp/gateway.asp?hr=/en/lp/spila/wlb/awlbc/01table_of_contents.shtml&hs=

Marshall, Katherine 1993. "Employed parents and the division of housework." *Perspectives on Labour and Income* (Statistics Canada, Catalogue No. 75-001-XPE) 5, 3 (Autumn): 23–30.

Palameta, Boris 2003. "Who pays for domestic help?" *Perspectives on Labour and Income* (Statistics Canada, Catalogue No. 75-001-XIE) (August), online edition.

The author would like to thank David Paton for his methodological assistance.

chapter fifteen

Gender at Work: Strategies for Equality in Neo-liberal Times

Gillian Creese and Brenda Beagan
(An original chapter written
for this volume.)

INTRODUCTION

Not long ago, working women were considered unusual, if not neglectful of home and family. Today, most women, like most men, are gainfully employed. In reality, of course, paid employment is only part of the work that most women do. Domestic labour is unpaid work that must be accomplished, usually on a daily basis, to sustain household members. In 2005, women aged 25 to 44 years with full-time jobs, and a male partner and children at home, performed 4.7 hours of domestic work each day; men performed significantly less domestic work each day, at 3.1 hours (Statistics Canada 2006a:37).[1] That time difference of 1.6 hours per day amounts to women working an additional 584 unpaid hours, or 73 additional eight-hour shifts, every year. That inequitable division of unpaid domestic work has a significant impact on inequalities experienced in the labour market. As governments across Canada engage in neo-liberal reforms that downsize the public sector, cut social programs and services, and privatize "caring work" back into individual households, gendered work disparities, both paid and unpaid, will likely grow. This chapter explores the major trends in women's paid work, identifies strategies to achieve greater equality, and considers the impact of neo-liberal reforms on gender equity in the workplace.

TRENDS IN WOMEN'S LABOUR FORCE PARTICIPATION

The number of women in the labour force has increased steadily since the Second World War, when only one in four women were employed (24% in 1951) (Calzavara 1993:312). In 2004, 58% of women over the age of 15 years were employed, with women making up 47% of the workforce[2] (Statistics Canada 2006b:103). Our grandmothers were most likely to be in the labour force prior to marriage and childbearing, perhaps returning once their children had grown up and left home. Today most women remain employed through their child-rearing years. Nearly 80% of women with children under 16 years of age are in the labour force, including 61% of those with children under the age of 3 (Statistics Canada 2006b:121). While women have increased their rates of labour force participation, the pattern for

men has gone in the opposite direction, from 84% in 1951 to 68% in 2004 (Calzavara 1993:312; Statistics Canada 2006b:103).[3] As a result of these twin trends, the participation rates of women and men are now more similar than different. The majority of women and men are employed (or seeking employment) throughout most of their adult lives.[4] One key difference that remains, however, is the likelihood of part-time versus full-time employment. In 2004, more than two million women, over one-quarter of the female labour force (27%), were employed part-time; only 11% of men worked part-time (Statistics Canada 2006b:124).[5]

It is worth noting some key variations in employment trends among different groups of women (see Table 15-1). Compared with immigrant women, especially more recent immigrants, Canadian-born women have higher rates of employment, lower levels of unemployment, and earn higher incomes. Full-time earnings for recent immigrants

TABLE 15-1	Employment, Unemployment, and Employment Income Differences among Women in Canada, 2000		
	Percent Employed	Percent Unemployed	2000 Average Employment Earnings*
Immigrant Women**	64%	8.1%	$34 500
Recent Immigrant Women***	58%	12.1%	$28 000
Canadian-born	70%	7.0%	$35 000
Visible Minority	63%	8.9%	$32 100
Not Visible Minority	70%	5.6%	$35 100
Aboriginal	47%	17%	28 851****
All women	56%	7%	34 892

*All incomes in this table are full-year, full-time employment earnings.

** Immigrant/non-immigrant and visible/non-visible minority data are for all women aged 25 to 64 years; Aboriginal/non-Aboriginal data are for all women over 15 years.

*** *Recent* refers to immigrants who arrived between 1991 and 2000.

**** Employment income for Aboriginal women compared to all women was compiled by Jackson (2005:116) based on Statistics Canada data.

Source: Statistics Canada, *Women in Canada*, various years; and Jackson 2005:116.

average only 80% of the earnings of Canadian-born women ($28 000 versus $35 000). Similarly, visible minority women experience lower rates of employment, higher levels of unemployment (9% versus 6%), and lower employment earnings than other women ($32 100 versus $35 100). Immigrant status and visible minority status overlap; 69% of visible minority women are immigrants (Statistics Canada 2006b:241).

Recent research suggests that there is a small income gap based on visible minority status among women who are born in Canada (Pendakur and Pendakur 2004:24). On the other hand, significant differences are evident between Aboriginal and non-Aboriginal women in Canada; Aboriginal women have more than double the unemployment rates (17% compared with 7%) and lower incomes than other women (see Table 15-1). Another notable division among women is tied to ability/disability status. Women with disabilities have much lower employment rates than those without disabilities (40% compared with 69% in 2001) (Statistics Canada 2006b:294).[6] Notwithstanding this great diversity among women, however, the gender gap between women and men is even more marked and continues to form a central feature of the Canadian labour market.

OCCUPATIONAL SEGREGATION AND THE INCOME GAP

Not only are more women employed today, but women are employed in a much broader range of occupations than at any time in the past. In the last three decades, women have made major inroads into such prestigious and traditionally "male" professions as medicine, dentistry, law, and corporate management. In spite of these success stories, occupational segregation on the basis of

gender remains firmly entrenched in the Canadian labour market. Compared with men, women work in a narrower range of occupations, and remain concentrated in those areas with lower pay and less social prestige.

A majority of women (53.5%) are employed in just two occupational sectors: clerical and administration (24.3%) and sales and service (29.2%) (see Table 15-2). When we add nursing (8.7%), we account for nearly two-thirds of all women in the labour force (62.2%). As Table 15-2 shows, most occupational sectors are either dominated by men or, less often, dominated by women. Men dominate the following fields: management (62.3%), especially senior management (77.9%); natural sciences, engineering, and mathematics (80.6%); primary industries (89.7%); trades, transport, and construction (93%); and processing, manufacturing, and utilities (68.9%). Together, nearly two-thirds of men work in these six occupational sectors (61.1%). In contrast, women predominate in only three areas: teaching (64.6%), nursing (87.2%), and clerical and administrative work (74.9%). Thus, while it is true that some women have made considerable occupational gains over the last two decades, most women continue to work in the "pink collar" or feminized occupations.

When women enter into an occupation previously dominated by men, one of two processes usually happens: The occupation becomes re-gendered, or subdivisions develop within the occupation. It is rarely the case that an occupation becomes truly integrated by gender. When an occupation re-genders, it is usually in the direction of feminization; what was "men's work" becomes redefined as "women's work" (Reskin and Padavic 1994). A job may lose its appeal for men due to declines in job security, wages, or prestige (Reskin and Roos 1990); as men lose interest, women

TABLE 15-2	Distribution of Employment in Canada, by Occupation and Gender, 2004		
Occupation	Women	Men	Women as a Percentage of Employment
Senior Management	0.3	1.0	22.1
Other Management	6.7	9.8	37.7
Total Managerial	7.0	10.8	36.6
Business/Finance	3.2	2.7	51.3
Natural Sciences/Engineering/Mathematics	3.0	9.7	21.2
Social Sciences/Religion	6.2	2.2	71.6
Teaching	5.2	2.5	64.6
Doctors/Dentists/Other Health	1.4	1.0	55.0
Nursing/Therapy/Other Health	8.7	1.1	87.2
Artistic/Literary/Recreational	3.3	2.6	52.8
Total Professional	31.0	21.8	55.6
Clerical/Administrative	24.3	7.2	74.9
Sales/Service	29.2	19.6	56.7
Primary	1.4	5.2	19.4
Trades/Transport/Construction	2.2	26.1	7.0
Processing, Manufacturing/Utilities	4.8	9.3	31.1
Total	100%	100%	46.8%

Source: Statistics Canada, *Women in Canada*, various years.

are more able to enter the job, driving wages and prestige down and causing men to lose interest more rapidly (Padavic 1991). Alternatively, as women enter an occupation, horizontal segregation may occur as women and men gravitate to different specialties, different sectors, or different types of clients (Roos and Reskin 1992). For example, while more than 50% of medical school graduates are female, women disproportionately enter family practice, pediatrics, obstetrics/gynaecology, and psychiatry, while the more highly paid medical specialties are still almost exclusively male (Association of Canadian Medical Colleges 2004).

Gendered occupational segregation might not be so noteworthy were it not for the marked economic consequences for most women. As Table 15-3 shows, women earn less than men within each occupational sector, even those in which women predominate. Overall, women employed full-time, full year in 2003 earned 70 cents for every dollar men earned ($36 500 compared with $51 700). When part-time workers are included, women's average earnings drop to 64 cents for every dollar men earned (Statistics Canada 2006b:152). Even women in clerical jobs, among the most "feminine" occupations, earned $8500 less per year than men in the same occupation (see Table 15-3)! As economic restructuring progressed through the 1990s, with the loss of many high-wage unionized jobs in predominantly male sectors of employment, the

TABLE 15-3	Average Annual Earnings, by Occupation and Gender, Full-Time, Full-Year Workers, 2003		
Occupation	Women	Men	Women's Earnings as a Percentage of Men's
Managerial	46 600	69 000	67.4
Administrative	35 500	55 700	63.7
Professions			
Business/Finance	55 800	80 400	69.3
Natural Sciences	55 300	66 500	83.1
Social Sciences/Religion	63 900	91 200	70.0
Teaching	47 500	63 300	75.0
Medicine/Health	61 100	116 300	52.5
Artistic/Recreational	33 600	41 900	80.0
Clerical	33 300	41 800	79.7
Sales/Service	24 100	43 300	55.7
Trades/Transportation	24 800	43 500	57.1
Primary	19 200	31 500	60.8
Manufacturing	26 200	45 100	58.1
Total	36 500	51 700	70.5

Source: Statistics Canada, *Women in Canada*, various years.

TABLE 15-4	Women's Earnings as a Ratio of Men's Earnings, Full-Time, Full-Year Workers
Year	Women's Earnings as a Percentage of Men's
1991	68.7
1996	72.3
2003	70.5

Source: Statistics Canada, *Women in Canada*, various years.

gendered wage gap fluctuated, though the general pattern remained fairly stable[7] (see Table 15-4).

As Table 15-5 illustrates, the gendered wage gap appears across all educational levels, ranging from a low of 57% of men's wages for women with some secondary schooling, to a high of 76% for those with some post-secondary training. In 2003, a woman with a university degree earned an average annual income of $53 400, considerably more than most female workers, but $24 100 less than the average man with a university degree. One reason for this is that occupational segregation cuts across educational levels. Most often, women and men with similar levels of education are trained in different fields and are not employed in the same jobs. While women are a majority of university students enrolled in bachelor's degrees in health professions (76%), education (78%), fine arts (67%), and humanities (61%), women are a

TABLE 15-5	Average Annual Earnings, by Education and Gender, Full-Time, Full-Year Workers, 2003		
Educational Attainment	Women	Men	Women's Earnings as a Percentage of Men's
Less than grade 9	21 700	31 200	69.4
Some secondary school	22 900	40 000	57.3
Secondary school graduate	30 500	43 000	71.0
Some post-secondary	31 500	41 600	75.6
Post-secondary certificate/diploma	34 200	49 800	68.6
University degree	53 400	77 500	68.9
Total	36 500	51 700	70.5

Source: Statistics Canada, *Women in Canada*, various years.

minority in the fields of science and mathematics (30%) and engineering (24%) (Statistics Canada 2006b:100). Differences in educational fields result in different occupational opportunities.

Even within identical occupations requiring specialized educational qualifications, however, a gendered wage gap remains. For example, one study found the following inequities within the professions: female judges earned 90.5%, doctors (general practitioners) 72.5%, doctors (specialists) 61.2%, dentists 63.7%, engineers 71.8%, lawyers 67.4%, and university professors 79.7% of what their male counterparts earned in 2000 (Krahn et al. 2007:192).Although women working in traditionally male-dominated professions are economically advantaged relative to other women, they remain disadvantaged relative to their male colleagues.

EVERYDAY INEQUALITIES ON THE JOB

As we have seen, women have entered formerly male occupations, but most are either in new female subspecialties or in occupations that become feminized; in either case, women typically continue to earn less than their male colleagues. Ensuring equality of access to diverse occupations is not enough to ensure equality on the job. Simply getting into an occupation or profession where women have historically been underrepresented does not ensure that women's experiences there will be the same as men's. There may still be significant barriers to full participation. When women enter a traditionally male workplace, they often face highly gendered workplace cultures. Men may engage in boundary "heightening," exaggerating gender differences to exclude women by increasing sexual banter (Reskin and Padavic 1994) or resorting to sexual harassment (Cockburn 1991).

More commonly, in traditionally male-dominated jobs, women may face "subtle sexism," an everyday kind of gender inequality that has been internalized "as 'normal,' 'natural,' or 'acceptable'" (Benokraitis 1997:11). For example, women lawyers have been found to face instances of hostile humour, isolation, diminishment, devaluation, and discouragement that cumulatively exclude them, rendering them less confident and less productive (Haslett and Lipman 1997). Women in medicine struggle to dress professionally while seeking to balance femininity, authority, comfort, and practicality; yet they are still often mistaken for nurses (Beagan 2002). Operating rooms are designed to fit typical male proportions: the operating tables, the clamps, the instruments—everything is built for a man's hand and a man's height. When a small woman is in the operating room, she faces physical problems, and may become seen as *being* a problem when she places extra demands on staff to accommodate her differences (Beagan 2002).

While any single incident or event may appear to be too trivial to confront, the power of these everyday forms of gender inequality lies in the "aggregate burden" they accumulate through daily repetition. Over time these micro-level inequities may "constitute a formidable barrier to performance, productivity, and advancement" (Haslett and Lipman 1997:51). Such daily gender practices, which occur at the level of everyday interactions between individuals, may be intentional or unintentional (Frehill 1997); nonetheless, they constitute the commonplace processes through which gender inequality is enacted and perpetuated at work (O'Brien 1998).

SEEKING SOLUTIONS: STRATEGIES FOR EQUALITY IN NEO-LIBERAL TIMES

There are four main strategies proposed to achieve greater gender equality in the labour market: (1) policies to hire more women in higher-paying jobs traditionally held by men (employment equity); (2) programs to raise the monetary value of work traditionally performed by women (pay equity); (3) attempts to organize a larger segment of the low-wage workforce (unionization); and (4) strategies to accommodate and, equally important, to redistribute domestic responsibilities linked to the household (domestic labour). Each of these strategies promises some improvement in the situation of women workers; each also has limitations;

and each initiative is currently being undermined by neo-liberal reforms.

Employment Equity

Given the depth of gendered occupational segregation, one of the most important policy initiatives is the incorporation of employment equity programs to eliminate barriers to employment and implement positive policies and practices to correct systematic disadvantages experienced by women, Aboriginal peoples, people with disabilities, and people in visible minority groups. The federal Employment Equity Act was passed in 1986 and revised in 1996. It requires public-sector and federally regulated private-sector employers with 100 or more employees to develop plans to ensure that their staff represents the qualified workforce available. For example, if women make up 40% of trained biologists, eventually 40% of biologists employed in a government department should be women. The Act applies to about 8% of the Canadian labour force (Treasury Board of Canada Secretariat 2002).

Seven provinces (British Columbia,[8] Manitoba, Saskatchewan, Quebec, Nova Scotia, New Brunswick, and Prince Edward Island) developed employment equity policies (not laws) that apply to the provincial public service. Ontario introduced employment equity legislation in 1994, under a New Democratic government. Grounded on a belief in the existence of systemic oppression requiring systemic remedies, it applied to most employers in the province. In 1995, a newly elected Progressive Conservative government made repealing the Act one of its first actions, arguing that "special measures" are themselves discriminatory (Bakan and Kobayashi 2000; Abu-Laban & Gabriel 2002).

By all reports, the success of employment equity in achieving its goals has been modest. Until the early 1990s, improvements were minimal; since 1996, stronger enforcement mechanisms have meant some improvements for women, particularly Aboriginal women, though people with disabilities are still significantly underrepresented and people from other visible minority groups have seen little improvement (Bakan and Kobayashi 2000). The increasing employment of women and Aboriginal peoples in the public sector has occurred as governments shifted drastically from permanent positions to term-contract and casual positions. Moreover, the target groups have been hired largely into administrative support and clerical positions (Bakan and Kobayashi 2000).

Several limitations of employment equity restrict its impact in equalizing job opportunities for women. First, it only covers a fraction of the workforce, almost entirely limited to the public service. Furthermore, recent neo-liberal policies in some provinces (for example, Ontario and British Columbia) have further reduced rather than expanded coverage. Second, at the federal level employment equity was very poorly enforced until the 1996 revisions. Even now, an employer cannot be required to take steps that would cause "undue hardship" on the employer (Treasury Board of Canada Secretariat 2002). Third, equality is defined as the proportion of women employed relative to the proportion of women available in the trained workforce. This fails to address systemic gender segregation, which, as we have seen, results in very small proportions of women qualified for some occupations.

Pay Equity

While employment equity policies seek to equalize women's representation in male-dominated occupations, pay equity policies seek to address the consistent underpaying of "women's jobs" relative to comparable "men's jobs." As early as the 1950s, legislation was passed in most provinces requiring equal pay for equal work, but occupational segregation meant that women and men seldom did the same work (Wilson 1996:129). Beginning in the late 1970s, the federal government and several provinces[9] introduced legislation that requires "equal pay for work of equal value"—meaning jobs that are comparable in terms of skill, effort, working conditions, and responsibility—which is usually assessed through complex systems of job evaluation. This process allows very different job categories to be compared across segregated occupations (for example, comparing male janitors and female receptionists working at a university, or female nurses and male lab technicians working at a hospital).

At the federal level, pay equity is addressed through the Canadian Human Rights Act, section 11, prohibiting wage discrimination between male and female employees performing work of equal value. It is a complaints-based model, in which pay practices only come under scrutiny if a complaint is made. Cases can take years to process, at enormous cost. The burden is on the workers who make the complaint to bear the cost of systemic change; in effect, only workers represented by large unions have recourse to this measure (Iyer 2002). Some provinces developed more proactive pay equity legislation. Ontario's 1987 Pay Equity Act requires all private- and public-sector employers with 10 or more employees to achieve and maintain pay equity by classing jobs as predominantly male or female and comparing the value of work done in each job class using a gender-neutral job comparison system (Iyer 2002). However, it is limited in that it only compares job classes, not male and female workers within job classes. Furthermore, there is little enforcement by the government.[10]

Though pay equity has led to significant pay settlements for some groups of women, at neither the federal nor provincial levels has it resulted in a significant reduction of the gendered wage gap (Iyer 2002). It is usually limited to comparisons within an individual workplace, so in predominantly female workplaces there may be no appropriate male comparators. Moreover, the majority of the workforce is not covered by pay equity legislation. Some provinces have never passed pay equity legislation, while others, such as British Columbia, have recently repealed these initiatives.[11] Iyer (2002) concludes that pay equity is of greatest benefit to women in large unionized workplaces who are employed full-time in specific sectors. The most economically vulnerable women, and those most likely to experience wage discrimination, are least likely to benefit from pay equity policies.

Unionization

Another potential solution is to increase rates of unionization in low-wage sectors, sectors that are also disproportionately female. On average, unionized workers enjoy higher wages and better benefits than their non-union counterparts, and the gap is greatest for part-time workers, the vast majority of whom are women. In 1998, the average hourly wage for unionized part-time workers was $16.71 compared with $9.76 for non-union part-timers; full-time unionized workers earned $19.01 an hour compared with $15.50 for non-union full-timers (Akyeampong 1998:42). Moreover, on average, "full-time unionized women earned 90% of their male counterparts' hourly wages" (Akyeampong 1998:34). Historically, unions were male preserves centred in blue-collar industries like manufacturing, construction, logging, and mining. Over the last four decades, large numbers of public-sector workers also formed unions, bringing civil servants, nurses, teachers, and postal workers into the labour movement. Today, employees in the public sector are more than three times as likely as those in the private sector to be members of unions (Akyeampong 1998:34). As a result of these changes in patterns of unionization, about half of all union members today are women (Statistics Canada 2006b:112).

Men and women are equally likely to be union members, 32% of each in 2004 (Statistics Canada 2006b:112). And while unionization does decrease the gendered wage gap for the same job, unions have not decreased gender segregation in the workplace. Moreover, unions have historically been male-dominated institutions and women still remain underrepresented in positions of leadership. Issues of gender equity are often not seen as union priorities. Women unionists have identified a number of strategies that would make unions more sensitive to gender equity. These include targeting union organizing among part-time and low-wage workers, pursuing solidarity bargaining so the gap between higher- and lower-paid workers becomes narrower,[12] and focusing on stronger bargaining for "women's issues" such as daycare, pay equity, employment equity, and policies on sexual harassment (Creese 1999:209–220).

Of course, most employees (nearly 70%) are not covered by collective agreements of any kind. And during the last decade, government policies to reduce employment in the public sector, contract out public services to private for-profit companies, and curtail the ability to organize unions and to strike have been adopted by governments across the country, most notably in Ontario, Alberta, and British Columbia. Such policies are intended to decrease rates of unionization, lower wages in the public sector, and generally limit the influence of unions. As long as these policies dominate the political agenda, it is less likely that unionization will provide a solution for most women seeking equality at work.

Domestic Labour

One of the most important dimensions of the gendered division of labour, as we noted earlier, is the uneven distribution of domestic labour in the household. In 2000, women were 2.5 times as likely as men to look after children for more than 30 hours a week, 2.9 times more likely to do 30 hours of housework a week, and 2.0 times more likely to spend more than 10 hours caring for an elderly person every week (Corman and Luxton 2007:269). Even when women work full-time in the labour force, most retain primary responsibility for child care, elder care, housework, shopping, and food preparation. This extra domestic work (73 additional 8-hour shifts every year for women with children at home) may limit women's ability to compete for jobs or promotions that demand long hours, to relocate for employment purposes, or to pursue further education to upgrade skills. The uneven division of labour in the household disadvantages women in the workplace, making it difficult to compete with male colleagues who often have a wife to shoulder the greater burden of domestic responsibilities. We need to recognize that workplaces have been structured around the experience of men who have someone else to care for home and hearth; as such, most workplaces allow little flexibility for employees to perform domestic tasks (Hessing 1992).

Unfortunately, neo-liberal policies are likely to intensify domestic work by downloading more responsibilities back to individual households (Armstrong and Armstrong 2001). Patients are released from hospital earlier to be cared for at home (usually by wives, mothers, or daughters). Home-care services are cut back for the elderly, who must turn to relatives for support (usually daughters or daughters-in-law). Public funding for daycare is cut and subsidies reduced, forcing some parents (usually mothers) out of the labour market or into lower-paying part-time jobs. Class sizes are increased and special-education teachers are reduced so more children require additional help at home (often from mothers). All of these policy decisions result in more domestic work that disproportionately falls on women's shoulders.

If we wish to level the playing field for women and men in the workplace, we need to support public programs designed to meet the needs of employed women and their families. Initiatives that will improve gender equity in the workplace include government-supported low-cost daycare and better maternity and paternity leave provisions; adequate social services in areas such as health, education, and home care; and "family friendly" employee programs such as on-site daycare, flex-time, family leave, and a work culture that does not demand excessive overtime or frequent relocation to qualify for promotions. These measures would improve the situation of all parents, especially single mothers, who head one in every five families with children (Statistics Canada 2006b:38). In the long run, however, men must also begin to take on a much larger share of domestic responsibilities. Although men are doing more domestic work today than in the past, the division of labour is still far from equal.

Without significant change on the domestic front, gender segregation in low-paying jobs will likely remain the reality for most women. Women who do pursue high-powered careers—for example, in areas like law—are still more likely to be single and/or childless (Hagan and Kay 1995; Reskin and Padavic 1994). Men do not have to make a choice between children and a successful career, and women should not have to either. Redefining the domestic division of labour may also help to break down the sharp gendered distinctions and social value attached to men's work and women's work. We might just begin to "do gender" differently at work if we also do it differently, and more equitably at home.

CONCLUSION

In the period since the Second World War, labour force participation rates of women and men have become more similar than different, but major differences remain in the gender segregation of occupations, in the wages earned by women and men, and in the uneven distribution of unpaid work in the household. Gender segregation and a significant income gap are not easy to overcome, and contemporary neo-liberal policies pose a significant barrier to achieving greater gender equity. Measures proposed to provide women with access to more and higher-paying jobs in the labour market include employment equity, pay equity, unionization, and various initiatives by governments, employers, and men in their individual households, to better support families and equalize responsibilities for domestic labour. Although none of these proposals alone provides a solution to existing forms of gender inequality, in combination these strategies could promise to substantially improve the situation of women in the workplace.

NOTES

1. In two-person households without children there was less domestic labour performed, but women still did the lion's share: women performed 3.0 hours of domestic labour each day, while men performed 2.4 hours (Statistics Canada 2000:111).

2. Labour force participation rates vary with economic conditions across the country, ranging from the lowest levels in Newfoundland (46.7% of women and 53.7% of men) to the highest levels in Alberta (64.7% of women and 76.1% of men) (Statistics Canada 2006b:119).

3. Reasons for the decline in men's labour force participation include the development of universal old age pensions, income security programs for ill and injured workers, and economic restructuring and job loss.

4. The unemployment rates for women and men have fluctuated during the last few decades but women are currently less likely than men to be unemployed. In 2004, the unemployment rate for adult women was 6.8%, and for men 7.5% (Statistics Canada 2006b:129).

5. Women are also less likely to be self-employed: 11% of women and 19% of men were self-employed in 2004 (Statistics Canada 2006b:129).

6. Yearly employment earnings are not available, but in 1998 women with disabilities aged 35 to 49 years earned a median hourly wage of $12.36 compared with $15.05 for women without disabilities (82%) (Canadian Council on Social Development 2002). Average annual income (from all sources) in 2000 was $17 200 for women with disabilities, $5000 less than for women without disabilities (Statistics Canada 2006b:296).

7. Two decades of job losses, mostly full-time unionized jobs, in the primary and secondary industries, and an increase of lower-wage, often part-time, jobs in the service sector have produced a notable decline in young men's wages (Morissette 1997:8-12). Given this, we might expect some narrowing of the gendered gap simply due to the decline in men's wages without reflecting a real increase in women's wages.

8. The Liberal government in British Columbia eliminated the employment equity policy in the public service. The policy had been implemented by the previous New Democratic government.

9. Manitoba, Nova Scotia, New Brunswick, Ontario, Prince Edward Island, and Quebec all have pay equity legislation. British Columbia, Newfoundland and Labrador, Saskatchewan, and the Yukon use human rights codes to address pay equity.

10. Failure to enforce legislation makes its value questionable. Iyer (2002) notes that among Ontario private-sector employers of 50 or fewer employees, non-compliance with the Pay Equity Act is as high as 90%.

11. A pay equity provision was added to the Human Rights Code by the NDP government in British Columbia just prior to the 2001 election, but was quickly repealed by the new Liberal government (Iyer 2002).

12. Traditionally, unions negotiate for percentage wage increases that, over time, increase the gap between higher- and lower-wage workers. Solidarity wage bargaining requires a commitment to raise the wages of workers at the bottom end of the pay scales (usually women) more than those at the top (usually men) to narrow the wage gap over time. This is a common practice in some countries—for example, in the Swedish labour movement—but uncommon in Canada.

REFERENCES

Abu-Laban, Yasmeen, and Christina Gabriel 2002. *Selling Diversity: Immigration, Multiculturalism, Employment Equity, and Globalization*. Peterborough, ON: Broadview Press.

Akyeampong, Ernest 1998. "The rise of unionization among women." *Perspectives on Labour and Income* 10, 4:30–43.

Armstrong, Pat, and Hugh Armstrong 2001. *Thinking It Through: Women, Work and Caring in the New Millennium*. Halifax: Healthy Balance Research Program.

Association of Canadian Medical Colleges 2004. *Canadian Medical Education Statistics* 26.

Bakan, Abigail, and Audrey Kobayashi 2000. *Employment Equity Policy in Canada: An Interprovincial Comparison*. Ottawa: Status of Women Canada (March).

Beagan, Brenda L. 2002. "Micro inequities and everyday inequalities: 'Race,' gender, sexuality and class in medical school." *Canadian Journal of Sociology* 26, 4:583–610.

Benokraitis, Nijole V. 1997. "Sex discrimination in the twenty-first century." In Nijole V. Benokraitis (ed.), *Subtle Sexism: Current Practice and Prospects for Change*, pp. 5–33. Thousand Oaks, CA: Sage.

Calzavara, Liviana 1993. "Trends and policy in employment opportunities for women." In James Curtis, Edward Grabb, and Neil Guppy (eds.), *Social Inequality in Canada* (2nd ed.), pp. 311–326. Toronto: Prentice Hall Canada.

Canadian Council on Social Development 2002. *Disability Information Sheet* Nos. 2 and 4. Retrieved May 27, 2002 (http://www.ccsd.ca/drip/research/dis4/index.htm).

Cockburn, Cynthia 1991. *In the Way of Women: Men's Resistance to Sex Equality in Organizations*. London: Macmillan.

Corman, June, and Meg Luxton 2007. "Social reproduction and the changing dynamics of unpaid household and caregiving work." In Vivian Shalla and Wallace Clement (eds.), *Work in Tumultuous Times: Critical Perspectives*, pp. 262–288. Montreal: McGill-Queen's University Press.

Creese, Gillian 1999. *Contracting Masculinity: Gender, Class and Race in a White-Collar Union, 1944–1994*. Don Mills, ON: Oxford University Press.

Frehill, Lisa M. 1997. "Subtle sexism in engineering." In Nijole V. Benokraitis (ed.), *Subtle Sexism: Current Practice and Prospects for Change*, pp. 117–135. Thousand Oaks, CA: Sage.

Hagan, John, and Fiona Kay 1995. *Gender in Practice: A Study of Lawyers' Lives*. New York: Oxford University Press.

Haslett, Beth Bonniwell, and Susan Lipman 1997. "Micro inequities: Up close and personal." In Nijole V. Benokraitis (ed.), *Subtle Sexism: Current Practice and Prospects for Change*, pp. 34–53. Thousand Oaks, CA: Sage.

Hessing, Melody 1992. "Talking on the job: Office conversations and women's dual labour." In Gillian Creese and Veronica Strong-Boag (eds.), *British Columbia Reconsidered: Essays on Women*, pp. 391–415. Vancouver: Press Gang Publishers.

Iyer, Nityz 2002. *"Working Through the Wage Gap": Report of the Task Force on Pay Equity*. Victoria, BC: Attorney General's Office.

Jackson, Andrew 2005. *Work and Labour in Canada: Critical Issues.* Toronto: Canadian Scholars' Press.

Krahn, Harvey, Graham Lowe, and Karen Hughes 2007. *Work, Industry & Canadian Society.* Toronto: Thomson, Nelson.

Morissette, René 1997. "Declining earnings of young men." *Canadian Social Trends* 46 (Autumn):8–12.

O'Brien, Jodi 1998. "Introduction: Difference and inequalities." In Jodi O'Brien and Judith A. Howard (eds.), *Everyday Inequalities: Critical Inquiries*, pp. 1–39. Malden, MA: Blackwell.

Padavic, Irene 1991. "Attractions of male blue-collar jobs for black and white women: Economic need, exposure, and attitudes." *Social Science Quarterly* 72, 1:33–49.

Pendakur, Krishna, and Ravi Pendakur 2004. "Colour my world: Has the majority–minority earnings gap changed over time?" Vancouver Centre of Excellence Research on Immigration and Integration in the Metropolis, Working Paper Series no. 04-11 (May).

Reskin, Barbara, and Irene Padavic 1994. *Women and Men at Work.* Thousand Oaks, CA: Pine Forge Press.

Reskin, Barbara, and Patricia Roos 1990. *Job Queues, Gender Queues: Explaining Women's Inroads into Male Occupations.* Philadelphia: Temple University Press.

Roos, Patricia, and Barbara Reskin 1992. "Occupational desegregation in the 1970s: Integration and economic equity?" *Sociological Perspectives* 34, 1:62–91.

Statistics Canada 2000. *Women in Canada 2000: A Gender-Based Statistical Report.* Ottawa: Minister of Industry (September).

Statistics Canada 2006a. *General Social Survey on Time Use: Overview of the Time Use of Canadians 2005.* Ottawa: Minister of Industry (July).

Statistics Canada 2006b. *Women in Canada: A Gender-Based Statistical Report* (5th ed.). Ottawa: Minister of Industry (March).

Treasury Board of Canada Secretariat 2002. "Overview of the Employment Equity Act (1996) from a Public Service Perspective." Retrieved May 8, 2002 (http://www.tbs.sct.gc.ca/Pubs_pol/TB_852/OVER1E.html).

Wilson, S.J. 1996. *Women, Families and Work* (4th ed.). Toronto: McGraw-Hill Ryerson.

The Ebb and Flow of Immigration in Canada

Monica Boyd and Michael Vickers
(Adapted and updated from Statistics Canada, *100 Years of Immigration in Canada*, from the Statistics Canada publication *Canadian Social Trends*, Catalogue 11-008, Autumn 2000, pp. 2–11. Reprinted with permission.)

INTRODUCTION

Record numbers of immigrants came to Canada in the early 1900s. During the First World War and the Depression years, numbers declined but, by the close of the twentieth century, they had again approached those recorded almost 100 years earlier. Despite the superficial similarities at the beginning and the end of a century of immigration, the characteristics of immigrants are quite different. This change reflects many factors: developments and modifications in Canada's immigration polices; the displacement of peoples by wars and political upheaval; the cycle of economic "booms and busts"

in Canada and other countries; Canada's membership in the Commonwealth; and the growth of communication, transportation, and economic networks linking people around the world.

These forces have operated throughout the twentieth century to alter the basic characteristics of Canada's immigrant population in five fundamental ways. First, the numbers of immigrants arriving each year have waxed and waned, meaning that the importance of immigration for Canada's population growth has fluctuated. Second, immigrants increasingly chose to live in Canada's largest cities. Third, the predominance of men among adult immigrants declined as family migration grew and women came to represent slightly over half of immigrants. Fourth, the marked transformation in the countries in which immigrants had been born enhanced the ethnic diversity of Canadian society. Fifth, alongside Canada's transition from an agricultural to a knowledge-based economy, immigrants were increasingly employed in the manufacturing and service sectors of the economy. This article provides an overview of these important changes over the last 100 years.

THE EARLY YEARS: 1900–1915

The twentieth century opened with the arrival of nearly 42 000 immigrants in 1900. Numbers quickly escalated to a record high of over 400 000 in 1913. Canada's economy was growing rapidly during these years, and immigrants were drawn by the promise of good job prospects. The building of the transcontinental railway, the settlement of the prairies, and expanding industrial production intensified demand for labour. Aggressive recruitment campaigns by the Canadian government to boost immigration and attract workers also increased arrivals: between 1900 and 1914, more than 2.9 million people entered Canada, nearly four times as many as had arrived in the previous 14-year period.

Such volumes of immigrants quickly enlarged Canada's population. Between 1901 and 1911, net migration (the excess of those arriving over those leaving) accounted for 44% of population growth, a level not reached again for another 75 years. The share of the overall population born outside Canada also increased in consequence, so that while immigrants accounted for 13% of the population in 1901, by 1911 they made up 22%.

Most of the foreign-born population lived in Ontario at the start of the century, but many later immigrants headed west. By 1911, 41% of Canada's immigrant population lived in the Prairies, up from 20% recorded in the 1901 Census. This influx had a profound effect on the populations of the western provinces. By 1911, immigrants represented 41% of people living in Manitoba, 50% in Saskatchewan, and 57% of those in Alberta and British Columbia. In contrast, they made up less than 10% of the population in the Atlantic provinces and Quebec, and only 20% in Ontario.

Men greatly outnumbered women among people settling in Canada in the first two decades of the twentieth century (Urquhart and Buckley 1965). The 1911 Census recorded 158 immigrant males for every 100 females, compared with 103 Canadian-born males for 100 females. These unbalanced gender ratios are not uncommon in the history of settlement countries such as Canada, Australia, and the United States. They often reflect labour recruitment efforts targeted at men rather than women, as well as the behaviour of immigrants themselves. In migration flows, particularly those motivated by economic reasons, men frequently precede women, either because the move is viewed as temporary and there is no need to uproot family members, or because the man intends to become economically established before being joined by his family. By the time of the 1921 Census, the gender ratio for immigrants had become less skewed, standing at 125 immigrant males for every 100 immigrant females. It continued to decline throughout the century, reaching 93 per 100 in 2001.

What You Should Know about This Study

This chapter draws on numerous data sources, with the principal sources being the 1901 to 2001 Censuses of Population, and immigration statistics collected by Citizenship and Immigration Canada. It also draws on research by historians and sociologists specializing in immigration issues.

Immigration: the movement of people into a country for purposes of legal settlement.

Net migration: the difference between immigration and emigration (the flow of people leaving the country permanently).

Immigrants/foreign born: principally people who are, or have been, landed immigrants in Canada. A landed immigrant is a person who has been granted the right to live in Canada permanently by immigration authorities. Some are recent arrivals; others have resided in Canada for many years.

Non-permanent residents: people from another country who live in Canada and have work, student, or Minister's permits, or claim refugee status. They are not included in the immigrant population after 1986, except in growth projections.

Refugee: according to the 1951 United Nations Convention on refugees, a refugee is a person who " . . . owing to well founded fear of being persecuted for reasons of race, religion, nationality, membership of a particular social group or political opinion, is outside the country of his nationality and is unable, or owing to such fear, is unwilling to avail himself of the protection of that country . . . " As a signatory to this convention, Canada uses the UN definition of a refugee in assessing who is eligible to enter Canada as a refugee.

Visible minority population: the Employment Equity Act defines visible minorities as "persons, other than Aboriginal peoples, who are non-Caucasian in race or non-white in colour." The visible minority population includes the following groups: blacks, South Asians, Chinese, Koreans, Japanese, Southeast Asians, Filipinos, Arabs and West Asians, Latin Americans, and Pacific Islanders.

Of course, women also immigrated for economic reasons in the early decades of the century. There was strong demand for female domestic workers, with women in England, Scotland, and Wales being most often targeted for recruitment. Between 1904 and 1914, "domestic" was by far the most common occupation reported by adult women immigrants (almost 30%) arriving from overseas. Men immigrating from overseas during that period were more likely to be unskilled and semi-skilled labourers (36%) or to have a farming occupation (32%) (Urquahart and Buckley 1965). Historians observe that, contrary to the image of immigrants being farmers and homesteaders, immigrants at the turn of the century were also factory and construction workers. And although many did settle in the western provinces, many also worked building railroads or moved into the large cities, fuelling the growth of industrial centres.

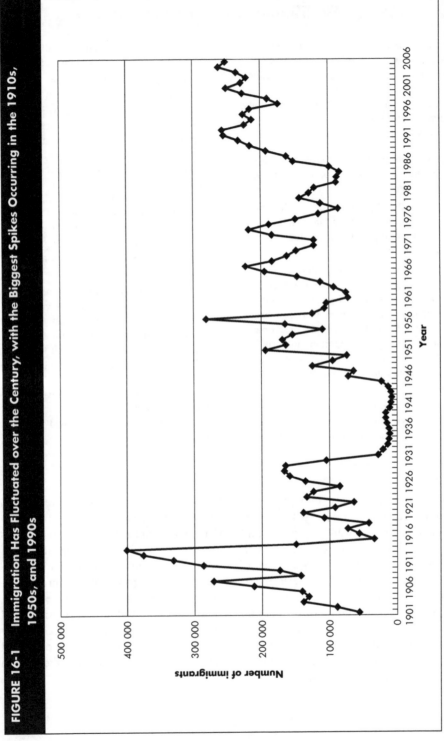

FIGURE 16-1 Immigration Has Fluctuated over the Century, with the Biggest Spikes Occurring in the 1910s, 1950s, and 1990s

Sources: Citizenship and Immigration Canada, *Facts and Figures 1998: Immigration Overview*; Citizenship and Immigration Canada, *Facts and Figures 2002*. (www.cic.gc.ca/english/pub/facts2002/immigration/immigration_1.html); Citizenship and Immigration Canada, *Facts and Figures 2006*. (www.cic.gc.ca/english/resources/statistics/facts2006/index.asp).

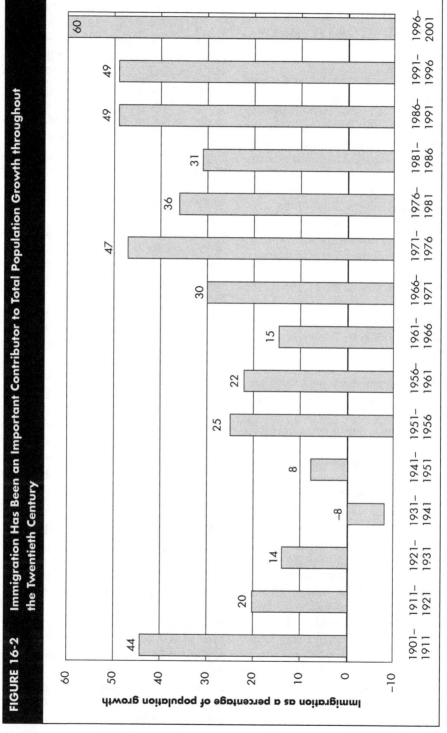

FIGURE 16-2   Immigration Has Been an Important Contributor to Total Population Growth throughout the Twentieth Century

Source: Statistics Canada, *Census of Population* (http://epe.lac-bac.gc.ca/100/205/301/statcan/canada_e-book-ef/05-01-21/www.statcan.ca/english/Pgdb/demo03.htm).

IMMIGRATION FROM OUTSIDE BRITAIN AND THE U.S. BEGINS TO GROW IN 1910S

At the start of the century, the majority of immigrants to Canada had originated in the United States or the United Kingdom. However, during the 1910s and 1920s, the number born in other European countries began to grow, slowly at first, and then rising to its highest levels in 1961 and 1971.

This change in countries of origin had begun in the closing decades of the nineteenth century, when many new groups began to arrive in Canada—Doukhobors and Jewish refugees from Russia; Hungarians; Mormons from the U.S.; Italians; and Ukrainians. This flow continued up until the First World War. It generated public debate about who should be admitted to Canada: For some writers and politicians, recruiting labour was the key issue, not the changing origins of immigrants; for others, British and American immigrants were to be preferred to those from southern or eastern European countries.

By comparison, immigration from Asia was very low at this time, in dramatic contrast to the situation at the end of the twentieth century. Government policies regulating immigration had been rudimentary during the late 1800s, but when legislation was enacted in the early 1900s, it focused primarily on preventing immigration on the grounds of poverty, mental incompetence, or on the basis of non-European origins. Even though Chinese immigrant workers had helped to build the transcontinental railroad, in 1885 the first piece of legislation regulating future Chinese immigration required every person of Chinese origin to pay a tax of $50 upon entering Canada. At the time, this was a very large sum. The "head tax" was increased to $100 in 1900, and to $500 in 1903. This fee meant that many Chinese men could not afford to bring brides or wives to Canada. As evidence of this fact, the 1911 Census recorded 2790 Chinese males for every 100 Chinese females, a figure far in excess of the overall ratio of 158 immigrant males for every 100 immigrant females.

The Act of 1906 prohibited the landing of persons defined as "feebleminded," having "loathsome or contagious diseases," "paupers," persons "likely to become public charges," criminals, and "those of undesirable morality." In 1908, the Act was amended to prohibit the landing of those persons who did not come to Canada directly from their country of origin. This provision effectively excluded the immigration of people from India, who had to book passage on ships sailing from countries outside India because there were no direct sailings between Calcutta and Vancouver. Also in the early 1900s, the Canadian government entered into a series of agreements with Japan that restricted Japanese migration (Calliste 1993; Kelley and Trebilcock 1998; Troper 1972). It should be noted that although Asians were the most severely targeted by efforts to reduce immigration by non-Europeans, other ethnic groups such as blacks from the United States and the Caribbean also were singled out.

THE WARS AND THE GREAT DEPRESSION: 1915–1946

With the outbreak of the First World War, immigration quickly came to a near standstill. From a record high of over 400 000 in 1913, arrivals dropped sharply to less than 34 000 by 1915. Although numbers rebounded after the war, they never again reached the levels attained before 1914. As a result, net immigration accounted for about 20% of Canada's population growth between 1911 and 1921, less than half the contribution made in the previous decade.

However, the influence of earlier foreign-born arrivals continued, reinforced by the more modest levels of wartime and post-war immigration: At the time of the 1921 Census, immigrants still comprised 22% of the population.

The number of immigrants coming to Canada rose during the 1920s, with well above 150 000 per year entering in the last three years of the decade. But the Great Depression and the Second World War severely curtailed arrivals during the 1930s and early 1940s—numbers fluctuated between 7600 and 27 500. Furthermore, there was actually a net migration loss of 92 000 as more people left Canada than entered between 1931 and 1941. The 1930s is the only decade in the twentieth century in which this occurred. By the time of the 1941 Census, the percentage of the total population that was foreign-born had fallen to just under 18%.

While more men than women had immigrated to Canada in the first three decades of the century, the situation was reversed when immigration declined in the 1930s and 1940s. During this period, women outnumbered men, accounting for 60% of all adult arrivals between 1931 and 1940, and for 66% between 1941 and 1945 (Urquahart and Buckley 1965). As a result of these changes, the overall gender ratio of the immigrant population declined slightly.

While lower numbers and the predominance of women among adult immigrants represented shifts in previous immigration patterns, other trends were more stable. The majority of immigrants continued to settle in Ontario, Manitoba, Saskatchewan, Alberta, and British Columbia. Increasingly, though, they gravitated to urban areas, foreshadowing the pattern of recent immigration concentration in large cities that became so evident in the last years of the century.

Britain was still the leading source of immigrants, but the arrival of people from other parts of the globe also continued. During the 1920s, the aftershocks of the

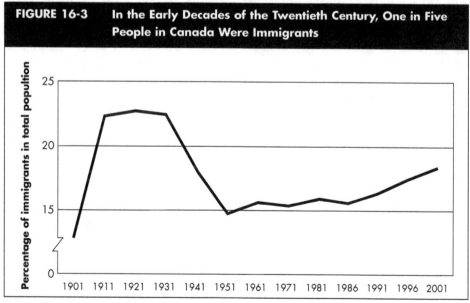

FIGURE 16-3   In the Early Decades of the Twentieth Century, One in Five People in Canada Were Immigrants

Sources: Statistics Canada, Catalogue No. 99-936 and Product No. 93F0020XCB; and *Canada's Ethnocultural Portrait: The Changing Mosaic.* 2001 Census: Analysis Series, p. 5. Catalogue No. 96F0030XIE2001008. Ottawa: Statistics Canada Census Operations Division. Retrieved October 9, 2007.(http://www12.statcan.ca/english/census01/products/analytic/companion/etoimm/pdf/96F0030XIE2001008.pdf).

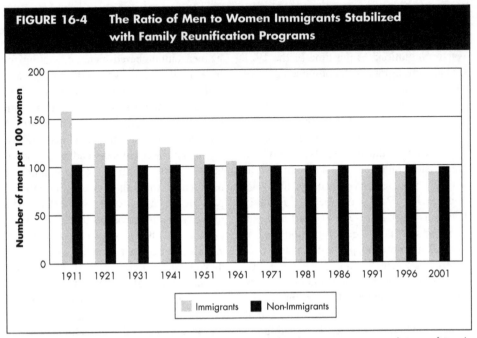

FIGURE 16-4   The Ratio of Men to Women Immigrants Stabilized with Family Reunification Programs

Sources: Statistics Canada, Catalogue Nos. 99-936, 93-155, 93-316, and Product No. 93F0020XCB; and *Census of Canada, 2001: Immigrant Status and Place of Birth of Respondent, Sex and Age Groups for Population.* Ottawa: Statistics Canada. Retrieved October 9, 2007.(http://prod.library.utoronto.ca:8090/datalib/datar/cc01/bct/357/95f0357xcb01001.ivt).

First World War and the Russian Revolution stimulated migration from Germany, Russia, Ukraine, and Eastern European countries including Poland and Hungary (Kelley and Trebilcock 1998). During the Depression, the majority of immigrants came from Great Britain, Germany, Austria, and Ukraine. Fewer than 6% were of non-European origin.

Public debate over whom to admit and the development of immigration policy to regulate admissions was far from over. Regulations passed in 1919 provided new grounds for deportation and denied entry to enemy aliens, to those who were enemy aliens during the war, and to Doukhobors, Mennonites, and Hutterites (Kalbach 1970). The 1923 Chinese Immigration Act restricted Chinese immigration still further (Avery 2000). Responding to labour market pressures following the Crash of 1929

and the collapse of the Prairie economy, farm workers, domestics, and several other occupational groups, as well as relatives of landed immigrants, were struck from the list of admissible classes. Asian immigration was also cut back again (Kalbach 1970).

Then, with the declaration of war on Germany on September 10, 1939, new regulations were passed that prohibited the entry or landing of nationals of countries with which Canada was at war. In the absence of a refugee policy that distinguished between immigrants and refugees, the restrictions imposed in the interwar years raised barriers to those fleeing the chaos and devastation of the Second World War. Many of those turned away at this time were Jewish refugees attempting to leave Europe (Abella and Troper 1982). War-related measures also included the forced relocation—often to detention camps—of Japanese Canadians living within a 100-mile area along the British Columbia coastline. It was argued that they might assist a Japanese invasion.

THE BOOM YEARS: 1946–1970

The war in Europe ended with Germany's surrender on May 6, 1945; in the Pacific, Japan surrendered on August 14. With the return of peace, both Canada's economy and immigration boomed. Between 1946 and 1950, over 430 000 immigrants arrived, exceeding the total number admitted in the previous 15 years.

The immediate post-war immigration boom included the dependants of Canadian servicemen who had married abroad, refugees, and people seeking economic opportunities in Canada. Beginning in July 1946, and continuing throughout the late 1940s, Orders-in-Council paved the way for the admission of people who had been displaced from their homelands by the war and for whom return was not possible (Kalbach 1970; Knowles 2007). The ruination of the European economy and the unprecedented boom in Canada also favoured high immigration levels.

Numbers continued to grow throughout most of the 1950s, peaking at over 282 000 admissions in 1957. By 1958, immigration levels were beginning to fall, partly because economic conditions were improving in Europe, and partly because, with the Canadian economy slowing, the government introduced administrative policies designed to reduce the rate of immigration. By 1962, however, the economy had recovered and arrivals increased for six successive years. Although admissions never reached the record highs observed in the early part of the century, the total number of immigrants entering Canada in the

1950s and 1960s far exceeded the levels observed in the preceding three decades.

During this time, net migration was higher than it had been in almost 50 years, but it accounted for no more than 30% of total population growth between 1951 and 1971. The population effect of the large number of foreign-born arrivals was muted by the magnitude of natural growth caused by the unprecedented birth rates recorded during the baby boom from 1946 to 1965.

Many of the new immigrants settled in cities, so that by 1961, 81% of foreign-born Canadians lived in an urban area, compared with 68% of Canadian-born. The proportion of the immigrant population living in Ontario continued to grow, accelerating a trend that had begun earlier in the century; in contrast, the proportion living in the Prairie provinces declined.

Such shifts in residential location went hand-in-hand with Canada's transformation from a rural agricultural and resource-based economy in the early years of the century to an urban manufacturing and service-based economy in the later years. Post-war immigrants were important sources of labour for this emerging economy, especially in the early 1950s. Compared with those arriving at the turn of the century, the post-war immigrants were more likely to be professional or skilled workers, and they accounted for over half of the growth in these occupations between 1951 and 1961.

Although the largest number of immigrants arriving after the Second World War were from the United Kingdom, people from other European countries were an increasingly predominant part of the mix. During the late 1940s and 1950s, substantial numbers also arrived from Germany, the Netherlands, Italy, Poland, and the U.S.S.R. Following the 1956 Soviet invasion of Hungary, Canada also admitted over 37 000 Hungarians, while the Suez Crisis of the same year saw the arrival of almost 109 000

British immigrants (Kalbach 1970; Kelley and Trebilcock 1998; Avery 2000; Hawkins 1972). During the 1960s, the trend increased. By the time of the 1971 Census, less than one-third of the foreign-born population had been born in the United Kingdom; half came from other European countries, many from Italy.

NEW POLICIES HELP DIRECT POST-WAR IMMIGRATION TRENDS

Much of the post-war immigration to Canada was stimulated by people displaced by war or political upheaval, as well as by the weakness of the European economies. However, Canada's post-war immigration policies also were an important factor. Because they were statements of who would be admitted and under what conditions, these policies influenced the numbers of arrivals, the types of immigrants, and the country of origin of new arrivals.

Within two years of the war ending, on May 1, 1947, Prime Minister Mackenzie King reaffirmed that immigration was vital for Canada's growth, but he also indicated that the numbers and country of origin of immigrants would be regulated. Five years later, the Immigration Act of 1952 consolidated many post-war changes to immigration regulations that had been enacted since the previous Act of 1927. Subsequent regulations that spelled out the possible grounds for limiting admissions included national origin; on this basis, admissible persons were defined to be those with birth or citizenship in the United States, the United Kingdom, Australia, New Zealand, the Union of South Africa, and selected European countries.

Children of Immigrants

One of the main reasons why people choose to uproot themselves and immigrate to another country is their desire to provide greater opportunities for their children. Thus, one of the main indicators used to measure the success of an immigrant's adaptation to Canadian society is the degree of success that their children achieve.

Such success is measured primarily in terms of socio-economic factors, such as increased educational attainment and level of occupational status, compared with the preceding generation. Analysis of data from the 1986 and 1994 General Social Surveys indicate that second-generation immigrants (Canadian-born children with at least one foreign-born parent) are generally more successful than their immigrant parents, and equally or more successful than third-generation children (both of whose parents are Canadian-born).

These findings are consistent with the "straight line" theory of the process of immigrant integration, which asserts that integration is cumulative: With each passing generation since immigration, the measurable differences between the descendants of immigrants and the Canadian-born are reduced until they are virtually indistinguishable. However, this theory's dominance has been challenged in recent years by analysts who argue that it is based primarily on the experiences of immigrants who were largely white and European, and whose children grew up during a period of unprecedented economic growth. They argue that this theory applies less well to more recent immigrants because it ignores changes in the social and economic structure of Canada in the latter half of the twentieth century. Also, it discounts the impact of barriers facing young immigrants, who are predominantly visible minorities, in their ability to integrate successfully.

Possible evidence of such barriers to the integration of the children of immigrants may be seen in an analysis of ethnic origin data for Canada's largest cities from the 1991 Census. This study found that among members of the so-called "1.5 generation"—the foreign-born children of immigrant parents—non-European ethnic origin groups were more likely to live in households that were more crowded and had lower per-capita household incomes than those with European origins.

For more information, see M. Boyd and E.M. Grieco 1998. "Triumphant transitions: Socioeconomic achievements of the second generation in Canada." *International Migration Review*; and M. Boyd 2000. "Ethnicity and immigrant offspring." *Race and Ethnicity: A Reader*.

In 1962, however, new regulations effectively removed national origin as a criterion of admission. Further regulations enacted in 1967 confirmed this principle and instead introduced a system that assigned points based on the age, education, language skills, and economic characteristics of applicants. These policy changes made it much easier for persons born outside Europe and the United States to immigrate to Canada.

The 1967 regulations also reaffirmed the right, first extended in the 1950s, of immigrants to sponsor relatives to enter Canada. Family-based immigration had always co-existed alongside economically motivated immigration, but now it was clearly defined. As wives, mothers, aunts, and sisters, women participated in these family reunification endeavours: Women accounted for almost half of all adult immigrants entering Canada during the 1950s and 1960s. As a result of this gender parity in immigration flows, gender ratios declined over time for the foreign-born population.

GROWTH AND DIVERSITY: 1970–2001

In the 1960s, changes in immigration policy were made by altering the regulations that governed implementation of the Immigration Act of 1952. But in 1978, a new Immigration Act came into effect. This Act upheld the principles of admissions laid out in the regulations of the 1960s: family reunification and economic contributions. For the first time in Canada's history, the new Act also incorporated the principle of admissions based on humanitarian grounds. Previously, refugee admissions had been handled through special procedures and regulations. The Act also required the minister responsible for the immigration portfolio to set annual immigration targets in consultation with the provinces. The most recent legislation, the Immigration and Refugee Protection Act, effective in June 2002, keeps these three criteria of admission; however, since the mid 1990s, economic migrants have outnumbered those entering on the basis of family reunification or humanitarian concerns.

From the 1970s through the 1990s, immigration numbers fluctuated. The overall impact, however, continued to be a significant contribution to Canada's total population growth that increased as the century drew to a close. With consistently high levels of arrivals after the mid 1980s, immigration accounted for about half of the population growth between 1986

FIGURE 16-5   **For Most of the Twentieth Century, Most Immigrants Settled in Ontario, British Columbia, and Quebec**

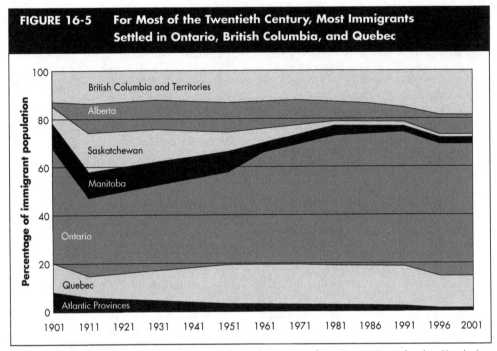

Sources: Statistics Canada, Product No. 93F0020XCB; 1901 Census of Population (Bulletin VIII); 1996 Census data: http://epe.lac-bac. gc.ca/100/205/301/statcan/canada_e-book-ef/05-01-21/www.statcan.ca/english/Pgdb/demo36c.htm; 2001 Census data: http://epe.lac-bac.gc.ca/100/205/301/statcan/canada_e-book-ef/05-01-21/www.statcan.ca/english/Pgdb/demo34d.htm. Accessed October 10, 2007.

and 1996 and 60% between 1996 and 2001. These percentages exceeded those recorded in the 1910s and the 1920s. The cumulative effect of net migration from the 1970s onward was a gradual increase in the percentage of foreign-born Canadians. By the time of the 2001 Census, immigrants comprised just over 18.4 % of the population, the largest proportion in more than 50 years.

Having an immigration policy based on principles of family reunification and labour market contribution also recast the composition of the immigrant population. It meant that people from all nations could be admitted if they met the criteria as described in the immigration regulations. The inclusion of humanitarian-based admissions also permitted the entry of refugees

from countries outside Europe. As a result, the immigrants who entered Canada from 1966 onward came from many different countries and possessed more diverse cultural backgrounds than earlier immigrants. Each successive census recorded declining percentages of the immigrant population that had been born in European countries, the United Kingdom, and the United States.

Meanwhile, the proportion of immigrants born in Asian countries and other regions of the world began to rise, slowly at first and then more quickly through the 1980s. By 2001, 36.5% of the immigrant population in Canada had been born in Asia and another 17% came from places other than the United States, the United Kingdom, or Europe. The top five places of birth for immigrants arriving between 1996 and 2001 were the People's Republic of China, India, Hong Kong, Pakistan, and the Philippines. Together, these five countries accounted for more than one-third of all immigrants who arrived in those six years.

IMMIGRATION THE LARGEST CONTRIBUTOR TO GROWTH OF VISIBLE MINORITY POPULATION

The visible minority population has grown dramatically in the last two decades. In 2001, 13.4% of Canada's population—almost 4 million people—identified themselves as members of a visible minority group, up from under 5% in 1981. Immigration has been a big contributor to this growth: About 7 in 10 visible minorities are immigrants, over three-quarters of whom have arrived since 1981.

Most immigrants live in Canada's big cities, with the largest numbers concentrated in the census metropolitan areas (CMAs) of Toronto, Montreal, and Vancouver. This continues the trend established earlier in the century. Proportionally more immigrants than Canadian-born have preferred to settle in urban areas, attracted by economic opportunities and by the presence of other immigrants from the same countries or regions of the world. In 2001, 87% of all immigrants lived in a CMA, compared with just 56% of the Canadian-born population. As a result, the largest CMAs have a higher concentration of immigrants than the national average of just over 18%. In 2001, 44% of Toronto's population, 38% of Vancouver's, and 19% of Montreal's were foreign-born.

The attraction to urban centres helps to explain the provincial distribution of immigrants. Since the 1940s, a disproportionate share has lived in Ontario and the percentage has continued to rise over time. By 2001, 55% of all immigrants lived in Ontario, compared with 18% in British Columbia and 13% in Quebec.

RECENT IMMIGRANTS' ADJUSTMENT TO LABOUR FORCE CAN BE DIFFICULT

Just as immigrants have contributed to the growth in Canada's population, to its diversity, and to its cities, so too have they contributed to its economy. During the last few decades, most employment opportunities have shifted from manufacturing to service industries, and immigrants are an important source of labour for some of these industries. However, compared with non-immigrants, they are more likely to be employed in the personal services industries, manufacturing, and construction. Moreover, the likelihood of being employed in one industry rather than another often differs depending on the immigrant's sex, age at arrival, education, knowledge of English and/or French, and length of time in Canada.

Living in a new society generally entails a period of adjustment, particularly when a person must look for work, learn a new language, or deal with an educational system, medical services, government agencies, and laws that may differ significantly from those in his or her country of origin. The difficulty of transition may be seen in the labour market profile of recent immigrants: Compared with longer-established immigrants and with those born in Canada, many may experience higher unemployment rates, hold jobs that do not reflect their level of training and education, and earn lower incomes. Further, studies of immigrant earnings indicate that recent arrivals are not doing as well as newly arrived groups that entered Canada in previous decades. Comparisons of the earnings of new arrivals across censuses since 1961 indicate that the relative entry earnings of those who arrived in the 1990s have declined over time. The earnings gap between immigrant and Canadian-born men widened from 11% in 1980 to 33% in 1995, before declining to 22% in 2000. Similar trends exist for the earnings gap between Canadian-born and immigrant women. The time necessary for the wages of new cohorts to catch up to those of the Canadian-born also is getting longer (Aydemir and Skuterud 2005; Frenette and Morissette 2005).

In the past, the disparities between recent immigrants and the Canadian-born have often disappeared over time, indicating that initial labour market difficulties reflect the adjustment process. The differences in the 1990s may also result from the diminished employment opportunities available during the recession, also a period of difficulty for the Canadian-born who were new entrants to the job market. Nevertheless, one review (Picot and Sweetman 2005) suggests that employers may be increasingly discounting foreign experience, treating immigrants as if they are new entrants to the labour force instead of being simply new arrivals in Canada.

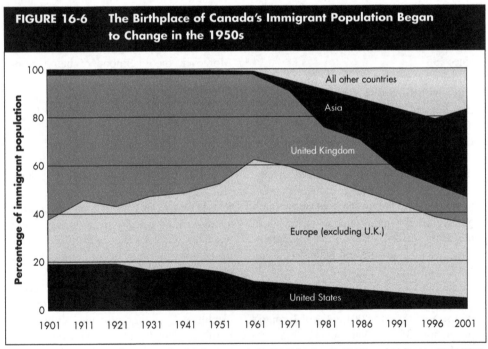

FIGURE 16-6   The Birthplace of Canada's Immigrant Population Began to Change in the 1950s

Sources: Statistics Canada, Catalogue Nos. 99-517 (Vol. VII, Part 1), 92-727 (Vol. I, Part 3), 92-913, and Product No. 93F0020XCB; 2001 data: http://epe.lac-bac.gc.ca/100/205/301/statcan/canada_e-book-ef/05-01-21/www.statcan.ca/english/Pgdb/demo34d.htm. Accessed October 10, 2007.

SUMMARY

Few would quarrel with the statement that the twentieth century in Canada was an era of enormous change. Every area of life, ranging from the economy to family to law, was altered over the course of a hundred years. Immigration was not immune to these transformative forces. The size and character of immigration flows were influenced by economic booms and busts, by world wars and national immigration policies, and indirectly by expanding communication, transportation, and economic links around the world.

The ebb and flow of immigration has presented the most volatile changes over the last 100 years. The twentieth century began with the greatest number of immigrant arrivals ever recorded. Thereafter, levels fluctuated, often with dramatic swings from one decade to the next. The lowest levels were recorded in the 1930s during the Depression. By the start of the new millennium, though, the number of immigrants arriving annually were again sufficiently large that net migration accounted for 60% of Canada's population growth.

Other changes in immigration are better described as trends, for they followed a course that was cumulative rather than reversible. The high ratio of men to women immigrants dropped steadily throughout the century. There were two main reasons for this decline. First, the number of men immigrating fell during the two world wars and the Depression; and second, the number of women immigrants increased in the last half of the century as a result of family reunification after the Second World War and of family migration, in which women, men, and their children immigrated together.

Even in the 1900s and 1910s, the foreign-born were more likely to live in urban areas. After the initial settlement of the Prairies in the early 1900s, the trend toward urban settlement accelerated. By 2001, the vast majority of recent immigrants were residing in census metropolitan areas, mainly those of Toronto, Vancouver, and Montreal.

Government policies regulating who would be admitted and under what conditions also evolved. Much of the effort during the first 50 years of the century focused on restricting immigration from regions of the world other than the U.S., Britain, and Europe. This position changed in the 1960s, when national origin was removed as a criterion for entry. The policies enacted thereafter entrenched the basic principles guiding admissions, such as family reunification, economic contributions, and humanitarian concerns. With these changes, the source countries of immigrants to Canada substantially altered. By the 2001 Census, over half of the foreign-born in Canada were from countries other than the UK, the U.S., and those in Europe.

As a result of these changes, Canada at the close of the twentieth century contrasted sharply with Canada 100 years before. Immigrants had increased the population; they had diversified the ethnic and linguistic composition of the country; and they had laboured in both the agrarian economy of old, and in the new industrial and service-based economy of the future.

REFERENCES

Abella, Irving, and Harold Troper 1982. *None Is Too Many: Canada and the Jews in Europe, 1933–1948.* Toronto: Lester & Orpen Dennys.

Avery, Donald 2000. "Peopling Canada." *The Beaver* 80, 1:28–38.

Aydemir, Abdurrahman, and Mikal Skuterud 2005. "Explaining the deteriorating entry earnings of Canada's immigrant cohorts,

1966–2000." *Canadian Journal of Economics* 38, 2:641–672.

Calliste, Agnes 1993 "Race, gender and Canadian immigration policy: Blacks from the Caribbean, 1900–1932." *Journal of Canadian Studies* 28, 4: 131–148.

Frenette, Marc, and René Morissette 2005. "Will they ever converge? Earnings of immigrant and Canadian-born workers for the last two decades." *International Migration Review* 39, 1:229–258.

Hawkins, Freda 1972. *Canada and Immigration: Public Policy and Public Concern.* Montreal: McGill-Queen's University Press.

Kalbach, Warren 1970. *The Impact of Immigration on Canada's Population.* Ottawa: Dominion Bureau of Statistics.

Kelley, Ninette, and M.J. Trebilcock 1998. *The Making of the Mosaic: A History of Canadian Immigration Policy.* Toronto: University of Toronto Press.

Knowles, Valerie 2007. *Strangers at Our Gates: Canadian Immigration and Immigration Policy, 1540–2006* (revised ed.). Toronto: Dundurn Press.

Picot, Garnett, and Arthur Sweetman 2005. "The deteriorating economic welfare of immigrants and possible causes: Update 2005." Statistics Canada: Analytical Studies Branch. Research Paper Series No. 262. (http://www.statcan.ca/english/research/11F0019MIE/11F0019MIE2005262.pdf)

Troper, Harold 1972. *Only Farmers Need Apply: Official Canadian Government Encouragement of Immigration from the United States, 1896–1911.* Toronto: Griffin House.

Urquhart, Malcolm, and Kenneth Buckley 1965. *Historical Statistics of Canada.* Toronto: Macmillan.

chapter seventeen

The Economic Integration
of Visible Minorities
in Contemporary Canadian
Society: Revisited

Feng Hou, T.R. Balakrishnan, and
Rozzet Jurdi
(An original chapter written
for this volume.)

INTRODUCTION

Ethnic or cultural diversity is a defining feature of Canadian society. A question that has attracted intensive attention among social researchers is whether ethnic affiliation matters in the formation of social classes in Canada. John Porter (1965) proposed that Canadian society was stratified along ethnic lines as a "vertical mosaic" in which the charter groups (English and French) positioned themselves on the top of the occupational hierarchy. He argued that other minority ethnic groups, because of their inferior socio-economic status upon arrival in Canada, had to work in a segmented labour market and had limited opportunities to achieve social mobility. This thesis has been referred to as the "ethnically blocked mobility" thesis. However, empirical evidence does not support Porter's assumption about an enduring connection between the ethnic hierarchy in socio-economic status and the entrance status of immigrant groups. Related studies in the 1970s and 1980s documented a convergence process in occupational status, as some minority ethnic groups outranked the charter groups in occupational standing (Darroch 1979; Herberg 1990; Isajiw et al. 1993; Pineo and Porter 1985; Reitz 1990; Shamai 1992). These studies also revealed a significant improvement in educational attainments among some minority ethnic groups over the charter groups.

While some minority ethnic groups have experienced significant upward mobility in educational and occupational attainment, a more recent concern has emerged about a "colour-coded vertical mosaic" of income disparity among racial groups (Herberg 1990; Li 1990; Lian and Matthews 1998; Reitz and Breton 1994). For instance, Lian and Matthews (1998) show that all major visible minority groups had below-average earnings at each educational level, while most groups of European ethnicity had above-average earnings. The disadvantage of some visible minority groups has been attributed to racial prejudice and discrimination, which limit their access to the full range of job opportunities and other socio-economic resources. In spite of their superior educational attainment, income equality may be harder to attain for these groups because of systemic discrimination in institutional settings and interpersonal relations.

Education, occupation, and earnings are three major indicators of socio-economic status. Inequality among racial/ethnic groups on these three dimensions may reflect different sources of social stratification. In North America, differences in education result from group differences in parents' socio-economic resources (educational, linguistic, and skill endowments, income and wealth), social capital (family structure, social networks, cultural orientation), and the context of reception and subsequent history of each ethnic community (Portes and MacLeod 2003). Differences in occupational attainment originate from group differences in human capital (schooling, field of study, on-the-job training, literacy, work experience, etc.), worker preferences, stereotyping, and discrimination. Differences in earnings could come from group differences in human capital, differences in occupational/industrial

distribution, and discrimination. Education is usually achieved early in life and is a major determinant of an individual's occupational attainment. Both educational and occupational qualifications are important determinants of earnings. Ethnic minority groups may not be disadvantaged on all three dimensions. Some groups can achieve high educational levels due to the selectivity of immigration and/or high aspirations and personal efforts. However, with the same educational level they may have lower occupational status and earnings than other groups. To examine how a minority group is being integrated economically into Canadian society, it is essential to look at all three dimensions and the connections among them—that is, the occupational returns from education, and the income return from educational and occupational qualifications relative to other groups.

Based on our analysis of the 1991 Census data, we showed in an earlier article that visible minorities and minority ethnic groups of European origin in Canada have experienced different and distinct economic integration processes (Hou and Balakrishnan 1996). We found that, for the European groups such as Poles, Portuguese, Italians, and Greeks, social mobility came first in earnings, then in education, and finally in occupation. These groups entered Canada with low human capital and had to attain a certain level of financial success before they could exploit the opportunities of educational and occupational mobility. These groups obtained much higher earnings relative to their educational and occupational achievements. The Canadian-born in these groups did achieve educational and occupational levels close to those of the British or the average for the total population. In contrast, the visible minorities came to Canada with a much higher educational attainment than the

European groups and the average for the total population. The Canadian-born and immigrants who came as children in these groups also attained much higher levels of education than the British and French "charter" groups and the average population. However, adjusting for educational attainment, visible minorities had a lower occupational status. And in spite of their accomplishments in education and occupation, visible minorities earned much less compared to European minority ethnic groups or the charter groups. In other words, the integration process for the visible minorities is the reverse of that of the non–visible minority groups.

It is not clear to what extent the pattern we observed with the 1991 Census still holds a decade later. The 1990s were noteworthy for changing immigration patterns. Though Canada has always been a country that attracted significant numbers of immigrants, the largest number of immigrants to come in one decade arrived in this period, reaching a total of 2.2 million persons. Further, there was a shift in major immigrant source regions from Europe to Asia, which started in the 1970s but was much more pronounced in the 1990s. About three-quarters of the immigrants who came to Canada in the 1990s were visible minorities, mainly from Asia and, to a lesser extent, from the Caribbean and Latin America. The majority of new arrivals came as independent immigrants who had higher educational qualifications than ever before. Meanwhile, the number of Canadian-born visible minorities has also increased dramatically. By 2001, about 45% of blacks, 29% of South Asians, and 25% of Chinese were born in Canada. Many of these Canadian-born visible minorities have even higher educational attainment than their immigrant counterparts and the Canadian-born with European origins. How Canadian-born

visible minorities fare in occupation and earnings would indicate the extent to which visible minority status remains an important factor in the society's socio-economic structure. Moreover, the decade from 1991 to 2001 was one of rapid economic growth in North America, and of globalization throughout the world. New opportunities in the labour market were being created due to economic and demographic causes such as sustained low fertility rates in the developed countries. Under these changing circumstances, it is important to re-examine whether the earlier findings for 1991 still hold true in 2001.

Our objective in this chapter is to update our earlier study on the differences in social mobility among selected racial/ethnic groups in contemporary Canadian society. We will compare the socio-economic attainment of Southern and Eastern European groups such as Italians, Poles, Greeks, and Portuguese, who immigrated mostly between the 1950s and the 1970s, with a range of visible minority groups, including blacks, Chinese, South Asians, and Filipinos, who immigrated in large numbers since the 1970s. By comparing the 1991 and 2001 findings, we wish to detect any changes in group differences in educational levels, occupational attainment, and employment earnings. It has been suggested that ethnic disparities in Canada have narrowed continuously, first in education and then in occupational attainment, over the last several decades, and that group differences in income might follow a similar trend (Herberg 1990). We will see whether we observe such a trend between 1991 and 2001.

DATA AND METHODS

The data for this paper are from the 1991 and 2001 three percent sample of individual files in the Canadian Census Public Use Sample. Most of the analysis will be based on the 2001 Census, as the 1991 Census results have already been analyzed in our earlier paper (Hou and Balakrishnan 1996). Where 1991 data are also used, it is mainly to highlight the differences between the two census dates. The ethnic groups specified for this study include the two charter groups—British and French—and five European groups: Italians, Greeks, Jews, Poles, and Portuguese. Five visible minority groups are also considered: Chinese, South Asians, Filipinos, blacks, and "other" visible minorities. The latter category includes Arabs and West Asians, Vietnamese, other East/Southeast Asians, Latin/Central/South Americans, etc. Only people 30 to 60 years of age were selected, based on the consideration that most people in this age range have completed their formal education and are likely to be employed and earning an income.

Simple cross-tabulations are used to show the educational and occupational attainments of ethnic groups by immigration status. Since our main interest is in explaining income differences among the ethnic groups, a more extensive analysis is carried out by looking at income differentials by immigration cohorts in the two census years, and performing multiple regression analyses with controls for the effects of age, duration of stay in Canada, education, occupation, home language, gender, and province of residence.

RESULTS

Educational Attainment

The relative difference in educational attainment among the ethnic groups is the result of three factors: educational attainment at the time of entry into Canada, subsequent schooling after arrival in Canada, and, in the case of second and later generations, schooling in Canada. Educational differences at the time of entry are influenced by the liberalization of Canadian immigration laws with their non-discriminatory clauses, by the needs of the labour market, and by the point system in the selection of new immigrants. These factors have favoured Asian immigrants in recent years (Beaujot et al. 1988). Therefore, it is important to control for year of immigration when comparing educational levels among ethnic groups. Educational attainment is a good indicator of entrance status. Hence, a comparison of the educational attainments of adult immigrants with those of the Canadian-born, taking into account the various periods when they arrived, should partially reveal the extent of blocked mobility.

Table 17-1 shows differentials in educational attainment among the selected ethnic groups. For each ethnic group, a proportional distribution of three educational levels is calculated for the whole group, for the Canadian-born among that group, and by time of immigration. Considerable heterogeneity exists, both among the selected groups of European origin and among the visible minorities. We will discuss each ethnic group first, and then identify some common patterns.

Among the five European groups, Jews have by far the highest education. About two-thirds of the adults in the age group 30 to 60 had university education, a proportion found among the Canadian-born Jewish population and for each of the various Jewish immigration cohorts. Poles are a distant second in educational attainment, higher than the British, the French, and the total population. Not only native-born Poles but also Polish immigrants in the various periods of immigration

TABLE 17-1   Population Size and Percentage Distribution of Educational Levels by Ethnicity and Immigration Status for Population Aged 30 to 60 Years, 2001

	British	French	Polish	Portuguese	Italian	Greek	Jewish	Chinese	South Asian	Filipino	Black	Other Visible	Total
Population Size													
Total	2 641 220	1 223 620	121 670	120 090	343 100	65 080	72 580	446 120	344 050	133 900	223 350	344 700	6 079 470
Canadian-born	2 302 770	1 185 080	41 780	16 820	189 400	25 370	44 330	30 540	9310	2330	17 480	18 580	3 883 790
Born outside Canada	338 460	38 540	79 890	103 270	153 700	39 710	28 250	415 580	334 730	131 570	205 870	326 120	2 195 690
Year of Immigration													
Before 1961	59 090	2660	6020	3580	46 460	4360	2950	3760	660	40	810	480	130 870
1961–1970	98 900	7240	5460	29 550	71 430	16 770	3880	21 630	16 580	4350	18 430	12 120	306 340
1971–1980	92 520	9210	6710	41 910	23 900	12 640	6680	77 670	82 060	26 450	60 890	55 940	496 560
1981–1990	42 570	5920	40 430	19 400	6620	3700	6430	103 680	82 930	32 600	51 040	98 340	493 640
1991–2000	28 610	10 140	20 720	7430	3770	1920	7130	204 030	145 080	64 030	66 570	142 240	701 670
Percent Distribution													
Educational Level													
<= High school	32.7	41.0	28.1	67.6	40.4	45.9	14.3	35.2	37.2	14.9	35.0	34.0	35.5
Some post-sec.	39.9	33.9	41.5	23.5	35.8	29.5	20.7	22.4	24.6	30.4	40.5	24.9	34.6
University & +	27.4	25.1	30.5	8.9	23.8	24.6	65.0	42.4	38.1	54.6	24.5	41.1	29.8
Canadian-born													
<= High school	33.5	41.7	31.3	40.2	27.0	21.4	13.8	13.9	24.2	30.2	39.8	24.9	35.2
Some post-sec.	39.4	33.9	38.7	41.3	41.3	39.1	18.8	29.0	32.1	33.3	38.9	30.4	37.5
University & +	27.1	24.4	30.0	18.5	31.7	39.5	67.4	57.1	43.7	36.5	21.4	44.7	27.3
Year of Immigration Before 1961													
<= High school	33.5	27.8	42.9	57.8	50.1	62.7	22.5	41.2	55.6	–	31.8	61.5	41.5
Some post-sec.	39.7	30.6	29.5	22.7	30.4	17.0	17.5	19.6	27.7	–	40.9	7.7	33.3
University & +	26.8	41.7	27.6	19.6	19.5	20.3	60.0	39.2	16.7	100.0	27.3	30.8	25.2
1961–1970													
<= High school	28.6	26.5	36.5	66.4	62.0	61.9	23.8	31.6	29.2	10.1	26.0	27.7	41.7
Some post-sec.	41.9	41.8	41.2	24.6	28.0	26.9	26.7	26.3	23.4	23.8	45.5	29.3	33.3
University & +	29.5	31.6	22.3	9.0	10.0	11.2	49.5	42.2	47.5	66.1	28.5	43.0	25.0

TABLE 17-1 (continued)

	British	French	Polish	Portuguese	Italian	Greek	Jewish	Chinese	South Asian	Filipino	Black	Other Visible	Total
1971–1980													
<= High school	26.7	22.5	27.5	75.6	60.0	65.5	16.6	33.5	30.3	16.1	32.1	33.9	35.8
Some post-sec.	46.1	31.7	38.5	19.7	27.8	20.8	24.3	29.6	31.9	33.4	45.4	29.8	34.2
University & +	27.2	45.8	34.1	4.7	12.2	13.7	59.1	36.9	37.8	50.5	22.5	36.2	30.1
1981–1990													
<= High school	24.4	14.4	23.0	76.8	50.3	54.0	15.0	43.3	42.8	15.4	37.2	41.9	37.9
Some post-sec.	45.7	37.5	44.2	17.0	33.0	25.0	29.9	24.1	26.3	33.9	43.4	27.7	31.4
University & +	29.9	48.1	32.8	6.3	16.8	21.0	55.2	32.6	30.9	50.7	19.5	30.4	30.6
1991–2000													
<= High school	20.5	15.3	24.4	68.1	41.2	42.3	6.2	35.2	38.9	14.3	36.3	30.9	32.2
Some post-sec.	41.7	31.0	46.9	18.9	34.3	25.1	19.2	17.6	19.9	27.8	34.7	20.7	23.4
University & +	37.7	53.7	28.7	12.9	24.5	32.7	74.6	47.3	41.2	57.9	29.0	48.4	44.4
Males													
<= High school	32.1	40.1	27.5	66.2	37.5	42.3	11.8	30.7	33.8	16.0	34.0	29.9	34.2
Some post-sec.	40.8	35.7	41.6	25.4	38.3	30.7	19.5	21.4	24.0	31.4	36.5	23.7	35.3
University & +	27.2	24.2	30.9	8.4	24.2	26.9	68.7	47.9	42.2	52.5	29.5	46.4	30.5
Females													
<= High school	33.3	41.9	28.6	68.9	43.4	49.4	17.0	39.3	40.9	14.3	35.9	38.1	36.9
Some post-sec.	39.0	32.1	41.3	21.8	33.2	28.4	21.8	23.3	25.4	29.9	43.8	26.2	34.0
University & +	27.7	26.0	30.0	9.4	23.3	22.3	61.3	37.4	33.7	55.8	20.3	35.7	29.1

Source: The 2001 Census Public Use Sample
Note: (1) "Other Visible" minorities here include Vietnamese, Korean, East/Southeast Asian, Arab and West Asian, and Latin/Central/South American. (2) Education: "less or equal to high school" includes high school graduates and below; "Some post-secondary" includes non-university education or without university certificate; "University & +" includes university certificate or diploma and above.

have relatively high levels of education. The overall education levels of the other three European groups—Italians, Portuguese, and Greeks—are the lowest among the European groups. Two-thirds of the Portuguese aged 30 to 60 had only high school education, and the proportion with university education was less than 10%. During the 1960 to 1990 period, when most of the Portuguese came to Canada, their education at the time of entry was low, with less than 10% having a university education. Those born in Canada had much higher education. That is, about 18.5% of Canadian-born Portuguese aged 30 to 60 had some university education and only 40.2% had less than high school education. This pattern suggests that, in spite of the low entrance status of Portuguese immigrants, their children do achieve education levels fairly close to the national average. Similar patterns can be observed for the Italians and Greeks, who have educational levels somewhat higher than that of the Portuguese. Their children also do better than their parents. Among the second and later generations, the educational attainments of Italians and Greeks are actually higher than the national average, and higher than those of native-born British or French.

Among the visible minorities, the Chinese, South Asians, Filipinos, and other visible minorities have much higher education levels than the British, the French, and the total population. This is true among both the Canadian-born and foreign-born segments. Since Canadian-born visible minorities aged 30 to 60 are mostly the children of those who immigrated to Canada before the 1970s, comparing the Canadian-born with their parents' generation in average educational attainment is a good indicator of intergenerational mobility. Like the European minority groups (Portuguese, Italians, and Greeks), Chinese and South

Asians clearly have achieved intergenerational upward mobility in educational attainment. For instance, about 57% Canadian-born Chinese completed a university education. This level is much higher than the average among Chinese immigrants who arrived before the 1970s.

In comparison, Filipinos and blacks seem to have experienced stagnation or downward mobility in university education across generations. Filipinos have been the fastest-growing group among immigrants in the last decade. Ever since their increased immigration during the 1960s, Filipinos have had the highest educational level at entry. More than half of Filipino immigrants had a university education. However, the second generation of Filipinos aged 30 to 60 had lower educational levels than their immigrant parents, although their levels are still higher than those for the European groups and the national average. Blacks have the lowest education level among the visible minorities. Only a quarter of blacks aged 30 to 60 had some university education. While this is not too different from the national average, or from the figures for the European groups, it is much lower than the level for the Chinese, South Asians, and Filipinos. A disturbing finding is that Canadian-born blacks do not fare any better than do immigrant blacks. The proportion with university education among Canadian-born blacks is only 21.4%, which is lower than that among black immigrants. This means that there is no evidence of upward mobility in education for this group.

With the exception of blacks, the blocked mobility thesis does not appear to apply to visible minorities or to the European groups considered here, at least with regard to education. Education has long been regarded as the prerequisite for gaining access to high-paying and prestigious jobs in Canada and other societies. The ambition to integrate and to get ahead in society may encourage members of ethnic minorities to acquire necessary educational credentials. Although some European immigrants, such as the Portuguese, Italians, and Greeks, came to Canada with low education, their children attained educational levels equal to or higher than the British or French charter groups and the national average. The low socio-economic status of these minority groups at entrance did not limit their children's mobility achievements in education. The Chinese, South Asians, and Filipinos who arrived with comparatively higher levels of education maintained their superiority in the second generation as well. The belief that education can eventually equalize social and economic opportunities may be the underlying reason for the overachievement in education of the children of immigrants among many minority groups.

Occupational Attainment

According to human capital theory in economics, occupational attainments in an industrial society such as Canada are determined largely by the training and experience a worker possesses, since training and experience are functionally related to the skills required in managerial and professional occupations (Wanner 2005). Inefficient allocation of labour because of discrimination based on such ascribed characteristics as race, ethnicity, immigrant status, class background, or gender should decrease in more industrialized societies, where the emphasis is on training and experience (Parsons 1970; Treiman 1970). Some studies in Canada have focused on the issue of whether occupational attainment has matched the

education and training of ethnic minorities and new immigrants. Boyd (1985) found that education had a greater influence on occupational outcomes for men born in Canada than for immigrant men, and that immigrant women had the lowest occupational status. She suggested that immigrants were handicapped because education received outside Canada was valued less in Canada (Boyd 1985).

In our earlier study of 1991 data, we found that, among the Canadian-born, the four minority European groups—Poles, Portuguese, Italians, and Greeks—were similar to the British in regard to their share of managerial and professional occupations (Hou and Balakrishnan 1996). Those born in Canada or those who came to Canada as children were generally more likely to be working in managerial and professional occupations than were adult immigrants. We also found that none of the three major visible minority groups—Chinese, blacks, and South Asians—was overrepresented in managerial occupations relative to British Canadians, although these groups were sometimes overrepresented in professional occupations. Hence, compared to the European groups, visible minorities had difficulty in attaining occupational mobility despite their superior educational levels.

In Table 17-2, we present the percentage distribution by occupation, for the various ethnic groups by immigration status for full-time employed workers aged 30 to 60 in 2001. Among the Canadian-born, groups with European origins are similar in their share of professional occupations, although the level is much higher for Jews and lower for the Portuguese. With the exception of the French, the proportion of other European groups working in managerial occupations is similar to or higher

TABLE 17-2 Percentage Distribution of Occupation by Ethnicity and Immigration Status for Full-Time Employed Workers Aged 30 to 60 Years, 2001

Occupation	British	French	Polish	Portuguese	Italian	Greek	Jewish	Chinese	South Asian	Filipino	Black	Other Visible	Total
Occupation													
Managerial	16.1	11.9	10.1	8.7	16.0	17.7	23.6	11.8	10.0	5.2	7.1	11.1	13.6
Professional	26.9	27.1	25.7	12.0	22.4	21.2	40.9	31.7	23.5	20.7	21.1	26.5	26.1
Sales, service, clerical	34.3	35.3	31.0	35.4	37.7	41.2	29.7	35.1	33.3	46.8	40.9	29.9	35.1
Craft, trade, manual	22.7	25.8	33.1	43.9	23.9	20.0	5.7	21.4	33.2	27.3	30.9	32.5	25.2
Canadian-born													
Managerial	15.6	11.8	14.7	14.9	17.4	22.1	25.3	17.1	16.1	11.1	14.4	14.5	14.7
Professional	26.5	26.6	28.6	19.3	26.3	28.3	39.8	40.5	35.0	40.0	19.4	36.6	26.8
Sales, service, clerical	34.6	35.4	34.3	37.9	38.4	38.0	30.6	32.2	31.5	28.9	46.9	30.0	35.1
Craft, trade, manual	23.2	26.2	22.5	27.9	17.9	11.6	4.3	10.2	17.5	20.0	19.3	18.8	23.4
Year of Immigration Before 1961													
Managerial	18.5	21.7	14.3	16.4	17.2	14.5	8.4	13.8	14.3	–	–	14.3	17.2
Professional	24.2	45.9	26.6	25.5	21.2	20.0	41.6	29.3	28.6	–	31.1	28.6	24.1
Sales, service, clerical	38.3	24.3	38.7	27.3	38.7	45.5	39.0	43.2	–	–	43.8	42.9	38.1
Craft, trade, manual	19.0	8.1	20.4	30.9	23.0	20.0	11.1	13.8	57.1	–	25.0	14.3	20.6
1961–1970													
Managerial	19.3	11.9	14.5	11.1	13.9	11.3	20.9	15.0	14.1	7.2	10.1	23.9	15.4
Professional	29.2	31.7	21.7	14.7	14.2	13.3	32.6	33.7	34.0	51.5	25.7	27.1	24.3
Sales, service, clerical	32.4	35.7	30.1	35.6	35.0	44.8	41.9	35.8	27.8	27.1	45.9	31.4	34.9
Craft, trade, manual	19.1	20.8	33.7	38.5	36.9	30.5	4.7	15.5	24.0	14.2	18.3	17.6	25.4
1971–1980													
Managerial	18.0	15.0	3.0	7.0	9.9	18.1	28.7	13.8	13.0	7.2	7.5	14.1	12.6
Professional	27.9	40.1	25.0	8.0	13.5	9.8	43.6	32.2	24.1	28.8	22.8	27.0	25.0
Sales, service, clerical	32.4	32.0	32.0	36.7	37.1	47.4	23.4	33.1	36.7	41.0	39.7	28.8	35.1
Craft, trade, manual	21.7	12.9	40.0	48.3	39.6	24.8	4.3	20.9	26.2	23.1	30.0	30.1	27.3
1981–1990													
Managerial	18.5	9.9	7.4	3.7	7.8	11.8	19.5	10.8	8.0	4.6	5.4	9.4	9.1
Professional	32.4	44.4	23.2	7.1	19.1	25.5	37.8	26.8	20.1	18.4	20.7	22.3	23.0
Sales, service, clerical	29.6	34.6	27.6	32.4	30.4	37.2	32.9	37.9	33.0	50.0	41.0	30.4	34.9
Craft, trade, manual	19.5	11.1	41.8	56.8	42.7	25.5	9.8	24.5	38.9	27.0	32.9	38.0	32.9

TABLE 17-2 (continued)

	British	French	Polish	Portuguese	Italian	Greek	Jewish	Chinese	South Asian	Filipino	Black	Other Visible	Total
1991–2000													
Managerial	19.9	13.0	5.5	3.0	6.8	16.7	18.0	9.6	8.1	4.6	4.8	8.2	8.3
Professional	39.1	43.5	26.4	11.9	20.5	29.2	49.5	32.3	22.9	16.1	18.6	27.3	26.1
Sales, service, clerical	25.5	32.6	29.8	32.7	45.4	29.1	21.3	34.7	32.2	47.6	38.2	30.3	34.8
Craft, trade, manual	15.4	10.9	38.4	52.5	27.2	25.0	11.2	23.4	36.8	31.8	38.4	34.2	30.8
Males													
Managerial	18.5	13.4	12.3	10.6	19.5	20.9	27.1	13.7	11.5	6.8	8.9	12.5	15.8
Professional	23.5	23.6	24.3	9.7	20.2	19.4	43.0	36.1	24.4	19.1	19.6	27.2	24.0
Sales, service, clerical	22.4	23.9	16.1	20.3	24.7	34.9	20.8	27.6	24.0	27.9	27.5	21.8	23.4
Craft, trade, manual	35.6	39.1	47.2	59.4	35.6	24.9	9.0	22.7	40.0	46.2	44.1	38.5	36.8
Females													
Managerial	12.8	9.7	7.5	6.3	11.2	13.8	18.9	9.6	7.7	4.0	5.4	8.8	10.7
Professional	31.5	31.8	27.5	14.9	25.3	23.3	38.2	26.6	22.1	21.8	22.6	25.5	29.0
Sales, service, clerical	50.1	50.9	48.9	54.9	55.4	48.7	41.7	43.9	47.5	60.4	54.3	42.7	50.2
Craft, trade, manual	5.6	7.6	16.2	23.9	8.1	14.1	1.2	19.9	22.7	13.9	17.7	23.0	10.1

Source: The 2001 Census Public Use Sample

Note: Occupation: Managerial (senior managers and middle and other managers); Professional (professionals and semi-professionals and technicians); Sales, services, clerical (supervisors, administrative and senior clerical personnel, skilled sales and service personnel, clerical personnel, intermediate sales and clerical personnel, other sales and clerical personnel); Other (supervisors: trades and crafts, skilled trades and crafts workers, semi-skilled manual workers, other manual workers).

than the national average. Canadian-born Poles, Italians, Greeks, and Portuguese are much more likely to work in the managerial and professional occupations than are their immigrant counterparts. On the whole, these minority European groups seem to be able to achieve occupational mobility, even though they came to Canada with low levels of education.

The experience of the visible minorities is heterogeneous. Canadian-born Chinese and South Asians did much better, with higher proportions in managerial and professional occupations than Canadian-born British and French, and the national population. Proportions in the professional occupations were especially high among the Canadian-born Chinese and South Asians, reflecting their high educational attainment. About 40.5% of Canadian-born Chinese and 35.0% of Canadian-born South Asians were in professional occupations, a figure that is much higher than the national average of 26.8% for all Canadian-born respondents, and higher than the figure for most of the European groups. The only Canadian-born group that did better than the Chinese and South Asians in managerial and professional employment was the Canadian-born Jewish group, with 25% in managerial occupations and 40% in professional occupations.

Filipinos and blacks fared much worse compared to other visible minorities. Filipinos, who are the highest-educated group at entry, did poorly even with an increased duration of stay in Canada. Fifty-eight percent of the Filipinos who came to Canada in the 1990s had university education, but only 4.6% were in managerial occupations and only 16.1% in professional occupations. This situation improves only marginally for the earlier immigrants. Even among the Filipinos who arrived in earlier decades, the proportions

in the higher-status occupations were much less than the national average. Clearly, occupational attainment does not keep pace with education for Filipino immigrants. However, among Canadian-born Filipinos there is some evidence of occupational mobility. The proportion in managerial occupations is 11.1%, although this is still less than the national average of 14.7% for the Canadian-born population. In contrast, the proportion in professional occupations is considerably higher (40.0%) than the national average, probably because of higher post-secondary education among Filipinos.

The case of black immigrants is similar to that of the Filipinos, except that their education level is much lower. Their proportion with a university education is lowest among the visible minorities. The proportion in managerial and professional occupations among black immigrants is close to that of the Filipinos. Blacks show improvement among the Canadian-born, but are still at levels below the national average.

To examine fully the ethnic differentials in occupational distribution, it is also necessary to do an analysis in which we control for other relevant variables, particularly because there are large group differences in educational attainment and immigrant status. The control variables are years since immigration, age, educational level, home language, province of residence, and gender. The regression analyses were done separately for 1991 and 2001 so that comparisons can be made over time. Since occupation is a dependent variable with four categories (managerial; professional; crafts, trades, and manual; and sales, service, and clerical), we use the polytomous regression model for this analysis. The sales, service, and clerical grouping is treated as the reference category and compared to both the managerial and the

TABLE 17-3　Polytomous Logistic Regression Showing Propensity (Odds Ratio) of Occupational Distribution (Managerial and Professional against Sales, Services, Clerical) for Full-Time Employed Workers Aged 30 to 60 Years, 2001

	1991		2001	
	Managerial	Professional	Managerial	Professional
Ethnic Origin				
British (ref)	1.00	1.00	1.00	1.00
French	0.80**	1.01	0.77**	0.95
Polish	0.76**	0.98	0.77**	0.96
Portuguese	0.68**	0.66**	0.74**	0.71**
Italian	0.96	0.80**	0.89*	0.74**
Greek	0.99	0.60**	0.97	0.65**
Jewish	0.96	0.90	1.08	0.89
Chinese	0.82**	0.92	0.86*	1.03
South Asian	0.51**	0.62**	0.61**	0.65**
Filipinos	0.14**	0.43**	0.23**	0.32**
Black	0.32**	0.74**	0.41**	0.62**
Other Visible	0.82**	0.87	0.81**	0.85**
Year of Immigration				
Canadian-born (ref)	1.00	1.00	1.00	1.00
Before 1961	1.13*	1.12*	1.10	1.03
1961–1970	1.09	1.19**	1.26**	1.19**
1971–1980	1.19**	0.97	1.19**	1.18**
1981–1990	0.83**	0.83**	0.91	1.06
1991–2000	–	–	0.77**	1.00
Current Age				
30–34 (ref)	1.00	1.00	1.00	1.00
35–39	1.18**	1.06*	1.10**	0.98
40–44	1.37**	1.17**	1.25**	0.99
45–49	1.45**	1.24**	1.21**	1.01
50–54	1.42**	1.19**	1.23**	1.06
55–59	1.20**	1.08	1.16**	0.98
Educational Level				
<=High school (ref)	1.00	1.00	1.00	1.00
Some post-sec.	1.57**	4.38**	1.43**	4.04**
University & +	5.81**	23.91**	4.79**	19.66**
Home Language				
English/French (ref)	1.00	1.00	1.00	1.00
Other	0.63**	0.80**	0.69**	0.81**
Province				
Ontario (ref)	1.00	1.00	1.00	1.00
Quebec	0.97	0.95	0.83**	1.00
Other	0.84**	0.88**	0.82**	0.85**
Gender				
Male (ref)	1.00	1.00	1.00	1.00
Female	0.25**	0.59**	0.34**	0.64**
Intercept	–1.09**	–1.87**	–0.93	-1.65
Log Pseudo Likelihood		31 795		37 500
Pseudo R^2		0.40		0.37

*Significant at the 0.05 alpha level. ** Significant at the 0.01 alpha level.
Source: The 2001 Census Public Use Sample.

professional categories. This allows us to calculate the "odds ratios" of being in managerial and professional occupations. Managerial and professional occupations are considered higher-status occupations and, hence, provide a gauge of relative success in the system of social inequality.

The results of this analysis are presented in Table 17-3. Beginning with managerial occupations, we see that when the effects of all selected control variables are taken into account, only the Greeks and Jews fared as well as the British (the reference group) in the likelihood of working in such jobs in 2001. Italians came close, with an odds ratio of 0.89, meaning that Italians were about 11% less likely to be in managerial occupations than were the British. The other European groups—French, Poles, and Portuguese—were, on average, 25% less likely to be in managerial occupations in comparison to the British. However, it is among the visible minorities that we find the largest differences relative to the British reference group. While the Chinese do reasonably well, with odds ratios of 0.82 and 0.86 in the two census years, South Asians, blacks, and Filipinos do much worse. The odds ratios of being in managerial occupations for South Asians were only 0.51 in 1991 and 0.61 in 2001. While the situation improved slightly during the 1991–2000 period, in 2001 a South Asian was still 40% less likely to be in a managerial position compared to someone of British origin when other factors such as education, home language, etc. are controlled. Blacks did even worse, with odds ratios of 0.32 and 0.41 in the two census years. By far the lowest-ranked group is Filipinos, with odds ratios of only 0.14 and 0.23. Compared to the British, a Filipino has only a one-fourth chance of being in a managerial occupation.

The pattern of odds ratios for professional occupations is similar to that for the managerial occupations, with the odds for European groups somewhat lower than for the British and visible minorities having much lower odds. However, when compared to odds ratios for managerial occupations, the odds ratios of visible minorities being in professional occupations seem to be higher. In other words, because of their higher educational levels and training, visible minorities are better able to get into professional occupations, but have less success with managerial occupations. On the whole, our findings seem to parallel our earlier findings from 1991, in showing that visible minorities have greater difficulty than other groups in achieving occupational attainments that are commensurate with their education levels, especially at the managerial level.

Ethnicity and Income

Many studies based on earlier census materials and survey data have shown that, even after controlling for various factors such as age, year of immigration, education, official language proficiency, etc., visible minorities earn less than their white European counterparts (Li 1990; Herberg 1990; Balakrishnan 1988; Kalbach and Richard 1988; Beaujot and Rappak 1988; Kazemipur and Halli 2000). In our earlier study (Hou and Balakrishnan 1996), we hypothesized that visibility and social distance will manifest themselves primarily in their effects on employment earnings. We predicted that European minority groups, such as Italians, Portuguese, and Poles, will have higher earnings than blacks, Chinese, South Asians, and other visible minorities with similar educational and occupational qualifications. Also, we expected that while the incomes of visible minorities would generally increase with

TABLE 17-4 Wage Income (in Year 2000 $) for Various Ethnic Groups According to Period of Immigration and Sex, by Year of Census, for Full-Time Employed Workers Aged 30 to 60

Period of Immigration	British Male 1990	British Male 2000	British Female 1990	British Female 2000	French Male 1990	French Male 2000	French Female 1990	French Female 2000	Polish Male 1990	Polish Male 2000	Polish Female 1990	Polish Female 2000	Portuguese Male 1990	Portuguese Male 2000	Portuguese Female 1990	Portuguese Female 2000
Before 1971	59 930	60 530	37 040	41 630	52 780	*	38 840	*	52 900	57 670	38 050	*	43 770	51 470	26 780	34 710
1971–1980	59 120	61 390	34 440	37 750	50 300	*	35 950	*	53 220	*	33 100	*	39 640	42 340	22 990	31 280
1981–1990	56 860	66 090	31 650	39 150	45 720	*	*	*	36 960	46 400	26 220	30 850	34 320	40 910	20 840	26 220
1991–2000	*	61 070	*	39 040	*	*	*	*	*	41 430	*	25 480	*	36 620	*	*
Canadian-born	50 540	55 890	33 210	40 990	45 050	51 130	30 900	38 130	51 720	56 180	35 560	41 500	*	51 210	*	38 940
Total	51 710	56 670	33 570	40 840	45 150	51 200	31 000	38 480	47 820	50 120	33 450	33 640	40 990	45 440	24 740	32 370

Period of Immigration	Italian Male 1990	Italian Male 2000	Italian Female 1990	Italian Female 2000	Greek Male 1990	Greek Male 2000	Greek Female 1990	Greek Female 2000	Jewish Male 1990	Jewish Male 2000	Jewish Female 1990	Jewish Female 2000	Chinese Male 1990	Chinese Male 2000	Chinese Female 1990	Chinese Female 2000
Before 1971	46 290	52 220	28 040	38 990	37 100	45 980	26 670	31 950	67 720	*	42 270	*	49 310	54 560	32 370	37 890
1971–1980	44 210	47 780	24 580	33 930	35 630	*	26 630	*	62 290	*	40 570	*	46 640	51 160	31 410	38 630
1981–1990	*	44 950	*	*	*	*	*	*	50 290	*	27 100	*	36 770	43 710	25 480	32 840
1991–2000	*	*	*	*	*	*	*	*	*	46 560	*	*	*	33 030	*	24 200
Canadian-born	50 570	56 100	36 250	43 390	49 880	51 040	*	46 880	68 870	78 690	44 530	58 490	47 660	55 170	38 040	46 170
Total	47 550	53 870	30 840	41 250	38 290	47 840	27 840	38 490	66 230	72 050	42 190	55 200	43 870	42 870	29 810	31 990

Period of Immigration	South Asian Male 1990	South Asian Male 2000	South Asian Female 1990	South Asian Female 2000	Filipino Male 1990	Filipino Male 2000	Filipino Female 1990	Filipino Female 2000	Black Male 1990	Black Male 2000	Black Female 1990	Black Female 2000	Other Visible Minorities Male 1990	Other Visible Minorities Male 2000	Other Visible Minorities Female 1990	Other Visible Minorities Female 2000
Before 1971	55 020	57 110	34 460	42 630	47 920	*	41 990	*	46 810	52 560	34 530	35 370	52 480	59 960	31 270	*
1971–1980	45 430	51 780	28 700	33 650	40 700	40 940	31 900	35 020	39 250	45 290	28 880	32 770	41 170	45 630	27 330	31 740
1981–1990	33 830	40 510	24 070	28 580	28 690	36 980	24 430	30 160	30 970	38 540	24 090	28 450	32 570	37 830	22 540	28 580
1991–2000	*	32 470	*	22 380	*	29 890	*	24 390	*	33 030	*	26 480	*	32 370	*	24 070
Canadian-born	*	53 100	*	*	*	*	*	*	38 270	43 540	31 410	33 500	57 460	57 420	38 520	40 200
Total	43 570	40 770	28 590	28 860	37 300	34 860	30 730	28 590	39 290	40 650	29 590	30 420	41 150	39 830	28 220	29 010

Source: Census Use Sample Tapes 1991 and 2001.
Notes: * less than 50 cases in the sample. All numbers have been rounded to the nearest 10.

duration of stay in Canada, such an increase would still be less than for European minority groups. The findings in our earlier study (1996) largely supported these hypotheses.

The 1990s are especially important for the study of income differentials among ethnic groups. In that decade, the absolute number and proportion of visible minorities increased to unprecedented levels. At entry, the educational levels and job skills of visible minority immigrants also went up. At the same time, a number of economic studies showed that the entry-level incomes of new immigrants in this decade went down drastically, raising the question of whether they will ever catch up in income with the Canadian-born population (Frenette and Morissette 2005; Baker and Benjamin 1994). Hence, we anticipate that the situation in 2000 may not be significantly better than it was 10 years earlier. However, some change might be expected, since the 1990s was also a period that saw considerable effort on the part of various governmental and community agencies to make multiculturalism work in terms of equality in employment, housing, and other resources available to new immigrants.

Table 17-4 presents the wage income of full-time employed workers aged 30 to 60 in 1990 and 2000 (expressed in 2000 dollars), for the various ethnic groups, broken down by period of immigration and gender. The 1990 income figures were adjusted for inflation during the decade by a factor of 1.22 to reflect increases in consumer prices. A number of important observations can be made.

First, real incomes, after adjusting for inflation, went up for all European groups during the decade, with increases ranging from about 6% for the British and French to around 10% for the Portuguese, Italians,

and Greeks. In contrast, the visible minority groups showed little change in real income.

Second, when visible minority groups are broken down by nativity and period of immigration, we find that Canadian-born Chinese and blacks increased their real income. Still, by 2000, Canadian-born black men on average earned 22% less than Canadian-born British men. Due to small numbers in the sample, we were not able to calculate the corresponding change among Canadian-born South Asians and Filipinos. We can see that recent visible minority immigrants made less than their European counterparts. Moreover, the gap in real income between those who came earlier and those who came more recently was larger. Although one should expect some gaps in real income for recent immigrants compared to earlier immigrants due to their shorter stay in Canada, the gaps for visible minorities are much greater than what we find for European groups. For example, Chinese males aged 30 to 60 who came in the period 1991–2000 earned $33 030, compared to $54 560 earned by Chinese males who came before 1971, a gap of 39%. Of course, those who came before 1970 were much older in 2000 and could be expected to earn more. The corresponding gap for South Asians is 43%. In contrast, the gaps are only 28% for the Portuguese and the Poles. Again, due to small sample sizes, we are not able to calculate the patterns for Italian and Greek immigrants. The comparisons above are based on group averages. One needs to control for various factors before valid, meaningful comparisons can be made of earnings. The purpose here is mainly to show, in a rather cursory way, not only that the earnings of visible minorities do seem to be lower than the European groups but also that their recent declines have been greater.

TABLE 17-5 **Multiple Regression Analysis Showing Wage Income Differentials (in Year 2000 $) for Full-Time Employed Workers Aged 30 to 60**

Predictors		1990		2000	
		ß	Stand. (ß)	ß	Stand. (ß)
Ethnic Origin	British (ref)	0	–	0	–
	French	−1790 **	−0.035	−1400 **	−0.020
	Polish	−440	−0.002	−40	0.000
	Portuguese	−2330 **	−0.011	−600	−0.003
	Italian	−1140 **	−0.010	−200	−0.002
	Greek	−5880 **	−0.021	−4210 **	−0.015
	Jewish	4590 **	0.020	6000 **	0.022
	Chinese	−2320 **	−0.017	−1610 **	−0.014
	South Asian	−5840 **	−0.036	−4090 **	−0.033
	Filipino	−8740 **	−0.040	−7480 **	−0.043
	Black	−8150 **	−0.046	−6850 **	−0.046
	Other Visible	−5900 **	−0.036	−4250 **	−0.031
Time in Canada	Canadian-born (ref)	0	–	0	–
	≥31 years	2560 **	0.020	1000 **	0.009
	21–30 years	2770 **	0.027	680	0.007
	11–20 years	1740 **	0.019	−1990 **	−0.020
	≤10 years	−3420 **	−0.030	−7290 **	−0.074
Age	30–34 (ref)	0	–	0	–
	35–39	3510 **	0.058	4150 **	0.058
	40–44	5550 **	0.091	6770 **	0.097
	45–49	6950 **	0.104	7550 **	0.106
	50–54	6590 **	0.087	8550 **	0.113
	55–59	5240 **	0.060	7340 **	0.077
Educational Level	<=High school (ref)	0	–	0	–
	Some post-sec.	4780 **	0.088	5050 **	0.087
	University & +	14 630 **	0.256	15 850 **	0.264
Occupation	Sales, service, clerical	0 780 **	– 0.014	0 1730 **	– 0.027
	Craft, trade, manual	8200 **	0.138	9890 **	0.155
	Professional Managerial	16 840 **	0.229	20 250 **	0.247
Home Language	English/French (ref)	0	–	0	–
	Other	−6030 **	−0.072	−5980 **	−0.078
Province	Ontario (ref)	0	–	0	–
	Quebec	−4210 **	−0.081	−6890 **	−0.098
	Other	−4310 **	−0.079	−4800 **	−0.080
Gender	Male (ref)	0	–	0	–
	Female	−14 A45620 **	−0.292	−13400 **	−0.237
Intercept		53050 **		50490 **	
R Squared		0.304	0.276		

Source: The 1991 and 2001 Census Public Use Sample.
Notes: * Significant at the 0.05 alpha level. ** Significant at the 0.01 alpha level. All coefficients have been rounded to nearest 10.

Table 17-5 presents the results of a regression analysis of wage income for full-time employed workers aged 30 to 60 in 1990 and 2000. The 1990 incomes are expressed in 2000 dollars, adjusted for inflation using consumer price indices. Control variables include duration of stay in Canada for the foreign-born, age, education level, occupation, home language, province of residence, and gender. When the various factors are controlled, we find that only Jews had higher incomes than the British in both 1990 and 2000. With the exception of Greeks, other European groups had incomes slightly lower than the British in 2000. The differences among them are not significant. During the 1990s, then, European minority groups narrowed their disadvantage in earnings relative to the British.

The situation for visible minorities is quite different. By 2000, all minority groups earned significantly less than the British. The earnings gaps were largest for blacks and especially for Filipinos. Filipinos earned $8740 less than the British in 1990 and $7475 less than the British in 2000, after relevant controls for other factors. The earnings of blacks were $8150 less than the British in 1990 and $6850 less in 2000. The income of South Asians was $5840 less than the British in 1990. By 2000, the difference had declined, but was still substantial at $4090. Among major visible minority groups, the Chinese had the smallest earnings gap: about $2320 less than the British in 1990 and $1610 less in 2000. The earnings gaps of visible minority groups relative to the British seem to have narrowed slightly in the 1990s.

While our primary interest is in ethnic income differentials, it is worthwhile also to look at some income differentials in control variables, as they may reveal possible causes of the ethnic differences.

A comparison of regression coefficients by time of stay in Canada is a case in point. In the 1991 sample, by the time immigrants had been in Canada for 10 years, they had caught up with the Canadian-born. The 2001 data show that it took immigrants 20 years to catch up with the Canadian-born. Not only did entry-level incomes decline for immigrants in the 2001 sample, but it also took a longer time for immigrants in this sample to catch up when compared with immigrants in the 1991 sample. This finding indicates that substantial income inequality persists between visible and non-visible groups, even after controlling for such factors as age, education, occupation, and gender. This pattern is a matter of concern because it suggests that there could be continuing problems with discriminatory practices in the labour market.

CONCLUSION

In this chapter, we have found that the conclusions arrived earlier by Hou and Balakrishnan (1996) still held true 10 years later. The integration processes for non-visible minorities and visible minorities continue to be different and distinct. In absolute numbers, immigration from Europe has decreased substantially compared to earlier decades. Those Europeans who did come to Canada continued to be less educated than visible minorities. Specifically, Poles, Portuguese, Italians, and Greeks aged 30 to 60 who came during the 1991–2000 period had much lower education levels than the Chinese, South Asians, Filipinos, or blacks. For example, among the Portuguese who came in that decade, only 13% had university education compared to 58% of Filipinos and 29% of blacks (recall Table 17-1).

The Canadian-born among the European minority groups did much better than their immigrant parents in educational attainment and were close to the British and French, and to the national average. However, European minorities were still well behind Canadian-born visible minority groups in regard to education. The selectivity of immigration has contributed only partly to the higher education levels of visible minorities, since their Canadian-born segments have attained even higher levels of education than their immigrant counterparts, except in the case of blacks and Filipinos.

Not only did the charter groups no longer maintain a superior position in educational attainment over minority groups, they were also surpassed by some minority groups in occupational attainment. Thanks in part to their high levels of education, by 2001 the Canadian-born Jewish, Greek, Chinese, and South Asian groups on average were more likely to work in managerial and professional occupations than the British and French. However, in terms of occupational returns from their education, the British were still at the top of the ethnic hierarchy. With the same educational level, only Greeks and Jews had likelihoods of working in managerial occupations that were similar to those of the British, and only Chinese had likelihoods of working in professional occupations that were similar to those of the British. The gap between the British and European groups in terms of occupational returns from education was generally smaller than that for visible minorities. Finally, visible minorities were more disadvantaged in transferring their education into managerial occupations than they were in the case of professional occupations.

Ethnic differences in socio-economic status were also evident in the area of earnings inequality. Although European groups, such as the Portuguese and Italians, have relatively lower education, their incomes were similar to the British when other factors were controlled. On the other hand, with similar qualifications the earnings of all visible minorities remained significantly lower than that of the British by 2001. Although the gaps seemed to narrow in the 1990s, they remained very large for Filipinos, blacks, and South Asians. With controls for differences in socio-demographic characteristics, Filipinos and blacks earned 14% to 15% less than the British. The important question that remains to be answered is why some European groups have been able to earn relatively high incomes while visible minority groups have not. For most members of ethnic minority groups, average incomes depend on the conditions of the labour market. Therefore, much of the income inequality that persists even after controlling for educational qualifications is probably related to discrimination. All visible minorities experienced a certain amount of income inequality in our findings, although the Chinese did a little better than the other groups. This outcome suggests that visibility has had an additional effect on income inequality. It appears that the disparate integration processes experienced by non-visible and visible minorities are not only determined by group differences in demographic factors, such as immigration status and language, or by differential motivations as manifested in the improvement of education, but also by structured social inequality. Some observers have assumed that with a longer stay in the country, especially for later generations, income inequality based on racial and ethnic background will disappear. Our research suggests that this assumption is dubious and that we cannot be complacent if we are serious about eradicating the effect of discrimination on the employment and income of Canada's ethnic minorities.

REFERENCES

Baker, M., and D. Benjamin 1994. "The performance of immigrants in the Canadian labour market." *Journal of Labour Economics* 12:369–405.

Balakrishnan, T.R. 1988. "Immigration and the changing ethnic mosaic of Canadian cities." *Report for The Review of Demography and Its Implications for Economic and Social Policy.* Ottawa: Health and Welfare Canada.

Beaujot, Roderic, K.G. Basavarajappa, and Ravi B.P. Verma 1988. *Income of Immigrants in Canada.* Ottawa: Ministry of Supply and Services Canada.

Beaujot, R., and Peter J. Rappak 1988 "The role of immigration in changing socioeconomic structures." *Report for the Review of Demography and Its Implications for Economic and Social Policy.* Ottawa: Health and Welfare Canada.

Boyd, Monica 1985. "At a disadvantage: The occupational attainment of foreign born women in Canada." *International Migration Review* 18:1091–1119.

Darroch, Gordon A. 1979. "Another look at ethnicity, stratification and social mobility in Canada." *Canadian Journal of Sociology* 4: 1–25.

Frenette, Marc, and René Morissette 2005. "Will they ever converge? Earnings of immigrant and Canadian-born workers over the last two decades." *The International Migration Review* 39:228–258.

Herberg, Edward N. 1990 "The ethno-racial socioeconomic hierarchy in Canada: Theory and analysis of the new vertical mosaic." *International Journal of Comparative Sociology* 31:206–221.

Hou, Feng, and T.R. Balakrishnan 1996 "The integration of visible minorities in contemporary Canadian society." *Canadian Journal of Sociology* 21:307–326.

Isajiw, Wsevolod W., Aysan Sever, and Leo Driedger 1993. "Ethnic identity and social mobility: A test of the 'drawback model.'" *Canadian Journal of Sociology* 18:177–196.

Kalbach, Warren E., and Madeline A. Richard 1988 "Ethnic-religious identity, acculturation, and social and economic achievement of Canada's post-war minority populations." *Report for The Review of Demography and Its Implications for Economic and Social Policy.* Ottawa. Health and Welfare Canada.

Kazemipur, A., and S.S. Hall 2000. *The New Poverty in Canada: Ethnic Groups and Ghetto Neighbourhoods.* Toronto: Thompson Educational Publishing.

Li, Peter S. 1990. *Ethnic Inequality in a Class Society.* Toronto: Thompson Educational Publishing.

Lian, Jason, and Ralph Matthews 1998. "Does the vertical mosaic still exist? Ethnicity and income in Canada, 1991." *Canadian Review of Sociology and Anthropology* 35, 4 (November): 461–482.

Parsons, Talcott 1970. "Equality and inequality in modern society, or social stratification revisited." In Edward O. Laumann (ed.), *Social Stratification: Research and Theory for the 1970s,* pp. 13–72. Indianapolis, IN: Bobbs-Merrill.

Pineo, Peter C., and John Porter 1985. "Ethnic origin and occupational attainment." In Monica Boyd, John Goyder, and Frank Jones (eds.), *Ascription and Achievement: Studies in Mobility and Status Attainment in Canada,* pp. 357–392. Ottawa: Carleton University Press.

Porter, John 1965. *The Vertical Mosaic.* Toronto: University of Toronto Press.

Portes. Alejandro, and Dag MacLeod 2003. "Educating the second generation: Determinants of academic achievement among children of immigrants in the United States." *Journal of Ethnic and Migration Studies* 25, 3: 373–396.

Reitz, Jeffrey 1990. "Ethnic Concentrations in Labour Markets and Their Implications for Ethnic Inequality." In Raymond Breton et al. (eds.),. *Ethnic Identity and Equality*, pp. 135–195. Toronto: University of Toronto Press.

Reitz, Jeffrey, and Raymond Breton 1994. *The Illusion of Difference: Realities of Ethnicity in Canada and the United States*. Toronto: C.D. Howe Institute.

Shamai, Shmuel 1992. "Ethnicity and educational achievement in Canada 1941–1981." *Canadian Ethnic Studies* 24:43–51.

Treiman, Donald J. 1970. "Industrialization and social stratification." In Edward O. Laumann (ed.), *Social Stratification: Research and Theory for the 1970s*, pp. 207–234. Indianapolis, IN: Bobbs-Merrill.

Wanner, Richard A. 2005 "Twentieth-century trends in occupational attainment in Canada." *Canadian Journal of Sociology* 30:441–469.

chapter eighteen

Racial Inequality, Social Cohesion, and Policy Issues in Canada

Jeffrey G. Reitz and Rupa Banerjee
(Abridged from Jeffrey G. Reitz and
Rupa Banerjee, "Racial Inequality, Social
Cohesion, and Policy Issues in Canada."
In Keith Banting, Thomas J. Courchene,
and F. Leslie Seidle (eds.), *Belonging?
Diversity, Recognition and Shared
Citizenship in Canada* (Montreal:
Institute for Research on Public Policy,
2007), pp. 489–545.
Reprinted with permission.

Immigration has substantially increased the racial diversity of the Canadian population. Since the 1960s, when discriminatory selection policies were eliminated, questions about immigration's impact on the cohesiveness of Canadian society have become more prominent. Although few predict a breakdown in social cohesion as a result of racial diversity, concerns about racial tensions have been expressed from a variety of political standpoints by a number of commentators, including advocates for minority rights (Lewis 1992; Omidvar and Richmond 2003) and advocates of reduction in immigration (Economics Council of Canada 1991; Stoffman 2002; Collacott 2002; Francis 2002). In this chapter, we review some research findings specifically related to racial inequality and discrimination in Canada as well as to the social integration of racial minorities in Canadian society; we then examine the relation between the two. Our review suggests that racial inequality is a significant issue in Canada, and that the extent of discrimination is a point of dispute between racial groups. This creates a potentially significant racial divide and prompts us to ask whether existing policy responses are adequate to bridge the gap.

The shift toward non-European sources of immigration to Canada after the late

1960s was marked. Immigrants arriving before 1970 were overwhelmingly from Europe, and in the 1950s and 1960s, many came from southern and Eastern Europe, as well as northern Europe, the United Kingdom, and the United States. Of those arriving in the 1960s or before, only 10.2% were racial or visible minorities (based on 2001 Census data). However, this figure rises dramatically to 51% for 1970s arrivals, 65.4% for 1980s arrivals, and nearly 75% for 1990s arrivals. As a result, racial or visible minorities have grown from constituting less than 1% of the population in 1971 to 13.4% in 2001. The largest groups are Chinese (3.4%), South Asians (3.1%) and blacks (2.2%).

The increasing impact of racial diversity in Canada is magnified because of the concentration of minorities in certain immigrant-intensive cities, especially Toronto and Vancouver. In the Toronto Metropolitan Area, racial minorities constituted only about 3% of the total population of 2.6 million in 1971, but by 2001 the figure had grown to 36.8% of 4.6 million. A recent Statistics Canada study has projected that by 2017, when racial minorities will make up 20% of the Canadian population, both Toronto and Vancouver will likely be "majority-minority" cities (Statistics Canada 2005b; see also Kalbach et al. 1993).

Ethnoracial diversity may adversely affect a society's cohesiveness in two ways. When diversity results in inequality, it may undermine the sense of fairness and inclusion among individuals and groups. Racial diversity may also weaken the commonality of values, commitments, and social relations among individuals and groups, thereby affecting their capacity to co-operate in the pursuit of common objectives. Each dimension is important in its own right, and they may have a combined effect on social cohesion.

Given the long history of ethnic and linguistic diversity in the Canadian population, both issues have always been of great significance. However, in many countries, breakdowns in interracial relations have most often been seen as linked to the former—racial inequality and discrimination. Witness the United States in the 1960s (Kerner Commission 1968) or Britain in the 1980s (Scarman 1986). And in Canada in recent years, responses to increasing racial diversity have gradually shifted; more attention is being paid to equality issues than to cultural commonalities. For example, although equality has always been an objective of Canada's multiculturalism initiative, it was sought initially through an emphasis on culture—specifically, recognition of the cultural contribution of various ethnic groups and the promise of government support for culture. This was intended to help break down barriers to equal participation in society (as Prime Minister Pierre Trudeau suggested in his speech announcing the policy [Canada House of Commons 1971:8545–8546]). But since the 1980s, multiculturalism has included an explicit antiracism component. Racial equality is now a focus of other policies, as well, such as the federal employment equity policy adopted in 1986.

In this chapter, we examine evidence of racial inequality and discrimination and consider their relation to the social integration of racial minorities in Canada. In doing so, we have used very helpful data from Statistics Canada's landmark Ethnic Diversity Survey (EDS).[1]

The analyses we present distinguish recent immigrants, immigrants with longer experience in Canada, and the children of immigrants—the so-called second generation. Most racial minorities in Canada are immigrants, but a born-in-Canada generation is emerging: by 2001, it constituted 29.4% of the racial minority population. As the children of relatively recent immigrants, most of these Canadian-born members of racial minorities are young: 63.3% are under 16; only 16.2% are over 25. Still, because they constitute an emerging young adult population with a perspective that differs from that of immigrants, this second generation is critical to an assessment of the long-term impact of immigration (Boyd 2000; Reitz and Somerville 2004). On the one hand, as Canadian-born, they will not confront many of the obstacles their parents faced as arriving immigrants. On the other hand, their expectation of social acceptance, economic opportunity and equal participation may be greater than that of their parents.

An analysis of the existing literature and EDS findings indicate that racial minority immigrants integrate into Canadian society relatively slowly, and that discriminatory inequalities are at least part of the reason. This prompts a consideration of existing Canadian policies on racial inequality and their adequacy to address this challenge to the cohesiveness of Canadian society.

RACIAL INEQUALITIES AND DISCRIMINATION

Overall Economic Situation and Employment of Racial Minorities

Generally speaking, visible minorities have much lower relative household incomes and higher poverty rates than do ethnic groups of European origin (Kazemipur and Halli 2001, 2000:107–109; Ornstein 2000; Reitz and Banerjee 2005). Data from the EDS (Table 18-1, column 1) show mean individual-equivalent household incomes for ethnic groups,[2] relative to the mean for the census metropolitan area of residence. For visible minorities, the incomes are $7686 less than the local average, while for whites, they are $1895 above the local average; thus, the gap is $9581. In relation to the national mean individual-equivalent household income of $41 330, this gap is 23.2%. Relative household incomes of virtually all racial minority

groups—including Chinese, South Asians, and blacks, as the largest groups—are substantially lower than those of almost all white groups (for further details, see Reitz and Banerjee 2005).[3] In 2001, the poverty rate for racial minorities was nearly double that for the rest of the population (Table 18-1, column 2, from census data) 26.6% compared with 14.2%; some racial minorities had higher rates than others.[4] White immigrant groups experience inequality as well, but not nearly to the same extent.

The main economic problem for new racial minority immigrants is, of course, finding adequate employment (Li 2000). There are a number of reasons they experience difficulties in doing so. Some of these difficulties—but by no means all—are associated with the period of adjustment or "entry effect" that all immigrants must confront. Entry problems may be particularly severe for immigrants arriving during a recession, as was the case for many in the early 1900s. Experience shows that all immigrants do better as they settle in and become more accustomed to their new environment. Furthermore, adverse experiences linked to economic recession may be offset by a later rebound in the economy, as the immigrants who arrived in the early 1980s discovered (Bloom et al. 1995; Grant 1999). In short, economic disadvantage and high rates of poverty may attenuate over time, and the entry effect will disappear.

There are a number of other reasons for immigrants' employment difficulties. Perhaps the most important are urban settlement, the discounting of qualifications, and race. With respect to the first reason, in seeking employment, immigrants find that any educational advantage they might have due to Canada's skill-selective immigration policy is offset by the fact that most settle in major urban areas where jobs are plentiful but competition is intense from new native-born labour market entrants, who tend to be young and also highly

TABLE 18-1 **Objective and Perceived Ethnoracial Inequality in Canada by Ancestry**

	IE Income (mean $1)[1]	Poverty Rate (%)[2]	Perceived Discrimination (%)	Perceived Vulnerability (%)	N
Non-visible Minorities (by Ancestry) [3]					
Canadian	1258.7	16.4	10.7	14.3	10 293
French	750.5	16.6	9.1	19.2	592
British	3386.1	11.8	10.7	15.0	1744
Northern and Western European	2238.2	12.5	10.0	11.2	4356
Russian and Eastern European	405.7	16.2	12.5	16.5	299
Other Southern European	−2778.6	14.3[†]	14.7	16.8	2098
Jewish	11 637.7	13.3[†]	20.0	38.7	276
Arab and West Asian	−6058.4	29.2	18.9	21.2	125
Latin American	−7416.6	25.1	24.2	23.8	5893
Greek	−617.4	16.3[†]	13.6	15.6	291
Italian	1278.0	12.2[†]	11.5	19.2	207
Portuguese	−5832.7	12.8[†]	8.9	15.9	568
Other European	9453.1	12.5	16.2	16.0	4109
Total Non-visible Minorities	1895.3	14.2	10.6	16.0	30 851
Visible Minorities (all ancestries)					
Chinese	−6730.2	26.9	33.2	33.6	513
South Asian	−5815.8	21.7	33.1	38.7	1424
Black	−10 607.2	31.1	49.6	43.0	2421
Filipino	−5063.5	16.4[†]	35.8	48.8	653
Latin American	−10 270.3	29.3	28.6	30.0	362
Southeast Asian	−6829.3	25.6	34.5	37.7	148
Arab and West Asian	−13 359.4	40.8	29.8	27.0	386
Korean	−17 145.0	40.8[†]	40.5	49.0	209
Japanese	4079.5	n/a	42.8	34.2	1892
Other Visible Minorities	−7114.5	23.7	33.3	36.8	331
Multiple Visible Minorities	−4304.2	n/a	41.5	28.7	283
Total Visible Minorities	−7686.4	26.6	35.9	37.3	8622
Total					39 473

Source: *Ethnic Diversity Survey 2002* (Ottawa: Statistics Canada, 2003).

[1] Individual-equivalent household income, relative to the census metropolitan area (CMA) mean. The individual-equivalent income adjusts household incomes for household size, and is calculated by dividing household income by the square root of household size.

[2] Data on poverty rates are from the 2001 Census Public Use Microdata File, 2.7 percent sample, for people aged 15 and over, and are based on Statistics Canada's low-income cutoff. In those data, visible minorities are identified only as black, South Asian, Chinese, and other visible minorities. In this table "other visible minorities" are further identified as Filipino, Latin American, Southeast Asian, Arab and West Asian, and Korean, based on ancestry.

[3] The origins of this group in the "non-visible minorities" category include Arab, West Asian and Latin American, and these also appear in the "visible minority" group. Those who are considered in the "non-visible minority" category described themselves as white in the visible minority question. Those who did not identify any ancestry or visible minority group or did not report household income or perceived inequality were excluded.

[†] Data exclude Maritime provinces.

educated (Reitz 2004b). In terms of the second reason, immigrants' skills tend to be discounted in the labour market, while those of the native-born are not (Reitz 2001a; Li 2001); as for the third reason, racial minority immigrants face more obstacles than immigrants of European origin or native-born workers (Pendakur and Pendakur 1998, 2002). Other possible reasons for employment difficulties include isolation in minority occupational enclaves and the fact that minority group social networks lack the linkages necessary to find good jobs.

The obstacles to immigrant success appear to have increased, and the greatest impact has been felt by those arriving most recently, even though the late 1990s and early 2000s were a period of strong labour demand. In fact, underlying the ups and downs of several business cycles, there has been a downward trend in the employment rates and earnings of successive cohorts of newly arrived immigrants, both male and female (Frenette and Morissette 2003; see also Baker and Benjamin 1994; Reitz 2001b). Whereas immigrant men arriving in the five-year period before the 1981 Census earned 79.6% of the earnings of native-born men, by 1996 this figure had dropped to 60%. For women, it dropped from 73.1% to 62.4%. By 2001, as a result of the improved labour demand of the late 1990s, relative earnings for the most recently arrived immigrants were higher than they had been in the mid 1990s, but they remained about 15 percentage points below 1970 levels (Frenette and Morissette 2003:7). Notably, despite earnings mobility experienced by immigrants as their time in Canada increases, the general trend toward declining earnings also affects immigrants who have been in Canada longer.

New immigrants have seen reduced employment success even though immigrant education levels are at an all-time high (Frenette and Morissette 2003; see also Statistics Canada 2003; Citizenship and Immigration Canada 1998). Marc Frenette and René Morissette (2003:4) show that the proportion of immigrant men arriving in the late 1990s who possessed at least the equivalent of a bachelor's degree was over 40%, more than twice the figure of 18.6 for native-born Canadian men; the corresponding figures for women were 37.5% and 21.7%. Yet, as we have mentioned, this has

not translated into employment success. Only some of the reasons for these trends are well understood. The shift towards immigrants originating from outside Europe, with the resulting change in the racial composition of immigration, explains some of the reduced employment success, particularly during the 1970s and 1980s. Abdurrahman Aydemir and Mikal Skuterud (2005:648–649) show that when we consider immigrant trends throughout the period following the policy changes of the 1960s focusing on earnings in relation to levels of education, we see that the decline in earnings to 2000 is as much as 50% for both men and women. As much as one-third of this decline stems from origin shifts and the disadvantages associated with racial minority status.

Broader labour market changes affect immigrants, as well—particularly racial minorities. David Green and Christopher Worswick (2004) have shown that, to some extent, the downward trend in immigrant employment parallels the trend among the native-born entering the workforce for the first time, in the sense that both groups fared worse in the 1990s than in earlier decades. While the causes of the trend may or may not be the same for immigrants and native-born, the consequences are greater for immigrants, since a larger proportion are pushed into poverty, and racial minorities are disproportionately affected.

Increased difficulties for immigrants may also be related to the move toward a knowledge economy, the transformation of the occupational structure and an overall increase in earnings inequality. One aspect of this is the rise in native-born education levels, which, since the 1970s, has been generally faster than the rise in immigrant education levels. Reitz (2001b) shows that the discounting of the foreign-acquired education of immigrants in the labour market compounds their difficulties in keeping pace. Furthermore, the increased earnings disadvantages of immigrants are related to their reduced access to professional-level employment (Reitz 2003b), and to their growing difficulty in obtaining well-paying jobs outside professional fields, where educational qualifications are becoming more important. Finally, there is a noticeable decline in the value of foreign experience in the labour market, though the origins of this decline are not yet known (Green and Worswick 2004; Aydemir and Skuterud 2005; Reitz 2006).

In addition, the economic situation of immigrants may be affected by broader institutional changes in Canadian society (Reitz 1998). Specifically, social services have been reduced, affecting immigrants who are in the early stages of settlement, and costs for public services are rising, including costs for retraining and educational upgrading.

Clearly, the racial dimension of economic inequality in Canada today is significant, and its social implications require scrutiny. In any society, a noticeable association of racial status and economic success over extended periods raises questions about social and political integration. A critical aspect of this, which we will now consider, is the significance of discriminatory treatment.

Perceptions of Racial Prejudice and Discrimination: A Racial Divide?

The fact that immigrants experience inequality and disadvantage may not in itself be divisive if it is regarded as the result of understandable circumstances—such as newcomer status, lack of sufficient language skills or training that does not match Canadian job requirements. Simply stated, inequality may not become a social problem if it is perceived as legitimate. However, racism, prejudice, and discrimination are another matter. Not

surprisingly, discriminatory treatment is more likely to be perceived as unjust and to lead to serious intergroup antagonism, as Gunner Myrdal has noted. In his classic—and prescient—examination of U.S. racial inequality, Myrdal (1944) points out the significance of the contradiction between the ideal of equal opportunity and the reality of inequality reinforced by discrimination.

But how significant is racial discrimination in Canada? Let us begin by considering the way this problem is perceived in Canadian society. Within certain minority groups, perceptions of racial discrimination are fairly widespread. In the 2002 Ethnic Diversity Study, which includes reports of personal experiences of racial and ethnic discrimination, respondents were asked, "In the past 5 years [or, for more recent immigrants, since arriving in Canada], do you feel that you have experienced discrimination or been treated unfairly by others in Canada because of your ethnicity, race, skin colour, language, accent, or religion?" To capture perceptions of vulnerability to discrimination, two other questions were asked. The first concerned the respondent feeling "uncomfortable or out of place in Canada" because of race or cultural background; the second concerned the respondent worrying about becoming a victim of a hate crime.[5]

As Table 18-1 shows, of the members of visible minorities who responded to this survey, 35.9% reported experiences of discrimination, compared with 10.6% of whites. The highest rate is for blacks, at 49.6%, but there are substantial rates also for the other visible minority groups, including Chinese at 33.2%, and South Asians at 33.1%. Among most white groups, experiences of discrimination are reported by fewer than 15%.[6] Experiences of perceived vulnerability are reported by 37.3% of visible minority groups and 16% of white groups. These are personal experiences and the EDS does not report perceptions of discrimination against the group as a whole. However, earlier surveys indicate that individuals are even more likely to perceive discrimination against their group as a whole than against themselves personally: over one-third of Chinese respondents felt that way, as did a clear majority of blacks.

Despite improvement in the economic circumstances of immigrants as they adjust to Canadian society and labour markets and the generally more positive employment experiences of the second generation, a racial gap in perception of discrimination is notable among immigrants with longer experience in Canada. This gap is even greater among the children of immigrants. Data from the EDS, reported in Table 18-2, show that among recent immigrants (those arriving during the previous 10 years), 33.6% of racial minorities report having experienced discrimination, compared with 19.2% of those of European origin. Among immigrants arriving earlier, perceptions of discrimination are less common for those of European origin; at a rate of 10.2%, it is about the same as it is for the children of European immigrants and for the broader Canadian population of third generation and greater. But among racial minority immigrants who arrived earlier, perceptions of discrimination are, if anything, more common, at 35.5%; and among the children of racial minority immigrants, the percentage experiencing discrimination is still greater, at 42.2%. The racial gap in perceptions of discrimination, which is 14.4% for recent immigrants, is 25.3% for earlier immigrants, and 31.3% for the children of immigrants. In other words, greater experience in Canada seems to lead to a larger racial gap in the perception of discrimination. This widening racial gap is observed among Chinese, South Asians, blacks, and other visible minority

groups. In these groups, the percentage of those born in Canada who report experiences of discrimination varies between 34.5% for Chinese, 43.4% for South Asians, and 60.9% for blacks, compared with 10.9% for the children of immigrants of European origin.

Members of minority groups also express serious concerns about the non-recognition of immigrant qualifications. In some cases, the educational qualifications may be equivalent to those of native-born Canadians yet not recognized by employers. Complaints about barriers to licensed trades and professions have been voiced for many years, and the first wave of the Longitudinal Survey of Immigrants to Canada, based on interviews with approximately 12 000 immigrants arriving between October 2000 and September 2001 and released in 2003 (Statistics Canada 2005a), shows that the lack of recognition of foreign credentials or experience is one of the most commonly reported employment problems—along with lack of Canadian job experience and official language knowledge. The earnings lost due to this long-standing problem are potentially quite large, amounting to about $2 billion annually (Reitz 2001a; Watt and Bloom 2001).

The broader Canadian population remains skeptical of the significance of racial discrimination affecting minorities, and there is a prevailing view that racism is marginal in Canada (Reitz and Breton 1994). Even so, many members of the majority population recognize that discrimination exists. A CRIC–*Globe and Mail* survey entitled *The New Canada* shows that about three in four Canadians—both white and visible minority—agree that "there is a lot of racism in Canada" (Centre for Research and Information on Canada [CRIC]–*Globe and Mail* 2003; see also Breton 1990:210–21). However, there are differences with respect to how significantly prejudice affects opportunities in

TABLE 18-2   Objective and Perceived Inequality by Origin, Immigration Cohort, and Generation, 2002

| | Immigrants | | Second Generation[3] | Third Generation and Higher[4] |
	Recent[1]	Earlier[2]		
IE Income (mean $)[5]				
White	−8467.5	2190.6	3497.2	3656.7
All Visible Minorities	−14 630.7	1535.2	−1.6	
Chinese	−16 500.8	1523.3	4670.0	
South Asian	−13 103.3	1938.1	417.9	
Black	−15 872.1	−6840.0	−3782.8	
Other Visible Minorities	−13 726.9	−3779.5	−1680.3	
Perceived Discrimination (percent)				
White	19.2	10.2	10.9	9.9
Visible Minorities	33.6	35.5	42.2	
Chinese	35.4	30.9	34.5	
South Asian	28.2	34.1	43.4	
Black	44.8	47.7	60.9	
Other Visible Minorities	32.5	34.8	36.2	
Perceived Vulnerability (percent)				
White	26.2	17.0	14.8	16.1
Visible Minorities	41.8	37.8	27.0	
Chinese	40.8	32.3	20.2	
South Asian	40.7	39.9	28.4	
Black	49.8	44.5	37.2	
Other Visible Minorities	41.0	37.6	25.2	

Source: *Ethnic Diversity Survey 2002* (Ottawa: Statistics Canada, 2003).

[1] Immigration between 1992 and 2002. N's (depending on the outcome measure): whites 740–770; Chinese 603–622; South Asians 455–479; blacks 174–181; other visible minorities 563–585; all visible minorities 1795–1867.

[2] Immigrated in 1991 and before. N's (depending on the outcome measure): whites 4992–5186; Chinese 758–769; South Asians 643–675; blacks 401–425; other visible minorities 999–1032; all visible minorities 2801–2928.

[3] N's (depending on the outcome measure): whites 11 949–12 069; Chinese 889–897; South Asian 713–723; black 677–691; other visible minorities 1062–1073; all visible minorities 3341–3384.

[4] N's for white of third generation and higher (depending on the outcome measure): 14 247–14 875. Third generation visible minorities are excluded.

[5] Mean individual-equivalent household income, relative to the census metropolitan area (CMA) mean: The individual-equivalent income adjusts household incomes for household size, and is calculated by dividing household income by the square root of household size.

key arenas such as employment. The survey shows that 42% of visible minorities think that prejudice affects opportunities, compared with 30% of whites. Moreover, the actual racial divergence in perceptions of the significance of discrimination is greater than is reflected in this difference in percentages, because some whites say it is whites who lose opportunities because of discrimination (17%)—sometimes called "reverse discrimination"—whereas this perception is less common among visible minorities (7%).

The view that racial discrimination is not a significant problem in Canada undoubtedly contributes to a belief that existing government policies on the subject are adequate, so that further action is not needed. Official policies on multiculturalism and human rights are seen as sufficient to maintain what most Canadians would describe as a favourable environment for immigrants and minority groups, particularly by international standards. Only a minority of the white population think that prejudice is something that the Canadian government should address with more determination.

Evidence of Discrimination against Racial Minority Immigrants

These are the perceptions, but what are the facts? In some ways, the research community is as divided as the general population. While the available research confirms that racial discrimination does exist, it allows for divergent interpretations of its significance.

Four types of evidence are cited in discussions of the extent of discrimination: prejudiced attitudes; evidence of discrimination in human rights cases; field tests of discrimination; and discrimination as revealed by statistical analysis of earnings gaps in labour market surveys. While each is useful, each is also problematic. Prejudiced attitudes could lead to discrimination, but not necessarily. Human rights case evidence may be persuasive, and the circumstances of a particular case may be suggestive of broader patterns, but it remains case-specific. Field trials show patterns of discrimination but not its consequences in the aggregate for minority inequality. Finally, statistical analyses of labour force data are open to diverse interpretations. However, when considered together, the four types of evidence suggest that the possibility of significant discrimination should be taken seriously. We deal with each in turn.

1. Attitude research reveals prejudice in Canada and a corresponding potential for discrimination. Not all attitudes toward minorities are negative, of course. Attitudes toward immigration in general tend to be more favourable in Canada than in societies receiving fewer immigrants (Simon and Lynch 1999). Gallup polls conducted almost every year between 1975 and 2001 have shown

majority support for either maintaining or increasing Canada's emphasis on immigration (the exception being 1982, a recession year [Reitz 2004a:111]). Yet research also makes it clear that racial boundaries are a reality of Canadian social life. For example, while most Canadians deny harbouring racial views, they maintain a "social distance" from minorities—that is, they say they prefer not to interact with members of other racial groups in certain social situations (Reitz and Breton 1994). Although an Environics Focus Canada poll showed that a large majority (93% in 2000) reject the proposal that "non-whites should not be allowed to immigrate to Canada" (Esses et al. 2002:72), there is much evidence that Canadians are more comfortable with groups of European origin than with non-European groups, and these preferences carry implications for group status (Angus Reid Group 1991; Berry and Kalin 1995; Esses and Gardner 1996).

Racism and racial bias help determine attitudes toward immigration (Henry et al. 1998; Satzewich 1998), and concerns about the threat to jobs are related to racial attitudes (Palmer 1991, 1996; Esses et al. 2001; Kalin and Berry 1994; Berry and Kalin 1995). Some research suggests that Canadians see immigrants as posing an economic threat, and this view fuels a prejudicial backlash (Esses et al. 2001). If the political acceptability of immigration derives from the economic success of immigrants, then a dip in that success rate could politically undermine the program of immigration. There is little evidence as yet that this is occurring in Canada, demonstrating that the economic problems of the newly arrived do not quickly affect the overall tone of intergroup relations.

The potential impact of racial attitudes on discrimination is complex, however. Although prejudicial attitudes do not necessarily lead to discriminatory behaviour, they may be associated with such behaviour. For example, psychological research by Victoria Esses, Joerg Dietz and Arjun Bhardwaj (2006) shows that assessments of foreign qualifications tend to be lower among persons who show other evidence of racial bias or prejudice. Discrimination may be displayed by persons who are not overtly prejudiced because of social pressure. For example, systemic discrimination arises when established practices in an organization exclude minorities. A complex phenomenon, systemic discrimination is only beginning to be understood, and its significance is being debated. A 1997 Canadian Human Rights Tribunal decision that found systemic racial discrimination in the federal public service illustrates the complex nature of evidence required for legal proof (Beck et al. 2002).

2. The Human Rights Tribunal decision just cited serves as an example of the kind of evidence we can draw from human rights complaints, but, while compelling, it is only one case. It involved allegations that there was a glass ceiling for minorities in a particular federal department—that is, that systemic discrimination was practised by those responsible for promoting staff to senior managerial positions. There was evidence of statistical underrepresentation of minorities at the senior management level; evidence derived from a survey on human resource practices of discrimination in the promotion process; and testimony about the attitudes of officials responsible for promotion decisions. The case is remarkable, partly because the respondent was a mainstream employer—the Government of Canada—generally considered an opponent of racial bias and discrimination.

3. Field tests have been conducted to find out if there is a variance in employer responses to people from different racial groups applying for the same jobs and presenting the same qualifications, and the results have offered persuasive evidence of discrimination. In Canada, the most cited study is still an early one conducted by Frances Henry and Effie Ginsberg (1985); their field tests reflected whites receiving three times as many job offers as blacks. The Economic Council of Canada repeated the field trials and produced different results: some interpret this as indicating a reduction in the significance of discrimination; others disagree (Reitz 1993; Reitz and Breton 1994:84). It is unfortunate that such information is not kept current and readily available. Arguably, such studies should be repeated regularly and on a larger scale, in the manner of the program organized by the International Labour Office in Geneva (Zegers de Beijl 2000). Yet even this program does not address the question of the extent to which discrimination accounts for the overall economic inequalities experienced by racial minorities.

4. A large number of statistical studies show that within the labour force as a whole—relative to measured job qualifications, such as education or work experience, and with differences in knowledge of official languages taken into account— visible minority immigrants have lower earnings than their European counterparts or native-born Canadian workers of European origin. Some studies are Canada-wide (Li 1992; Boyd 1992; Christofides and Swidinsky 1994; Baker and Benjamin 1994); others are specific to immigrant-intensive settings, such as Toronto (Reitz 1990; Reitz and Sklar 1997). In either case, the amount of earnings disadvantage varies among minority groups and between genders. For immigrant men, it varies between 10% and 25%. Inequalities are greater for blacks than for some Asian groups. Earnings disadvantages exist for

immigrant women, although the amounts are less, as the comparison group is native-born Canadian women, themselves a disadvantaged group compared with men.

Such analyses are useful in identifying potential discriminatory earnings gaps, but the earnings disadvantages of minorities are open to interpretation not just in terms of discrimination but also in terms of deficiencies in qualifications that cannot be measured in the survey data. Foreign-acquired educational qualifications might be lower quality, foreign experience might not be relevant in Canada or language skills might be deficient in subtle but significant ways.

Education and Employment for the Children of Immigrants

The education and employment experiences of Canadian-born children of immigrants (or of immigrant who arrive so young that their formative experiences occur in Canada) are regarded as critical to the long-term integration of racial minorities. In fact, their experiences may be a better test of the prevalence of racial discrimination. Earnings disadvantages for immigrants, even when controls for years of formal education or experience are applied, may be attributed to differences in the quality of Canadian relevance of foreign-acquired education or experience, or to language difficulties that are difficult to measure. Hence, several studies of discrimination have focused on experiences of racial minorities born in Canada, as their labour market experiences would not be affected by such characteristics.

Overall, the education levels of the racial minority second generation in Canada are fairly high—even relative to parental education levels—despite complaints of cultural and racial bias in Canadian schools, including universities. Since the federal government introduced multiculturalism as

a policy framework, provincial authorities responsible for education have addressed this issue with multicultural, and then antiracist, policies (Davies and Guppy 1998; Dei 2000). While education researchers still point to racial biases among teachers and in the curriculum (Henry et al. 1998; James 1998), Scott Davies and Neil Guppy (1998:136) show, using the 1991 Census, that among persons 20 years of age and older, both immigrant and native-born visible minorities have significantly higher rates of high school graduation than the majority population.

It is important, however, to distinguish descriptive findings on educational attainment from findings that bear on equality of opportunity in the school system. The emerging second generation are children of relatively well-educated immigrants, many of whom arrived with the earlier minority immigrant cohorts of the 1970s and, despite difficulties, earned relatively high incomes. The education levels attained by their children do not necessarily reflect equality of opportunity, and barriers hidden in the analyses may subsequently come to light.[7]

Possible variations in educational attainment by origin group may be important. For example, Davies and Guppy (1998:134–140) suggest that black men have lower educational attainment. Alan Simmons and Dwaine Plaza (1998) conducted an age-specific analysis in Toronto of the university attendance of young adult immigrants and the native-born, distinguishing blacks, South Asians, and others. Whereas rates for the mainstream population are about 40% for women and 36% for men, for blacks born in Canada, the figures are 40% and 27%; for South Asians, they are 72% and 67%. Simmons and Plaza conclude that young black men in Canada show a modest disadvantage.

Regarding the critical question of employment discrimination, analysis of the employment experiences of the children of immigrants has been hampered by statistical problems. One such problem stems from the small size of the second-generation population (de Silva 1992; Wanner 1998). Derek Hum and Wayne Simpson (1999) suggest that among native-born racial minorities, only black men suffer employment discrimination. By contrast, Krishna Pendakur and Ravi Pendakur (1998, 2002) have found that the racial disadvantage for native-born racial minorities is significant, albeit less so than for racial minority immigrants (see also Li 2000; Reitz 2001a).

The net earnings disadvantages of native-born visible minorities grew for both men and women from 1971 to 1996, leading Pendakur and Pendakur (2002:510) to conclude that "inequality is seen to be on the rise." Robert Swidinsky and Michael Swidinsky (2002) use the same 1996 data but a smaller public-use sample, a different model in which the criterion is weekly wages, and a different group of control variables, not including occupation. They find less discrimination and a different pattern of group differences. While the differences between the two studies illustrate the complexities of analysis, it is useful to note that in both, black males experience the greatest earnings disadvantages, and this is the group that most often reports discrimination in interview studies.

Summary

Among the various ethnic groups in Canada, racial minorities have the lowest incomes and highest rates of poverty, and many members of these groups believe they have experienced discrimination based on their minority racial origins. Although the economic situation is somewhat better for those who have been in Canada longer and for the Canadian-born generation, the perception that they have been affected by discrimination is more widespread among the latter two groups. In fact, there is a racial divide over perceptions of discrimination. In this context, the research on the extent of discrimination—although it does not conclusively point to discrimination as a significant cause of racial inequality—does not conclusively resolve the questions.

SOCIAL COHESION AND THE SOCIAL INTEGRATION OF RACIAL MINORITIES

Analysis of the social consequences of racial inequality and perceptions of discrimination may have many different aspects. Ultimately, our concern in this chapter is with the cohesion of society and the impact of minorities on that cohesion. Here, "cohesion" refers to the capacity of society to set and implement collective goals. Lack of cohesion may be reflected in conflict, sometimes violent conflict. Instances of civil disorder involving immigrants or minorities in other countries—most recently, France and the United Kingdom—have reinforced these concerns. We should remember, however, that conflict does not necessarily detract from cohesion: it may actually help resolve problems of intergroup relations and, hence, be an essential part of social life in a cohesive society. Finally, lack of social cohesion is manifested in other less dramatic but equally important ways, including lack of participation in decision making, withdrawal of support for decisions, and lack of organizational capacity to participate in constructive social activities.

The following discussion focuses on the integration of racial minorities as an important aspect of the Canadian social fabric. It also considers the impact of inequality and discrimination on minority social integration. Here, "social integration" refers to the extent to which individual members of a group form relationships with people outside the group—relationships that help them to achieve individual economic, social, or cultural goals. Social integration, in this sense, is relevant to the broader question of social cohesion: groups whose members look to the broader society as a means to private ends are more likely to become engaged in common objectives; similarly, groups that are well integrated into society become resources for the constructive resolution of conflicts.

In the Ethnic Diversity Survey, which provides data on individuals, the analysis focuses on those attitudes and behaviours that are expected to reflect integration into society. Three of these seem especially relevant here: strength of individual ties to the group, overall satisfaction with life (presumably a reflection of a sense of having achieved personal goals) and extent of civic participation.

Several EDS survey questions tap into these aspects. Regarding individual ties to Canadian society, there are measures of sense of belonging to Canada, trust in others, self-identification as Canadian, and acquisition of Canadian citizenship. Regarding the second aspect—overall life satisfaction—there is a single question. The third aspect—civic participation—is reflected in the following two items: participation in voluntary organizations and voting in federal elections. The survey question on participation in voluntary organizations probes deeper than simple membership, asking whether the respondent contributes on a voluntary basis to the activities of the organization. The question on voting asks about federal elections. Voting is a meaningful indicator of participation in the Canadian community, but as citizenship is a prerequisite to voting, and acquisition of citizenship reflects various circumstances, it is important to restrict analyses of voting to an examination of those who are Canadian citizens and were eligible to vote in the last federal election prior to the survey date.

Table 18-3 compares the results for all seven indicators for whites and visible minorities. On six of the seven indicators, visible minorities appear less integrated. The greatest gap between visible minorities and whites is in self-identification as Canadian (30.7 percentage points). There are also significant gaps in citizenship (18.3 percentage points) and in voting (11.1 percentage points). The gap in citizenship undoubtedly reflects, at least in part, the significantly higher proportion of immigrants among visible minorities. There are smaller racial gaps in life satisfaction (5.5 percentage points) and volunteering (7.2 percentage points). On two indicators—sense of belonging and trust in others—there does not appear to be a significant overall racial difference. Visible minorities, in fact, express a somewhat stronger sense of belonging than whites.

Some of these generalizations apply to most visible minorities; others do not. The most pervasive pattern affecting all visible minorities is the substantially lower level of Canadian identity and voting. All also have lower rates of citizenship. Regarding life satisfaction and trust, there are clear variations among groups. Lower life satisfaction affects Chinese in particular, while the other groups are closer to the white average. Less trust in others affects blacks, while South Asians and other visible minorities are near the white average; Chinese are more than 10 percentage points above the white average. Some groups have lower levels of integration in most aspects, particularly blacks and Chinese. Blacks have the highest rate of volunteer work, followed by South Asians and other visible minorities; Chinese are lower than whites.

Recency of Immigration and the Second Generation

Findings from the Ethnic Diversity Survey also permit us to make a systematic assessment of the effects of immigration and generational status on the integration of visible minorities. We can summarize our

TABLE 18-3   Integration of Visible Minorities into Canadian Society, 2002 (percent)

	Belonging[1]	Trust[1]	Canadian Identity[1]	Citizenship[1]	Life Satisfaction[1]	Volunteering[1]	Voted in Federal Election[2]
Whites	54.8	49.9	64.3	97.30	47.2	33.8	81.9
All Visible Minorities	58.6	47.9	33.6	78.96	41.7	26.6	70.8
Special Minority Origins							
Chinese	52.7	60.1	40.5	83.90	30.8	20.7	68.1
South Asian	64.9	49.0	30.5	73.30	48.4	29.1	76.1
Blacks	60.6	30.6	29.0	80.80	43.5	34.6	71.8
Other Visible Minorities	58.3	45.5	32.0	78.00	45.2	26.1	69.5

Source: *Ethnic Diversity Survey 2002* (Ottawa: Statistics Canada, 2003).

[1] *N*'s (depending on the outcome measure): whites 31 341–32 660; all visible minorities 8149–8622; Chinese 2267–2421; South Asians 1755–1892; blacks 1347–1424; other visible minorities 2757–2885.

[2] The analysis of voting is restricted to eligible voters, namely, citizens and those at least 20 years old. *N*'s: whites 28 250; all visible minorities 5581; Chinese 1646; South Asians 1159; blacks 888; other visible minorities 1888.

findings under three points. (For complete details and statistics, see Reitz and Banerjee 2007.) First, whites who have greater experience in Canada are better integrated into society than their visible-minority counterparts. The negative effects on visible minorities of greater experience living in Canada are most pronounced with regard to their self-identification as Canadian and their voting, but are also found in their sense of belonging, trust in others, and life satisfaction. Still, visible minorities are more likely than whites to become citizens, and there are no major differences in volunteering.

Second, although visible minority immigrants have lower earnings than whites at an individual level, low earnings in and of themselves contribute little or nothing to these trends in social integration. Rather, negative trends in integration reflect more pronounced experiences of discrimination and vulnerability, which become, or remain, pronounced for the second generation.

Third, many of the most important trends affect all visible minorities. Perhaps most significantly, in the second generation, all visible minority groups are more negative on all indicators. Nevertheless, some groups consistently show more negative patterns than others. In the second generation, blacks and South Asians are least likely to self-identify as Canadian; blacks and other visible minorities are least likely to vote; blacks, Chinese, and other visible minorities are least likely to have a sense of belonging in Canada.

In sum, improvement in immigrants' earnings may contribute to successful integration, but higher earnings alone do not smooth the path to integration. The analysis here suggests that experiences of discrimination and vulnerability remain, slowing the social integration of minorities. Furthermore, these effects may be intensified for the children of immigrants,

whose expectation of equality may be greater than was the case for their parents.

Among visible minorities, blacks consistently experience the greatest inequality, and their integration into Canadian society is slower. However, the fact that none of the indicators of inequality fully explains the slower integration of visible minorities suggests that the awareness of one's group standing as problematic may affect how individuals feel about society, even those not focusing on specific disadvantages.

POLICY ISSUES: MANAGING DIVERSITY UNDER CONDITIONS OF INEQUALITY

Our findings on racial inequality and the social integration of minorities carry implications for broader issues of multiculturalism and pluralism in Canada. We may well ask whether existing policies are adequate to address potential threats to social cohesion. The following discussion points to one feature of existing policy that may affect potential threats—namely, policy goals and the processes of setting them.

Goals of Canadian Multiculturalism and Antiracism

Multiculturalism is the centrepiece of Canada's policy on interethnic relations, and its focus is on broad ideals rather than specific goals and objectives. Canada has been an innovator in multiculturalism policies, which have been embraced at all levels of government since their initial proclamation in 1971 (Quebec does not embrace the label "multiculturalism," even though its policies have similar goals). The initial formulation articulated very broad equity objectives (Canada,

House of Commons 1971:8545–8546), but there were few specifics. Reactions to the policy of multiculturalism have been varied: some have supported it as the essence of modern conceptions of equality (Kymlicka 1995); other have criticized it as divisive (Bissoondath 1994; Schlesinger 1992). Despite the lack of consensus, since the Canadian policy has developed with the passage of explicit legislation and the multicultural character of the country is protected in the Constitution, the emphasis on broad ideals has held firm.

Racial barriers have been identified across a range of institutions in Canada, and many policy arenas touch on this issue of race relations. These include immigration and settlement policy; human rights policy; employment policy, including that which addresses discrimination and recognition of immigrant qualifications; policies for minority equality in public services; and policies for policing and the administration of justice in minority communities. But policies designed to address the special needs of visible minorities and to promote racial equality have been developed without an emphasis on specifics and with perhaps an even smaller consensus on objectives. When race relations was introduced under the rubric of multiculturalism in the 1980s, it was not recognized in principle as a separate concern.

Governments have responded to race issues as they have arisen, but with little coordination or continuity. Recently, *A Canada for All: Canada's Action Plan against Racism* has attempted to coordinate existing policies directed at racial equality rather than initiate new ones (Department of Canadian Heritage 2005). Like previous efforts, this one has very broad goals and offers few specifics.

Policy related to racial minorities is spread throughout agencies and levels of government. One example of lack of coordination is the policies that address the deteriorating employment situation of newly arrived immigrants (Reitz 2005). A number of relevant policies are in place, but they have not been developed in a coordinated way. At the federal level, Citizenship and Immigration Canada is responsible for immigrant selection and settlement; Canadian Heritage, Human Resources and Social Development Canada and various other departments are responsible for related policies. Most policies involve activities for which responsibility is divided among various levels of government, and the responsible parties have taken approaches that are in some respects complementary and in others diverse—even contradictory. A recent example is the federal plan, announced by the Harper government, to create an agency to assess foreign-acquired credentials; it takes little account of existing provincial agencies. Instead, we need a comprehensive policy initiative that addresses such issues as immigrant employment, settlement programs, recognition of immigrant qualifications, bridge training and employment discrimination. And all of this should be considered in relation to the ongoing success of the immigration program. Coordination might be enhanced by the creation of a unit within the federal government (perhaps directed by a cabinet minister) responsible for immigration-related policies and with the authority to initiate discussions with provincial and municipal governments to promote greater consistency and effective policy-making.

Provincial governments have not considered race relations in a consistent manner. In Ontario, an Anti-racism Secretariat advisory group within the Minister of Citizenship was abolished by the Harris government, which also abolished the provincial Employment Equity Act on the grounds that it gave undue preference to racial minorities. Similarly, a network of Toronto municipal committees on community and race relations functioned for many years but disappeared in the wake of municipal amalgamation and budget reductions mandated by the province in the late 1990s.

Illustrative of the lack of policy specificity regarding goals is the absence of provision for their formal evaluation. Evaluation requires explicit goals, and these are not in place. Multiculturalism policy itself has never been evaluated in the specific social sciences sense of the word, which implies direct observation of program impact. Jeffrey Reitz and Raymond Breton (1994) have shown that intergroup relations involving immigrants (including racial minority ones) in Canada are not markedly different from those in the U.S., a finding that casts doubt on the notion that Canada's multiculturalism has a dramatic impact. In fact, a perception of multiculturalism as largely symbolic and incapable of creating a major social impact has been reinforced by the fact that program expenditures are very small.

Public Information and Goal Setting

Canadians agree on the primacy of equal opportunity in principle but differ on the question of putting it into practice. The gap between the widespread perception among racial minorities of problems with equal opportunity and skepticism among political leaders about the need to address such problems is, to some extent, a gap in perception of fact; hence, consensus might be assisted by clarification of relevant facts. In this context, the lack of credible research information on which to base political decision making poses difficulties.

Universities, research centres, public foundations, and interest groups could provide an adequate research base from which to address these needs, but university-based research on immigration and race relations is a low-priority activity, often conducted

with few resources. And the recently established network of immigration research centres (part of the Metropolis Project) provides resources for only small-scale research. In the past, royal commissions have focused attention on topics of national priority, and the Commission on Systemic Racism in the Ontario Criminal Justice System made significant contributions to knowledge, though follow-up reforms have been slow.

Political Participation

Immigrants have high rates of citizenship acquisition, but minority access to electoral office has been limited (Black 2000, 2001). Their small size in any political constituency and low voting rates contribute to this. Avenues of access to political decision-making for minority groups include the ethnic community itself—through its leaders' connections to individual politicians—or advisory groups established to provide minority input into decision making (Breton 1990). The effectiveness of such means of representation is debated.

These problems of access may be related to the low rates of voting among racial minorities, as shown by the EDS data cited earlier. If racial minorities experience distinctive problems but have difficulty gaining a voice within Canada's political institutions, then proactive measures are needed to ensure that their viewpoints are reflected in decision making. Here, a national advisory council would be useful. Such a council could address concerns about the impact of immigration on race relations and social cohesion. An effective council would have the means for independent fact-finding, which would allow it to explore the most divisive issues in an authoritative manner. One such issue is racial discrimination.

CONCLUSIONS

This discussion has combined existing research on racial inequality in Canada with an analysis of the social integration of racial minorities based on the 2002 EDS, raising questions about Canadian policies directed at racial minorities and arriving at three basic conclusions. First, the rapidly growing racial minority populations in Canada experience much greater inequality than do traditional European-origin immigrant groups, and discrimination is a widespread concern for racial minorities. The debate among researchers over the significance of racial discrimination, so far inconclusive, is paralleled by a broader debate across society, and this debate seems to divide racial groups.

Second, social integration into Canadian society for racial minorities is slower than it is for immigrants of European origin, partly as a result of their sense of exclusion, represented by perceived discrimination. It is striking that indications of lack of integration into Canadian society are so significant for second-generation minorities, since they are regarded as the harbinger of the future. Educational and employment success for many within these racial minority groups may not be the only matter of social and political relevance. The evidence suggests that economic integration does not guarantee social integration, although it may contribute to such integration.

Third, based on a brief overview, we conclude that it is far from clear that existing policies are adequate to address the evident racial divide in Canadian society. Policies have emphasized the laudable ideals of equal opportunity and opposition to racism, but they lack the features that would enable them to effectively bridge that racial divide. More specifically, existing policies are weakened by their failure to present clear objectives, reflecting a lack of interracial consensus on the significance of the problem of discrimination and a lack of will to create such a consensus. These policies also lack the means to ensure effective implementation, intergovernmental coordination, or evaluation.

Underlying these circumstances is a lack of effective participation by racial minorities themselves in the political decision-making process. Given the salience of equality issues for these groups, such issues may require more attention in the future. Without a new recognition of the significance of racial equality issues within the majority population, the most important precondition for improved policy may be the creation of more effective means for minority group participation.

NOTES

1. The Ethnic Diversity Survey was a post-census telephone survey conducted between April and August of 2002 using a sample of 41 695 persons aged 15 and over, excluding Aboriginal persons.

2. Individual-equivalent household incomes adjust household incomes for household size and are calculated by dividing household incomes by the square root of household size.

3. Among racial minorities, Japanese are the sole exception in having relatively high incomes. Of these identifying as white, the ones belonging to either a Latin American group or an Arab/West Asian group have relatively low incomes. In these two categories, the majority actually do not identify as white. In the census data, these two groups appear both as white and as visible minorities.

4. Rates of poverty are relatively high for the largest visible minorities—blacks (44.6%), Chinese (29.4%) and South Asians (34.6%)— but they are highest for Ethiopians, Ghanaians, Afghans, and Somalis, among whom poverty rates reach 50% to 80% and higher (Ornstein 2000).

5. The respondent was read the following "Using a scale from 1 to 5, where 1 is not worried at all and 5 is very worried, how worried are you about becoming the victim of a crime in Canada because of someone's

hatred of your ethnicity, culture, race, skin colour, language, accent or religion?"

6. One exception is the Jewish group. 20% reported experiences of discrimination. The other exceptions are Latin Americans and Arab/West Asians.

7. A few studies have focused on educational opportunity and the accessibility of education to the second generation. The studies suggest that educational opportunities for native-born racial minorities in Canada are comparable to those for the native-born population in terms of levels of education attained (Boyd and Grieco 1998, based on the General Social Survey. Boyd 2002, based on the Survey of Labour and Income Dynamics), academic performance based on parent and teacher assessments, and formal testing (Worswick 2001, based on the National Longitudinal Survey of Children and Youth).

REFERENCES

Angus Reid Group 1991. *Multiculturalism and Canadians: Attitude Study 1991*. Ottawa: Multiculturalism and Citizenship Canada.

Aydemir, Abdurrahman, and Mikal Skuterud 2005. "Explaining the deteriorating entry earnings of Canada's immigrant cohorts, 1966–2000." *Canadian Journal of Economics/ Revue canadienne d'économique* 38, 2:641–672.

Baker, Michael, and Dwayne Benjamin 1994. "The performance of immigrants in the Canadian labour market." *Journal of Labour Economics* 12, 3:369–405.

Beck, J. Helen, Jeffrey G. Reitz, and Nan Weiner 2002. "Addressing systemic racial discrimination in employment: The Health Canada case and implications of legislative change." *Canadian Public Policy/Analyse de poliques* 28, 3:373–394.

Berry, John W., and Rudolf Kalin 1995. "Multicultural and ethnic attitudes in Canada: An overview of the 1991 survey." *Canadian Journal of Behavioural Science* 27, 4:17–49.

Bissoondath, Neil 1994. *Selling Illusions: The Cult of Multiculturalism in Canada*. Toronto: Penguin Books.

Black, Jerome 2000. "Ethnoracial minorities in the Canadian House of Commons: The case of the 36th Parliament." *Canadian Ethnic Studies* 32, 2:105–114.

Black, Jerome 2001. "Immigrants and ethnoracial minorities in Canada: A review of their participation in federal electoral politics." *Electoral Insight* 3, 1:8–13.

Bloom, David E., Gilles Grenier, and Morely Gunderson 1995. "The changing labour market position of Canadian immigrants." *Canadian Journal of Economics/Revue canadienne d'économique* 28, 4b:987–1005.

Boyd, Monica 1992. "Gender, visible minority and immigrant earnings, inequality: Reassessing an employment equity premise." In Vic Satzewich (ed.), *Deconstructing a Nation: Immigration, Multiculturalism and Racism in the 1990s Canada*. pp. 279–321. Toronto: Garamond Press.

Boyd, Monica 2000. "Ethnicity and immigrant offspring." In Madeline A. Kalbach and Warren E. Kalbach (eds.), *Perspectives on Ethnicity in Canada*. pp. 137–154. Toronto: Harcourt Canada.

Boyd, Monica 2002. "Educational attainments of immigrant offspring: Success or segmented assimilation? *International Migration Review* 36, 4:1037–1060.

Boyd, Monica, and Elizabeth M. Grieco 1998. "Triumphant transitions: Socioeconomic achievements of the second generation in Canada." *International Migration Review* 32, 4:521–551.

Breton, Raymond 1990. "The ethnic group as a political resource in relation to problems of incorporation: Perceptions and attitudes." In Raymond Breton, Wsevolod W. Isajiw, Warren E. Kalbach, and Jeffrey G. Reitz (eds.), *Ethnic Identity and Equality: Varieties of Experience in a Canadian City*. pp. 196–255. Toronto: University of Toronto Press.

Canada, House of Commons 1971 *House of Commons Debates*, 3rd sess. 28th Parliament, October 8, vol. 8. Ottawa: Queen's Printer.

Centre for Research and Information of Canada (CRIC)–*Globe and Mail* 2003. *The New Canada*. Montreal and Toronto. CRIC, Globe and Mail, Canadian Opinion Research Archive.

Christofides, Louis N., and Robert Swidinsky 1994. "Wage determination by gender and visible minority status: Evidence from the 1989

LMAS." *Canadian Public Policy/Analyse de politiques* 22,1:34–51.

Citizenship and Immigration Canada 1998. *The Economic Performance of Immigrants: Immigration Category Perspective.* IMDB Profile Series. Ottawa: Citizenship and Immigration Canada. December.

Collacott, Martin 2002. *Canada's Immigration Policy: The Need for Major Reform.* Vancouver: Fraser Institute.

Davies, Scott, and Neil Guppy 1998. "Race and Canadian education." In Vic Satzewich (ed.), *Racism and Social Inequality in Canada: Concepts, Controversies and Strategies of Resistance*, pp. 131–156. Toronto: Thompson Educational Publishing.

de Silva, Arnold 1992. *Earnings of Immigrants: A Comparative Analysis.* Ottawa: Economic Council of Canada.

Dei, George J. 2000. *Removing the Margins: The Challenges and Possibilities of Inclusive Schooling.* Toronto: Canadian Scholars' Press.

Department of Canadian Heritage 2005. *A Canada for All: Canada's Action Plan against Racism: An Overview.* Ottawa: Minister of Public Works and Government Services Canada.

Economic Council of Canada 1991. *Economic and Social Impacts of Immigration.* Ottawa: Supply and Services Canada.

Esses, Victoria M., Joerg Dietz, and Arjun Bhardwaj 2006. "The role of prejudice in the discounting of immigrant skills." In Ramiswami Mahalingam (ed.), *Cultural Psychology of Immigrants*, pp. 113–130. Mahwah, NJ: Lawrence Erlbaum.

Esses, Victoria M., John F. Dovidio, and Gordon Hodson 2002. "Public attitudes toward immigration in the United States and Canadian response to the September 11, 2001: 'Attack on America.'" *Analysis of Social Issues and Public Policy* 2:69–85.

Esses, Victoria M., John F. Dovidio, Lynn M. Jackson and Tamara L. Armstrong 2001. "The immigration dilemma: The role of perceived group competition, ethnic prejudice, and national identity." *Journal of Social Issues* 57, 3:389–412.

Esses, Victoria M., and Robert C. Gardner 1996. "Multiculturalism in Canada: Context and current status." *Canadian Journal of Behavioural Science* 28, 3:145–152.

Francis, Diane 2002. *Immigration: The Economic Case.* Toronto: Key Porter Books.

Frenette, Marc, and René Morissette 2003. *Will They Ever Converge? Earnings of Immigrant and Canadian-Born Workers over the Last Two Decades.* Analytical Studies Branch Research Paper Series. Cat. No. 11F0019MIE B no. 215. Ottawa: Statistics Canada

Grant, Mary L. 1999. "Evidence of new immigrant assimilation in Canada." *Canadian Journal of Economic/Revue canadienne d'économique* 32, 4:930–955.

Green, David, and Christopher Worswick 2004. "Earnings of immigrant men in Canada: The roles of labour market entry effects and returns to foreign experience." Accessed November 7, 2006. (http://www.econ.ubc.ca/green/chrfexp4.pdf)

Henry, Frances, and Effie Ginsberg 1985. *Who Gets the Work? A Test of Racial Discrimination in Employment.* Toronto: Urban Alliance on Race Relations, Social Planning Council of Metropolitan Toronto.

Henry, Frances, Carol Tator, Winston Mattis, and Tim Rees 1998. *The Colour of Democracy: Racism in Canadian Society* (2nd ed.) Toronto: Harcourt Brace.

Hum, Derek, and Wayne Simpson 1999. "Wage opportunities for visible minorities in Canada." *Canadian Public Policy/Analyse de politiques* 25, 3:379–394.

James, Carl 1998. "'Up to no good': Black on the streets and encountering police." In Vic Satzewich (ed.), *Racism and Social Inequality in Canada* pp. 157–176. Toronto: Thompson Educational Publishing.

Kalbach, Warren E., Ravi Verma, M.V. George, and S.Y. Dai 1993. *Population Projections of Visible Minority Groups, Canada, Provinces and Regions, 1991–2016.* Ottawa: Statistics Canada. Working Group on Employment Equity Data, Population Projections Section, Demography Division.

Kalin, Rudolf, and John W. Berry 1994. "Ethnic and multicultural attitudes." In John W. Berry and Jean A. Laponce (eds.), *Ethnicity and Culture in Canada: The Research Landscape* pp. 293–321. Toronto: University of Toronto Press.

Kazemipur, Abdolmohammad, and Shiva S. Halli 2000. *The New Poverty in Canada:*

Ethnic Groups and Ghetto Neighbourhoods. Toronto: Thomson Educational Publishing.

Kazemipur, Abdolmohammad, and Shiva S. Halli 2001. "Immigrants and new poverty: The case of Canada." *International Migration Review* 35, 4:1129–1156.

Kerner Commission 1968. *Report of the National Advisory Commission on Civil Disorders.* Toronto: Bantam.

Lewis, Stephen 1992. *Report to the Office of the Premier.* Toronto: Government of Ontario.

Li, Peter S. 1992. "Race and gender as bases of class fractions and their effects on earnings." *Canadian Review of Sociology and Anthropology* 29, 4:488:510.

Li, Peter S. 2000. "Earnings, disparities between immigrants and native-born Canadians." *Canadian Review of Sociology and Anthropology* 37, 3:289–311.

Li, Peter S. 2001. "The market worth of immigrants' educational credentials." *Canadian Public Policy/Analyse de politiques* 27, 1: 23–38.

Myrdal, Gunner 1944. *An American Dilemma: The Negro Problem and Modern Democracy.* New York: Harper and Row.

Omidvar, Ratna, and Ted Richmond 2003. *Immigrant Settlement and Social Inclusion in Canada.* Laidlaw Foundation Working Papers Series, Perspectives on Social Inclusion. Toronto: Laidlaw Foundation.

Ornstein, Michael 2000. *Ethnoracial Inequality in Metropolitan Toronto: Analysis of the 1996 Census.* Toronto: Institute for Social Research: York University.

Palmer, Douglas 1991. "Prejudice and tolerance in Canada. In *Social and Economic Impacts of Immigration*, pp. 103–119. Ottawa: Economic Council of Canada.

Palmer, Douglas 1996. "Determinants of Canadian attitudes towards immigration. More than just racism?" *Canadian Journal of Behavioural Science* 28, 3:180–192.

Pendakur, Krishna, and Ravi Pendakur 1998. "The colour of money: Earnings differentials among ethnic groups in Canada." *Canadian Journal of Economics/Revue canadienne d'économique* 31, 3:518–548.

Pendakur, Krishna, and Ravi Pendakur 2002. "Colour my world: Have earnings gaps for Canadian-born ethnic minorities changed over time?" *Canadian Public Policy/Analyse de politiques* 28, 4:489–512.

Picot, Garnett, and Feng Hou 2003. *The Rise in Low-Income Rates among Immigrants in Canada.* Analytical Studies Branch Research Paper Series. Catalogue No. 11F001MIE B no. 198. Ottawa: Statistics Canada.

Reitz, Jeffrey G. 1990. "Ethnic concentrations in labour markets and their implications for ethnic inequality." In Raymond Breton, Wsevolod W. Isajiw, Warren E. Kalbach, and Jeffrey G. Reitz (eds.), pp. 135–195. Toronto: University of Toronto Press.

Reitz, Jeffrey G. 1993. "Statistics on racial discrimination in Canada." *Policy Options* 14, 2:32–36. Montreal: IRPP.

Reitz, Jeffrey G. 1998. *Warmth of the Welcome: The Social Causes of Economic Success for Immigrants in Different Nations and Cities.* Boulder, CO: Westview Press.

Reitz, Jeffrey G. 2001a. "Immigrant skill utilization in the Canadian labour market: Implications of human capital research." *Journal of International Migration and Integration* 2, 3:347–378.

Reitz, Jeffrey G. 2001b. "Immigrant success in the knowledge economy: Institutional change and the immigrant experience in Canada, 1970–1995." *Journal of Social Issues* 57, 3:577–611.

Reitz, Jeffrey G. 2003a. "Educational expansion and the employment success of immigrants in the United States and Canada, 1970–1990." In Jeffrey G. Reitz (ed.),*Host Societies and the Reception of Immigrants*, pp. 151–180. San Diego: Center for Comparative Immigration Studies, University of California.

Reitz, Jeffrey G. 2003b. "Occupational dimensions of immigrant credential assessment: Trends in professional managerial, and other occupations, 1970–1996." In Charles Beach, Alan Green, and Jeffrey G. Reitz (eds.), *Canadian Immigration Policy for the 21st Century*, pp. 469–506. Kingston: John Deutsch Institute for the Study of Economic Policy, Queen's University.

Reitz, Jeffrey G. 2004a. "Canada: Immigration and nation-building in the transition to a knowledge economy." In Wayne A. Cornelius, Philip L. Martin, James F. Hollifield, and Takeyuki Tsuda (eds.), *Controlling Immigration: A Global Perspective* (2nd ed.), pp. 97–133. Stanford: Stanford University Press.

Reitz, Jeffrey G. 2004b. *Social Risks for New-comers to Canada: Issues Respecting the Role of Government in Ontario.* Panel on the Role of Government in Ontario Research Paper 11. Accessed November 7, 2006. (http://www.law-lib.utoronto.ca/investing/reports/rp11.pdf)

Reitz, Jeffrey G. 2005. "Tapping immigrants' skills: New directions for Canadian immigration policy in the knowledge economy." *IRPP Choices* 11, 1:1–18.

Reitz, Jeffrey G. 2006. "Recent trends in the integration of immigrants in the Canadian labour market: A multi-disciplinary synthesis of Research." Unpublished paper. Accessed December 12. (http://www.utoronto.ca/ethnicstudies/trends.pdf)

Reitz, Jeffrey G. and Rupa Banerjee 2005. "Racial inequality and social cohesion in Canada: Findings from the Ethnic Diversity Survey." Paper presented at the Canadian Ethnic Studies Association meeting "Social Trends and Social Justice: Analysis of the EDS Survey," October 13–16, Ottawa.

Reitz, Jeffrey G. and Rupa Banerjee 2007. "Racial inequality and social cohesion in Canada." In Keith Banting, Thomas Courchene, and F. Leslie Seidle (eds.), *Belonging? Diversity, Recognition and Shared Citizenship in Canada,* pp. 489–545. Montreal: Institute for Research on Public Policy.

Reitz, Jeffrey G. and Raymond Breton 1994. *The Illusion of Difference: Realities of Ethnicity in Canada and the United States.* Toronto: C.D. Howe Institute.

Reitz, Jeffrey G. and Sherilyn M. Sklar 1997. "Culture, race, and the economic assimilation of immigrants." *Sociological Forum* 12, 2:233–277.

Reitz, Jeffrey G. and Kara Somerville 2004. "Institutional change and emerging cohorts of the 'new' immigration for the integration of racial minorities in Canada." *Journal of International Migration and Integration* 5, 4:385–415.

Satzewich, Vic, (ed.) 1998. *Racism and Social Inequality in Canada: Concepts, Controversies and Strategies of Resistance.* Toronto: Thompson Education Publishing.

Scarman, Leslie George 1986. *The Brixton Disorders: 10–12 April 1981. The Scarman Report: Report of an Inquiry by the Right Honourable the Lord Scarman.* Harmondsworth, UK: Penguin Books.

Schlesinger, Arthur M. Jr. 1992. *The Disuniting of America: Reflections on a Multicultural Society.* New York: W.W. Norton.

Simmons, Alan, and Dwaine Plaza 1998. "Breaking through the glass ceiling: The pursuit of university training among African-Caribbean migrants and their children in Toronto." *Canadian Ethnic Studies* 30, 3:99–120.

Simon, R.J. and J.P. Lynch 1999. "A comparative assessment of public opinion toward immigrants and immigration policy." *International Migration Review* 33, 2:445–467.

Statistics Canada 2002. *Ethnic Diversity Survey B User Guide.* Ottawa: Statistics Canada.

Statistics Canada 2003. *Earnings of Canadians: Making a Living in the New Economy.* 2001 Census Analysis Series Catalogue No. 96F00-30XIE2001013. Ottawa: Statistics Canada.

Statistics Canada 2005a. "Longitudinal survey of immigrants to Canada: A portrait of early-settlement experiences." Catalogue No. 89-614-XIE. Ottawa: Statistics Canada.

Statistics Canada 2005b. *Population Projections of Visible Minority Groups, Canada, Provinces and Regions, 2001 to 2017.* Catalogue no. 91-541-XIE. Ottawa: Statistics Canada.

Stoffman, Daniel 2002. *Who Gets In: What's Wrong with Canada's Immigration Program—and How to Fix It.* Toronto: Macfarlane Walter and Ross.

Swidinsky, Robert, and Michael Swidinsky 2002. "The relative earnings of visible minorities in Canada: New evidence from the 1996 Census." *Relations industrielles/Industrial Relations* 5, 4:630–659.

Wanner, R.A. 1998. "Prejudice, profit, or productivity: Explaining returns to human capital among male immigrants to Canada." *Canadian Ethics Studies* 30, 3:24–55.

Watt, Douglas, and Michael Bloom 2001. *Exploring the Learning Recognition Gap in Canada: Phase 1 Report. Recognizing Learning: The Economic Cost of Not Recognizing Learning and Learning Credentials in Canada.* Ottawa: Conference Board of Canada.

Worswick, Christopher 2001. *School Performance of the Children of Immigrants in Canada, 1994–98.* Research Paper 178 Catalogue No. 11F0019MIE. Ottawa: Statistics Canada.

Zegers de Beijl, Roger 2000. *Documenting Discrimination against Migrant Workers in the Labour Market: A Comparative Study of Four European Countries.* Geneva: International Labour Office.

chapter nineteen

First Nations, Inequality, and the Legacy of Colonialism

Charles R. Menzies
(An original chapter written
for this volume.)

INTRODUCTION

. . . it would not be accurate to assume that even pre-contact existence in the territory was in the least bit idyllic. The plaintiffs' ancestors had no written language, no horses or wheeled vehicles, slavery and starvation was not uncommon, wars with neighbouring peoples were common, and there is no doubt, to quote Hobbes, that Aboriginal life in the territory was, at best, "nasty, brutish and short."

B.C. Supreme Court Chief Justice, Allan McEachern, *Delgamuukw: Reasons for Judgment*, 1991.

Racism is racism, and racism stings. All the good intentions in the world do not take away the sting and do not take away the pain.

Patricia Monture-Angus,
Thunder in My Soul, 1995.

The First Nations' response to Justice Allan McEachern's decision (quoted above) was angry and tearful. For the First Nations people living in the Gitksan and Wet'suwet'en Territories, the four-year-long court case was about the right to live as they and their ancestors had for millennium upon millennium. From the point of view of the governments of British Columbia and Canada, a large tract of land full of crucial economic resources was at stake and had to be defended. By opening their box of stories and experience to a court, the Gitksan and Wet'suwet'en people, elders, and chiefs had placed their trust in an institution they saw as foreign. In return, they felt that they had been repaid with insult and disdain. While McEachern's decision stands out from recent court rulings and was to a certain extent overturned in appeal,[1] his basic interpretations of First Nations people as having existed without "real" social organization or culture until the arrival of Europeans in the Americas is itself a product of the colonial encounter.

Canada is built upon a colonial system in which Aboriginal lands have been expropriated, Aboriginal institutions banned, and Aboriginal peoples relegated to marginal sectors of the mainstream economy. Put simply:

> Colonialism involves a relationship which leaves one side dependent on the other to define the world. At the individual level, colonialism involves a situation in which one individual is forced to relate to another on terms unilaterally defined by the other. (McCaskill 1983:289)

Five hundred years of European settlement in the Americas is painfully and tragically represented in standard indices of social pathologies such as high rates of suicide, un- and under-employment, and substance abuse. This is not to deny impressive and important examples of successful First Nations people. Rather, it is important to underline the fact that the structure of social inequality experienced by First Nations people is directly linked to the processes of colonialism and government policies directed at undermining Aboriginal institutions and social organization. In this chapter, I describe the contemporary structure of inequality, outline the general process of colonialization and

expropriation of First Peoples in Canada, and suggest strategies for improving the current situation.

STORIES TO CRY OVER

Social inequality cannot simply be captured in a set of cold, apparently objective numbers (although you will see some numbers below). Think of the everyday stories we tell among friends, in school, or at work. These stories form the basis of our regular communication. They are important sources of knowledge and cultural codes. For the social scientist, these stories are also important places to search out experiences and expressions of inequality. Who is telling the story? Where is it being told? Who is excluded from the audience? We recognize that some stories are not public, that they are in some sense restricted to special places or social settings.

An important part of my writing details the semi-private stories of Euro-Canadian men and the role their story-telling plays in the maintenance of colonial structures.[2] These are emotionally wrenching stories. While one may wish to deny or ignore them, it is more important to listen to these stories. How does it feel to be the target, the butt of the joke, the object of ridicule? A cousin told me, some years after I had given her a copy of *Stories from Home* (Menzies 1994), that the stories of hate I had recounted made her cry.

"I know these men, or men just like them. My husband has worked alongside of them. We raised our children in the same community as them. To hear how they talk about us [First Nations people] in your paper still makes me cry," she said. The telling of these stories is important to my cousin, even though they are painful to hear. They reveal, more than any graph, the everyday experience of racism and inequality. Here is a version of a story I first heard while sitting on the deck of a fishing boat one summer afternoon in a northern British Columbia port.

A small gathering of men were relaxing in the quiet time between the end of work and heading up town or home for the night. Ed, a crewmember from an adjacent boat, joined our circle and began to talk about his exploits of the previous evening. He had spent most of his time participating in a twentieth-year high school reunion—by all accounts it had been a smashing success.

Ed is a respected member of the local fishing community,[3] an accomplished storyteller, and an effective public speaker (the public here being a group of predominantly Euro-Canadian fishermen). I began to tune out—I'd heard this story before, at least versions of it—drink, party, and drink. . . . I had almost decided to leave when Ed's story took an unexpected turn.

"Jim had all this paint up at his place, so we loaded it into my car and drove back downtown. Parked off Third, took a look for the cops and then went to it."

"Doing what?" I asked.

"Hey? What do you think we were doing?"

"Painting the town red," somebody said to a chorus of laughs.

"No," said Ed, "we were painting the town white. Yeah, we painted a bloody white crosswalk from the Belmont [Hotel] right into the Empress. Help all those drunken Indians make it across the street."

"I wonder'd who did that when I came down to the boat this morning," I said. "But why is it so jagged? It's crooked."

"That's the beauty of it," said Ed. "It's designed just right. Your Indian stumbles out of the bar, into the street. 'Hey, look,'

he says, 'a crosswalk.' And he's right over into the other bar. First class."

The irony of Ed's own drunkenness seemed to have escaped him. He plays up a popular explanation of the so-called "Indian problem": the drunken Indian. Yet his story is only one example in a multitude of narratives of colonialism in which the disparate threads of racial superiority and intolerance are wound. Ed's story is part of the day-to-day experience of social inequality felt by people of Aboriginal descent.

THE CONTEMPORARY STRUCTURE OF INEQUALITY

Social scientists typically measure inequality using social indicators such as income level, rate of participation in employment and education, and quality of life measures such as health and housing. To demonstrate inequality objectively, it is necessary to show that significant differences between groups of people do in fact exist. In this section, statistics concerning income, health, and justice are presented. You will notice that although there are some very successful First Nations individuals (in business, entertainment, politics), many are relatively impoverished when compared with mainstream Canadian society. Social statistics are often produced in an ad hoc manner, and coordination among producers of social statistics seems to be insufficient, resulting in inconsistent statistics. In updating this article, I found the issue of classifications that appeared to change depending on the agenda of the producer to be one difficulty. Some statistics are available for all First Nations people, some only for on-reserve or urban populations. Further distinctions may be made between Inuit, Metis, and Registered Indian populations. The most recent and comprehensive statistics were available from the 2001 Census and the next release from the 2006 Census will not take place until April 2008. This makes gathering of timely and comprehensive data difficult.

Income

Data reported by Indian and Northern Affairs (2000) show significant discrepancies between income levels of First Nations people and those of other Canadians. In 1995, the average individual income for Registered Indians (on- or off-reserve) was 60% of that for other Canadians. In terms of median family income, First Nations families earned about 61% of the national average ($25 602 versus $41 898). Maxim et al. (2001:469–471) report similar results for 1995, using data from the 1996 Census of Canada Public Use Microdata File. Based on the wage and salary incomes of people who had some income, and who were between 18 and 64 years old, these researchers found that, on average, all major categories of Aboriginal Canadians made significantly lower incomes than did non-Aboriginals. The biggest gap was for Registered Indians, who made 62% of the non-Aboriginal average. Inuit earnings were at 65%, Metis at 72%, and non-Registered Indians at 77% of the non-Aboriginal average. Even among full-time workers, there is a significant gap: Grabb (2008:138) has reported that, based on 2001 Census data, the annual incomes of First Nations peoples who worked full-time, full-year were only about 87% of the Canadian average. Another way to look at income is to examine the data for Low Income Cut-Offs. Almost half of Registered Indian families live at or below the LICOs, compared with about 17% of all Canadian families.

In examining income data, one must consider more than just how much people earn. The source of income also provides important information about the structure of inequality. For the majority of Canadians over the age of 15 (Aboriginal and non-Aboriginal), earned income is a major source of income. However, Aboriginal people (especially those on-reserve) receive a higher portion of their income in the form of government transfers. About 77% of all Canadians derive their income from employment. However, only 24% of all Canadians receive the bulk of their income in the form of government transfers, compared with 42% of Aboriginal people. For on-reserve populations, the figures show 55% of the income coming from employment and 45% from government transfers.

Health

Although the basic health of First Nations people has improved over the last several decades, significant differences remain between the health of Aboriginal people and members of mainstream Canadian society (Statistics Canada 1995). Illnesses resulting from poverty, overcrowding, and poor housing have led to chronic and acute respiratory diseases, which take a heavy toll among Aboriginal people. According to Indian and Northern Affairs (2002), the average age of death for Aboriginals in 2000 had improved considerably but was still 6.3 years below that of the average for non-Aboriginal Canadians. The rate of infant mortality is almost twice the Canadian average (11.6 per 1000 versus 6.1 per 1000). More than 33% of all Aboriginal deaths are related to violence, compared with 8% in Canada generally. These statistics highlight a significant discrepancy between non-Aboriginal and Aboriginal Canadians.

The Law

The interaction between First Nations people and Canadian law occurs at a collective and individual level. Collectively, particular social institutions (such as the feast or potlatch system on the northwest coast) have been banned or restricted. The right to vote in federal elections was denied to all status Indians until 1960. Between 1927 and 1951, activity related to land claims (e.g., protesting) was illegal (Tennant 1990; Cole and Chaikin 1990). And many Aboriginal children were forcibly removed from their home communities and placed in residential schools (Haig-Brown 1988). The impact of these assimilationist policies on First Nations individuals is clearly seen in the overrepresentation of First Nations people incarcerated in the criminal justice system.

As of 2001, Aboriginal people accounted for slightly less than 3% of the total Canadian population. However, they accounted for 18% of federal and 14% of provincial admissions to prison. In western Canada, the percentage of the in-prison population who are Aboriginal ranged between 20% and 76%, depending on the province (Correctional Services Canada 2001). The ratio of Aboriginal people incarcerated in Canadian jails has been increasing steadily over the course of the twentieth century. In Saskatchewan, for example, the percentage of the prison population of Aboriginal descent has gone from 5% in the 1920s to 76% in 2001 (Correctional Services Canada 2001). In Manitoba, 59% of prisoners are of Aboriginal descent.

Patricia Monture-Angus (1996:335) highlights an important difficulty with this statistical picture: "The overrepresentation of Aboriginal people in the system of Canadian criminal justice is all too often seen as an Aboriginal problem (that is, a problem with Aboriginal people)." In a careful examination of all aspects of the Canadian criminal justice system, Ponting and Kiely (1997:155) conclude that "each stage of the judicial process is punctuated with a disproportionate number of Aboriginal people. [Their data] suggest that Aboriginal people are victims of a discriminatory criminal justice system."

EXPLAINING INEQUALITIES: COLONIALISM'S LEGACY

The socio-economic context of First Nations people is one that is clearly disadvantaged in comparison with mainstream society. Popular explanations of this imbalance of power and resources typically blame the victim. Such explanations fail to take into account the rich, vibrant way of life that pre-existed European arrival in the Americas, or the many examples of individual and community success (more on this below). By focusing on individuals, popular explanations deny the overpowering dominance of European traditions and economic processes that were forced on Aboriginal peoples. An important and powerful set of explanations roots social inequality in the historical and cultural phenomena of colonialism, the expropriation of First Nations land and resources, and government policies designed to undermine Aboriginal social institutions.

COLONIAL HISTORY: A NORTHWEST COAST ILLUSTRATION

On the northwest coast of British Columbia, people of European and First Nations descent have come together and separated over the years as the result of the historical movement of capital. Initial contact revolved around the exchange of commodities such as fur, iron, beads, or other trade goods.

In British Columbia, a maritime-based fur trade structured the early contacts between Europeans and First Nations

(1774–1858). In this period, a European-based mercantile capitalism interacted with an indigenous kin-ordered mode of production,[4] in which the control over labour power and the production of trade goods remained under the control of the Native American traders who were for the most part "chiefs." They "mobilized their followers and personal contacts to deliver . . . otter skins, and [their] power grew concomitantly with the development of the trade" (Wolf 1997 [1982]:185). The merging of these two modes of production—one based on the family and one based on European capitalism—produced new wealth and intense inflation for both First Nations and Europeans (Fisher 1977:8–20; Codere 1961:443–467; Wolf 1997 [1982]: 184–192). However, as Europeans prospered from this fur trade and developed industrial enterprises, First Nations people lost control over trade and were displaced by a settler-based industrial capitalism.

This was also a period of massive demographic transition whereby non-indigenous diseases such as smallpox, measles, and flu lead to what can only be describe as waves of death washing along the coast and interior of the province (Campbell et al. 2003). Understanding the social changes that followed requires that we take into account, in a serious manner, the devastation to communities caused by this microbial form of colonialism. In many cases, European settlers in British Columbia took land that had been "cleared" of people by disease. In other cases, diseases erupted from what were at best callousness, or at worst intentional spread of disease. The survival and active participation in the developing industrial economy of the colony of British Columbia is a testament to the power and reliance of First Nations society and culture.

As European settlement extended into First Nations territories, marriages between Euro-Canadian businessmen and First Nations women became increasingly common. According to several commentators, these early marriages followed customary First Nations practices and were ostensibly designed to facilitate trade and co-operation between groups (Fisher 1977).

Vancouver Island, and British Columbia more generally, began the change from colonies in which Europeans exploited indigenous labour power to colonies of settlement in the 1850s following the discovery of gold in the interior of the province. With the exception of the fishing industry, First Nations' labour power "was only of marginal significance in the economic concerns of the Europeans" (Fisher 1977:96, 109). Mining, forestry, and fishing supplanted the fur trade and became the backbone of British Columbia's economy.

The extension of industrial capitalism into this region fundamentally altered the basis for alliance. No longer valued as trading partners, First Nations were slotted into the developing resource economy as a subordinate part of the growing industrial labour force in which workers were segregated by race and gender. Union organizers and social activists have attempted, with little success, to overcome these structural divisions.

By the mid 1880s, indigenous control of commercially valuable land and resources was almost completely destroyed through a variety of legal (and extra-legal) measures introduced by Canada and the provinces (McDonald 1994). One of the most insidious changes was the creation of the legal category of "food fishing" in the 1880s, which prohibited Aboriginal fishers from catching fish without a permit from the federal government (Newell 1993). At the same time, First Nations people were integrated "into virtually every major resource industry in [British Columbia] as workers and owner-operators" (Knight 1996:10).

Alliances between First Nations and non-Aboriginal resource workers have played a major role in shaping British Columbia's union movement, especially in the fishing industry. Although union organizers have attempted to include them in pan-racial organizations, First Nations workers ultimately found themselves in conflict with many of their Euro-Canadian co-workers. The major point of contention between non-Aboriginal and First Nations resource workers has been the issue of land claims. Despite their common confrontation with capital as workers, non-Aboriginal workers' associations have not been able to develop a united policy on redressing the expropriation of First Nations territories or Eurocentric attacks against First Nations social institutions. While unions have been successful in addressing some aspects of First Nations experiences as workers, they seemed incapable of effectively confronting and overcoming the racism and segregation of twentieth-century industrial society.

ASSIMILATION AND GOVERNMENT POLICIES

Colonialism is not simply an economic process. It also involves social policy and regulation. In Canada, the underlying premise of most twentieth-century social policies directed at Aboriginal people has been assimilation, and the central instrument of assimilationist policy was the residential school. "By taking children away from the old ways and 'civilizing' them into European ways, so the argument ran, 'the Indian problem' would be solved" (Barman 1996:273). However, residential schools did not fulfill their stated goals. Instead, they "served as vehicles for marginalizing generations of young men and women from the Canadian mainstream

and from home environments" (Barman 1996:273).

In the early 1900s, attempts were also made to assimilate mobile Aboriginal people by settling them into agricultural communities. From the government point of view, forcing nomadic First Nations people into settlements would allow other instruments of assimilation, such as local government, church, and school, to be more easily brought into effect. Settlement also freed up large tracts of land that could then be developed by non-Aboriginal people.

SUCCESS STORIES

The story of First Nations is not all social pathology and economic disadvantage. First Nations people have maintained a strong sense of their social identity and their place within their traditional territories. On the northwest coast of Canada, for example, First Nations cultural institutions have been maintained despite concerted attacks from missionaries, government offices, and economic interests to dislodge them. The Nisga'a, Tsimshian, Gitksan, and Haida in north-coastal British Columbia have persisted in asserting their Aboriginal rights and title from the moment Europeans first arrived to occupy their land.

Examples of political organization are not restricted to British Columbia. The James Bay Cree, for example, won an important battle against the government of Quebec, which guaranteed them their homeland. The Native Women's Association of Canada fought for a redress of sexual discrimination under the Indian Act and played an important role in the passage of Bill C-31, which reinstated status to First Nations women (and their children) who had married non-Aboriginals (Frideres 1998).

The Calder case, named after Frank Calder (an important Nisga'a leader and former member of the B.C. legislature for the New Democratic Party), began the legal process in British Columbia that led the way to the important 1995 Agreement in Principle between the Nisga'a, Canada, and British Columbia. Throughout the 1980s, the Gitksan and Wet'suwet'en people waged a strategic struggle for the recognition of their Aboriginal rights, a struggle that included tactical blockades, legal actions, and economic restraints. Taken together, the concerted political action of First Nations people has forced Canada and non-Aboriginal Canadians to take notice (as witnessed, for example, by the apology to First Peoples in January 1998 by the federal government of Canada).

STRATEGIES FOR THE FUTURE

In *What Is the Indian Problem?*, Noel Dyck (1991:162) cogently argues that "the only way to rectify the ravages that Indian bands have suffered is to stop looking for 'experts' and 'masterplans' and to refuse to accept the presumption that Indians do not know what is in their best interests." Mainstream Canadian society has to accept its collective responsibility for the legacy of colonialism. An important first step is to accelerate the process of treaty negotiations and finally to dismantle the colonial apparatus of the Canadian state.

Self-determination is not a panacea for all of the past wrongs. It is, however, an important place to start. But, for self-determination to have any meaningful remedial effect on the experience of First Nations' social inequality, it must be built upon a solid economic and resource base. The 1997 Supreme Court of Canada ruling on the Delgamuukw case lays the basis for a fundamental change in Canadian law that could vastly improve the economic situation of First Nations. The court found that Aboriginal people have a right to fair compensation for lands expropriated by the Canadian state, that they have a right to use their traditional lands as they see fit, and that their oral traditions should be accorded the same evidentiary weight as written sources in cases concerning Aboriginal rights and title. This decision may well usher in a new era of economic and political co-operation between First Nations and the non-Aboriginal peoples of Canada. At the very least, it can be read as the beginning of a process of national reconciliation in which mainstream Canada finally accepts its complicity in the process of colonialism.

NOTES

1. In 1997, the Supreme Court of Canada decided that Aboriginal rights have not been extinguished and that McEachern's decision was flawed because he did not accept the Gitksan and Wet'suwet'en adaawk (oral history).

2. See, for example, Menzies 1994, 1997.

3. The physical location of this fishing community is not specifically relevant to the main issue of this chapter. Nor does this one man's storytelling necessarily reflect widespread opinion within the larger community.

4. The kin-ordered mode of production is one in which access to and control of labour power is mediated by relations of kinship. For an elaboration of this concept see Wolf (1997 [1982]:88–96).

REFERENCES

Barman, Jean 1996. "Aboriginal education at the crossroads: The legacy of residential schools and the way ahead." In David Alan Long and Olive Patricia Dickason (eds.), *Visions of the Heart: Canadian Aboriginal Issues*, pp. 271–303. Toronto: Harcourt Brace and Company.

Campbell, Kenneth, Charles R. Menzies, and Brent Peacock 2003. *B.C. First Nations Studies*. Victoria, BC: B.C. Ministry of Education.

Codere, Helen 1961. *Fighting with Property: A Study of Kwakuitl Potlatching and Warfare 1729–1930*. American Ethnological Society Monograph No. 18. New York: J.J. Augustin.

Cole, Douglas, and Ira Chaikin 1990. *An Iron Hand upon the People*. Vancouver: Douglas & McIntyre.

Correctional Services Canada 2001. Aboriginal Offender Statistics. Retrieved September 3, 2002 (http://www.csc-scc.gc.ca/text/prgrm/correctional/abissues/know/4_e.shtml).

Dyck, Noel 1991. *What Is the Indian Problem? Tutelage and Resistance in Canadian Indian Administration*. St. John's, NL: ISER, Memorial University of Newfoundland.

Fisher, Robin 1977. *Contact and Conflict: Indian-European Relations in British Columbia, 1774–1890*. Vancouver: University of British Columbia Press.

Frideres, James S. 1998. *Aboriginal Peoples in Canada: Contemporary Conflicts* (5th ed.). Scarborough, ON: Prentice Hall Allyn and Bacon Canada.

Grabb, Edward G. 2008. "Social inequality." In W.E. Hewitt, J. White, and J. Teevan (eds.), *Introduction to Sociology: A Canadian Focus*, pp. 119–149. Toronto: Pearson Education Canada.

Haig-Brown, Celia 1988. *Resistance and Renewal: First Nations People's Experiences of the Residential School*. Vancouver: University of British Columbia Press.

Indian and Northern Affairs 2000. *Comparison of Social Conditions, 1991 and 1996*. Catalogue no. R32-163/2000. Retrieved September 3, 2001 (http://www.ainc-inac. gc.ca/pr/sts/hac/socl_e.pdf).

Indian and Northern Affairs Canada 2002. Basic Departmental Data 2001. Catalogue no. R12-712001E. Retrieved September 3, 2001 (http://www.ainc-inac.gc.ca/pr/sts/bdd01/bdd01_e.pdf).

Knight, Rolf 1996. *Indians at Work* (2nd ed.). Vancouver: New Star Books.

Maxim, Paul S., Jerry P. White, Dan Beavon, and Paul C. Whitehead 2001. "Dispersion and polarization of income among Aboriginal and non-Aboriginal Canadians." *Canadian Review of Sociology and Anthropology* 38, 4:465–476.

McCaskill, D. 1983. "The urbanization of Indians in Winnipeg, Toronto, Edmonton, and Vancouver: A comparative analysis." *Culture* 1:82–89.

McDonald, James A. 1994. "Social change and the creation of underdevelopment: A northwest coast case." *American Ethnologist* 21, 1: 152–175.

McEachern, Justice Allen 1991. *Delgamuukw: Reasons for Judgment*. B.C. Supreme Court.

Menzies, Charles R. 1994. "Stories from home: First Nations, land claims, and Euro-Canadians." *American Ethnologist* 21, 4: 776–791.

Menzies, Charles R. 1997. "Indian or White? Racial identities in the British Columbian fishing industry." In Anthony Marcus (ed.), *Anthropology for a Small Planet: Culture and Community in a Global Environment*, pp. 110–123. St. James, NY: Brandywine Press.

Monture-Angus, Patricia 1995. *Thunder in My Soul: A Mohawk Woman Speaks*. Halifax: Fernwood Publishing.

Monture-Angus, Patricia 1996. "Lessons in decolonization: Aboriginal overrepresentation in Canadian criminal justice." In David Alan Long and Olive Patricia Dickason (eds.), *Visions of the Heart: Canadian Aboriginal Issues*, pp. 335–354. Toronto: Harcourt Brace and Company.

Newell, Diane 1993. *Tangled Webs of History: Indians and the Law in Canada's Pacific Coast Fisheries*. Toronto: University of Toronto Press.

Ponting, J. Rick, and Jerilynn Kiely 1997. "Disempowerment: 'Justice,' racism, and public opinion." In J. Rick Ponting (ed.), *First Nations in Canada: Perspectives on Opportunity, Empowerment, and Self-Determination,* pp. 152–192. Toronto: McGraw-Hill Ryerson.

Statistics Canada 1995. *Profile of Canada's Aboriginal Populations.* Ottawa: Statistics Canada.

Tennant, Paul 1990. *Aboriginal Peoples and Politics: The Indian Land Question in British Columbia, 1849–1989.* Vancouver: University of British Columbia Press.

Wolf, Eric R. 1997 [1982]. *Europe and the People without History* (2nd ed.). Berkeley, CA: University of California Press.

chapter twenty

Age-based Inequalities
in Canadian Society

Neil Guppy and Robin Hawkshaw
(An original chapter written
for this volume.)

INTRODUCTION

Age defines many of our rights and privileges. For instance, obtaining a driver's licence before the age of 16 is impossible, and many large car rental firms will not lease vehicles to anyone under 25. As another example, children cannot begin formal public schooling before the age of 5, but once enrolled in school, attendance is mandatory until 16. Age also shapes certain aspects of our working lives. Provincial wage laws often contain clauses allowing employers to pay lower minimum wages to workers under 18 than to adults. A Canadian Human Rights Tribunal recently agreed that it was permissible for Air Canada to require pilots to retire at age 60 (see CHRT, 2007), even though some

wanted to continue working. Both minimum wage laws and mandatory retirement provisions may seem unfair because one or two years of age makes little difference to how effectively most people can perform at work. However, just as with the right to drive or go to school, age may be used as an automatic trigger affecting both wages and retirement.

In these examples, age is used as an inflexible criterion for making decisions about what we can or cannot do. This process, often called "age-grading," can seem very unfair. Determining access to rights and privileges based solely on age, despite individual merit or ability, runs strongly against the premise of equal opportunity and merit-based decision making. Using chronological age to fix a date in our lives at which point we can (or cannot) be counted on to act reliably or responsibly makes a huge assumption. This presumption applies to a host of formal rights, ranging from voting or running for public office, through to serving in the armed forces or drinking alcoholic beverages.

Sometimes age can be a barrier to rights and privileges, not because of laws but through social convention. In the workplace, for example, mere seniority often takes precedence over performance or merit in determining pay (e.g., in teaching), layoffs (e.g., last hired, first fired), or promotions (e.g., where loyalty is often reward). Less formally, such activities as leaving home, having children, or investing in retirement savings plans may be constrained by age. This constraint occurs because people come to believe that these and other behaviours typically *should* take place at certain stages in the life course, but not at others.

Whether resulting from legal regulations or social norms, such age-based delineations of human behaviour are primarily social creations. In other words, while aging can be partly understood as a physiological process, it is also a social process. Age, in this latter sense, is used as a socially constructed criterion for classifying and ranking people (age-grading), a process with significant implications for generating and sustaining patterns of inequality.

AGE, PUBLIC POLICY, AND HUMAN RIGHTS

The Canadian Charter of Rights and Freedoms was designed to ensure that all Canadians enjoy equal access to fundamental opportunities and rewards. Equal rights for people of all ages is a key Charter principle:

> Every individual is equal before and under the law and has the right to the

> equal protection and equal benefit of the law without discrimination and, in particular, without discrimination based on race, national or ethnic origin, colour, religion, sex, age or mental or physical disability." (Section 15.1)

The wording of Section 15.1 suggests that using age to decide the rights and privileges of individual Canadians is discriminatory. How, then, can age be used as an automatic trigger effectively barring someone from obtaining a driver's licence at the age of 14 or voting in provincial elections at 15? Similarly, if someone is not hired for a job simply because she/he is too young or too old, this would clearly seem to contravene the Charter, as would forcing an airline pilot to retire at age 60. However, this latter policy of forced retirement is still applied because it is believed that under certain conditions age restrictions are justifiable.

Typically, when age-grading determines rights and privileges, the argument is that these practices place *reasonable limits* on people's activity. In obtaining a driver's licence or renting a car, for example, age-grading is justified as a reasonable criterion to invoke by citing the higher accident rates of younger drivers. Age restrictions on buying alcohol are similarly justified. Alcohol consumption impairs judgment, and so restricting access to alcohol for young people is viewed as reasonable.

Unequal access is thought to be justified in these circumstances because the infringement of individual rights and privileges is beneficial for the whole of society. In special circumstances, the rights of the individual are given lower priority than the rights of the community, and this too is reflected in the Canadian Charter, which

> guarantees "the rights and freedoms set out [herein] subject only to such *reasonable limits* prescribed by law as can

be *demonstrably justified* in a free and democratic society." (Section 1, emphasis added)

In a previous edition of this volume, we noted that with the aging of the Canadian population there would be challenges to age-related legislation such as mandatory retirement. In fact, mandatory retirement is now completely illegal in Quebec, Ontario, and Manitoba. It is no longer allowed in Prince Edward Island, New Brunswick, Alberta, Yukon, Nunavut, and the Northwest Territories unless it is a requirement of a pension plan. Nova Scotia, Newfoundland, Saskatchewan, and British Columbia have all passed legislation that will eliminate mandatory retirement before this volume is published. The Government of Canada doesn't practise mandatory retirement but does allow it in federally regulated industries such as transportation, communications, and banking. Mandatory retirement is allowed, under the Canadian Human Rights Act, in special circumstances. Mandatory retirement is still allowable if it has been determined that a normal age of retirement, for a particular occupation, has been established by law, usual practice, or bona fide requirements (BFR) for the performance of duties (for more information, see Human Resources and Social Development Canada 2007).

Reflecting again on Section 15.1 of the Charter, notice that of all the categories listed (e.g., sex, race), age is fundamentally different. Age is the only universal attribute. Aging happens to everyone and, therefore, any age restrictions eventually apply to us all. Unless succumbing to a premature death, all Canadians experience every age category, whereas in our lifetime normally we occupy only one category of sex, race, and so on.

Despite this difference between age and the other attributes listed in Section 15.1, age is, like most of the others, an *ascribed* characteristic. Ascribed characteristics are determined at birth, rather than being chosen or achieved (as is religion or education, for example). Our age is something we cannot change. To the extent that other people use ascribed attributes to make judgments about us, our opportunities and rewards may be diminished (e.g., we are too old or too young to be doing something) or enhanced (e.g., our age is taken to signal maturity or good judgment).

AGE AND DEPENDENCY

Age-grading is also related to dependency (Turner 1988). The judgments others hold of us, or the entitlements others grant us, depend on whether we are believed to be responsible citizens, capable of making rational decisions about the welfare of ourselves and others. Ariès (1962 [1960]) has argued that childhood, as a recognizable feature of the life course, only began to emerge in European societies through the late 1600s. Children came to be seen as a group with special needs, especially susceptible to poverty, vagrancy, and social and moral corruption. Various child protection laws were thus enacted at this time to safeguard children.

Debate continues over children's rights. In the Canadian justice system, for example, policy-makers have attempted to grant special rights to young offenders (aged 12 to 17), while also requiring young persons to be accountable for their actions (see Department of Justice [2002] for a discussion of the new Youth Criminal Justice Act).

The elderly, as a group, are also frequently defined as dependent. Partially, this is a consequence of degenerative diseases, such as Alzheimer's, that erode an individual's ability to function independently (see Gilmour and Park 2006). However, the social arrangements of work and family are also consequential for relations of dependency or independence. As discussed below, retirement and pension arrangements may make it difficult for many Canadians, especially women, to support themselves economically in their later years. Many elderly people also find that their traditional support systems (e.g., children, other relatives) no longer live in close enough proximity to provide substantial care.

DIMENSIONS OF ECONOMIC INEQUALITY OVER THE LIFE COURSE

Dependency is common at both ends of the age spectrum. As we mature, we gradually acquire more and more individual autonomy until, in our later years, dependency increases again. This ebb and flow in dependency is illustrated by examining how aging relates to various dimensions of inequality.

Figure 20-1 shows the average individual incomes, from all sources, that women and men receive at different periods in their lives. Average incomes increase for men to a peak at the age of 45, and decline throughout later life. Women's average incomes are always lower, rising only moderately to a plateau from ages 35 to 54 and declining moderately through their senior years. The contrasting nature of the two curves for women and men reflects the greater continuity of occupational careers for men and the greater variability of women's attachment to the labour force (Jones et al. 1990).

While the wages of young workers are still lower than those of older workers, the situation has improved in the last decade. Youth employment from 1997 to 2004 grew faster for young workers than it did

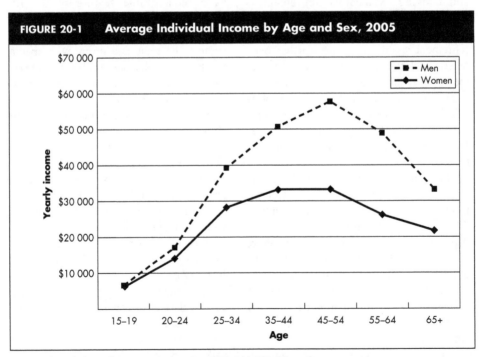

FIGURE 20-1   Average Individual Income by Age and Sex, 2005

Source: Author calculations from CANSIM Series V25655870, Table 202-407.

for workers over 25, and wages increased as well. Wages increased for teens largely because they worked more hours, but the 19 to 24 age group actually saw an increase in hourly earnings of 4.6% over those years (Usalcas 2005). Teens typically work part-time in minimum-wage retail and food service jobs. As these workers become older and gain experience and education, they often move on to full-time jobs and better wages.

Annual income is a good indicator of cash flow, but it says little about an individual's net worth or asset holdings. Home ownership is a good measure of the latter since this is a principal source of wealth for most Canadians (Statistics Canada 2005a). Between the ages of 45 and 55, approximately 75% of women and men live in a home they own (typically a family home, if married).

Living arrangements, especially as related to the family home, also shed light on dependency, which can be understood through the lens of home leaving. Recent changes have been fairly dramatic. The 2001 Census shows that 41% of Canadian young adults aged 20 to 29 live with their parents, a jump of 14% in 20 years (from 27% in 1981; Statistics Canada 2002). The 2001 Census also shows that 28% of young women and 33% of young men aged 20 to 29 have returned to their parents' home once after an initial departure (Statistics Canada 2002). Employment trends, educational aspirations, socio-economic status, ethnicity, and gender all influence the age at which a young person will leave home permanently (see Mitchell 2006). For instance, young women leave home slightly earlier than do young men because they tend to marry or cohabit at a younger age (Beaupré et al. 2006).

For men and women, the likelihood of living in a family-owned home peaks between the ages of 65 to 74. In 2001, 35%

of women and 61% of men aged 65 and over lived with a spouse or a partner (Statistics Canada 2003). This is a significant difference between the sexes. For unattached seniors, the likelihood of living in their own home declines to 53% for women and 56% for men (Statistics Canada 2005a). Women tend to live longer than men and men often marry younger women. As a result, women are much more likely than men to live their final years in relative isolation from family members, a pattern likely to intensify even more in the future. This means that "when men get older and frailer, most of them have built-in housekeepers and nurses—their wives. Women are not so fortunate" (National Council of Welfare 1990).

As noted in the chapter on poverty, however, one area in which government social programs have been especially effective is with respect to low income among the elderly. Many elderly people are still poor. In fact, in 2005, 242 000 Canadians over age 65 lived in poverty (using the Low Income Cut-Off after-tax figures). Nevertheless, that was fewer people than in 1996 (see Table 20-1). Indeed, whereas 21.3% of all seniors lived in poverty in 1980, that percentage dropped to 9.8% in 1996 and 6.1% in 2005.

Elderly women are still at much greater risk than elderly men, but retirement income for women has been changing recently. Women now spend more time in the workforce and consequently they have higher levels and more varied sources of pension income (see Division of Aging and Seniors 2002). Even with these improvements, though, in 2005 unattached elderly women (20.3%) are still twice as likely to be living with low income as unattached elderly males (13.4%; see Table 20-1). Because women live longer than men on average, older age groups contain many unattached women, and unattached people

TABLE 20-1 Canadians with Low Income (1992 LICO After-Tax Base)						
	1980		**1996**		**2005**	
	Number	**%**	**Number**	**%**	**Number**	**%**
Seniors (over age 65)	462 000	21.3	330 000	9.8	242 000	6.1
Senior couples	88 000	6	65 000	2.8	34 000	1.2
Senior unattached females	283 000	53.5	213 000	27.3	167 000	20.3
Senior unattached males	88 000	47	52 000	19.8	41 000	13.4
Children (under 18)	818 000	12	1 304 000	18.6	788 000	11.7

Source: Author calculations from CANSIM TABLE 2020802.

having only one income have higher poverty rates than couples. Not only do many elderly women live alone or in an institution, but they also do so in poverty.

For elderly unattached men, the picture is still bleak, although proportionately not quite as desperate. About 13.4% of these men live below the poverty line. Note, too, that as fewer seniors over time were living in poverty, children became the largest group numerically among the poor. In 2005, 11.7% or 788 000 children were poor, while the poverty rate for seniors fell to 6.1% or 242 000.

INCOME AND THE OLD AGE SECURITY SYSTEM

Why has the poverty rate declined for seniors? After accounting for the effect of inflation, the average income of senior couples has risen substantially (18%) from 1980 to 2003 (Statistics Canada 2006a). As noted by Baker and Gunderson (2006), their average real income (2003 dollars) rose from approximately $20 000 in 1980 to $25 146 in 2003, an increase of about 20%. A variety of government programs for seniors have been of major benefit.

The basic retirement income system for elderly Canadians works as follows (see also Human Resources and Social Development Canada 2005; Oderkirk 1996). Virtually all Canadians age 65 and over

receive taxable Old Age Security (OAS) payments (the maximum annual benefit was $5973.96 per person in 2007). As well, 35% of elderly Canadians receive the Guaranteed Income Supplement (GIS), an income-tested[1] benefit designed to help the elderly poor (in July 2007, the maximum monthly benefit for a single pensioner was $628.36). As well, most provinces provide additional income supplements and special tax breaks for the elderly. However, despite these support programs, the monies provided are not enough to keep many elderly Canadians out of poverty (see Table 20-1).

In addition to these age-related pension packages, there are two important employment-related components of the elderly income security system. One employment-related component is the Canada Pension Plan/Quebec Pension Plan (CPP/QPP), while the other is the private occupational pension plans to which some Canadians subscribe. Since 1966, all Canadians who have been members of the paid labour force, either as employees or self-employed, have been required by law to contribute to the CPP/QPP. Upon retirement, a pension equal to 25% of a person's average "pensionable earnings" is paid,[2] to a maximum ceiling of about $10 365 annually (Human Resources and Social Development Canada 2007). (By 2003, 85% of women aged 65 to 69 were receiving CPP/QPP benefits, up from 34.8% in 1980. Additionally, 53%

had some income from a private pension. Still, the percentage of women receiving pensions was lower than that of men. Ninety-five percent of men were receiving CPP/QPP income, and 69.8% had private pensions [Statistics Canada 2006b]).

CPP/QPP pension income is low for everyone. It is, however, especially low for people who only held labour force jobs intermittently (many women) and for people who earned low incomes even when they did work (again, many women, as well as many members of Canada's First Nations and the disabled population). And, of course, CPP/QPP income is zero for those who never held a labour force job.

Private occupation-based pension plans are also available and increasing numbers of Canadians, especially those in secure management jobs or union members, benefit from these funds. As of January 1, 2006, about 40% of paid workers were enrolled in one of these plans. In 2000, 55.1% of those covered were men and 44.9% were women, but by 2006 the numbers had begun to even out with men at 52.3% and women at 47.7%. Table 20-2 shows a comprehensive breakdown of not only the percentage of people receiving income from private pensions but also the dollar amounts. The decline in pension recipients apparent in the early 1990s has reversed. In 2003, 53.0% of women and 69.8% of men received some income from

employer pension plans and other retirement savings plans.

Although many elderly Canadians continue to live in poverty, there has been recent improvement in the overall picture. As we have shown, this improvement is due in large part to a strengthening of the income security system in the past two decades. Pensions now cover more Canadians (see Figure 20-2) and, since 1971, age-related pension increments have generally kept pace with or bettered inflation. The significance of this trend is that transfer payments still represent a crucial, albeit declining, portion of the total income the elderly receive. In fact, in 2003, 55% of the income for elderly women and 41.1% of the income for elderly men came in the form of government transfer payments (Statistics Canada 2006b).[3]

However, as the proportion of Canadians over the age of 65 continues to grow, there is now concern that the income security system for the elderly probably cannot withstand this growth. The head of Statistics Canada has asked, "Can we afford an aging society?" (Fellegi 1988) and has answered affirmatively. CPP reforms in 1997 included increases in contribution rates and a more aggressive policy with respect to the investment of surplus funds. According to the CPP Investment Board, "the CPP fund is sustainable at current contribution rates for at least the next 75 years" (Canada Pension

TABLE 20-2	Seniors' Income from Private Pension and Other Private Sources			
	Men		Women	
	1980	2003	1980	2003
Percentage	39.8	69.8	19.7	53.0
Average Amount	$10 700	$17 900	$6900	$10 200

Source: Adapted from the Statistics Canada publication *Women in Canada*, various years.

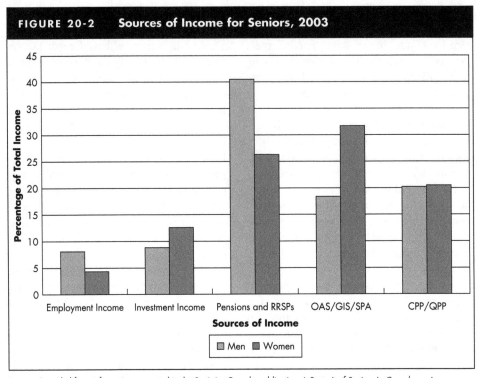

FIGURE 20-2   **Sources of Income for Seniors, 2003**

Source: Compiled from information presented in the Statistics Canada publication *A Portrait of Seniors in Canada*, various years.

Plan Investment Board 2006). Nevertheless, opinions are divided, especially because some projections show that, among industrialized countries, Canada will have one of the highest dependency ratios by 2030 (Chawla 1991; Gee and Gutman 2000). Statistics Canada has several hypothetical projections for differing levels of population growth (low, moderate, and high) but in all scenarios "the demographic dependency ratio—the number of children (aged 0 to 14 years) and seniors (65 years and over) per 100 working-age people (15 to 64 years)—would increase rapidly until 2031. It would be about 61 in 2031, compared with 44 in 2005" (Statistics Canada 2005b).

If these projections about the size of the dependent population in Canada are correct, severe pressure could be brought to bear on social benefits. Some have argued that "Canadians will most likely have to choose between increasing tax rates and social security contributions or lower levels of social benefits" (Burke 1991:8). However, this too is contested hotly. Myles (1989) argues that the root of the crisis in Old Age Security lies not in the numbers of elderly (what he calls the "demographic imperative"), but in the political alignments between capital and labour in the welfare state. Public pensions, health care, and income tax are the largest programs sensitive to population aging. For future long-term planning, policies need to be based on a set of rules or principles on which individuals can rely permanently, further arguing the importance of political agendas (Wolfson and Rowe 2006).

AGE-BASED CONFLICT
AND STRAIN

Age is correlated with the *distribution* of inequality and especially income derived from social programs. Seniors are vulnerable to moving into poverty because of this dependence on government transfers and the fact that many are very close to the poverty line. In addition, though, the privileges and rewards of different age groups are also *relational* in nature. Age-group relations entail issues of intergenerational equity or justice (McDaniel 2001). Tension between generations occurs when the rights and privileges favouring one age group impinge or are perceived to impinge on the opportunities or fortunes of another age group. However, as the Law Commission of Canada (2004) argues "one of the myths that characterizes discussion about the dependency ratio is that youth and older adults are a drain on society's resources and are not contributors." Older generations make contributions to the social fabric of any society through actions such as child care, mentoring, volunteering, and financial assistance. Many young people also contribute by volunteering and the provision of physical and social support.

Generational disputes can have lasting consequences. The 1960s is one historic period when intergenerational conflict led to significant social change, from policies on the Vietnam War to procedures for student involvement on many college and university committees. More recently, with the growth in the number of elderly Canadians, concern has been focused on another intergenerational trade-off. Can we continue to provide adequate funding for childhood education in the face of escalating medical costs for the care of the elderly (Foot 1996; Wolfson and Rowe 2006)?

Population aging also induces strain within institutions. For example, institutional strain due to aging occurs in health care. The medical system is oriented more toward treating acute illness (e.g., kidney transplants) than coping with chronic ailments. However, medical patients increasingly are elderly Canadians who are much more likely to suffer from chronic ailments (e.g., arthritis) that the system is least able to handle (Rosenberg and Moore 1997). Social strain due to age composition also occurs in the workplace when organizations must reduce their size. Tindale (1987) has documented the age-based conflicts among younger and older teachers in Ontario that resulted from the government's decision to reduce the number of teachers in the school system. Seniority, not ability, was used as the criterion to dismiss individuals, and this led to intense struggles across age groups as teachers fought to save their jobs.

However, the extent of age-based conflict must not be exaggerated. Conflict between generations has never been as prominent as have tensions between religious or ethnic groups, for example (see Davis and van den Oever 1981). While there is no denying the existence of intergenerational conflicts within families, allegiances to kin temper these disputes, thereby dampening antagonism, as do rules of inheritance and support.[4] Also, the universal nature of age mentioned earlier means that one cannot maintain a lifelong identification with a specific age group. Being a member of an "adolescent gang" all of one's life is impossible. Furthermore, even though teenage "rebellion" occurs, such rebellion only rarely leads to a long-term disintegration of family solidarity. Age-based conflict of a relational nature is thus not as significant a force in Canadian society as are other conflicts based on different ascriptive factors.

CONCLUSION

Age-grading practices affect our access to rights and opportunities. Age is often an automatic trigger overriding merit or ability in determining the citizenship rights a person can, or cannot, enjoy. Several dimensions of inequality, especially income, home ownership, and living arrangements, vary significantly across the age spectrum. The distribution of inequality, we have argued, is related to dependency. This dependency is illustrated most graphically by the number of young and old Canadians who live in, or on the edge of, poverty (see Table 20-1).

Although the income security system in Canada has improved the economic circumstances of elderly Canadians, substantial numbers of people over the age of 65 still live in poverty. The risk of living in poverty is especially acute when age intersects with other risk factors for inequality. Thus, women, the disabled, and immigrant and/or Aboriginal elderly are more likely to live in poverty. Exacerbating the economic misfortunes of many women is the likelihood that they will live alone or in an institution during their final years of life. Even when living in poverty, older men are much more likely to have at least the comfort of a spouse to share the burden of later life.

The ability of taxpayers to support the swelling ranks of the aged has also been noted. Especially if immigration levels are kept low, the proportion of Canadians over the age of 65 will rise substantially in the next few decades. This trend will in turn add pressure to Canada's social welfare system. The ability of the welfare state to manage this pressure will depend, in part, on accommodations reached between labour and business (Myles 1989; Wolfson and Rowe 2006).

We have also briefly noted other issues of intergenerational tension and have reviewed how changes in the age composition of the population can cause strains for the social system. Issues of dependency and interdependency affect us at both ends of the age spectrum.

NOTES

1. Whether or not a person receives GIS income depends on the total amount of income an individual receives. As total income rises, GIS income declines. The GIS was instituted to help the elderly poor. It is significant that 35% of all seniors receive the GIS, and that there is a serious problem of undersubscription (National Advisory Council on Aging 2006)

2. Numerous technical details influence exact CPP/QPP payments (see Human Resources and Social Development Canada 2005 for a useful primer). CPP/QPP income is indexed to average lifetime earnings, which means that low-wage earners in the labour force also will be low-pension recipients in retirement.

3. Government transfer payments include all social welfare payments from federal, provincial, and municipal governments, including Child Tax Benefits, Old Age Security and Guaranteed Income Supplements, Spouse's Allowances, Canada and Quebec Pension Plan benefits, Employment Insurance, worker's compensation, training allowances, veterans' pensions, social assistance, and pensions to the blind and persons with disabilities. Refundable tax credits and Goods and Services Tax credits are included as income.

4. Families can be violent, but frequently such violence is not age-related.

REFERENCES

Ariès, P. 1962 [1960]. *Centuries of Childhood: A Social History of Family Life.* R. Baldick, trans. New York: Alfred A. Knopf.

Baker, M., and M. Gunderson (2006). *Seniors' Income Adequacy.* Paper prepared for the Expert Roundtable on Seniors. Ottawa: Human Resources and Social Development Canada.

Beaupré, Pascale, Pierre Turcotte, and Anne Milan 2006. "When is junior moving out? Transitions from the parental home to independence" Retrieved July 5, 2007 (http://www.statcan.ca/english/freepub/11-008-XIE/2006002/main_junior.htm).

Burke, Mary Anne 1991. "Implications of an aging society." *Canadian Social Trends* (Spring):6–8.

Canada Pension Plan Investment Board 2006. News release, June 12. Retrieved August 25, 2007 (http://cppib.ca/News_Room/News_Releases/nr_06120601.html).

Canadian Human Rights Tribunal 2007 (August). *Vilven v. Air Canada*. Retrieved August 20, 2007 (http://www.chrt-tcdp.gc.ca/search/view_html.asp?doid=862&lg=_e&isruling=0).

Chawla, Raj 1991. "Dependency ratios." *Canadian Social Trends* (Spring):3–5.

Davis, Kingsley, and P. van den Oever 1981. "Age relations and public policy in advanced industrial societies." *Population and Development Review* 7, 1:1–18.

Department of Justice 2002. "New youth justice law receives royal assent." News release, February 19. Retrieved May 7, 2002 (http://www.canada.justice.gc.ca/en/news/nr/2002/doc_29883.html).

Division of Aging and Seniors 2002. "Canada's aging population." Retrieved August 22, 2007 (http://www.phac-aspc.gc.ca/seniors-aines/pubs/fed_paper/fedreport3_02_e.htm).

Fellegi, Ivan 1988. "Can we afford an aging society?" *Canadian Economic Observer* (October):4.1–4.34.

Foot, David 1996. *Boom, Bust, and Echo.* Toronto: Macfarlane, Walter, and Ross.

Gee, Ellen M., and Gloria M. Gutman (eds.) 2000. *The Overselling of Population Aging: Apocalyptic Demography, Intergenerational Challenges, and Social Policy.* Toronto: Oxford University Press.

Gilmour, Heather, and Jungwee Park 2006. "Dependency, chronic conditions and pain in seniors" Retrieved August 15, 2007 (http://www.statcan.ca/english/freepub/82-003-SIE/2005000/pdf/82-003-SIE20050007443.pdf).

Human Resources and Social Development Canada 2005. "Canadian retirement income system." Retrieved August 21, 2007 (http://www.hrsdc.gc.ca/en/lp/spila/wlb/aw/29retirement_system.shtml).

Human Resources and Social Development Canada 2007. "Mandatory retirement in Canada: Legislation of General Application." Retrieved August 20, 2007 (http://www.hrsdc.gc.ca/cgi-bin/hrsdc-rhdsc/print/print.asp?Page_Url=/en/lp/spila/clli/eslc/19Mandatory_Retirement.shtml).

Jones, Charles, Lorna Marsden, and Lorne Tepperman 1990. *Lives of Their Own: The Individualization of Women's Lives.* Toronto: Oxford University Press.

Law Commission of Canada 2004. "Does age matter? Law and relationships between generations." Retrieved August 30, 2007 (http://dsp-psd.pwgsc.gc.ca/Collection/JL2-23-2003E.pdf).

McDaniel, Susan 2001. "Born at the right time? Gendered generations and webs of entitlement and responsibility." *Canadian Journal of Sociology* 26, 2:193–214.

Mitchell, Barbara 2006. "The boomerang age from childhood to adulthood: Emergent trends and issues for aging families." Retrieved August 23, 2007 (http://www.canpopsoc.org/journal/CSPv33n2p155.pdf).

Myles, John 1989. *Old Age in the Welfare State: The Political Economy of Public Pensions.* Lawrence, KS: University Press of Kansas.

National Advisory Council on Aging 2006. "Seniors in Canada 2006 report card." Retrieved September 13, 2007 (http://dsp-psd.pwgsc.gc.ca/Collection/HP30-1-2006E.pdf).

National Council of Welfare 1990. *Women and Poverty Revisited.* Ottawa: Minister of Supply and Services.

Oderkirk, Jillian 1996. "Government sponsored income security programs for seniors: Old Age Security." *Canadian Social Trends* 40 (Spring):3–7.

Rosenberg, Mark, and Eric Moore 1997. "The health of Canada's elderly population: Current status and future implications." *Canadian Medical Association Journal* 57, 8: 1025–1033.

Statistics Canada 2002. *2001 Census: Profile of Canadian Families and Households: Diversification Continues.* Retrieved August 19, 2007 (http://www12.statcan.ca/english/census01/products/analytic/companion/fam/contents.cfm).

Statistics Canada 2003. *2001 General Social Survey Cycle 16: Caring for an Aging Society.* Retrieved August 19, 2007 (http://www.statcan.ca/english/freepub/89-582-XIE/89-582-XIE2003001.pdf).

Statistics Canada 2005a. "The wealth of Canadians: An overview of the results of the survey of financial security." Retrieved August 22, 2007 (http://www.statcan.ca/english/research/13F0026MIE/13F0026MIE2006001.pdf).

Statistics Canada 2005b. "Population projections for Canada, provinces and territories 2005–2031." Retrieved September 21, 2007 (http://www.statcan.ca/english/freepub/91-520-XIE/0010591-520-XIE.pdf).

Statistics Canada 2006a. "A portrait of seniors in Canada" Retrieved May 26, 2007 (http://www.statcan.ca/bsolc/english/bsolc?catno=89-519-X).

Statistics Canada 2006b. "Women in Canada (5th ed.): A gender-based statistical report." Retrieved September 17, 2007 (http://www.statcan.ca/english/freepub/89-503-XIE/0010589-503-XIE.pdf).

Tindale, Joseph 1987. "Age, seniority and class patterns of job strain." In V. Marshall (ed.), *Aging in Canada: Social Perspectives*, pp. 176–192. Toronto: Fitzhenry and Whiteside.

Turner, Bryan 1988. "Ageing, status politics and sociological theory." *British Journal of Sociology* 40, 4:588–606.

Usalcas, Jeannine 2005. "Youth and the labour market." *Perspectives on Labour and Income* 17, 4: 28–33.

Wolfson, Michael, and Geoff Rowe 2006. "Aging and intergenerational fairness: A Canadian analysis" Retrieved September 20, 2007 (http://www.iariw.org/papers/2006/wolfson.pdf).

chapter twenty-one

Postponed Adulthood: Dealing with the New Economic Inequality

John Myles
(This paper is part of the Canadian Council on Social Development's New Social Architecture Series. Reprinted with permission.)

The comments developed in this paper are the product of a joint collaboration with the Canadian Council on Social Development. I especially want to acknowledge the contributions of Andrew Jackson from the Canadian Labour Congress and Katherine Scott from the Canadian Council on Social Development.

INTRODUCTION

Two decades ago, political scientist Hugh Heclo (1988) pointed out that the great debate over intergenerational "class war" and equity in the U.S. had largely passed Europe by. The difference, he speculated, has to do with Europeans' greater inclination toward "life course" thinking when tackling issues about inequality: childhood and old age are simply *different moments in the lives of the same people*. Americans, he argued, are more inclined to consider the elderly and children as more or less static, distinct social groups that, in turn, divide into yet other groups based on race, disability status, and so forth. For Americans, thinking about childhood and old age as raising a distributional problem over a single life course seems distinctly foreign.

Whether Heclo captured the true mindset of Americans and Europeans correctly is not important. What matters is the way we approach the issue of redesigning Canada's social architecture—that is, from a life course perspective. But what exactly does that mean? To illustrate, consider an example well known to all of us.

Looking back to the 1950s and 1960s, most old people in most industrial democracies were poor. Moving ahead to the present day, comparatively few old people are poor. Why is that? Back then, of course, people didn't have the Canada Pension Plan (CPP), the Guaranteed Income Supplement (GIS), occupational pensions, or all of the other good stuff we have today. But that's only part of the answer.

The elderly cohorts of the 1950s were poor because they had poor lives. Born at the close of the nineteenth century, their youth was marred by the First World War and their working years straddled the Great Depression and the Second World War. They were poor not only because public retirement plans were ungenerous, and private plans underdeveloped, but also because they were "unlucky" generations.

By comparison, today's retirees are relatively affluent mainly because they had good lives. They are the children of high industrialism. Their early careers straddled the booming post-war decades. They generally enjoyed job security and rising real wages over most of their lives, and as a result, accumulated substantial savings and resources, not just CPP benefits. Compared to their parents, today's retirees, these children of high industrialism, had "good lives."

The objective of redesigning our social architecture is to ensure that today's children and the young adults now entering the labour market also have good lives—as children, as young adults, during middle age, and in their retirement years. So let's think about the potential life courses of today's post-industrial cohorts and their children. That's not so hard. The cohorts who will reach age 65 in the year 2040 are already with us. In fact, they will turn 30 in 2005. How will their lives differ from those of their industrial-age predecessors, today's retirees who entered the booming labour markets of the 1950s and 1960s when the foundations of the contemporary welfare state were put in place? What new risks do they face?

POST-INDUSTRIAL LABOUR MARKETS

A leading suspect in the new risk structure is the labour market. A standard assumption is that post-industrial economies have produced a new post-industrial, low-wage proletariat of fast-food and other service workers. It is true that Canada has the dubious distinction of having a lot of low-wage jobs. As shown in Table 21-1, almost a quarter of full-time workers in Canada earn less than two-thirds of median earnings, compared to 13% in Germany and only 5% in Sweden.

But this is not new. Despite all of the discussion of wage polarization, the low-wage character of the Canadian economy has always been with us (see Table 21-2). In short, the good old days of high industrialism

TABLE 21-1	Percentage of Full-Time Workers Earning Less Than 65% of Median Earnings, 1994		
Country	**All**	**Men**	**Women**
United States	25%	20%	33%
Canada	24%	16%	34%
Germany	13%	8%	25%
Sweden	5%	3%	8%

Source: OECD, *Employment Outlook*, 1996.

TABLE 21-2	Percentage of Full-Time Workers, Aged 25 to 54, Earning Less Than Two-Thirds of Total Median Income, Canada, 1971–2001		
	Total	**Male**	**Female**
1971	22%	14%	50%
1981	22%	14%	40%
1991	22%	15%	34%
2001	24%	18%	31%

Source: Census of Canada Master Files, 1971–2001.

were not all that good. Our low-wage economy is undoubtedly a major flaw in our social architecture, but this has always been so.

What has changed are the ways in which earnings are distributed over the life course and among households.

THE SECOND DEMOGRAPHIC TRANSITION AND POSTPONED ADULTHOOD

The most dramatic difference between today's young cohorts and their industrial-age predecessors is when, and how, they begin their adult lives.

For the cohorts of high industrialism—today's retirees—the transition to adulthood occurred early in their lives. Industrializing economies were relatively benign places for muscular young men and unmarried women, and from the turn of the last century through the 1960s, the main age markers of reaching social and economic maturity fell decade after decade. By the 1950s and 1960s, young adults were leaving home, getting married, and having their first child much sooner than any of the cohorts that had preceded them.

But all of that has changed. Since the 1960s, all of the age markers of social adulthood have been rising. As Rod Beaujot (2004) has documented, over 40% of young adults in their twenties are living

at home, up from 20% in 1970. Marriage and first childbirth now occur in the late twenties—just about the time people are beginning to establish themselves in real career jobs.

The reasons for these changes are not difficult to fathom. Post-industrial economies are knowledge-based economies. Rising demands for educational credentials mean that "real" work careers start much later in life. More importantly, the changing demands of the labour market now affect women as much as men. High female employment is a defining feature of our post-industrial world.

The consequences of starting adulthood later have been compounded by the most important shift in the wage distribution of the past quarter century—when they do enter the labour market, the relative earnings of young adults have been falling for over two decades. Postponed adulthood combined with declining entry-level wages mean that both the cumulative earnings and the accumulated wealth of adults in their mid-thirties have fallen dramatically since the end of the 1970s. By 1999, the median wealth of Canadian-born families (where the highest earner was aged 25 to 34) was down 26% from 1984 and among young foreign-born families, it was down 44% (Morissette et al. 2002).

Why does this matter? We've all seen the sitcom *Friends* and living like an adolescent at age 30 isn't so bad, or is it?

First, postponed adulthood and the declining earnings of young adults are the main reasons we have made such little progress in reducing child poverty. For while the social and economic life course has changed, biology hasn't. Because of biology, young adults (that is, those under age 35) still comprise the vast majority of parents of our young children, and no social policy can change that.

Given the incredible changes in the behaviour of today's young parents, the remarkable fact about child poverty is that it has not disappeared. Today's young parents are much better educated than parents of a generation ago and most mothers are employed. In the past, child poverty was associated with large families, but large families have disappeared into the mists of history.

Postponed adulthood is also important since it is the major driver of the low fertility equilibrium that is characteristic of almost all post-industrial societies. As such, it is a major cause of the huge social policy challenge that lies ahead—namely, population aging. Indeed, the revolution in life course patterns of young adults over the past 40 years—the "second demographic transition"—is as much a part of the phenomenon of "population aging" as is the much-vaunted arrival of the baby-boom generation.

The fact that current fertility levels in no way reflect the fertility preferences of our young adults has largely been ignored as a welfare issue. When asked about the number of children they would like to have, the most frequent response of young Canadians is two; the second most frequent response is three. It seems that young parents and would-be parents are simply not achieving their ideal family size.

Quite simply then, post-industrial economies—characterized by long periods of juvenile dependency that now extend into young adulthood and where both

women and men must build their careers—are not family-friendly places.

NEW LIFE COURSE INEQUALITIES

But let's move on and imagine how the lives of our post-industrial thirtysomethings will evolve as they move through their working years toward retirement in 2040. As with any major change, there is good news for some and bad news for others.

The first cohort divide in a world of dual-earner families is between single-adult households with comparatively little labour to sell and those with two or more adult earners. While the earnings of young adults have been falling overall, family earnings for many young families have been rising as a result of higher female employment. By contrast, single-earner households—with or without children—are at greater risk and their numbers have been rising. The percentage of single adult (aged 25 to 54) households in the population has doubled, from 10% in 1971 to 20% today. A recent U.S. study estimates that the share of never-married and divorced among the elderly poor will rise from 33% today to 48% by the time the baby-boomers retire (Butrica, Iams and Smith, 2003:46).

The second divide that will persist over the working lives of these current cohorts has two sources: the division between the educationally advantaged and disadvantaged, and the multiplier effect of marital homogamy in a world of high female labour force participation. Well-educated men and women tend to marry one another, forming families that have high earnings and few risks of unemployment. Less well-educated couples tend to have lower wages and they are far more likely to experience periods without work. Marital selection based on education has risen and it is unlikely to abate. In the 1950s, there were few highly educated women to marry. The doctor married his nurse or his secretary. Today he is more likely to be married to another doctor, a lawyer, or an advertising executive.

Morrisette and Johnson (2004) show that while the growth in the earnings gap among *individual* workers with more or less education has been modest in Canada, the corresponding gap in family earnings rose substantially. Between 1980 and 2000, couples with two university graduates saw their average annual earnings rise by 14%, to 22%, while couples where both had high school education or less had stagnant or declining earnings.

The cumulative effect of these trends over the last quarter-century is the long-term secular increase in earnings inequality among families (shown in Figure 21-1). This is a conservative estimate, as it excludes lone parents and unattached individuals. And we know from other sources that this trend has been accelerating, not abating, in recent years (Frenette, Green and Picot, 2004). Until the early 1990s, the tax-transfer was able to keep pace with these changes so that the final distribution of family incomes remained relatively stable. Since then, however, it has been losing the battle against rising inequality in family earnings.

The point is that today, our thirtysomethings are entering a world that is very different from the one their young cohorts of a quarter-century ago encountered. A new high-inequality equilibrium in the distribution of family earnings has emerged, and it appears to be a relatively permanent feature of our post-industrial world.

Finally, our post-industrial cohorts will face an additional constraint that neither today's retirees nor the baby-boomers encountered: the necessity of financing the consumption of an aging population when the baby-boomers begin to retire.

WHAT IS TO BE DONE?

Consider first the financing side. As Tom Kent has insisted, we need to be thinking about taxation, not just spending. If the new high-inequality equilibrium in family earnings is a relatively permanent feature of Canadian society, the case for progressively financed income transfers and services is stronger than it ever was for our industrial-age predecessors.

The case for progressive financing is even stronger when we consider the second

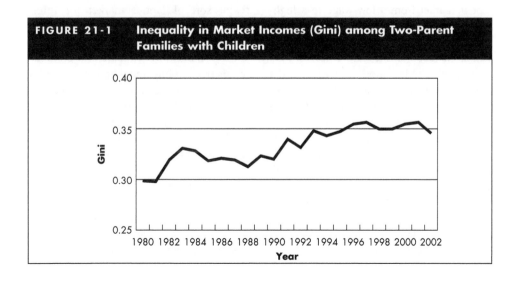

FIGURE 21-1   Inequality in Market Incomes (Gini) among Two-Parent Families with Children

great change in the post-industrial life course—the fact that we are living longer. But this post-industrial longevity bonus is unequally distributed. The highly educated and well-paid are experiencing the greatest longevity gains. As a result, they will absorb a disproportionate share of future pension and health care costs, just as they absorbed a disproportionate share of education costs when they were young.

What about spending? Our post-industrial cohorts, and especially those in the bottom third, face two problems simultaneously. The first is an income problem and the second is the servicing or caring problem that results from high levels of female employment.

To address the income problem, we need two sets of basic income guarantees.

The first set of guarantees would apply to persons who cannot reasonably be expected to participate in the paid work force, either temporarily or on a continuing basis, such as single-parent families with very young children, and persons with severe mental or physical disabilities.

For the employed, there are two strategies: one for the long-term and a second for the intermediate term.

The first best strategy for the longer term is one that aims to transform the Canadian labour market from a low-wage to a high-wage economy in ways that do not reduce total employment. Canada's large low-wage labour market indicates the presence of a large number of low-productivity jobs and a large number of firms habituated to a low-wage, low-productivity equilibrium. This could reflect the presence of a large pool of low-skilled workers, a large number of jobs that are undercapitalized, or some mix of the two. In either case, it is undesirable for both economic and social reasons.

If, as is often assumed, the problem lies on the supply side (i.e., inadequate skills), then new investments in human capital development that are targeted to the bottom third of the learning distribution—especially early in life—offer a solution. There is a strong case to be made for more and better early childhood education, but these investments will only begin to bear fruit 20 to 30 years in the future.

To the extent that there is a demand-side problem, the available strategies are equally long-term. Cross-national differences in wage structures of the current magnitude are, in part, the product of long-standing historical differences in wage-bargaining systems and labour market regulation. Institution building and reform, however, is almost by definition a long-term project. It is high time to revisit minimum wage legislation in Canada, but very large, short-term increases sufficient to induce dramatic changes in employer behaviour would undoubtedly reduce demand, and hence jobs, at the lower end of the labour market in the short run. As with early childhood education, however, a longer-term, gradualist approach that allows time for, and creates expectations of, employer adjustment may be feasible. Fatalism about what is possible in the long run is our worst policy enemy. A good policy starting point for the twenty-first century, then, would be to invest resources in developing a long-term strategy for a different sort of labour market for future generations.

But what of the intermediate term? What of the cohorts who are now completing their schooling and who will be paying for the pensions and health care when the baby-boom generation retires? For the foreseeable future, they are more or less stuck with our low-wage economy. This leaves us with only one, albeit second-best, solution.

In combination with a legislated wage floor, low-wage economies like that of Canada require a system of earnings subsidies for all low-wage earners. Essentially, we require a system of refundable tax credits or negative income tax (NIT) along the lines of the Earned Income Tax Credit in the U.S. or the Working Tax Credit in the UK. Importantly, such a strategy passes the litmus test of political feasibility. Ottawa has both the legislative authority and the long historical experience with NIT-style programs dating back to the Guaranteed Income Supplement and, more recently, the National Child Benefit.

What about services and especially early childhood education? The wage subsidy strategy and the servicing strategy are sometimes pitted against one another as though we were faced with a zero-sum trade-off between the two. I think this is wrong. Like health insurance, investments in children and other caring services also represent an earnings subsidy to low-wage families. Not only do they offset some significant share of child-rearing and caring costs, they also help raise female employment levels and family earnings.

Where will the money for all of this come from? What about the impending increase in retirement and health costs when the baby boomers retire? I think the answers to both questions are connected. The second distinctive feature of the post-industrial life course is that we are living longer and healthier than our industrial-age predecessors.

According to the anthropologists, the evolutionary reason for human longevity relative to other primates is related to the long period of juvenile dependency we require in order to acquire the complex skills we need to survive on our own. Instead of dying shortly after we finish reproducing, post-reproductive males and females provide the surplus goods and services that make extended juvenile

dependency possible. Someone has to be around to help the kids finance their first mortgage.

The period of so-called juvenile dependency has now moved well into young adulthood. But as yet, we have not taken advantage of our longevity gains to offset this development. The retirement age has been falling, despite increased longevity. I, for one, agree with the strategy advocated by the OECD to take steps to reverse that trend and encourage later retirement. Moving the average retirement age back toward age 65 not only saves on the expenditure side, but also would help create the additional output required to finance a refurbished social architecture for Canada.

The aim of social policy reform is to make our children's lives better over the whole of their life course, from childhood to old age. The post-industrial life course poses new challenges; it also provides new opportunities to meet those challenges.

REFERENCES

Beaujot, Rod 2004. *Delayed Life Transitions: Trends and Implications*. Ottawa: The Vanier Institute of the Family.

Heclo, Hugh 1988. "Generational politics." In John Palmer, Timothy Smeeding, and Barbara Torrey (eds.), *The Vulnerable*. Washington, DC: The Urban Institute, 1988.

Morissette, R., and A. Johnson 2004. *Earnings of Couples with High and Low Levels of Education, 1980–2000*. Research Paper No. 230, Analytical Studies Branch. Ottawa: Statistics Canada.

Morissette, René, Xuelin Zhang, and Marie Drolet 2002. *The Evolution of Wealth Inequality in Canada, 1984–1999*. Research Paper No. 187, Analytical Studies Branch. Ottawa: Statistics Canada.

chapter twenty-two

Regional Inequality:
Causes and Consequences

Catherine Corrigall-Brown and Fred Wien
(An original chapter written
for this volume.)

INTRODUCTION

In 1936, Canada's longest-serving prime minister, William Lyon Mackenzie King, famously said, "If some countries have too much history, we have too much geography." Canada is vast; there are significant natural and social barriers separating one region from another, and considerable differences in population, resources, and industrial structure. While these differences contribute to the unique and dynamic nature of our country, they also pose significant challenges for both provincial and federal governments.

Benjamin Higgins, a long-time student of regional development planning in North America, claims that "there is probably no advanced country where regional disparities play so great a role, economically, socially, and politically, as they do in Canada" (Higgins 1986:132; also see Higgins 1998). These regional disparities are evident in differences in the economic and social well-being of Canadians living in the various provinces. In addition to these objective inequalities, there are regional disparities in the subjective feelings of frustration among many citizens regarding their region's place in the Canadian federation. The Québécois have concerns about their language and cultural protection, Atlantic Canadians face continued economic uncertainty, and those in the western provinces feel politically alienated from the core of the country.

While regional inequality is important, it does not always occupy a central place among Canada's political concerns. In times of economic expansion, when all regions are registering economic growth, people are likely to hear less about these disparities, and this is also the case when important national and international issues dominate the political agenda. Since the 1960s, governments have sought to alleviate the hardship faced by the unemployed and the poor, and to create conditions of socio-economic development on a regionally equitable basis. Optimists hoped that these long-standing problems could be resolved by government intervention. However, after extensive efforts to reduce regional disparities in Canada, inequalities still exist. Much has been learned, especially about what not to do and the ineffectiveness of certain policy options. At the same time, new issues, such as free trade with the United States and Mexico, the rapid movement to a technology-based post-industrial society, and the changing patterns in the ownership and investment of capital in the world economy, pose new challenges whose implications for regional inequalities are not yet clear.

In this chapter, we review the debate on regional inequality in Canada. In particular, we examine the following questions: What is the extent of regional inequality in Canada? How do social scientists explain these inequalities? What have governments, especially at the federal level, tried to do about the problem? How successful have these measures been and, finally, what lessons can be drawn from this experience as we look ahead?

THE DIMENSIONS OF REGIONAL INEQUALITY

Regionalism is based on situations of politically relevant divisiveness and territorial cleavages, often accompanied by a consciousness on the part of residents that they have unique, regionally based interests (Schwartz 1974). While there is general agreement on the importance of regionalism and regional inequality in Canada (e.g., Brodie 1997; Skogstad 2000), the definition of region remains an important problem for assessing changes in inequality over time and for implementing policy. In the last few decades, successive governments have applied quite different interpretations of what constitutes a disadvantaged region. These definitional decisions are based as much on political grounds as on a rational analysis of pertinent social and economic characteristics.

The issue is as follows. The larger the area encompassed by the term *region*, the more likely that it will include significant internal variations or disparities. For example, the provinces within the western region (Manitoba, Saskatchewan, Alberta, and British Columbia) have some characteristics in common, but also enormous diversities. Similarly, the Atlantic provinces are often grouped together, but they differ considerably in such areas as their potential for the development of agriculture, forestry, manufacturing, or energy. In addition, there can be vast differences in social and economic well-being within provinces. It is not uncommon, even in a small province, to have large differences in, for example, unemployment rates. Such is the case in Nova Scotia where Halifax, in 2007, had lower levels of unemployment (5.6%) than the province as a whole (8.1%) (Statistics Canada 2007).

On the other hand, if a small, localized area is targeted (for example, a census district or a disadvantaged area within a province), policy solutions may be hindered because the underlying conditions contributing to the problem may require consideration of a broader geographic area. Can the problems of Cape Breton be resolved in isolation from the mainland of Nova Scotia? Can stagnation in eastern or northern Ontario be considered outside the context of developments in Toronto, Ottawa, or Montreal?

In practice, the province is most often used as the unit defining a region because data are most readily available at the provincial level, and less so for municipalities and other units. This approach is also occasioned by Canada's federal nature and by the political and constitutional significance of provincial governments.

What are some indicators of regional inequality in Canada, using provincial-level data? Typically, economic measures are used and, among these, income and unemployment rates are most prevalent. Other economic measures often cited include rates of poverty and the productive capacity of each province (e.g., provincial gross domestic product per capita, which measures the value of goods and services produced per person). Additional social indicators describe the educational level of the population, the

health of the population (e.g., infant mortality rates), or living standards (e.g., a crowding index with respect to housing). Some contemporary data measuring regional inequality are shown in Table 22-1.

The figures in Table 22-1 show substantial inequalities among the provinces on all measures reported. Median market income, which is the sum of earnings from employment income, investment income, and private retirement income before taxes, varies substantially among the provinces. In Newfoundland, median market income in 2005 was $45 900, or just 64% of what it was in Alberta. The unemployment rate and the likelihood of having families living under the low-income threshold (i.e., families spending more than 70% of their income on shelter, food, and clothing) also vary sharply

TABLE 22-1	Measures of Regional Inequality in Canada, by Province, Recent Years		
Province	**Median Market Income 2005**	**Unemployment Rate 2006**	**Low Income 2001**
Newfoundland	45 900	14.8	21.4
Prince Edward Island	51 700	11.0	15.2
Nova Scotia	55 000	7.9	18.8
New Brunswick	53 500	8.8	19.0
Quebec	55 900	8.0	23.4
Ontario	70 000	6.3	17.7
Manitoba	59 800	4.3	20.6
Saskatchewan	55 900	4.7	18.3
Alberta	71 700	3.4	18.4
British Columbia	62 200	4.8	19.6
Canada	57 700	6.3	19.7
Disparity Ratio (highest/lowest)	1.56	4.39	1.54

Sources: Median Market Income 2005: Includes all families with two or more people. Market income is the sum of earnings from employment income, investment income, and private retirement income. It is also called income before taxes and transfers. Statistics Canada, *Income in Canada.* Catalogue 75-202-XIE.
Unemployment Rate 2006: Statistics Canada, *Labour Force Characteristics 2006.* Catalogue 71-001-PIB.
Low Income 2001: Percentage of families spending more than 70% of their income on shelter, food, and clothing. Statistics Canada, Catalogue 13-569-XIB.

among the provinces. From these figures, it is obvious that social and economic outcomes for both individuals and families differ significantly by region. Just as it makes a difference into what family one is born, so too does it matter where that family resides.

EXPLANATIONS OF REGIONAL INEQUALITY

There are a number of competing theoretical explanations of regional inequality. Below we examine three major perspectives. Each of these seeks to explain why inequalities exist, and suggests what policies might remedy the situation. However, because these explanations are based on different theoretical interpretations, they point to different strategies for dealing with inequalities, some of which are not compatible with one another. Many analysts feel that no single explanation accounts fully for the patterns of regional inequality found in Canada, and so these writers pragmatically suggest that some wisdom is found in most, if not all, of the alternatives. They may also argue that some explanations are better at explaining the origin of disparities in previous decades, while other approaches are more useful under contemporary conditions.

The Staples Approach

The staples approach posits that regional inequality develops largely because of differences in the endowments of natural resources across areas, and in the economies and policies created to support the development of these resources. Staples are "raw or semi-processed materials extracted or grown primarily for export markets" (Marchak 1985: 674). In view of Canada's historic reliance on staple production and export, it is not surprising that Canadian social scientists would emphasize their role in regional development and, hence, regional inequality. The

roots of the staples approach originate with the work of Mackintosh (1923), Innis (1930, 1940, 1956), and others who examined successive staples, such as furs, cod, timber, and wheat, in order to understand their social, political, and economic impacts.

There are many conditions under which a given staple can become the engine of economic growth. Simply discovering a valued resource may be the key. A change in technology or transportation may also make it economical to produce a staple that has already been discovered, but not yet exploited. As well, the demand (and price) for a resource may increase, depending on such factors as the level of need in importing countries or the availability from other suppliers. In any case, if the conditions are favourable, capital and labour will flow into the region to develop and export the staple.

More contemporary interpretations attempt to specify the theory more clearly and delimit the conditions under which staples lead to economic development (e.g., Scott 1978; Watkins 1977). Watkins, in particular, suggests that staple theory, as elaborated in the earlier writings, only has explanatory value if applied to "new" countries such as Australia, New Zealand, or Canada. These countries historically have had few people in relation to their land and other resources, and few inhibiting traditions. In this context, it is argued, a region's prosperity depends not only on the availability and marketability of its natural resources, but also on the region's success in using the production or extraction of the staple in developing the rest of its economy. In other words, a region will prosper if it has a valued resource that can be profitably marketed abroad, and if it can extend appropriate linkages to other economic sectors (manufacturing, services, etc.) so that they receive a stimulus from the export sector.

For example, if a lot of equipment is required to extract or produce the staple, and if that equipment can be manufactured locally, then the manufacturing sector will be stimulated. Also, if the natural resource can be processed locally rather than being exported in a raw state, then the regional economy will gain jobs and income. As well, if labour is attracted to the export sector and receives high wages, then a local demand for consumer goods will be created. The region's long-term economic development, therefore, depends on the extent to which the stimulus provided by the exploitation of the staple can be generalized to diversify the economy. Provincial governments can actively encourage this by investing surpluses created from the exploitation of natural resources into other areas of the economy.

Unfortunately, it is in the nature of staple production that the demand for a given staple, and therefore its price, may eventually decline. Consumer preferences may change, new synthetic alternatives may be found, resources may be exhausted, production costs may increase, or other regions or countries may take over an established market. If the region has diversified its economy, the decline in the staple exporting sector is less of a problem. Labour and capital freed up in the declining sector can be redeployed to other productive uses. Some migration outside the region can also be expected, depending on factors such as government policy and opportunities elsewhere. It is more likely, however, that dependence on the staple production will continue and there will be a reluctance to adjust to the situation. Attempts may be made to subsidize and protect the declining industry, rather than encourage a search for alternative sources of economic growth. For example, the coal and steel industries in Cape Breton were the recipients of substantial subsidies over several decades, which sustained them long after they were economically viable. Governments may also seek to retain their population base, rather than encourage

migration from the region. Unless a new staple can be found and developed, the region may stagnate and decline.

There are two additional features of staple theory as it has been developed by Canadian political economists. First, the importance of staple production for a region or country is not restricted to its narrowly economic implications. Each staple, including the way its production is organized, leaves its imprint politically, socially, and culturally on the region. For example, the transition in Alberta, from an economy dominated by farming to one dominated by energy production and export, sped up the urbanization trend in the province, encouraged the development of a large managerial/entrepreneurial class, and replaced a populist-agrarian political regime with one more responsive to the new urban elite (Mansell 1986). Second, writers such as Innis (1956), Drache (1976), and Watkins (1977) have emphasized the negative implications of a staple economy—notably, the dependence on a foreign industrial centre through market and trade relations that are exploitative and constraining, the periodic crises and boom/bust periods, and the economic distortions induced in an area that lacks a diversified, self-reliant, and self-regulated economic base. We will return to these themes when we discuss dependency theory in a later section.

Critics of the staples approach often suggest that this perspective provided important insights historically, when regional economies were centred on the fur trade, the cod fishery, or wheat growing. They suggest, however, that staple production has receded in importance over time, although energy production continues to be important in some provinces such as Alberta and Newfoundland. Buckley (1958), in fact, dates the decline of the utility of the approach to as early as 1820. The Economic

Council of Canada (1977:8) concludes that "the maturing Canadian economy has reached the point where resources and transportation are no longer, as in the past, the only important determinants of regional variations in the well-being of Canadians, and we now have productive processes that are more complex and utilize natural resources somewhat differently."

The Modernization Model

Examination of the underdevelopment of Third World countries in the 1950s and 1960s led to the creation of the modernization or development model. This model suggested that important characteristics of the traditional sector in a given country needed to be overcome if development was to proceed. The source of change, and the model for development, was the modern, urban, industrial sector of the country. The modernization approach suggested that the social relationships, culture, political institutions, and social structures appropriate to modern industrial society would spread from the (modern) centre to the (traditional) periphery. This spread was to result primarily from the competition mechanism of the free market. Increased mobility of individuals between country and city, mass communications and transportation, formal education, and the development of a modern state would all serve to disseminate rational, income-maximizing behaviours that would eventually be common to all members of society.

The development perspective was also applied to explain regional underdevelopment in advanced industrial societies. It was not transferred without modification, however. While it is difficult to speak of development in Latin American countries without dealing with the overwhelming significance of the agriculture sector and the need for land reform, such is not the case in Canada. The debate in Canada also does not dwell as much on differences in progressive or traditional attitudes, values, and social structures between different parts of the country.

It is argued, however, that some regions of Canada are underdeveloped because their deficiencies stand in the way of improving their relative levels of employment and income in relation to other regions. Several factors have been identified as causing this underdevelopment: location in relation to markets and the resulting burden of transportation costs; lower rates of capital investment; shortcomings in infrastructure, such as roads, harbours, and hospitals; lower levels of investment in education and training of the workforce (human capital); inferior managerial quality; and lower levels of investment in new productive technology. Most of these factors contribute to the productivity of industry and thus to income and employment levels in the region.

Education may be particularly important in leading to the underdevelopment of certain regions. Learning societies can be defined as places where a large proportion of the population and organizations permanently perform knowledge-based activities; moreover, many actors need and are able to upgrade their skills as well as their awareness of scientific and technological changes (Sutz 2003). Learning is, of course, related to the acquisition of knowledge through teaching and research, but it also depends critically on opportunities to apply creatively what has been learned.

At a global level, the emergence of the knowledge economy implies that inequalities among countries are increasingly related to different capabilities to participate in knowledge-demanding tasks. Developed countries and regions have high educational averages and are also rich in interactive learning spaces, including educational institutions and the research and development

TABLE 22-2	Social Indicators of Regional Inequality, by Province, Recent Years					

Province	Education, 2001			Health, 2004		
	Less than high school	High school graduate	Bachelor's degree or higher	Infant Mortality (per 1000)	Life Expectancy (Male)	(Female)
Newfoundland	44.17	46.30	11.53	5.1	75.8	81.3
Prince Edward Island	39.50	49.07	11.43	4.3	76.8	81.6
Nova Scotia	37.27	48.71	14.02	4.6	76.5	81.6
New Brunswick	38.91	49.79	11.30	4.3	77.0	82.2
Quebec	32.84	53.20	13.96	4.6	77.5	82.6
Ontario	31.51	50.90	17.59	5.5	78.3	82.7
Manitoba	40.66	46.32	13.02	7.0	76.4	81.4
Saskatchewan	41.80	47.14	11.06	6.2	76.6	82.1
Alberta	33.42	51.51	15.07	5.8	77.8	82.6
British Columbia	30.59	53.29	16.12	4.3	78.7	83.1
Canada	33.20	51.37	15.43	5.3	77.8	82.6
Disparity Ratio (highest/lowest)	1.44	1.15	1.59	1.63	1.04	1.02

Sources: Education, 2001: Calculated from Statistics Canada, *2001 Census.* Catalogue 97F0024XIE.
Health, 2004: Statistics Canada, *Health Indicators.* Catalogue 82-221-XIE.

components of business and government agencies. Underdeveloped countries and regions have fewer interactive learning spaces and a lower average level of education. We also find clear regional differences in educational attainment among the provinces of Canada (see Table 22-2). In addition, some provinces are more likely to have government and private research facilities in their region, enabling the use of learned knowledge.

The modernization model assumes that, under free market conditions, workers would move from areas with low incomes and few educational possibilities to areas with higher incomes and more opportunities for education. However, artificial impediments prevent this "natural" equalization from occurring. It is suggested that if the minimum wage in poorer regions is higher than it should be, or if employment insurance

payments are more generous in amount and duration and the terms for accessing them are more lenient, then the incentives to leave the region are reduced. The same result occurs if the actions of unions, governments, or corporations keep wages unnaturally high.

As these examples illustrate, the deficiency identified by modernization theorists is not limited to the disadvantaged area, but is also built into the policies and practices of national governments, unions, or corporations in interaction with the poorer region. Courchene (1994) concludes that, because the natural adjustment mechanisms of the market are not free to work as they should, provincial governments increasingly depend on federal transfers to sustain themselves, which exacerbates the problem. He suggests that the various problems interact: if wages are prevented from moving downward in a poor province, then unemployment remains high. This triggers an influx of federal funds (e.g., for employment insurance). However, the more money that flows in, the less incentive there is for the province or region to worry about the adequacy of wage adjustment, as well as labour and capital mobility. The result is a "vicious cycle" of inequality (Courchene 1986:35; also see Courchene 1994).

Dependency Theory

Dependency theory first appeared in the late 1960s, and generated considerable intellectual excitement because it directly challenged the main tenets of modernization theory (Frank 1972; Wallerstein 1982). Articulated primarily by Latin American intellectuals, the approach contains two main arguments.

First, dependency theory suggests that underdevelopment is the result of exploitation by capitalist metropolitan centres. Far from being models of modernity to be emulated, the "developed" areas prosper at the expense of the "traditional" regions. Further, the exploitative relationship between, for example, the United States and Latin America is reproduced within both developed and underdeveloped countries, thus accounting for regional and racial inequality. One early application of the dependency perspective to Canada, by A.K. Davis (1971), divided the country into metropolitan areas (e.g., the urban industrial core) and satellite/hinterland areas (e.g., the North, the West, and Atlantic Canada). Davis argued that the metropolis continuously dominates and exploits the hinterland, but groups in the hinterland tend to fight back against their metropolitan exploiters.

The second argument is that underdevelopment occurs when resources are drained from peripheral areas to a centre that controls the terms of trade. Thus, raw materials are exported from satellite regions at prices below their true value, and manufactured goods from the central area are sold back to

the periphery at exorbitant prices. Richer areas concentrate on exporting industrial goods to the rest of the world while the poorer areas focus on trading primary commodities. However, over time, there is a tendency for the price of primary products to decline relative to the higher value-added industrial products (Greig et al. 2007). Hence, poorer countries and regions must export more primary products over time to purchase the same amount of industrial goods (Keily 1998:8; Preston 1996), and this keeps the poorer regions unable to catch up to the richer regions.

Financial institutions and multinational corporations play an important role in this process. Banks headquartered in core areas drain the peripheral regions of their savings and invest them elsewhere, while labour is attracted to the core when needed, but sent back to the periphery when not required. Often, the multinational corporation is regarded as the chief agent of exploitation, and the relationship between core and periphery is seen as uniformly negative. In other versions of this theory, multinationals located in a peripheral area and producing goods for a local market can be acknowledged as a source of growth and dynamism, since they need to create some internal prosperity in order to sell their consumer goods. However, while some local wealth is generated, substantial losses of capital resources from the area occur through profit remittances, interest payments, and royalties. If the result is not uniform underdevelopment in the peripheral region, it is at best uneven development or dependent development (Cardoso 1972).

Numerous Canadian studies in the dependency tradition emphasize these themes. Gidengil (1990) finds that while central regions often show autonomous growth, peripheral regions only show growth in response to expansion at the centre. Other studies of particular regions in Canada support these findings, including examinations of the deindustrialization of the Atlantic provinces from 1890 to 1920 and their continuing underdevelopment (Acheson 1977; Forbes 1977; House 1981); agriculture and oil development on the prairies (Fowke 1968; Knuttila and McCrorie 1980); and First Nations–white interactions in the context of resource development in the Canadian North (Elias 1975; Kellough 1980).

In social terms, dependency theory focuses on the class structure of the metropolitan and satellite areas. While different analysts of particular regions or countries identify various kinds of social class constellations, all analyses identify dominant elites and subordinate labourers in both centre and periphery. Parts of the periphery elite are linked to the centre elite and serve as its agent in the satellite area (Matthews 1980; Stavenhagen 1974). In the Canadian context, for example, Clement (1983) argues that a portion of the economic elite of Canada's periph-eral regions has been bought out by central Canadian and American business interests, and serves those interests in the region.

Dependency theory as an explanation for regional inequality in Canada has numerous critics. Some question the applicability to the Canadian context of a model articulated initially to explain underdevelopment in the Third World. In contrast to Third World countries, Canada is not generally characterized by low returns for labour (i.e., low wages), low returns for exported resource products, or a large traditional population sector (Marchak 1985). Others have questioned whether the theory has much to add to what has already been articulated, perhaps more appropriately for Canada, by staple theorists such as Innis and Watkins. In many ways, the debate has moved to larger questions and broader perspectives due to dissatisfaction with the rather simplistic dyadic relationships of dependency theory (Friedman and Wayne 1977).

PUBLIC POLICY MEASURES

Regional issues are of ongoing importance in Canada. Perhaps the earliest policies explicitly directed to alleviating regional disparities were the measures undertaken to counter the drought and depression experienced by Canada in the 1930s. The Second World War intervened and shifted attention to the need for mobilization in support of the war effort, and to national reconstruction when the war ended.

In more recent decades, however, regional disparities have been important considerations in government policy. This has been due to less favourable economic circumstances during certain periods and to a more interventionist approach by governments in resolving social and economic problems. Perceptions of the issue also changed with the growing recognition that the relative gap between regions was the important consideration, and not their absolute level of poverty or well-being or their current rates of economic growth or stagnation.

In examining the policies pursued, one is struck by the variety of measures implemented and the frequent changes in approach. There are myriad policies designed to promote regional development or reduce disparities. And, while some policies are clearly and explicitly directed at the problem, others have only indirect implications and can frustrate the intent and effect of the more explicit approaches. The frequent changes in policy occur, in part, because regional development programs are important for voter support and, therefore, each successive government wants to put its stamp on regional development efforts. In addition, approaches change because conditions change. Policies appropriate during a period of economic growth may be inappropriate in a period of decline.

One of the central problems in dealing with regional inequality in Canada is that our Constitution does not assign to either level of government the explicit responsibility for economic development or for combating regional disparities. Provincial governments have a major function in economic development because they own natural resources and control most determinants of human resources and land use. The federal government has created for itself a major role, essentially on the basis of its spending power. Equalization payments, income transfers, and shared cost agreements with the provinces all derive from Ottawa's spending power. In addition, the federal government holds jurisdiction over such matters as foreign and interprovincial trade and shares jurisdiction with the provinces over agriculture, fishing, forestry, and immigration (Savoie 2003). Thus, from a constitutional perspective, close federal–provincial coordination is required simply because both levels of government have assumed important roles in regional development.

The federal government has hardly needed to impose itself on the provinces in the regional development field. Indeed, several provinces, notably the four Atlantic provinces, have over the years insisted that Ottawa play a leading role in regional development. The pressure to include a new provision in the 1982 Constitution Act, committing Parliament and the Government of Canada to the principle of equalization payments and to the promotion of equal opportunities and economic development throughout the country, came from the provinces and not from the federal government. In the face of such pressures, federal officials now report that they have set out to contain provincial demands by insisting that any constitutional provisions for equalization or regional development be written in the broadest terms. To this end, section 36 of the 1982 Constitution Act merely commits the federal government to the principle of equalization (Savoie 2003).

The major kinds of initiatives that have been undertaken by the federal government, sometimes in co-operation with the provinces and sometimes unilaterally, are as follows:

1. Investments in infrastructure such as roads, harbours, schools, hospitals, wharves, and railroads.

2. Human capital investments and personal adjustment. These investments work to provide education, training, and mobility grants for unemployed people who wish to change careers or move to a region that offers better opportunities.

3. Policies of industrial assistance. These have included tax exemptions, tax credits, loan guarantees, or cash grants to individual firms to encourage them to locate in depressed areas. The same measures have been used to help new firms get started or to help existing firms expand, diversify, or export more of their products. Much debate has taken place about the effectiveness of industrial assistance policies. Policies have been criticized for supporting capital-intensive (rather than employment-intensive) establishments, and for attracting "footloose" industries to a region (i.e., firms with few backward and forward linkages and with little commitment to staying in their new location).

4. Policies directed to resource and sectoral development. The federal government, under its Department of Regional Economic Expansion in the 1970s, and more recently under other auspices, has signed general development agreements with the provinces. The agreements have provided federal financial support for the development of fields such as forestry, agriculture, or tourism. In the early 1980s, attention was given to stimulating the economy through investments in energy-sector mega-projects such as the extraction of coal in British Columbia and oil in Alberta. In the late 1990s, major new oil and natural gas developments off the east coast also attracted government support.

5. Compensatory and transfer policies. By far the greatest amount of federal money in support of the provinces and their residents is spent not for explicit development policies, but as cash transfers to the provinces and to individuals or families. Equalization grants, funds for hospitals, medical care, and post-secondary education, as well as payments for employment insurance and family allowances, make up the bulk of these transfers. In fact, these transfers greatly overshadow the budgets of the explicit regional development programs mentioned above. The grants to the provinces have made the provincial governments in the poorer regions very dependent on federal transfers for their total spending budget. As shown in Table 22-3, the dependence of individuals on personal transfer income is also substantial in the poorer provinces.

Because of the importance of federal transfer payments for understanding regional development in Canada, we should consider some of the ways in which these programs have changed over time. Before 1977–78, the federal and provincial governments applied a principle of equally sharing the costs of health care, post-secondary education, employment insurance, and other programs. Subsequently, however, the federal government became concerned with the escalating costs of these programs, which were administered by the provinces. For this reason, from 1972 to 1977, there was a transition to what is referred to as block funding, a program in which funding assistance comes in one lump sum and is not designated for specific uses.

To this end, from 1977 to 1995, the federal government transferred money to the provinces through Established Program Financing (EPF) with block funding. The period after 1997 saw the EPF system replaced with Canadian Health and Social Assistance Transfers (CHST). The CHST encompasses both the old EPF and Canada Assistance Plan (CAP) transfers, which were

TABLE 22-3	Average Value per Capita and Share of Government Transfers in Income of Working-Age Census Families	
Province	**Average Government Transfer**	**Percentage of Family Income from Government Transfers**
Newfoundland	7450	14.3
Prince Edward Island	6250	11.1
Nova Scotia	4944	8.6
New Brunswick	5403	9.8
Quebec	4451	7.2
Ontario	3309	4.3
Manitoba	3827	6.2
Saskatchewan	4138	7.0
Alberta	3396	4.6
British Columbia	3806	5.6
Canada	3904	5.6
Disparity Ratio (highest/lowest)	2.25	3.33

Source: Statistics Canada, *Income of Canadian Families, Provinces and Territories, 2000.* Catalogue 96F0030XIE.

used to provide income assistance to Canadians in need.

In 2004, the Canada Health and Social Transfer was divided into two programs: the Canada Social Transfer (CST) and the Canada Health Transfer (CHT). The programs were made independent to allow for greater accountability and transparency in federal funding. The CHT is composed of both cash and tax transfers. In 2006–07, CHT cash transfer payments from the federal government to the provinces and territories totalled $20.1 billion. Payments are not allocated on an equal per capita basis, but instead on the basis of provincial tax points. The value of a tax point represents the amount of revenue that is generated by one percentage point of a particular tax (in the case of the CHT and the CST, the personal income tax or the corporate income tax). Since provinces have different economies and, therefore, have unequal capacities to raise tax revenues, a tax point is worth more in a wealthy province than in a poorer province. Currently, Alberta and Ontario, the two provinces with the highest ability to raise revenue, receive lower per capita CHT cash payments than the other provinces.

In addition to the funding that the federal government gives the provinces through transfers, a variety of programs have been established to stimulate regional development directly. These policies have been pursued within several organizational frameworks. In the late 1950s and for much of the 1960s, discrete policies, such as the Federal Fund for Rural Economic Development, were administered by a variety of federal departments. The Trudeau administration, beginning in 1969, tried to consolidate all relevant programs under the newly created Department of Regional Economic Expansion (DREE). DREE was disbanded in 1982, however, in favour of an approach that provided for a federal coordinator's office in each region and the consideration of regional implications by Cabinet for all economic policies, not just those explicitly directed to regional development.

The current structure of regional development policy dates from 1987, when the federal Progressive Conservative government created four new federal agencies to deal with issues of regional inequality. First, the Atlantic Canada Opportunities Agency (ACOA) is responsible for coordinating economic development in Atlantic Canada; acting as an advocate for the region in the development of national economic policy; aiding in the establishment, expansion, and modernization of small and medium-sized enterprises; funding programs to provide employment replacements for the declining fishery; and promoting government co-operation with private-sector institutions. The second agency is the Federal Office of Regional Development–Quebec (FORD–Q), which defines the overall direction of regional policy in Quebec and negotiates intergovernmental agreements designed to assist the long-term economic development of regions in Quebec with low incomes, slow economic growth, or high unemployment. Third, the Federal Economic Development Initiative in Northern Ontario (FedNor) funds research and development, business creation, expansion, and modernization in northern Ontario. Finally, Western Economic Diversification Canada (WD) seeks to move the western economy away from traditional natural resource–based activities, gives repayable contributions to business and specific sectors or activities that are risky or innovative, and helps western Canadian businesses obtain federal contracts (Skogstad 2000).

In June 2000, Prime Minister Jean Chrétien went to Halifax to unveil a new approach to regional development. He gave ACOA $700 million of new money to be invested in research and development, training, and community economic development. However, Chrétien was less interested in partnerships with provinces than with private-sector partnerships. He also established a new advisory board to guide federal government spending in the new economy. The role of the provinces, it appears, would be determined on an ad hoc or as-needed basis (Savoie 2003).

More recently, Stephen Harper's Conservative government has addressed the issue of regional inequality. Harper is famously quoted as saying that Atlantic Canada's "have-not" status is a result of its "defeatism," its citizens' loss of faith in their own abilities and talents, and the region's reliance on Ottawa and its transfer programs (Atlantic Institute for Market Solutions 2002). However, once in government, Harper maintained much of the infrastructure for dealing with regional development that had been established by those before him. He has maintained ACOA, FedNor, and WD. The former Federal Office of Regional Development–Quebec is now called Canada Economic Development for Quebec Regions.

REGIONAL DISPARITIES OVER TIME

There is widespread agreement among experts about the major patterns and trends in regional inequality. First, based on median market income, the gap between the richest and the poorest provinces has decreased over time. In Table 22-4, we see that the poorest provinces improved their relative median incomes from 1961 to 2006. For example, Newfoundland and Prince Edward Island went from having median incomes under 60% of the national average in 1961 to 80% and 90%, respectively, in 2006. Two of the richer provinces, Ontario and Alberta, also experienced an increase in relation to the national average in the 1961–2006 period, with Ontario rising slightly, from 118% to 121%, and Alberta rising significantly, from 100% to 124%. Another affluent province, British Columbia,

TABLE 22-4	Median Market Income, by Province, 1961–2006 (Relative to the National Average, Canada = 100)					
Province	1961	1971	1980	1990	1999	2006
Newfoundland	58	64	64	71	68	80
Prince Edward Island	59	64	71	74	73	90
Nova Scotia	78	77	79	82	81	95
New Brunswick	68	72	71	77	81	93
Quebec	90	89	95	93	88	97
Ontario	118	117	107	113	111	121
Manitoba	94	94	90	87	91	104
Saskatchewan	71	80	91	80	87	97
Alberta	100	99	112	99	101	124
British Columbia	115	109	111	101	113	108
Canada	100	100	100	100	100	100
Disparity Ratio (highest/lowest)	2.03	1.84	1.74	1.59	1.66	1.56

Sources: Adapted from Polese (1987), with 1990 data from Statistics Canada, *Annual System of National Accounts, 1991.* Catalogue 13-201; 1996 data from Statistics Canada, *Provincial Economic Accounts, 1996.* Catalogue 13-213; and 1999 and 2006 data from Statistics Canada, Income in Canada. Catalogue 75-202-XIE.

has seen some relative decline in median income during this period. In most provinces, however, there has been improvement over time, with declining market income inequality since 1961.

Incomes in some provinces are boosted by federal government transfers. Table 22-3 shows the average government transfer per province and the resulting effect of these transfers on family incomes. It is clear that federal transfers help to reduce some of the inequality among the provinces. In 2000 in Newfoundland, for example, 14.3% of the average family's income came from federal transfers. These transfers were significantly larger than the average transfers in Ontario and Alberta, where they represented only 4.3% and 4.6% of the average family's income, respectively. Without these federal transfers, income inequality among the provinces would be much higher.

While regional income inequality is declining over time in Canada, changes in unemployment rates are much less encouraging. Table 22-5 compares unemployment rates in each province with the national average. We see increased disparity between 1971 and 1981, reduced disparity in the subsequent decade, and then increased inequality again between 1991 and 2006. In fact, inequality in unemployment rates in 2006 was higher than at any time since 1966.

Although it is important to examine the economic indicators of regional inequality, it is also important to study its social indicators. Inequality can manifest itself in many ways that are external to the economy, such as in the social and political spheres of life. An examination of these domains provides additional insight into the patterns of regional inequality in Canada. One social indicator of regional inequality is education level. Data on average provincial education levels

TABLE 22-5 Provincial Unemployment Rate, by Province, 1966–2006 (Relative to the National Average, Canada = 100)

Province	1966	1971	1976	1981	1986	1991	1996	2001	2006
Newfoundland	171	135	189	186	208	178	201	213	234
Prince Edward Island	–	–	135	150	140	163	152	155	174
Nova Scotia	138	113	134	134	140	116	130	125	125
New Brunswick	156	98	155	154	150	123	121	143	140
Quebec	121	118	123	137	115	115	122	121	127
Ontario	76	87	87	87	73	93	93	86	100
Manitoba	82	92	66	79	80	85	77	59	68
Saskatchewan	44	56	55	61	80	71	68	78	75
Alberta	74	92	56	50	102	79	73	64	54
British Columbia	135	116	121	88	131	96	92	121	76
Canada	100	100	100	100	100	100	100	100	100
Disparity Ratio (highest/lowest)	3.88	2.41	3.43	3.72	2.85	2.50	2.96	3.61	4.33

Sources: 1966 to 1996 data from Statistics Canada, *The Labour Force*; 2001 and 2006 data from Statistics Canada, *Labour Force Characteristics*. Catalogue 71-001-PIB.

reveal that "have-not" provinces tend to display not only economic disadvantages, but also lower general levels of education (see Table 22-2). In these provinces, a relatively larger proportion of the population has attained less than a high school diploma, while a comparatively smaller proportion has completed post-secondary education. The disparity in education levels among the provinces in turn suggests that some regions have increased social and political power. For example, lower social capital in terms of educational attainment may contribute to the relatively lower voting rates found in the Atlantic provinces.

Examining health indicators of inequality, such as life expectancy, reveals that people residing in the provinces that are most disadvantaged economically are also those who tend to have the shortest life expectancy. This is the case even though, in theory, health care is universally accessible in all provinces. Infant mortality rates, however, are an interesting anomaly. Although we would expect these rates to be highest in the Atlantic provinces, for example, we find that the Atlantic provinces, particularly Prince Edward Island and New Brunswick, have relatively low infant mortality rates, even lower than the rates for the economically advantaged provinces, such as Ontario and Alberta. This evidence suggests that, while it is clear that certain regions are disadvantaged in many economic and social domains, this is not an all-encompassing phenomenon and there can be interesting and important deviations from this overall tendency.

REGIONAL INEQUALITY IN COMPARATIVE PERSPECTIVE

We began this chapter by suggesting that regional inequality is a substantial and persistent problem in Canada, which makes it notable among advanced industrial or post-industrial societies. With this in mind, let

us briefly assess the similarities and differences between the experiences of Canada and the United States, in order to gain some comparative perspective on the issue of regional inequality.

The influence of geography on regional inequality is extensive. While Canada has significant natural resources, the United States has the added advantage of a wide dispersion of good agricultural land, mineral resources, and forests. The American population is also more evenly distributed and its urban centres are more balanced in size and location at various points along the coast and in the interior. By contrast, much of the Canadian population is concentrated in the Toronto to Montreal corridor, as is the preponderance of Canada's manufacturing capacity and financial and corporate institutions. The greater concentration in Canada is explained not only by the advantages of a central location to serve the more peripheral areas of the country, but also by the fact that most foreign (especially American) investment is located in southern Ontario, close to the major American markets and head offices. Thus, the overwhelming importance of the United States in trade and investment exerts its influence on the regional distribution of productive resources and population in Canada (Carroll 2004; McDougall 2006; Semple 1987). The United States has no similar relationship to a foreign power. Canada is also much more dependent on resource exports and is therefore more subject than the United States to the distortions, uncertainties, and pitfalls that this kind of economic development brings, as the staple and dependency theorists have described.

Another significant difference between Canada and the United States is the cultural makeup and distribution of the two populations. In Canada, the large concentration of the French-speaking population in Quebec and adjacent areas overlaps with regional disparities. In the United States, the significant ethnic and racial minorities are less concentrated in one region. Higgins (1986) argues that the United States has had an extraordinary mobility of labour and capital, and that this has helped to even out regional disparities. In comparison, the attachment of Canadians to their cultural communities is said to have reduced mobility.

As a result of these factors, regional disparities are less significant in the United States, and less entrenched. In the United States, there have been some significant reductions in regional disparities over time and some regions have declined (as New England did in the 1970s) while others have grown rapidly (as did the so-called Sunbelt in the same period). However, problems of localized underdevelopment seem to be associated with the problems of decay, neglect, and exploitation of core areas within large urban centres, rather than within larger geographic regions.

It is also important to note that regional inequality in both Canada and the United States is not solely represented by examining inter-provincial differences. One must also examine the inequalities within provinces that arise from urban–rural differences. As noted earlier, Davis (1971) describes the Canadian experience as a tension between metropolis and hinterland, which can characterize the relationships both between and within provinces. Social policies have tended to reinforce metropolis–hinterland power imbalances and inequalities, so much so that some authors refer to areas of northern and rural Canada as a domestic Third World (see Graham et al. 2000).

The general trend is that, with increased community size, there is an increase in average family income within each region. As a result, provinces whose populations are relatively concentrated in smaller cities and rural regions, such as the Atlantic provinces and Saskatchewan, tend to have lower per capita employment incomes. For these provinces, the population distribution across cities and rural regions accounts for at least half of their income disparities from

the national average. For example, earned income per capita in Nova Scotia was $3616 below the national average in 2001. Of this disparity, $2007 was due to the province's urban–rural composition and $1609 to other factors (Statistics Canada 2005). In Newfoundland and Labrador, the urban–rural composition of its population accounted for about 48% of its income disparity from the national level. In Saskatchewan, fully 84% of its income disparity can be attributed to the concentration of its population in smaller urban and rural areas (Statistics Canada 2005).

There are many reasons why urban–rural inequalities arise. First, corporate and economic power resides primarily within large cities, where head offices are situated. Political power is also concentrated in large urban centres, especially in provincial and federal capital cities. Finally, ideological power is centred in urban areas in a number of ways, including the concentration of mass media organizations—major newspapers, television and radio networks, publishing companies, etc.—and the centres of higher learning and research, as represented in major universities and institutes. These are certainly important factors in the Atlantic region where there is significant urban–rural inequality as a result of differing economic bases. In the urban areas, public-sector employment and retail dynamism create strong economies. At the same time, the economies of rural areas in the region tend to focus on natural resources, which are declining and shedding labour.

POLITICAL OUTCOMES OF REGIONAL INEQUALITY

Inequality across the regions of Canada is important for a variety of reasons. Beyond our concerns about regional inequality for its own sake, it has many political consequences. Inequality, or the perception of inequality, affects the ways in which Canadians identify politically, and also the political party structure and electoral outcomes of the nation as a whole.

It is clear that Canadians have a variety of ways in which they can identify, either with their province, with their country, or in some other way. These subjective attachments can have real political implications. Canadians in general positively identify with both the national and the provincial political communities (Simeon 2004). In a recent survey, 81% of Canadians outside Quebec felt "profoundly attached" to Canada and 59% felt the same way about their province (Mendelson 2003). In comparison, in Quebec, 46% of the population identified themselves as Québécois first or Québécois only, while 30% identified as Canadians and Quebecers equally and only 22% as Canadians first or only.

Westerners tend to value both Canadian and provincial identifications equally, but often perceive themselves as excluded from power at the centre. In a survey in 1997, the Environics Research group found that more than 50% of the respondents from the four western provinces strongly agreed with the statement, "The West usually gets ignored in national politics because the political parties depend mostly upon the voters in Quebec and Ontario" (Henry 2002). In fact, since 1979, at no time has the proportion of western Canadians agreeing (somewhat or strongly) with this statement fallen below 80%. Residents of the largest province, Ontario, identify most with the national government, where they exercise significant political influence. Interestingly, citizens in the poorer Atlantic provinces have similar views, no doubt influenced by the recognition that their well-being continues to depend heavily on financial support from Ottawa (Beauchamps et al. 1999).

The effects of these identities and attitudes are seen in Canada's political party system and electoral outcomes. Canada's party system lost its pan-Canadian veneer in the 1990s. In particular, the elections of

1993, 1997, and 2000 produced a distribution of seats in the House of Commons with stronger regional parties than Canadians had seen for generations, and more distinctive regional blocks of MPs from hitherto national parties. On the surface, at least, Canadian politics has seldom been so regionalized. Two regional parties formed in the 1990s and both held the position of official opposition in the federal Parliament: the sovereigntist Bloc Québécois after the 1993 election and the Western-based Reform Party/Canadian Alliance after the 1997 and 2000 elections.

The federal-level Bloc Québécois manifests the most extreme version of regionalism: the desire to have Quebec secede from the country. This initiative is closely linked to the separatist provincial party, the Parti Québécois, which was elected to govern Quebec for the first time in 1976. The level of nationalist sentiment has varied since then, but there is some indication of an increase. For example, in the first referendum on Quebec sovereignty or separation, in 1980, only 40% of Quebecers voted in favour; in the second referendum, in 1995, that figure rose to 49% (Young and Archer 2002).

In the case of the Western-based Canadian Alliance, it merged with the federal Conservative party before the 2004 election, but this did not eliminate the strong regional political sentiments in the West. For example, the 2006 election produced a minority Conservative government, which was elected with 124 seats. The Liberals became the official opposition (103 seats), with the Bloc Québécois receiving 51 seats and the NDP 29 seats. The regional divisions in this election are shown in the regional concentration of most of these parties, especially the predominance of the Bloc Québécois in Quebec, but also the over-representation of Conservatives in the West and Liberals in Ontario and the Atlantic region. Such electoral outcomes underscore the importance of regional disparities, or the perception of such disparities, in Canada.

CONCLUSION

Despite the changes we have outlined in this chapter, the stability of regional inequality patterns in Canada is still impressive. This is not to say that policy measures have failed, since there is improvement in some areas and, in any event, because the situation could have worsened without these measures. Also, much has been learned in the process. For example, it is now clear that transferring funds to provincial governments and to families and individuals reduces inequalities in regional median incomes, and is defensible on equity grounds. The debate continues, however, about whether these transfers have a negative effect on the economic development of the region, by interfering with adaptive processes.

The key issue is perhaps clearer now than it was before: how to bring about self-sustaining, indigenous economic development in the disadvantaged regions. The role of global economic developments should also be taken into account in new regional programs. One example is the Asia-Pacific Gateway and Corridor Initiative. The purpose of this initiative is to strengthen Canada's competitive position in international commerce by providing a system of transportation infrastructure, which includes British Columbia's Lower Mainland and Prince Rupert ports, road, and rail connections. This structure will reach across western Canada and into the economic heartlands of North America, as well as to major airports and border crossings. To this end, the initiative provides an integrated set of investment and policy measures focused on trade with the Asia-Pacific Region, in order to establish Canada's Asia-Pacific Gateway and Corridor as the best transportation network facilitating global supply chains

between North America and Asia (Transport Canada 2007).

Other innovative programs, such as the Atlantic Innovation Fund (AIF), seek to support entrepreneurial endeavours in disadvantaged regions. This fund is run by the Atlantic Canada Opportunities Agency and works to develop innovative products and services. To receive funding through this program, individuals or companies must be based in Atlantic Canada, have a potential commercial value, and include a large research and development component. The latter criterion emphasizes the recognized importance of education and research in long-term regional development.

Despite these innovative programs, the federal government has generally retreated from regional development issues in recent years. This is evident in the absolute level of spending budgeted by the federal government on these issues, as well as in shifts in government ideology, which stresses a renewed faith in the workings of the market and, therefore, promotes a smaller federal role in regional equalization. Consistent with this trend are the federal government's concessions to provincial demands for more control over regional projects. Finally, regional development has become a lower priority because national issues, such as free trade and global conflicts, currently dominate the agenda.

The future of Canada's disadvantaged regions will continue to be shaped in large part by events and trends impinging on the regions from outside, as well as by internal dynamics. For example, there is still considerable debate surrounding the issue of how the North American Free Trade Agreement (NAFTA) of 1994 will affect Canada's regions and regional politics. Two main effects have been noted.

First, the relative success of the regions increasingly depends on how they integrate into continental and global markets, rather than the national market. As regional economies become inserted differently into the global economy, their links with the outside world will become more important relative to their economic linkages within Canada. In this sense, Canada becomes less able to act as the giant "mutual insurance company." Global pressures, the argument goes, will increasingly constrain federal policy instruments, including monetary, fiscal, trade, and redistributive policies. In such a political economy it may well become harder to sustain the political commitment of wealthier provinces to inter-regional redistribution (Savoie 2003).

In addition, NAFTA further constrains the capacity of the federal government to deal with issues of regional inequality, because the federal government must conform to international trade rules under the agreement before it can address the concerns of the Canadian regions. Such considerations indicate that the study of regional inequality in Canada may be at a turning point. Perspectives and policies that have been prevalent for many years are increasingly being questioned, especially with respect to their results and usefulness in dealing with present and future issues.

REFERENCES

Acheson, T.W. 1977. "The Maritimes and 'Empire Canada.'" In D.J. Bercuson (ed.), *Canada and The Burden of Unity*. Toronto: Macmillan.

Atlantic Institute for Market Solutions 2002. (http://www.aims.ca)

Beauchamps, Patrick, Tim Dugas, and Frank L. Graves 1999. "Identity and national attachments in contemporary Canada." In Harvey Lazar and Tom McIntosh (eds.), *Canada: The State of the Federation 1998–9*. Kingston: Institute of Intergovernmental Relations.

Brodie, Janine 1997. "The new political economy of regions." In Wallace Clement (ed.), *Understanding Canada: Building on the New Canadian Political Economy*. Montreal and Kingston: McGill-Queen's University Press.

Buckley, Kenneth 1958. "The role of staple industries in Canada's economic development." *Journal of Economic History* 18 (December):439–450.

Cardoso, Fernando 1972. "Dependency and development in Latin America." *New Left Review* 74, 14 (July–August):83–95.

Carroll, William K. 2004. *Corporate Power in a Globalizing World: A Study in Elite Social Organization*. Don Mills, ON: Oxford University Press.

Clement, Wallace 1983. *Class, Power, and Poverty: Essays on Canadian Society*. Toronto: Methuen.

Courchene, Thomas 1986. "Avenues of adjustment: The transfer system and regional disparities." In Roger Savoie (ed.), *The Canadian Economy: A Regional Perspective*. Toronto: Methuen.

Courchene, Thomas 1994. *Social Canada in the Millennium: Reform Imperatives and Restructuring Principles*. Ottawa: Renouf Publishing.

Davis, A.K. 1971. "Canadian society and history as hinterland versus metropolis." In R.J. Ossenberg (ed.), *Canadian Society: Pluralism, Change and Conflict*. Scarborough, ON: Prentice Hall.

Drache, Daniel 1976. "Rediscovering Canadian political economy." *Journal of Canadian Studies* 11, 3 (August):3–18.

Economic Council of Canada 1977. *Living Together: A Study of Regional Disparities*. Ottawa: Supply and Services Canada.

Elias, Peter 1975. *Metropolis and Hinterland in Northern Manitoba*. Winnipeg: The Manitoba Museum of Man and Nature.

Forbes, Ernest 1977. "Misguided symmetry: The destruction of regional transportation policy for the Maritimes." In D.J. Bercusson (ed.), *Canada and the Burden of Unity*. Toronto: Macmillan.

Fowke, Vernon 1968. "Political economy and the Canadian wheat grower." In Norman Ward and Duff Spafford (eds.), *Politics in Saskatchewan*. Toronto: Longmans Canada.

Frank, Andre Gunder 1972. "Sociology of development and underdevelopment of sociology." In James Cockcroft et al. (eds.), *Dependence and Underdevelopment: Latin Americas Political Economy*. New York: Doubleday.

Friedman, Harriet, and Jack Wayne 1977. "Dependency theory: A critique." *Canadian Journal of Sociology* 2, 4 (Winter):399–416.

Gidengil, Elisabeth 1990. "Centres and peripheries: The political culture of dependency." *The Canadian Review of Sociology and Anthropology* 27, 1:23–48.

Graham, John R., Karen J. Swift, and Roger Delaney 2000. *Canadian Social Policy: An Introduction.* Scarborough, ON: Prentice Hall Allyn and Bacon.

Greig, Alastair, David Hulme, and Mark Turner 2007. *Challenging Global Inequality: Development Theory and Practice in the 21st Century.* New York: Palgrave MacMillan.

Henry, Shawn 2002. "Revisiting western alienation: Towards a better understanding of political alienation and political behaviour in western Canada." In Lisa Young and Keith Archer (eds.), *Regionalism and Party Politics in Canada.* Don Mills, ON: Oxford University Press.

Higgins, Benjamin 1986. "Regional development planning: The state of the art in North America." In Donald Savoie (ed.), *The Canadian Economy: A Regional Perspective.* Toronto: Methuen.

Higgins, Benjamin 1998. *Employment without Inflation.* New Brunswick, NJ: Transaction Publishers.

House, Douglas 1981. "Big oil and small communities in coastal Labrador: The local dynamics of dependency." *Canadian Review of Sociology and Anthropology* 18, 4 (November): 433–452.

Innis, Harold 1930. *The Fur Trade in Canada.* Toronto: University of Toronto Press.

Innis, Harold 1940. *The Cod Fisheries.* Toronto: University of Toronto Press.

Innis, Harold 1956. *Essays in Canadian Economic History.* Edited by Mary Q. Innis. Toronto: University of Toronto Press.

Keily, Ray 1998. *Industrialization and Development: A Comparative Analysis.* London: UCL Press.

Kellough, Gail 1980. "From colonialism to economic imperialism." In J. Harp and J. Hofley (eds.), *Structured Inequality in Canada.* Scarborough, ON: Prentice Hall.

Knuttila, K.M., and J.N. Mccrorie 1980. "National policy and prairie agrarian development: A reassessment." *Canadian Review of Sociology and Anthropology* 17, 3 (August):263–272.

Mackintosh, W.A. 1923. "Economic factors in Canadian history." *Canadian Historical Review* IV, 1 (March):12–25.

Mansell, Robert 1986. "Energy policy, prices and rents: Implications for regional growth and development." In William Coffey and Mario Polese (eds.), *Still Living Together: Recent Trends and Future Directions in Canadian Regional Development.* Montreal: The Institute for Research on Public Policy.

Marchak, Patricia 1985. "Canadian political economy." *Canadian Review of Sociology and Anthropology* 22, 5 (December):673–709.

Matthews, Ralph 1980. "The significance and explanation of regional differences in Canada: Towards a Canadian sociology." *Journal of Canadian Studies* 15, 2:43–61.

McDougall, John C. 2006. *Drifting Together: The Political Economy of Canada–U.S. Integration.* Peterborough, ON: Broadview Press.

Mendelson, Matthew 2003. *Quebecers' National Identities.* (http://www.queensu/cora/trends)

Polese, Mario 1987. "Patterns of regional economic development in Canada: Long term trends and issues." In William Coffey and Mario Polese (eds.), *Still Living Together: Recent Trends and Future Directions in Canadian Regional Development.* Montreal: The Institute for Research on Public Policy.

Preston, P.W. 1996. *Development Theory: An Introduction.* Oxford: Clarendon Press.

Savoie, Donald J. 2003. "Regional development: A policy for all seasons and all regions." In François Rocher and Miriam Smith (eds.), *New Trends in Canadian Federalism.* Peterborough, ON: Broadview Press.

Schwartz, Mildred A. 1974. *Politics and Territory: The Sociology of Regional Persistence in Canada.* Montreal and Kingston: McGill-Queen's University Press.

Scott, A.D. 1978. "Policy for Declining Regions: A Theoretical Approach." In H. Lithwick (ed.), *Regional Economic Policy: The Canadian Experience.* Toronto: McGraw-Hill Ryerson.

Semple, R. Keith 1987. "Regional analysis of corporate decision making within the Canadian economy." In William Coffey and Mario Polese (eds.), *Still Living Together: Recent Trends and Future Directions in Canadian Regional Development*. Montreal: The Institute for Research on Public Policy.

Simeon, Richard 2004. "Canada: Federalism, language, and regional conflict." In Ugo M. Amoretti and Nancy Bermeo (eds.), *Federalism and Territorial Cleavages*. Baltimore: The Johns Hopkins University Press.

Skogstad, Grace 2000. "Regional development policy." In Dietmar Braun (ed.), *Public Policy and Federalism*. Burlington, VT: Ashgate.

Statistics Canada 2005. "Study: Urban and provincial income disparities." *The Daily*. July 21.

Statistics Canada 2007. "Unemployment rates." Catalogue No. 71-001-XIE.

Stavenhagen, Rodolfo 1974. "The future of Latin America: Between underdevelopment and revolution." *Latin American Perspectives* 9, 1 (Spring):124–148.

Sutz, R. Arocena 2003. "Inequality and innovation as seen from the South" *Technology and Society* 25:171–182.

Transport Canada 2007. "Canada's Asia-Pacific Gateway and Corridor Initiative." (http://www.tc.gc.ca/majorissues/APGCI/menu.htm)

Young, Lisa, and Keith Archer (eds.) 2002. *Regionalism and Party Politics in Canada*. Don Mills, ON: Oxford University Press.

Wallerstein, I. 1982. "The rise and future demise of the world capitalist system: Concepts for comparative analysis." In H. Alavi and T. Shamin (eds.), *An Introduction to the Sociology of 'Developing Societies.'* Basingstoke, UK: Macmillan.

Watkins, Mel 1977. "The staple theory revisited." *Journal of Canadian Studies* 12 (Winter):83–95.

FURTHER REFERENCES— SECTION 3: ASCRIPTION AND SOCIAL INEQUALITY

Gender

Calliste, Agnes, and George Dei (eds., with the Assistance of Margarida Aguiar) 2000. *Power,*

Knowledge and Anti-Racism Education: A Critical Reader. Halifax: Fernwood. An examination of social spaces through the lens of an anti-racist feminist scholarship and practice.

Cossman, Brenda 1997. *Bad Attitudes on Trial: Pornography, Feminism, and the Butler Decision.* Toronto: University of Toronto Press. Legal battles over what is and what is not pornography are the focus of this collection. It raises key issues related to inequality and the legal system.

Nelson, Adie 2006. *Gender in Canada* (3rd ed.). Don Mills, ON: Pearson Education Canada. This text covers a broad range of topics in the area of gender studies, including theoretical perspectives on gender and discussions of such issues as sex-role socialization, gender and the family, women in the workplace, same-sex marriage, and transgenderism.

Policy Action Research List (PAR-L) (http://www.unb.ca/par-l/index.htm). An electronic network of individuals and organizations interested in women-centred policy issues in Canada. They maintain a good list of feminist resources.

Ross, Becki 1995. *The House That Jill Built: A Lesbian Nation in Formation.* Toronto: University of Toronto Press. A historical account of the rise of the lesbian movement in Canada.

Statistics Canada 2006. *Women in Canada 2005: A Gender-Based Statistical Report* (5th ed.). Ottawa: Statistics Canada. Available free online at http://www.statcan.ca/english/freepub/89-503-XIE/0010589-503-XIE.pdf.

Status of Women in Canada. (http://www.swc-cfc.gc.ca/). Status of Women Canada (SWC) is the federal government agency that promotes gender equality and the full participation of women in the economic, social, cultural, and political life of the country. SWC focuses its work in three areas: improving women's economic autonomy and well-being, eliminating systemic violence against women and children, and advancing women's human rights.

Warner, Tom 2002. *Never Going Back: A History of Queer Activism in Canada.* Toronto: University of Toronto Press. Using interviews and archival material, the author presents a history of gay and lesbian liberation in a Canadian context.

Young, Lisa 2000. *Feminists and Party Politics.* Vancouver: University of British Columbia

Press. This book examines the effort to bring feminism into the formal political arena through established political parties in Canada and the United States.

Ethnicity, Race, and Ancestry

Assembly of First Nations 2007 (http://www. afn.ca/). This website promotes co-operation between First Nations peoples and the people of Canada.

Banting, Keith, Thomas Courchene, and F. Leslie Seidle (eds.) 2007. *Belonging? Diversity, Recognition, and Shared Citizenship in Canada*. Montreal: Institute for Research on Public Policy. This collection of studies explores approaches to understanding and accommodating ethnic differences and cultural diversity in Canadian society. Some papers assess the sense of belonging that citizens feel and express, and how this may be related to their ethnic and racial backgrounds. Some analyses also consider the approaches that other countries have applied when addressing this important question.

Breton, Raymond 2005. *Ethnic Relations in Canada: Institutional Dynamics*. Edited and with an introduction by Jeffrey Reitz. Montreal and Kingston: McGill-Queen's University Press. This collection of works by Raymond Breton covers a wide array of important theoretical and empirical studies of ethnic inequality in Canada. Special attention is given to the topics of French–English relations, the Quebec independence movement, linguistic cleavages in Canada, multiculturalism, and ethnic political and community organization.

Canadian Race Relations Foundation 2007 (http:// www.crr.ca/). This organization provides a national framework for fighting racism.

Elliott, Jean Leonard, and Augie Fleras 2007. *Unequal Relations* (5th ed.). Toronto: Pearson Prentice Hall Canada. This source offers a useful introduction to patterns of racial and ethnic group inequalities and racial/ethnic group relations in Canada.

First Nations Statistics (http://www.firststats.ca/ home.asp). The First Nations Statistical Institute (FNSI) is a not-for-profit statistical service organization dedicated to putting First Nations information to use. At the time of writing it is not yet operational but would

be a worthwhile link to monitor for future reference.

Frideres, James, and René Gadacz 2007. *Aboriginal Peoples in Canada: Contemporary Conflicts* (7th ed). Toronto: Pearson Prentice Hall. This book assesses both historical and contemporary issues pertaining to social inequality among Canada's Aboriginal peoples. Related topics include the problem of land claims, government policy toward native peoples, and the prospects for Aboriginal self-determination.

Kalbach, Madeline A., and Warren E. Kalbach (eds.) 2000. *Perspectives on Ethnicity in Canada: A Reader*. Toronto: Harcourt Canada. This classic collection looks at a diverse set of issues in the study of ethnicity, including the definition of ethnicity and race, changes in the ethnic composition and identity of the Canadian population, and problems of inequality, prejudice, and discrimination.

Li, Peter S. 2003. *Destination Canada: Immigration Debates and Issues*. Don Mills, ON: Oxford University Press. This volume offers a critical analysis of contemporary immigration issues, as well as providing extensive information on patterns of immigration in Canada over time, the economic benefits of immigration, and the socio-economic backgrounds and attainments of immigrant groups.

Maaka, Roger, and Augie Fleras 2005. *The Politics of Indigeneity: Challenging the State in Canada and Aotearoa New Zealand*. Dunedin, NZ: University of Otaga Press. This book compares the problems of inequality and injustice faced by indigenous peoples in Canada and New Zealand, and considers the potential solutions to these problems through political action and the pursuit of Aboriginal self-government.

Satzewitch, Vic, and Nikolaos Liodakis 2007. *"Race" and Ethnicity in Canada: A Critical Introduction*. Don Mills, ON: Oxford University Press. This text begins with a review of theoretical perspectives on the concepts of ethnicity and race, and then considers a number of important aspects of ethnic and racial inequality in Canada. These include French–English relations, multiculturalism, the inequalities faced by Aboriginal peoples, the role of immigration, and the general problem of racism.

Statistics Canada 2008. Census 2006 Release No. 5: Tuesday, January 15, 2008. Aboriginal peoples (http://www12.statcan.ca/english/census06/). Topic-based census data from the 2006 Census.

Age

Children and Youth (http://www.hrdc-drhc.gc.ca/menu/youth_child.shtml). Links to Human Resources Development Canada's and other government child and youth programs, services, and research.

Division of Aging and Seniors (http://www.hc-sc.gc.ca/seniors-aines). A site supported by Health Canada devoted to issues of seniors and aging.

Gee, Ellen M., and Gloria M. Gutman (eds.) 2000. *The Overselling of Population Aging: Apocalyptic Demography, Intergenerational Challenges, and Social Policy.* Toronto: Oxford University Press. A collection of papers dealing with implications of population aging.

Health Canada 2002. *Canada's Aging Population.* Ottawa: Minister of Public Works and Government Services. A reflection on the impact of aging on Canada.

McMullin, Julie 2004. *Understanding Social Inequality: Intersections of Class, Age, Gender, Ethnicity, and Race in Canada.* Don Mills, ON: Oxford University Press. In this analysis, the author explores how various forms of social inequality, including age, class, gender, race, and ethnicity, all intersect and simultaneously shape the power structure, the ideological system, and the distribution of resources in Canada.

Novak, Mark W., and Lori Campbell 2001. *Aging and Society: A Canadian Perspective* (4th ed.). Toronto: Nelson Canada. A recent state-of-the-art treatment of aging in Canadian society.

Social and Economic Dimensions of an Aging Population 2007. (http://socserv.socsci.mcmaster.ca/sedap/). Papers on aging from a Canadian multi-disciplinary research program.

Region

Amoretti, Ugo, and Nancy Bermeo (eds.) 2004. *Federalism and Territorial Cleavages.* Baltimore: The Johns Hopkins University Press. This edited volume examines issues of federalism and regionalism in a comparative perspective. Case studies of advanced industrial democracies as well as developing democracies contextualize the Canadian experience.

Barry, Donald, and Ronald C. Keith (eds.) 1999. *Regionalism, Multilateralism and the Politics of Global Trade.* Vancouver: UBC Press. This book analyzes the relationship between regionalism and globalism. A discussion of regional issues in other countries, as well as interregional relationships, is offered. This text also examines the Canadian government's various responses to regionalism.

Braun, Dietmar (ed.) 2000. *Public Policy and Federalism.* Burlington, VT: Ashgate. The third chapter of this book, by Grace Skogstad, offers an overview of Canadian regional development policy.

Canadian Institute for Research on Regional Development (http://www.umoncton.ca/icrpap/index_icrdr.html). The mandate of this non-profit organization is to promote informed public debate on regional development and disseminate objective analyses and information on the subject. Its main focus is the Maritime region.

Clarke, Harold, Allan Kornberg, and Peter Wearing 2000. *A Polity on the Edge: Canada and the Politics of Fragmentation.* Peterborough, ON: Broadview Press. This book provides a discussion of six critical events in Canadian politics from the 1988 federal election to the 1998 re-election of the Parti Québécois. It provides an interesting examination of regional issues in relation to Canadian politics and considers the impact of these events for regional politics in Canada.

Clement, Wallace (ed.) 1997. *Understanding Canada: Building on the New Canadian Political Economy.* Montreal and Kingston: McGill-Queen's University Press. The chapter by Brodie provides an excellent overview of the issues surrounding regionalism in Canada. She examines the bases of regionalism and provides an overview of the national policies that deal with these issues.

Poshmann, Finn 1998. "Where the money goes: The distribution of taxes and benefits in Canada." *C.D. Howe Institute Commentary* 105 (April). This paper provides an analysis of federal transfers to individual and regions and a discussion of various specific types of transfers, such as education and health.

Rocher, Francois, and Miriam Smith (eds.) 2003. *New Trends in Canadian Federalism* (2nd ed.). Peterborough, ON: Broadview Press. This edited volume explores a variety of contemporary issues surrounding Canadian federalism, including constitutional development, political identity, and public policy.

Savoie, Donald 2000. *Community Economic Development in Atlantic Canada: False Hope or Panacea?* National Library of Canada: The Canadian Institute for Research on Regional Development. This book provides a discussion of past efforts in community economic development in Atlantic Canada from the 1960s through the 1990s. Case studies are used to illustrate particular development policies.

Stevenson, Garth 2004. *Unfulfilled Union: Canadian Federalism and National Unity.* Montreal and Kingston: McGill-Queen's University Press. In this book, Stevenson examines a variety of issues relating to Canadian federalism, including the origins of the Canadian confederation, fiscal federalism, and federal–provincial conflicts.

Young, Lisa, and Keith Archer (eds.) 2002. *Regionalism and Party Politics in Canada.* Don Mills, ON: Oxford. This text offers an examination of overall theoretical approaches to the study of regionalism as well as a discussion of the contemporary Canadian party system as it relates to regional issues.

Some Consequences
of Social Inequality

The preceding three sections have described this country's main patterns of social inequality with respect to social class, income/occupation/education, and social ascription. Also, various interpretations have been offered for the patterns of inequality. Further, some of the *effects* or *consequences* of social inequality received considerable attention, especially the ways in which the struggles between classes and between elites have resulted in certain social trends. For example, all of the selections in Section 1, particularly those by Grabb and Hwang, Brym, and Carroll, suggest how the economic structure of this country has changed as a result of both the interplay between capitalists and the state elite and the struggle between classes. The same is true of several selections in other sections (e.g., Urmetzer and Guppy's chapter on income, and Creese and Beagan's analysis of gender relations). It is difficult to describe Canada's unequal class and elite relations without spelling out how aspects of history have been determined by them.

There is a second important type of consequence of social inequality, though, that was not featured in Sections 1, 2, or 3. This concerns the *consequences for the experiences of individuals*, which flow from the many different forms of social inequality. Here the focus is on how the day-to-day living of Canadians is affected, as opposed to how the society is changing or not changing with time. In this instance, *consequences* refer to any aspects of the experiences of individuals that are influenced by differences in social inequality, including people's life chances, beliefs, and patterns of behaviour.

Our purpose in Section 4 is to portray this second type of consequence. There are a vast number of such consequences, because social inequality touches so many aspects of people's lives. Thus, the six selections in this section do not provide the last word on the consequences of social inequality, but do serve as enlightening examples. To suggest how broad the range of consequences of social inequality for individuals can be, we can recall the views of Hans Gerth and C. Wright Mills (1953:313), who wrote that they "include everything from the chance to stay alive during the first year after birth, to the chance to view fine arts, the chance to remain healthy and grow tall, and if sick to get well again quickly, the chance to avoid becoming a juvenile delinquent . . . and . . . the chance to complete a university or higher educational grade." These observations are no less true for Canadian society now than they were for the United States when they were written so many years ago.

The selections here are limited to three categories of consequences of social inequality: (1) people's differences in *life chances*; (2) their differences in *ways of thinking* concerning social inequality; and (3) their differences in *lifestyle and orientation to social interaction*.

We shall first deal with the issue of differences in *life chances*. We start with an aspect of life chances that involves the toughest of definitions: that of health and life expectancy. This is "toughest" in the sense that good health and continued life are among the prized possessions in Canadian society, and undoubtedly *the* most prized possession for many Canadians. Hence, the criterion of good health/life expectancy provides us with a strong test of our society's system of inequality.

The first selection in this section, by Gerry Veenstra, offers an extensive review of recent evidence on the effects that various forms of social inequality have on the health of Canadians. His analysis shows that, to varying degrees, social class, gender, race, and sexual orientation are all significant predictors of a broad range of health outcomes and life chances. These include life expectancy, incidence of chronic disease, and self-reported health, among others. The chapter also considers possible explanations for how and why social inequality has such a consistent impact on health in Canada.

The next selection in this section asks us to consider another serious problem of life chances. The author, Tracy Peressini, reminds us that most people take for granted certain basic comforts of life—a roof over their heads and three meals per day—even if they are quite poor. Peressini emphasizes that a small but growing category of Canadians does not have access to these life comforts. The author reviews attempts to estimate the number of homeless people in this country, and discusses what we know about their social background, personal characteristics, and life circumstances. Also discussed are explanations of how people arrive at the dismal circumstance of homelessness. Explanations for homelessness vary from social structural reasons to individual-level factors. Each avenue of explanation accounts for some but not all cases of homelessness. Whatever the appropriate explanation for particular people, the homeless almost always end up being very poor and unable to afford housing. Peressini goes on to discuss public policy, emphasizing that the major problem of affordable housing is left largely in local municipal or provincial hands, and is not a federal government responsibility. Thus, there have been few sustained, country-wide initiatives directed at the problem.

The second type of consequence of social inequality addressed in this section has to do with differences in *ways of thinking*. Here we could start by recalling Karl Marx's famous observation that it is not the consciousness of men that determines their being, but rather their social being, primarily their location in the class structure, that determines their consciousness. We can ask to what extent this view is correct for

Canada today. Are the different social classes and social status groups aware of their differences? Do individuals try to safeguard or promote their class or group interests? Going further, we can ask whether the different classes and status groups develop still other differences in beliefs and behaviour over time.

Questions of this type, designed to probe the degree and extent of class and status consciousness, or common thinking by classes and strata, raise problems of great significance for understanding the dynamic aspect of Canada's structure of social inequality. For example, a class consciousness based on common interests has existed at many times and places, and has at times led to organized class action and class struggles that changed the whole structure of societies (see, e.g., the discussions in the selections by Conley and Brym in Section 1). However, class consciousness does not follow automatically from objective class differences. People may have a class position that differs markedly from that of others without being particularly aware of this difference. Thinking and conduct are not determined merely by objective position in the economic or social order, but also depend in part on the way in which people perceive and interpret their social circumstances. For example, socialization through the education system and the media probably has an effect on people's thinking about their class or status position and its meaning. Also, a person has, simultaneously, the experiences of a class position, a level of education achieved, an occupation, a certain level of income, an ethnic or racial status, a gender, and an age group. It is sometimes difficult to know which of these sets of experiences will most influence the person's perceptions of social inequality.

The third selection in Section 4, by Edward Grabb and Monica Hwang, provides recent evidence concerning people's beliefs about inequality and how these beliefs are related to the social statuses or social backgrounds of Canadians. The analyses show that Canadians tend toward an "individualistic" view on issues of inequality, with the average person accepting such ideas as the positive effects of competition, the need for people to take responsibility for themselves, and the fairness of income differences based on individual performance or effort. There is some support for the conclusion that more advantaged people, including those with higher income and higher occupational status, are more likely to hold such beliefs. However, these effects are not strong, and suggest that people's social backgrounds have at most a limited impact on whether they subscribe to the individualistic perspective on inequality that tends to dominate in Canadian society.

The third category of consequences of social inequality explored in this section has to do with *effects upon lifestyles and social interaction*. The selection by Robert Andersen and Scott Milligan examines one aspect of this important issue. They assess the relationship between social inequality and the level of acceptance or intolerance that people have toward certain groups in society. More specifically, the authors consider recent Canadian survey data to see whether people who are in deprived or disadvantaged circumstances, as judged by such measures as income, occupation, education, race, gender, and region, are more or less willing to have as their neighbours individuals from three designated groups: homosexuals, immigrants, and people with a different racial background. Their findings are especially relevant for assessing some claims in the literature that people of lower- or working-class background are less tolerant of so-called "outgroups" than are other people. Their research also reveals interesting patterns over time within Canada and shows how the Canadian level of tolerance toward the three groups compares with that found in 30 other countries.

The next selection, by James Curtis, Edward Grabb, Tom Perks, and Tina Chui, considers the potentially important linkages between different forms of social inequality, on the one hand, and the motivation or capacity of people to engage in political and community activity, on the other hand. The authors ask whether Canadians who are higher in regard to various social statuses—majority versus minority ethnic group members, immigrants versus non-immigrants, middle-aged versus the young and old, men versus women, those with high education versus those low in education, those with higher versus lower incomes, and so on—are also higher in involvement in political and associational behaviour. Contrary to the view that there is full openness regarding political participation, people's social statuses were sometimes found to be related to forms of political involvement. The "haves" were sometimes more involved than others, but this was not always the case, and the patterns often were not strong. The authors emphasize that socio-economic status and ascriptive social statuses are stronger predictors of other more intensive forms of political activity, such as running for and achieving political office. That is, while the "mass" political activities are structured in only a modest way by social status, there is evidence of a more marked degree of inequality for achieving higher levels of political power.

The final chapter, by Neil Guppy and Scott Davies, looks at another important consequence of social inequality in Canada. The specific focus of this selection is on the structure of the Canadian education system and the traditional inclusion of the long summer vacation break in the organization of the standard school calendar. Guppy and Davies show how the school calendar can have an unexpected and systematically different effect on the educational success or failure of students from lower- and higher-class backgrounds. This effect provides us with an excellent example of the surprising, and often hidden, consequences that social structures can impose on individuals who occupy different locations in the system of social inequality.

REFERENCES

Gerth, Hans, and C. Wright Mills 1953. *Character and Social Structure: The Social Psychology of Social Institutions.* New York: Harcourt Brace and World.

chapter twenty-three

Social Inequality and Health

Gerry Veenstra
(An original chapter written
for this volume.)

INTRODUCTION

Social inequality in its various forms can have a multitude of detrimental effects on people's lives. Such inequalities can potentially influence a host of important life chances, including the probability of obtaining a university degree, getting a good job, adopting a child, or being victimized by crime. The purpose of this chapter is to explore the degree to which social inequalities in Canada affect one of the most fundamental life chances of all: people's health. The main focus of the analysis is the relationship between gender, race, social class, and sexual orientation, on the one hand, and a range of significant health outcomes, on the other

hand. The discussion deals with a variety of arguments and explanations that populate the social determinants of health literature, and offers an indication of the degree to which health researchers have provided sound empirical evidence to assess these arguments and explanations.

The first section of the chapter describes associations between gender and health in Canada, delineating historical gender differences in life expectancy and contemporary gender differences in mortality and in various dimensions of physical and mental health (morbidity). The next section describes associations between race and health. Experiences of interpersonal and institutionalized racism, as well as the potentially intervening effects of social class and cultural differences in lifestyle practices, are particularly relevant to these associations. A description of the strong association between social class and health comes next, accompanied by explanations that address material, psychosocial, and behavioural factors. The final section of the chapter describes some of the health effects of sexual orientation, effects that may be at least partly explained by the presence of homophobia and heterosexism in Canadian society. While the gender-health and class-health associations have been extensively researched in Canada, less conclusive work has been done to date on the effects of race and sexual orientation in this country. As a result, the race and sexuality sections of this chapter are more speculative than definitive.

GENDER AND HEALTH

Before the advent of industrial capitalism, Canadian men and women had very similar life expectancies (Clarke 2000). As recently as 1921, life expectancy was 60.6 years for women and 58.4 years for men, a difference of only 2.2 years. By the 1950s, the gender gap had widened to about 4.5 years in favour of women. By 1996, life expectancy was 81.4 years for women and 75.7 years for men, representing a major improvement in length of life for all Canadians over the preceding 75-year period, but with a resulting gender gap in life expectancy of 5.7 years. The gender gap subsequently narrowed a little to 5.3 years as of 2000 (Trovato and Nirannanilathu 2007). At present, Canadian women clearly hold the edge over Canadian men when it comes to length of life.

Among causes of death, the rank ordering for the top 15 causes, as reported in Canadian health statistics in 1997, was almost the same for men and women. This pattern suggests that men and women are dying for largely the same reasons. However, for 14 of these causes of death, the age-standardized mortality rate for men

was higher than the corresponding rate for women. Only for mortality from psychoses was the rate marginally higher for women. In particular, the cancer, cardiovascular disease, unintentional injuries, and suicide mortality rates were much higher for men than for women. Trovato and Nirannanilathu (2007) showed that death from heart disease was the major contributor to the gender gap in life expectancy in 2000, followed by other cancers, accidents/violence, and lung cancer. Other circulatory diseases, breast cancer, prostate cancer, cirrhosis of the liver, and suicide made substantially smaller contributions to gender differences in mortality. In regard to unintentional injuries, motor vehicle accidents were especially important in accounting for higher mortality among men—especially young men—than among women (Segall and Chappell 2000). During the teenage and young adult years, young men are much more likely than young women to die as the result of an accident, and even elderly men are more likely than elderly women to die from accidents due to falls, poisoning, drowning, choking, guns, or electrocution (Clarke 2000). Throughout the past century the large majority of deaths in the workplace were male deaths. In short, men appear to be more likely than women to die from nearly all of the major causes of death.

Various explanations have been posed to account for these gendered health inequalities. The "social acceptability" hypothesis suggests that women are more willing to accept the sick role than are men, by admitting sickness to others and accepting help from friends, family, and the health care system (Gee and Kimball 1987). Women may also be more attentive to bodily sensations, more willing to talk about them, and more likely to seek care for each episode of an illness. A greater attention to minor signs and symptoms and a greater willingness to take preventive and healing actions may mean that health problems for women are less severe than for men of the same age (Clarke 2004).

Alternatively, the "risk" hypothesis suggests that men are socialized to engage in risky behaviours such as hang-gliding, drinking and driving, and so forth. One U.S. government project concluded that the prevalence of risk behaviours among adults was more common among men than among women for all but 3 of the 14 risk behaviours studied. Some of these behaviours included smoking, drinking and driving, failing to use safety belts, not getting health screenings, and not being aware of medical conditions (Powell-Griner et al. 1997). A related explanation, the "healthy behaviours" argument, asserts that women are more likely than men to engage in healthful behaviours and lifestyles (Courtenay 2000). For example, women may be more likely to exercise, to control their weight, and to consume vitamin and mineral supplements. All of the explanations noted above are implicitly embedded in theories of masculinity and femininity, and essentially argue that adherence to popular norms of hegemonic masculinity and femininity is lethal for men's health and beneficial for women's health.

Although the gender and mortality storyline in Canada suggests that males are more at risk than females, the gender and morbidity storyline is quite different. For example, based on data from the National Population Health Survey (NPHS) of 1994–95, Denton et al. (2004) reported significantly poorer health scores for Canadian women with regard to distress, self-rated health, functional health, and the presence of a chronic condition. McDonough and Walters (2001) used data from the 1994–95 NPHS and also showed more distress and chronic conditions among women. Similarly, Janzen and Muhajarine (2003) analyzed data from the 1994–95 and 1996–97 waves of the NPHS to demonstrate poorer self-rated health and chronic conditions scores

for women; the second of these associations persisted after stratifying the sample by age. Veenstra's (2007) analysis of data from the Canadian Community Health Survey of 2003 also showed a slightly higher risk of reporting fair or poor self-rated health for women than for men, after controlling for age, although a second measure of health in that study, hypertension, was not significantly associated with gender.

Overall, then, the empirical evidence is consistent in showing that Canadian women tend to be more likely than Canadian men to report psychological distress, poor self-rated health, and the presence of a chronic condition. Various theories from the sociological literature on health inequalities have been employed to explain such gender differences in health. For instance, the "multiple roles" hypothesis suggests that, among women, taking on numerous duties (e.g., as parent, employee, sibling, caretaker, secretary for the choir) can result in role overload, role conflict, and excessive demands on time and energy that can contribute to higher levels of psychological distress and poorer physical health (Waldron et al. 1998). Similarly, the "nurturant" hypothesis suggests that women may experience more ill health than men due to excessive primary caregiver responsibilities, which typically fall to women in a patriarchal society. Providing care for others can lead to role strain, along with stress and time constraints that can lead women to neglect their own health needs (Segall and Chappell 2000).

Proponents of another hypothesis, the "socio-economic status" argument, claim that men tend to rank higher than women on measures of socio-economic status, such as income and occupational prestige, with subsequent negative effects for women's health. The reasons for such socio-economic differences are structural in nature and pertain to the history of patriarchy in Canada and elsewhere. Evidence indicates, for example, that women are not always rewarded in the marketplace for doing the same work as men; women often confront a "glass ceiling" that limits the status they can attain in a given organization; traditional "male" occupations tend to be of higher status than traditional "female" occupations; and so on. Women are also more likely to work at part-time jobs without benefits and opportunities for advancement and in jobs with less control over their hours of work and their own duties. In light of the strong evidence for associations between socio-economic status and health in Canada, which are described later in this chapter, it is reasonable to conclude that gender differences in socio-economic status may at least partly explain gender differences in health.

Another hypothesis focuses on the "biased nature of medical research" argument. It suggests that women's health may tend to be worse than men's because much medical research has stemmed from male researchers studying male subjects. In previous generations, women's bodies were assumed to be similar to men's bodies but harder to research because of the additional complications introduced by menstruation, menopause, and pregnancy. Consequently, women have been traditionally under-studied in medical research, with treatments being developed for men that may not always apply to women.

Finally, there is the "under-reporting" hypothesis, which asserts that in many household surveys women are more likely to speak for the household as a whole than are men, which means that the morbidity characteristics of men are often under-reported (Clarke 2000). Prevalent norms of masculinity may also make men less likely to record for themselves the presence of an illness and/or report an illness to a survey researcher. The under-reporting explanation essentially suggests that survey data sometimes provide an inaccurate portrayal of health among men, and that what may appear to be poorer health scores for women are not the case in reality.

Not all of these explanations have been subject to rigorous empirical investigation based on nationally representative Canadian data. Veenstra (2007) showed a reduction in the effect of gender on self-rated health after controlling for educational attainment and household income, suggesting that socio-economic status may mediate this gender-health association. Denton et al. (2004) explored the degree to which various influences mediate the association between gender and health. These influences included structural factors (e.g., living alone, being a single parent, being of low income, working double days, and working in lower-status occupations), behavioural factors (e.g., smoking, drinking, and being obese), and psychosocial factors (e.g., stressful life events, childhood trauma, chronic stress in life domains, self-esteem, mastery, and coherence). While some of these factors did help to account for the association between gender and self-rated health, most of the gender differences in functional health, distress, or chronic conditions were not explained by them. McDonough and Walters (2001) engaged in a similar investigation and concluded that differential exposure to stressors played a small role in explaining gender differences in psychological distress, but had no effect on gender differences in self-rated health or chronic conditions. Finally, using the NPHS dataset, Janzen and Muhajarine (2003) sought to determine whether "breadth" of social role occupancy differentially affected the health of men and women. That is, these authors considered whether single, double, or triple role occupancy (involving various combinations of being married, having children at home, and working in the labour market) accounted for gender differences in health. The researchers found, however, that men were more likely than women to hold *both* single *and* triple roles, so that the role overload hypothesis could not be substantiated in their analysis.

In summary, Canadian research based on nationally representative data reveals a somewhat higher risk of some forms of mental and physical illness for women than for men. In contrast, studies pertaining to mortality indicate the existence of higher death rates for men than for women for nearly every major cause of death. Most of the explanations for gender differences in the health determinants literature have not yet been conclusively validated in the Canadian context. Nevertheless, theoretical perspectives that focus on contemporary manifestations of norms of masculinity and femininity seem especially promising.

RACE AND HEALTH

Race is a social and political construct that has been used to distinguish among people on the basis of pheno-typical (visible) physical characteristics such as skin colour and facial structure. The word *race* appeared in the English language in the early seventeenth century, but it was not until the eighteenth century that it began to be used in Europe and North America as a way to name and explain differences between human populations. In the nineteenth century, there were generally thought to be three broad racial categories: Caucasians, Mongoloids, and Negroids. It turns out that the physical features that were used to distinguish these racial categories do not correlate well with geno-typical differences (differences in genetic makeup), nor are there sizable systematic differences among these categories in regard to personality, intelligence, and so forth. Race has therefore proved to be an extremely poor scientific construct. As a result, the term *race* is often placed in quotation marks by sociologists in order to draw explicit attention to this problematic and to make it clear that racial groupings are inherently social, rather than biological, constructions.

How might "race" influence the health of Canadians? Individuals who do not belong to the economically and politically ascendant group of a society—in Canada, the ascendant group is whites of Western European descent—often possess discernible characteristics, such as language and dress, that more or less clearly locate them within a minority racial group and thus can lead to experiences of racism. Racist experiences can affect health directly via the negative physical and psychological consequences of the interpersonal racial discrimination incurred during the course of everyday life. Racial oppression can become internalized in the mind and self, damaging self-esteem and potentially compromising and reducing the amount of social support available. Health can also be affected in indirect fashion via processes of institutional racism, whereby minority groups who are identified and defined as biologically and culturally different are systematically excluded from certain social, political, and economic worlds (Karlsen and Nazroo 2002). In short, racism can influence how people are treated in many aspects of their lives, limiting their job, educational, recreational, marital, and family choices and chances. All of these experiences and restrictions have the potential to affect health. Unfortunately, explanations predicated on the occurrence of either interpersonal or institutional racism are not easily verified empirically. There are inherent difficulties in recording experiences of discrimination that are not always recognized as such by survey respondents.

Another explanation for an association between race and health is the well-known "immigrant health effect," which refers to the tendency for many immigrants who arrive in Canada with excellent health to experience a decline toward the national health average over time (Dunn and Dyck 2000; Newbold 2005; Newbold and Danforth 2003). McDonald and Kennedy (2005) have speculated that the initial good health of immigrants is attributable to their healthier behaviours in the home country, health screening by immigration officers, and immigrant self-selection, whereby the healthiest and wealthiest are most likely to migrate. However, many immigrants see their health scores decline because of their subsequent adoption of Canadian behaviours related to diet and exercise, increased exposure to common environmental factors, under-reporting of chronic conditions by recent immigrants, and persistent language, cultural, and economic barriers to the use of health services. To the degree that some racial groups are more likely than others to be composed of recent immigrants to Canada, the immigrant health effect may contribute to explaining racial differences in health. Other explanations for racial differences in health focus on cultural variations in dietary practices and certain health behaviours; these factors may influence health but are not necessarily predicated on racism and experiences of discrimination. The latter explanations are relatively easy to test empirically, due to the numerous indicators measuring immigration history and lifestyle practices available in many nationally representative survey datasets.

Even so, the body of existing research on race and health in Canada is not large (Clarke 2004). With respect to mortality differences in Canada by race, Sheth et al. (1999) examined total and cause-specific mortality from cardiovascular disease and cancer among Canadians from European, South Asian, and Chinese backgrounds, using data on age-standardized mortality rates from 1979 to 1993 for people aged 35 to 74. Mortality from ischemic heart disease was highest among South Asians and Europeans and lowest among Chinese. Mortality from cancer was highest for Europeans, intermediate for Chinese, and lowest among South Asians, while mortality from diabetes was highest for South Asians and lowest for Chinese, and mortality from chronic obstructive pulmonary disease was highest for Europeans.

Mortality rates from all causes combined were highest for Europeans, intermediate for South Asians, and lowest for Chinese. Lower rates for South Asians were primarily due to lower death rates from cancer, while lower rates for Chinese were primarily due to lower death rates from ischemic heart disease. In short, most mortality rates were *highest* for European Canadians, suggesting that race-health explanations pertaining to cultural differences in lifestyles or the immigrant health effect may be more relevant here than are explanations founded on racism and discrimination. Unfortunately, Sheth et al. (1999) were unable to explain their findings because of the lack of suitable data at their disposal.

A substantial body of other mortality research has demonstrated the health circumstances of First Nations people in Canada. Shah (2004) notes that life expectancy in 2000 for Aboriginal peoples—Status Indians, non-Status Indians, Metis, and Inuit—was 68.9 years for males (versus 76.3 years for Canadian males) and 76.3 years for females (versus 81.5 years for Canadian females). The deficits in length of life between Aboriginals and other Canadians were somewhat narrower than they had been in previous decades but were still substantial. As for specific causes of death, data for 1996 indicated that First Nations and Inuit people were 6.5 times more likely than the total Canadian population to die from injuries or poison, while evidence from 1994 showed that the suicide rate for Aboriginals aged 15 to 24 was eight times higher than that of any other group of Canadian youth (Shah 2004). Deaths from diabetes among Aboriginal peoples are also especially high in comparison with the Canadian population (Young et al. 2000). It is apparent that life expectancies for First Nations peoples are among the very lowest of all racial groups in Canada.

In regard to racial differences in morbidity, Veenstra (2007) used data from the Canadian Community Health Survey of 2003 to describe higher risks of fair/poor self-rated health for East Asians and Aboriginals relative to whites, and higher risks of high blood pressure for blacks and Aboriginals relative to whites, after controlling for age and immigrant status. He found that socio-economic status, as measured by educational attainment and household income, mediated some of the association between Aboriginal affiliation and the two health indicators. These findings suggest that social and economic inequities pertaining to education, employment, and poverty may explain a significant portion of the health differential faced by Aboriginal peoples in Canada.

Wu et al. (2003) used data from the National Population Health Survey of 1996–97 to predict depression. They found that, compared with English Canadians, respondents in the Chinese, East Asian, and Southeast Asian groups showed lower levels of depression, while respondents in the Aboriginal, French Canadian, Jewish, and "other white" categories experienced higher levels. The researchers also found that socio-economic status and social resources (in the form of various types of social support) did *not* mediate the association between racial/ethnic affiliation and depression. Marital status did mediate the association, however, with non-English Canadians being more likely to be unmarried. The authors speculated that marital relationships are a rich source of emotional and instrumental support and that these relationships tend to encourage good health care practices and oblige individuals to refrain from engaging in health-damaging behaviours. Again using the 1996–97 NPHS, Wu and Schimmele (2005) compared the worse functional health scores of Aboriginals, Arabs, West Asians, and "mixed-race" Canadians, as well as the worse self-rated health scores of Aboriginals, to the national average. When health behavioural and socio-economic status factors were controlled, only the functional health disadvantage experienced by Arabic and West Asian Canadians disappeared, suggesting that socio-economic status and health behaviours do not explain the majority of the race-health associations identified in their analyses.

To assess the immigrant health effect, Kobayashi (2003) used data from the 1996–97 NPHS, and found that Asian-born Canadians were less likely than native-born Canadians to report the presence of a chronic condition. Similarly, using 1994–95 data from the NPHS, Wang et al. (2000) found that the risk of arthritis was significantly lower among Asian immigrants than North American–born Canadians, after controlling for age, gender, socio-economic variables, and the body mass index.

In summary, data on mortality rates and life expectancy indicate that Aboriginals in Canada suffer higher mortality rates than virtually all other Canadians, and that Chinese and South Asian Canadians appear to have comparatively low mortality rates from major causes of death, such as cancer, ischemic heart disease, and chronic obstructive pulmonary disease. Research on morbidity again demonstrates exceptionally poor health outcomes for Aboriginal peoples, and shows that this result is at least partly explained by socio-economic factors. Studies also reveal better health scores for Canadians from some Asian backgrounds, although this pattern may or may not persist above and beyond the healthy immigrant effect. In general, then, explanations for the race-health effect that point to class differentials and experiences of racism or discrimination seem especially pertinent to Aboriginal health in Canada. However, explanations predicated on cultural differences in lifestyle practices and on the immigrant health effect seem more pertinent for understanding the relatively good health of members of other ethnic or racial minority populations.

SOCIAL CLASS
AND HEALTH

Health research that uses the idea of social class, especially as conceived within the classical Marxist and Weberian sociological traditions (Marx and Engels 1970, 1976; Weber 1968), is well developed in European nations such as the United Kingdom. However, no nationally representative study in the United States or Canada has used such conceptions of social class when assessing health patterns. Instead, virtually all of the North American research on social class and health has relied on socio-economic status measures (especially income, education, and occupation) in place of social class, and has used the terms *social class* and *socio-economic status* interchangeably. Socio-economic status indicators like income, education, and occupation are typically employed as continuously graded scales that serve to stratify individuals rather than groups (see, e.g., Grabb 2007). Education, as measured by highest educational level attained or number of years of education, is the most common indicator of socio-economic status in the health literature, in part because measures of education are easy to collect and because, beyond a certain age, formal educational credentials generally remain constant. Education also has a relatively low refusal rate on questionnaires (Liberatos et al. 1988). Annual income or wealth is also used frequently in health research, although these variables are far more difficult to measure. For example, questions about income have a high refusal rate on questionnaires (Liberatos et al. 1988) and income or wealth can be unstable over the life course (Benzeval and Judge 2001).

It is apparent that socio-economic status and social class should be clearly differentiated from one another, both conceptually and empirically, because they can manifest distinct, though often interrelated, associations with health. Since class relations

privilege some groups in the labour market and then reward the members of these groups and their families with better incomes, greater opportunities for educational attainment, and/or jobs with higher prestige, socio-economic status likely intervenes between class position and health. However, to the extent that class relations influence the health of the members of some class groupings by pathways other than the accumulation of socio-economic resources, then class position and socio-economic status will be distinct determinants of health. Unfortunately, the degree to which social class and socio-economic status are distinct and complementary determinants of health in Canada is not known. The relationship between socio-economic status and health has been extensively researched in this country, however, and many explanations for it can be found in the health literature.

Possible explanations for the association between socio-economic status and health include the "spuriousness" argument, which suggests that some prior genetic cause such as physical size or intellectual capacity influences both socio-economic status and health. Adler et al. (1994) note, however, that some studies have controlled for height and find little evidence indicating that intelligence is related to health. Alternatively, the "drift" hypothesis suggests that illness starts a downward trajectory on the socio-economic status ladder (i.e., that causality goes from illness to socio-economic status rather than in the other direction). As Adler et al. (1994) show, two comprehensive reviews of the literature conclude that drift accounts for only a small proportion of the relationship between socio-economic status and health. A third hypothesis is the "level of analysis" argument, which proposes that wealthy people congregate spatially in neighbourhoods that tend to have *other* characteristics that can have an influence on the health of everyone who lives there, including lower crime rates, more green space, fewer bars, and more supermarkets. This explanation essentially argues that the association between socio-economic status and health reflects this higher-level contextual relationship, and so is not truly causal. Like the preceding explanations, this hypothesis has yet to receive much empirical support in the literature.

Most explanations, however, do accept the existence of a causal link of some kind from socio-economic status to health. Some researchers offer a "psycho-social" explanation that focuses on non-material factors associated with social status. According to this argument, because people are generally aware of where they stand relative to others in society, those who are of low standing in everyday social interactions across multiple social contexts incur deleterious emotional and biological effects related to their health. Researchers who adopt a materialist perspective argue that poor health reflects such material phenomena as adverse housing characteristics, bad environmental exposures, poor nutrition, and limited access to medical care, all of which stem from people's low economic standing (Lynch et al. 2004). There is also an "education" argument, which suggests that better-educated people tend to have more accurate information about what influences their health, and the related "health behaviours" argument, which claims that people of higher socio-economic status tend to engage in more healthful practices with regard to smoking, physical activity, dietary choices, substance abuse, and so on. However, Adler et al. (1994) note that the relationship between socio-economic status and health appears to persist even after controlling for such health behaviours.

Whatever the explanation, an abundance of evidence demonstrates that socio-economic status is strongly related to health in Canada. This is true for a wide variety of health indicators pertaining to mortality, morbidity (including heart diseases, cancers, cardiovascular diseases, etc.), functional

ability, and self-perceptions of health. Some research has shown that the socio-economic status effect is particularly strong for young and middle-aged adults (Segall and Chappell 2000). Health researchers have also observed that individuals toward the top of the social "ladder" tend to have better health than those immediately below them at all stages of the ladder, but that this relationship weakens in strength as status increases (Wolfson et al. 1999).

Only two of the many studies that investigate relationships between socio-economic status and health in Canada are touched upon here. Veenstra (2007) used the Canadian Community Health Survey of 2003 to report strong effects of both educational attainment and household income on self-rated health and on the presence of hypertension. Indeed, of the four dimensions of inequality explored in this investigation, socio-economic status was by far the strongest predictor of health. Race also had an effect, while gender and sexual orientation made minimal contributions to explaining health variability in Canada. This study illustrates the power of socio-economic status, relative to other major dimensions of social inequality, as a predictor of health.

Studies focusing on psychosocial explanations for the effect of socio-economic status on health have recently captured the interest of many health researchers. Dunn et al. (2006) used a national survey sample collected by the Institute for Social Research at York University to assess the association between health and several socio-economic status measures. These measures included educational attainment, household income, personal income, perceived social standing relative to other Canadians and to Canadians of a previous generation, and actual social standing relative to others in the respondents' neighbourhoods of residence. As expected, results showed that socio-economic status was strongly associated with self-rated health. In support of the psychosocial argument, the researchers also found that perceived status relative to other Canadians was a strong predictor of self-rated health after controlling for age and gender (although perceived status relative to the previous generation was not related to health). Actual relative status was also strongly associated with self-rated health, particularly for comparisons with other neighbourhood residents located at the top of the income ladder. Dunn et al. could not control for socio-economic status when exploring the latter relationships, however, and so could not clearly distinguish between the relative strengths of the materialist and psychosocial explanations.

In summary, social class, at least as indicated by various socio-economic status measures, is clearly among the strongest inequality-based determinants of health in Canada. The especially steep slope of the relationship between socio-economic status and health at the lower end of the status ladder provides support for a materialist perspective. On the other hand, the absence of a clearly identifiable status "cut-point," a point at which the relationship between socio-economic status and health disappears, supports the viability of the psychosocial perspective. It should also be noted that behavioural explanations are undoubtedly important when it comes to understanding the health effects of socio-economic status.

SEXUAL ORIENTATION AND HEALTH

Negative attitudes toward people with non-heterosexual orientations range from homophobia to heterosexism. Homophobia refers to "any belief system that supports negative myths and stereotypes about homosexual people, or any of the varieties of negative attitudes that arise from fear or dislike of homosexuality" (Banks 2004:6).

Heterosexism refers to "a belief system that values heterosexuality as superior to and/or more natural than homosexuality; does not acknowledge the existence of non-heterosexuals; and assumes that all people are heterosexual" (Banks 2004:6). Processes of homophobia and heterosexism can stratify people socially, economically, and politically by sexual orientation, and hence can have an effect on the health of non-heterosexual Canadians.

Banks (2004) has identified several ways in which homophobia and heterosexism manifest themselves, all of which have the potential to explain health differences that separate gay, lesbian, and bisexual (GLB) people from the heterosexual population. First, internalized homophobia refers to learned biases that people— including GLB people themselves— incorporate into their own belief systems. External homophobia refers to observed and experienced expressions of internal biases, such as avoidance or verbal abuse. Institutional homophobia refers to discriminatory actions on the part of societal institutions, including governments, educational institutions, and businesses, that adversely affect non-heterosexual people. Finally, cultural homophobia or heterosexism refers to social standards and norms that portray heterosexuality as "normal" or "moral" and that, as a result, more or less overtly depict non-heterosexual orientations as "deviant" or "abnormal." Such norms and negative depictions can be found almost everywhere in the media, in educational settings, and in religious systems, and can lead to the social exclusion of GLBs.

Banks (2004) has delineated a series of ways in which experiences of homophobia and heterosexism might affect the health of GLBs. Many negative health effects arise from the chronic stress that results from repeatedly experiencing social stigmatization. For instance, GLBs may be less likely than heterosexuals to possess strong familial social support and a strong sense of community, leaving GLBs with fewer coping skills and resources for confronting and adapting to chronic stressors. GLBs may suffer emotional distress from internalizing the negative attitudes toward homosexuality that are propagated in society, from the pressure to conceal their sexual identity, and from their fear of stigmatization. "Coming out" to their families, friends, and communities can be a stressful experience that leads to shame, anxiety, and social rejection.

Other explanations for the association between sexual orientation and health focus on health-relevant behaviours. For instance, certain self-destructive behaviours, such as risky sexual behaviours, violence-based behaviours, and suicide attempts, may be more prevalent among GLB populations than among other Canadians. Substance abuse, which may be one means of coping with stress or painful emotional issues, also has negative health consequences. In addition, external homophobia can lead to verbal and physical attacks on GLBs that have direct health effects. Finally, experiences of discrimination in regard to employment, insurance, housing, and legal representation, ultimately can have indirect health effects, especially since these experiences are connected to socio-economic disadvantage.

There are some studies of the health of gay, lesbian, and bisexual people in Canada, although these analyses have generally been limited by geographic area and sample selection. For instance, one study of young gay males in Vancouver has provided important insights into the possible health effects of sexual orientation (Botnick et al. 2002). Findings revealed that suicide attempts were high in this group, probably because of their relatively low levels of social support, socio-economic status, and self-esteem. Another study, by Low-Beer et al. (2002), compared heterosexual, gay,

and bisexual men living in the West End of Vancouver and found higher levels of HIV/AIDS in the non-heterosexual groups. Additional research by Myers et al. (1996), based on an analysis of a purposive sample of gay men from across Canada, revealed a relatively high incidence of sexual behaviours that placed the respondents at risk of poor health outcomes. However, given the somewhat selective nature of the samples involved, the results from these studies cannot be generalized to gay, lesbian, and bisexual people in Canada as a whole.

The first nationally representative Statistics Canada survey to ask a question about sexual orientation was the Canadian Community Health Survey. Veenstra (2007) used the 2003 version of this dataset to investigate associations between sexual orientation and health at the national level. He found that homosexual, and especially bisexual, Canadians were more likely than heterosexual respondents to report fair or poor self-rated health. However, problems encountered in the course of his investigation illustrate how difficult it can be to generate trustworthy empirical insights into this issue. For example, in the survey sample of respondents aged 25 and older, only 0.9% of respondents selected the homosexual option and only 0.5% chose the bisexual option. These proportions are lower than those reported in similar studies from the United States (Cochran et al. 2003), Australia (Jorm et al. 2002), and the Netherlands (Bakker et al. 2006), where between 2% and 3% of the general population report being homosexual or bisexual. In fact, all of the survey research on this issue probably underestimates the proportion of people with non-heterosexual orientations, due to fear of stigmatization among survey respondents. Indeed, Banks (2004) has suggested that the actual proportion of non-heterosexuals in the population may be as high as 10%. Veenstra (2007) compared the educational attainments and incomes of heterosexual, homosexual, and bisexual respondents in his sample, and speculated that wealthy and well-educated homosexual respondents may have been more willing than poor and less-educated homosexuals to report their actual sexual orientation in the CCHS. This outcome suggests that the sample of non-heterosexuals in the CCHS, which is supposed to be nationally representative, probably does not accurately represent the non-heterosexual population in Canada.

To summarize, the limited evidence available in Canada supports the contention that experiences of homophobia and encounters with heterosexism on the part of gay, lesbian, and bisexual Canadians are detrimental to various aspects of their mental and physical well-being. Further research along these lines is needed to understand more precisely how and for whom social inequality based on sexual orientation influences health in this country.

CONCLUSION

Health in Canada is an expensive business: in 2005, Canada spent fully 10.4% of its Gross Domestic Product (about $142 billion) on health care. Most Canadians associate the quality of the health care system with the health of the population, implicitly assuming that the first strongly influences the second. However, when we consider that the biggest causes of death in Canada today are degenerative diseases such as cardiovascular disease and cancer, rather than the infectious diseases that were leading causes of mortality a century earlier, it becomes apparent that the nature and quality of Canada's health care system may not play as large a role in promoting the health of Canadians as it once did. Preventive measures such as immunization and sanitation undoubtedly have had a tremendous positive effect in lowering mortality

rates from infectious disease. Nevertheless, preventive measures for heart disease and cancer are not so easily enacted by a health care system that focuses most of its attention on treating infectious diseases.

One of the major obstacles to any further increase in the life expectancy of Canadians is the continuing existence of social inequality. As shown in this chapter, inequalities based on gender, race, socioeconomic status, and sexual orientation have an important impact on the health and well-being of many people in this country. Especially problematic are the negative health effects incurred by Aboriginal Canadians, people with lower education, and those who have lower incomes. Forms of social inequality that translate into health disparities are among the most egregious and inequitable of all. Many Canadians pay for these inequities with their health, and even with their lives.

The obstacles to ameliorating these problems may be difficult to overcome (Frankish et al. 1999). First, better theoretical models and better evidence are required in order to understand more fully the nature of the causal mechanisms that link social inequality to health in Canada. At the same time, though, it could be that causal models that are complex and multifaceted are more likely to deter changes in policy than to stimulate them. This is because the time frames necessary for addressing and ameliorating social inequality do not always fit nicely into the limited time windows that seem inherent to government electoral cycles and to changing political priorities. Another problem is identifying the appropriate levels of government (municipal, provincial, federal) and divisions (social services, housing, taxation) that should take responsibility for initiating and sustaining real change. It could also be that too many Canadians see health care and health as the same thing, with the result that not enough of us are ready to rally behind a movement toward reducing social inequality itself, which would in turn improve the aggregate health of Canadians in general. Recognizing the close links between social inequality and health should be one of the highest priorities for those policy-makers who seek a substantial improvement in the health of all Canadians.

REFERENCES

Adler, Nancy, Thomas Boyce, Margaret Chesney, Sheldon Cohen, Susan Folkman, Robert Kahn, and Leonard Syme 1994. "Socio-economic status and health." *American Psychologist* 49, 1:15–24.

Bakker, Floor, Theo Sandford, Ine Vanwesenbeeck, Hanneke Van Lindert, and Gert Westert 2006. "Do homosexual persons use health care services more frequently than heterosexual persons? Findings from a Dutch population survey." *Social Science and Medicine* 63:2022–2030.

Banks, Christopher 2004. *The C$st of Homophobia: Literature Review on the Economic Impact of Homophobia on Canada.* Saskatoon, SK: Community-University Institute for Social Research.

Benzeval, M., and K. Judge 2001. "Income and health: The time dimension." *Social Science and Medicine* 52:1371–1390.

Botnick, Michael, Katherine Heath, Peter Cornelisse, Steffanie Strathdee, Stephen Martindale, and Robert Hogg 2002. "Correlates of suicide attempts in an open cohort of young men who have sex with men." *Canadian Journal of Public Health* 93, 1: 59–62.

Clarke, Juanne Nancarrow 2000. *Health, Illness, and Medicine in Canada* (3rd ed.). Don Mills, ON: Oxford University Press.

Clarke, Juanne Nancarrow 2004. *Health, Illness, and Medicine in Canada* (4th ed.). Don Mills, ON: Oxford University Press.

Cochran, Susan, J. Greer Sullivan, and Vickie Mays 2003. "Prevalence of mental disorders, psychological distress and mental health services use among lesbian, gay, and bisexual adults in the United States." *Journal of Consulting and Clinical Psychology* 71, 1: 53–61.

Courtenay, Will 2000. "Constructions of masculinity and their influence on men's well-being: A theory of gender and health." *Social Science and Medicine* 50:1385–1401.

Denton, Margaret, Steven Prus, and Vivienne Walters 2004. "Gender differences in health: A Canadian study of the psychosocial, structural and behavioural determinants of health." *Social Science and Medicine* 58:2585–2600.

Dunn, James, Gerry Veenstra, and Nancy Ross 2006. "Psychosocial and neo-material dimensions of SES and health revisited: Determinants of self-rated health in a Canadian national survey." *Social Science & Medicine* 62, 6: 1465–1473.

Dunn, James R., and Isabel Dyck 2000. "Social determinants of health of Canada's immigrant population: Results from the National Population Health Survey." *Social Science and Medicine* 51:1573–1593.

Frankish, C. James, Gerry Veenstra, and Glen Moulton 1999. Population health in Canada: Issues and challenges for policy, practice and research." *Canadian Journal of Public Health* 90:S1, S71–S75.

Gee, Ellen, and M. Kimball 1987. *Women and Aging.* Toronto: Butterworths.

Grabb, Edward 2007. *Theories of Social Inequality* (5th ed.). Toronto: Thomson Nelson.

Janzen, B., and Nazeem Muhajarine 2003. "Social role occupancy, gender, income adequacy, life stage and health: A longitudinal study of employed Canadian men and women." *Social Science and Medicine* 57:1491–1503.

Jorm, Anthony, Ailsa Korten, Bryan Rodgers, Patricia Jacomb, and Helen Christensen 2002. "Sexual orientation and mental health: Results from a community survey of young and middle-aged adults." *British Journal of Psychiatry* 180:423–427

Karlsen, Saffron, and James Nazroo 2002. "Agency and structure: The impact of ethnic identity and racism on the health of ethnic minority people." *Sociology of Health and Illness* 24:1–20.

Kobayashi, Karen 2003. "Do intersections of diversity matter? An exploration of the relationship between identity markers and health for mid- to later-life Canadians." *Canadian Ethnic Studies* XXXV, 3:85–98.

Liberatos P., B. Link. and J. Kelsey 1988. "The measurement of social class in epidemiology." *Epidemiologic Reviews* 10:87–121.

Low-Beer, S., K. Bartholomew, A. Weber, K. Chan, M. Landolt, D. Oram, A. Schilder, and R. Hogg 2002. "A demographic and health profile of gay and bisexual men in a large Canadian urban setting." *AIDS Care* 14, 1: 111–115.

Lynch J., G. D. Smith, S. Harper, M. Hillemeier, N. Ross, G. A. Kaplan, and M. Wolfson 2004. "Is income inequality a determinant of population health? Part 1: A systematic review." *Milbank Quarterly* 82, 1:5–99.

Marx, Karl, and Friedrich Engels 1970 (1846). *The Communist Manifesto*. New York: Washington Square Press.

Marx, Karl, and Friedrich Engels 1976 (1846). "The German ideology." In *Marx/Engels Collected Works, Vol. 5*. New York: International Publishers.

McDonald, James, and Steven Kennedy 2005. "Is migration to Canada associated with unhealthy weight gain? Overweight and obesity among Canada's immigrant." *Social Science and Medicine* 61:2469–2481.

McDonough, Peggy, and Vivienne Walters 2001. "Gender and health: Reassessing patterns and explanations." *Social Science and Medicine* 52, 4:547–559.

Myers, T., G. Goden, J. Lambert, L. Calzavara, and D. Locker 1996. "Sexual risk and HIV testing behaviour by gay and bisexual men in Canada." *AIDS Care* 8, 3:297–310.

Newbold, K. Bruce 2005. "Self-rated health within the Canadian immigrant population: Risk and the healthy immigrant effect." *Social Science and Medicine* 60:1359–1370.

Newbold, K. Bruce, and Jeff Danforth 2003 "Health status and Canada's immigrant population." *Social Science and Medicine*. 57:1981–1995.

Powell-Griner, E., J. Anderson, and W. Murphy 1997. "State-and sex-specific prevalence of selected characteristics: Behavioural risk factor surveillance system, 1994 and 1995." *Morbidity and Mortality Weekly Report, Centers for Disease Control, Surveillance Summaries* 46, 3:1–31.

Segall, Alexander, and Neena Chappell 2000 *Health and Health Care in Canada*. Toronto: Prentice Hall.

Shah, Chandrakant P. 2004. "The health of aboriginal peoples." In D. Raphael (ed.), *Social Determinants of Health: Canadian Perspectives*, pp. 267–280. Toronto: Canadian Scholars' Press.

Sheth, Tej, Cyril Nair, Mukund Nargundkar, Sonia Anand, and Salim Yusuf 1999. "Cardiovascular and cancer mortality among Canadians of European, South Asian and Chinese origin from 1979 to 1993: An analysis of 1.2 million deaths." *Canadian Medical Association Journal* 161, 2:132–161.

Trovato, Frank, and Lalu Nirannanilathu 2007. "From divergence to convergence: The sex differential in life expectancy in Canada, 1971–2000." *Canadian Review of Sociology* 44, 1:101–122.

Veenstra, Gerry 2007. "A test of intersectionality theory." Unpublished paper.

Waldron, I., C. Weiss, and M. Hughes 1998. "Interacting effects of multiple roles on women's health." *Journal of Health and Social Behavior* 39:216–236.

Wang, Peizhong, Renée Elsbett-Koeppen, G. Geng, and Elizabeth Badley 2000 "Arthritis prevalence and place of birth: Findings from the 1994 Canadian National Population Health Survey." *American Journal of Epidemiology* 152, 5:442–445.

Weber, Max 1968 (1922). *Economy and Society, Volumes 1–3*. New York: Bedminster Press.

Wolfson, Michael, George Kaplan, John Lynch, Nancy Ross, and Eric Backlund 1999. "The relationship between income inequality and mortality: An empirical demonstration." *BMJ* 319:953–957.

Wu, Zheng, Samuel Noh, Violet Kaspar, and Christoph Schimmele 2003. "Race, ethnicity and depression in Canadian society." *Journal of Health and Social Behaviour* 44, 3:426–441.

Wu, Zheng, and Christoph Schimmele 2005. "Racial/ethnic variation in functional and self-reported healh." *American Journal of Public Health* 95, 4:710–716.

Young, T. Kue, Jeff Reading, Brenda Elias, and John O'Neil 2000. "Type 2 diabetes mellitus in Canada's First Nations: Status of an epidemic in progress." *Canadian Medical Association Journal* 163, 5:561–566.

chapter twenty-four

Persistent Inequalities:

Homelessness in Canada

Tracy Peressini
(An original chapter written
for this volume.)

INTRODUCTION

Beginning in the mid 1980s, homelessness was deemed to be a major social problem that required immediate attention and social action (Bogard 2001). While there has been no shortage of attention given to the issue over the last two decades, very little has been accomplished to reduce the number of homeless persons in Canada, or to address their housing and service needs. The lack of progress is partly because Canadian advocates and government officials continue to debate such issues as definitions and numbers, the reasons for homelessness, who is responsible for addressing the problem, and how the problem should be addressed (see, e.g., Laird 2007; Shapcott 2005). Advocates typically argue for quick action, while government officials and policy analysts favour measured responses based on reliable and valid knowledge about the size and scope of the problem. This difference is evident in the varying approaches proposed by the City of Toronto (2006) and the Toronto Disaster Relief Committee (2007). Regardless of which position is correct, researchers maintain that the homeless are one of the fastest growing segments of the population (e.g., Nunez and Fox 1999) and that this signals growing inequality between the rich and the very poor (Wright 2000). Now that we have entered the twenty-first century, the consensus among social scientists and policy analysts is that, like poverty, homelessness has become an all-too-persistent feature of society (Hoch 2000). Therefore, it is essential that we understand the nature and extent of the problem of homelessness in Canada.

This chapter examines the politics of homelessness that are rooted in definitions and counts of the population, because these considerations have had a major impact on the types of research that have been conducted and the public policy and program responses to homelessness. Next, some of the reasons for and explanations of homelessness are described and evaluated. The chapter concludes with a discussion of current social policies aimed at helping the homeless.

THE POLITICS OF HOMELESSNESS: DEFINITIONS AND COUNTS

The most contentious and controversial issue associated with homelessness is determining how many homeless Canadians there are. To date, we have no reliable estimate of the size or scope of the problem in Canada (HRDC 2007; Laird 2007). There have been two attempts to estimate the size of the homeless population in Canada, one in 1987 by the Canadian Council on Social Development (see McLaughlin 1987) and the other during the 1991 Canadian Census (see Begin et al. 1999). The 1987 count produced a national estimate of between 130 000 and 250 000 homeless. The findings from 1991 were never released. One other study by Statistics Canada (2002) reported that 14 145 Canadians were counted in shelters for persons lacking a fixed address, other shelters and lodging, and rooming with assistance services. Advocates

have argued that the exact numbers do not matter, in any event, but that people do. Their view is that we should focus our time and efforts on responding to the problem, not on counting the population. Government officials, however, contend that in order to respond effectively, the size and scope of the problem must be measured accurately, so that appropriate policies and sufficient resources can be allocated to address it. These conflicting positions, which define the politics of homelessness in Canada, have dominated the discussion and undermined researchers' attempts to understand the problem since the 1980s.

There is also a lack of agreement as to who the "homeless" are, so much so that the inconsistency across definitions and counts has been referred to as the "homeless muddle" (Ellickson 1990:45). The disagreement reflects the disparate and incompatible agendas and politics of the key players involved with the problem. On the one hand, social advocates and service providers prefer definitions that address the full spectrum of homelessness. These definitions can be so broad as to include anyone who is at risk of homelessness (e.g., those who have some form of housing, but are at imminent risk of losing it, or the hidden homeless). On the other hand, government officials and policy analysts prefer definitions that are restricted to those who currently do not have a permanent place to live, typically those actually living on the street and/or living in shelters for the homeless. For example, using a broad definition of homelessness, American social advocates in the 1980s estimated that the homeless population was in excess of one million people (Hombs and Snyder 1982). In contrast, the American government, counting only street people and those in shelters, estimated that between 250 000 and 350 000 people were homeless (U.S. Department of Housing and Urban Development 1984).

A comparison of Canadian counts (McLaughlin 1987) and American figures (Burt and Cohen 1989) demonstrates how the size of the population expands and contracts with the definition of homelessness. This comparison, while controlling for the difference in the size of the national population in each country, indicates that there were 4.5 times as many homeless Canadians as Americans in 1987. In other words, 9 in every 1000 people were homeless in Canada, compared with an American rate of 2 in 1000 (Peressini and McDonald 2000). However, the difference in these rates is attributable to the definition of the homeless and how they were counted. The Americans based their estimate on a physical count of the shelter users and street people in 20 cities with populations over 100,000 (Burt and Cohen 1989), while the Canadians asked for estimates of numbers from key informants.

Clearly, then, how we define homelessness directly affects the size of the population that is counted, which in turn determines the degree of social response needed to address the problem (Fitzgerald et al. 2001:121). The estimated size and composition of the homeless population guide government officials and policy analysts in estimating the amount of funding that should be allotted for programs and services to address the social, economic, and health needs of the homeless (Springer 2000). Definitions, therefore, not only specify who will be counted, but also determine who "counts." In other words, the act of defining who is homeless results in a political and moral statement about who is worthy of public assistance and resources and who is not (Rossi 1989).

While there are differences of opinion about numbers and rates, we have made some headway regarding definitions. Most researchers and social advocates now agree that the United Nations' definition of homelessness is the ideal definition. According to the UN definition, persons are homeless if they meet one of two criteria. First, they have no home and live either outdoors or in emergency shelters or hostels. Second, they live in homes that do not meet the UN's standards for a minimal home, which include protection from the elements, access to safe water and sanitation, affordable price, secure tenure and personal safety, and accessibility to employment, education, and health care (Springer 2000). In practice, however, many studies employ a variant of the narrower definition stipulated in the United States under the Stuart B. McKinney Homeless Assistance Act (U.S. Congress, House of Representatives 1987). The Act defines homeless individuals as persons who lack a fixed, regular, and adequate nighttime residence; or persons who have a primary nighttime residence that involves one of the following: a supervised or publicly operated shelter designed to provide temporary living accommodations (including welfare hotels, congregate shelters, and transitional housing for the mentally ill), an institution that provides temporary residence for individuals intended to be institutionalized, or a public or private place not designed for, or ordinarily used as, a regular sleeping accommodation for human beings (see Hirschl 1990:444–445).

Because of the absence of a reliable national estimate of the number of homeless Canadians, many Canadian cities began to conduct regular censuses of their homeless populations. Unfortunately, no consistent procedure has been used in the counts. Also, the accuracy of the counts varies considerably across Canada's cities and from one year to the next, mainly because of changes in how the homeless are defined and how the counts are conducted. The City of Toronto, however, uses a Homeless Management Information System (HMIS), a computerized database that monitors the number of people staying in their emergency and transitional shelters. In addition, the city can collect personal and demographic information from nightly shelter users, and it allows them to track usage over time. Based on data collected over the past decade, Toronto reports that the yearly number of people staying in emergency shelters increased from approximately 27 000 to 32 000 (City of Toronto 2003). Regardless of the procedures used, and whatever the absolute numbers, several major cities have reported that the number of people staying in emergency and temporary shelters, as well as those living on the streets, has increased. Some reported increases are 193% in the Greater Vancouver Area (2002–2005), 21% in Toronto (1990–2002), 19% in Edmonton (2004–2006), and 32% in Calgary (2004–2006).

THE FACE OF HOMELESSNESS IN CANADA

Most experts agree that the face of homelessness has changed over the last 20 years. Today's homeless population is comparatively more diverse. The homeless now come from all classes and demographic groups, including men and women, children and youth, families, students, seniors, immigrants, Aboriginal people, and people from Canada's various ethnic communities. They have experienced problems with poverty, unemployment, family violence, child abuse, divorce, mental illness, depression, physical disabilities, substance abuse, and deviance. They are present in every city, region, and province across Canada. However, the images of bag ladies,

beggars, squeegee kids, and skid-row alcoholics have prevailed and are the impressions that most often come to mind when the issue of homelessness is raised. While street people are the most visible of the homeless, researchers have found that they make up less than 10% of the population in the U.S. (Dennis and Iachan 1993) and between 12% and 19% of the population in Canada (City of Calgary 2006; City of Toronto 2006). In fact, most homeless persons do not actually live on the street; instead, they live in temporary and emergency shelters, with friends and family, in their cars, indoors in public spaces, and in abandoned buildings. They also move into and out of public institutions such as group homes, psychiatric wards, shelters, and prisons. They are the invisible poor, and most of them do not ever cross our paths as we move around the community. As one homeless sole-support parent in Calgary recently told a local reporter, "You can see me on the street and not know I'm homeless" (Slobodian 2002:B2).

The reality of homelessness is that, for many, it is a complex process of exits from and returns to homelessness. Researchers in the U.S. have found that the majority of the homeless population experiences multiple spells of homelessness, with initial spells being of a relatively short duration (usually from 7 to 30 days) and subsequent spells of progressively longer duration (Piliavin et al. 1993). For most people, homelessness is not a lasting condition, but a short-term situation that they move into and out of as they lose and regain their housing. Certainly, virtually no one chooses to be homeless, but extreme poverty offers little economic stability and it only takes a personal crisis—such as the loss of a job, a missed child support payment, or an illness—to cause people to lose their housing. That many of the homeless quickly recover their housing is a testament to their resilience and resourcefulness. Sadly, though, the fact that they experience recurring episodes of homelessness is a reflection of the wide-ranging cuts in federal support of Canada's social safety net over the last few decades.

In part, the rapid turnover rate in the homeless population prevents us from seeing the many different types of persons affected by homelessness. Another factor that limits the visibility of the homeless is the availability of shelters, programs, and services for some of them. For example, women, particularly those with children, tend to have access to a highly developed and well-coordinated system of short- and long-term shelters and services that is very effective in preventing them from having to stay on the streets (Bogard 2001; Passaro 1996). There generally is no adequate system of shelter and services for homeless men. The only services available to men, who are expected to find a job and support themselves, are drop-in centres and overnight homeless shelters. The shelters provide refuge on a nightly basis but force users onto the street the very next morning. Thus, men tend to be more often associated with the street population, and more visible, because they have no place to stay during the day (Passaro 1996).

Not only are men the most visible of Canada's homeless, they also constitute the largest demographic group among homeless persons. This is one of the facts about the homeless that is least recognized by some policy-makers. Virtually every study of homelessness in Canada has found that men make up between 70% and 90% of the population (Layton 2000), and yet the problem of male homelessness is often addressed only through the provision of overnight shelters.

The gender bias in public and policy responses to homelessness can be seen in the greater attention paid to homelessness among women, children, and families. Homeless families, in particular, have drawn a great deal of attention. Even though we do not know how many homeless one- and two-parent families there are in Canada, many government researchers and social advocates single out these categories and note their rapid growth in the last decade. For example, using data from the shelter user database, the City of Toronto, in its 2001 Report Card on Homelessness, highlighted that between 1988 and 1999, the number of two-parent families looking for shelter in Toronto rose from 320 to 2070; an increase of more than 600%. This increase, however, is not nearly as impressive when the number of homeless families is compared with the number of single homeless persons. Of the 30 000 people seeking shelter in Toronto in 1999, just over 1700 consisted of families, compared with more than 24 000 single persons, the majority of whom were men (City of Toronto 2001:3). It is also notable that, more recently, the City of Toronto has reported a decline of almost 50% in the number of two-parent families seeking shelter between 2001 and 2002 (City of Toronto 2003:38). The point of these examples is not to diminish the plight of homeless families, but to demonstrate that there is a selective perception and assessment of the level of need among the homeless based on their demographic characteristics.

It is also important to remember that the experience of homelessness is devastating and demoralizing for everyone who experiences it. As Koegel et al. (1990) have noted, homelessness involves a levelling process, in which personal and demographic characteristics have no observable impact on a person's ability to adapt and to survive on the streets. To be homeless is to be truly disadvantaged, regardless of age, sex, ethnic background, or any other demographic characteristic. With this in mind, a brief overview of the research findings on selected social and demographic characteristics of Canada's homeless is presented below.

Local studies from across Canada indicate that, in most cases, the age of the homeless ranges between 18 and 34 (Laird 2007), although the number of homeless youth may be on the rise. For example, between 1998 and 2000, the proportion of youth (aged 15 to 24) using the shelter system in Toronto increased moderately, from 20% to 23% (City of Toronto 2001) and, as of 2003, this age group represented 22% of all shelter users in Toronto (City of Toronto 2003). The number of immigrants and refugees who are homeless appears to be on the rise as well. The City of Toronto reported a 6% increase in the number of refugees and immigrants seeking admission to its shelter system over a two-year period, with the majority being families (City of Toronto 2001). Findings from an earlier study conducted in Calgary indicated that the homeless had an average of 10 years of education, which was slightly lower than the Canadian average, and usually had worked at some time during the year previous to being interviewed (Peressini 1995). Although the evidence is mostly anecdotal, it appears that sizable proportions of the homeless population in some of Canada's cities are Aboriginal persons, ranging as high as 75% in some cases (Beavis et al. 1997; Begin et al. 1999).

Finally, there is some limited information on other personal issues and problems among Canada's homeless, including mental illness, drug and alcohol abuse, criminal behaviour, and physical health. In Khandor and Mason's (2007:46) study of men and women using Toronto's Street Health Clinic, 71% of those surveyed said that they used drugs other than alcohol

regularly (three or more times per week), with 15% reporting using prescription opioids. These researchers also found that 75% of their respondents reported some form of chronic health problem, such as arthritis, allergies, asthma, diabetes, and epilepsy, and 1 in 7 were in severe pain (Khandor and Mason 2007:4). Breton and Bunston (1991), in their study of single homeless women in Toronto, found that 44% of their sample reported using drugs and alcohol prior to the survey. More than 70% of the women said they had contracted or received treatment for some form of physical illness, while roughly 40% reported treatment for some form of emotional or mental illness. Khandor and Mason (2007:4) found that, in 2006, 1 in 10 of their homeless respondents had attempted suicide, with 30% stating they had no one to rely on in an emotional crisis. Other researchers have determined that the severity and likelihood of having emotional, mental, and physical health problems increases with the duration of homelessness. For example, Peressini (1995) found that a sample of chronically homeless men in Calgary was 10 times more likely to suffer from and receive treatment for emotional, psychological, or substance abuse than were the newly homeless in the study.

EXPLAINING HOMELESSNESS

One version of how people become homeless focuses on the individual's social, behavioural, emotional, and psychological deficits, and emphasizes the role that personal pathology and disabilities play in the process of homelessness. From this perspective, homelessness occurs because of personal limitations, or because there is something "wrong" with the individual. The causes of homelessness are identified as mental or physical illness, physical disability, social alienation, social deviance and social disaffiliation (e.g., criminal behaviour, juvenile delinquency, drug and alcohol abuse), and human capital deficits (e.g., little education, low or inappropriate job skills and work experience). Thus, researchers have argued that homelessness is the result of people's inability to take care of themselves, either through incapacitation, choice, or a lack of social and personal resources (Bogard 2001; Hoch 2000).

Studies carried out over the last two decades support these types of explanation for homelessness. For example, research in the United States has shown that mental illness is correlated with homelessness, although this factor explains homelessness for only 10% to 30% of the population (Piliavin et al. 1993; Linhorst 1992). What is the source of homelessness for the remaining 70% to 90% of the population? Only some people with health problems become homeless, some with alcohol and drug abuse problems become homeless, and some of those released from prison end up on the street.

There are people who become homeless who do not experience these types of personal problems. To account for these other cases, some researchers argue that homelessness should be understood as a consequence of the social, political, and economic structures of society, which limit or restrict access to resources and opportunities. Homelessness in this case is viewed as the result of increased poverty and unemployment, declines in social and affordable housing, cuts to welfare and health care programs, and the shift from a manufacturing economy to a service economy (Devine and Wright 1997). According to such explanations, homelessness occurs when people cannot afford housing because they are unemployed, are

on welfare, or work in minimum-wage jobs. Homelessness also occurs when the costs of housing increase due to market demand (e.g., when low vacancy rates combine with little new housing construction). Roth and Bean (1986) found that almost a quarter of their sample listed unemployment as the major reason given for their homelessness. Elliott and Krivo (1991), in a study of variations in the rates of homelessness across 60 major U.S. metropolitan areas, found inconsistent effects of housing availability and affordability on the rates of homelessness. A study by Tucker (1990) showed no significant correlation between the rate of homelessness and the rates of poverty and unemployment for the various cities in his sample.

The findings in the current research literature suggest that both individual and structural explanations for homelessness shed some light on the problem. For many people, homelessness results from one or more non-economic personal troubles; these must be addressed first, so that individuals can then acquire the functional skills and abilities to live independently and to keep their housing. On the other hand, structural factors, such as the lack of low-cost housing, often limit the ability of Canada's extremely poor to find a place that they can afford. Each avenue of explanation suggests a different set of strategies for the individual, the community, and the state. Homelessness cannot be understood fully by focusing on one or the other of the theories. Hence, designing effective homelessness prevention and reduction policies and programs will require an integrated approach that considers and incorporates both individual- and structural-level explanations.

While each type of explanation of homelessness has some merit, for the most part, the existing theories and explanations of homelessness are "post hoc" explanations. Researchers conduct a study, describe the incidence and prevalence of socio-demographic characteristics (e.g., age, gender, ethnic and racial background, education, health, employment history, etc.), and then devise an explanation that fits the data.

SOCIAL POLICY AND HOMELESSNESS

In a country where the government does not set an official poverty line, it should come as no surprise that Canada has long had no national legislation, policy, or program that addresses the problem of homelessness (Daly 1996:25). In 1999, however, the federal government did establish the National Homelessness Initiative (NHI), a program that provided $753 million over three years to support community programs and services designed to reduce and alleviate homelessness across Canada (HRDC 2007). The corner-stone of the NHI had been the Support-ing Communities Partnership Initiative, which offers limited funds to build and expand emergency and transitional shel-ters and services to the homeless across the country. In 2007, the NHI was replaced by the new Homelessness Partnering Strategy (HPS) (see HRDC 2007). This new strategy, which started on April 1, 2007, "provides $269.6 million over two years to prevent and reduce homelessness" (HRDC 2007), which rep-resents a 54% reduction in funding for structures and supports for Canada's homeless.

The Homelessness Partnership Initiative (HPI) is the foundation of the HPS. It advo-cates the "housing first approach," whereby the housing needs of the homeless are provided first, and, once housed, their health, education, employment, and parent-ing needs are then addressed. The HPI has four components: designated communities; outreach communities; Aboriginal commu-nities; and federal horizontal pilot projects. In short, this "new federal response" to homelessness is intended to piggyback on regional and provincial initiatives, and take on a peripheral role in developing homeless-ness policies and programs.

Currently, programs and services for the homeless operate in two ways. First, community and faith-based groups offer programs and services; these are almost always under-funded, and the groups com-pete with each other for what little funding is available at the provincial and municipal levels. Second, charitable organizations such as the United Way or the Salvation Army provide services and programs. The existing system of services and programs for the homeless is a skeletal system of emergency and stop-gap measures that rarely amount to much more than "three hots and a cot" (Feins and Fosburg 1999:9–1). At present, much of the HPS funding is allocated to three initiatives. These include the previously discussed Homeless Partnership Initiative (HPI); the Homelessness Accountability Network (HAN), which is designed to enhance linkages and networks among the desig-nated communities making up the HPI; and the Surplus Federal Real Property for Homelessness Initiative (SFRPHI), which provides surplus federal properties to com-munities for use in their homelessness reduction strategies. The funding provided through the HPS will definitely have a pos-itive impact on the lives of homeless women, children, and families, and will help to strengthen the existing system of emergency programs and services for them. Nevertheless, it is doubtful that the HPS will help in significantly reducing rates of homelessness for men, who constitute the majority of the homeless population.

One of the most controversial aspects of the federal government initiative is that neither poverty reduction nor the construction of new affordable housing is part of the HPS mandate. By focusing on the support of existing programs and services, and piggybacking on community initiatives, the HPS reinforces the traditional stereotype that homelessness is a product of individual choice, incompetence, failure, or pathology, and is not the result of inadequacies and inequalities in the welfare system and the availability of housing. This is a sore spot for many social advocates and service providers, who have consistently pointed to cuts and freezes in Canada's social programs— including welfare, employment insurance, health care, and the building of social housing—as the prime sources of the rising rates of homelessness.

For all of the differences observed across the homeless population, the homeless have two characteristics in common: a lack of housing, and a lack of economic resources to secure and retain housing. In Canada, two main programs of poverty reduction and income support are designed to stabilize household incomes: welfare and employment insurance. In 1995, the federal government transformed the Canada Assistance Plan (CAP) into the Canadian Health and Social Transfer (CHST) and reduced federal contributions to post-secondary education, public health, and social assistance by $7 billion (Yalnizyan 1998). The CHST is a transfer payment from the federal government to the provinces. The provinces then apply these funds as they see fit to cover the costs of education, health care, and welfare. This change in social policy has directly affected welfare

rates, shelter allowances, and eligibility requirements in virtually every province. For example, between 700 000 and 800 000 people in Ontario had their incomes slashed when the Ontario government cut welfare cheques by 21.6% in 1995 (Yalnizyan 1998). Prior to these cuts, the maximum amount received by a single employable person in Ontario was $663 per month. Because of the rate cuts, maximum shelter allowances were set at $320 per month, with a living allowance of $195, reducing the maximum amount to $515 per month (Yalnizyan 1998). In addition, cuts to employment insurance since 1991 have doubled the number of unemployed people who do not qualify for benefits and who, therefore, have no form of income. The result is that, in Ontario alone, more than a million people lost not only their source of income, but also their ability to keep their housing.

Attacks on income security programs provide only half of the story of increased homelessness in Canada. Since the 1980s, the federal government has withdrawn from the social housing market and downloaded the responsibility for building new social housing to the provinces. Social housing provides the working poor, those on fixed incomes, and those on welfare with decent and affordable housing. Rents are either subsidized or geared to an individual's or a family's income. Social housing programs also provide assisted or supportive housing to mentally ill and physically disabled Canadians, and play an essential role in preventing people from losing their housing and becoming homeless. The Federation of Canadian Municipalities has estimated that a minimum of 45 000 new rental units must be built per year for the next 10 years, with at least half being affordable units, if we are to meet current demands for new and social housing. Unfortunately, cuts in the CHST have meant that provincial governments not only have had to cut income security programs, but also have had to make up the shortfall in funding out of their own budgets, leaving them with little funding for social housing. As a result, since the 1980s there has been a freeze on new social housing starts in most provinces.

By abdicating responsibility for reducing poverty rates, and without targeting funds for new affordable and subsidized housing, the federal government's homelessness initiative is unlikely to have much impact in reducing the number of homeless in Canada. Homelessness cannot be addressed until the criteria for public expenditures and program development are based on the needs and requirements of all Canadians, including those living and dying on Canada's streets. As Wright (2000:27) has argued, "ending homelessness is about creating a truly democratic human society beyond the barbarism of the current stock of social inequalities and economic and political violence." Only when our elected officials take responsibility for providing all Canadians with decent and affordable housing, stable and well-paying jobs, and universal health care will we see the end of homelessness (Wright 2000).

REFERENCES

Beavis, M., N. Klos, T. Carter, and C. Douchant 1997. *Literature Review: Aboriginal Peoples and Homelessness.* Ottawa: Canada Mortgage and Housing Corporation.

Begin, P., L. Casavant, and N.M. Chenier 1999. *Homelessness.* Ottawa: Parliamentary Research Branch, Library of Parliament (PRB 99-1E).

Bogard, C. 2001. "Advocacy and enumeration." *American Behavioral Scientist* 45, 1:105–120.

Breton, M., and T. Bunston 1991. *Single Homeless Women: A Report on Their Quality of Life.* Ottawa: Health and Welfare Canada.

Burt, M.A., and B.E. Cohen 1989. *America's Homeless: Numbers, Characteristics, and Programs That Serve Them.* Washington, DC: The Urban Institute Press.

City of Calgary 2006. *Count of Homeless Persons in Calgary.* Calgary: City of Calgary.

City of Toronto 2001. *The Toronto Report Card on Homelessness, 2001.* Toronto: City of Toronto.

City of Toronto 2003. *The Toronto Report Card on Homelessness, 2003.* Toronto: City of Toronto.

City of Toronto 2006. *2006 Street Needs Assessment: Results and Key Findings.* Toronto: City of Toronto.

Daly, G. 1996. *Homeless: Policies, Strategies and Lives on the Street.* New York: Routledge.

Dennis, M.L., and R. Iachan 1993. "A multiple frame approach to sampling the homeless and transient population." *Journal of Official Statistics* 14, 5:1–18.

Devine, J.A., and J.D. Wright 1997. "Losing the housing game: The leveling effects of substance abuse." *American Journal of Orthopsychiatry* 67, 4:618–631.

Edmonton Joint Planning Committee on Housing 2006. *Out in the Cold: A Count of Homeless Persons in Edmonton.* Edmonton: Edmonton Joint Planning Committee on Housing.

Ellickson, R.C. 1990. "The homelessness muddle." *Public Interest* 99:45–60.

Elliott, M., and L.J. Krivo 1991. "Structural determinants of homelessness in the United States." *Social Problems* 38, 1:113–131.

Feins, J.D., and L.B. Fosburg 1999. "Emergency shelter and services: Opening a front door to the continuum of care." In *Practical*

Lessons: The 1998 National Symposium on Homelessness Research, pp. 9-1 to 9-36. Washington, DC: U.S. Department of Housing and Urban Development.

Fitzgerald, S.T., M.C. Shelley, and P.W. Dail 2001. "Research on homelessness." *American Behavioral Scientist* 45, 1:121–148.

Hirschl, T. 1990. "Homelessness: A sociological research agenda." *Sociological Spectrum* 10: 443–467.

Hoch, C. 2000. "Sheltering the homeless in the U.S.: Social improvement and the continuum of care." *Housing Studies* 15, 6:865–876.

Hombs, M.E., and M. Snyder 1982. *Homelessness in America: A Forced March to Nowhere.* Washington, DC: Community for Creative Non-Violence.

Human Resources Development Canada (HRDC) 2007. *Homelessness Partnering Strategy.* Retrieved October 2007 (http://www.homelessness.gc.ca/home/index_e.asp). Ottawa: Government of Canada.

Khandor, E., and K. Mason 2007. *The Street Health Report.* Toronto: Street Health.

Koegel, P., A. Burnam, and R.K. Farr 1990. "Subsistence adaptation among homeless adults in the inner city of Los Angeles." *Journal of Social Issues* 16, 4:83–107.

Laird, G. 2007. *Homelessness in a Growth Economy: Canada's 21st Century Paradox.* Calgary: Sheldon Chumir Foundations for Ethics in Leadership.

Layton, J. 2000. *Homelessness: The Making and Unmaking of a Crisis.* Toronto: Penguin.

Linhorst, D.M. 1992. "A redefinition of the problem of homelessness among persons with a chronic mental illness." *Journal of Sociology and Social Work* 17, 4:43–56.

McLaughlin, MaryAnn 1987. *Homelessness in Canada: The Report of the National Inquiry.* Ottawa: Canadian Council on Social Development.

Nunez, R., and C. Fox 1999. "A snapshot of family homelessness across America." *Political Science Quarterly* 114, 2:289–307.

Passaro, J. 1996. *The Unequal Homeless: Men on the Streets, Women in Their Place.* New York: Routledge.

Peressini, T. 1995. *Disadvantage, Drift and Despair: A Study of Homelessness in Canada.* Unpublished dissertation. Waterloo, ON: The University of Waterloo.

Peressini, T., and L. McDonald 2000. "Urban homelessness in Canada." In T. Bunting and P. Filion (eds.), *Canadian Cities in Transition* (2nd ed.), pp. 523–543. Don Mills, ON: Oxford University Press.

Piliavin, I., M. Sosin, A.H. Westerfelt, and R.L. Matsueda 1993. "The duration of homeless careers: An exploratory study." *Social Service Review* (December):576–597.

Rossi, P.H. 1989. *Down and Out in America: The Origins of Homelessness.* Chicago: The University of Chicago Press.

Roth, D., and G. Bean 1986. "New perspectives on homelessness: Findings from a statewide epidemiological study." *Hospital and Community Psychiatry* 37, 7:712–719.

Shapcott, M. 2005. *Toronto's Proposed Street Count Won't Count for Much at All.* Toronto: Centre for Urban Community Studies, University of Toronto.

Slobodian, L. 2002. "A helter-shelter life: Hope, but no home." *Calgary Herald*, June 8.

Social Planning and Research Council of BC 2005. *On Our Streets and in Our Shelters: Results of the 2005 Greater Vancouver Homelessness Count.* Vancouver: Social Planning and Research Council of BC.

Springer, S. 2000. "Homelessness: A proposal for a global definition and classification." *Habitat International* 24:475–484.

Statistics Canada 2002. *2001 Census: Analysis Series—Collective Dwellings.* Ottawa: Statistics Canada. Catalogue No. 96F0030XIE2001004.

Toronto Disaster Relief Committee (TDRC) 2007. *TDRC-Online.* Retrieved October 2007 (http://www.tdrc.net/). Toronto: Toronto Disaster Relief Committee.

Tucker, W. 1990. *The Excluded Americans: Homelessness and Housing Policies.* Washington, DC: Regnery Gateway.

U.S. Congress, House of Representatives 1987. *Stewart B. McKinney Homeless Assistance Act.* Conference report to accompany H.R. 558, 100th Congress, 1st Session. Washington, DC: U.S. Government Printing Office.

U.S. Department of Housing and Urban Development (HUD), Office of Policy Development and Research 1984. *A Report to the Secretary on the Homeless and Emergency Shelters.* Washington, DC: Department of Housing and Urban Development.

Wright, T. 2000. "Resisting homelessness: Global, national and local solutions." *Contemporary Sociology* 29, 1:26–43.

Yalnizyan, A. 1998. *The Growing Gap: A Report on Growing Inequality between the Rich and Poor in Canada.* Toronto: Centre for Social Justice.

chapter twenty-five

The Effects of Social Status on Beliefs about Individualism and Inequality in Canada

Edward Grabb and Monica Hwang
(An original chapter written
for this volume.)

INTRODUCTION

Canada is widely thought to be one of the best societies in the world in which to live. This perception is reflected in the country's consistently high rankings on the annual United Nations Human Development Index, which compares the overall quality of life in different nations, based on such measures as average life expectancy, educational attainment, and material standard of living. According to the UN index, Canada held the number-one rating of all countries during the 1990s and, despite a recent decline, still ranked among the top six nations in the world as of 2006 (United Nations 1996, 2000, 2006).

However, notwithstanding the very positive image that Canada appears to have around the globe, it is also evident that Canadian society has some notable shortcomings when it comes to providing for the well-being of all of its citizens. As we know from many of the chapters in this book, individuals often face significant problems of inequality on the basis of their race, gender, class background, and a range of other factors.

In this chapter, our purpose is to consider how Canadians feel about the role of the individual and the nature of inequality in their own society. How does living in such a prosperous and yet unequal society shape popular views about such questions as whether inequality is acceptable or justifiable and whether the government should intervene to assist individuals who are in need? One of the main goals of our analysis is to explore the relationship between the social backgrounds of Canadians and their beliefs about these and other similar issues.

INDIVIDUALISM AS A DOMINANT VALUE

Sociologists have long been interested in understanding the dominant system of values, or "dominant ideology," that prevails in different societies. Some writers use the concept of dominant ideology in a manner similar to that of Karl Marx, to indicate the core beliefs that are held by the most powerful class or dominant group in society (Marx and Engels 1846, 1848; for discussion, see Abercrombie et al. 1980). Other analysts have used the term to indicate the values that are embraced or accepted, not only by the most privileged or dominant groups but also by the population in general (Williams 1960:409; Mann 1970; Grabb and Curtis 2005:67, 261).

Regardless of which usage is preferred, however, there is little doubt that among the ideas that are generally thought to be central to the dominant ideology of democratic societies like Canada, none is more important than the belief in "individualism." The concept of individualism has been subject to varying definitions by social scientists. In the present context, however, it refers to the fundamental belief that all people have (or should have) the right, the freedom, and the responsibility to make their own way in society. There is some debate as to whether individualism in this sense is as strongly emphasized by Canadians as it is by other peoples, especially Americans; nevertheless, there is no question that individualism is a core element in Canada's system of dominant values (for some debate and

discussion, see Marchak 1988; Lipset 1990, 1996; Olsen 2002; Adams 2003; Grabb and Curtis 2005; Reutter et al. 2006).

The strong emphasis on individualism in contemporary democracies is evident in research that has been conducted in Canada and elsewhere on a variety of interrelated attitudes and beliefs. Some of these studies have considered the extent to which people believe that each individual has or should have an equal opportunity to succeed in life. For example, one analysis from the 1990s showed that 98% of Americans believed that everyone *should* have equal opportunity to get ahead (Inkeles 1997:379). Several early studies in the United States found that about three-quarters of the population believed that equal, or at least considerable, opportunity actually did operate in their society (e.g., Mizruchi 1964; Huber and Form 1973; Kluegel and Smith 1986). More recent American evidence suggests some decline in this belief, although the findings reveal that, as of 2006, about 67% of respondents still agree that all or most Americans have "an opportunity to succeed" in their country (Campbell Public Affairs Institute 2006).

Some Canadian research has assessed people's views on why individuals succeed or get ahead in life. This research showed that more than 80% of Canadians emphasized personal qualities such as ambition and hard work (along with getting a good education) as the main reasons for success, and saw background characteristics like class background, race, or gender as generally unimportant factors (Pammett 1996:72–73; Curtis and Grabb 2004:399). These findings are similar to the results of earlier Canadian studies (e.g., Johnstone 1969:8–11; *Maclean's* 1998; Sniderman et al. 1996:97–100) and to evidence reported in recent American surveys (Campbell Public Affairs Institute 2004, 2006).

Other studies have looked at the necessity or justifiability of individual inequality as an incentive for personal excellence and societal progress. For example, research in the United States has generally found that most people see income inequality as an important motivation for individuals to work hard and achieve in life (e.g., Kluegel and Smith 1986:106–107; Kelley and Evans 1993). Such attitudes are also evident in Canada, though to a lesser degree (Pammett 1996:74–77; see also Osberg and Smeeding 2006).

Another body of research has considered people's attitudes about the relative merits of government assistance versus individual self-reliance when addressing problems of inequality. The results of several studies indicate somewhat greater support for self-reliance rather than government intervention among Canadians. For example, using data from the early 1990s, one study found that less than half (43%) of a national sample agreed that the government should act to reduce income differences between high-income and low-income Canadians (Olsen 2002:110). A more recent analysis showed that this proportion had increased slightly, to 48%, by 2002 (Centre for Research and Information on Canada 2002:7). Although most evidence indicates that the emphasis on self-reliance is somewhat lower in Canada than in the United States (see Perlin 1997:80–90; Olsen 2002:110; Grabb and Curtis 2005:180–182), it seems clear that Canadians also tend to take an individualistic perspective on this question, and on most other issues pertaining to inequality in their society.

THE EFFECTS OF SOCIAL STATUS

The next question to address is the possible effect that social background has on the extent to which people adopt an individualistic view of the problem of inequality. In other words, does being in a position of relative advantage or disadvantage in society, as judged by the different ranked social statuses that people occupy, have an impact on such beliefs as the necessity of inequality and the value of personal responsibility?

Conflicting predictions can be posed about this question. On the one hand, it could be that Canadians in privileged social positions, such as those with higher incomes or prestigious occupations, for example, would tend to be sympathetic or altruistic about the plight of disadvantaged individuals, and so would favour such policies as reducing inequality and increasing government assistance to help those less fortunate than themselves. An alternative hypothesis, however, is that individuals with higher social statuses are more likely than other people to believe that individual differences in privilege or well-being are appropriate, and should not be altered through government intervention or other initiatives. This hypothesis follows from the assumption that advantaged people tend to see their own high positions as justifiable rewards for their personal industry and achievement, with inequality being a natural consequence of individual differences in effort, ability, acquired skills, and so on.

Previous studies indicate some support for the latter hypothesis, although the pattern is generally not as strong or as consistent as might be expected. Early research in the United States found, for example, that members of disadvantaged groups, such as racial minorities, women, and those with lower incomes, were usually somewhat less likely than more privileged people to believe that inequality was based mainly on individual differences in effort or motivation (Huber and Form 1973:97–104; Kluegel and Smith 1986:100–102). More recent American survey data from 2006 also show a significant though modest relationship between income level and belief in equal opportunity, with 58% of those earning less than $50 000 per year agreeing that the United States is a society of opportunity, compared with 67% of respondents earning $100 000 per year or more (Campbell Public Affairs Institute 2006). An analysis of Canadian survey data from 2002 found a similarly modest effect for income, this time in regard to support for increasing government assistance to individuals; the data showed that about 50% of people with household incomes below $40 000 per year were in favour of more government services, compared with 42% of those with household incomes above $80 000 per year (Centre for Research and Information on Canada 2002:6). The same study (2002:6, 11) also showed some other social status effects, with women being more supportive than men of increased government services, and Quebecers being somewhat more in favour of reducing income differences compared with other Canadians (see also Johnstone 1969). Finally, in perhaps the most detailed Canadian assessment to date, Curtis and Grabb (2004) found a surprisingly weak relationship between social background and commitment to individualist values. This analysis revealed that most Canadians, regardless of their position on a range of social status indicators (including income, employment status, education, gender, region, and others), believed that individual factors such as hard work and ambition were far more important for getting ahead in Canada than were background characteristics like race, gender, or having wealthy parents (Curtis and Grabb 2004:401–403).

Given the results of these earlier studies, the present chapter reconsiders the question of Canadian beliefs about individualism and inequality. We rely on recent survey evidence and assess the effects of a more extensive set of social status measures than has been used in previous studies.

DATA AND METHODS

Sample

The data for this analysis come from a national survey of adult Canadians that was conducted in 2000. The data were collected as part of the World Values Surveys, a set of international sample surveys involving more than 60 countries (see Inglehart et al. 2004). The Canadian sample, which was weighted to make it representative of the national population, includes 1931 respondents.

Measuring Beliefs about Individualism and Inequality

Five items from the survey were selected to assess Canadians' beliefs about individualism and inequality. Four of the items use a format in which respondents are asked to rate their relative position on 10-point scales in regard to two contrasting statements, with a score of 1 meaning "you agree completely with the statement on the left" and a score of 10 meaning "you agree completely with the statement on the right"; any number between 1 and 10 could be chosen if the respondents' beliefs fell somewhere between the two extremes. The wordings of these four items are as follows:

1. "The government should take more responsibility to ensure that everyone is provided for" versus "People should take more responsibility for themselves."

2. "Competition is harmful. It brings out the worst in people" versus "Competition is good. It stimulates people to work hard and develop new ideas."

3. "Government ownership of business and industry should be increased" versus "Private ownership of business and industry should be increased."

4. "Incomes should be made more equal" versus "We need larger income differences as incentives for individual effort."

Item number 5 involves a different format, with respondents being asked to consider a hypothetical situation in which "two secretaries of the same age, doing practically the same job," are paid differently because one secretary "is quicker, more efficient, and more reliable at her job." Respondents then indicate whether they think it is "fair or not fair that the one secretary is paid more than the other."

Items 1, 2, and 3 are used as indicators of individualism in the present analysis, with respondents who support personal responsibility, who think competition is good, and who favour increased private business ownership considered to have a more individualistic outlook than other respondents. Items 4 and 5 assess the respondents' views about inequality, with those seeing larger income differences as an incentive for individual effort, and those believing it is fair to pay the more efficient and reliable secretary more money, considered to be stronger supporters of individual inequality.

Measures of Social Status

We wish to determine whether people who have relatively more advantaged or privileged social statuses are more likely than other Canadians to adopt an individualistic orientation to the problem of inequality. In the present analysis, we consider the effects of nine different social status measures. The first five of these measures deal with economic or socio-economic status: (1) *education*, which refers to the respondent's highest level of educational attainment, and is a rank-ordered measure with the following categories: grade school or less, some high school, high school graduate, some post-secondary, and post-secondary graduate; (2) *income*, which refers to

total household income from all sources and is grouped approximately into fifths or quintiles, ranked from lowest to highest; (3) *occupational status*, which is based on an eight-category measure that ranges from unskilled manual workers to employers/owners; (4) *employment status*, which includes the unemployed, as well as part-time, full-time, and self-employed workers; and (5) *subjective class identification*, which asks respondents to indicate the social class to which they think they belong, and which involves four categories: lower class, working class, lower middle class, and upper middle class or higher. The other social status variables we consider are: (6) *race*, dichotomized to distinguish between non-white and white respondents; (7) *gender*, which compares males and females; (8) *language*, grouped into francophone, anglophone, and allophone; and (9) *region*, which includes five categories: the Atlantic provinces, Quebec, Ontario, the Prairie provinces, and British Columbia.

RESULTS

Overall Patterns

Table 25-1 shows the results of our analysis. The initial finding to note concerns the first row of numbers, which shows the average score for all respondents on each of the five attitude questions. Here we see that Canadians tend to take an individualistic perspective on the questions about personal responsibility, the benefits of competition, and support for increased private-sector business ownership. That is, on all three of these items, the average responses are above the midpoint on each 10-point scale. This is especially true of the question about competition, with a score of 7.5 out of 10. The score on the private ownership item is also high, at 7.1 out of 10, while the average score on the personal responsibility measure is 6.2 out of 10.

TABLE 25-1	Comparison of Responses to the Five Inequality Items by the Various Social Status Characteristics of the Respondents				
	People Responsible for Selves	Competition Is Good	Private Ownership Should Increase	Income Differences a Good Incentive	Fair to Pay Better Secretary More
All Respondents	6.2/10	7.5/10	7.1/10	5.4/10	84%
Social Statuses					
Education					
< Grade School	6.4	7.7	7.3	5.3	78%
Some High School	6.2	7.2*	7.2	5.4	80
High School Grad	6.2	7.5	7.1	5.3	82
Some Post-sec.	6.1	7.9	7.6	5.7	95***
Post-sec. +	6.1	7.5	6.7*	5.7	89**
R-square	0.0%	0.7%	1.1%	0.4%	1.8%
F	0.7	3.4**	5.5***	1.8	8.7***
Income					
Lowest 1/5	5.8	7.1	6.9	5.2	79%
Fourth	6.1	7.4*	7.0	5.1	79
Third	6.4***	7.6**	7.2*	5.4	84
Second	6.3**	7.5*	7.3*	5.6	88***
Highest 1/5	6.6***	7.9***	7.4***	6.1***	91***
R-square	1.2%	1.1%	0.7%	1.5%	1.3%
F	5.8***	5.5***	3.5**	7.1***	6.5***
Occupation					
Unskilled Manual	6.0	7.3	7.0	5.2	79%
Semi-skilled Manual	5.7	7.7	7.0	4.8	71*
Skilled Manual	6.3	7.3	7.0	5.5	83
Forepersons	5.8	8.2*	7.8*	6.0*	90*
Non-manual Workers	6.1	5.5	7.3	7.0	86*
Non-manual Supervisors	6.7*	7.5	7.2	5.7	87
Professional	6.1	5.5	7.5	7.0	89*
Employer/Owner	6.6*	7.9**	7.9***	6.0***	86
R-square	1.0%	1.0%	1.6%	1.3%	1.7%
F	2.8**	2.8**	4.5***	3.5***	4.7***
Employment					
Unemployed	5.8	6.9	6.9	5.1	72%
Part-time	5.8	7.4*	6.9	5.2	81*
Full-time	6.3*	7.6***	7.2	5.5	86***
Self-employed	6.4	7.5*	7.5*	5.5	87**
All Others	6.1	7.5**	7.1	5.5	83***
R-square	0.6%	0.7%	0.5%	0.3%	1.1%
F	3.1*	3.5**	2.2	1.6	5.4***

TABLE 25-1   (continued)

	People Responsible for Selves	Competition Is Good	Private Ownership Should Increase	Income Differences a Good Incentive	Fair to Pay Better Secretary More
Subjective Class					
Lower Class	5.6	7.3	7.2	5.3	75%
Working Class	6.1*	7.5	7.3	4.9	82*
Lower Middle	6.2*	7.2	6.8	5.5	82*
Upper Middle +	6.3**	7.8*	7.2	5.9*	88***
R-square	0.5%	0.9%	0.8%	2.0%	1.0%
F	3.2*	5.7***	4.9**	6.3***	12.8***
Race					
Non-white	5.9	7.6	6.4	5.5	76%
White	6.2	7.5	7.2***	5.4	85**
R-square	0.2%	0.1%	1.0%	0.0%	0.5%
F	3.0	1.2	20.0***	0.1	9.5**
Gender					
Female	6.1	7.3	6.9	5.3	80%
Male	6.2	7.7***	7.3***	5.6***	88***
R-square	0.0%	0.8%	0.8%	0.5%	1.0%
F	0.2	15.4***	15.1***	10.2***	20.1***
Language					
Francophone	5.9	6.7	6.5	5.4	79%
Anglophone	6.3*	7.7***	7.4***	5.4	86***
Allophone	5.9	7.9***	6.8	5.7	74
R-square	0.6%	3.9%	2.9%	0.1%	1.1%
F	5.8**	39.3***	28.2***	0.6	11.0***
Region					
Quebec	5.9	6.7	6.5	5.4	76%
Atlantic	6.1	7.4**	7.4***	5.2	80
Ontario	6.2	7.8***	7.2***	5.3	86***
Prairies	6.5***	7.9***	7.6***	5.6	88***
British Columbia	6.3	7.7***	7.5***	5.8	88***
R-square	0.7%	3.9%	3.4%	0.4%	1.5%
F	3.2*	19.6***	16.5***	1.8	7.4***
N =	(1912)	(1912)	(1895)	(1910)	(1901)

Notes: * indicates $p<.05$; ** indicates $p<.01$; *** indicates $p<.001$. For the first four items, scores are on a scale from 1 to 10. For the fifth item, the percentage is for respondents agreeing with the statement.

For the other two items, which deal more explicitly with people's attitudes about inequality, we get somewhat mixed results. The question about the secretaries' pay suggests a high level of support for the idea that inequality is acceptable to Canadians, provided it is based on individual performance.

Here we see that 84% of respondents say that the better-performing secretary should be paid more than the other secretary. On the other hand, for the question about the need for larger income differences to provide incentives for individual effort, respondents are split, with an average score of 5.4, which is right in the middle of the 1-to-10 scale. Nevertheless, the latter question is probably the most extreme question among the five attitude items, since respondents are not simply asked whether existing levels of income inequality are acceptable but whether such inequality should be increased even further. Seen in this light, this result indicates a comparatively high level of support for individual inequality. Overall, then, the findings are generally consistent with previous research in showing that Canadians embrace a relatively individualistic viewpoint when it comes to the problem of inequality and related issues such as competition, personal responsibility, and government involvement.

Social Status and Beliefs about Individualism and Inequality

Our main concern in Table 25-1 is to assess the extent to which the nine social status measures are related to the five attitude items. In particular, we wish to determine whether people with more advantaged backgrounds are more likely than less advantaged Canadians to take an individualistic perspective. If so, we should find that such a perspective is relatively more prevalent among the following groups: the more highly educated, those with higher incomes, individuals with higher occupational status, employed respondents, those who have a higher subjective class identification, men, whites, anglophones, and people from more prosperous regions (e.g., Ontario, the Prairies, and British Columbia).

The results shown in Table 25-1 are based on a statistical technique known as dummy-variable regression, in which the least advantaged category of each social status measure (e.g., those with less than grade school education for the education variable) is selected as the reference category. This group is then compared with each of the more advantaged categories of that variable, and a test of statistical significance is applied

to determine whether any of the other categories are significantly higher or lower than the reference group on each attitude item.

We see that, for some of the social status measures, there is consistent support for the hypothesis that privileged Canadians hold more individualistic views about inequality and related issues than do their less privileged counterparts. This is especially true for three of the socio-economic status indicators: income, occupation, and subjective class location. That is, on all five attitude questions, we find that people with higher incomes, higher occupational statuses, and higher subjective class identifications are significantly more likely than other respondents to take an individualistic viewpoint. The differences, while consistent, are generally not large. For example, on the question about whether competition is good, respondents in all five income categories tend to agree, although it is true that respondents in the highest category do have the highest score, at 7.9 out of 10, and respondents in the lowest income category do have the lowest score, at 7.1 out of 10. Similarly, most respondents in all income categories favour paying the better-performing secretary more money, although the highest support (91%) is found among the highest income group and the lowest (79%) is found among the lowest income group.

We find that employment status has a relatively weak effect on people's attitudes, with notable differences evident for only two questions: the unemployed are significantly less likely than other groups to believe that competition is good, and are also less likely to favour paying more money to the better-performing secretary. One possibly surprising result among the socio-economic status measures is the effect of education. Here we see that only on the secretary question do highly educated Canadians appear to be more likely than others to express an individualistic perspective. On the other four attitude items, the more highly educated respondents are either no different from, or less individualistic than, the less educated respondents. These patterns, however, may not be that unexpected if we consider that some previous research has shown similar results. Earlier studies have attributed this outcome to the liberalizing effects of education, which may make people more aware of the problems faced by the poor and more willing to believe that inequality is not just an individual problem (see, e.g., Kluegel and Smith 1986:101; Kelley and Evans 1993:106; Reutter et al. 2006:15).

The results for the other social status measures indicate some mixed support for the hypothesis that privileged groups hold a comparatively more individualistic attitude about inequality. For region, we find, as expected, that respondents from the most prosperous regions, including British Columbia, Ontario, and especially the Prairies, are the most in favour of competition, private ownership, and paying the two secretaries different incomes. Atlantic residents, who live in the poorest region of Canada, tend to be less supportive of these attitudes, but it is Quebecers who voice the least support. A related pattern occurs for language group, in that francophones, the large majority of whom reside in Quebec, are the least in favour of competition, private ownership, and unequal pay for the two secretaries; anglophones are typically the most supportive of such attitudes. The effects of gender are also evident for four of the five items, with relatively small but statistically significant differences showing that males have more individualistic views about inequality than do females. Finally, there is a significant effect for race on only two of the attitude questions: whites are somewhat more likely than non-whites to favour increased private ownership and to believe that the two secretaries should receive different pay.

Another way to assess the effects of social status on people's responses to the five attitude questions is to consider the R-square values reported in Table 25-1. These values indicate how much of the variability in any of the attitude questions can be accounted for, or explained, by the effects of any particular social status measure. The results show that *none* of the nine social status measures by itself has a very strong impact on any of the five attitude questions. That is, none of the R-square values is as high as 4%, out of a possible 100%, and almost all of the values are below 2%. These findings mean that the vast majority of the variability in people's attitudes about individualism and inequality in our analysis is not due to the different social statuses of the respondents. Although it is not reported in the table, we also did a multivariate analysis, in which we looked at the combined effects of all nine social status measures in accounting simultaneously for people's responses to each of the five attitude items. The combined R-square values ranged from a low of 4.7% for the personal responsibility question to a high of 8.1% for the question about increasing private rather than government business ownership in Canada. In other words, these results again suggest that, while social status differences play some role in explaining people's views about individualism and inequality, their impact is relatively minor in comparison with other explanations.

CONCLUSION

The results of our analysis are generally consistent with earlier research that has considered the dominant belief system of Canadians, especially regarding the value of individualism and the nature of inequality in our society. Like most previous studies, the findings presented in this chapter show that Canadians tend toward an individualistic perspective concerning these issues, with the average person accepting such ideas as the positive effects of competition, the need for more private ownership of business, the importance of people taking personal responsibility for themselves, and the fairness of income differences based on individual performance.

Our results also follow the findings of earlier research in suggesting that people with more advantaged social backgrounds, at least on some measures, are more likely to embrace these beliefs about individualism and inequality than are people with less privileged status characteristics. This outcome is especially clear when comparing individuals with higher and lower socio-economic status, as judged by such measures as income, occupation, and subjective class location. The same pattern is also apparent to a lesser degree for other social status measures, with anglophones, males, and those living in more prosperous regions of Canada (especially outside Quebec) being comparatively more likely than other Canadians to adopt an individualistic outlook.

Even so, while we have seen that the effects of social status are often significant, one of our most important findings is that these effects are not strong, a result that is again consistent with previous research (recall, e.g., Centre for Research and Information on Canada 2002; Curtis and Grabb 2004). That is, even for Canadians who are relatively disadvantaged, whether the criterion is socio-economic status, gender, race, language, or region, people's views in most cases lean toward the individualistic end of the continuum. Moreover, even when all of the social status influences are considered in combination, they account for only a small proportion of the variability in attitudes that Canadians express about individualism and inequality.

In other words, the findings reported here suggest that people's beliefs about these topics are *dominant* in both senses of the term noted at the beginning of this paper. That is, these views tend to be widely held, both by the more privileged members of Canadian society and by the population as a whole. Most would seem to agree, then, with the idea that inequality is acceptable in Canada, and is in many ways a matter of individual effort and personal responsibility.

Such attitudes can be seen as lending ideological support to maintenance of the status quo—existing arrangements by which the dominant groups should continue to do comparatively well. These beliefs also imply that, in most people's minds, the system works largely as it should, and that there is little reason to want to change it. One other possibility, of course, is that most Canadians tend to adopt the dominant ideology, with its emphasis on individualism and the justifiable nature of inequality, because most people are basically happy with their current situation. As noted at the beginning of this chapter, Canada has consistently been named by the United Nations as one of the best countries in the world in which to live, primarily because of our comparatively high level of material affluence and our generally good quality of life. Thus, perhaps for this reason, the relatively strong support we have seen for the dominant value system is to be expected. Even so, there is clear evidence of structurally based inequalities and injustice in much of the existing research on Canada, including many of the chapters appearing in this book. Therefore, there is considerable room to wonder why more Canadians, especially those who face problems of poverty or discrimination, do not voice a higher level of discontent about the problems of disadvantage and structural inequality in their society.

REFERENCES

Abercrombie, Nicholas, Stephen Hill, and Bryan S. Turner 1980. *The Dominant Ideology Thesis.* London: George Allen and Unwin.

Adams, Michael 2003. *Fire and Ice: The Myth of Value Convergence in Canada and the United States.* Toronto: Penguin Canada.

Campbell Public Affairs Institute 2004. *The Maxwell Poll: Civic Engagement and Inequality.* Syracuse, NY: Maxwell School of Syracuse University.

Campbell Public Affairs Institute 2006. *The Maxwell Poll: Civic Engagement and Inequality*. Syracuse, NY: Maxwell School of Syracuse University.

Centre for Research and Information on Canada 2002. *Portraits of Canada 2002*. Montreal: The Canadian Unity Council.

Curtis, James, and Edward Grabb 2004. "Social status and beliefs about what's important for getting ahead." In James Curtis, Edward Grabb, and Neil Guppy (eds.), *Social Inequality in Canada: Patterns, Problems, Policies* (4th ed.), pp. 393–409. Toronto: Pearson Education Canada.

Grabb, Edward, and James Curtis 2005. *Regions Apart: The Four Societies of Canada and the United States*. Don Mills, ON: Oxford University Press.

Huber, Joan, and William Form 1973. *Income and Ideology*. New York: The Free Press.

Inglehart et al. 2004. *World Values Surveys and European Values Surveys, 1999–2001*. Ann Arbor, MI: Inter-University Consortium for Political and Social Research [computer file].

Inkeles, Alex 1997. *National Character: A Psycho-Social Perspective*. New Brunswick, NJ: Transaction Publishers.

Johnstone, John C. 1969. *Young People's Images of Canadian Society*. Studies of the Royal Commission on Bilingualism and Biculturalism, No. 2. Ottawa: Queen's Printer.

Kelley, Jonathan, and M.D.R. Evans 1993. "The legitimation of inequality: Norms on occupational earnings in nine nations." *American Journal of Sociology* 99, 1:75–125.

Kluegel, James, and Eliot Smith 1986. *Beliefs about Inequality*. New York: Aldine de Gruyter.

Lipset, S.M. 1990. *Continental Divide: The Values and Institutions of the United States and Canada*. New York: Routledge Press.

Lipset, S.M. 1996. *American Exceptionalism*. New York: Norton.

Maclean's 1998. "Taking the pulse of a nation." *Maclean's* 110, 52 (January 5).

Mann, Michael 1970. "The social cohesion of liberal democracy." *American Sociological Review* 35:423–439.

Marchak, Patricia 1988. *Ideological Perspectives on Canada* (3rd ed.) Toronto: McGraw-Hill Ryerson.

Marx, Karl, and Friedrich Engels 1846. *The German Ideology*. In *Marx Engels Collected Works*, Vol. 5. New York: International Publishers, 1976.

Marx, Karl, and Friedrich Engels 1848. *The Communist Manifesto*. New York: Washington Square Press, 1970.

Mizruchi, Ephraim 1964. *Success and Opportunity*. New York: The Free Press.

Olsen, Gregg M. 2002. *The Politics of the Welfare State: Canada, Sweden, and the United States*. Toronto: Oxford University Press.

Osberg, Lars, and Timothy Smeeding 2006. "'Fair' inequality? Attitudes to pay differentials: the United States in comparative perspective." *American Sociological Review* 71:450–473.

Pammett, Jon 1996. "Getting ahead around the world." In Alan Frizzell and Jon Pammett (eds.), *Social Inequality in Canada*, pp. 67–86. Ottawa: Carleton University Press.

Perlin, George 1997. "The constraints of public opinion: Diverging or converging paths?" In Keith Banting, George Hoberg, and Richard Simeon (eds.), *Degrees of Freedom: Canada and the United States in a Changing World*, pp. 71–149. Montreal and Kingston: McGill-Queen's University Press.

Reutter, Linda, Gerry Veenstra, Miriam Stewart, Dennis Raphael, Rhonda Love, Edward Makwarimba, and Susan McMurray 2006. "Public attributions for poverty in Canada." *Canadian Review of Sociology and Anthropology* 43:1–22.

Sniderman, Paul, Joseph Fletcher, Peter Russell, and Philip Tetlock 1996. *The Clash of Rights: Liberty, Equality, and Legitimacy in Pluralist Democracy*. New Haven, CT: Yale University Press.

United Nations 1996. *Human Development Report 1996*. New York: United Nations Development Programme.

United Nations 2000. *Human Development Report 2000*. New York: United Nations Development Programme.

United Nations 2006. *Human Development Report 2006*. New York: United Nations Development Programme.

Williams, Robin M., Jr. 1960. *American Society*. New York: Alfred A. Knopf.

chapter twenty-six

Inequality and Intolerance: Canada in Cross-national Perspective

Robert Andersen and Scott Milligan
(An original chapter written
for this volume.)

INTRODUCTION

Social tolerance has long been considered a desirable trait for a democratic society (Jones 2007). It is not surprising, then, especially given Canada's diversity, that the Canadian state places great importance on the acceptance of individual or group differences (White 2003; Merchant and Rich 2004; Mulder and Krahn 2005). Partly for this reason, many Canadians see tolerance as a hallmark of our national identity (Howard-Hassman 1999). Nevertheless, this does not mean that all groups are accorded the same level of acceptance, or that acceptance is equally distributed among all groups, in Canadian society. Of interest in this respect is the impact of inequality, particularly given

growing evidence that income inequality is on the rise in most modern societies (Nielsen and Alderson 1995; Firebaugh 2000; Goesling 2001), including Canada (Barrett and Pendakur 1995; Kazempiur and Halli 2000).

The goal of this chapter is to assess whether social inequality, especially inequality related to social class, affects intolerance toward racial minorities, immigrants, and gays and lesbians, both in Canada and elsewhere. We address four research questions: (1) Is there a relationship between inequality and intolerance across countries? (2) How does intolerance in Canada compare to intolerance in other countries? (3) Does inequality within Canada have implications for intolerance?

(4) Have overall levels of intolerance in Canada changed over time? We answer these questions by exploring survey data from the World Values Surveys (Inglehart et al. 2001). Before turning to our analysis, we discuss some theoretical rationales for and against the argument that inequality affects intolerance.

INTOLERANCE OF "OUTGROUPS"

Although no single process sufficiently explains it (Gibson 1986; Chong 1993), there is significant evidence that intolerance is related to the perception that an "outgroup" poses a threat, whether real or imaginary, to the way of life of the majority. (See, for example, Sullivan et al. 1982.) It is relatively straightforward to apply this idea to the impact of social inequality: Those in lower economic positions have less economic security than those in higher economic positions, and hence feel more vulnerable to people from groups other than their own (cf. McClosky and Brill 1983). There are a number of arguments for how this vulnerability could lead to intolerance, including: (1) a perceived threat due to intergroup conflict, (2) parochialism and ignorance, (3) working-class "authoritarianism" or conformism, and (4) relative deprivation. Nevertheless, several theoretical perspectives also lead to a different conclusion—that is, that economic inequality has no relationship with tolerance in modern democracies. First, many argue that it is education, not economic position, that affects tolerance; research that shows otherwise typically either neglects the role of education or employs social status measures that are at least partly based on education. Additional theories, such as the individualization thesis and the post-materialist thesis, suggest that economic conditions were once important

for predicting social and political attitudes and actions, but that they are no longer relevant in advanced modern democracies. We discuss these various viewpoints in greater detail below.

Arguments for an Effect of Socio-economic Position on Intolerance

Social Identity Theory and Intergroup Conflict

Social identity theory suggests that the relationship between economic position and intolerance is driven largely by intergroup conflict (Tajfel 1974). Although social identity theory is concerned only with how perceived threats shape attitudes (i.e., it does not assess whether these perceptions are justified), in some circumstances intergroup conflict has real implications. Those in the lower classes are more likely to experience, or believe that they experience, negative consequences due to the presence of other groups. For example, those in the working class might tend to be intolerant of immigrants because they perceive—rightly or wrongly—that immigrants are more willing to work longer hours, in poorer conditions, and for less pay, all of which could give immigrants a competitive advantage in the labour market. In other words, intolerance among working-class people could stem from a fear that immigrants will take their jobs. At the same time, we might expect that those in the middle classes are more accepting of immigrants because they are less concerned that they will have to compete with immigrants for their jobs. Although this argument is not typically discussed with respect to social identity theory, it is often used to explain working-class support of extreme right-wing parties in Europe. (See, for example, Andersen and Evans 2003; Andersen and Zimdars 2003.)

Parochialism and Ignorance

Unjustified perceptions of threat can result from a lack of knowledge of the "outgroup" (Gibson 1986, 2006; Chong 2003; Weldon 2006). Based on studies of social networks, we might expect that people with many social ties outside of their own group will have better knowledge of other groups (cf. Granovetter 1973). Merton's (1957) distinction between "localite" and "cosmopolitan" individuals is also relevant in this regard. Localites are people who are largely in contact with others who are similar to themselves. In contrast, cosmopolitan individuals see themselves as belonging to a larger world. While Merton's work refers specifically to those living in larger urban centres, it is relatively straightforward to extend the idea to those with generally more diverse networks. We might expect localites to be more likely to be intolerant because they have less contact with people who have views different from their own. (For findings consistent with this idea, see Andersen and Yaish 2003; Money 1999.)

There is ample evidence that those in lower socio-economic positions tend to have less diverse and less far-reaching social networks than those from higher socio-economic positions (Parkin 1967; Teather 1997; Eckstein 2001; Woldoff 2002; Entwisle et al. 2007). Although the gap has certainly narrowed over the past few decades, working-class people tend to travel less, either for work or for leisure (Katz-Gerro 2002; Tomlinson 2003); to participate less in voluntary associations (Wilson and Musick 1997; Curtis, Baer, and Grabb 2001; Andersen, Curtis, and Grabb 2006); and to have fewer close contacts outside their workplace (cf. Erickson 1996; Andersen and Heath 2002; Andersen, Yang, and Heath 2006). As a result of these attributes, individuals in lower socio-economic positions have less exposure to, and probably less knowledge about, people who differ from themselves, at least when compared with those in higher socio-economic positions.

Working-Class Authoritarianism and Conformism

The most famous theory predicting that the working class is less tolerant than other groups is Lipset's working-class authoritarianism thesis (Lipset 1959, 1960; see also Grabb 1979; Grabb 1980; Billiet et al. 1996). Lipset suggested that certain predispositions can arise in some individuals because of their social contexts. He argued that the social and economic insecurity, and resulting family tension, that is found disproportionately in the working class can result in isolation from dominant political and cultural values, which in turn inhibits the development of sophisticated views about social and political issues. This lack of sophistication leads to a preference for simple solutions to political and social problems and hence to traditionalism, moral conservatism, and hostility toward outgroups. More recent adaptations of this theory suggest that the working class is not necessarily more authoritarian, but rather more "conformist" than other social classes (Svallfors 2006; see also Kohn 1977). Kohn (1977:201) states that working-class individuals are less willing than other people to "allow others to step out of narrowly confined limits of what is proper and acceptable."

The working-class authoritarianism thesis has been heavily criticized, with much evidence suggesting that the working class is no more authoritarian than any other class, once other factors are taken into consideration. For example, many argue that education, not social class itself, is largely responsible for differences in attitudes (Lipsitz 1965; Grabb 1979; Dekker and Ester 1987; Houtman 2003). Other research suggests that it is small business owners, not those in the working class, who are most likely to hold authoritarian views (Scheepers et al. 1989). Lipset himself acknowledged the theory's limitations in later work when he suggested that education, not class, plays the crucial role. More specifically, he stated that "a consistent and continuing research literature has documented relationships between low levels of education and racial and religious prejudice, opposition to equal rights for women, and with support of, and involvement in, fundamentalist religious groups" (Lipset 1981:478). At the very least, these findings show the need to consider other aspects of socio-economic status, such as education, rather than focusing on social class alone.

Relative Deprivation

Unlike the other theories we have examined, relative deprivation is concerned with the relative, rather than the absolute, position of the working class. From this view, those in lower social class positions can enjoy a relatively high standard of living and economic security and yet still be less accepting of outgroups than those in higher social classes. In fact, some argue that relative differences in economic conditions have more important consequences than absolute economic conditions (Runciman 1966; Griffin 1988). The term *relative deprivation* was originally coined by Stouffer (1949). It refers to the discontent that is felt by individuals or groups who subjectively feel they are unfairly disadvantaged compared to other groups whom they view as enjoying unjust rewards. The concept was expanded by Merton (1957), who used it as the basis for his conception of anomie. Merton argued that the high rates of social mobility characteristic of developed societies raise people's expectations about their social and economic standing. Those who fail to reach their expectations are prone to feelings of dissatisfaction with society, which lead them to protest against their situation. The

concept of relative deprivation has been used to explain many social phenomena, including racial conflict (Vanneman and Pettigrew 1972), radical politics (Runciman 1966; Walker and Pettigrew 1984), and criminal activity (Lea and Young 1984; Box 1987; Young 1999).

Arguments against the Link between Economic Position and Intolerance

The Liberalizing Role of Education

As already mentioned, many argue that education, not social class, is the primary socio-economic predictor of tolerance (Stouffer 1955; Prothro and Grigg 1960; McClosky 1964; Davis 1975; McCutcheon 1985). These writers contend that social class effects are found only or primarily when the effects of education are neglected or when measures of social class are partly based on education. The rationale for an education effect is compelling. Higher education is said to expose people to a more diverse range of cultures, ideas, and ways of life, with the result that highly educated individuals are presumed to be relatively more open-minded about social diversity. It is not completely clear whether education actually liberalizes people's beliefs or simply leads to better knowledge of social norms and values, resulting in "appropriate" liberal answers to survey questions (Jackman 1972). Nevertheless, it is important to take into account the role of education when assessing the effects of class on tolerance.

The positive association between education and acceptance has been found for a wide variety of outgroups, including those that we consider in this chapter. For example, Jackman (1978) found that the more educated were more in favour of racial integration and ethnic equality than were the less educated (also Bobo and Zubrinski

1996; Pedersen 1996; Gay 2006). Similarly, Quillian (1995) and Coenders and Scheepers (1998) demonstrated that highly educated individuals are much more likely than the less educated to express tolerance of immigrants (also Pedersen 1996; Semyonov et al. 2006; Haubert and Fussell 2006). A similar education effect has been found with respect to beliefs about gender equity (Ainsworth and Roscigno 2005; Cotter et al. 1999) and tolerance of homosexuality, both in Canada (Andersen and Fetner, 2008) and elsewhere (Overby and Barth 2002; Hicks and Lee 2006; Embrick et al. 2007).

Individualization and the "End of Class Politics"

There has been much debate over the past few decades about the declining importance of economic position—more specifically, of social class—as an explanation for social and political attitudes and actions in modern capitalist societies (see the volume edited by Evans 1999). Some argue that class is "dead" while others argue that class remains important, although in ways that are different from the past. More generally, "post-modern" explanations (e.g., Pakulski 1993; Pakulski and Waters 1996) argue that individualism has taken the place of class identities. Those who adhere to the individualization thesis see several societal changes as being responsible for the declining significance of class. These include improved living standards for the working class, greater social and geographical mobility, increased opportunities for individual lifestyle choices, and the growth of mass communications, which have led to weaker and more diffuse patterns of personal interaction and a reduced reliance on locally-based networks of support. Nevertheless, other writers, while agreeing that such structural changes have taken place, contend that economic position still matters for the everyday lives

of individuals. From this perspective, it is now more difficult to observe class effects on attitudes and behaviours because the changing class structure has made old measures of class no longer suitable (Weeden and Grusky 2005), and/or because political parties are less likely to cater to class interests (Andersen and Heath 2003).

Postmaterialism: The Role of Democracy and Economic Development

Exploring the role of inequality among countries can also shed light on patterns of intolerance in Canada. Inglehart's (1971, 1990, 1997) post-materialist thesis provides some insight into this question. The post-materialist thesis argues that there has been considerable change in attitudes in modern democracies, with a shift away from material interests and toward so-called "postmaterialist" values (Inglehart and Baker 2000). The thesis holds that as societies democratize, modernize, and obtain a high level of economic development, most people live economically secure lives, and are thus freed from material concerns. Postmaterialists argue that, as a result, individuals have moved away from collective material interests based on social class to more individualistic concerns related to lifestyle and freedom of expression, and thus have become more accepting of others. The theory implies that economic position has little impact on intolerance because even the less advantaged are comparatively free from material concerns.

The post-materialist thesis leads to two expectations: (1) Given Canada's highly developed economy and degree of democratization, Canadians should exhibit relatively high levels of overall acceptance when compared to other national populations, and (2) Because Canadians generally enjoy considerable wealth or affluence, post-materialism should be widespread, and so socio-economic status should have little impact on intolerance in Canada. There is some existing research supporting both of these findings (Nevitte et al. 1989; Butovsky 2002; Brym et al. 2004). Nevertheless, there are also reasons to believe that post-materialism is less widespread than its proponents assume. First, as other chapters in this volume have shown, the benefits of economic prosperity are not equally distributed throughout the population of Canada, so not everyone experiences the freedom from material concerns that is so important to the post-materialist thesis. Second, economic inequality appears to be rising in many countries, suggesting that even if the post-materialist thesis is correct, the tide may be turning back in the other direction (see Milanovic 2005). Third, even if most Canadians are relatively free from serious concerns about their material well-being, inequalities continue to persist and these inequalities could still lead to differences in attitudes stemming from relative deprivation.

We turn now to our own analysis of the impact of social inequality on intolerance in Canada. In the next section, we discuss the data and variables that we employ. We then explore overall levels of intolerance, specifically toward other races, immigrants, and gays and lesbians in Canada and other countries, and take into consideration the role of economic inequality across countries. We end with an assessment of the relationship between various measures of socio-economic position and intolerance within Canada.

DATA AND VARIABLES

Data Sources

Our analysis uses survey data from the World Values Surveys (Inglehart et al. 2001). For our comparative analysis of intolerance in Canada and other countries, we employ data collected in 2000 from 31 nations. We also use information on the GDP per capita of these 31 countries compiled by the United Nations (2005). For the analysis of intolerance within Canada, we employ the 2000 WVS, as well as data collected in the 1980 and 1990 waves of the WVS. All of the national samples that were collected were designed to be representative of the adult population in each country.

Dependent Variables

We explore the impact of inequality on three dependent variables that tap the acceptance of outgroups. All three variables stem from a single question in the WVS that was worded as follows: "On this list are various groups of people. Could you please sort out any that you would not like to have as neighbours?" We focus on three specific groups among the 10 groups presented to respondents: "People of a different race," "Immigrants/ foreign workers," and "Homosexuals." Respondents were given two possible response choices—that is, they could either mention or not mention the group as one that they would not want to have as neighbours. Those who mentioned a group were assumed to be expressing intolerant attitudes, while those who did not mention a group were assumed to have relatively tolerant views about the group in question.

Measures of Social Inequality

We consider the effects of six different measures of social inequality or social status on intolerance: household income, occupation, education, race, gender, and region. *Household income* is divided into quintiles. *Occupation* is grouped into eight categories: unskilled manual labour, semi-skilled manual labour, skilled manual labour, forepersons, routine non-manual labour, non-manual supervisors, professionals, and employers/owners. *Education* is divided into five categories: less than grade school, some high school, a high school diploma, some post-secondary school, and post-secondary completion. Due to limitations in the dataset, race is simply divided into white versus other. Finally, we divide the sample into five regions: the Atlantic provinces, Quebec, Ontario, the Prairie provinces, and British Columbia.

RESULTS

Canada in Cross-National Perspective

We start by comparing the overall level of intolerance exhibited by Canadians with the levels expressed by people in other countries. As noted earlier, the post-materialist thesis suggests that acceptance of other groups should be positively related to economic development and democracy, or conversely that intolerance should be negatively related to these variables. Given that Canada is highly developed and also has a long democratic tradition, we should expect levels of acceptance in Canada to be relatively high when compared to acceptance in other nations. To this end, Figure 26-1 plots the proportion of respondents in each country who would *not* want as neighbours someone from a different race, immigrants, and homosexuals, and relates these proportions to the country's GDP per capita (in U.S. dollars). New democracies, which are defined as countries having less than 20 years of continuous democratic rule, are indicated by open circles, while old democracies are indicated by solid circles. Also shown are the fitted lines from simple regressions of average intolerance on GDP per capita, and their corresponding correlation coefficients.

Several noteworthy findings are evident in Figure 26-1. First, for all three of the designated groups, the average level of intolerance is negatively related to GDP per capita; that is, in keeping with expectations, as economic development rises, intolerance decreases. The correlation coefficients indicate that the relationships are quite strong for all three designated groups, but that the effect of GDP per capita is strongest for attitudes toward homosexuals ($r = -0.87$). Second, regardless of GDP per capita and democratic tradition, intolerance of homosexuals tends to be more pronounced than intolerance for the other two groups. Third, people living in the new democracies (the vast majority of which are less developed economically than the old democracies) are, on average, less tolerant than those living in the old democracies. Finally, compared with other peoples, Canadians exhibit a very low level of intolerance regarding other races and immigrants, both overall and among those nations with similar levels of democratization and economic development; in contrast, however, Canadian attitudes about homosexuals, while still being more liberal than those of people living in the new democracies, are only about average when compared with people living in the old democracies.

Table 26-1 provides the same information as Figure 26-1, but identifies the 31 countries. Except for Sweden (with 2.6%), Canada has the smallest percentage of respondents (3.8%) stating that they wouldn't want someone of a different race as a neighbour. Canada is similarly liberal with respect to immigrants (4.5%), with only Portugal (2.6%) and Sweden (2.9%) exhibiting lower scores among the 31 countries. On the other hand, almost 18% of Canadian respondents claimed that they would not want a gay or lesbian person as a neighbour. As already noted, this result indicates that Canada is in the middle of the pack among modern industrial societies in regard to people's views about homosexuals. It is interesting that the

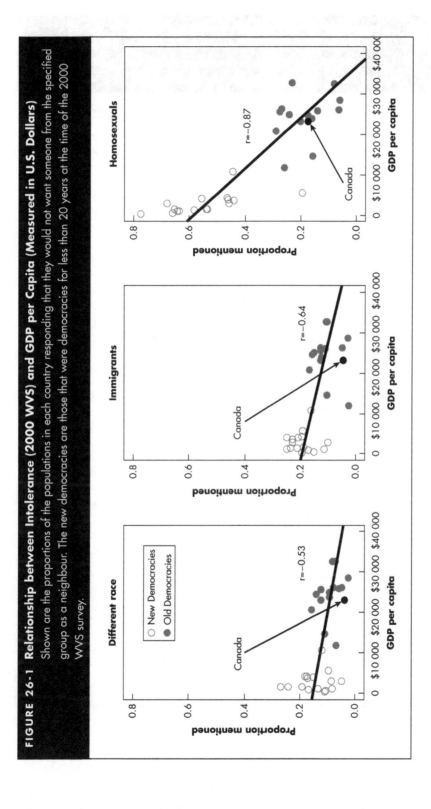

FIGURE 26-1 Relationship between Intolerance (2000 WVS) and GDP per Capita (Measured in U.S. Dollars)

Shown are the proportions of the populations in each country responding that they would not want someone from the specified group as a neighbour. The new democracies are those that were democracies for less than 20 years at the time of the 2000 WVS survey.

TABLE 26-1   **Percentage of Respondents Indicating That They Would *Not* Like to Have a Neighbour Who Is from a Different Race, an Immigrant, or a Homosexual (From the 2000 WVS), and GDP per Capita, for 31 Countries**

Country	Different race	Immigrants	Homosexuals	GDP per capita
Austria	7.9	12.7	26.7	26 341
Belarus	16.5	17.1	63.3	1039
Belgium	13.9	15.7	17.5	24 705
Bosnia Herzegovina	13.2	24.8	64.2	1229
Bulgaria	26.7	23.4	53.4	1609
Canada	3.8	4.5	17.2	23 280
Croatia	17.3	19.3	46.4	4393
Czech Republic	9.6	19.1	19.3	5744
Denmark	7.4	10.6	8.0	32 708
Estonia	14.8	20.7	45.8	4043
Finland	12.1	12.7	20.1	23 290
France	9.1	12.1	15.8	23 967
Germany	5.9	11.0	14.0	26 056
Ireland	12.3	12.5	27.5	25 748
Italy	15.6	16.5	28.7	20 834
Latvia	4.8	9.8	45.5	3019
Lithuania	8.5	22.7	67.8	3078
Macedonia	19.1	18.6	53.6	1705
Moldova	11.0	19.4	77.3	392
Netherlands	5.0	5.0	6.2	26 282
Poland	18.1	24.8	55.4	4255
Portugal	6.7	2.6	25.6	11 955
Romania	24.2	21.1	65.2	1602
Russia	8.2	11.2	58.2	1332
Slovakia	17.0	22.8	44.0	3781
Slovenia	12.0	16.0	44.3	10 836
Spain	11.0	10.2	15.7	14 770
Sweden	2.6	2.9	6.0	28 621
Ukraine	10.5	14.8	65.6	636
United Kingdom	9.2	15.1	24.1	25 057
United States	8.1	10.2	22.9	32 767

Netherlands and the Scandinavian countries are far more liberal on this issue, despite having only slightly higher GDP per capita than Canada. The proportions reporting that they would not want homosexuals as neighbours was only 6.2% in the Netherlands, 6.0% in Sweden, and 8.0% in Denmark.

Inequality and Intolerance within Canada

The previous analysis provides tentative support for the post-materialist thesis in showing that acceptance of the three outgroups that we are considering is highest among countries that are rich and have a long democratic tradition. In other words, there is evidence that inequality across nations might account for at least some of the differences in intolerance. As yet, however, we have not assessed the post-materialist idea that the high level of acceptance in rich nations reflects a general acceptance that is widespread *within* these nations. Therefore, we now turn to an assessment of the levels of intolerance within Canada alone. Given our finding that economic development has its strongest effect on attitudes toward homosexuality, we expect inequality within each country to have its strongest effect on acceptance of this group as well. In Canada, we might also expect weaker effects of social class on attitudes toward immigrants and people of a different race, since immigrants and non-whites are among the most likely to have lower socio-economic status (Pendakur and Pendakur 1998, 2007; Kazempiur and Halli 2001). In other words, immigrants and those of other races are perhaps less likely than homosexuals to be perceived as "outgroups."

Table 26-2 assesses the bivariate relationships between each of the three tolerance/intolerance measures and all of the independent variables. The chi-square

statistic in the last row for each variable indicates whether there is a statistically significant relationship with the dependent variable in question. We start with the two variables that most closely tap social class position: household income and occupation. The chi-square tests suggest that household income and occupation are significantly related to Canadians' attitudes about homosexuals, but that neither of these predictors has an effect on attitudes about immigrants, while occupation has a significant but very weak effect on attitudes about people of a different race. As expected, those with lower incomes and working-class occupations tend to be less favourable than those in middle-class positions to having homosexuals as neighbours. Even this finding requires some qualification, however, since employers/owners tend to be just as intolerant on this question as is the manual working class. It is professionals and other white-collar workers who tend to be the most accepting. Overall, these data suggest that it may be the type of work people do, or perhaps the level of education needed for their occupation, that affects attitudes, rather than the economic rewards associated with the job.

We also see in Table 26-2 that, for all three groups, education has the predicted effect on intolerance. That is, the proportion of respondents who do not want the three groups as neighbours generally decreases as the level of education increases. Using race as a predictor reveals that this variable has no significant relationship to people's attitudes about having immigrants or people of another race as neighbours; these findings are notable, given the large proportion of both immigrants and racial minorities living in Canada. At the same time, though, we do find a significant race effect for homosexuals, with non-whites expressing significantly less acceptance than whites. There is no gender difference in regard to attitudes about neighbours who are immigrants or of

TABLE 26-2 **Percentage Indicating That They Would *Not* Like to Have a Neighbour Who Is from a Different Race, an Immigrant, or a Homosexual, by Various Social Status Characteristics, Canadian Respondents to the 2000 WVS**

	Different race	Immigrants	Homosexuals
All respondents	3.8	4.5	17.2
Income			
Lowest 1/5	4.2	4.8	23.1
Fourth	4.3	5.6	13.5
Third	2.7	4.4	17.1
Second	2.1	2.8	10.7
Highest 1/5	2.7	3.1	13.7
Chi-square (4 degrees of freedom)	4.03	4.27	21.00***
Occupation			
Unskilled Manual	0.6	2.6	18.6
Semi-skilled Manual	4.5	3.8	18.0
Skilled Manual	6.0	7.1	19.0
Forepersons	0	0	21.4
Routine Non-manual Labour	2.2	3.1	14.2
Non-manual Supervisors	3.1	5.2	14.6
Professionals	2.4	3.6	7.2
Employers/Owners	3.8	4.8	20.2
Chi-square (7 degrees of freedom)	16.87*	12.89	21.99**
Education			
< Grade School	10.7	9.7	33.0
Some High School	2.3	4.3	20.7
High School Graduate	3.1	4.5	14.3
Some Post-secondary	3.6	2.9	14.4
Post-secondary +	2.0	2.4	7.2
Chi-square (4 degrees of freedom)	20.25***	10.75*	47.40***
Race			
Non-white	6.0	4.3	27.6
White	3.1	4.3	14.7
Chi-square (1 degree of freedom)	2.96	0	13.53***
Gender			
Female	2.6	3.8	12.7
Male	4.1	4.9	19.7
Chi-square (1 degree of freedom)	2.64	1.37	13.83***
Region			
Quebec	6.1	8.1	11.8
Atlantic	2.6	3.1	19.4
Ontario	2.4	3.0	15.9
Prairies	2.0	2.4	14.6
British Columbia	1.4	2.8	17.4
Chi-square (4 degrees of freedom)	10.75*	20.08***	9.22
N	1520	1520	1520

*P-value < 0.05; **P-value < 0.01; ***P-value < 0.001

a different race, but there is a tendency for females to be more accepting than males of homosexuals. Finally, region has a statistically significant effect on intolerance of immigrants and other races, but not on intolerance toward homosexuals. More specifically, people in Quebec stand out from those in other regions in tending to be less accepting of neighbours who are immigrants or who are from a different race. Compared to those from other regions, Quebecers and residents of British Columbia may be slightly more accepting of homosexuals, but here the region effect is not statistically significant.

Thus far we have explored only the bivariate relationships between each of our predictors and the three dependent variables. We have tentative support for the hypothesis that intolerance is related to social class. This is especially the case for attitudes about gay and lesbian people, with both income and occupational status significantly related to intolerance. There is also some indication that occupation affects intolerance of people of a different race. It is important to note, however, that education is highly related to the acceptance levels expressed in regard to all three

outgroups. Given that education is also strongly related to income and occupation, it is possible that, once education is controlled, income and occupation will no longer be related to intolerance. To test this proposition, we have fitted logit models, which allow us to assess the partial effects of each of the predictors on the dependent variables. In other words, these models enable us to control for the effects of all other variables when assessing the impact of any one predictor. Chi-square tests for the effects of each of the six predictor variables are displayed in Table 26-3. The findings suggest that occupation has no impact on any of the dependent variables, including intolerance of people of a different race, once education is controlled. Nevertheless, the income effect on attitudes about gays and lesbians remains statistically significant with controls. In other words, even when looking within particular education categories, we find a positive relationship between income and acceptance of gays and lesbians as neighbours.

Before ending our analysis, it is interesting to explore Canadian trends in intolerance over time. Figure 26-2 plots the

TABLE 26-3 Type II Chi-Square Tests for Social Status Characteristics When All Are Included in Logistic Regression Models

These are tests for the effect of each social status indicator controlling for all others.

Social status indicator (degrees of freedom)	Dependent variable		
	Different race	*Immigrants*	*Homosexuals*
Income (4)	1.41	1.16	11.60*
Occupation (7)	11.86	10.92	6.21
Education (4)	9.62*	6.35	28.74***
Race (1)	3.64	0.13	19.44***
Gender (1)	1.65	0.84	14.76***
Region (4)	9.50*	12.08*	9.32

*P-value < 0.05; **P-value < 0.01; ***P-value < 0.001

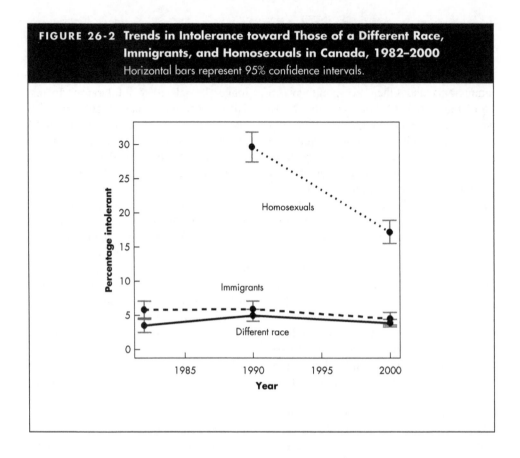

FIGURE 26-2   Trends in Intolerance toward Those of a Different Race, Immigrants, and Homosexuals in Canada, 1982–2000
Horizontal bars represent 95% confidence intervals.

proportion of respondents who would not want someone from the three groups as a neighbour for different time periods. For attitudes toward immigrants and other races, we have data for 1980, 1990, and 2000. For attitudes toward homosexuals, we have data only for 1990 and 2000. The horizontal bars surrounding the proportions represent 95% confidence intervals. The findings in this graph are quite striking: intolerant attitudes toward immigrants and other races have remained very stable over time, while intolerance toward homosexuals dropped significantly from 1990 to 2000. We suspect that the change in attitudes toward gays and lesbians partly reflects the increased public attention regarding gay rights over the past two decades (see Walters 2001; Andersen and

Fetner, in press). This hypothesis, of course, is consistent with the notion that knowledge about an issue can affect level of acceptance.

CONCLUSIONS

Our exploration of intolerance in cross-national perspective has found support for the post-materialist thesis, as we have determined that the average intolerance toward different groups within countries is related to the level of economic development of the countries being compared. In addition, however, economic development, as measured by GDP per capita, appears to have stronger effects for some issues than for others. More specifically, GDP per capita has a much stronger effect on average acceptance of gays and lesbians than on acceptance of immigrants and people of a different race. It is also important to note that, in every country we examined, the average level of acceptance of homosexuals was lower than that shown toward the other two groups. Our findings revealed much more variability in tolerance regarding homosexuals, however, which helps to explain the stronger relationship between GDP per capita and this variable. Our results also indicate that Canada tends to be far more accepting of other races and immigrants than one would expect given the country's level of economic development. At the same time, however, Canadian attitudes toward gays and lesbians, while highly accepting in comparison with the levels of acceptance found in most nations, are only at the average among countries with similarly high levels of democratization and economic development.

While we can only speculate based on the present analysis, the relatively high acceptance that Canadians express for immigrants and people of other races may stem from the fact that, compared with people in most other nations, Canadians have a better knowledge of and more exposure to such groups in their daily lives. We would expect this greater knowledge and experience, simply because Canada is among the most ethnically diverse nations in the world, and has one of the largest foreign-born populations (see, e.g., Li 2003). Especially in large centres, it would be nearly impossible for Canadians to avoid contact with immigrants or people from racial groups that are different from their own. This relatively high level of contact and interaction may help to enhance intergroup understanding and reduce perceptions of threat, which in turn would promote decreased intolerance. Compared with other countries, Canada's position regarding overall acceptance of homosexuals is also consistent with this line of thought. Assuming that there are not vast international differences in the size of

the gay and lesbian populations, especially in developed societies, we would not expect that Canadians would have greater contact with gays and lesbians than would people from other countries. This could partly explain our finding that Canadians do not differ from people in other developed countries in regard to their acceptance of homosexuals as neighbours.

As with the cross-national findings, our findings within Canada are mixed regarding the impact of social inequality on intolerance. Variables directly related to social class (i.e., income and occupation) appear in our data to have little or no effect on acceptance of immigrants and people of other races. Although we have found that intolerance of other races is related to occupation, this relationship is rendered statistically insignificant when other variables, such as education, are controlled. On the other hand, income affects intolerance of homosexuals, both with and without controls. Our results also confirm previous research in showing that education has a consistent and positive relationship with acceptance of outgroups.

Our finding that social class does not appear to affect people's acceptance of immigrants or other races casts doubt on those theories suggesting that inequality affects intolerance. Our results are more consistent with the post-materialist thesis. Nevertheless, in the case of attitudes toward gays and lesbians, we found evidence that social class does matter. It is possible that the same line of reasoning, which we used to explain cross-national differences in the effects of social class on intolerance toward the various groups, also applies within Canada as well. That is, given that most immigrants to Canada start with working-class jobs (Driedger 2003) and are increasingly non-white (Statistics Canada 2003), working-class Canadians are likely to have a familiarity with immigrants and people of different races. On the other hand, contact with gays and lesbians is apt to be rarer for those in the working class than for those in other social classes (Barrett and Pollack 2005; Embrick et al. 2007). Therefore, we suggest that differences in the amount of contact that working-class people have with homosexuals, as opposed to the other two groups we have considered, could at least partly explain the different class effect regarding attitudes about homosexuals. Simply put, compared with gays and lesbians, immigrants and people of other racial backgrounds may be less likely to be perceived as "outgroups." Our evidence is buttressed by other comparative research employing more sophisticated analyses on the same topic (Andersen and Fetner 2008). Our findings are also consistent with cross-national research on social trust, which indicates that inequality within countries is more important for predicting trust than is economic development per se (Uslaner 2002; Uslaner and Brown 2002).

Before concluding, we should also make it clear that our results by themselves are not definitive. As is true of most research, the present study is not without certain limitations. In particular, our dependent variables amount to quite restrictive measures of intolerance. For example, it is possible that people who would be willing to have neighbours belonging to various outgroups would still not want to associate with such groups on a regular basis. On the other hand, it is likely that some of the respondents who would not want certain outgroups as neighbours would, nevertheless, strongly support the belief that such groups should have the same fundamental rights as everyone else. Another point to note is that our results might differ significantly from those we would have found if other outgroups were considered in the analysis. Unfortunately, the data that we employ do not enable us to assess these possibilities. Despite these limitations, however, the results presented here provide a useful if partial snapshot of the relationship between inequality and intolerance in Canada society, and suggest possible avenues for future research in this important area.

REFERENCES

Ainsworth, James, and Vincent Roscigno 2005. "Stratification, school-work linkages, and vocational education." *Social Forces* 84, 1: 257–284.

Andersen, Robert, and Jocelyn A.J. Evans 2003. "Values, cleavages, and party choice in France, 1988–1995." *French Politics* 1, 1:83–114.

Andersen, Robert, and Tina Fetner 2008. "Cohort differences in tolerance of homosexuality: Attitudinal change in Canada and the United States, 1981–2000." *Public Opinion Quarterly* 72, 2.

Andersen, Robert, James Curtis, and Edward Grabb 2006. "Trends in civic association activity in four democracies: The special case of women in the United States." *American Sociological Review* 71, 3:376–400.

Andersen, Robert, and Anthony Heath 2002. "Class matters: The persisting effects of contextual social class on individual voting behaviour in Britain, 1964–97." *European Sociological Review* 18, 2:125–138.

Andersen, Robert, and Anthony Heath 2003. "Social identities and political cleavages: The role of political context." *Journal of the Royal Statistical Society, Series A* 166, 3:301–327.

Andersen, Robert, and Meir Yaish 2003. "Social cleavages, electoral reform and party choice: Israel's 'natural' experiment." *Electoral Studies* 22, 3:399–423.

Andersen, Robert, Min Yang, and Anthony Heath 2006. "Class politics and political context in Britain, 1964–97: Have voters become more individualized?" *European Sociological Review* 22:125–138.

Andersen, Robert, and Anna Zimdars 2003. "Class, education and extreme party support in Germany, 1991–98." *German Politics* 12, 2: 1–23.

Barrett, Donald, and Lance Pollack 2005. "Whose gay community? Social class, sexual self-expression, and gay community involvement." *The Sociological Quarterly* 46, 3:437–456.

Barrett, Garry, and Krishna Pendakur 1995. "The asymptotic distribution of the generalized Gini indexes of inequality." *Canadian Journal of Economics* 28, 4B:1042–1055.

Billiet, Jaak, Rob Eisinga, and Peer Scheepers 1996. "Ethnocentrism in the Low Countries: A comparative perspective." *Journal of Ethnic and Migration Studies* 22, 3:401–416.

Bobo, Lawrence, and Camille Zubrinsky 1996. "Attitudes on residential integration: Perceived status differences, mere in-group preference, or racial prejudice?" *Social Forces* 74, 3: 883–909.

Box, Steven 1987. *Recession, Crime and Punishment.* London: Macmillan.

Brym, Robert J., John W.P. Veugelers, Jonah Butovsky, and John Simpson 2004. "Postmaterialism in unresponsive political systems: The Canadian case." *Canadian Review of Sociology and Anthropology* 41, 3: 291–318.

Butovsky, Jonah 2002. "The salience of post-materialism in Canadian politics." *Canadian Review of Sociology and Anthropology* 39, 4: 471–484.

Chong, Dennis 1993. "How people think, reason, and feel about rights and liberties." *American Journal of Political Science* 37, 3: 867–899.

Coenders, Marcel, and Peer Scheepers 1998. "Support for ethnic discrimination in the Netherlands 1979–1993: Effects of period, cohort, and individual characteristics." *European Sociological Review* 14, 4:405–422.

Cotter, David, Joan Hermsen, and Reeve Vanneman 1999. "Systems of gender, race, and class inequality: Multilevel analyses." *Social Forces* 78, 2:433–460.

Curtis, James, Douglas Baer, and Edward Grabb 2001. "Nations of joiners: Explaining voluntary association membership in democratic societies." *American Sociological Review* 66, 6:783–805.

Davis, James A. 1975. "Communism, conformity, and categories: American tolerance in 1954 and 1972–73." *American Journal of Sociology* 81, 3: 491–514.

Dekker, Paul, and Peter Ester 1987. "Working-class authoritarianism: A re-examination of the Lipset thesis." *European Journal of Political Research* 15, 4:395–415.

Driedger, Leo 2003. "Changing boundaries: Sorting space, class, ethnicity, and race in Ontario." *Canadian Review of Sociology and Anthropology* 40, 5:593–621.

Eckstein, Susan 2001. "Community as gift-giving: Collectivist roots of volunteerism." *American Sociological Review* 66, 6:829–851.

Embrick, David, Carol Walther, and Corrine Wickens 2007. "Working class masculinity: Keeping gay men and lesbians out of the workplace." *Sex Roles* 56, 11–12:757–766.

Entwisle, Barbara, Katherine Faust, Ronald Rindfuss, and Toshiko Kaneda 2007. "Networks and contexts: Variation in the structure of social ties." *American Journal of Sociology* 112, 5:1495–1533.

Erickson, Bonnie 1996. "Culture, class, and connections." *American Journal of Sociology* 102, 1:217–251.

Evans, Geoffrey (ed.) 1999. *The End of Class Politics? Class Voting in Comparative Context.* Oxford: Oxford University Press.

Firebaugh, Glenn 2000. "The trend in between-nation income inequality." *Annual Review of Sociology* 26:323–339.

Gay, Claudine 2006. "Seeing difference: The effect of economic disparity on black attitudes toward Latinos." *American Journal of Political Science* 50, 4:982–997.

Gibson, James 1986. "Pluralistic intolerance in America: A reconsideration." *American Politics Quarterly* 14, 4:267–293.

Gibson, James 2006. "Do strong group identities fuel intolerance? Evidence from the South African case." *Political Psychology* 27, 5: 665–705.

Goesling, Brian 2001. "Changing income inequalities within and between nations: New evidence." *American Sociological Review* 66, 5:745–761.

Grabb, Edward 1979. "Working-class authoritarianism and tolerance of outgroups: A reassessment." *Public Opinion Quarterly* 43,"1:36–47.

Grabb, Edward 1980. "Marxist categories and theories of class: The case of working-class authoritarianism." *Pacific Sociological Review* 23, 4:359–376.

Granovetter, Mark 1973. "The strength of weak ties." *American Journal of Sociology* 78, 6: 1360–1380.

Griffin, David R. 1988. *Spirituality and Society: Postmodern Visions.* Albany, NY: State University of New York Press.

Haubert, Jeannie, and Elizabeth Fussell 2006. "Explaining pro-immigrant sentiment in the US: Social class, cosmopolitanism, and perceptions of immigrants." *International Migration Review* 40, 3:489–507.

Hicks, Gary, and Tien-tsung Lee 2006. "Public attitudes toward gays and lesbians: Trends and predictors." *Journal of Homosexuality* 51, 2: 57–77.

Houtman, Dick 2003. "Lipset and 'Working-class authoritarianism.'" *The American Sociologist* 34, 1–2:85–103.

Howard-Hassman, Rhoda 1999. "'Canadian' as an ethnic category: Implications for multiculturalism and national identity." *Canadian Public Policy* 25, 4:523–537.

Inglehart, Ronald 1971. "The silent revolution in Europe: Intergenerational change in postindustrial societies." *American Political Science Review* 65:911–1017.

Inglehart, Ronald 1990. *Culture Shift in Advanced Industrial Society.* Princeton, NJ: Princeton University Press.

Inglehart, Ronald 1997. *Modernization and Postmodernization: Cultural, Economic, and Political Change in 43 Societies.* Princeton, NJ: Princeton University Press.

Inglehart, Ronald, et al. 2001. "World Values Surveys and European Values Surveys, 1981–1984, 1990–1993, 1995–1997, and 1999–2000 [Computer file]. ICPSR version. Ann Arbor, MI: Institute for Social Research [producer]. Ann Arbor, MI: Inter-university Consortium for Political and Social Research [distributor].

Inglehart, Ronald, and Wayne Baker 2000. "Modernization, cultural change, and the persistence of traditional values." *American Sociological Review* 65, 1:19–51.

Jackman, Mary 1978. "General and applied tolerance: Does education increase commitment to racial integration?" *American Journal of Political Science* 22, 2:302–324.

Jackman, Robert 1972. "Political elites, mass publics, and support for democratic principles." *Journal of Politics* 34, 3:753–773.

Jones, Peter 2007. "Making sense of political toleration." *British Journal of Political Science* 37, 3:383–402.

Katz-Gerro, Tally 2002. "Highbrow cultural consumption and class distinction in Italy, Israel, West Germany, Sweden, and the United States." *Social Forces* 81, 1:207–229.

Kazempiur, Abdolmohammad, and Shiva Sitall Halli 2000. "Neighbourhood poverty in Canadian cities." *Canadian Journal of Sociology* 25, 3:369–381.

Kazempiur, Abdolmohammad, and Shiva Sitall Halli 2001. "Immigrants and 'new poverty': The case of Canada." *International Migration Review* 35, 4:1129–1156.

Kohn, M.L. 1977. *Class and Conformity: A Study in Value.* Chicago: University of Chicago Press.

Lea, John, and Jock Young 1984. *What Is to Be Done about Law and Order?* Harmondsworth, UK: Penguin.

Li, Peter 2003. *Destination Canada: Immigration Debates and Issues.* Don Mills, ON: Oxford University Press.

Lipset, Seymour Martin 1959. "Democracy and working-class authoritarianism." *American Sociological Review* 24, 3:482–502.

Lipset, Seymour Martin 1960. *Political Man: The Social Bases of Politics.* Garden City, NY: Doubleday.

Lipset, Seymour Martin 1981. *Political Man: The Social Bases of Politics* (expanded ed.). Baltimore, MD: Johns Hopkins University Press.

Lipsitz, Lewis 1965. "Working-class authoritarianism: A re-evaluation." *American Sociological Review* 30, 1:103–109.

McClosky, Herbert 1964. "Consensus and ideology in American politics." *American Political Science Review* 58, 2:351–382.

McClosky, Herbert, and Alida Brill 1983. *Dimensions of Tolerance: What Americans Believe about Civil Liberties.* New York: Basic Books.

McCutcheon, Allan L. 1985. "A latent class analysis of tolerance for nonconformity in the

American public." *Public Opinion Quarterly* 49, 4:474–488.

Merchant, David, and Paul Rich 2004. "Canada and the Commonwealth: Does the Commonwealth have a future as well as a past?" *American Behavioural Scientist* 47, 10:1319–1328.

Merton, Robert 1957. *Social Theory and Social Structure*. Glencoe, IL: The Free Press.

Milanovic, Branko 2005. *Worlds Apart: Measuring International and Global Inequality*. Princeton, NJ: Princeton University Press.

Money, Jeannette 1999. *Fences and Neighbors: The Political Geography of Immigration Control*. Ithaca, NY: Cornell University Press.

Mulder, Marlene, and Harvey Krahn 2005. "Individual and community-level determinants of support for immigration and cultural diversity in Canada." *Canadian Review of Sociology and Anthropology* 42, 2:421–444.

Nevitte, Neil, Herman Bakvis, and Roger Gibbins 1989. "The ideological contours of 'new politics' in Canada: Policy, mobilization and partisan support. *Canadian Journal of Political Science* 22, 3:475–503.

Nielsen, François, and Arthur S. Alderson 1995. "Income inequality, development, and dualism." *American Sociological Review* 60, 5: 674–701.

Overby, Marvin, and Jay Barth 2002. "Contact, community context, and public attitudes toward gay men and lesbians." *Polity* 34, 4:433–456.

Pakulski, J. 1993. "The dying of class or of Marxist class theory?" *International Sociology* 8, 3:279–292.

Pakulski, J., and M. Waters 1996. *The Death of Class*. London: Sage.

Parkin, Frank 1967. "Working class Conservatives: a theory of political deviance." *British Journal of Sociology* 18:278–290.

Pedersen, Willy 1996. "Working class boys at the margins: Ethnic prejudice, cultural capital, and gender." *Acta Sociologica* 39, 3: 257–279.

Pendakur, Krishna, and Ravi Pendakur 1998. "The colour of money: Earnings differentials among ethnic groups in Canada." *Canadian Journal of Economics* 31, 3:518–548.

Pendakur, Krishna, and Ravi Pendakur 2007. "Minority earnings disparity across the distribution." *Canadian Public Policy* 33, 1:41–61.

Prothro, J.W., and C.W. Grigg 1960. "Fundamental principles of democracy: Bases of agreement and disagreement." *Journal of Politics* 22, 2: 276–294.

Quillian, Lincoln 1995. "Prejudice as a response to perceived group threat: Population composition and anti-immigrant and racial prejudice in Europe." *American Sociological Review* 60, 4: 586–611.

Runciman, W.G. 1966. *Relative Deprivation and Social Justice:. A Study of Attitudes to Social Inequality in Twentieth Century England*. Berkeley, CA: University of California Press.

Scheepers, Peer, Rob Eisinga, and Leo Van Snippenburg 1989. "Klassepositie en autoritarisme: Hernieuwde toets van een klassieke hypothese" [Class position and authoritarianism: Renewed test of a classical hypothesis]. *Acta Politica* 24:337–346.

Semyonov, Moshe, Rebeca Raijman, and Anastasia Gorodzeisky 2006. "The rise of anti-foreigner sentiment in European societies, 1988–2000." *American Sociological Review* 71, 3:426–449.

Statistics Canada 2003. "Selected demographic and cultural characteristics." Topic-based tabulation number 97F0010XCB2001044.

Stouffer, Samuel 1949. *The American Soldier*. Princeton, NJ: Princeton University Press.

Stouffer, Stephen A. 1955. *Communism, Conformity, and Civil Liberties: A Cross-Section of the Nation Speaks its Mind*. New York: Doubleday.

Sullivan, John, James Piereson, and George Marcus 1982. *Political Tolerance and American Democracy*. Chicago: Chicago University Press.

Svallfors, Stefan 2006. *The Moral Economy of Class*. Stanford, CA: Stanford University Press.

Tajfel, Henri 1974. "Social identity and intergroup behaviour." *Social Science Information* 13, 2:65–93.

Teather, Elizabeth 1997. "Voluntary organizations as agents in the becoming of place." *Canadian Geographer* 41, 3:226–235.

Tomlinson, Mark 2003. "Lifestyle and social class." *European Sociological Review* 19, 1: 97–111.

United Nations 2005. *UN Statistics Division Online Database.* (http://unstats.un.org/unsd/cdb/cdb_dict_xrxx.asp?def_code=63)

Uslaner, Eric 2002. *The Moral Foundations of Trust.* Cambridge, UK: Cambridge University Press.

Uslaner, Eric, and Mitchell Brown 2002. "Inequality, trust, and civic engagement." *American Politics Research* 33, 6:868–894.

Vanneman, Reeve, and Thomas Pettigrew 1972. "Race and relative deprivation in the urban United States." *Race* 13, 4:461–486.

Walker, Iain, and Thomas Pettigrew 1984. "Relative deprivation theory: An overview and conceptual critique." *British Journal of Social Psychology* 23 (November):301–310.

Walters, Suzanna Danuta 2001. *All the Rage: The Story of Gay Visibility in America.* Chicago: University of Chicago Press.

Weeden, Kim A., and David Grusky 2005. "The case for a new class map." *American Journal of Sociology* 111, 1:141–212.

Weldon, Steven 2006. "The institutional context of tolerance for ethnic minorities: A comparative multilevel analysis of Western Europe." *American Journal of Political Science* 50, 2: 331–349.

White, Linda 2003. "Liberalism, group rights, and the boundaries of toleration: The case of minority religious schools in Ontario." *Canadian Journal of Political Science* 36, 5:975–1003.

Wilson, John, and Marc Musick 1997. "Who cares? Toward an integrated theory of volunteer work." *American Sociological Review* 62, 5: 694–713.

Woldoff, Rachel 2002. "The effects of local stressors on neighborhood attachment." *Social Forces* 81, 1:87–116.

Young, Jock 1999. *The Exclusive Society: Social Exclusion, Crime and Difference in Late Modernity.* Thousand Oaks, CA: Sage.

chapter twenty-seven

Political Involvement, Civic Engagement, and Social Inequality

James Curtis, Edward Grabb,
Thomas Perks, and Tina Chui
(An original chapter written
for this volume.)

INTRODUCTION

In the popular media and public discussions, Canada is normally portrayed as a free and democratic society, where all citizens have the right to influence political decisions, and where everyone is encouraged to engage in different forms of civic participation and community or collective action. In such a society, we might expect that people are relatively similar in their levels of involvement in the formal political process, and in the "parapolitics" that occurs among local organizations and community interest groups. Presumably, then, most Canadians should participate to about the same degree in such activities as voting, discussing politics, trying to influence others, joining political parties and community groups, making

public protests, and supporting social movements.

In other words, we might think that, for these types of behaviours, members of more privileged status groups do not have an advantage over other people. In fact, we might even reason that the disadvantaged have more to protest about than other people and, therefore, are more highly represented than the advantaged in public protest activities, such as signing petitions or joining in demonstrations.

Some social scientists have questioned, however, whether there really is such a broad base to political and civic engagement in Canada and other democratic countries. In particular, these researchers have doubted that individuals who rank lower on various social status dimensions have as great an opportunity or inclination to participate in these types of activities. This question is clearly an important one for students of social inequality to consider, because political action and interest group involvement are normally seen as fundamental to our basic human rights and civil liberties.

Research in Canada and other societies, especially extensive work in the United States, has shown that there is in fact a relationship between achieved and ascribed statuses and level of involvement in both politics and community or civic activities (see, e.g., Curtis 1971; Smith 1975; Curtis and Lambert 1976; Milbrath and Goel 1977; McPherson and Lockwood 1980; Palisi and Palisi 1984; Knoke 1986; Kay et al. 1987; Curtis et al. 1989; Curtis, Grabb, and Baer 1992; Curtis, Baer, and Grabb 2001; Baer et al. 2001; Curtis and Grabb 2002). These studies have found, for example, that persons with higher occupational status, education, and income are more likely than other people to join and participate in voluntary organizations of various kinds.

Some studies also indicate that disadvantaged racial and ethnic groups, such as American blacks, are less likely to be involved in voluntary associations than are groups higher in the ethnic stratification system. However, other research also suggests that these ethnic or racial differences may be partially the result of socio-economic inequalities, rather than racial or ethnic differences per se (e.g., Smith 1975; Grabb and Curtis 1992).

Along similar lines, research indicates that middle-aged people are more likely to participate in voluntary organizations than are older and younger people, and males are more likely to do so than are females (e.g., Curtis 1971; Smith 1975; Cutler 1976; McPherson and Lockwood 1980; Edwards et al. 1984; Palisi and Palisi 1984; Knoke 1986; Curtis et al. 1992; Curtis et al. 2001; Corrigall-Brown

2002). It should be noted that, with regard to gender, one apparent exception to the general pattern concerns "new" voluntary associations, which focus on support for so-called "new social movements," including animal rights groups, women's organizations, peace groups, and environment and conservation organizations. Canadian research indicates that, in these types of voluntary associations, women are more active than men (Curtis and Grabb 2002). Otherwise, however, there is a general tendency for men to participate more often, not only in voluntary associations, but also in formal politics, such as voting, political party membership, and political interest (e.g., Curtis and Lambert 1976; Milbrath and Goel 1977; Chui et al. 1993; Curtis et al. 2001; Curtis and Grabb 2002).

These differences have been explained in a number of ways. One well-known early explanation suggested that such patterns are largely accounted for by the "relative centrality" of different groups in society (see, e.g., Milbrath and Goel 1977; Chui et al. 1993). According to this perspective, some people are more centrally positioned in important social networks. Persons from the higher socio-economic strata and from the more privileged or established racial, ethnic, gender, and age groupings are perhaps the best examples. These individuals generally have more power and resources at their disposal than others do. They also tend to have greater knowledge, information, and awareness about how various organizations operate in their community and elsewhere. For these reasons, it is argued, people of higher rank or social status are more likely to be active participants in the political processes that help to shape their society.

More recently, writers have applied a different, though related, perspective that focuses on the concept of "social capital." Although the definitions of this concept vary somewhat (see, e.g., Coleman 1988; Putnam 1995, 2000; Lin 2000), social capital can basically be thought of as a resource, or a form of social power, that arises from and is represented by people's locations in key social networks. From this perspective, as well, it is argued that those groups and individuals who are in advantaged or dominant positions in the class, gender, ethnic, and other hierarchies of society tend to be more actively engaged in political and civic affairs, both in their local communities and in society generally.

Involvement and interest in politics and other civic activities can stem from various motivations. A belief in the value of individual participation in a free society and a wish to contribute to the welfare and progress of one's community and country are two examples. It is likely, however, that the tendency for members of more prosperous and powerful status groups to be more engaged in such activities is also due to their own private or special interests. In particular, people from advantaged groups may be more highly motivated to take part in political and community life out of a desire to maintain their superior position in the stratification system, by working in and having greater control over those organizations that help decide on important policies in the community or the wider society (see, e.g., Olson 1965; Lin 2000; Putnam 2000).

In this paper, we examine recent information dealing with the relationship between social inequality and political or community activity in Canada. We consider the relationship between people's positions on a number of different dimensions of inequality, on the one hand, and a wide range of measures of political involvement, civic engagement, and community participation, on the other hand.

DATA SOURCES AND PROCEDURES

We have used two data sources for our analyses for this chapter: one from responses to a national survey conducted in 1991 and the other from responses to a national survey in 2000. The first data source provides us with much more detailed information, so we shall begin with a discussion of that study, its procedures, and its results. We will turn to the 2000 study following our discussion of the first study.

STUDY ONE

Data Source

A national sample of adult Canadians was interviewed as part of the larger World Values Survey in 1991–1993, an international survey of more than 40 countries conducted by Ronald Inglehart and associates (for details, see Inglehart et al. 1994). The present analyses are limited to the Canadian respondents aged 21 and older. Some younger respondents, aged 18 to 21, were excluded from the analyses because many were still in school and, therefore, may not have been able to give as much time to political activities as older people.

Measures of Respondents' Political and Organization Activities

Five measures of political activities were used: discussing politics,[1] attempting to persuade people on issues,[2] interest in politics,[3] expecting to vote in the next election,[4] and political group activity.[5] Table 27-1 shows the response categories for each of these types of activity. In addition, we used a measure of public protest activity, based on responses to the following questions:

> Now I would like you to look at this card. I'm going to read out some different forms of political action that people can take, and I would like you to tell me, for each one, whether you have actually done any of these things, whether you might do it, or would never, under any circumstances, do it: *signing a petition, joining a boycott, attending lawful demonstrations, joining strikes, or occupying buildings or factories.*

The responses for each of these activities were given scores as follows: "Have actually done" = 3; "Might do it" = 2; and "Would never" = 1. These scores were then summed for each respondent to give her or him a measure of *participation in public protest activity*. This measure ranged from 6 (low protest activity) to 18 (high protest activity).

The survey also yielded information on the respondent's stated *support for social movements*; whether or not they were a member of organizations working for these movements. Respondents were asked:

> There are a number of groups and movements looking for public support. For each of the following movements, which I read out, can you tell me whether you approve or disapprove of this movement?: *ecology or nature protection* movement; *anti-nuclear energy* movement; *disarmament* movement; *human rights* movement (at home and abroad); *women's* movement; and *anti-apartheid* movement.

For present purposes, the response categories for each of the six movements were assigned scores as follows: "Approve strongly" = 4; "Approve somewhat" = 3; "Disapprove somewhat" = 2; and "Disapprove strongly" = 1. Then the respondents' support ratings for the six social movements were summed for a measure with a range of 6 (low support) to 24 (high support).

These six social movements have been referred to by others as "new social movements." Although some of these movements are tied to causes or issues that are not precisely new (e.g., women's rights and equality), they are called "new" because they typically have enjoyed renewed prominence in recent years. In addition, they are also seen to operate outside or independently of more traditional movements, such as the labour union movement and early suffrage movements (see Carroll 1992; Larana et al. 1994).

Finally, we also used a measure that gauged the *voluntary organization activity* of respondents. First, each respondent reported his or her memberships in community organizations, in answer to the following question: "Which, if any, of the following do you belong to?" A checklist of 16 possible organization categories was supplied: charities and social welfare, churches or religious organizations, education or arts groups, trade unions, political parties or groups, community action groups, human rights organizations, conservation or environmental groups, animal welfare groups, youth work groups, sport and recreation organizations, professional associations, women's groups, peace groups, health organizations, and "others." People were also asked, "And do you currently do any unpaid voluntary work for any of them?" Each respondent was given a score of 1 for each organization in which she or he was a member only, and a score of 2 for each working membership. These scores were then summed across all types of organizations, to produce a scale of voluntary organization activity. The measure ranged from 0 (no involvement) to 32 (high involvement).

Social Status Measures

Nine different measures of inequality or social status were examined for their possible relationship to the political and community activity measures. Tables 27-4 and 27-5 later in this chapter provide details on the exact categories used for each of the social status variables. Because of the international nature of the World Values Survey, *education* had to be measured using an indirect indicator, which was the respondent's age at completion of schooling; the 10 values for this measure ranged from finished school "at 12 years of age or earlier" to finished school "at 21 years of age or older." Respondent's *occupational status* was measured using a set of 11 different categories that were roughly rank-ordered from high to low status. *Age* was grouped into six categories, with values ranging from younger (age 21–29) to older (70 or more). *Gender* was divided simply into female versus male. *Household income* had 10 levels, from a low of less than $5000 per year to a high of $50 000 or more. *Language group* was divided into English versus French. The available race measure produced a fourfold classification: whites, blacks, Chinese, and all others. Respondents were also divided into two categories according to *nativity* or country of birth: Canadian-born versus foreign-born. *Region* was a seven-category measure, running east to west, from the Atlantic region to British Columbia.

Overall Involvement in Political and Organizational Activities

Tables 27-1, 27-2, and 27-3 show the overall involvement of the respondents in the various political and organizational activities. Starting with Table 27-1, we see that a relatively large proportion of people, close to 72%, indicated that they would vote if an election were held tomorrow. This proportion is very similar to the voter turnouts in recent Canadian elections; these ranged from 69% to 75% in the 1980–1993 period, for example (Elections Canada 1993:Table 4). In addition, almost 60% said that they were either "very" interested (20%) or "somewhat" interested (39%) in politics. Close to 20% discussed politics "often," and another 57% did so "occasionally"). However, only 14% tried regularly to persuade fellow workers, friends, or family members concerning political issues. If we consider involvement in groups that are identified by the respondent as "political parties or groups," only 8% reported such involvement, with 5% saying they were simply a member of such a group, and another 3% also doing volunteer work for the group.

If we look at the other end of the scale, non-involvement, we see that 13% of the sample said they "never" attempted to persuade others of their views; almost one-quarter (23%) of the respondents never discussed politics; about 40% reported that they were "not very" interested or "not at all" interested in politics; 28% did not intend to vote; and 92% were not involved in political groups in any way.

When we turn to participation in all types of voluntary groups in the community (Table 27-1), we find that 60% had one or more memberships and about 43% were doing work in one or more organizations. About 53% had multiple memberships, and about 23% were working in more than one organization.

Overall, then, we find little evidence of mass involvement in political activity in Canada. It is true that a sizable majority of Canadians vote federally, express some political interest, and at least occasionally engage in political discussion. However, very few are members of political parties or politically oriented organizations, and

TABLE 27-1	Levels of Involvement in Various Types of Political and Organizational Activities: Overall National Adult Sample		
Type of Activity and Level of Involvement	**Percentage of Sample**	**Type of Activity and Level of Involvement**	**Percentage of Sample**
Discuss Politics		**Political Group Involvement**	
Often	19.7	None	92.2
Occasionally	57.1	Member, No Work	4.6
Never	23.2	Working Member	3.3
(N=)	(1618)	(N=)	(1620)
Persuade Friends		**Voting**	
Often	13.9	No	28.5
Time to Time/Rarely	73.0	Yes	71.5
Never	13.1	(N=)	(1625)
(N=)	(1619)		
		Voluntary Organization Involvement	
Political Interest		Member of None	35.9
Very	20.2	One	20.8
Some	39.3	Two	16.4
Not Very	26.2	Three Plus	26.9
Not at All	14.3	(N=)	(1625)
(N=)	(1619)	Working for None	56.7
		One	20.1
		Two	11.4
		Three Plus	11.8
		(N=)	(1625)

even fewer do volunteer work for such organizations. There is stronger evidence of community participation if we look at the proportion of people who belong to at least one voluntary organization of whatever type, though even here the proportion of people who are not only members, but also actively involved, is less than half of the total sample.

In Table 27-2 we consider rates of involvement in the various types of public protest actions. Here we see, once more, that involvement levels are generally low, with the exception of signing petitions. Seventy-seven percent of respondents report signing a petition, while another 14% think they might do so sometime in the future, and only 8% say they would never do so.

However, for joining a boycott, only about one-quarter (24%) have ever done this, and 34% say they never would do so. For attending demonstrations the parallel figures are 22% ("Have done") and 36% ("Would never do"). The rates of involvement are even lower for "Joining a lawful strike," with only 7% doing this, and 66% saying they would never do it. Finally, only 3% have occupied facilities, and 78% would never do so. If we sum the responses across these activities, to create an Index of Public Protest Activities ranging from 8 to 15, the overall sample has an average score of only 9.1.

In Table 27-3 we see that reasonably large proportions of respondents express

TABLE 27-2   Levels of Involvement in Five Types of Public Protest Activity: Overall National Adult Sample

Level of Involvement	Types of Protest Actions				
	Sign Petition %	Join Boycott %	Attend Demonstration %	Join Strike %	Occupy Facility %
Have Done	77.3	24.1	21.6	7.3	3.0
Might Do	14.4	41.8	42.0	26.4	18.6
Would Never Do	8.3	34.1	36.4	66.3	78.4
Total	100%	100%	100%	100%	100%

(N = 1625)

TABLE 27-3   Levels of Approval for Six Social Movements: Overall National Adult Sample

Social Movement	Approval Level					
	Approve Strongly %	Somewhat %	Disapprove Somewhat %	Strongly %	(N)	Total
Ecology	53.5	41.3	3.9	1.3	(1590)	100%
Anti-nuclear	32.3	41.8	19.9	6.0	(1549)	100%
Disarmament	39.3	39.8	14.8	6.1	(1555)	100%
Human Rights	57.8	35.7	5.1	1.3	(1579)	100%
Women's	35.8	48.1	12.7	3.4	(1577)	100%
Anti-apartheid	46.5	36.8	11.5	5.2	(1439)	100%

support for each of the six new social movements. Well over one-half of the sample approve "strongly" or "somewhat" with each social movement. The "strong" support ranges from a high of 58% for the human rights movement and 54% for the ecology movement to 47% for anti-apartheid, 39% for disarmament, 36% for the women's movement, and 32% for the anti-nuclear movement. When we sum the responses across all six types of social movement, producing an Index of Social Movement Support with a range of 6 to 24, we find a high average score for the overall sample of 19.6.

Social Status and Political Activity

We now consider the key question of whether or not social status is related to level of involvement in the various political and community activities. In other words, do all categories of Canadians get involved more or less equally, or do people from more advantaged groups get involved more than others?

Table 27-4 provides data on the relationship between the five forms of political participation listed in Table 27-1 and the nine different measures of social status.

TABLE 27-4	**Social Statuses and Average Scores for Involvement in Five Types of Political Activities**

Social Status Categories		Type of Activity				
	N	**Discuss Politics**	**Persuade Friends**	**Political Interest**	**Voting**	**Political Group Activity**
Total Sample	1625	(1.96)	(2.01)	(2.65)	(0.72)	(0.11)
Years of Schooling						
<12 years	32	1.84	1.97	2.35	0.66	0.06
13	20	1.85	1.80	2.40	0.50	0.05
14	73	1.68	1.88	2.45	0.62	0.05
15	82	1.73	1.87	2.93	0.59	0.04
16	170	1.77	1.86	2.42	0.66	0.08
17	172	1.87	2.00	2.52	0.76	0.05
18	297	1.90	1.99	2.61	0.72	0.12
19	137	1.91	2.04	2.58	0.69	0.10
20	93	2.04	2.02	2.74	0.78	0.09
21+ years	519	2.18	2.10	2.88	0.76	0.15
eta		(0.25)	(0.17)	(0.18)	(0.13)	(0.10)
significance		‡	‡	‡	†	*
Occupational Level						
Owner > 10 employees	47	2.17	2.32	3.13	0.75	0.38
Owner < 10 employees	63	2.06	2.05	2.83	0.71	0.05
Professional	289	2.20	2.07	2.90	0.74	0.18
Middle Manager	143	2.12	2.08	2.86	0.76	0.12
Lower Manager	191	1.88	1.94	2.52	0.70	0.05
Supervisor	39	2.14	2.08	2.95	0.73	0.15
Skilled Lab	117	1.85	1.93	2.53	0.76	0.07
Semi-skilled	234	1.81	1.97	2.47	0.68	0.09
Unskilled	228	1.78	1.97	2.38	0.68	0.07
Farmers	79	2.04	2.03	2.84	0.75	0.19
All Others	175	1.87	1.94	2.54	0.69	0.07
eta		(0.25)	(0.15)	(0.23)	(0.06)	(0.16)
significance		‡	‡	‡	n.s.	‡
Income Level						
<$5000	71	1.75	1.96	2.27	0.62	0.03
$5000–10 000	90	1.99	1.97	2.69	0.74	0.10
10 000–15 000	98	1.88	1.94	2.55	0.69	0.04
15 000–20 000	109	1.88	1.99	2.53	0.63	0.02
20 000–25 000	152	1.89	1.97	2.58	0.70	0.14
25 000–30 000	224	1.99	1.99	2.66	0.77	0.14
30 000–35 000	189	1.96	2.04	2.71	0.75	0.09
35 000–40 000	173	2.07	2.03	2.78	0.84	0.11
40 000–45 000	103	2.19	2.05	2.83	0.82	0.17
50 000+	178	2.19	2.16	2.92	0.79	0.19
eta		(0.17)	(0.13)	(0.16)	(0.15)	(0.13)
significance		‡	†	‡	‡	†

TABLE 27-4	(continued)					

Social Status Categories — Type of Activity

	N	Discuss Politics	Persuade Friends	Political Interest	Voting	Political Group Activity
Age						
21–29	308	1.81	2.03	2.44	0.70	0.08
30–39	457	1.95	2.02	2.58	0.73	0.11
40–49	315	2.01	2.05	2.70	0.73	0.14
50–59	207	2.03	2.02	2.84	0.76	0.15
60–69	191	2.11	1.95	2.90	0.71	0.09
70 & over	147	1.93	1.88	2.67	0.60	0.09
eta		(0.14)	(0.09)	(0.15)	(0.09)	(0.05)
significance		‡	†	‡	*	n.s.
Gender						
Male	807	1.95	2.02	2.75	0.73	0.14
Female	818	1.94	2.00	2.56	0.70	0.09
eta		(0.05)	(0.03)	(0.10)	(0.04)	(0.06)
significance		n.s.	n.s.	‡	n.s.	†
Language Group						
English	1251	1.98	2.00	2.71	0.74	0.11
French	374	1.90	2.04	2.46	0.62	0.10
eta		(0.05)	(0.03)	(0.11)	(0.11)	(0.02)
significance		n.s.	n.s.	‡	‡	n.s.
Race						
Whites	1499	1.96	2.01	2.67	0.73	0.11
Blacks	15	2.13	2.00	2.47	0.53	0.13
Chinese	48	1.83	1.98	2.51	0.56	0.13
All Others	63	1.90	1.95	2.33	0.54	0.11
eta		(0.05)	(0.02)	(0.08)	(0.11)	(0.01)
significance		n.s.	n.s.	*	‡	n.s.
Nativity						
Not Born in Canada	281	2.09	2.01	2.79	0.69	0.12
Born in Canada	1344	1.94	2.01	2.63	0.72	0.11
eta		(.09)	(0.01)	(0.06)	(0.03)	(0.02)
significance		†	n.s.	†	n.s.	n.s.
Region						
AT	133	1.81	1.88	2.37	0.64	0.15
QU	403	1.93	2.04	2.50	0.63	0.11
ON	611	1.99	2.01	2.74	0.75	0.09
MA	59	1.90	2.03	2.50	0.69	0.15
SK	74	1.97	1.97	2.82	0.74	0.12
AB	171	2.02	2.03	2.70	0.74	0.20
BC	174	2.04	2.02	2.88	0.74	0.05
eta		(0.09)	(0.08)	(0.16)	(0.14)	(0.09)
significance		†	n.s.	‡	‡	†

n.s. = Not a statistically significant difference. † Significant at $p < 0.01$.
* Significant at $p < 0.05$. ‡ Significant at $p < 0.001$.

Based on the relative centrality and social capital perspectives, we would expect the following groups to be higher in political involvement than their less advantaged counterparts: the more highly educated, those with higher incomes, those with higher occupational status, English speakers, whites, the native-born, males, the middle-aged, and those living in the more economically powerful regions of the country, especially Ontario.

Overall, the findings confirm many, though not all, of these expectations. As predicted, education and income have statistically significant relationships with all five measures of political participation, and in the expected direction. That is, the more highly educated respondents and those with higher incomes are more likely than other people to vote, to be involved in political groups, to show interest in politics, to discuss politics, and to attempt to influence others concerning political issues.

Age, occupation level, and region are significantly related to four of the five political activity measures. As expected, the middle-aged are more involved in voting, express greater political interest, discuss politics more, and attempt to influence the opinions of others more, at least compared with younger people and (particularly) older people. Occupational status is related in the expected way to all political activities except voting, where there is no statistically significant pattern. As for region, residents of the powerful or more prosperous regions, especially Ontario and the western provinces, tend to be higher on political interest, discussing politics, and voting. Respondents from the western regions also show higher levels of political group involvement.

Moving on to the other ascribed statuses (Table 27-4), we see that language group is related to discussing politics, political interest, and voting, with English speakers higher than French speakers, which is again consistent with the relative centrality and social capital perspectives. One caution here, though, is that voting pertains to federal elections and not provincial elections. If the voting question dealt with provincial elections, it is likely that the proportions of French speakers and Quebecers voting would be more similar to those of other Canadians. Race appears to be related to only two of the five measures of political activity; for political interest and voting, whites, as expected, are more active than other groups. Finally, in the case of nativity, we find no evidence of the expected pattern: The native-born are *less* involved than the foreign-born in political interest and political discussions, and there are no significant differences by place of birth for the other three political activity measures.

In Table 27-5, we relate the nine social status variables to three different indices of activity: *political protest, social movement support*, and *community organization involvement*. Most of the relationships in Table 27-5 are statistically significant, and in the expected direction. In general, advantaged groups tend to be more involved in the three types of activity. The exceptions are that race and nativity are not significantly related to public protest and social movement support, and income is related to public protest and organization involvement, but not to support for social movements. As we would expect, those higher in education are more involved in public protest, in community interest groups, and in supporting social movements than are their less educated counterparts. The same is true for males compared with females, the middle-aged compared with other age groups, and those with higher incomes and occupational statuses

TABLE 27-5 Social Statuses and Involvement in Public Protest, Social Movements, and Voluntary Community Organizations

Social Status Categories		Average Level of Involvement				
	N	Public Protest	N	Support Movements	N	Community Groups
Total Sample	1625	9.07	1625	19.60	1625	2.66
Years of Schooling						
<12 years	29	6.83	19	17.90	32	1.75
13	20	8.35	13	17.31	20	2.45
14	67	7.66	48	19.13	73	1.60
15	75	7.91	67	18.76	82	2.15
16	153	8.19	138	19.25	170	1.69
17	158	8.46	143	19.69	172	2.23
18	271	9.12	251	19.55	297	2.48
19	120	9.23	114	19.65	137	2.42
20	89	9.35	86	19.95	93	2.77
21+ years	479	9.96	460	19.93	519	3.56
eta		(0.33)		(0.12)		(0.21)
significance		‡		†		‡
Occupational Level						
Owner > 10 employees	45	9.64	44	19.43	47	3.98
Owner < 10 employees	59	9.10	57	19.58	63	1.94
Professional	265	10.15	259	20.06	289	4.03
Middle Manager	131	9.32	124	19.17	143	3.04
Lower Manager	175	8.79	151	19.66	191	2.36
Supervisor	54	8.98	48	18.44	59	2.41
Skilled Lab	107	9.42	94	19.06	117	2.09
Semi-skilled	219	8.90	193	19.83	234	2.10
Unskilled	211	8.61	198	19.38	228	3.27
Farmers	73	8.47	66	18.08	79	2.21
All Others	161	7.99	132	18.96	175	2.65
eta		(0.25)		(0.18)		(0.23)
significance		‡		‡		‡
Income Level						
<$5000	62	7.77	53	19.57	71	1.94
$5000–10 000	82	8.37	70	19.56	90	2.27
10 000–15 000	89	7.91	77	19.21	98	1.63
15 000–20 000	100	8.68	86	19.76	109	2.31
20 000–25 000	145	8.86	124	19.23	152	2.88

TABLE 27-5	(continued)

Social Status Categories		Average Level of Involvement				
	N	Public Protest	N	Support Movements	N	Community Groups
25 000–30 000	211	9.03	192	19.28	224	2.65
30 000–35 000	177	9.52	170	19.58	189	2.94
35 000–40 000	163	9.77	154	19.63	173	2.73
40 000–45 000	95	9.88	94	19.87	103	3.21
50 000+	170	10.04	161	19.91	108	3.76
eta		(0.28)		(0.08)		(0.17)
significance		‡		n.s.		†
Age						
21–29	275	9.35	255	20.16	308	2.19
30–39	423	9.65	392	20.18	457	2.67
40–49	288	9.51	278	19.72	315	3.11
50–59	196	8.56	173	19.34	207	3.02
60–69	172	8.05	165	8.21	191	2.69
70 & over	136	7.32	103	18.15	147	2.34
eta		(0.21)		(0.24)		(0.11)
significance		‡		‡		†
Gender						
Male	757	9.34	701	19.22	807	2.57
Female	733	8.78	665	19.97	878	2.79
eta		(0.09)		(0.13)		(0.03)
significance		‡		‡		n.s.
Language Group						
English	1142	8.95	1058	18.33	1251	2.80
French	348	9.44	308	20.47	374	2.28
eta		(0.12)		(0.17)		(0.08)
significance		‡		‡		†
Race						
Whites	1385	9.08	1261	19.59	1499	2.69
Blacks	11	8.00	14	21.00	15	2.00
Chinese	40	8.63	40	19.70	48	3.33
All Others	54	9.09	51	19.06	63	2.14
eta		(0.09)		(0.08)		(0.06)
significance		n.s.		n.s.		n.s.

TABLE 27-5 *(continued)*

Social Status Categories	Average Level of Involvement					
	N	Public Protest	N	Support Movements	N	Community Groups
Nativity						
Not Born in Canada	254	8.96	240	19.46	281	2.83
Born in Canada	1236	9.08	1126	19.62	1344	2.65
eta		(0.03)		(0.02)		(0.06)
significance		n.s.		n.s.		n.s.
Region						
AT	125	8.08	112	19.63	133	2.61
QC	374	9.51	332	20.48	403	2.36
ON	564	8.78	526	19.70	611	2.70
MB	50	9.16	47	19.21	39	3.45
SK	69	8.86	68	18.25	74	2.61
AB	150	9.25	127	18.68	171	2.19
BC	158	9.69	154	19.73	174	2.67
eta		(0.22)		(0.20)		(0.09)
significance		‡		‡		*

n.s. = Not a statistically significant difference.
* Significant at $p < 0.05$.
† Significant at $p < 0.01$.
‡ Significant at $p < 0.001$.

compared with others. One exception concerns the relationship between gender and support for new social movements, where we find, as other research suggests, that women are slightly higher in support than are men. Another possible exception concerns occupation, where we find that skilled workers, despite being relatively low in occupational status, have higher involvement levels on the three activity indices than might otherwise be expected. This is perhaps because of their links to labour organizations.

In the case of language group and region, the results are not entirely consistent with either the relative centrality or the social capital perspectives. We find that the French and Quebec respondents are comparatively high in public protest activity and social movement support, although residents of Alberta and British Columbia rank high on both of these measures as well. The results for voluntary association activity more closely follow the predicted pattern, with the English and people from Ontario being higher on this measure.

We also conducted some multivariate analyses, using a technique called multiple classification analysis (MCA). This technique allowed us to look at the relationship between any one of the social status variables and the activity measures, while simultaneously controlling for the effects of all other social status variables.

These analyses are not reported in tables here, to conserve space. However, the results are largely the same as those shown in Tables 27-4 and 27-5. These results suggest that the patterns found in Tables 27-4 and 27-5 do not change in direction, even with the inclusion of controls, although some of the relationships are no longer statistically significant after controls. Thinking of the relationships in Table 27-4, first, we find that, with controls, one of the effects of occupational status (for political discussions) is no longer significant. The effect before controls may have been largely due to the strong joint effect of educational status on both occupation and the political discussion measure. The same change occurs for the effects of income on both political discussion and political persuasion. These appear to have resulted mainly from the effects of educational status differences. Also, one effect of race (on political group involvement), one effect of language group (on voting), and one effect of nativity (on political group involvement) are not statistically significant after controls for the effects of education, occupation, and income, suggesting that it is differences resulting from these three achieved characteristics that make for the differences in political involvement by the ascribed characteristics.

Controls produce few changes in the statistical significance of the results reported in Table 27-5 for the indices of public protest, support of social movements, and involvement in community groups. The exceptions are involvement in public protest and community organizations by language group, where the language group differences are found not to be significant after controls; however, the pattern of higher involvement by Quebec residents persisted with controls.

SUPPLEMENTAL ANALYSES FROM A SECOND STUDY

The data for our second study are from the 2000 National Survey of Giving, Volunteering, and Participating (NSGVP). This survey was conducted by Statistics Canada through telephone interviews with a representative sample of Canadians aged 15 and over. We chose as a working subsample from the NSGVP data only respondents aged 25 and over (N = 15 912). Statistics Canada placed all respondents under the age of 24 together in the same 10-year category (aged 15–24) in the data, at least for the coding in the public-use data file. Therefore, respondents in their teens could not be separated from respondents in their early twenties. The age restriction of 25 and older for the working sample was chosen to ensure that respondents in our analyses had completed their schooling.

We chose four alternative measures of *current adult community participation* for our analyses. These measures were not represented well in Study One, and we wanted to determine whether the pattern of findings in the first study extended to these other measures of community activities. The measures (with the ranges given in parentheses) were total number of organizations volunteered with over the past 12 months (coded as 0 to 20),[6] total number of voluntary association memberships held last year (coded from 0 to 7, the latter for seven or more associations),[7] the number of recent elections voted in, counting the last federal, provincial, and, municipal elections (0 to 3),[8] and an index of attention to current affairs, based on responses to three questions.[9]

The social status characteristics that we used as predictors in the analyses were largely the same as in Study One. They were as follows: current employment status (full-time, part-time, or not working); personal income (Statistics Canada provided five categories, which included none, up to $19 999; $20 000–$39 999; $40 000–$59 999; and $60 000 and over); level of education completed (less than high school graduation, high school graduate, some post-secondary education, and university degree); age group (coded into 10-year categories between 25 and 64 years, with a final category of 65 years and over); gender; language of interview (English or French); nativity (native-born or foreign-born); and region (the Atlantic provinces, Quebec, Ontario, the Prairies, and British Columbia). We again used MCA as our main analysis procedure.

To conserve space, we do not provide tables of results for Study Two. Most of the patterns of results were similar to those already discussed for Study One, but they were not entirely the same. First, the results for the achieved social statuses were as follows. The higher the education level, the higher the amount of voting over the three elections, the higher the voluntary activity (on both measures), and the greater the attention to current affairs. Income level showed very much the same patterns of direct relationships with the activity measures, in that those with higher incomes were more involved in each case. There was no occupational status measure, but there was an employment status measure. Those who were employed were more involved than those not in the workforce, although it is interesting as well that, for three of the four activity measures, people working part-time were somewhat more involved than people working full-time. (The one exception was the index of attention to current affairs.) These findings suggest that available free time for pursuing political and community activities is a factor affecting how involved one can become, among those who are working part-time or full-time.

The results for the ascribed social status predictors were as follows. Age showed the expected curvilinear pattern with activity, except that following current affairs did not tail off among those aged 55–64 and 65 or older. This particular activity does not require strong effort outside the home when compared with voluntary association activity per se, because attending community events and meetings is not necessary. Thus, it makes sense that there would be little problem for older people to continue to follow current affairs. There was very little difference between the activity levels of females and males, or between the French and English language groups. The foreign-born were less involved than the native-born in voting activity, perhaps because some of the foreign-born might not yet have been eligible to vote, but the two groups were quite similar on the other three forms of activity. Surprisingly, in a reversal of the patterns of findings from the other study, people from the Atlantic provinces and Quebec were slightly more involved in voting and voluntary association activity than were people from Ontario, the Prairies, or British Columbia. The above patterns also held with controls for the effects of the other predictor variables.

The present study used a more detailed measure of voting than the first study, including all three types of elections: municipal, provincial, and federal. Only federal voting was referred to in the question used in Study One. The results by region in Study Two suggest that there may be more active "local" politics in the two higher-activity regions—the Atlantic region and Quebec—and this is reflected in the results. Such patterns may not be evident when the interviewer asks only about federal voting activity. The measure of voluntary association activity was also a more detailed one than that used from the earlier study. For both of these forms of activity we must be cautious about drawing firm conclusions concerning regional patterns until we have still further evidence on the matter.

The NSGVP survey used in Study Two also contained six questions on the respondents' level of community activity in youth. Each of the items asked for a "yes" or "no" response. The six questions asked whether, during their "school years," the respondents were participants in "organized team sports"; were members of "a youth group"; did "some kind of volunteer work"; went "door-to-door to raise money"; were "active in student government"; or were "active in religious organizations." Interestingly, for these six items taken separately, and for an index composed of responses to all six questions, the categories of respondents who were currently more active in the community also had higher levels of involvement in their youth. In other words, those adult individuals who currently were higher in education, higher in income, employed, and in the more middle-aged cohorts were the most likely to have been involved in community activity when they were in their school-age years. In addition, being involved in voluntary activities as young people made them more likely to be involved in the community in their adulthood, and this finding held both before and after controls for the effects of the social status predictors (Curtis and Perks 2002). These results suggest that part of the explanation for people's levels of community activity as adults lies in their acquiring contact with and experience in voluntary community activities earlier in the life course. It is possible, as well, that those who were active in their youth had parents who were also active and who consequently provided encouragement, rewards, and role modelling for being active in the community.

CONCLUSION

We have examined recent Canadian data on the question of who participates in political and community affairs in Canadian society. Drawing from previous research and theory on the subject, we began with the premise that those groups that enjoy more social power, because of their higher "relative centrality" and greater "social capital" relative to other people in our society, would have higher levels of political involvement, civic engagement, and community activity. These advantaged groups include, for example, those with higher education and socio-economic status, people who speak English rather than French, males, the Canadian-born, and the middle-aged. Our predictions receive partial support in the results. The strongest support is found for education, occupational status, income, and age. For some types of activity, there is support for the effects of gender and language group. In Study Two, we also determined that individuals who were involved with community activity in their youth were generally more likely to be involved in voluntary associations as adults.

The patterns of results for race and nativity are much less consistent with, and sometimes even contradict, our expectations based on relative centrality and social capital theory. Moreover, controlled analyses show that some of the effects of race and nativity, before controls, occur because of differences in education, occupation, and income across these two characteristics. However, this latter set of findings may not so much call into question the relative centrality and social capital arguments, as suggest an important specification of them. Namely, the results may demonstrate that power and resource differences that are rooted in achieved statuses, including socio-economic status and particularly education, are the key explanations for why ascribed statuses such as race and nativity are correlated with political activity. The findings appear to cast doubt on any *comprehensive* claims about the relationship between political involvement and civic engagement, on the one hand, and social capital or relative centrality, on the other hand. Instead, a more complex set of processes seems to be at work in accounting for why individuals are more likely than others to join and participate in various political and community activities.

The patterns for region were also more complex than suggested by our working hypothesis, and do not lend themselves to easy generalizations. Perhaps our finding of higher involvement of Ontarians and people from the western provinces can be traced to relatively greater socio-economic advantages in these regions, in which case there may be some support here for the relative centrality and social capital perspectives. Nevertheless, Quebecers were found to be somewhat more involved in political protests and in support for new social movements than other Canadians, yet Quebec has traditionally been a relatively disadvantaged province judging by most economic indicators. The Quebec results, however, could represent a special set of circumstances, because of the typically higher levels of political unrest in that province, which stem from issues such as Quebec separatism or sovereignty and the continuing debate over Canada's constitution.

In general, we have found that, apart from voting in federal elections and a few other exceptions, it is rare that a majority of Canadians becomes involved in various types of social action or political activity. Perhaps the low level of involvement in behaviours such as public protest activity is an indication that most Canadians are relatively happy about the way things are in their country and, therefore, feel no strong need to participate in political or social change. Nevertheless, to the extent that political and community activities are structured by social status, it is apparent, as well, that those who are higher in social status also tend to be the people who are most involved in such actions. Because we would assume that these individuals should be happier about the status quo than those who are lower in social status, this pattern may seem surprising. One possibility is that such actions on the part of those in advantaged situations are mainly directed toward helping and promoting the interests of others less fortunate than themselves. An alternative interpretation for the greater political and civic involvement of more privileged groups is that they have a stronger desire to protect their own interests through such activities, and also possess the material and other resources necessary for participation.

We also should consider the possibility that social capital or relative centrality may explain some kinds of political and organizational involvement better than others. To some theorists, the existence of a wide range of voluntary political and community activities, as well as broad involvement by less powerful groups, may be indicative of a democratic and "pluralist" power structure in our society (e.g., Dahl 1982). A different view, however, must also be considered: It may be that people with greater social power are simply being strategic and selective when deciding which activities they choose to pursue and which organizations they choose to join. Some writers argue that voluntary organizations serve as the representatives of competing or conflicting interest groups, some of which have a much greater capacity than others to ensure that their particular policy preferences are implemented (e.g., Hayes 1978, 1983). From this perspective, we would expect that people with higher social capital and greater relative centrality, in pursuing their own desire to have access to power, would concentrate on truly influential organizations and activities, rather than on the whole range of activities.

Evidence from other research does suggest that such a pattern may be at work. For example, individuals with higher social status are significantly more likely than other people to run for political office. Moreover, they are even more likely to be successful in being elected to Parliament, and even more likely still to serve as senior ministers in government (see, e.g., Forcese and de Vries 1977; Guppy et al. 1988). Over the years, those with higher social status have also been far more likely to occupy powerful positions in Canada's system of "elites," both in public or government organizations and in the private economic and social spheres (e.g., Porter 1965; Clement, 1975, 1977; Olsen 1980; Nakhaie 1997). Therefore, while the present study gives some indication of a relatively broad base to political and community group involvement in Canada, the findings do not mean that those with privileged social statuses are rivalled by less advantaged groups or individuals in the overall power structure.

NOTES

1. "When you get together with your friends, would you say you discuss politics frequently, occasionally, or never?"

2. "When you, yourself, hold a strong opinion, do you ever find yourself persuading relatives or fellow workers to share your views? If so, does it happen often, from time to time, or rarely?"

3. "How interested would you say you are in politics: very interested, somewhat interested, not very interested, or not at all interested?"

4. "If there were a general election tomorrow, which party would you vote for?" Responses were divided into "would vote" and named choice versus "would not vote."

5. "Please look carefully at the following list of voluntary organizations and activities and say which, if any, you belong to—political parties or groups—and which if any are you currently doing unpaid voluntary work for."

6. The question was simply, "For how many organizations did you volunteer in the past 12 months?"

7. Total number of voluntary association memberships currently held was the number of memberships reported in response to a set of questions concerning "a service club or fraternal association; a political organization; a cultural, education, or hobby organization; a religious affiliated group; a neighbourhood, civic, or community association or school group; any other organization."

8. The voting measure was based on three questions that asked, "Did you vote in the last federal election?"; "Did you vote in the last provincial election?"; and "Did you vote in the last municipal election?" Each affirmative answer was given a score of 1, and the scores were summed.

9. Attention to current affairs was based on three questions: "How frequently do you follow news and current affairs that are local and regional?"; "How frequently do you follow news and current affairs that are national?"; and "How frequently do you follow news and current affairs that are international?" Responses to each were coded as Rarely or never = 1; Several times each month = 2; Several times each week = 3; and Daily = 4. The responses to the three questions were summed.

REFERENCES

Baer, Douglas, James Curtis, and Edward Grabb 2001. "Has voluntary activity declined? Cross-national analyses for fifteen countries." *Canadian Review of Sociology and Anthropology* 38:249–274.

Carroll, William (ed.) 1992. *Organizing Dissent: Contemporary Social Movements in Theory and Practice.* Toronto: Garamond.

Chui, Tina, James Curtis, and Edward Grabb 1993. "Who participates in community organizations and politics?" In James Curtis, Edward Grabb, and Neil Guppy (eds.), *Social Inequality in Canada: Patterns, Problems and Policies* (2nd ed.), pp. 524–538. Scarborough, ON: Prentice-Hall.

Clement, Wallace 1975. *The Canadian Corporate Elite.* Toronto: McClelland and Stewart.

Clement, Wallace 1977. *Continental Corporate Power.* Toronto: McClelland and Stewart.

Coleman, James S. 1988. "Social capital in the creation of human capital." *American Journal of Sociology* 94:S95–S120.

Corrigall-Brown, Catherine 2002. "What do politics have to do with me? An analysis of political alienation among young Canadians." Unpublished master's thesis, University of Western Ontario.

Curtis, James 1971. "Voluntary association joining: A cross-national comparative note." *American Sociological Review* 36:872–880.

Curtis, James, Douglas Baer, and Edward Grabb 2001. "Nations of joiners: Explaining voluntary association membership in democratic societies." *American Sociological Review* 66:783–805.

Curtis, James, and Edward Grabb 2002. "Involvement in the organizational base of new social movements in English Canada and French Canada." In Douglas Baer (ed.), *Political Sociology: Canadian Perspectives,* pp. 164–181. Toronto: Oxford University Press.

Curtis, James, Edward Grabb, and Douglas Baer 1992. "Voluntary association membership in fifteen developed countries: A comparative analysis." *American Sociological Review* 57:139–152.

Curtis, James, and Ronald Lambert 1976. "Voting, political interest, and age: National survey findings for French and English Canadians." *Canadian Journal of Political Science* 9:293–307.

Curtis, James, Ronald Lambert, Steven Brown, and Barry Kay 1989. "Affiliating with voluntary associations: Canadian-American comparisons." *Canadian Journal of Sociology* 14: 143–161.

Curtis, James, and Thomas Perks 2002. "Early experiences with voluntary community activities and adult community involvement." Unpublished paper.

Cutler, Steven T. 1976. "Age differences in voluntary association membership." *Social Forces* 55:43–58.

Dahl, Robert 1982. *Dilemmas of a Pluralist Democracy.* New York: Oxford University Press.

Edwards, Patricia K., John N. Edwards, and Alan DeWitt Watts 1984. "Women, work, and social participation." *Journal of Voluntary Action Research* 13:7–22.

Elections Canada 1993. *Official Voting Results: Thirty-Fifth General Election.* Ottawa: Elections Canada.

Forcese, Dennis, and John de Vries 1977. "Occupational and electoral success in Canada: The 1974 federal election." *Canadian Review of Sociology and Anthropology* 14: 331–340.

Grabb, Edward, and James Curtis 1992. "Voluntary association activity in English Canada, French Canada and the United States: Multivariate analyses." *Canadian Journal of Sociology* 17:371–388.

Guppy, Neil, Sabrina Freeman, and Shari Buchan 1988. "Economic background and political representation." In J. Curtis, E. Grabb, N. Guppy, and S. Gilbert (eds.), *Social Inequality in Canada: Patterns, Problems, Policies* (1st ed.), pp. 394–404. Scarborough, ON: Prentice-Hall Canada.

Hayes, M.T. 1978. "The semi-sovereign pressure groups: A critique of current theory and an alternative typology." *Journal of Politics* 40: 134–161.

Hayes, M.T. 1983. "Interest groups: Pluralism or mass society?" In A.J. Cigler and B.A. Loomis (eds.), *Interest Group Politics,* pp. 110–125. Washington, DC: CQ.

Inglehart, Ronald, et al. 1994. *World Values Survey, 1991–1992: Individual and Aggregate*

Level Codebook. Ann Arbor, MI: University of Michigan, Institute for Social Research.

Kay, Barry, Ronald Lambert, Steven Brown, and James Curtis 1987. "Gender and political activity in Canada: 1965–1984." *Canadian Journal of Political Science* 20:851–863.

Knoke, David 1986. "Associations and interest groups." *Annual Review of Sociology* 12:1–21.

Larana, Enrique, Hank Johnston, and Joseph Gusfield (eds.) 1994. *New Social Movements: From Ideology to Identity.* Philadelphia: Temple University Press.

Lin, Nan 2000. "Inequality in social capital." *Contemporary Sociology* 29:785–795.

McPherson, J.M., and W.G. Lockwood 1980. "The longitudinal study of voluntary association memberships: A multivariate analysis." *Journal of Voluntary Action Research* 9:74–84.

Milbrath, Lester, and M.L. Goel 1977. *Political Participation* (2nd ed.). Chicago: Rand McNally.

Nakhaie, M. Reza 1997. "Vertical mosaic among the elites: The new imagery revisited." *Canadian Review of Sociology and Anthropology* 34:1–24.

Olsen, Dennis 1980. *The State Elite.* Toronto: McClelland and Stewart.

Olson, Marvin E. 1965. *The Logic of Collective Action.* Cambridge, MA: Harvard University Press.

Palisi, Bartolomeo J., and Rosalie J. Palisi 1984. "Status and voluntary associations: A cross-cultural study of males in three metropolitan areas." *Journal of Voluntary Action Research* 13:32–43.

Porter, John 1965. *The Vertical Mosaic.* Toronto: University of Toronto Press.

Putnam, Robert 1995. "Bowling alone: America's declining social capital." *Journal of Democracy* 6:65–78.

Putnam, Robert 2000. *Bowling Alone: The Collapse and Revival of American Community.* New York: Simon and Schuster.

Smith, David Horton 1975. "Voluntary action and voluntary groups." *Annual Review of Sociology* 1:247–270.

chapter twenty-eight

School's Out for the Summer: Should It Be?

Neil Guppy and Scott Davies
(An original chapter written
for this volume.)

When school's over for another year, students often rejoice: "No more testing, no more books, no more teachers' dirty looks." Teachers rejoice too: they're just as happy without the dirty looks and they relish a few weeks not having to grade tests. However, new research suggests that both groups are wrong to rejoice, as the long summer holiday is counterproductive to learning. It undermines the success of our school system and has the worst effect on the students who need help the most.

Anecdotally, any good music teacher can explain the problem: if students studying piano or violin take long breaks, bad things happen. Scales are forgotten, habits are broken, progress is reversed. So the best music schools organize only short breaks—nothing like schooling's extended summer hiatus. Skilled athletes know this same principle. Practice, and by that they mean a steady diet of practice, aids performance.

Recent school research has generated parallel findings, ones that are especially important for children from less privileged economic backgrounds. Evidence shows that when schools are out for summer, learning recedes (see Downey et al. 2004; Chin and Phillips 2004). Just like piano students who don't practise, students on holiday see their cognitive skills erode.

But here's the kicker. The effect of the summer setback differs by social class. Students from less privileged backgrounds—those "at risk"—see their progress slide much more dramatically than do students from affluent families. While there are learning gaps between economic groups during the school year, they are modest compared to those that occur during breaks. Furthermore, these summer learning setbacks or gaps have cumulative, lasting consequences (Alexander et al. 2007).

Schooling, it turns out, is an important equalizer. Outside of school, where children spend most of their time, the quality of children's surroundings varies widely. On measures like frequency of reading, amount and quality of verbal communication, and availability of cultural resources in the home, there is a sharp disparity between a child living in poverty and a child living with two professional parents (Hertzman 2000).

Schools, on the other hand, differ relatively little in library resources, quality of teaching, and learning material. In Canada, operating budgets for schools are much more equal than are housing prices or income differences between school neighbourhoods. Schooling therefore provides a more equitable environment, but this environment disappears during the summer break (Davies and Guppy 2006).

This is exactly why Principal Caroline Krause and the staff at Vancouver's Grandview/?Uuqinak'uuh Elementary School are lobbying for a reorganized school year. Krause argues that her inner-city students "desperately need a new school calendar." The school is seeking a "balanced" calendar, not an increase in total instructional days. Most simply, this might entail shrinking the summer break to five weeks and redistributing the

remaining holiday time to other parts of the school year. Students would lose less ground during the summer, and would gain instructional time in September—time that is now lost to review. As well, both students and teachers would enjoy strategic breaks distributed throughout the school year. (For an overview of school calendar reorganization, see Shields and Oberg 2000.)

Schools have been remarkably progressive institutions. For example, Canada's school system is less stratified by gender than the church, the workplace, and even the family. Success also crosses racial and ethnic lines. From historically separate schools for black and Asian students, we now find an open system in which multiculturalism is a core part of the curriculum. Partly as a result of this openness, the 2001 Canadian Census shows that young visible-minority Canadians are more likely to graduate from university than are young non-visible-minority Canadians.

Not all ethnic, racial, and ancestral groups have benefited from the changes in the organization and social practices of schooling. Aboriginal and black youth, in particular, have not prospered in the education system. However, in many settings there is a high correlation between being an inner-city youth, experiencing poverty, and being black or Aboriginal. Indeed, this confluence is one of the key factors propelling the Grandview/?Uuqinak'uuh Elementary School to seek change.

Nevertheless, success in promoting equality by gender, race, and ethnicity has come from hard work. We have fought—and mostly succeeded—to reduce gender stereotyping in textbooks, to value equally the voices of girls and boys, to deter anti-racist language and graffiti, and to trim Eurocentrism from the curriculum (see Davies and Guppy 2006).

We have been far less successful in supporting the learning successes of students from different social classes and certain racial/ancestral backgrounds. Children from less affluent families fare the worst in learning outcomes. It could and should be different.

The current school calendar is a relic of our agricultural past. In a knowledge economy, the time for a new organizational clock is here. We need positive changes that will help to make schooling more successful for all.

REFERENCES

Alexander, Karl L., Doris R. Entwisle, and Linda Steffel Olson 2007. "Lasting consequences of the summer learning gap." *American Sociological Review* 72, 2:167–180.

Chin, Tiffani, and Meredith Phillips 2004. "Social reproduction and child-rearing practices: Social class, children's agency, and the summer activity gap." *Sociology of Education*, 77, 3:185–210.

Davies, Scott, and Neil Guppy 2006. *The Schooled Society: An Introduction to the Sociology of Education.* Toronto: Oxford University Press

Downey, Douglas B., Paul T. von Hippel, and Beckett A. Broh 2004. "Are schools the great equalizer? Cognitive inequality during the summer months and the school year." *American Sociological Review* 69, 5:613–635.

Hertzman, Clyde 2000. "The case for an early childhood development strategy." *ISUMA: Canadian Journal of Policy Research* (Autumn):11–18.

Shields, Caroline, and S.L. Oberg 2000. *Year-round Schooling: Promises and Pitfalls.* Lanham, MD: Scarecrow/Technomics.

FURTHER REFERENCES— SECTION 4: CONSEQUENCES OF SOCIAL INEQUALITY

Allahar, Anton, and James Cote 1998. *Richer and Poorer: The Structure of Inequality in Canada.* Toronto: Copp Clark. The authors use a framework that centres on the role of dominant ideology to examine social inequality in Canada, with a special focus on issues of class, gender, age, and race/ethnicity. A key claim in this analysis is that Canadians are in a state of denial about the existence of major inequalities in their society.

Breton, Raymond, Norbert Hartmann, Jos Lennards, and Paul Reed 2004. *A Fragile Social Fabric? Fairness, Trust, and Commitment in Canada.* Montreal and Kingston: McGill-Queen's University Press. In this study, the authors provide research findings from a national survey of Canadians. Much of the analysis deals with the effects of ethnic, class, gender, and regional inequality on Canadian attitudes about such issues as trust, community involvement, and their sense of belonging in Canadian society.

Canadian Institute for Health Information 2007. *Health Care in Canada 2007* (http:// secure.cihi.ca/cihiweb/products/hcic2007_e. pdf). This report has been published annually since 2000, in conjunction with Statistics Canada, to provide current information about the status of the health care system and the health of Canadians.

C.D. Howe Institute (http://www.edhowe.org). This organization is a social policy research institution. It provides analyses of such policy issues of national interest as trade, the environment, health care, and culture.

Centre for Policy Alternatives (http://www. policyalternatives.ca). This organization currently provides critical analyses of the impact on Canada and Canadians of developments in the Canadian public education system, free trade, and electricity privatization, among other topics.

Grabb, Edward, and James Curtis 2005. *Regions Apart: The Four Societies of Canada and the United States.* Toronto: Oxford University Press. This book compares Canadians and Americans on a number of topics related to social inequality, including tolerance of ethnic and racial minorities, beliefs about personal freedom and individual rights, and views about the role of government in the two nations. The researchers also show that people's values and attitudes are shaped by important regional differences involving English Canada, Quebec, the American North, and the American South.

Green, David, and Jonathan Kesselma (eds.) 2006. *Dimensions of Inequality in Canada.*

Vancouver: University of British Columbia Press. This collection brings together a number of studies that explore the important causes and consequences of social inequality. Patterns of inequality in such areas as income and wages, material consumption, employment, political participation, and community involvement are among the topics considered.

Hagan, John, and Bill McCarthy 1997. *Mean Streets: Youth Crime and Homelessness.* Cambridge: Cambridge University Press. The authors present information on (1) the lives of homeless youth on the street; (2) how the youths came to be there; and (3) how they leave the streets. The social class dimensions of these phenomena are explored, along with other factors. Theories put forward in the previous literature are critiqued, and alternative theoretical interpretations are offered. The study is based on qualitative data gathered in two Canadian cities.

Ornstein, Michael, and Michael Stevenson 2003. *Politics and Ideology in Canada.* Montreal and Kingston: McGill-Queen's University Press. This book examines the question of ideological power in Canada. The analysis compares the perspectives of Canada's elite leadership with those of the general public on a range of important issues, including such topics as state power and support for government welfare programs.

Statistics Canada. *Perspectives on Labour and Income* and *Canadian Social Trends.* These two quarterly publications are very useful sources, offering relatively brief and straightforward presentations of up-to-date information on income and jobs, social problems, health, education, demographic processes, and many other topics. Frequently, the pieces show how people's achieved and ascribed social statuses are related to the issue in question. These sources are also available online through the Statistics Canada website (http://www.statcan.ca). Catalogue nos. 11-008-XIE and 75-001-XIE.

Statistics Canada. 2006. *Measuring Violence against Women: Statistical Trends.* (http://www.swc-cfc.gc.ca/pubs/measuring/index_e.html). This statistical document on violence against women was produced by Federal/Provincial/Territorial Ministers Responsible for Status of Women. Statistical data are presented to describe the dimensions and nature of violence against women, the impacts and consequences, societal responses and supports for victims, and women's use of criminal justice and other services. Catalogue no. 85-570 XIE 2006001.

Tepperman, Lorne, James Curtis, and Albert Kwan 2007. *Social Problems: A Canadian Perspective* (2nd ed.). Don Mills, ON: Oxford University Press. This text reviews research on numerous topics of concern to students of social inequality. These include poverty and economic inequality, homelessness, race and ethnic relations, gender inequality, sexism, and ageism.

Index

A

Aboriginal peoples. *See* First Nations peoples
ACOA. *See* Atlantic Canada Opportunities Agency (ACOA)
adulthood, 319–320
affluence. *See* wealth (affluence)
age(ism), 195, 305–306
    community involvement and, 422
    conflict, 313–314
    dependency, 307–308
    political involvement and, 422–424
    voluntary work and, 410
Air Canada, 32, 305
Alcan, 23
Alger, Horatio, 116
Anti-Inflation Board, 69
Assembly of First Nations, 192
assimilation, 299, 301
Atlantic Canada Opportunities Agency (ACOA), 335, 336
Australia,
    income distribution in, 88
    social mobility in, 128, 129
authoritarianism, working-class, 391, 392–393

B

Bank of Montreal, 22
Bank of Nova Scotia, 22
Bannerji, Himani, 39
BCNI. *See* Business Council on National Issues (BCNI)
Beagan, Brenda, 193
Bell, Daniel, 134
Bloc Québecois, 340
Block, Fred, 30
Bourdieu, Pierre, 161, 164, 165
Bridges, William, 133
British Columbia Hydro and Power Authority, 25
Bronfman, Charles, 35
Burgess, Bill, 34
Business Council on National Issues (BCNI), 36, 37, 41, 68

C

Caisse dépôt et placement du Québec, 25
Calder, Frank, 302
Canada Assistance Plan (CAP), 334, 375
Canada Economic Development for Quebec Regions, 336
Canada Health Transfer (CHT), 335

Canada Pension Plan/Quebec Pension Plan (CPP/QPP), 93, 142, 310, 311, 318
Canada Post, 25
Canada Savings Bonds, 93
Canada Social Transfer (CST), 335
Canada Trust, 22
Canada,
    concentration of capital in, 31–32, 40
    corporate structures in, 20
    economy, 18, 20, 23–26
    foreign ownership in, 20, 23
    GDP in, 23
    homelessness in, 368–372
    immigration to, 237–238, 242
    income distribution in, 79–80
    income inequality in, 83–85, 90
    intolerance in, 390–392, 393–394
    intolerance trends in, 395–396
    mortality rates in, 353, 354, 355, 358, 359, 364
    occupational structure in, 117–118, 120, 122
    petty bourgeoisie in, 46–49, 50, 51, 54
    post-secondary tuition fees in, 160, 164, 166
    poverty definition in, 107, 108, 109
    regional inequality in, 325–327
    school system in, 430
    social mobility in, 116–117
    state involvement in economy, 20, 24–25
    trade with US, 34
    unemployment in, 141
    unionization in, 55–56
    US transnational companies in, 23, 26
    wealth distribution in, 95–97, 101, 102, 103
Canadian Alliance for Trade and Job Opportunities (CATJO), 68
Canadian Alliance Party, 340
Canadian Auto Workers, 44
Canadian Census Public Use Sample, 256
Canadian Charter of Rights and Freedoms, 306, 307
Canadian Community Health Study (CCHS) (2003), 364
Canadian Council of Chief Executives, 41
Canadian Health and Social Assistance Transfers (CHST), 334, 375, 376

Canadian Human Rights Act (1977), 231, 307
Canadian Human Rights Commission, 192
Canadian Human Rights Tribunal, 282
Canadian Imperial Bank of Commerce, 22
Canadian Labour Congress, 44
Canadian Manufacturers Association, 36
Canadian Mobility Study (CMS) (1973), 117, 118, 119, 120
Canadian Mortgage and Housing Corporation, 25
Canadian National Railways (CNR), 32
Canadian Pacific Railway, 30
Canadian Wheat Board, 25
CanWest Global, 22
CAP. *See* Canada Assistance Plan (CAP)
capitalism, global, 18, 40, 41, 191–192, 200, 201, 203
    Marxist analysis of, 44–46
CATJO. *See* Canadian Alliance for Trade and Job Opportunities (CATJO)
CCHS. *See* Canadian Community Health Study (CCHS) (2003)
Census of Canada Public Use Microdata File (1996), 298
Census of Population (1901), 238
Census of Population (1911), 238, 242
Census of Population (1921), 238, 243
Census of Population (1941), 243
Census of population (1971), 246
Census of Population (1991), 238, 247, 254
Census of Population (2001), 248, 251, 298, 430
Centre for Research and Information on Canada (CRIC), 279
China,
    immigration from, 249
Chinese Immigration Act (1923), 244
Chrétien, Jean, 25, 335
Chrysler Canada, 23
CHST. *See* Canadian Health and Social Assistance Transfers (CHST)
CHT. *See* Canada Health Transfer (CHT)
CHUM Television, 22
Citizenship and Immigration Canada, 239

Clarica Life Insurance, 22
Clarkson, Stephen, 33
class. *See* middle class, working class
class conflict, 45, 47–48, 57
class consciousness, 52, 54–55
class inequality,
    gender inequality and, 203–205
class structure, 46
    polarization of, 47–50
Clement, Wallace, 19
CMS. *See* Canadian Mobility Study
    (CMS) (1973)
CNR. *See* Canadian National
    Railways (CNR)
collective bargaining, 64, 67, 69, 70
colonialism, 296–297, 299
    assimilation of First Nations peo-
      ples, 299, 301
    First Nations peoples and,
      295–298, 299
concentration,
    economic, 18–22, 25, 30–31
    geographic, 30–31
Conference Board of Canada, 36
Conservative Party, 335, 336, 340
Constitution Act (1982), 333
continentalism, 33–34
corporations,
    Canadian, 33–34
    democratization of, 39–41
    privately-owned, 18, 26, 32
CPP Investment Board, 311
CPP/QPP. *See* Canada Pension Plan/
    Quebec Pension Plan (CPP/QPP)
Creese, Gillian, 193
CRIC. *See* Centre for Research and
    Information on Canada (CRIC)
CST. *See* Canada Social Transfer
    (CST)
CTV Broadcasting, 22
cultural capital, 161–162, 172, 175,
    181, 185
Curtis, Jim, 198
cybercapitalism, 33

D

d'Aquino, Thomas, 37
Daimler Chrysler Canada, 23
Davies, Sandstrom, Shorrocks, and
    Wolff report (2006) (DSSW), 97,
    98
Davis, Wade, 41
Davis, William, 38
de Tocqueville, Alexis, 113
democratization (of corporations),
    39–41
Department of Regional Economic
    Expansion (DREE), 335
deregulation, 32, 38
Desmarais, Paul, 20, 21
dialectical materialism, 203
Dicken, Peter, 31, 35
Doukhobors, 242, 244

DREE. *See* Department of Regional
    Economic Expansion (DREE)
DSSW. *See* Davies, Sandstrom,
    Shorrocks, and Wolff report
    (2006) (DSSW)
dummy-variable regression, 386
Durkheim, Emile, 45, 57
Dyck, Noel, 302

E

Economic Council of Canada, 282,
    329
Edmonton School-Work Transition
    Study, 173
    1985 sample, 173–174
    1992 sample, 185
    1999 sample, 179–180
EDS. *See* Ethnic Diversity Study
    (EDS)
education values,
    intolerance and, 391–394
    SES and, 174–178
    underdevelopment and, 329
education,
    as tolerance role, 391–394
    for children of immigrants,
      283–284
    inequality and, 80–81
    inequality in from contexts, 159,
      166
    inequality in from resources, 158,
      159
    social inequality in, 150–151, 154
    socio-economic effects on,
      151–153
educational aspirations,
    SES and, 174–178
educational attainment,
    cultural effect on, 161–162, 165
    ethnicity and, 151–152, 155–156
    First Nations peoples and,
      155–156
    gender and, 154
    trends in, 159
    visible minority, 254–255, 260,
      267, 269, 270
educational expectations, 160, 162,
    163, 164–166
educational streaming, 163–164, 167,
    168
elite, economic, 20
    changes to, 29–31
    development of, 31–32
    families, 20, 31, 35
    moral reform of, 32, 38, 39
    women as part of, 38, 39
employment, 134
    changing patterns of, 134,
      137–138, 145
    equity programs, 230
    equity, 230–231
    for children of immigrants,
      283–284

gender inequalities, 224, 226,
    227, 228, 229, 230
    gender-segregated, 140, 143–145,
      146
    pay equity programs, 231–232
    quality of, 142, 146
    segregation, 226–229
    social status and, 382, 383, 386
    training for, 135, 136, 142, 143,
      146
    women in, 224, 225–226
Engels, Friedrich, 200–201
entrepreneurs, 20, 21
EPF. *See* Established Program
    Financing (EPF)
Established Program Financing
    (EPF), 334
Ethnic Diversity Study (EDS), 274,
    275, 279, 285, 289, 290
ethnic diversity, 38, 39, 40
    immigration and, 281–283
ethnicity, 194–195
    and occupations, 255, 256,
      260–265
    gender and, 194–195
    income and, 265–269
    voluntary work and, 410
ethnoracial diversity, 274
Eurocentrism, 430
European Union, 23

F

Falconbridge, 23
family, 217, 218
    division of labour within,
      213–218
FDI. *See* foreign direct investment
    (FDI)
Federal Economic Development
    Initiative in Northern Ontario
    (FedNor), 335, 336
Federal Fund for Rural Economic
    Development, 335
Federal Office of Regional
    Development - Quebec (FORD-
    Q), 335
Federation of Canadian
    Municipalities, 375
FedNor. *See* Federal Economic
    Development Initiative in
    Northern Ontario (FedNor)
feminism, second-wave, 197
Financial Post, 22, 23
First Nations peoples,
    colonialism, 296–299
    educational attainment, 155–156
    grievances, 191
    health of, 298
    income of, 298
    legal system and, 298–299
    LICO and, 298
    life expectancy for, 358
    prison percentage of, 299

racial injustice towards, 192, 195, 207
residential schools and, 299, 301
self-determination, 302
schools and, 430
social identity of, 301
social inequality structures, 296
social inequality writings of, 296–297
women in employment, 226, 230, 231
First World War,
immigration before, 237, 242–245
Forbes magazine, 97
Ford of Canada, 23
FORD-Q. *See* Federal Office of Regional Development - Quebec (FORD-Q)
foreign direct investment (FDI), 31
Fraser Institute, 36, 67
Sarlo line, 109, 110
Fukuyama, Francis, 39

G
gay, lesbian, and bisexual (GLB) people, 362–363
GDP. *See* gross domestic product (GDP)
GDPpc. *See* gross domestic product per capita (GDPpc)
gender inequality, 192–193
class inequality and, 203
complexities of, 207–208
ethnicity and, 194–195
explanations for, 199, 200, 202, 206, 208, 209
health and, 354–357
homelessness, 371, 374
in labour force, 229, 230, 234
mortality and, 353–354, 357, 358
multiple identities and, 208, 209
race and, 191–192
social movements and, 410–411
gender, 193
conceptualization of, 198–199
roles, 193
schoolbook stereotyping, 430
stratification study bias, 197–198
General Motors of Canada, 23
General Social Survey (GSS), 119, 120, 127, 246
genetics, 171
Georgietti, Ken, 44
GICs. *See* guaranteed investment certificates (GICs)
GIS. *See* Guaranteed Income Supplement (GIS)
GLB. *See* gay, lesbian, and bisexual (GLB) people
globalization, 29–30, 34, 35, 39, 40, 41
corporate, 40–41
Globe and Mail, The, 22, 279

GNP. *See* gross national product (GNP)
Goodman, Leo, 126
Goods and Services Tax (GST), 87
governance reforms, 32, 34, 37, 38, 39
Grandview/?Uuqinak'uuh Elementary School, 430
Great Britain,
immigration from, 244
income distribution in, 85
income inequality in, 85
social mobility in, 128
wealth inequality in, 98
Great Depression, 83
immigration during, 237, 242–245, 251
Great West Life Insurance, 22
gross domestic product (GDP), 23, 34, 395, 396
in Brazil, 98
in China, 98
in India, 98
in South Africa, 98
intolerance and, 395, 396, 399, 402, 403
gross domestic product per capita (GDPpc), 61, 62, 71
gross national product (GNP), 31
GSS. *See* General Social Survey (GSS)
GST. *See* Goods and Services Tax (GST)
Guaranteed Income Supplement (GIS), 310, 318
guaranteed investment certificates (GICs), 92

H
HAN. *See* Homelessness Accountability Network (HAN)
Hargrove, Buzz, 44
Harper, Stephen, 336
privatization by, 25
Harvey, David, 32
health inequalities,
gendered, 354–357
homelessness and, 369, 372, 373
race and, 357–359
sexual orientation and, 362–364
social class and, 360–362
Heclo, Hugh, 317
hegemony, 29, 33, 37, 40
heterosexism, 362–363
Higgins, Benjamin, 324, 339
Hitler, Adolf, 191
HIV/AIDS, 363
HMIS. *See* Homeless Management Information System (HMIS)
Homeless Management Information System (HMIS), 370
Homelessness Accountability Network (HAN), 374

Homelessness Partnering Strategy (HPS), 374, 375
Homelessness Partnership Initiative (HPI), 374
homelessness, 367–368
definitions of, 368–370
diversity of, 370–372
gender of, 371
numbers of, 368–370
public policy for, 374–376
reasons for, 372–374
homophobia, 354, 362, 363, 364
housework, 214
men and 214–218
HPI. *See* Homelessness Partnership Initiative (HPI)
HPS. *See* Homelessness Partnering Strategy (HPS)
human capital theory (of labour markets), 135
Hutterites, 244
Hydro Québec, 25

I
ideology,
dominant, 380–381
IMF. *See* International Monetary Forum (IMF)
immigrant health effect, 352, 357, 358, 359
Immigration Act (1952), 246, 247
Immigration Act (1978), 247
Immigration and Refugee Protection Act (2002), 247
immigration, 237–238
1900–1915, 238–241
1915–1946, 242–245
1946–1970, 245–246
1970–2001, 247–249
adjustment by, 249–251
attitudes towards, 281–283
children, 246–247
community involvement and, 424
definition of, 239
education for children of, 283–284
employment for children of, 283–284
gendered, 238, 243, 247
health and, 359
intolerance and, 390, 391, 394, 395, 396
landed, 239, 244
net, 238, 239, 242, 243, 245, 248, 251
post-war policies, 246–247
racial diversity and, 273–274
regulations, 244, 246, 247, 248
Imperial Oil, 23
Inco, 23
income distribution, 79–80, 83, 84
ethnicity and, 265–269
First Nations peoples, 298

gendered wage gap, 228–229, 232
misconceptions, 82
quintiles, 84–86
sources of information on, 94, 97
income taxes, 87
income, market, 86, 89–90
individualism, 379–380
class conflict and, 394–395
definitions of, 380–381
inequality measures of, 383
research into, 380, 381, 386, 387
social status and, 381–382
inequality,
education, 80–81
income, 83–85
occupation, 80
socio-economic bases of, 80, 81
Institute for Social Research, York
University, 361
institutional environment, 64–65
Insurance Corporation of British
Columbia (ICBC), 25
intergroup conflict, 391, 403
individualization and, 394
International Labour Office, 282
International Monetary Forum (IMF),
37, 41
intolerance,
education and, 391, 392, 393–394
GDP and, 395, 396, 399, 402, 403
immigration and, 390, 391, 394,
395, 396
regionalism and, 395, 396, 401
social class and, 390, 392, 393,
394, 399, 401, 403, 404

J
Japan,
immigration from, 242, 245

K
King, Martin Luther, Jr., 191
Krause, Caroline, 430

L
labour market segmentation theory,
135–136
post-industrial, 318–320, 322
labour markets, 133, 134
definition of, 134
discrimination in, 146–147
human capital theory of, 135
internal, 136
part-time, 136, 138, 139–140
restructuring of, 137, 140, 146
segmentation theory, 135–136
labour,
domestic, 224, 230, 233–234
dual-earners, 218–219
high-earning women, 219–220
increase in, 214, 219, 221
parenting as, 220
women's, 213–214

Liberal Party of Canada, 340
privatization by, 25
LICO. *See* Low Income Cut-Off
(LICO)
life expectancy, 350, 353, 354, 358,
359, 364
LIM. *See* Statistics Canada, Low
Income Measure (LIM)
Lipset, Seymour Martin, 116, 118
London Life Insurance, 22
Longitudinal Survey of Immigrants to
Canada (2003), 279
Lougheed, Peter, 38
Low Income Cut-Off (LICO),
109–110, 111
First Nations peoples and, 298

M
Mackenzie King, William Lyon, 246,
324
Magna International, 21
Marshall, Katherine, 193
Marx, Karl, 44, 45–46, 47, 48, 50, 52,
53, 54, 55, 57, 118, 201–203, 380
mass media, ownership of, 22
MCA. *See* multiple classification
analysis (MCA)
McEachern, Allan, 295
Mennonites, 244
meritocracy, 38, 39
middle class, 46–48, 49–50, 54, 55,
57
minority ethnic groups, 253–255
European origin, 255, 256, 259,
260, 265, 266, 270
Monture-Angus, Patricia, 295, 299
Mulroney, Brian,
privatization by, 25
multiculturalism, 39, 274, 280, 283,
287–289, 430
multiple classification analysis
(MCA), 421, 423
Myles, John, 134

N
NAFTA. *See* North American Free
Trade Agreement (NAFTA)
NASDAQ. *See* National Association
of Dealers Automated Quotation
System (NASDAQ)
National Action Committee on the
Status of Women, 192
National Advisory Council on Aging,
192
National Association of Dealers
Automated Quotation System
(NASDAQ), 33
National Child Benefit, 323
National Homelessness Initiative
(NHI), 374
National Policy, 30
National Population Health Study
(NPHS) (1994), 355, 356, 359

National Survey of Giving,
Volunteering, and Participating
(NSGVP) (2000), 422, 424
National Trust Company, 22
Native Womens' Association of
Canada, 301
NDP. *See* New Democratic Party
(NDP)
negative income tax (NIT), 323
neo-conservatism, 67–69
neoliberalism, 29, 32, 36, 37, 40
New Canada, The, 279
New Democratic Party (NDP), 55, 56
free trade, 68
New York Stock Exchange (NYSE), 33
NHI. *See* National Homelessness
Initiative (NHI)
NIT. *See* negative income tax (NIT)
Nortel Networks Corp., 33, 38
North American Free Trade
Agreement (NAFTA), 34
NPHS. *See* National Population
Health Study (NPHS) (1994)
NSGVP. *See* National Survey of
Giving, Volunteering, and
Participating (NSGVP) (2000)
NYSE. *See* New York Stock
Exchange (NYSE)

O
OAS. *See* Old Age Security (OAS)
occupation inequality, 80
by gender, 229–230, 234
occupation(s),
changing, 133, 137
in post-industrial society, 134, 136
non-standard, 139–141
political involvement and, 418,
421, 422
occupational aspirations,
SES and, 174–178
visible minority, 254–256
occupational distribution, 254, 260, 263
occupational outcomes,
SES and, 174–178
Old Age Security (OAS), 310
Ontario Lottery Corporation, 25
*Origins of the Family, Private
Property and the State, The,* 200
outgroups, 391, 393, 395, 399, 401
ownership, economic, 21–22
foreign, 22–24
forestry, 22
in financial sector, 22
mining, 22

P
parochialism, 391, 392
Pay Equity Act (1987) (Ontario), 231
political involvement, 409–411
age and, 411, 418
occupation level and, 418, 422
race and, 413, 422

regionalism and, 418
social status and, 411, 415–422
Porter, John, 19, 192, 253
postmaterialism, 394–395
poverty, 77, 78, 79–80, 82, 83, 85, 90, 307
absolute, 108–109
definitions of, 107, 108–109, 110, 113
homelessness and, 368, 370, 373, 374, 375, 376
measuring, 107, 108, 109–113
patterns, 112
reasons for measuring, 113, 114
reduction, 107, 113–114
relative, 108, 109
seniors and, 309–310, 311, 313, 314
welfare programs for, 113–114
Power Corporation, 20, 21, 22
power, corporate, 29–30
movement of, 36, 41
transnational practices, 30–35, 37, 38–41
private business, foreign-owned, 22–24
Progressive Conservative Party,
back-to-work legislation, 69
free trade, 68
privatization by, 25
property, ownership of, 17–18
Provincial Sales Tax (PST), 87
PST. See Provincial Sales Tax (PST)
Public Sector Compensation Restraint Act (1982), 69

Q
Quebec,
nationalism, 192
Québecois, 340
identification of, 340

R
race,
health and, 357–359
mortality rates and, 358–359
political involvement and, 413, 418, 422, 424
racial discrimination, 194, 279–280
evidence, 281–283
health and, 357, 358, 359
Rae, Bob, 69
Reform Party, 340
refugee, 239
regional inequality,
dependency theory of, 331–332
dimensions of, 325–327
government initiatives for, 333, 335, 340, 341
in US, 338–339
intolerance and, 395, 396, 401
life expectancy in, 338
modernization model of, 329–331

political outcomes from, 339–341
social factors in, 325, 327, 329, 332, 339
staples approach to, 327–329
theories of, 327, 328, 331, 332, 338
trends in, 336, 341
regionalism, 195–196, 324–325
political activity and, 413, 418, 421, 423
social movements and, 423, 424
social status and, 382, 383, 386, 387, 388
registered pension plans (RPPs), 96
registered retirement income funds (RRIFs), 95
registered retirement savings plan (RRSP), 41, 96
registered savings plans (RSPs), 92
Reich, Robert, 134
Relations of Ruling, 204
relative centrality, 410, 418, 421, 424
relative deprivation, 391, 393–395
Rifkin, Jeremy, 133
risk hypothesis (for mortality rates), 355
Royal Bank of Canada, 22
Royal Commission on Bilingualism and Biculturalism (1968), 39
Royal Commission on the Status of Women (1970), 153, 154
RPPs. See registered pension plans (RPPs)
RRIFs. See registered retirement income funds (RRIFs)
RRSP. See registered retirement savings plan (RRSP)
RSPs. See registered savings plans (RSPs)

S
sales taxes, 87–88
see also Goods and Services Tax (GST), Provincial Sales Tax (PST)
Sarlo, Christopher, 109, 110
SCF. See Survey of Consumer Finance (SCF)
schools,
social inequality and, 429–431
Scott, Bill, 198
Second World War, 23
immigration after, 245, 246–247, 251
immigration during, 242–245
social movements after, 191, 201
wages after, 50
Sennett, Richard, 133
SES. See socio-economic status (SES)
SFRPHI. See Surplus Federal Real Property for Homelessness Initiative (SFRPHI)

SFS. See Survey of Financial Security (SFS)
Siltanen, Janet, 193
Smith, Adam, 108
social capital, 163
social class,
health and, 360–362
individualization and, 391, 394–395
intolerance and, 390, 392, 393, 394, 399, 401, 403, 404
life chances and, 171–173
research methods, 173–174
SES and, 352, 355, 356, 359, 360–362
social identity theory, 391
social inequality,
age, 305–306, 314
dependency, 307–308, 309, 312, 314
effects of, 349, 350, 353, 362
First Nations writings, 296–297
measures of, 393, 394, 395–396
post-industrial solutions, 322–323
post-industrial, 318–320, 321
schools and, 166–167, 429–431
social status and, 381–382
social tolerance and, 390, 391–394, 395
structures, 296–298
tolerance and, 391–394
social mobility,
Canadian studies, 119, 128, 129
definitions of, 117–119, 129
education and, 150
gender and, 126, 129
models, 118, 122, 126–128, 129
occupational, 117–120
patterns of, 120, 126–128, 129
research techniques for, 117–118, 126, 128, 129
tables, 117–118, 120, 122, 125–126
social movements,
regionalism and, 423, 24
social status, 381–382
achieved, 410, 422, 423, 424
ascribed, 410, 418, 422, 423, 425
employment and, 382, 383, 386
individualism, 386–387
inequality and, 380, 381, 382–383
measures of, 383, 413
political activity and, 411, 415–422
regionalism, 382, 383, 386, 387, 388
SES and, 386–387
Social Stratification: Canada, 198
social tolerance, 390–391
education and, 391–394
postmaterialism and, 394–395
social inequality and, 390, 391–394, 395

socio-economic status (SES), 158, 159, 160, 161, 162, 163, 164, 165, 166, 167, 174, 253, 254, 270
    educational aspirations and, 176–178
    education values, 175–176
    health and, 360–362
    high school performance and, 174–175
    occupational aspirations and, 183–184
    occupational outcomes and, 181–183
    school-work transitions and, 180–181
    social class and, 352, 355, 356, 359, 360–362
    women's health and, 354–357
South Africa,
    apartheid, 192
state involvement (in economy), 24–25
Statistics Canada, 94, 95, 96, 97, 109, 110, 112, 113, 118, 119, 120, 128, 140, 274, 311, 312, 363, 422
    Low Income Measure (LIM), 110, 112
status groups, 46–47, 53, 57
Stories from Home, 296
stratification analysis, 197–198
    women's place in, 198–199, 202
strikes,
    affluence and, 61–64
    business cycle and, 64–66
    research into, 64–66
    unemployment and, 61–64
Stuart B. McKinney Homeless Assistance Act (1987) (US), 369
Sun Life Insurance, 22
Supporting Communities Partnership Initiative, 374
Surplus Federal Real Property for Homelessness Initiative (SFRPHI), 374
Survey of Consumer Finance (SCF), 94, 95, 96, 97
Survey of Financial Security (SFS), 94, 95, 96, 97
Sweden,
    strike frequency in, 65, 71, 72
    wealth inequality in, 98
Switzerland,
    wealth inequality in, 97, 98

T
tax system, 79, 86, 87
Thomson Company, 22
Thomson, David, 97
Thunder in My Soul, 295

TNCs. *See* transnational corporations (TNCs)
Toronto Disaster Relief Committee, 367
Toronto Stock Exchange, 39, 135
Toronto's Street Health Clinic, 372
Toronto, City of, 367
    homelessness in, 370, 371, 372
Toronto-Dominion Bank, 22
transnational corporations (TNCs), 30–32, 34, 37, 38–41
    Canadian-based, 33, 35
    Japanese-based, 31, 35
    US-based, 34
Trilateral Commission, 37
Trudeau, Pierre Elliott, 335

U
UN Human Development Report (2002), 40
UN University's World Institute for Development Economics Research (WIDER), 97
UN. *See* United Nations (UN)
unemployment rate, 61–64
    strikes and, 61–62
unionization, 55–56, 65, 71, 230, 232
United Kingdom. *See* Great Britain
United Nations (UN),
    homelessness definition, 369
United Nations Conference on Trade and Development (2006), 23
United Nations Convention on Refugees (1951), 239
United Nations Human Development Index, 379
United States of America (US),
    civil rights movement in, 191, 192
    General Social Surveys in, 128
    homelessness in, 369, 373
    immigration from, 242, 247, 248
    income distribution in, 79
    income inequality in, 88
    poverty definition in, 109
    regional inequality in, 331, 338, 339
    social mobility in, 128, 129
    trade with Canada, 34–35
    wealth inequality in, 93, 94, 98
Universal Declaration of Human Rights, 191
university corporationization, 37
Useem, Michael, 36

V
visible minority, 239, 254–256
    educational attainment, 267
    immigrants as, 249
    incomes of, 254, 269, 275

occupational attainment, 253–254, 277, 284
    occupational disadvantages, 278, 282
volunteerism,
    age and, 413, 414
    ethnicity and, 424

W
wage and price controls, 67–69
WD. *See* Western Economic Diversification Canada (WD)
wealth (affluence), 61–64, 83–84
    definition of, 92–94
    distribution factors, 98–102
    distribution, 94–97
    income sources, 99–100
    inequality, 95–97
    inherited, 99–100
    mobility, 102–103
    strikes and, 61–64
    world distribution of, 97–98
Weber, Max, 44, 45, 46–47, 48, 50, 51, 53, 54, 57, 118
welfare state, 79, 83, 87, 88, 89, 90
    in Sweden, 88
Western Economic Diversification Canada (WD), 335, 336
Weston, Galen, 97
What is the Indian Problem?, 302
WIDER. *See* UN University's World Institute for Development Economics Research (WIDER)
Winnipeg General Strike (1919), 66
WLB. *See* work-life balance (WLB)
Wood, Ellen, 40
work-life balance (WLB), 213, 220
working class, 45–48
    authoritarianism, 391, 392–393
    characteristics of, 48
    ethnicity of, 53–54
    gender of, 53–54
    homogenization of, 46, 47, 50–53
    immigration and, 53
    polarization of, 50
World Bank, 41
    poverty and, 108, 114
World Economic Forum, 37
World Trade Organization (WTO), 34, 37
World Values Surveys (WVS), 395, 411, 413
WTO. *See* World Trade Organization (WTO)
WVS. *See* World Values Surveys (WVS)

Y
Yalnizyan, Armine, 85